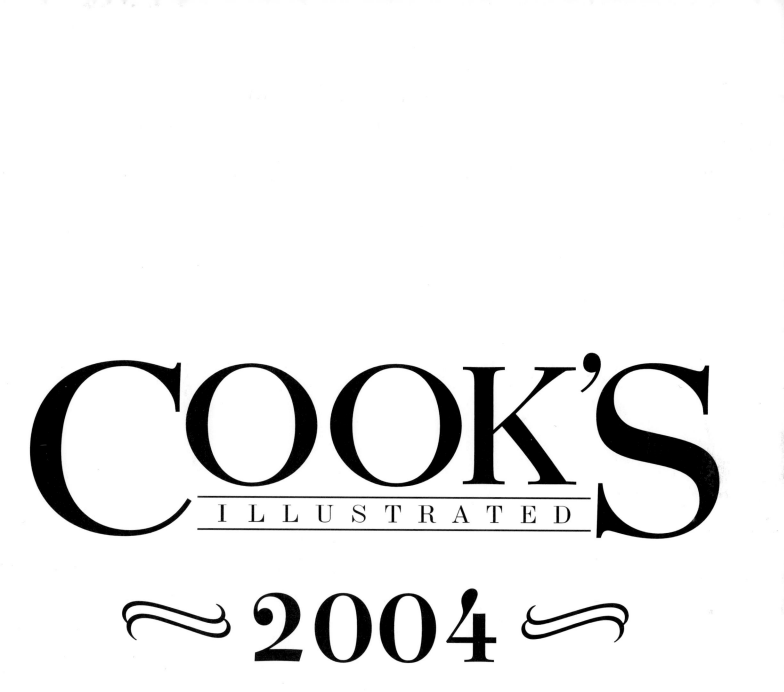

COOK'S
ILLUSTRATED

~ 2004 ~

$29.95

Published by
America's Test Kitchen
17 Station Street
Brookline, MA 02445

ISBN: 0-936184-83-3
ISSN: 1068-2821

To get home delivery of *Cook's Illustrated*, call 800-526-8442 inside the U.S., or 515-247-7571 if calling from outside the U.S., or subscribe online at www.cooksillustrated.com.

In addition to Annual Hardbound Editions available from each year of publication (1993–2004), *Cook's Illustrated* offers the following cookbooks:

The Best Recipe Series
Cover & Bake
The New Best Recipe
Steaks, Chops, Roasts & Ribs
Baking Illustrated
Restaurant Favorites at Home
Perfect Vegetables
The Quick Recipe
Italian Classics
American Classics
Soups and Stews
Grilling and Barbecue

The America's Test Kitchen Series (companion cookbooks to our hit public television series)
America's Test Kitchen Live!
   (2005 season companion cookbook)
Inside America's Test Kitchen
   (2004 season companion cookbook)
Here in America's Test Kitchen
   (2003 season companion cookbook)
The America's Test Kitchen Cookbook
   (2002 season companion cookbook)

Additional books from the editors of *Cook's Illustrated* magazine
The Cook's Bible
The Yellow Farmhouse Cookbook
The Dessert Bible
The Cook's Illustrated Complete Book of Poultry
The Cook's Illustrated Complete Book of Pasta and Noodles
The Best Kitchen Quick Tips
The Kitchen Detective
1993–2004 Master Index

The How to Cook Master Series
How to Make a Pie
How to Make an American Layer Cake
How to Stir-Fry
How to Make Ice Cream
How to Make Pizza
How to Make Holiday Desserts
How to Make Pasta Sauces
How to Make Salad
How to Grill
How to Make Simple Fruit Desserts
How to Make Cookie Jar Favorites
How to Cook Holiday Roasts and Birds
How to Make Stew
How to Cook Shrimp and Other Shellfish
How to Barbecue and Roast on the Grill
How to Cook Garden Vegetables
How to Make Pot Pies and Casseroles
How to Make Soup
How to Sauté
How to Cook Potatoes
How to Make Quick Appetizers
How to Make Sauces and Gravies
How to Cook Chinese Favorites
How to Make Muffins, Biscuits, and Scones
How to Cook Chicken Breasts

To order any of our cookbooks listed above, give us a call at 800-611-0759 inside the U.S., or at 515-246-6911 if calling from outside the U.S.

You can order subscriptions, gift subscriptions, and any of our books by visiting our online store at www.cooksillustrated.com

BC=Back Cover

COOK'S ILLUSTRATED INDEX 2004

COOK'S ILLUSTRATED INDEX 2004

NUMBER SIXTY-SIX

JANUARY & FEBRUARY 2004

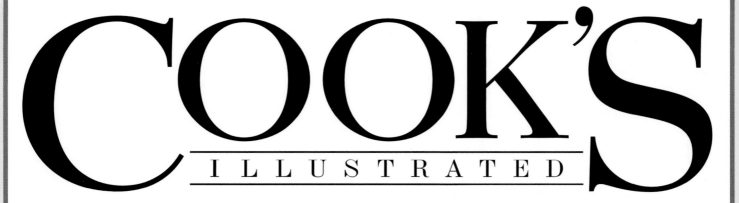

COOK'S
ILLUSTRATED

Garlic-Rosemary
Roast Chicken

Best Oven Fries
As Good as French Fries

Chocolate
Bundt Cake
Rich, Moist, Chocolatey

Eggplant Parmesan
Light
No Frying, No Grease, Great Flavor

Tasting Dijon
Mustard
Check the Expiration Date?

Hearty Lentil Soup

Rating Fat Separators
Does Type Really Matter? Yes!

Better Apple Brown Betty
Pasta with Sun-Dried Tomatoes
Perfect Fish Meunière
Homemade Stock 101

www.cooksillustrated.com

$5.95 U.S./$6.95 CANADA

0   74470 62805   7

0 2>

CONTENTS

January & February 2004

www.cooksillustrated.com

HOME OF AMERICA'S TEST KITCHEN

Founder and Editor	Christopher Kimball
Executive Editor	Jack Bishop
Senior Editors	Adam Ried
	Dawn Yanagihara
Director of Editorial Operations	Barbara Bourassa
Editorial Manager, Books	Elizabeth Carduff
Art Director	Amy Klee
Test Kitchen Director	Erin McMurrer
Senior Editors, Books	Julia Collin Davison
	Lori Galvin-Frost
Senior Writer	Bridget Lancaster
Associate Editors	Matthew Card
	Rebecca Hays
Science Editor	John Olson
Web Editor	Keri Fisher
Copy Editor	India Koopman
Test Cooks	Erika Bruce
	Keith Dresser
	Sean Lawler
	Diane Unger-Mahoney
Assistant Test Cooks	Garth Clingingsmith
	Nina West
Assistant to the Publisher	Melissa Baldino
Kitchen Assistants	Laura Courtemanche
	Nadia Domeq
	Ena Gudiel
Contributing Editor	Elizabeth Germain
Consulting Editors	Shirley Corriher
	Jasper White
	Robert L. Wolke
Proofreader	Jean Rogers

Vice President Marketing	David Mack
Retail Sales Director	Jason Geller
Corporate Sponsorship Specialist	Laura Phillipps
Sales Representative	Shekinah Cohn
Marketing Assistant	Connie Forbes
Circulation Manager	Larisa Greiner
Products Director	Steven Browall
Direct Mail Director	Adam Perry
Customer Service Manager	Jacqueline Valerio
Customer Service Representative	Julie Gardner
E-Commerce Marketing Manager	Hugh Buchan

Vice President Operations and Technology	James McCormack
Production Manager	Jessica Lindheimer Quirk
Assistant Production Manager	Mary Connelly
Production Assistants	Ron Bilodeau
	Jennifer McCreary
Systems Administrator	Richard Cassidy
WebMaster	Aaron Shuman
Production Web Intern	Miles Benson

Chief Financial Officer	Sharyn Chabot
Controller	Mandy Shito
Office Manager	Elizabeth Wray
Receptionist	Henrietta Murray
Publicity	Deborah Broide

For list rental information, contact: ClientLogic, 1200 Harbor Blvd., 9th Floor, Weehawken, NJ 07087; 201-865-5800; fax 201-867-2450.
Editorial Office: 17 Station St., Brookline, MA 02445; 617-232-1000; fax 617-232-1572.
Postmaster: Send all new orders, subscription inquiries, and change of address notices to: Cook's Illustrated, P.O. Box 7446, Red Oak, IA 51591-0446.

PRINTED IN THE USA

EXOTIC CITRUS

EXOTIC CITRUS The more far-flung members of the citrus family come in all sizes and run the gamut from puckery sour to pleasingly sweet. The pomelo is the largest of all citrus, growing up to 10 inches in diameter. Its thick skin encloses yellow- to coral-colored flesh; it is less acidic than the common grapefruit and can be eaten as such. A cross between a pomelo and a grapefruit, the melogold has few seeds and is also sweeter than a grapefruit. The juicy, thin-skinned Meyer lemon, a milder, sweeter version of a regular lemon, is favored by pastry chefs. Small and sour, Key limes hail from the Florida Keys and are best known for their namesake pie. Sweet limes, juiced or eaten out of hand, taste more like lemons and can be very sweet at the peak of ripeness. The diminutive orange kumquat is tangy and full of seeds but can be eaten whole, rind and all. The lumpy citron, with its sparse and extremely sour flesh, is valued for its thick, aromatic peel. Also used exclusively for its rind is the Buddha's Hand, or fingered citron, a symbol of prosperity in Eastern cultures.

COVER: Elizabeth Brandon, BACK COVER (*Exotic Citrus*): John Burgoyne

MOVING DAY

Tom and Nancy have been close neighbors ever since we built our farmhouse in 1987. That was the same year that Jean put up her place across the valley, her white clapboard home peering down on us like an old farmer checking to see who just drove by. At that time, John and Lucille still lived in their one-room camp across the way, Mickey Smith was still alive, driving his VW Rabbit about half as fast as a lame horse, and most of our open land was tired, old corn fields.

Tom and Nancy's weathered blue farmhouse sits right on the road, and you would often see the two of them sitting on the front porch with a cup of coffee in the early morning and Tom with a can or two of beer at night. The house was haunted, perhaps by the ghost of a woman who died years ago in an upstairs bedroom. She hadn't been seen for a few days, so the young Harley Smith (Harley was a student at the schoolhouse next door) was given the job of climbing a ladder to check on her. She was dead alright and thereafter made the occasional ghostly appearance in the stairwell.

In those early days, their kids were still young. Josceline did our babysitting, and Nate was always doing chores with his dad: loading wood into the basement, feeding the pigs and beefer, boiling sap out back on an open fire. There were graduation parties, cookouts, Crockpot spaghetti sauces, venison steaks, squirrel stew, long days and nights in the sap house, deer hung from the rafters in the shed, skating parties on the pond with a Thermos of hot chocolate, turkey hunting, stories of tracking wounded deer late at night through the mountains, and afternoons in front of the TV watching Nascar. One night Tom and Nancy came home from a fishing trip and found a baker's dozen of bats in the house. Tom hid upstairs while Nancy chased the bats out of the house with a badminton racquet.

Tom (honorary president of The Old Rabbit Hunter's Association) and I hunted every fall for rabbits, meeting down at his place to grab Bucket, his beagle. We'd walk out his back door, march across Lincoln's Christmas tree farm, through the old barns behind Betty's, and then down through the swamp and back across the road toward my place. The first time I tried rabbit hunting I was so excited that I went through close to a dozen shotgun shells. Tom smiled and asked impishly, "Need more ammo?"

Last summer their house went on the market, and I didn't think much of it. But real estate was hot, and they got their asking price. Much to our surprise (and maybe theirs as well), they signed the contract and were set to move out on Labor Day. Josceline came up from Savannah to clean out the attic. Adrienne and I and the kids helped move furniture into a long storage trailer. The workroom and barn had to be cleaned out, too—trash compactors, table saws, a Model A windshield, chop saws, ice saws, deer antlers, nails, screws, kerosene heaters, old jugs—just about anything one could collect in more than 20 years of living in one place. An antiques dealer bought off the smaller pieces, the backup beagle (the one who never learned to track a rabbit) was given away to a neighbor, and the sap house was stripped of its arch and storage tanks. Harley, now in his 70s, came over and sat in a big chair next to his pickup, like a circuit judge. When some lumber or old tool went by that he liked, he simply nodded up and down and it was loaded onto his flatbed. A nod to the side and it was put in the junk pile.

Just before moving, Bucket, the good rabbit dog, died; he had lived through a bad eye infection last fall but didn't make it to another season. Their black mutt, Sam, got run over by a truck in late August. Their three large apple trees were full, but the rest of the place looked empty. The vegetable garden, usually a picture-perfect plot of beans, lettuce, corn, squash, and tomatoes, was

Christopher Kimball

now left half-tended. Then they were gone.

In our small town, those of us who have been around awhile can pick out a spot in the trees where the dance hall used to be or the house that the Woodcocks lived in or maybe the place where the old red barn once stood—the one where Charlie Bentley and I used to do the milking. These days, most folks don't remember Marie Briggs, the town baker; Minor Heard's General Store; or the old town road that used to go up through our property over to Tate Hill Road. Some day all will be forgotten—the sound of Tom sighting in his rifle in late October, the sight of Whitney on a bike, headed down the dirt road for the first time, or the plume of smoke that shot up from Nate's sap house and hung like fog over our valley. When the last barn is gone, the last child has packed and left for school, and the last neighbor moved on to another town, we are left behind like characters from an old book. We wait for the sound of a truck or the jangle of the phone. We eagerly promise to keep the home fires burning, the jug of cider in the root cellar, and the wood cookstove started early on cold mornings so the smoke can be seen from the road. Yet those of us still at home find happiness in this place, where foundations tell stories, and where nobody much looks to the future. We all suspect that it isn't half as good as the past, the place where we first met as neighbors, where our children were born, and where we lived the stories that we now tell to strangers.

Leavings are bitter and homecomings are bittersweet. But I have faith that our children and neighbors will be close by once again. I think I can hear them, from time to time, in the driveway, walking up to the back porch. I go to make the coffee and biscuits, knowing that even ghosts deserve a bit of small-town hospitality.

FOR INQUIRIES, ORDERS, OR MORE INFORMATION:

www.cooksillustrated.com

At www.cooksillustrated.com you can order books and subscriptions, sign up for our free e-newsletter, or check the status of your subscription. Join the Web site and you'll have access to 10 years of Cook's recipes, cookware and ingredient testings, and more.

COOKBOOKS

We sell more than 40 cookbooks by the editors of Cook's Illustrated. To order, visit our bookstore at www.cooksillustrated.com or call 800-611-0759 or 515-246-6911 from outside the U.S.

COOK'S ILLUSTRATED Magazine

Cook's Illustrated magazine (ISSN 1068-2821), number 66, is published bimonthly by Boston Common Press Limited Partnership, 17 Station Street, Brookline, MA 02445. Copyright 2004 Boston Common Press Limited Partnership. Periodicals postage paid at Boston, Mass., and additional mailing offices, USPS #012487. POSTMASTER: Send address changes to Cook's Illustrated, P.O. Box 7446, Red Oak, IA 51591-0446. For subscription and gift subscription orders, subscription inquiries, or change-of-address notices, call 800-526-8442 in the U.S., 515-247-7571 from outside the U.S., or write us at Cook's Illustrated, P.O. Box 7446, Red Oak, IA 51591-0446.

Is a Floating Egg a Rotten Egg?

I learned a lot from the "Eggs 101" article in your March/April 2003 issue, but I was surprised that it did not include a way of testing the freshness of eggs without cracking them open (when, for example, you want to hard-cook them). This is what I've usually followed as advice: Put the egg in a bowl of cold tap water. If it lies flat on the bottom, it's fresh; if it stands up and bobs on the bottom, it's not as fresh, though still OK; if it floats to the surface, it's bad. Is this accurate, to your knowledge? Is there a better way?

CYN CHANDLER
PINEHURST, N.C.

➤ We received a couple of letters from readers recommending slight variations on the theory that "fresh eggs sink in water, spoiled eggs float," and we decided to test it with three cartons of eggs with sequential expiration dates exactly one month apart. Our results matched your description of the eggs' behavior based on the age of the carton they came from: Most of the eggs from the freshest carton sank, most of those from the next freshest carton bobbed, and all of those from the oldest carton floated. Based on our tests in "Eggs 101," however, we can say that an older egg is not necessarily a spoiled egg.

SINK, BOB, OR FLOAT
The fresher the egg, the more likely it is to sink when placed in water.

We found minimal performance differences in eggs that were fresh and eggs that were up to three months old. A floating egg is, however, an egg with a good-sized air cell, and that's why it floats. Eggs take in air and lose carbon dioxide and water as they age. A large air cell indicates that the egg is at least a month or two old.

Baking with Splenda

Could you try the sugar substitute called Splenda in baking? The manufacturer says it tastes like sugar and can be substituted for sugar cup for cup.

HAROLD JOHNSON
WORCESTER, MASS.

➤ Splenda is the brand name of a product sweetened by means of sucralose, a substance derived from sucrose, better known as table sugar. Making sucralose involves changing the structure of the sugar molecules by substituting three chlorine atoms for three hydrogen-oxygen, or hydroxyl, groups. According to manufacturer McNeil Nutritionals, part of Johnson & Johnson, sucralose provides no calories because the body doesn't metabolize it as sugar. McNeil also says that the granulated form of Splenda (the Splenda available in packets is not the same) can be used cup for cup to replace sugar. We tested this assertion in our recipes for sugar cookies and blueberry cobbler.

The sugar cookies made with Splenda had a texture that was markedly different from those made with granulated sugar, being so soft as to almost melt in your mouth in the way cookies made with confectioners' sugar do. The cookies made with regular sugar were more substantial and had a definite chew. The Splenda cookies also looked different; they didn't brown at all, and they were puffy. The "real" sugar cookies browned nicely around the edges and, compared with the Splenda batch, were fairly flat. Flavorwise, the Splenda cookies tasted, well, sweet. On a negative note, they were lacking in the caramel flavor that developed in the regular sugar cookies as they browned. On a positive note, the cookies made with Splenda were also lacking the artificial flavors that just about every other sugar substitute brings with it.

Tasters noticed similar differences in the cobblers, although this time differences in the level of sweetness were more notable. As with the sugar cookies, the biscuits in the cobbler made with Splenda didn't brown, but they also tasted less sweet and were not as tender as the biscuits made with sugar. The berry filling made with Splenda also tasted less sweet, and it was more liquidy. Even though in this case the flavor differences were more marked, tasters were again pleasantly surprised at not being able to detect artificial flavors in the cobbler made with Splenda.

Overall, then, the cookies and cobbler made with Splenda were not on a par with those made with sugar—differences in texture and color were the most significant—but for someone on a sugar-restricted diet, we thought they would be better than no cookies or cobbler at all. We appreciated the fact that Splenda added sweetness without adding other, undesirable flavors. It bears noting, though, that Splenda does add another thing that most other sugar substitutes don't add: calories.

How can a product that calls itself a "No Calorie Sweetener" have calories? Because it meets the U.S. Food and Drug Administration's technical definition of a "no-calorie" food, which for sugar substitutes means having no more than 5 calories per serving. According to the manufacturer, 1 cup of Splenda contains 96 calories. In contrast, 1 cup of granulated sugar (the amount used in our sugar cookies) contains 768 calories.

Tastes like, but doesn't quite bake like, sugar.

But if the body doesn't recognize Splenda in the way it does sugar, as the manufacturer says, where do the calories come from? In the case of granulated Splenda, the answer is maltodextrin, a bulking agent similar to cornstarch. Without it, sucralose is 600 times sweeter than sugar.

Saying Yes to the Garlic Press

What, if any, substantive difference exists between minced and pressed garlic?

LIZA Q. WIRTZ
CAMBRIDGE, MASS.

➤ Since we tested garlic presses in the March/April 2001 issue of the magazine, we've been recommending the use of minced or pressed garlic in our recipes. In various recipes, our tasters couldn't tell the difference between properly minced garlic and pressed garlic. While chefs may well be able to produce piles of perfectly minced garlic in no time flat, we've found that home cooks often don't mince garlic as finely as many recipes require. A garlic press produces not only a very fine mince (almost a puree) but an evenly fine mince, which ensures even distribution of flavor throughout the dish. The winner of our test was the Zyliss Susi DeLuxe Garlic Press, available at many kitchen stores for $12.99.

Best–Buy Knife "Set"

I've been looking to buy a knife set. What's the least (amount of money and number of knives) I can get away with?

JANET SPEERS
CAMBRIDGE, MASS.

➤ Years of carving, slicing, mincing, and dicing have taught us that three knives will nicely carry us through most kitchen jobs. First on our list would be a chef's knife, which can be used for everything from carving a roast to chopping vegetables to mincing parsley. Second would be a paring knife for things like coring apples, peeling and sectioning oranges, stemming mushrooms—all jobs for which a chef's knife is just too big. Third would be a bread (or serrated) knife. Nothing works better than a bread knife for slicing cleanly through tough-skinned tomatoes, not to mention all manner of breads, delicate pastries, and dense and chewy bagels.

If you're looking for a "best buy" on these knives—that is, optimum performance at a modest price—we can recommend three that placed either first or second in past tests, all of them made by Forschner: the 8-inch chef's knife ($31.00), the 3¼-inch paring knife ($5.95), and the 10¼-inch bread knife ($36.00). For information on where to purchase these knives, see Resources, page 32.

Storing Oyster-Flavored Sauce

We have been doing a lot of stir-fry meals, many using oyster-flavored sauce. On the bottles we get, there is no instruction on what to do after opening them. Our last bottle was kept in the refrigerator but was clogged up when we went to use it. What is the best place to keep it?

DR. AND MRS. RONALD S. GREEN
CHEYENNE, WYO.

➤ In its publications on food safety, the National Restaurant Association recommends a maximum storage period of two years, unrefrigerated, for unopened bottles of salty condiments. We could find no guidelines for such products once opened, but in a search of oyster-flavored sauces in an Asian grocery store, we checked labels and found that most brands do recommend refrigeration after opening. The thickness you noticed was likely caused by the low temperature, as oyster-flavored sauce becomes viscous when refrigerated. Bringing the oyster sauce to room temperature before using it should help, and a small amount of water can be added to sauce that remains thick once brought to room temperature.

Rocking with a Mezzaluna

Knifework is not exactly my forte in the kitchen, so I was intrigued by the mezzaluna you suggested as an alternative to a chef's knife in your July/August 2003 issue. You said it's good at mincing herbs. What else can I use it for?

URSULA TUCHAK
ALBERTA, CANADA

➤ We discovered the advantages of the crescent-shaped knife called a mezzaluna (Italian for "half moon") when testing it along with several other (and much less functional) herb choppers. The mezzaluna made quick work of basil, parsley, and rosemary, producing a fine and even mince as we mastered the technique of rocking the blade back

WHAT IS IT?

In my travels I've seen two salt containers of similar design, either of which I would love to own. They both looked like—the best I can describe it—a hooded bowl. The top was easy to grab to pour from the bowl, and the front was open so it was easy to get a measuring spoon in. The first one I saw was custom-designed pottery, the second made of glass. Have you ever come across such as these, and, if so, do you know where I could get one?

JOE MORGAN
BEAVER, PA.

➤ We believe that the object you're describing is a salt pig, pictured above. While we found this one at the Web site for King Arthur Flour, a search of the Web turned up ceramic vessels identical in shape and differing only in color. This one, about 4 inches wide and 5 inches tall, holds about half a pound of salt. The sites we checked indicated that the knob on top is for carrying and that the large, round opening provides easy access to the salt. It's also thought that the hooded shape keeps moisture from collecting on the salt. One of our editors left this salt pig out on her kitchen counter for a couple of months last summer (which included a couple of very humid weeks) and the salt did indeed remain dry, with no clumping whatsoever. Its hood distinguishes the salt pig from the salt cellar, which is generally a small, open bowl.

We couldn't help but wonder how the salt "pig" got its name and so contacted a couple of lexicographers, one of whom—George H. Goebel, an editor of the *Dictionary of American Regional English* at the University of Wisconsin, Madison—made his way to the *Scottish National Dictionary*. This reference indicated that this use of "pig" is an old one found mostly in Scots and northern English dialect, where it means an earthenware vessel, specifically "a pot, jar, pitcher, [or] crock," which of course fits the notion of a salt pig very nicely. (A couple of the Web sites ventured that the hooded opening looks like a pig's snout.) Goebel added that according to the same dictionary, "pig" or "penny pig" can mean "an earthenware money-box, now sometimes made in the form of the animal 'pig,'" while the "piggy" in "piggy bank" originally meant "made of earthenware." The pig shape was apparently a visual pun. To purchase the salt pig pictured here, see Resources, page 32.

A "piggy bank" for salt.

and forth over the cutting board. What else can a mezzaluna do? To find out, we used ours to mince or chop more than a dozen different foods, and we liked the results we got with most of them.

A mezzaluna is as well suited to mincing garlic as it is herbs. Onion, ginger, bell and Thai chile peppers, olives, and pickles also chopped up nicely (for the onion, cut into ¼-inch slices first, then mince with the mezzaluna). Celery and carrots did not fare well, the thickness and crunchiness of both providing lots of resistance to the curved blade. Almonds, peanuts, pecans, and walnuts, on the other hand, were pretty easy to handle. We found it best to first chop them into large pieces by raising and lowering the blade in a chopping motion; they could then be "rocked" into a finer chop. Last on our list were baking chocolate and raisins. For the chocolate, we found it best to ease the blade into the side of the block with a few slow strokes to break it up; we then rocked away, easily

NOT JUST FOR ITALIANS
The mezzaluna is a good alternative to a chef's knife or food processor when mincing herbs, garlic, or ginger or when chopping small amounts of nuts, raisins, or chocolate.

producing a mound of chopped chocolate. Raisins were a bit sticky, but less so than when we chopped them with a chef's knife.

Errata

➤ Although in cooking and eating most of us treat peanuts more like a nut than like a legume, they are in fact a member of the pea family and as such qualify as a legume—as a couple of readers pointed out after seeing the back cover of the November/December 2003 issue, which is labeled "Nuts."

➤ Step 4 of the Spiced Pumpkin Cheesecake recipe on page 22 of the November/December 2003 issue directs the cook to remove the sides of the springform pan while the cheesecake remains in the water bath. At this point, a paring knife should be used to loosen the sides of the cake from the pan, but the sides of the pan should not be removed until the cake has been chilled in the refrigerator for a minimum of four hours.

SEND US YOUR QUESTIONS We will provide a complimentary one-year subscription for each letter we print. Send your inquiry, name, address, and daytime telephone number to Notes from Readers, Cook's Illustrated, P.O. Box 470589, Brookline, MA 02447, or to notesfromreaders@bcpress.com.

Quick Tips

⇒ COMPILED BY REBECCA HAYS AND NINA WEST ⇐

Flavored Sugars

Cinnamon sugar is commonplace, but Ann Budreski of Montpelier, Vt., keeps more unusual sugars on hand for stirring into coffee and tea, sprinkling onto fresh fruit, and decorating cookies, muffins, or homemade doughnuts. She uses the food processor to make ginger, vanilla, chocolate, citrus, and cinnamon sugars.

For ginger or vanilla sugar: Process 2 teaspoons minced candied ginger or ¼ fresh vanilla bean with 1 cup sugar in the workbowl of a food processor for 45 seconds to 1 minute.

For chocolate, citrus, or cinnamon sugar: Add 2 teaspoons cocoa powder, 2 teaspoons grated fresh zest from one lemon, lime, grapefruit, or orange, or ½ teaspoon ground cinnamon to 1 cup sugar and pulse 20 times in the workbowl of a food processor.

Store the chocolate and cinnamon sugars at room temperature in sealed containers for several months. Store the ginger, vanilla, and citrus sugars in the refrigerator for up to one week.

Reheating French Toast

After a big weekend breakfast, there are inevitably a few uneaten pancakes or slices of French toast. Instead of discarding the leftovers, Sean Sweeney of Brookline, Mass., has come up with this method of reheating them.

1. Layer parchment paper between the cooked French toast slices or pancakes, wrap portions in plastic wrap and then in foil, and store in the freezer.
2. To reheat, unwrap and heat the French toast or pancakes for 10 to 12 minutes on a baking sheet in a 350-degree oven and serve with hot maple syrup. The breakfast treats can also be reheated in a toaster oven.

Quick Compound Butter

Compound butter is generally prepared by softening butter, mixing in flavoring ingredients, shaping the mixture into a log, and then rechilling or freezing the butter so that it can be sliced and served as a savory topping for steak, chops, or fish. Cecily Ward of San Francisco, Calif., saves time by using a whole stick of salted butter straight from the refrigerator.

1. Unwrap the butter, halve it lengthwise, and roll each piece directly in the seasonings, whether chopped fresh herbs, hot red pepper flakes, chili powder, or grated citrus zest.
2. Slice and serve—no mixing or rechilling is necessary.
3. Wrap leftovers in the original butter wrapper and freeze for future use.

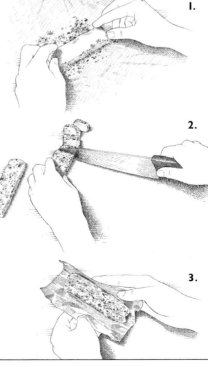

Roasted Garlic Paste

Roasted garlic cloves are great for spreading on bread or stirring into soups and stews for extra flavor, but it can take some time and patience to extrude the roasted cloves from their papery skins. Jenny Buechner of Madison, Wis., found a way to streamline the process. After dry-toasting individual garlic cloves on the stovetop, she passes the unpeeled cloves through a garlic press. This creates a perfectly smooth paste, and the garlic peel is easily removed from the press.

Reviving Crystallized Honey

All honey hardens and crystallizes over time, but it need not be discarded. To bring honey back to its translucent, liquid state, Janet Reynolds of Dedham, Mass., uses a pot of simmering water, although you could also use a microwave. Once cooled, use the honey or screw the lid back on for storage. The honey will eventually recrystallize, but it should flow freely for several weeks.

Place the opened jar of honey in a saucepan filled with about an inch of water and place over very low heat, stirring the honey often, until the crystals melt. Alternatively, heat the opened jar in the microwave on high power in 10-second increments, stirring intermittently, until it has liquefied.

Impromptu Bowl Cover

Plastic wrap is the usual choice for covering leftovers for storage, but Kim Waters of Gainesville, Ga., discovered another option. A clean, unused shower cap (often found in complimentary toiletry packs in hotel rooms) makes a perfect bowl cover. It is big enough to fit most large mixing bowls and creates a more reliable seal than most plastic wraps.

Grating Small Amounts of Cheese

When a Microplane rasp-style grater (our favorite tool for grating small amounts of hard cheese) isn't handy, Nancy Milker of Willits, Calif., reaches for a serrated steak knife to grate Parmesan or Asiago over bowls of pasta or risotto. Holding the cheese in one hand and a small serrated steak knife in the other, she lightly scrapes the cheese directly over the food.

Edible Spoon Rest

A spoon rest is a nice extra to have in the kitchen, but many cooks don't want to bother with them. Julian Lewis of Burlington, Vt., came up with an alternative. Instead of a ceramic or metal spoon rest, she uses a slice of bread. The bread catches bits of food and soaks up juices, in the process becoming a savory treat for the family dog (or the cook).

New Use for Stovetop Grates

Michael Drury of Harwich, Mass., was preparing to roast a chicken at his vacation home and realized at the last minute that the kitchen wasn't equipped with a V-rack. With some quick thinking, he built his own rack using the grates from his gas stove and aluminum foil.

1. Wrap two light-gauge stovetop grates with foil and use a paring knife or skewer to poke large holes in the foil so that juices can drip down into the pan as the bird roasts.
2. Place the grates in the roasting pan, resting them against the sides of the pan so that the bottoms of the grates meet to create a V-shape. Roast the chicken (or turkey) as directed in the recipe.

No-Fuss Wrapper Storage

Opened boxes of aluminum foil and plastic wrap often catch on the kitchen drawer frame, causing it to jam. Robert Ziff of Loris, S.C., offers this simple preventive measure. When you return a box of foil or plastic wrap to its storage drawer, turn the box lid-side down. The next time you open the drawer, no lids stick up and catch to prevent the drawer from opening.

Dotting with Butter

Recipes often instruct the cook to "dot" the top of casseroles, fruit pies, and other baked desserts with butter for extra richness and browning. Rather than cutting butter into small pieces and then sprinkling them over the dish with warm hands (a messy proposition), Jane Ashworth of Beavercreek, Ohio, came up with this tip.

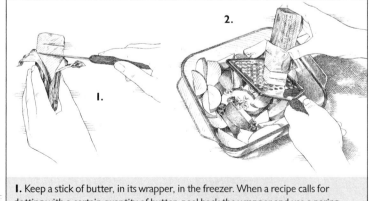

1. Keep a stick of butter, in its wrapper, in the freezer. When a recipe calls for dotting with a certain quantity of butter, peel back the wrapper and use a paring knife to mark the proper amount.
2. Using the large holes of a flat grater, grate the butter directly over the baking dish, distributing it evenly.

Keeping Fish Extra-Fresh

Fresh fish and shellfish are best purchased and served on the same day. If fish must be stored, even briefly, it is best kept on ice. Instead of keeping seafood in a messy container of melting ice, Laura Bueermann of Cambridge, Mass., recommends the following.

Place a layer of sealed frozen ice bricks (the kind used in picnic coolers) along the bottom of the meat drawer in the refrigerator. Place the wrapped fish on top of the ice bricks. For firm-fleshed fish and shellfish, place additional ice bricks on top. Replace melted ice bricks with fully frozen bricks as necessary.

Cleaning Tough Tea Stains

If you brew a fresh pot of tea every morning, you know that tannin stains build up quickly on ceramics. Jennifer Pade of New York, N.Y., found this easy way to remove them.

Fill the stained teapot, teacup, or any tainted piece of ceramic with water and drop in a denture cleansing tablet. Let soak for 2 or 3 hours, then wash with dishwashing liquid and hot water. Light stains will disappear, leaving the cup or pot looking as good as new. Heavier stains may need several treatments followed by a scrubbing with hot soapy water.

Resurrecting Pot-au-Feu

A French boiled dinner seems hopelessly out of date, but we thought it was worth revisiting. Could we bring this one-dish classic back from the brink of extinction?

≳ BY BRIDGET LANCASTER AND NINA WEST ≲

Not long after man discovered fire, he (or she) discovered the boiled dinner. This primal and simplest of cooking methods requires nothing more than simmering meat and vegetables in a pot of water, and the technique is used around the world, from Mongolian hotpot to New England corned beef and cabbage. Literally translated as "pot on fire" (referring to the stovetop simmering method and not some unfortunate cooking accident), pot-au-feu is the French version. The resulting broth is often elegant enough to serve as its own course with crusty bread, followed by the sliced, meltingly tender beef and an assortment of vegetables, all of which are presented family-style, with condiments such as horseradish and mustard.

As exotic ingredients and chef-inspired recipes have taken hold of American cooks, traditional recipes such as pot-au-feu have fallen out of favor. But there is something appealing about this relic from the golden age of French country cooking. Pot-au-feu is straightforward fare that uses neither strange ingredients nor complicated cooking methods, and, although it requires a substantial investment of time (it takes hours to make tough, cheap meat tender), this recipe can produce a spectacular complete meal for a crowd. This being company food, our goal was to make the best pot-au-feu possible.

Because there are neither potent ingredients nor a sauce to mask mistakes, pot-au-feu has to be perfectly executed. If the meat is tough or if the vegetables are bloated from overcooking, the dish has little appeal. We reasoned that choosing the right ingredients—from the cut of beef to the proper vegetables—would greatly enhance the flavor of the dish. When to add the ingredients and how long they should cook would also be key.

Meat Matters

To offer a mix of meat textures, pot-au-feu uses at least two types of beef, usually a boneless roast as well as a bone-in cut such as short ribs or beef shanks. For the roast, we tested cuts from

With tender beef, well-seasoned vegetables, and a rich broth, pot-au-feu turns simple ingredients into a complete meal for a crowd.

the round (leg) and chuck (shoulder) as well as brisket and preferred the chuck roasts, which get their big flavor and velvety texture from the good amount of fat and collagen running through them. All of the chuck roasts tested were good, but the chuck-eye was our favorite. As for bony cuts, we loved the richly decadent meat from short ribs, but this cut didn't add much flavor to the broth. Beef shanks are packed with flavorful marrow that melted into the broth, but shank meat was not as satisfying as that from the short ribs. We decided to include both bony cuts to produce a beefy broth and rich-tasting meat.

Vegetable Season

As for which vegetables to include, tasters were most comfortable with more conservative additions, such as carrots, parsnips, new potatoes, and green beans, although pearl onions, fennel, cabbage, leeks, turnips, butternut squash, and sweet potatoes were also well received. A few

vegetables were disliked. Zucchini and summer squash were watery and spongy, and broccoli was too pungent. Most recipes call for adding the vegetables to the broth all at once, but this produced overcooked vegetables every time. We discovered that batch cooking—potatoes go in for a few minutes, then the carrots and parsnips, then the green beans—ensures that each vegetable cooks perfectly.

Perfectly cooked—but, unfortunately, also perfectly bland. In addition, the pounds of vegetables made the broth taste like vegetable soup. We decided to cook the vegetables separately from the beef in highly salted water (2 tablespoons of salt per 4 quarts of water), hoping that this would season the vegetables sufficiently. And did it ever! Each vegetable now tasted brighter and cleaner, and the whole dish took a giant leap forward.

Sweat the Small Stuff

While we weren't looking for vegetable soup, we admitted that the broth could use a little more flavor. We found that a few bay leaves, peppercorns, and whole cloves gave the broth depth, while parsley and thyme added freshness. A whole head of garlic improved things greatly, but we still wanted more flavor.

We added carrot, celery, and onion back to the broth (not enough to overpower the beef), and the flavor definitely improved. We tried sweating the vegetables in a little oil until they began to exude their juices. This step took all of 10 minutes, but now the broth tasted full and complex. And yet . . . we still wanted a richer, more concentrated flavor.

Like many pot-au-feu recipes, ours now called for about 7 quarts of water, enough to cover the beef and vegetables. Since we had decided to cook our vegetables separately, however, we realized that this was probably too much water. We cut 1 quart and knew we were on the right track. We cut another, and though the water now barely covered the meat, this was no problem; the once sizable roast reduced in mass as it cooked. With the lid left off the pot, our 5 quarts of water reduced down to 3 quarts of rich broth.

With our heady broth ladled over the fall-

Steady (And Not So Slow) Wins

We found that the rate at which the pot-au-feu cooks can greatly influence the end product and simmering time. The best choice is a steady simmer, which is strong enough to cook the meat in about 3½ hours but gentle enough not to damage the meat or broth.

GENTLE SIMMER: 198°–205°
Cooking time: 6 hours
Very few bubbles break the surface of the broth, appearing mostly around the sides of the pot. Broth is perfectly clear.

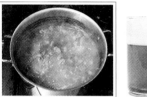

STEADY SIMMER: 206°–211°
Cooking time: 3½ hours
Larger bubbles break the surface of the broth at a more rapid rate, especially around the sides of the pot. Broth is fairly clear.

RAPID BOIL: 212°
Cooking time: 1½ hours
Large bubbles appear all over the surface and begin to "roll over." Violent churning breaks apart meat and turns broth cloudy.

apart-tender roast, melt-in-your-mouth ribs and shanks, and perfectly cooked and seasoned vegetables, our pot-au-feu was now simple cooking at its best. This French classic didn't seem that dated anymore. In fact, with its emphasis on presenting each ingredient in its most natural form, it was downright chic—well, almost.

POT-AU-FEU
SERVES 8 TO 10

A stockpot with at least a 12-quart capacity is necessary for this recipe. Cheesecloth is ideal for straining the broth, although a quadruple layer of paper towels will do in a pinch. Once the beef braise reaches a boil, reduce the heat to maintain a steady simmer; if left to boil, the resulting broth will be murky. For serving, arrange the components on a large warmed platter and give diners individual shallow soup bowls in which to plate their portions. It is not compulsory to serve all of the condiments listed below; mustard and cornichons are traditional choices.

Beef Braise

- 1 medium celery rib, chopped medium
- 2 medium carrots, chopped medium
- 2 medium onions, chopped medium
- 2 teaspoons vegetable oil
- 1 beef chuck roast (about 3 pounds), preferably chuck-eye, tied according to illustration below
- 3 pounds beef short ribs (about 5 large ribs), trimmed of excess fat and tied according to illustration below
- 2 pounds beef shanks (each about 1½ inches thick), tied according to illustration below
- 5 quarts water
- 3 large bay leaves
- 1 teaspoon whole black peppercorns
- 5 whole cloves
- 1 large garlic head, outer papery skins removed and top third of head cut off and discarded
- 10 fresh parsley stems
- 8 sprigs fresh thyme
- 1 tablespoon salt

Vegetables

- 2 pounds small red new potatoes, scrubbed and halved if larger than 1½ inches
- 2 tablespoons salt
- 1½ pounds carrots (about 7 medium), halved crosswise, thicker half quartered lengthwise, thinner half halved lengthwise
- 1½ pounds parsnips (4 to 5 medium), halved crosswise, thicker half quartered lengthwise, thinner half halved lengthwise
- 1 pound green beans, stem ends trimmed

Garnishes and Condiments

- ¼ cup chopped fresh parsley leaves
- 1 baguette, thickly sliced
  Dijon or whole-grain mustard
  Sea salt
  Cornichons
  Prepared horseradish

1. **FOR THE BEEF BRAISE:** Stir together celery, carrots, onions, and oil in 12-quart stockpot; cook, covered, over low heat, stirring frequently, until vegetables are softened but not browned, 8 to 10 minutes. (If vegetables begin to color before softening, add 1 tablespoon water and continue to cook.) Add beef roast, ribs, shanks, water, bay leaves, peppercorns, and cloves; increase heat to medium-high and bring to boil, using large shallow spoon to skim any foam and fat that rise to surface. Reduce heat to low and simmer, uncovered, for 2½ hours, skimming surface of fat and foam every 30 minutes.

2. Add garlic, parsley stems, thyme, and salt. Simmer until tip of paring knife inserted into meats meets little resistance, 1 to 1½ hours.

3. Using tongs, transfer roast, ribs, shanks, and garlic to large cutting board and tent with foil. Strain broth through mesh strainer lined with double layer cheesecloth into large container (you should have about 3 quarts liquid). Let broth settle for at least 5 minutes, then skim off fat using large shallow spoon.

4. **FOR THE VEGETABLES:** While broth settles, rinse out stockpot and add potatoes, salt, and 4 quarts water; bring to boil over high heat; boil 7 minutes. Add carrots and parsnips and cook 3 minutes longer. Add green beans and cook 4 minutes longer. Using slotted spoon, transfer vegetables to large warmed serving platter, arranging as desired; tent with foil.

5. **TO SERVE:** Using tongs, squeeze garlic cloves out of skins and into small serving bowl. Remove twine from roast and separate roast at its seams; cut roast across grain into ½-inch-thick slices and arrange on platter with vegetables. Remove twine from shanks and ribs and arrange on platter. Ladle about 1 cup broth over meat and vegetables to moisten; sprinkle with parsley. Serve, ladling broth over individual servings and passing garlic, baguette, and condiments separately.

STEP-BY-STEP | TYING THE MEAT

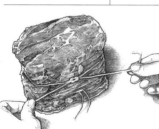

Chuck roast: Cut two 2-foot pieces of butcher's twine. Wrap one piece around roast about 1 inch from bottom and tie with double knot. Snip off excess and repeat with second piece about 1 inch from top.

Short ribs: Cut two 1-foot pieces of butcher's twine for each rib. Wrap one piece about 1 inch from top and tie with double knot. Snip off excess and repeat with second piece about 1 inch from bottom.

Shanks: Cut four 1-foot pieces of twine for each shank. Wrap each piece of twine around shank and tie in center.

Lighter, Quicker Eggplant Parmesan

Traditional recipes fry breaded eggplant in copious amounts of oil. Could we eliminate the frying, streamline the dish, and make it taste better than the original?

⇒ BY REBECCA HAYS ⇐

There's a first—and a last—time for everything. When it comes to eggplant Parmesan, my first attempt at this dish was also my last. The reason is manifest to anyone who has fried notoriously spongy eggplant in generous amounts of oil. This combination is almost certain to produce a heavy, greasy conclusion to a long day in the kitchen. What's to like about time-consuming and greasy?

Despite my misgivings about giving this classic but insipid recipe another try, I cooked a sampling of eggplant Parmesans, ranging from traditional to "new wave." The main objection I had to most of the recipes was their requirement to fry the eggplant in four or five tedious batches. It took an attentive eye to keep the oil at just the right temperature, making the risk of greasy eggplant great. After a full day of breading, frying, and tomato-sauce making, I was predictably tired and disappointed. Most of the casseroles were left uneaten, with tasters having described them as "oily," "dense," "supergreasy," and "messy." I was now determined to reinvent this dish by baking the eggplant rather than frying it; I wanted a fresher, lighter take on the classic Italian version.

Before I could get started, I had to tackle a recurring issue. Most recipes call for purging (salting) eggplant to expel bitter juices (see "A Spoonful of Salt," page 9) and prevent the porous flesh from soaking up excess oil. To double-check this theory, I baked some unsalted eggplant. Oil absorption wasn't a problem, but the eggplant did taste bitter, and it had a raw, mealy texture. Thirty minutes of salting remedied the problem. For efficiency's sake, I chose good-sized globe eggplants; I didn't want to multiply the number of slices I'd have to prepare. For the best appearance, taste, and texture, I settled on unpeeled, ¼-inch-thick crosswise slices, not lengthwise planks.

Eggplant is a sponge when it comes to oil. The secret to lighter eggplant Parmesan is to limit its access to oil.

Shake 'n Bake

In my first effort to sidestep deep-frying, I dispensed with the breading altogether, baking naked, salted eggplant slices on a baking sheet coated with cooking spray. (This method is often employed in low-calorie recipes for eggplant Parmesan.) The resulting eggplant earned negative comments from tasters: "nontraditional," "atypical," and, more directly, "nasty!" I concluded that breading was essential and ticked off a list of possibilities. Flour alone wasn't substantial enough. Eggplant swathed in mayonnaise and then bread crumbs turned slimy. Eggplant coated in a flour and egg batter and then bread crumbs was thick and tough. A standard single breading (dipping the eggplant first in egg, then bread crumbs) was too messy—the egg slid right off the eggplant, leaving the crumbs nothing to adhere to.

A double, or bound, breading proved superior. Dipping the eggplant first in seasoned flour, then egg, then bread crumbs created a substantial (but not heavy) and crisp coating that brought the mild flavor and tender, creamy texture of the eggplant to the fore. The initial coating of flour in a bound breading creates a dry, smooth base to which the egg can cling. I seasoned the bread crumbs with generous amounts of Parmesan, salt, and pepper.

I'd been using fresh bread crumbs and wondered whether I should toast them to improve their flavor or if I could get away with using store-bought crumbs. The answers were "no" and "no." Toasted crumbs baked up too hard and tended to burn, and store-bought crumbs were so fine that they disappeared under blankets of tomato sauce and cheese.

After considerable experimentation, I found that the best way to achieve a crisp coating is to bake the breaded slices on two preheated baking sheets, each coated with a modest 3 tablespoons of vegetable oil (olive oil tasted sour), rotating the pans and flipping the slices partway through. At 425 degrees, the slices sizzled during cooking and became fully tender in 30 minutes. Using this technique, I turned out crisp, golden brown disks of eggplant, expending a minimum of effort (and using very little oil). And now (seeing that I wasn't busy frying up four batches of eggplant in hot oil), I had time to grate cheese and whip up a quick tomato sauce while the eggplant baked.

Creating a Casserole

Eggplant Parmesan couldn't be called such without Parmesan cheese, so that was a given. I'd already used some for breading the eggplant,

TEST RECIPES: Following a Trail of Crumbs

BAKED NAKED	FLOUR ALONE	MAYO & CRUMBS	BATTER & CRUMBS	EGGS & CRUMBS
"Nasty"	"Insubstantial"	"Slimy"	"Thick and tough"	"Too messy"

We prepared eggplant in nearly a dozen ways. Above are some failed samples, with tasters' harsh comments.

• A WINNING COMBINATION •

FLOUR, EGGS, & CRUMBS

Dipping the eggplant in flour, then egg, then bread crumbs created a substantial (but not heavy) and crisp coating.

and a little extra browned nicely on top of the casserole. Mozzarella is another standard addition. A modest amount (8 ounces) kept the casserole from becoming stringy.

A few cloves of minced garlic, a sprinkling of hot red pepper flakes, and some olive oil started off a quick tomato sauce, followed by three cans of diced tomatoes, with just two of them pureed in the food processor to preserve a chunky texture. A handful of fresh basil leaves (I reserved some basil for garnish, too) plus salt and pepper were the final flourishes.

Because breading softens beneath smothering layers of sauce and cheese, I left most of the top layer of eggplant exposed. This left me with about one cup of extra sauce, just enough to pass at the table. Another benefit of this technique was that without excess moisture, the casserole would be easy to cut into tidy pieces. With the eggplant fully cooked, the dish needed only a brief stay in a hot oven to melt the cheese.

In the end, I had drastically reduced the amount of oil and attention required to make this dish, and I had done it without compromising flavor. Now there will never be a "last" time for eggplant Parmesan.

EGGPLANT PARMESAN
SERVES 6 TO 8

Use kosher salt when salting the eggplant. The coarse grains don't dissolve as readily as the fine grains of regular table salt, so any excess can be easily wiped away. To be time-efficient, use the 30 to 45 minutes during which the salted eggplant sits to prepare the breading, cheeses, and sauce.

Eggplant

- 2 pounds globe eggplant (2 medium eggplants), cut crosswise into ¼-inch-thick rounds
- 1 tablespoon kosher salt
- 8 slices high-quality white sandwich bread (about 8 ounces), torn into quarters
- 1 cup grated Parmesan cheese (about 2 ounces)
    Salt and ground black pepper
- 1 cup all-purpose flour
- 4 large eggs
- 6 tablespoons vegetable oil

Tomato Sauce

- 3 cans (14½ ounces each) diced tomatoes
- 2 tablespoons extra-virgin olive oil
- 4 medium garlic cloves, minced or pressed through garlic press (about 1 generous tablespoon)
- ¼ teaspoon red pepper flakes
- ½ cup coarsely chopped fresh basil leaves
    Salt and ground black pepper

- 8 ounces whole milk or part-skim mozzarella, shredded (2 cups)
- ½ cup grated Parmesan cheese (about 1 ounce)
- 10 fresh basil leaves, torn, for garnish

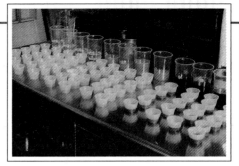
1. FOR THE EGGPLANT: Toss half of eggplant slices and 1½ teaspoons kosher salt in large bowl until combined; transfer salted eggplant to large colander set over bowl. Repeat with remaining eggplant and kosher salt, placing second batch in colander on top of first. Let stand until eggplant releases about 2 tablespoons liquid, 30 to 45 minutes. Arrange eggplant slices on triple layer paper towels; cover with another triple layer paper towels. Firmly press each slice to remove as much liquid as possible, then wipe off excess salt.

2. While eggplant is draining, adjust oven racks to upper- and lower-middle positions, place rimmed baking sheet on each rack, and heat oven to 425 degrees. Pulse bread in food processor to fine, even crumbs, about fifteen 1-second pulses (you should have about 4 cups). Transfer crumbs to pie plate and stir in 1 cup Parmesan, ¼ teaspoon salt, and ½ teaspoon pepper; set aside. Wipe out bowl (do not wash) and set aside.

3. Combine flour and 1 teaspoon pepper in large zipper-lock bag; shake to combine. Beat eggs in second pie plate. Place 8 to 10 eggplant slices in bag with flour; seal bag and shake to coat eggplant. Remove eggplant slices, shaking off excess flour, dip in eggs, let excess egg run off, then coat evenly with bread crumb mixture; set breaded slices on wire rack set over baking sheet. Repeat with remaining eggplant.

4. Remove preheated baking sheets from oven; add 3 tablespoons oil to each sheet, tilting to coat evenly with oil. Place half of breaded eggplant on each sheet in single layer; bake until eggplant is well browned and crisp, about 30 minutes, switching and rotating baking sheets after 10 minutes, and flipping eggplant slices with wide spatula after 20 minutes. Do not turn off oven.

5. FOR THE SAUCE: While eggplant bakes, process 2 cans diced tomatoes in food processor until almost smooth, about 5 seconds. Heat olive oil, garlic, and red pepper flakes in large heavy-bottomed saucepan over medium-high heat, stirring occasionally, until fragrant and garlic is light golden, about 3 minutes; stir in processed and remaining can of diced tomatoes. Bring sauce to boil, then reduce heat to medium-low and simmer, stirring occasionally, until slightly thickened and reduced, about 15 minutes (you should have about 4 cups). Stir in basil and season to taste with salt and pepper.

6. TO ASSEMBLE: Spread 1 cup tomato sauce in bottom of 13 by 9-inch baking dish. Layer in half of eggplant slices, overlapping slices to fit; distribute 1 cup sauce over eggplant; sprinkle with half of mozzarella. Layer in remaining eggplant and dot with 1 cup sauce, leaving majority of eggplant exposed so it will remain crisp (see illustration below); sprinkle with ½ cup Parmesan and remaining mozzarella. Bake until bubbling and cheese is browned, 13 to 15 minutes. Cool 10 minutes, scatter basil over top, and serve, passing remaining tomato sauce separately.

TECHNIQUE
SAUCE WITH CAUTION

To prevent the crisp eggplant slices from becoming soggy, use a minimum of tomato sauce to dot the top layer, leaving most of the eggplant exposed.

Garlic-Rosemary Roast Chicken

What is the secret to moist, tender roast chicken with robust—not raucous—garlic and rosemary flavor?

⇒ BY DAWN YANAGIHARA ⇐

A perfectly roasted chicken is winsome: rich, flavorful, simple, and satisfying. It is a rarity, however, and worthy of a standing ovation because, despite its uncomplicated nature, it requires skill to accomplish, a deft coordination of the doneness of the white and dark meat. In the Tuscan tradition, garlic and rosemary add flavor to a roast chicken. Indeed, they render it heady and robust, but garlic and rosemary are often bullies, overly aggressive and assertive. This explains why an exceptional garlic and rosemary roast chicken is even more of a rarity than a plain one.

An assessment of several recipes revealed a nearly universal approach to this dish: the simple application of a garlic-rosemary mixture beneath the skin before roasting. The recipes that I tried yielded, for the most part, overroasted chickens with tough, parched breast meat, and just one bite filled the mouth with the astringent, resinous flavor of rosemary and a vaguely raw and very sharp garlickiness that could be tasted for days. The task at hand was to harness the flavors of garlic and rosemary and unite them with a perfectly roasted chicken with tender and moist breast and thigh meat.

Roasting Rites

Good garlic-rosemary roast chicken begins with the roasting method. The test kitchen has routinely found that brining, or soaking in a salt-water solution, adds moisture and seasoning that penetrates the meat. This garlic-rosemary chicken was no different. For a 4-pound bird, brining in ½ cup of salt and 2 quarts of water for one hour was the right formula, producing roast chicken that was moist and well seasoned. Next, I made a flavored brine to see if it would have any meritorious effects on the flavor of the bird. I crushed 10 garlic cloves and three sprigs of rosemary with the salt, stirred the mixture into a pint of hot tap water to allow the flavors to bloom, then added cold water to cool the mixture before adding the chicken. The difference was notable. This roast chicken was subtly flavored and perfumed with garlic and rosemary.

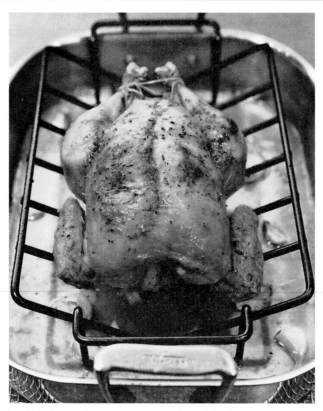

Liquid in the roasting pan prevents scorching of the drippings, which are later used to make a light jus.

Past kitchen tests have shown that starting a bird breast-side down helps with even cooking (the legs get heat exposure and a head start, while the breast is shielded), and my findings concurred with these tests. I also agreed that dividing the roasting time (about one hour for a 4-pound bird) between two oven temperatures (375 and 450 degrees) yielded tender, moist meat and nice browning, two antithetical objectives. But I reversed the order. I started the chicken breast-side down at 450 and finished it breast-side up at 375. This way, the part of the bird that bore the brunt of the heat was the sturdier dark meat of the legs, not the delicate white breast meat, which proved to be more tender when exposed to more moderate temperatures.

Tasters agreed that a jus (a light sauce) was essential for adding more garlic and rosemary flavor to this dish. Liquid added to the roasting pan at the halfway point prevented the drippings from scorching so that a jus could be made from them.

I made a minor adjustment by adding a greater amount of liquid to reduce the risk of complete evaporation and then singeing. Though the liquid could be added at the outset instead of at the midpoint, it was unnecessary simply because it was not until the latter portion of roasting that the drippings tended to burn. Liquid in the roasting pan meant that the skin would not be ultracrisp, but there seemed little point in crisping the skin when a sauce would be moistening it just before serving.

Flavor Boosters

Applying a garlic and rosemary mixture beneath the skin in the style of most recipes is the best method of incorporating flavor (tossing whole garlic cloves and rosemary sprigs into the cavity did not work), but questions remained. First, should the garlic-rosemary mixture include a fat element, either butter or olive oil? It should. A fruity, aromatic olive oil (butter seemed out of place) helped in the distribution of the garlic and rosemary and also added flavor. I next tried preparing the garlic for the paste in a few different ways. To my surprise, the simplest method—calling for a modest 2 teaspoons of raw garlic—was pleasantly punchy and the uncontested favorite. Responding to comments that the rosemary was too pungent and piney, I pared it back to just 2 teaspoons minced and made the necessary adjustments to the amounts of olive oil, salt, and pepper. I distributed just a portion of this modest amount of aromatic paste under the skin of the breast and thigh areas. The remainder I rubbed into the cavity of the chicken to season the drippings that gathered within, which would flavor the jus. This judicious seasoning was key— the chicken met with success.

The chicken was good, but the resulting jus was lacking in depth. Chicken broth and a small amount of white wine helped, but, in keeping with the theme of this dish, a bit of garlic and rosemary was also required. Once again, I prepared the garlic in a number of different ways: I toasted it, sliced and sautéed it, minced and sautéed it, and incorporated raw garlic into the jus. Sweet, mellow slowly roasted garlic mashed to a paste took the honors. To circumvent roasting the garlic separately under its own cover, I tried tossing unpeeled cloves (about 10) into the roasting pan and roasting them beneath the chicken. There they became soft and creamy, and because they sat for some time in the liquid and drippings, their flavors permeated the jus. The only problem was that the garlic cloves were too darkly colored in spots, but that was easily remedied by adding the cloves to the roasting pan 15 minutes into cooking, giving them just 15 minutes of dry heat to brown before adding the liquid. As for the rosemary, one sprig added to the simmering liquid and discarded before serving provided just the right amount of flavor.

As a final jus enrichment, I whisked in a couple of tablespoons of butter, expecting it to add smooth, sweet flavor. Instead, it was an awkward addition, just as it had been earlier in testing. The jus was far better off without it. A mere sprinkling of fresh black pepper and my work was done. Here was a garlic-rosemary roast chicken with greatness and gusto, but not one that would outstay its welcome.

GARLIC-ROSEMARY ROAST CHICKEN WITH JUS
SERVES 3 TO 4

If the roasting pan is considerably larger than the chicken, keep an eye on the pan drippings; the greater surface area may mean more rapid evaporation and a risk of burnt drippings. Add water to the pan as necessary if the liquid evaporates.

Chicken and Brine
- 1/2 cup salt
- 10 unpeeled garlic cloves
- 3 rosemary sprigs
- 1 whole chicken (about 4 pounds), giblets discarded

Garlic-Rosemary Paste
- 2 teaspoons minced fresh rosemary leaves
- 2 medium garlic cloves, minced or press through garlic press (2 teaspoons)
- 1/8 teaspoon salt
  Ground black pepper
- 1 tablespoon extra-virgin olive oil, plus extra for brushing chicken

Jus
- 10 medium-large unpeeled garlic cloves
- 1/2 teaspoon extra-virgin olive oil
- 1 3/4 cups low-sodium chicken broth
- 1/2 cup water
- 1/4 cup dry white wine or vermouth
- 1 sprig fresh rosemary
  Salt and ground black pepper

1. FOR THE CHICKEN AND BRINE: Combine salt, garlic, and rosemary in zipper-lock bag; seal, pressing out air. Pound with meat pounder or rolling pin until garlic cloves are

crushed. Transfer mixture to large container or stockpot and stir in 2 cups hot tap water; let stand 10 minutes to release flavors. Add 1½ quarts cold tap water and stir until salt is dissolved. Submerge chicken in brine and refrigerate 1 hour.

2. Remove chicken from brine and pat dry with paper towels. Adjust oven rack to lower-middle

position and heat oven to 450 degrees. Set V-rack in small roasting pan and lightly spray rack with nonstick cooking spray.

3. FOR THE PASTE: Stir together rosemary, garlic, salt, ¼ teaspoon pepper, and 1 tablespoon oil in small bowl. Rub about 1½ teaspoons of paste in cavity of chicken. Carefully loosen skin

---

STEP-BY-STEP | APPLYING THE PASTE

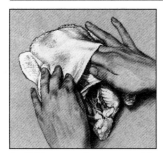 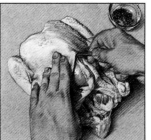 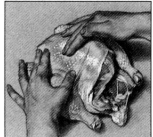

1. With your fingers, carefully loosen skin over breast and thigh.

2. Spoon some garlic-rosemary paste under skin on each side of breast.

3. With your fingers on top of skin, work paste to distribute it over breast and thigh.

SCIENCE: ## Why Brining Works

Many have attributed the added juiciness of brined chicken to osmosis—the flow of water across a barrier from a place with a higher water concentration (the brine) to a place with a lower one (the chicken). I decided to test this explanation. If osmosis is in fact the source of the added juiciness of brined meat, I reasoned, then a bucket of pure unsalted water should add moisture at least as well as a brine, because water alone has the highest water concentration possible: 100 percent. After soaking one chicken in brine and another in water for the same amount of time, I found that both had gained moisture, about 6 percent by weight. Satisfied that osmosis was indeed the force driving the addition of moisture to meat during brining, I roasted the two birds, along with a third straight out of the package. I would soon discover that osmosis was not the only reason why brined meat cooked up juicy.

During roasting, the chicken taken straight from the package lost 18 percent of its original weight, and the chicken soaked in water lost 12 percent of its presoak weight. Remarkably, the brined bird shed only a mere 7 percent of its starting weight. Looking at my test results, I realized that the benefit of brining could not be explained by osmosis alone. Salt, too, was playing a crucial role by aiding in the retention of water.

Table salt is made up of two ions, sodium and chloride, that are oppositely charged. Proteins, such as those in meat, are large molecules that contain a mosaic of charges, negative and positive. When proteins are placed in a solution containing salt, they readjust their shape to accommodate the opposing charges. This rearrangement of the protein

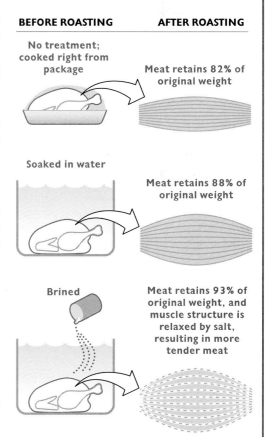

BEFORE ROASTING   **AFTER ROASTING**

No treatment; cooked right from package

Meat retains 82% of original weight

Soaked in water

Meat retains 88% of original weight

Brined

Meat retains 93% of original weight, and muscle structure is relaxed by salt, resulting in more tender meat

molecules compromises the structural integrity of the meat, reducing its overall toughness. It also creates gaps that fill up with water. The added salt makes the water less likely to evaporate during cooking, and the result is meat that is both juicy and tender.

—John Olson, Science Editor

RECIPE SHORTHAND: CARVING MADE EASY

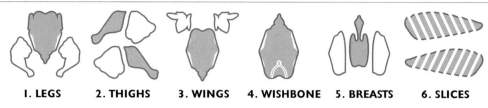

I. LEGS   **2. THIGHS**   **3. WINGS**   **4. WISHBONE**   **5. BREASTS**   **6. SLICES**

I. Legs: Cut legs from body. **2. Thighs:** Cut thighs from drumsticks at joints. **3. Wings:** Pull wings out from body and cut. **4. Wishbone:** Lift neck skin and cut out wishbone. **5. Breasts:** Cut along breastbone and remove breasts. **6. Slice:** Cut breasts crosswise into ½-inch slices.

over breast and thigh on each side; slip half of remaining paste under skin on each side of breast, then, using fingers, distribute paste over breast and thigh by rubbing surface of skin (see illustrations 1 through 3, page 11). Tie ends of drumsticks together with kitchen twine and tuck wings behind back. Rub all sides of chicken with 2 teaspoons oil and season with pepper. Set chicken breast-side down on prepared V-rack and roast 15 minutes.

4. **FOR THE JUS:** While chicken is roasting, toss garlic cloves with ½ teaspoon oil; after chicken has roasted 15 minutes, scatter cloves in pan and continue to roast 15 minutes longer.

5. Remove roasting pan from oven; decrease oven temperature to 375 degrees. Using tongs or wads of paper towels, rotate chicken breast-side up; brush breast with 1 teaspoon oil. Add 1 cup broth and ½ cup water to pan and continue to roast until chicken is medium golden brown and instant-read thermometer inserted into thickest part of breast and thigh registers about 160 and 175 degrees, respectively, adding more water to roasting pan if liquid evaporates. Tip V-rack to allow juices in cavity to run into roasting pan. Transfer chicken to large plate.

6. Remove garlic cloves to cutting board. Using wooden spoon, scrape up browned bits in roasting pan and pour liquid into 2-cup liquid measuring cup. Allow liquid to settle; meanwhile, peel garlic and mash to paste with fork. Using soup spoon, skim fat off surface of liquid (you should have about ⅔ cup skimmed liquid; if not, supplement with water). Transfer liquid to small saucepan, then add wine, rosemary sprig, remaining ¾ cup broth, and garlic paste; simmer over medium-high heat, until reduced to about 1 cup, about 8 minutes. Add accumulated juices from chicken and discard rosemary sprig; adjust seasonings with salt and pepper to taste. Carve chicken and serve with jus.

GARLIC-ROSEMARY ROAST CHICKEN WITH POTATOES

In this variation, the jus is omitted and the potatoes roast in the flavorful drippings. The roasted garlic cloves can be spread on bread and eaten alongside the chicken.

Follow recipe for Garlic-Rosemary Roast Chicken with Jus through step 3, omitting jus ingredients (and step 4). During first 15 minutes of roasting, quarter 1½ pounds 2-inch red or Yukon Gold potatoes; toss potatoes, 10 medium-large unpeeled garlic cloves, 1½ tablespoons extra-virgin olive oil, and ¼ teaspoon each salt and pepper in medium bowl. After chicken has roasted 15 minutes, scatter potatoes and garlic in single layer in roasting pan; roast for another 15 minutes. Continue with recipe from step 5, omitting the addition of liquid to roasting pan and stirring potatoes after rotating chicken; when chicken is done, do not tip V-rack with roast chicken to allow juices to run into roasting pan. While chicken rests, transfer potatoes and garlic to large paper towel–lined plate and pat with additional paper towels. Carve chicken and serve with potatoes and garlic.

TESTING EQUIPMENT: Countertop Rotisserie Ovens

Disembodied meat rotating slowly and mechanically in an illuminated vitrine smacks of the macabre. Conveniently, a countertop rotisserie oven can serve up, it seems, both dinner and a show. A more compelling sales pitch, I suppose, would be that of the manufacturers. They herald rotisserie ovens as the easy means to flavorful, juicy, perfectly cooked, lower-fat, and generally glorious food. Skeptics like us are not easily sold, however, so we got our hands on five countertop rotisserie ovens to see what they were capable of.

In each oven, we roasted a whole brined chicken, a 4-pound beef rib roast, and a pork tenderloin. Then we selected one recipe from the instruction manual that came with each machine and cooked it in its respective oven. While we found that the two ovens with a horizontal spit did a better job roasting chickens than did vertical roasters (the chickens seemed more moist and more flavorful), overall we could find little to recommend a countertop rotisserie oven of any type.

The two horizontal roasters were the George Jr. Rotisserie and the Ronco Showtime Jr. (both available for $100). The chickens cooked in these ovens were decent, but the lurid, ashen pork tenderloins were entirely unappetizing and nearly tasteless. The beef rib roasts browned beautifully, but when cut into revealed egregiously uneven cooking: The perimeters were well done, while the very core of each roast was medium. Demerits were given to the George Jr. oven for making loading and cleaning very difficult, for directing us to secure our 4-pound beef rib roast in an 8-inch-square by 2¼-inch-deep basket (an impossible fit; the roast had to go directly on the spit), and for proffering a lousy recipe for Dijon mustard steaks. Because the Ronco Showtime Jr. did a slightly better job roasting the chicken, because it was easier to load, unload, and clean, and because Ron's Spicy Lemon Pepper Chicken Wings were surprisingly good, we thought it the best of the lot.

The others, all vertical roasters, were the Betty Crocker BCF6000 Vertical Rotisserie Vertisserie Plus ($100), the Farberware Vertical Rotisserie ($75), and the Sunbeam Carousel Rotisserie ($80). The first two looked surprisingly similar and were the simplest to use, while the Sunbeam was the most awkward. None of these three excelled at any cooking task or equaled the performance of the Ronco or George Jr. models. The Sunbeam, however, provided entertainment: Several spectators were positively captivated by the pirouetting "spit-roasted cobra"—baby-back ribs—threaded on the central skewer in a serpentine "S" shape. —D.Y.

Best in Show
RONCO Showtime Jr.

Second Best
GEORGE JR.
Rotisserie

A Flawed Contestant
BETTY CROCKER BCF6000
Vertisserie Plus

Another Flawed Contestant
FARBERWARE Vertical
Rotisserie

An Entertaining Loser
SUNBEAM Carousel
Rotisserie

Pasta with Sun-Dried Tomatoes

Sun-dried tomatoes can be dry and overpowering. We set out to solve both problems.

BY ERIN MCMURRER

A child star of the 1990s, the sun-dried tomato rarely finds its way onto restaurant menus these days. That's a shame, because at their best, sun-dried tomatoes are meaty, sweet, chewy, and bright tasting. Unfortunately, most people remember them as parched and leathery or overmarinated and overpowering. I wanted to see if I could breathe some life (and moisture) into this handy source of tomato flavor and pair it with pasta.

Sun-dried tomatoes are available dried, like raisins, or packed in oil with flavorings. Many of the dried tomatoes, which, like dried mushrooms, must be hydrated in hot water before being used, tasted too salty, bitter, strong, or musty, and their texture was either mushy or tough. The jarred contestants had a pleasant chewy consistency, similar to that of plump raisins, but got low marks for the poor quality of their packing oil, the heavy hand taken with the spices, or their astringent flavor. All in all, however, the jarred tomatoes were superior to the jerky-like dried versions.

The first step was to drain and rinse the tomatoes to rid them of their universally unpleasant marinades. Even rinsed of marinade, sun-dried tomatoes pack a lot of flavor and so are best partnered with equally assertive ingredients, such as olives, garlic, anchovies, arugula, and capers. Rich cheeses and good olive oil balance these feisty flavors. I also cut the tomatoes into small pieces to tame their presence.

PASTA WITH SUN-DRIED TOMATOES, RICOTTA, AND PEAS

SERVES 4 TO 6

Oil-packed sun-dried tomatoes are sold in jars of different sizes. One 8½-ounce jar is enough for any of the following recipes.

- 1 pound medium shells
- Salt
- 1 cup (4 ounces) frozen peas
- 2 medium garlic cloves, minced or pressed through garlic press (2 teaspoons)
- 2 tablespoons olive oil
- ¼ teaspoon red pepper flakes
- 12 ounces (1½ cups) whole milk ricotta
- 1 cup drained oil-packed sun-dried tomatoes (one 8½-ounce jar; see note), rinsed, patted dry, and chopped coarse
- ¼ cup grated Parmesan, plus additional for serving
- 2 teaspoons chopped fresh mint leaves
- Ground black pepper

1. Bring 4 quarts water to rolling boil, covered, in stockpot. Stir in pasta and 1 tablespoon salt; cook until al dente, adding peas in last 15 seconds of cooking. Drain, reserving ¾ cup cooking water, and return pasta and peas to stockpot.

2. Meanwhile, heat garlic, oil, and red pepper flakes in small skillet over medium heat; cook until sizzling but not browned, about 1 minute. Set skillet aside to cool slightly. Stir together ricotta, sun-dried tomatoes, Parmesan, mint, ½ teaspoon salt, ¼ teaspoon pepper, and garlic/oil mixture in bowl. Stir pasta cooking water into ricotta mixture; add ricotta mixture to pasta in pot and stir well to combine. Serve immediately, passing additional Parmesan separately.

PASTA WITH ARUGULA, GOAT CHEESE, AND SUN-DRIED TOMATO PESTO

SERVES 4 TO 6

Crisp fried capers make an excellent garnish for this dish. See Kitchen Notes, page 30, for instructions.

- 1 cup drained oil-packed sun-dried tomatoes (one 8½-ounce jar), rinsed, patted dry, and chopped very coarse
- 6 tablespoons extra-virgin olive oil
- ¼ cup walnuts, toasted in small dry skillet over medium heat until fragrant, about 6 minutes
- 1 small garlic clove, minced or pressed through garlic press (about ½ teaspoon)
- ¾ ounce (½ cup) grated Parmesan
- Salt and ground black pepper
- 1 pound campanelle or farfalle
- 1 medium bunch arugula (about 10 ounces), washed, dried, stemmed, and cut into 1-inch lengths (about 6 cups)
- 3 ounces goat cheese

1. In food processor, pulse sun-dried tomatoes, oil, walnuts, garlic, Parmesan, ½ teaspoon salt, and ⅛ teaspoon pepper until smooth, about fifteen 2-second pulses, scraping down bowl as needed. Transfer to small bowl and set aside.

2. Bring 4 quarts water to rolling boil, covered, in stockpot. Stir in pasta and 1 tablespoon salt; cook until al dente. Drain, reserving ¾ cup cooking water, and return pasta to stockpot; immediately stir in arugula until wilted. Stir pasta cooking water into pesto; stir pesto into pasta. Serve immediately, dotting individual bowls with ½-inch pieces goat cheese.

PASTA WITH GREEN OLIVE–SUN-DRIED TOMATO SAUCE AND TOASTED BREAD CRUMBS

SERVES 4 TO 6

- 2 slices (about 2 ounces) white sandwich bread, crusts removed, bread torn into quarters
- 1 teaspoon plus 2 tablespoons extra-virgin olive oil
- 1 pound spaghetti
- Salt
- 3 medium garlic cloves, minced or pressed through garlic press (about 1 tablespoon)
- ¼ teaspoon red pepper flakes
- 3 anchovy fillets, chopped fine
- 1 can (14½ ounces) diced tomatoes, drained, ½ cup juice reserved, tomatoes chopped fine
- 1 cup drained oil-packed sun-dried tomatoes (one 8½-ounce jar), rinsed, patted dry, and chopped fine
- 1 cup finely chopped green olives
- 1 tablespoon chopped fresh parsley leaves

1. Process bread in food processor to evenly fine crumbs, about 10 seconds (you should have about 1 cup); transfer to medium nonstick skillet and toss with 1 teaspoon oil. Set skillet over medium heat and cook, stirring occasionally, until crisp and golden, about 6 minutes. Transfer to small bowl; wipe out skillet.

2. Bring 4 quarts water to rolling boil, covered, in stockpot. Stir in pasta and 1 tablespoon salt; cook until al dente. Drain and return pasta to pot.

3. Meanwhile, combine remaining 2 tablespoons oil, garlic, red pepper flakes, and anchovies in now-empty skillet; set over medium-low heat and cook, stirring frequently, until garlic is fragrant but not browned, about 3 minutes. Stir in canned tomatoes and cook, stirring frequently, until slightly thickened and dry, about 5 minutes. Stir in sun-dried tomatoes, olives, and reserved tomato juice; cook until heated through, about 1 minute. Stir sauce and parsley into pasta in pot. Serve immediately, sprinkling individual bowls with portion of bread crumbs.

COOK'S EXTRA gives you free recipes online. For Pasta with Sun-Dried Tomatoes, Cauliflower, and Thyme-Infused Cream, visit www.cooksillustrated.com and key in code 1041. It will be available until February 15, 2004.

Hearty Lentil Soup

Does a bowl of lentil soup sound about as inspiring as a serving of instant oatmeal? We set out to put the taste and texture back into this simple dish.

⇒ BY ELIZABETH GERMAIN ⇐

Run-of-the-mill lentil soup always reminds me of the scene from the film *Oliver!* when Oliver Twist begs, "Please, sir, may I have some more?" The problem, of course, is that no one who isn't truly, deeply hungry would ask for a second helping of the thin slop or flavorless mud that often passes for this common soup. Even a picture-perfect bowlful of lentil soup can be an illusion because it still may have no flavor whatsoever. Yet this earthy dish ought to be a winner. It's cheap, it's quick, and it tastes just fine—maybe even better—the next day. I was determined to develop a master recipe for my cold weather repertoire that would be a keeper. I wanted a hearty lentil soup worthy of a second bowl.

I started by preparing five representative recipes, and two discoveries quickly came to light. First, garlic, herbs, onions, and tomatoes are common denominators. Second, texture is a big issue. None of my tasters liked the soup that was brothy or, at the other extreme, the one that was as thick as porridge. They also gave a big thumbs down to those that looked like brown split pea soup. Consequently, recipes that included carrots, tomatoes, and herbs were rewarded for their brighter colors (and flavors). There was also a clear preference for the subtle, smoky depth meat provides. The next step was to determine which lentils to buy and how to cook them.

Lentil Lessons

Brown, green, and red lentils are the most common choices on supermarket shelves. At specialty markets and natural food stores, you can also find black lentils and French green lentils (lentils du Puy), the latter being the darling of chefs everywhere. In addition to color differences, lentils can be divided according to their size—large or small—and to whether they are split, like peas, or not. Ordinary brown and green lentils are large, while red, black, and lentils du Puy are small. Red lentils are often sold split and are used most frequently in Indian dishes such as dal.

A bowl of lentil soup can actually be inspiring—that is, if you know the secret to preserving the texture of the lentils.

To make some sense of all of this, I made five pots of lentil soup, each one using a different colored lentil. Red lentils were out—they disintegrated when simmered. All four of the remaining choices produced an acceptable texture, but tasters preferred, as expected, the earthy flavor and firm texture of the lentils du Puy. To our surprise, however, the larger green and brown lentils fared reasonably well, exceeding the low expectations of the test kitchen. (For more details on this tasting, see "Lentils 101" at right.)

Next, I set out to test cooking methods. Some recipes call for soaking the lentils for a few hours before cooking. Not only did I determine that this step was entirely unnecessary—lentils cook up rather quickly—but I also discovered that soaking increases the likelihood of a mushy texture. Even without soaking, some varieties, especially the large brown and green lentils, have a greater tendency to fall apart if overcooked,

TASTING: **Lentils 101**

Lentils come in various sizes and colors, and the differences in flavor and texture are surprisingly distinct. I asked tasters to evaluate five kinds of lentils in my soup, rating them in terms of taste, texture, and appearance. Here's what we found, with the lentils listed in order of preference. –E.G.

Lentils du Puy These lentils are smaller than the more common brown and green varieties. While they take their name from the city of Puy in central France, they are also grown in North America and Italy. Dark olive green, almost black, in color, with mottling, these lentils were praised for their "rich, earthy, complex flavor" and "firm yet tender texture."

Black Lentils Like lentils du Puy, black lentils are slightly smaller than the standard brown lentils. They have a deep black hue that tasters likened to the color of caviar. In fact, some markets refer to them as beluga lentils. Tasters liked their "robust, earthy flavor" and "ability to hold their shape while remaining tender." A few tasters found the color of the soup made with them "too dark and muddy."

Brown Lentils These larger lentils are the most common choice in the market and are a uniform drab brown. Tasters commented on their "mild yet light and earthy flavor." Some found their texture "creamy," while others complained that they were "chalky." But everyone agreed that they held their shape and were tender inside.

Green Lentils Another larger lentil, this variety is the same size as the brown lentil and is greenish-brown in color. Although tasters accepted the "mild flavor" of these lentils and liked the way they "retain their shape while being tender," most complained that the soup made from them was "a bit anemic looking."

Red Lentils These small orange-red lentils "completely disintegrate when cooked." They made a soup that looked "anemic."

even for just a few minutes. Searching for a way to avoid this problem, I employed a common Indian culinary trick: sweating the lentils in a covered pan with aromatic vegetables prior to adding the liquid. Using brown lentils, I cooked up two batches and, bingo, I had solved the problem! The sweated lentils remained intact, while the unsweated lentils had broken down.

To better understand this phenomenon, I set up a series of tests with our staff science editor, John Olson. We sweated one batch of lentils with just onions and carrots. In the second batch, we added salt, and in the third batch we added vinegar to test the role of acids. The results were clear. The first batch—without any salt or acid—was the worst, with a very mushy texture. The lentils sweated with salt were the most intact; the vinegar helped keep the lentils firm, but it was not as effective as the salt (at least in amounts that would taste good). Why did we get these results? When legumes are cooked, pectin-like compounds break down into a gelatinous goo similar to jam. Salt and acids (such as those found in vinegar or canned tomatoes) reinforce the original insoluble pectic compounds and retard their conversion to gel. Sweating lentils with bacon, canned tomatoes, and salt (as well as aromatic vegetables and herbs) not only ensured an ideal texture but boosted the flavor of the legumes as well.

One issue concerning texture remained. Tasters wanted a chunkier soup and did not like the brothy base. I tried pureeing a few cups of the soup and then adding it back to the pot. Tasters praised the contrast of the now creamy base with the whole lentils and found the entire soup more interesting.

Flavor Development

Pork was the meat of choice in all of the recipes I examined. I found that the lentils cooked too quickly to extract the smoky flavor that a ham bone or hock can impart. Prosciutto and pancetta were too mild. Tasters preferred the smoky flavor of bacon and liked the textural addition of the bacon bits. Another advantage bacon offered was rendered fat. I used it to sauté the vegetables and aromatics, which further infused the soup with smoky flavor.

From early testing, I knew that onions, carrots, garlic, and tomatoes were a given for flavor and color. When crushed or pureed tomatoes were added to the pot, the soup took on the dispiriting color of tomato sauce. Tasters preferred drained diced tomatoes, which allowed the lentils to remain center-stage. Turnips were out of place, and potatoes were too starchy. Tasters also rejected celery, saying its flavor was too prominent. Bay leaves, thyme, and parsley rounded out

the other flavors and added a touch of bright green to the pot.

Last, but not least, was the question of liquids. I prepared two batches, one with water and one with chicken broth. Neither was ideal. Water produced a soup that was not as rich in flavor as desired, while the broth-only version tasted too much like chicken soup. After several more tests, I concluded that a mix of 3 parts broth to 1 part water produced a hearty depth of flavor without being overpowering.

Now the flavor of my soup was good, but it was missing that final extra touch. I turned to ingredients to brighten the soup and found that dry white wine worked wonders. Because the acidic wine had noticeably improved the soup, I tried one final adjustment. Many recipes call for the addition of vinegar or lemon juice just before the soup is served. I stirred a touch of balsamic vinegar into the pot at completion, and tasters gave this soup a perfect 10.

With my master recipe complete, I developed a few variations. Stirring a hefty amount of spinach into the pot at the end of cooking created a popular version: lentil soup with greens. For a spicier and more exotic rendition, I added some of the aromatic spices used in North African cooking—cumin, coriander, cinnamon, and cayenne—and substituted cilantro for the parsley and lemon juice for the vinegar. Now my tasters came up and asked, "Please, Elizabeth, may I have some more?"

HEARTY LENTIL SOUP
MAKES ABOUT 2 QUARTS, SERVING 4 TO 6

Lentils du Puy, sometimes called French green lentils, are our first choice for this recipe, but brown, black, or regular green lentils are fine, too. Note that cooking times will vary depending on the type of lentils used. Lentils lose flavor with age, and because most packaged lentils do not have expiration dates, try to buy them from a store that specializes in natural foods and grains. Before use, rinse and then carefully sort through the lentils to remove small stones and pebbles. The soup can be made in advance. After adding

the vinegar in step 2, cool the soup to room temperature and refrigerate it in an airtight container for up to 2 days. To serve, heat it over medium-low until hot, then stir in the parsley.

3	slices bacon (about 3 ounces), cut into ¼-inch pieces
1	large onion, chopped fine (about 1½ cups)
2	medium carrots, peeled and chopped medium (about 1 cup)
3	medium garlic cloves, minced or pressed through garlic press (about 1 tablespoon)
1	can (14½ ounces) diced tomatoes, drained
1	bay leaf
1	teaspoon minced fresh thyme leaves
1	cup (7 ounces) lentils, rinsed and picked over
1	teaspoon salt
	Ground black pepper
½	cup dry white wine
4½	cups low-sodium chicken broth
1½	cups water
1½	teaspoons balsamic vinegar
3	tablespoons minced fresh parsley leaves

1. Fry bacon in large stockpot or Dutch oven over medium-high heat, stirring occasionally, until fat is rendered and bacon is crisp, 3 to 4 minutes. Add onion and carrots; cook, stirring occasionally, until vegetables begin to soften, about 2 minutes. Add garlic and cook until fragrant, about 30 seconds. Stir in tomatoes, bay leaf, and thyme; cook until fragrant, about 30 seconds. Stir in lentils, salt, and pepper to taste; cover, reduce heat to medium-low, and cook until vegetables are softened and lentils have darkened, 8 to 10 minutes. Uncover, increase heat to high, add wine, and bring to simmer. Add chicken broth and water; bring to boil, cover partially, and reduce heat to low. Simmer until lentils are tender but still hold their shape, 30 to 35 minutes; discard bay leaf.

2. Puree 3 cups soup in blender until smooth, then return to pot; stir in vinegar and heat soup over medium-low until hot, about 5 minutes. Stir in 2 tablespoons parsley and serve, garnishing each bowl with some of remaining parsley.

HEARTY LENTIL SOUP WITH SPINACH

Follow recipe for Hearty Lentil Soup, replacing parsley with 5 ounces baby spinach. Continue to heat soup, stirring frequently, until spinach is wilted, about 3 minutes; serve.

HEARTY LENTIL SOUP WITH FRAGRANT SPICES

Follow recipe for Hearty Lentil Soup, adding 1 teaspoon ground cumin, 1 teaspoon ground coriander, 1 teaspoon ground cinnamon, and ¼ teaspoon cayenne along with garlic; substitute lemon juice for balsamic vinegar and minced fresh cilantro for parsley.

A Good Sweat (Makes a Difference)

FIRM LENTILS   MUSHY LENTILS

Sweating the lentils in the presence of salt and acids (from canned tomatoes) retards the conversion of pectin-like compounds to a gel. Once sweated, these lentils easily remain intact during a long simmer in broth (as seen on the left) while becoming tender on the inside. Lentils simmered without first being sweated fall apart (as seen on the right) if overcooked.

Better & Quicker Homemade Stock

We devised a formula for great homemade stock that won't take an entire day to make. BY REBECCA HAYS

Restaurant chefs adhere to time-consuming, involved routines for making chicken and beef stocks. Bones, meat, and mirepoix (onions, carrots, and celery) are first oven-roasted or sautéed on the stovetop. A bouquet garni (a bundle of several fresh herbs) and water are added, and the stock simmers, uncovered, for hours, with the cook periodically skimming off impurities. For clarity, a raft (beaten egg whites and sometimes ground meat) might be added to trap sediment. Finally, the stock is strained, cooled, and defatted.

This method is fine for professional cooks with the inclination to tend to a simmering pot all day, and it does yield rich, deeply flavored stock. But most home cooks don't want (or need) to follow such a complicated regimen. We've developed new techniques and helpful tips for making stock with great flavor while requiring fewer ingredients, less work, and less time than the classic method.

USING THE RIGHT EQUIPMENT

You don't need to make a huge investment in equipment to produce a good stock, but a few tools make the process easier.

Strainer: A stock made with hacked bones will contain minute bone particles and splinters and must be strained. A fine-mesh strainer is ideal for this job. Liquids must be strained into a clean bowl or pot. The sturdy, deep, relatively narrow bowl of a standing mixer is a perfect receptacle.

Dutch oven or stockpot: Stock should be made in a pot large enough to accommodate plenty of bones, meat, aromatics, and water. Whether you use a Dutch oven or stockpot, choose a lidded pot with a capacity of at least 8 quarts.

Colander: Before straining the stock, transfer bones and large pieces of meat to a colander. This helps to prevent splashing when pouring the liquid through the strainer. Any type of colander will do—just be sure to place it over a bowl.

Meat cleaver: Hacking chicken parts into small pieces allows their flavorful juices to release quickly into the stock, significantly reducing the total simmering time. Rather than risk damaging your chef's knife, use a meat cleaver, which is designed to cut through bones.

Skimmer: A skimmer is a wide, flat, perforated spoon with a long handle. It is the best tool for skimming impurities and foam that rise to the surface of a stock as it cooks. If a skimmer is not available, a large slotted spoon works well, too.

ILLUSTRATION: JOHN BURGOYNE

USING THE RIGHT INGREDIENTS

Choosing Chicken

In kitchen tests, we found that stocks made with kosher or premium chickens (we like Bell & Evans) tasted better and had more body than stocks made with mass-market birds. Our advice: If you have a favorite chicken for roasting, use it for stock.

Cutting Up Chicken Parts: Chicken hacked into small pieces with a meat cleaver will give up its flavor in record time. To cut through bone, place your hand near the far end of the meat cleaver handle, curling your fingers securely around it in a fist. Handle the cleaver the way you would a hammer, holding your wrist stiff and straight and letting the weight of the blade's front tip lead the force of the chop.

Choosing Beef

We made six stocks with six different cuts of beef, including the chuck, shanks, the round, arm blades, oxtails, and short ribs. We added marrowbones to the boneless cuts to establish an equal meat-to-bone ratio in each pot and simmered the bone-in cuts as is. Tasters liked the stock made from shanks best. In addition to using the right cut, we found that the best stock is made with a lot of beef. Most recipes skimp on the beef but we found that a full six pounds of shanks is required to make two quarts of rich-tasting stock.

Cutting Meat from Shank Bones: Cut the meat away from the shank bone into large 2-inch chunks.

QUICKER CHICKEN OR BEEF STOCK, STEP BY STEP

1. Sauté. Onions are a must for any stock, but cooking tests proved that carrots and celery aren't vital.

2. Sweat. Browning the chicken or beef and then sweating it (cooking over low heat in a covered pot) allows the meat to quickly release its rich, flavorful juices and greatly reduces the simmering time.

3. Simmer. Add boiling water (to jump-start the cooking process), bay leaves (other herbs don't add much flavor), and salt.

4. Skim. Skimming away the foam that rises to the surface of beef stock significantly improves its flavor. Skimming chicken stock will make it clearer, but the flavor improvement is less noticeable.

5. Strain. Once the flavor has been extracted from the stock ingredients, a skimmer or slotted spoon can be used to remove them to a colander. Then pour the stock through a fine-mesh strainer or a colander lined with cheesecloth.

6. Defat. After stock has been refrigerated, the fat hardens on the surface and is very easy to remove with a spoon. To defat hot stock, we recommend using a ladle or a fat separator (see pages 28–29).

FREEZING STOCK EFFICIENTLY

Ladle cooled stock into nonstick muffin tins and freeze. When the stock is frozen, twist the muffin tin just as you would twist an ice tray. Place the frozen blocks in a zipper-lock plastic bag and seal it tightly.

1. An alternative is to pour stock into a coffee mug lined with a quart-sized plastic zipper-lock bag.
2. Place the filled bags flat in a large, shallow roasting pan and freeze. Once the stock is solidly frozen, the bags can be removed from the pan and stored in the freezer.

STOCK RECIPES

Both of the following stocks can be refrigerated in airtight containers for up to 4 days or frozen for 4 to 6 months. Each recipe makes about 2 quarts.

QUICK CHICKEN STOCK

- 1 tablespoon vegetable oil
- 1 medium onion, chopped medium
- 4 pounds whole chicken legs or backs and wingtips, cut into 2-inch pieces
- 2 quarts boiling water
- ½ teaspoon salt
- 2 bay leaves

INSTRUCTIONS:
Heat oil in large stockpot or Dutch oven over medium-high heat until shimmering but not smoking; add onion and cook until slightly softened, 2 to 3 minutes. Transfer to large bowl. Brown chicken in 2 batches, cooking on each side until lightly browned, about 5 minutes per side; transfer to bowl with onions. Return chicken and onion to pot and reduce heat to low; cover and sweat until chicken releases juices, about 20 minutes. Increase heat to high; add boiling water, salt, and bay leaves. Bring to boil, then reduce heat to low; cover and simmer slowly until stock is rich and flavorful, about 20 minutes, skimming foam off surface, if desired. Strain; discard solids. Before using, defat stock.

RICH BEEF STOCK

Red wine, used to deglaze the pan after browning the beef, adds an extra layer of flavor. To extract maximum flavor and body from the meat and bones, beef stock must be simmered much longer than chicken stock.

- 2 tablespoons vegetable oil
- 1 large onion, chopped medium
- 6 pounds beef shanks, meat cut from bone in large chunks, or 4 pounds beef chuck, cut into 3-inch chunks, and 2 pounds small marrowbones
- ½ cup dry red wine
- 2 quarts boiling water
- ½ teaspoon salt
- 2 bay leaves

INSTRUCTIONS:
Heat 1 tablespoon oil in large stockpot or Dutch oven over medium-high heat until shimmering but not smoking; add onion and cook, stirring occasionally, until slightly softened, 2 to 3 minutes. Transfer to large bowl. Brown meat and bones on all sides in 3 or 4 batches, about 5 minutes per batch, adding remaining oil to pot as necessary; do not overcrowd pot. Transfer browned meat and bones to bowl with onion. Add wine to empty pot; cook, scraping up browned bits with wooden spoon, until wine is reduced to about 3 tablespoons, about 2 minutes. Return browned beef and onion to pot, reduce heat to low, cover, and sweat until meat releases juices, about 20 minutes. Increase heat to high, add boiling water, salt, and bay leaves; bring to boil, then reduce heat to low, cover, and simmer slowly until meat is tender and stock is flavorful, 1½ to 2 hours, skimming foam off surface. Strain and discard bones and onion; reserve meat for another use, if desired. Before using, defat stock.

Fish Meunière

This simple French restaurant classic deserves a place in the repertoire of any good home cook. . . . Or does it?

⋗ BY ELIZABETH GERMAIN ⋖

Fish meunière is a deceptively easy French restaurant dish that ought to serve as a model recipe for home cooking. Ideally, fillets are dredged lightly in flour (no need for eggs or bread crumbs) and cooked on the stovetop until a golden crust forms, leaving the inside moist and flavorful. A brown butter sauce seasoned with lemon is then poured over the fish. What could be simpler, more delicious, or better suited to a Tuesday night dinner? That's what I thought, too, before I cooked a few test batches to get a handle on the technique for making this dish. What I got were plates of pale, soggy fillets in pools of greasy sauce—that is, if the fish hadn't stuck to the pan or fallen apart as I tried to plate it. Despite these failures (or maybe because of them), one thing did become clear. The simplicity of this dish makes it imperative that everything be prepared and cooked just so.

Taking a closer look at my initial meunière recipes (the term *meunière* refers to "miller's wife," a nod to the flour in the recipe), it was no wonder that I had found little success at the stove. Some recipes called for almost two sticks of butter for 2 pounds of fish. Who wants to eat fish literally swimming in fat? My tasters didn't. Other recipes failed in browning the fish, and the resulting fillets were soggy and white. It was time to go back to basics.

Preparing the Fish

Whole Dover sole—a variety of white flatfish—is the most authentic choice, but this fish is hard to come by and prohibitively expensive when it can be had, and a whole fish is hard to prepare. I opted instead for filleted white flatfish that would be available in most markets, thinking that sole or flounder would be the best choice. That said, I soon became aware of a veritable parade of choices—gray sole, lemon sole, yellowtail flounder, southern flounder, summer flounder, winter flounder, petrale sole, rex sole, rock sole, and starry flounder. After cooking 20 pounds of flatfish, I discovered that variety didn't much matter (tasters approved of them all); what counted were the thickness of the fillet and its freshness. If the fillet was thinner than ⅜ inch, it was nearly

This quick fish dish—served with a browned butter and lemon sauce—relies on precise technique and timing.

impossible to brown it without overcooking the inside. Fillets that were ⅜ inch thick or slightly more were perfect. They weighed 5 to 6 ounces each, and their length fit easily into a large skillet. Fillets weighing 7 to 10 ounces were acceptable, although they required cutting and trimming.

Tiny things can make a big difference, I learned, as I focused next on preparing the fish for the pan. For one, a thin coat of flour speeds up the browning, which is a particularly useful thing to know when you've got thin fish that cooks quickly. Straight from the fishmonger's wrapping paper, fish fillets are pretty wet. They must be patted dry or the flour will become thick and gluey. Simply dredging the dried fillets in flour presented problems. Excess flour fell off the fish and into the pan, where it burned. Shaking off the extra flour before cooking solves this problem. Still, even after a quick shake, the fillets cooked up with blotchy, browned crusts that did nothing for the flavor of the fish.

I then tried a technique used by Julia Child,

who recommends seasoning the fillets with salt and pepper and letting them sit before dredging. After 5 minutes, the fillets had begun to glisten with moisture. I then dredged them with flour, shook off the excess, and cooked them. "Perfectly seasoned and evenly coated" was the uniform thumbs-up response from tasters. Why does letting the seasoned fish rest for five minutes make such a difference? The salt extracts water from the fish, not so much as to make it wet but just enough to give it a thin coating of moisture that helps to ensure a perfectly even coating of flour. Without "bald spots" in the flouring, the fish browns evenly and tastes better.

Pan-Frying

The technique of pan-frying employs a heavy skillet and a good amount of fat. The food is cooked in a single layer as the cook waits patiently for it to brown, turning it once and then waiting again. The temptation is to lift up the food and take a peek, but it is essential to resist this impulse. For maximum browning (and to keep the fish from falling apart), the fish must be left alone as it cooks.

I found that traditional skillets did not work well. No matter how much fat I used, the fish had a tendency to stick. Nonstick skillets, on the other hand, worked well every time, producing beautifully browned fillets without sticking. A 12-inch skillet is a must, I discovered, and even then I could fit only two fillets at a time without having them overlap. I wanted my recipe to serve four, but using two skillets side-by-side seemed unreasonable. Instead, I opted to cook the fish in two batches, using a warmed plate in a 200-degree preheated oven to keep the first batch hot.

Clarified butter, or butter with the milk solids removed, is the traditional fat used by the French. Not only does clarified butter lend a rich flavor to the fish, but it has a higher smoking point (and thus burns less easily) than whole butter. Clarifying butter is easy, but it is too lengthy a process for a quick midweek entrée. Would tasters notice its absence? I cooked one batch with canola oil and another with clarified butter, and even my least discerning tasters noticed the difference. Whole butter burned, but a mixture of oil

FLIPPING FISH FILLETS

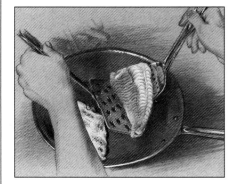

To easily turn fish fillets without breaking them, use two spatulas—a regular model and an extrawide version especially designed for fish. (In the test kitchen, we use a spatula that is 8½ inches wide by 3¼ inches deep for this job.) Using the regular spatula, gently lift the long side of the fillet. Then, supporting the fillet with the extrawide spatula, flip it so that the browned side faces up.

and butter, a classic combination, did the trick.

Next, I experimented with the amount of fat. Although recipes ranged from 1 to 6 tablespoons (for two fillets), I found that 2 tablespoons were ample, especially in a nonstick skillet. At this point, because I was using so little fat, I was technically sautéing rather than pan-frying. I began by cooking the fillets over low heat, but the results were mediocre at best; they did not brown but instead poached in the fat, and the taste was lackluster. High heat turned out to be equally problematic. By the time the interior of each fillet had cooked, some of the exterior had scorched and tasted bitter and unappealing. My next try was a winner. I heated the pan over high heat and then lowered it to medium-high as soon as I added the fish. The exterior browned beautifully, while the inside remained succulent.

For fillets that were the ideal thickness of ⅜ inch, three minutes on the first side and about two minutes on the second side achieved both a flavorful, nutty tasting exterior and a moist, delicate interior. Because the side that is cooked first is the most attractive, I found it best to stick to the hard and fast rule of cooking for three minutes on the first side and then adjusting the time for the second side. (With flatfish, the side of the fillet that is cooked first also matters. See "Anatomy of a Flatfish" at right.) The question was, how could I tell when a thin fillet was done? Restaurant chefs press the fillets with their fingers—a good technique, but one that requires practice. Observation eventually told me that the fillet was done when opaque. Because the fish continues to cook off the heat of the stovetop (and in the gentle heat of the preheated oven), it is imperative to remove it slightly before it's fully done. Instead of using

the tip of a knife, a method that tends to damage the fillet, I found that a toothpick inserted into a thick edge worked well. Now just one last cooking problem remained.

Finishing Touches

Traditionally, the sauce served with meunière is *beurre noisette,* or brown butter, with the addition of lemon and parsley. Crucial to the flavor of the sauce—which adds a rich nuttiness to the fish—is proper browning of the milk solids in the butter, a task that is not easily accomplished in a nonstick skillet. The problem is that the dark surface of the pan makes it nearly impossible to judge the color of the butter. The solution was simple: Brown the butter in a medium-size stainless steel skillet; its shiny bottom makes it easy to monitor the color. I then added lemon juice to the browned butter, sprinkled the fish with parsley, and poured the sauce over the fish. Now I could invite even Julia Child over for dinner.

FISH MEUNIÈRE WITH BROWNED BUTTER AND LEMON
SERVES 4

Try to purchase fillets that are of similar size, and avoid those that weigh less than 5 ounces because they will cook too quickly. A nonstick skillet ensures that the fillets will release from the pan, but for the sauce a traditional skillet is preferable because its light-colored surface will allow you to monitor the color of the butter as it browns.

Fish
- ½ cup all-purpose flour
- 4 sole or flounder fillets, each 5 to 6 ounces and ⅜ inch thick, patted dry with paper towels
  Salt and ground black pepper
- 2 tablespoons vegetable oil
- 2 tablespoons unsalted butter, cut into 2 pieces

Browned Butter
- 4 tablespoons unsalted butter, cut into 4 pieces
- 1 tablespoon chopped fresh parsley leaves
- 1½ tablespoons juice from 1 lemon, plus 1 lemon, cut in wedges for serving

1. FOR THE FISH: Adjust oven rack to lower-middle position, set 4 heatproof dinner plates on rack, and heat oven to 200 degrees. Place flour in large baking dish. Season both sides of each fillet generously with salt and pepper; let stand until fillets are glistening with moisture, about 5 minutes. Coat both sides of fillets with flour, shake off excess, and place in single layer on baking sheet. Heat 1 tablespoon oil in 12-inch nonstick skillet over high heat until shimmering, then add 1 tablespoon butter and swirl to coat pan bottom; when foaming subsides, carefully place 2 fillets in skillet, bone-side down (see photo below). Immediately reduce heat to medium-high and cook, without moving fish, until edges of fillets are opaque and bottom is golden brown, about 3 minutes. Using 2 spatulas, gently flip fillets (see illustration at left) and cook on second side until thickest part of fillet easily separates into flakes when toothpick is inserted, about 2 minutes longer. Transfer fillets, one to each heated dinner plate, keeping bone-side up, and return plates to oven. Wipe out skillet and repeat with remaining 1 tablespoon each oil and butter and remaining fish fillets.

2. FOR THE BROWNED BUTTER: Heat butter in 10-inch skillet over medium-high heat until butter melts, 1 to 1½ minutes. Continue to cook, swirling pan constantly, until butter is golden brown and has nutty aroma, 1 to 1½ minutes; remove skillet from heat. Remove plates from oven and sprinkle fillets with parsley. Add lemon juice to browned butter and season to taste with salt; spoon sauce over fish and serve immediately with lemon wedges.

FISH MEUNIÈRE WITH TOASTED SLIVERED ALMONDS

Follow recipe for Fish Meunière with Browned Butter and Lemon, adding ¼ cup slivered almonds to skillet when butter has melted in step 2.

FISH MEUNIÈRE WITH CAPERS

Follow recipe for Fish Meunière with Browned Butter and Lemon, adding 2 tablespoons drained capers along with lemon juice in step 2.

Anatomy of a Flatfish Fillet

Flatfish fillets have two distinct sides, and it makes a difference which one goes into the pan first. The side of the fillet that was facing the bones in the whole fish browns best and makes the most attractive presentation on the plate. The side of the fillet that was facing the skin is darker and doesn't brown as well. When cooking, start the fillets bone-side down, then flip them once a nice crust has formed. When the fillets are cooked through, slide them, bone-side up, onto heated dinner plates.

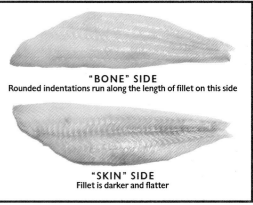

"BONE" SIDE
Rounded indentations run along the length of fillet on this side

"SKIN" SIDE
Fillet is darker and flatter

Ultimate Oven Fries

The savings in calories and fat are no reason to eat an oven fry—it has to taste good.
With its leathery crust and mealy interior, the typical oven fry needs work.

⇒ BY JULIA COLLIN DAVISON ⇐

Low fat is never a good excuse for lousy food, and oven fries should be no exception. Abysmal flavor and texture just aren't worth the savings in calories, especially when these "lite" fries taste like overroasted potatoes with thick, leathery crusts and hollow interiors. In other cases, they are limp, whitish, mealy, and bland—a complete failure in all respects. Yet easy and clean oven cooking—as opposed to deep-frying in a pot of hot, splattering oil—is such an engaging proposition that I decided to enlist temporarily in the low-fat army to see if I could make an oven fry worth eating on its own terms. If it didn't have a golden, crisp crust and a richly creamy interior, I was going back to the deep fryer.

I started off by baking five recipes from "healthy" cookbooks. The simplest called for cutting the potatoes into wedges and tossing them with oil before spreading them on a baking sheet. Other recipes called for cutting the potatoes more precisely into squared fries and then took off in different directions, leading me to toss the fries in egg whites, rinse them under running water, soak them in ice water, or steam them on the stovetop before baking. Yet another recipe called for preheating the baking sheet to crisp the crusts (and caused me two forearm burns). Yet no matter what the technique, these recipes produced fries that were either pale, soggy, and hopelessly stuck to the pan or incredibly crusty and tough. Still, aspects of each held promise. Some of the sickly looking examples had creamy interiors, while the tougher ones were perfectly golden and slid effortlessly off the pan. I decided that the place to start was at the beginning: what type of potato to use and how to cut it.

The Rudimentary Fry

First off, I tested russet, Yukon Gold, and boiling potatoes. Tasting wimpy and sporting spotty crusts, both the Yukon Gold and boiling potatoes couldn't hold a candle to the russets, with their hearty flavor and facility for turning golden brown. Equally obvious were the results of the peeled-versus-unpeeled-potato test. The unpeeled fries were tougher and had the distinct flavor of baked

These oven fries are as good as french fries and a lot less messy to prepare.

potatoes, whereas the peeled fries—unanimously preferred by tasters—had a clean and more characteristically "french" fry flavor. Tasters also liked the ample size and easy preparation of potatoes cut into wedges as opposed to the fussy and wasteful option of trimming potatoes down into squared, fast-food-fry wannabes.

Next I tried baking the fries at 400, 425, 450, 475, and 500 degrees. At lower temperatures, the fries didn't brown sufficiently. The 500-degree oven was a bit too hot and burned the fries at the edges. Baking at 475 degrees was best, but the fries still needed a deeper golden color and a crispier texture. Adjusting the oven rack to the lower-middle position was only moderately helpful, but moving it to the lowest position made for a significant improvement in the fries. The intense heat from the bottom of the oven browned them quickly and evenly, which, in turn, prevented the interiors from overcooking and melding into the crust (thereby becoming the unlikable hollow fry). Lightweight baking sheets can't handle this extreme temperature, so a heavy pan is a must (see "A Weighty Matter" below).

Up until now, I had been simply tossing the potatoes with oil, salt, and pepper before spreading them out on the baking sheet. Turning my attention to the amount of oil, I found the differences between 1 and 6 tablespoons to be astounding. Any fewer than 5 tablespoons left some of the fries uncoated and caused them to bake up dry and tough; any more than 5 tablespoons made them disagreeably greasy. Exactly 5 tablespoons, however, ensured that each wedge was evenly coated with oil as it baked. To guarantee even distribution of oil, I found it best to spread 4 tablespoons on the baking sheet and to toss the raw fries with the fifth. Slightly glistening as they emerge from the oven, the fries require a brief drain on paper towels to keep them from tasting oily. Although 5 tablespoons is much less oil than the couple of quarts or more called for when deep-frying potatoes, I felt my oven fries no

A Weighty Matter

LIGHTWEIGHT PAN: SPOTTY BROWNING

HEAVYWEIGHT PAN: EVEN BROWNING

The right pan makes all the difference when baking oven fries. A lightweight pan yields fries that are either pale or burnt. A heavy-duty baking sheet conducts heat better and ensures that the fries color evenly and deeply.

TASTING: Are Frozen Fries Worth Eating?

When several members of our staff confessed to buying frozen french fries on occasion (for their children, they insisted), we were intrigued. Could frozen fries hold a candle to homemade? We gathered five popular brands of steak fries to find out. The good news: Differences between brands were minimal. The bad news: All the brands (with one modest exception) were third-rate.

Alexia Oven Fries were the only fry with real potato flavor. Not surprisingly, these fries had the shortest ingredient list, with just potatoes, olive oil, sea salt, and dextrose (a form of sugar). The last-place finisher, McCain, featured all of that (with nonhydrogenated canola oil in lieu of the olive oil) plus sodium acid pyrophosphate, caramel, and oleoresin turmeric. Our verdict? Make your own or, at the very least, stick with ingredients you can pronounce. —Keri Fisher

ALEXIA: THE BEST OF THE BUNCH

PASSABLE IN A PINCH

ALEXIA Gourmet Quality Oven Fries
➤ "Not awful" was the highest praise tasters could muster.

NOT RECOMMENDED

ORE-IDA Steak Fries
➤ These "soggy" fries had a pronounced "processed flavor."

TRADER JOE'S Pacific Northwest Crinkle Wedge Potatoes
➤ Tasters thought these "pasty" fries tasted "like old potatoes."

STOP & SHOP Steak Fries
➤ "Very bad in every way."

MCCAIN Steak Cut French Fried Potatoes
➤ Comments ranged from "bland" to "horrible."

SCIENCE: The Power of Soaking

Experts agree (just ask McDonald's or our test cooks) that russet potatoes are the best variety for frying—either in a vat of bubbling oil or on a baking sheet in the oven. Unlike other potato varieties, russets produce fries with light, ethereal centers. But they are not perfect.

Russets can produce excessively thick crusts and somewhat dry interiors. The thick crust is caused by the browning of simple sugars in the russet, and the best way to remove some of the surface sugar is to soak the potatoes in water. The water has an added benefit. Potato starches gelatinize completely during cooking. The water introduced during soaking improves the creaminess and smoothness by working its way between the strands of gelatin starch. The final result is a fry that has a good surface crunch married to a smooth interior. —John Olson, Science Editor

A HOT BATH WORKS WONDERS

longer qualified as "low fat." Then again, neither did they qualify as pale, soggy, or dry.

Olive oil tasted slightly bitter and out of place, while the mild flavor of vegetable oil and the slight nuttiness of peanut oil (which we prefer to use when deep-frying) both worked well. Although the fries were now sticking to the pan far less than before, I was still plagued by the occasional stuck-on fry until I discovered one last trick. Rather than tossing the potatoes with salt and pepper, I sprinkled the seasonings over the oiled baking sheet. Acting like little ball bearings, the grains of salt and pepper kept the potatoes from sticking to the pan without getting in the way of browning.

Soaked, Steamed, and Pampered

Even though I had nailed down the basic method for cooking the fries, they were still beset with crusts that were too thick and interiors that were unappealingly mealy. Wondering what would happen if I steamed the fries before baking them (a technique I'd seen in a few other recipes), I steamed one batch on top of the stove in a steamer basket and another in the oven by covering the baking sheet tightly with foil. Little did I suspect that this seemingly odd method would deliver just the thing I had been after: an oven fry with the creamy, smooth core of an authentic french fry. Steaming on the stovetop had been a counter-clogging, time-consuming affair, but wrapping a baking sheet with foil was easy. The foil trapped the potatoes' natural moisture as they steamed themselves in the oven, and it then came off so the crusts could crisp for the balance of cooking. Five minutes of steaming was just right, turning the dry, starchy centers of the fries to a soft, creamy consistency without interfering with browning.

Now the only problem remaining was the crust. Steaming, although beneficial for the interior, turned the already thick crust even tougher; this was a far cry from the thin, brittle crust of a good french fry. To solve this problem, I decided to try the techniques of rinsing and soaking, which are often employed when making french fries. Rinsing the raw fries under running water made for a slightly more delicate crust, but soaking them for about an hour in cold tap water was pure magic. Slowly turning the water cloudy as they soaked, the fries emerged from the oven with thin, shatteringly crisp crusts and interiors more velvety than any oven fry I had tasted (for more information see "The Power of Soaking" above). But perhaps the biggest surprise came when I tried soaking the fries in water at different temperatures: ice cold, cold from the tap, and hot from the tap. The ice water took hours to become cloudy, the cold tap water took about 1 hour, and the hot tap water a convenient 10 minutes, which meant that I could peel, cut, and soak the potatoes in roughly the same time it took to heat up the oven.

With an ultracrisp shell, a velvety smooth core, and a nearly authentic french-fry flavor, these excellent oven fries were nearly indistinguishable from their deep-fried counterparts. I fooled several people in the test kitchen, and I know I won't

be heating up 2 quarts of peanut oil the next time I get a hankering for fries.

OVEN FRIES
SERVES 3 TO 4

Take care to cut the potatoes into evenly sized wedges so that all of the pieces will cook at about the same rate. Although it isn't required, a nonstick baking sheet works particularly well for this recipe. It not only keeps the fries from sticking to the pan but, because of its dark color, encourages deep and even browning. Whether you choose a nonstick baking sheet or a regular baking sheet, make sure that it is heavy duty. The intense heat of the oven may cause lighter pans to warp.

3 russet potatoes (about 8 ounces each), peeled, each potato cut lengthwise into 10 to 12 evenly sized wedges
5 tablespoons vegetable or peanut oil
   Salt and ground black pepper

1. Adjust oven rack to lowest position; heat oven to 475 degrees. Place potatoes in large bowl and cover with hot tap water; soak 10 minutes. Meanwhile, coat 18 by 12-inch heavy-duty rimmed baking sheet (see note) with 4 tablespoons oil and sprinkle evenly with ¾ teaspoon salt and ¼ teaspoon pepper; set aside.

2. Drain potatoes. Spread potatoes out on triple layer of paper towels and thoroughly pat dry with additional paper towels. Rinse and wipe out now-empty bowl; return potatoes to bowl and toss with remaining 1 tablespoon oil. Arrange potatoes in single layer on prepared baking sheet; cover tightly with foil and bake 5 minutes. Remove foil and continue to bake until bottoms of potatoes are spotty golden brown, 15 to 20 minutes, rotating baking sheet after 10 minutes. Using metal spatula and tongs, scrape to loosen potatoes from pan, then flip each wedge, keeping potatoes in single layer. Continue baking until fries are golden and crisp, 5 to 15 minutes longer, rotating pan as needed if fries are browning unevenly.

3. Transfer fries to second baking sheet lined with paper towels to drain. Season with additional salt and pepper to taste and serve.

The Best Chocolate Bundt Cake

Tired of great-looking chocolate Bundt cakes that are bland and boring? So were we.
Our ideal cake would be moist, rich with chocolate flavor, and attractive.

> BY ERIKA BRUCE

A Bundt cake is the pinnacle of cake-baking simplicity. With its decorative shape, this cake doesn't require frosting or fussy finishing techniques. What chocolate Bundt cakes do require, it turns out, is a major boost in flavor. Despite their tantalizing looks, most of these cakes have at best a muted chocolate presence. I wanted a cake that would deliver that moment of pure chocolate ecstasy when the first bite stops time. A chocolate Bundt cake should taste every bit as good as it looks, with a fine crumb, moist texture, and rich flavor.

Unfortunately, these sweet masters of disguise disappointed us so often in our initial taste tests that we almost relegated this recipe to the dustbin. Moist but pale, many of the cakes were devoid of any chocolate flavor. Others looked appealingly dark and mysterious but managed to capture only flat, bitter nuances of chocolate. An overly sweet, walnut-studded "tunnel of fudge" cake with a gummy, underbaked center was hardly worth the calories. A cake similar to a pound cake had great texture—dense and moist owing to the addition of sour cream—but the only thing that told tasters it was chocolate was its brown color.

A good Bundt cake is so attractive and moist that it doesn't need any frosting. The cake on the bottom rack has cooled fully and been dusted with confectioners' sugar for serving.

Searching for Chocolate Flavor

Because the pound cake made with sour cream had come closest to my textural ideal, I started with a working recipe using roughly the same proportions of butter, sugar, eggs, and flour and using the traditional method of creaming the butter and sugar (beating them together) before adding the other ingredients. I then focused on boosting the virtually nonexistent chocolate flavor. The recipe included a small amount of cocoa powder, so I thought that a good dose of melted chocolate would be in order. I started with unsweetened chocolate, which has the most intense flavor. The resulting cake tasted bitter, and its texture was chalky, reminiscent of third-rate brownies. Trying both semisweet and bittersweet, I noticed an improvement in texture, as both of these chocolates have added sugar and stabilizers that make them smoother and creamier than unsweetened.

Tasters found the semisweet chocolate too sweet; the bittersweet added the right chocolate edge.

Now I had more chocolate flavor, but I wanted a deeper, more complex taste. This time, more cocoa powder seemed like a logical solution. I replaced a portion of the flour in my recipe with an equal amount of cocoa powder. I had to choose between Dutch-processed cocoa powder and natural cocoa powder. (The first is "alkalized"—treated so as to reduce acidity—and is thought to provide a smoother chocolate flavor with an intensely dark color. The second, natural or regular cocoa powder, is slightly acidic and has a lighter, reddish hue.) Tasters preferred the cakes made with natural cocoa. Its assertive flavor with fruity undertones stood up better to the sour cream in the recipe.

I came upon the real trick to developing the chocolate flavor of this cake, however, when I

tried a technique that the test kitchen had earlier developed for devil's food cake. I poured boiling water over the cocoa and chocolate to dissolve them, a step that not only disperses the cocoa particles throughout the batter but also blooms the flavor.

Finessing Texture and Flavor

Now I had great, complex chocolate flavor, but I also had a new problem—the cake was too dry. To remedy this, I first tried decreasing the flour by ½ cup. Now the cake was more moist but still not moist enough, and I could not remove more flour without compromising its structure. I tried increasing the butter, but this merely made the cake greasy. I added an extra egg (most recipes call for just four; I went up to five), and that helped. Finally, I switched from granulated to light brown sugar, which not only added moistness but dramatically improved flavor.

But even after all of these amendments to the recipe, I was still falling short of my goal of a really moist cake. I decided to review the quantity of sour cream. When I increased it, the cake became greasy and overly acidic. I went back to my original recipes and found that many of them used either milk or buttermilk, which have a higher water content than sour cream. This tipped me off to a simple way to solve the problem: increasing the amount of boiling water added with the cocoa powder and chocolate. The resulting batter was looser and the baked cake significantly more moist—moist enough to finally satisfy my goal.

To finish the recipe, I dissolved a small amount of espresso powder along with the chocolate and cocoa and also added a healthy tablespoon of vanilla extract. Both flavors complemented the floral nuances of the chocolate. With the right pan and a ready batter, I baked my cake at temperatures

---

DON'T CHANGE PANS!

Don't be tempted to make the cake in another pan. Its heavy batter was designed to work in a Bundt pan that has a center tube to facilitate baking. When we baked the same batter in a 13 by 9-inch rectangular pan, the center collapsed.

ENSURING AN EASY RELEASE

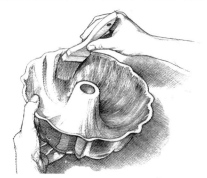

A Bundt cake is attractive only if you get it out of the pan in one piece. A simple paste made from melted butter and cocoa powder and painted into the grooves of the pan with a pastry brush worked wonders in helping to release our chocolate Bundt cake. We much preferred this tidy method over the standard technique of greasing and flouring, which left an unsightly pasty white film on the cake's exterior.

of 325, 350, and 375 degrees. At the highest temperature, the cake developed a thick upper crust and uneven crumb. Finding little difference in the cakes baked at the other two temperatures, I opted for the quicker baking time at 350. At long last, I had reached chocolate heaven.

CHOCOLATE SOUR CREAM BUNDT CAKE
SERVES 12 TO 14

Natural (or regular) cocoa gives the cake a fuller, more assertive chocolate flavor than does Dutch-processed cocoa. In addition, Dutch-processed cocoa will result in a compromised rise. The cake can be served with just a dusting of confectioners' sugar but is easily made more impressive with Tangy Whipped Cream and Lightly Sweetened Raspberries (recipes follow). The cake can be made a day in advance; wrap the cooled cake in plastic and store it at room temperature. Dust with confectioners' sugar just before serving.

Cake Release
- 1 tablespoon butter, melted
- 1 tablespoon cocoa

Cake
- ¾ cup (2¼ ounces) natural cocoa (see note)
- 6 ounces bittersweet chocolate, chopped
- 1 teaspoon instant espresso powder (optional)
- ¾ cup boiling water
- 1 cup sour cream, room temperature
- 1¾ cups (8¾ ounces) unbleached all-purpose flour
- 1 teaspoon salt
- 1 teaspoon baking soda
- 12 tablespoons (1½ sticks) unsalted butter, room temperature
- 2 cups (14 ounces) packed light brown sugar

- 1 tablespoon vanilla extract
- 5 large eggs, room temperature
- Confectioners' sugar for dusting

1. **FOR THE PAN:** Stir together butter and cocoa in small bowl until paste forms; using a pastry brush, coat all interior surfaces of standard 12-cup Bundt pan. (If mixture becomes too thick to brush on, microwave it for 10 to 20 seconds, or until warm and softened.) Adjust oven rack to lower-middle position; heat oven to 350 degrees.

2. **FOR THE CAKE:** Combine cocoa, chocolate, and espresso powder (if using) in medium heatproof bowl; pour boiling water over and whisk until smooth. Cool to room temperature; then whisk in sour cream. Whisk flour, salt, and baking soda in second bowl to combine.

3. In standing mixer fitted with flat beater, beat butter, sugar, and vanilla on medium-high speed until pale and fluffy, about 3 minutes. Reduce speed to medium and add eggs one at a time, mixing about 30 seconds after each addition and scraping down bowl with rubber spatula after first 2 additions. Reduce to medium-low speed (batter may appear separated); add about one third of flour mixture and half of chocolate/sour cream mixture and mix until just incorporated, about 20 seconds. Scrape bowl and repeat using half of remaining flour mixture and all of remaining chocolate mixture; add remaining flour mixture and beat until just incorporated, about 10 seconds. Scrape bowl and mix on medium-low until batter is thoroughly combined, about 30 seconds. Pour batter into prepared Bundt pan, being careful not to pour batter on sides of pan. Bake until wooden skewer inserted into center comes out with few crumbs attached, 45 to 50 minutes. Cool in pan 10 minutes, then invert cake onto parchment-lined wire rack; cool to room temperature, about 3 hours. Dust with confectioners' sugar, transfer to serving platter, and cut into wedges; serve with Tangy Whipped Cream and raspberries, if desired.

TANGY WHIPPED CREAM

- 1 cup cold heavy cream
- ¼ cup sour cream
- ¼ cup packed light brown sugar
- ⅛ teaspoon vanilla extract

With electric mixer, beat all ingredients, gradually increasing speed from low to high, until cream forms soft peaks, 1½ to 2 minutes.

LIGHTLY SWEETENED RASPBERRIES

- 3 cups fresh raspberries, gently rinsed and dried
- 1–2 tablespoons granulated sugar

Gently toss raspberries with sugar, then let stand until berries have released some juice and sugar has dissolved, about 15 minutes.

Bundt Pans

We tested eight so-called Bundt pans with a minimum capacity of 12 cups. In addition to preparing our chocolate Bundt cake in each pan, we baked vanilla pound cakes to test for evenness and depth of browning. All of the chocolate cakes released easily, but some of the pound cakes did stick, most notably in the Kaiser, Calphalon, and Nordic Ware Bubble.

(**Cook's Extra** gives you free additional information online. For the full results of our Bundt pan testing, visit www.cooksillustrated.com and key in code 1042. This information will be available until February 15, 2004.)

BEST PAN
NORDIC WARE Platinum Series $27.99
➤Thick, durable, cast aluminum produced even browning and a clean, well-defined shape.

BEST BUY
BAKER'S SECRET Non-Stick Fluted Tube Pan, $11.99
➤This inexpensive pan outperformed most others.

THE OTHER CONTENDERS

NORDIC WARE "Colors," Bubble Non-Stick, $9.99
➤This flimsy pan had a nice shape but lost points in release tests.

EXETER Fluted 10" Pan, $14.99
➤This poorly designed pan had decent browning but some sticking problems.

KITCHENAID Fluted Cake Pan, $24.99
➤A wide rim made for easy handling, but the exterior was very slippery.

KAISER Noblesse Bundform, $17.99
➤Cakes clung to this light-weight pan with barely detectable ridges.

CALPHALON Crown Bund Pan, $24.99
➤Cakes stuck seriously to this weighty pan, and they also failed to brown evenly.

SILICONE ZONE Bundform Pan, $19.99
➤This pliable pan was hard to handle and produced cakes with flattened tops.

Reinventing Apple Brown Betty

This combination of apples, sugar, and buttered bread crumbs inevitably results in a soggy mess of a dessert. It was time to give "Betty" a serious makeover.

≥ BY SUSAN LIGHT ≤

No doubt the creation of Colonial forebears reluctant to let anything go to waste, apple brown betty is a simple baked fruit dessert traditionally made with apples and leftover bread. Butter and sugar were added to enrich and sweeten the mixture, but the original recipe was plain by design. Although apple brown betty recipes abound in both old and new American cookbooks, rarely does the dish make it off the page and into the kitchen. Modern cooks instead choose cobblers and crisps. In a patriotic mood and charmed by the dessert's simplicity in an era of complicated culinary creations, I set out to rejuvenate this rustic classic.

In its most basic form, apple brown betty contains only four ingredients: apples, bread crumbs, sugar, and butter. Variations on this theme abound, however, so to begin my testing I made a range of recipes. Some were basic (buttered bread crumbs atop sweetened pieces of apple). Others were more complicated (one recipe had 14 ingredients, including cake crumbs, oat bran, Calvados, and raisins). To my dismay, tasters were neither comforted by the simple versions nor impressed by the elaborate ones. Each had soggy, mushy bread crumbs. Most were overly seasoned with spices, while others tasted bland and flat.

At this point, I made a few decisions. First, I would stick with the traditional (and short) ingredient list. Modern recipes with lots of add-ons seemed antithetical to this basic recipe. Second, I would try to coax as much flavor as possible from these core ingredients. Last, I had to do something about the texture: Soggy and mushy just would not cut it with the test kitchen.

The Crumb Conundrum

Because betties get much of their flavor from the crumbs, I figured I would start there. I tried a wide range of homemade bread crumbs—processed from white and wheat sandwich bread, English muffins, cinnamon-raisin bread, brioche, pound cake, angel food cake, sourdough, and baguettes—as well as store-bought dried bread crumbs. Crumbs made from cake and rich breads were out of place in this simple dessert, and sourdough and

After a makeover, our apple brown betty has a rich caramelized apple flavor and a crisp, buttery topping.

wheat bread crumbs were too strongly flavored. Store-bought crumbs were highly seasoned and too finely processed. In keeping with the straightforward nature of the dish, tasters preferred white sandwich bread pulsed in the food processor until coarsely ground. I used Pepperidge Farm Sandwich White, but any supermarket loaf with a sturdy, fairly dense crumb will work (a fluffy, airy loaf is not recommended).

Although I had concluded that crumbs made from sandwich bread were the most authentic, most convenient, and therefore best choice, they were awfully plain. Toasting the bread crumbs in a skillet with some butter seemed like a good way to enrich their flavor and improve their texture. One test cook suggested adding some of the sugar, which is usually tossed with the apples. This not only sweetened the crumbs but caused them to crisp and slightly caramelize. Mixing the bread slices—crusts attached—with 4 tablespoons butter and 2 tablespoons sugar in the food processor was easy enough, and the lot could then be added to a cold, regular skillet (no

need to preheat the pan and no need for a nonstick skillet) and cooked over medium heat until deep golden brown. I then spread the mixture on a paper towel–lined plate to cool. The paper towels absorbed excess butter and kept the crumbs crisp, with a slight chew.

Goldens and Grannies

With the flavor and texture of the crumbs greatly improved, it was time to start testing apples. I decided to limit my tests to varieties widely available throughout the year in major supermarkets: Granny Smith, McIntosh, Gala, Golden Delicious, and Braeburn, as well as various combinations thereof. I ultimately determined that a blend of two apples was better than one in terms of both texture and flavor. In the end, tasters preferred a combination of Granny Smith and Golden Delicious, with the sweeter flavor of the Goldens complementing the tartness of the Grannies. Tasters preferred apples cut roughly into ½-inch chunks, which gave them a forkful of apples and crumbs with each bite. Apple slices were too large and, as one taster said, a small dice made the betty look too much like stuffing.

Out of the Oven and into the Pan

In a nod to tradition, I baked the apples, butter, sugar, and bread crumbs together in a foil-covered dish; the results were varied, but none were very good. By sprinkling some of my tasty crumbs into the apple mixture (to thicken the juices) and reserving the rest to sprinkle over the apples just before serving, I was able to keep the topping crisp. But tasters complained (fairly loudly) that the apples were still bland. I could add spices to the mix, but I first wanted to coax more flavor from the apples, butter, and sugar. Eyeing the empty skillet I had used to toast the crumbs, I had a thought. Why not caramelize the apples and sugar on top of the stove in a hot skillet slicked with butter?

My first attempt at preparing a "skillet" brown betty was not wholly successful. Although I was able to fit all of the apples in the pan, they did not cook evenly; those crowded together on the bottom of the skillet cooked faster than the others. I

TEST RECIPES: **Betties Gone Bad**

TOO DRY

TOO MUSHY

TOO SOUPY

During testing, we prepared a lot of unpalatable betties. Here are three particularly bad versions. Firm apples held their shape nicely but were too dry and overwhelmed by an excess of crumbs (top). McIntosh apples became mushy when cooked and resembled applesauce (center). This soupy recipe called for too much liquid and not enough bread crumbs (bottom).

solved this problem by quickly cooking the apples in two batches. After the second batch of apples was done, I returned the first batch to the skillet and finished the dish by sprinkling the rest of the crumbs over the top. This method was much preferable. The apples cooked uniformly and turned an even golden brown. At this point I also tested different kinds and combinations of sugar and found that light brown sugar worked best with both the apples and the crumbs. Granulated sugar was too bright and sweet; dark brown sugar too rich and apt to burn in the skillet.

Cooking the apples in the skillet had improved their flavor greatly. They tasted richer, deeper, and slightly caramelized—something baked betties could never achieve. I still had two problems, however. The apples were just a tad too firm, and the dessert was a bit dry. The crumbs were more like stuffing and needed some juices to help them meld with the apples. I had come a long way from soggy and mushy; I had actually made a betty that was too dry and crunchy!

After much testing, I discovered that the solution was to add cider to the pan with the sautéed apples and then reduce it by half, a process that took just a few minutes. In addition to making the finished dessert saucier, the extra liquid helped to cook the apples until they were soft but still firm enough to hold their shape— exactly the texture I was looking for. The cider also deglazed the bottom and sides of the pan, picking up every bit of caramelized flavor and returning it to the dish. Finally, the sugars in the cider gave the dish a syrupy consistency and a deep apple flavor.

I stirred in ½ cup of my buttered, sugared, and toasted crumbs to thicken the betty and then sprinkled the rest on top to keep them crisp. I tweaked the flavor by adding just ¼ teaspoon each of ground cinnamon and ginger (along with the sugar at the outset of the

sautéing process) and by adjusting the sweet/tart balance with a little lemon juice just before serving. This betty's makeover was now complete. It came together even more quickly than the original and, in the opinion of the test kitchen, was much improved as well. The soggy bread crumbs had been replaced by a crisp topping, and the apples had gone from bland and pedestrian to lightly spiced and caramelized, with their flavor enhanced by the reduced cider. Now I had a simple apple dessert that was both frugal and delicious.

SKILLET APPLE BROWN BETTY
SERVES 6 TO 8

If your apples are especially tart, omit the lemon juice. If, on the other hand, your apples are exceptionally sweet, use the full amount. A scoop of vanilla ice cream is the perfect accompaniment to this dish. Leftovers can be refrigerated in an airtight container; topped with vanilla yogurt, they make an excellent breakfast.

Bread Crumbs
- 4 large slices (about 4 ounces) white sandwich bread, each slice torn into quarters
- 2 tablespoons packed light brown sugar
- 4 tablespoons unsalted butter, cut into 4 pieces

Apples
- 3 tablespoons packed light brown sugar
- ¼ teaspoon ground ginger
- ¼ teaspoon ground cinnamon
  Pinch salt
- 2 tablespoons unsalted butter
- 1½ pounds Granny Smith apples (about 3 medium), peeled and cut into ½-inch cubes (about 4 cups)
- 1½ pounds Golden Delicious apples (about 3 medium), peeled and cut into ½-inch cubes (about 4 cups)
- ¾ cup apple cider
- 1–3 teaspoons juice from 1 lemon (see note)

1. **FOR THE BREAD CRUMBS:** Pulse bread, sugar, and butter in food processor until coarsely ground, about six 2-second pulses. Transfer

mixture to 12-inch skillet; cook over medium heat, stirring constantly, until crumbs are deep golden brown, about 5 minutes. Transfer to paper towel–lined plate; wipe out skillet.

2. **FOR THE APPLES:** Combine sugar, spices, and salt in small bowl. Heat 1 tablespoon butter in now-empty skillet over medium-high heat; when foaming subsides, stir in 4 cups apples and half of sugar mixture. Distribute apples in even layer and cook, stirring two or three times, until medium brown, about 5 minutes; transfer to medium bowl. Repeat with remaining butter, apples, and sugar mixture, returning first batch of apples to skillet when second batch is done. Add apple cider and scrape bottom and sides of skillet with wooden spoon to loosen browned bits; cook until about ⅓ cup liquid remains and apples are tender but not mushy, 2 to 4 minutes. Remove skillet from heat; stir in lemon juice, if using, and ½ cup toasted bread crumbs. Using wooden spoon, lightly flatten apples into even layer in skillet and evenly sprinkle with remaining toasted bread crumbs. Let cool 5 minutes. Spoon warm betty into individual bowls and serve with vanilla ice cream, if desired.

SKILLET APPLE BROWN BETTY WITH PECANS AND DRIED CRANBERRIES

Follow recipe for Skillet Apple Brown Betty, adding ½ cup pecans to food processor along with bread, sugar, and butter and processing as instructed, then adding ½ cup dried cranberries to apple mixture with cider.

SKILLET APPLE BROWN BETTY WITH GOLDEN RAISINS AND CALVADOS

Any applejack, or even brandy, can be used in place of the Calvados.

Follow recipe for Skillet Apple Brown Betty, substituting ¼ cup Calvados or brandy for an equal amount apple cider and adding ½ cup golden raisins to apples along with cider/Calvados mixture.

STEP-BY-STEP | BETTY GETS A MAKEOVER–AND A SKILLET

1. Cook bread crumb mixture until crumbs are deep golden brown. Cool mixture on paper towel–lined plate.

2. Melt butter in empty skillet and cook apples and sugar mixture (in two batches) until golden brown.

3. Return all apples to pan. Add cider and cook until syrupy. Stir in some bread crumbs to thicken mixture.

4. Flatten apple mixture with spoon and sprinkle with remaining crumbs. Cool 5 minutes and serve.

Is French Dijon Mustard Best?

Can Grey Poupon, made by Nabisco, compete with made-in-France Dijon?

≥ BY ERIKA BRUCE AND ADAM RIED ≤

Ask most Americans how they use mustard, and they will report smearing it on a ballpark or backyard barbecue hot dog—a pretty humble proposition. Dijon mustard from France, however, is considered anything but humble. A lofty version of a common condiment, real Dijon mustard has culinary clout, and some are as revered as a great wine.

Numerous Dijon mustards, however, are actually manufactured here in the United States. (Grey Poupon, for example, is produced in this country by Nabisco.) Many cooks assume that real French mustard must be superior to its made-in-America brethren, a notion that we set out to confirm or deny. We placed a call to Barry Levenson, founder and curator of the Mount Horeb Mustard Museum, who helped us assemble nine popular samples of Dijon mustard from France and America to taste—twice, by the end of our saga—in blind tests. The results were, to say the least, an education in the mysteries of mustard.

Hot Stuff

First, a word about how mustard is made. Mustard comes by its characteristic heat naturally. The plant that produces mustard seeds, the basis of all mustard, belongs to the *Cruciferae* family, in the genus *Brassica*. So do horseradish, turnips, radishes, cabbage, and watercress, all noted in varying degrees for their sharp flavor.

Three types of mustard seeds are used to make mustard: yellow (*Brassica hirta*), black (*Brassica nigra*), and brown (*Brassica juncea*). Black and brown seeds are hotter, so they produce spicier condiments. Real Dijon mustard is based on brown, or sometimes black, seeds, which are almost identical chemically. Milder yellow seeds are used to make American, or ballpark-style, yellow mustard.

While mustard preferences are largely subjective (some like it hot and some don't), tasters did agree on the importance of several characteristics. With regard to flavor, we all thought that pungency, acidity, and saltiness should be well balanced and that any aftertaste should be clean, melodious, and free of any "off" flavors that tasters could perceive as musty, plasticky, metallic, artificial, or fishy. Tasters also sought a smooth texture that was neither too thick nor too thin. In terms of heat, even the most sensitive palates sought a moderate to assertive level. According to our tasters, insufficient or excessive spiciness was grounds for poor ratings.

Now to answer our initial question about whether real Dijon mustard—the stuff that is made in France—is better than American products such as Nabisco's Grey Poupon. The answer is an unequivocal no. After tallying our results, we found that we could recommend five brands, and only two of them, Roland Extra Strong and Delouis Fils, were French. The other three—Grey Poupon (maybe the guys in the limos in the Grey Poupon ads know something after all), French's Napa Valley Style Dijon, and Barhyte—were American-made. Of the four brands that we could not recommend, two were French and two were American.

To explain this bizarre outcome, we turned to our food lab, which analyzed all of the samples for heat level by measuring the quantity of *allyl isothiocyanate,* the active ingredient in Dijon mustard that gives it heat. Three of the four lowest rated mustards—Maille, Plochman's, and Roland organic—lost points for lack of bite, and their allyl isothiocyanate content ranged from fewer than 20 to just 30 milligrams per kilogram (mg/kg). The fourth, Inglehoffer, offered more spice (although still less than the top-rated mustards) at 120 mg/kg, but it was downgraded for excessive sweetness (oddly, this American brand contains sugar and balsamic vinegar). The recommended brands were spicier: Even the least spicy of the bunch—French's Napa brand—had an allyl isothiocyanate level of 100 mg/kg.

The Slippery Slope of Spice

Shortly after this tasting, we learned that spiciness—a key variable in a mustard's rating—diminishes with age. That means that two jars of the same product, one manufactured last month and the other manufactured last year, will have different levels of spice even if the jars have not been opened. Because we did not allow for the relative age of the mustards in our initial tasting, we went back to square one, where we took a crash course in how to decode mustard labels to determine date of manufacture.

Our first step was to call the companies, and we found that the shelf life of mustard is roughly six to 18 months, depending on the packaging material and storage conditions. Delouis Fils prints a lot number on its labels. Barhyte, Maille, and Grey Poupon print a "best if used by" date, and the remaining four brands, French's, Roland, Inglehoffer, and Plochman's, include codes designating the date of manufacture. Reviewing the

jars from our taste test, we immediately discovered that two of the "not recommended" brands near the bottom of the heat scale, Plochman's and Roland organic, were indeed well past their recommended shelf lives. At the time of our tasting, they were nearly two years old and 14 months old, respectively.

It seemed that in ignoring freshness, we may have invalidated our tasting results. The obvious remedy was to purchase fresh mustards and do a second tasting and heat analysis. This is exactly what we did and found that the fresher samples were, for the most part, spicier. Two brands, Barhyte and Plochman's, remained consistent from the first sample to the second, while the Delouis Fils, the only brand whose manufacture dates we could not accurately determine, slipped a little in terms of heat. The allyl isothiocyanate levels in the remaining brands, however, increased from the first sample to the second. The most dramatic example was the Inglehoffer, which skyrocketed from a tame 120 mg/kg to an explosive 1690 mg/kg.

Did the changes in heat level have a significant effect on our recommendations? Interestingly, no. Despite increased spiciness in all of the "not recommended" brands but one (Plochman's), flavor and/or texture flaws kept them at the bottom of the ratings in both tastings. (Plochman's was consistently perceived as too mild to recommend.) All of the recommended mustards retained their rank from the first tasting to the second, largely by dint of their good balance of flavors and favorable texture.

The Consumer Challenge

What should you look for, then, when purchasing Dijon mustard? First of all, forget about American versus French. Both our "recommended" and "not recommended" mustards included both French and American products. Second, because mustard quickly loses its heat, a fresher product is always better. Although reading labels is confusing at best, Grey Poupon, the number two mustard in our tasting, does include a "best if used by" date on the label, which gives you a fighting chance at finding the freshest sample on the shelf.

No matter what mustard you choose, though, try not to store it at home for long periods (even our test cooks have been known to store jars of Dijon for years in the refrigerator). Purchase small jars and replace them frequently.

TASTING DIJON MUSTARD

Twenty *Cook's Illustrated* staff members tasted the Dijon mustards listed below on two different occasions. Tasted first were samples purchased at local supermarkets or ordered online (just as any consumer would) without regard to freshness. The second tasting comprised fresher samples, ordered directly from the manufacturer whenever possible. Allyl isothiocyanate levels, which measure heat, are listed for both tastings. During tastings, samples were tried in a different order by different tasters to eliminate any effects of palate fatigue. Also, one sample was repeated in tastings to function as a control. The samples are listed in order of preference.

RECOMMENDED

ROLAND Extra Strong Dijon Mustard [FRANCE]
➤ **$3.59 for 13 ounces**
Sample 1 allyl isothiocyanate: Unavailable for first tasting.
Sample 2 allyl isothiocyanate: 420 mg/kg
An American brand manufactured in France, this cross-national hybrid was widely praised for its excellent flavor balance, having acidity, salt, and heat in pleasing proportions to one another. The heat level was moderate, with the mustard displaying "a nice horseradish flavor" that struck many tasters as just "the right amount of spice." The thick, smooth texture also won accolades.

GREY POUPON Dijon Mustard [U.S.A.]
➤ **$2.69 for 10 ounces**
Sample 1 allyl isothiocyanate: 240 mg/kg
Sample 2 allyl isothiocyanate: 840 mg/kg
This mustard is manufactured stateside by Nabisco in accordance with the original recipe from Dijon. Tasters praised its "well-rounded flavor," "nice balance," and "smooth," "creamy" texture. The flavor was "tangy," with a "slight bitterness" and "bite" recalling horseradish. Grey Poupon scored consistently in both tastings.

DELOUIS FILS Moutarde de Dijon [FRANCE]
➤ **$4.50 for 7 ounces**
Sample 1 allyl isothiocyanate: 210 mg/kg
Sample 2 allyl isothiocyanate: 110 mg/kg
This mustard exhibited a multidimensional, deep, well-balanced flavor. Tasters detected sufficient heat, with salt and acidity at levels that pleased them, using phrases such as "straightforward," "pungent," and "tangy." Oddly, some tasters picked up a mild sweetness, while others observed the texture to be slightly "chalky."

FRENCH'S Napa Valley Style Dijon Mustard [U.S.A.]
➤ **$3.29 for 12 ounces**
Sample 1 allyl isothiocyanate: 100 mg/kg
Sample 2 allyl isothiocyanate: 360 mg/kg
Somewhere between powerhouse and wimp when it came to heat, this self-described "truly American Dijon" was indeed deemed friendly to American palates. The majority of tasters received it well, noting its "mild" flavor, "slowly developing heat," and "smooth texture." A few detractors countered with comments such as "boring," "tame," and "not remarkable." Overall, however, a solid citizen.

BARHYTE SELECT Dijon Mustard [U.S.A.]
➤ **$4.00 for 9 ounces**
Sample 1 allyl isothiocyanate: 410 mg/kg
Sample 2 allyl isothiocyanate: 400 mg/kg
This American newcomer from Oregon made friends and foes. Enthusiasts raved that it was "all-around delicious," with "great balance" and a "true mustard taste," while detractors picked up on "harsh acidity" and a "bitter aftertaste." According to the lab analysis, the heat level remained remarkably consistent from the first sample to the second. The consistency was a bit "soupy" for some.

NOT RECOMMENDED

MAILLE Dijon Originale [FRANCE]
➤ **$2.99 for 13.4 ounces**
Sample 1 allyl isothiocyanate: 20 mg/kg
Sample 2 allyl isothiocyanate: 160 mg/kg
Several tasters swore by this highly esteemed French mustard before stepping into the tasting room, but opinions changed quickly, evidenced by comments such as "dull," "no depth," "pasty," and "soapy aftertaste." While most agreed that "it could be hotter" and detractors claimed the texture was "gluey," a few defenders countered with descriptors such as "smooth" and "fresh."

PLOCHMAN'S Premium Dijon [U.S.A.]
➤ **$2.89 for 9 ounces**
Sample 1 allyl isothiocyanate: <20 mg/kg
Sample 2 allyl isothiocyanate: <20 mg/kg
Definitely the mildest sample of the bunch, with tasters repeatedly likening it to plain yellow "ballpark" or "hot dog" mustard. Many tasters picked up on a "fruity sweetness" like that of "cider vinegar" as well as a lingering "pickle" flavor. This mustard's ultrasmooth consistency led one taster to note that it "seems whipped."

ROLAND Organic Extra Strong Dijon Mustard [FRANCE]
➤ **$2.99 for 7 ounces**
Sample 1 allyl isothiocyanate: 30 mg/kg
Sample 2 allyl isothiocyanate: 250 mg/kg
Despite its French heritage and roots shared with the winning mustard, few considered this organic product to be a good choice. Repeatedly cited as "salty," it did indeed have one of the highest sodium levels of all of the mustards tasted. It also lost favor for having an "odd," "clumpy," "mushy" texture and a "harsh" and "metallic" flavor.

INGLEHOFFER Hot Dijon Mustard [U.S.A.]
➤ **$2.49 for 8 ounces**
Sample 1 allyl isothiocyanate: 120 mg/kg
Sample 2 allyl isothiocyanate: 1690 mg/kg
The overbearing heat of the second sample (twice as hot as the next hottest sample) was variously described as "crazy," "wicked," "searing," and "painful." Also overbearing was the sweetness, attributed to the sugar and balsamic vinegar listed among the ingredients.

Label Sleuthing

Freshness matters when buying mustard, especially if you want a spread with heat. Some labels clearly indicate a use-by date, while others rely on cryptic manufacture dates or lot numbers.

Get out your reading glasses and, in some cases, code-cracking manual to figure out if the mustard is fresh or not.

Eventually, we cracked these codes, but our advice is to buy one of our recommended brands with a use-by date, choosing a jar with the most distant date.

Separation Anxiety

Excess fat ruins stocks and sauces. But do fat separators really work? We tested eight models—from pitchers to ladles to "fat mops"—to find out.

⇒ BY ADAM RIED ⇐

Church and state. Wheat and chaff. Dross and gold. What do these pairs have in common? They must be separated, just as the liquid fat must be separated from the drippings of a roast before making gravy or from a pot of hot stock before turning it into soup. Luckily, separating liquid fat is easy to do with a specially designed fat separator, aka gravy strainer or soup strainer. Three formats dominate the category: pitcher-type measuring cups with sharply angled spouts opening out from the base of the cup; ladles with slots around the perimeter; and "fat mops," brushes with long, soft bristles made from plastic fibers. Such extreme design differences raise the obvious question—which kind works best? A few days in the test kitchen spent defatting gallons of greasy chicken broth quickly parted the winners from the losers.

Conventional wisdom regarding the best defatting method is to chill already cooled liquid until the fat rises to the top and solidifies. Then you simply lift off the cap of solid fat and discard it, leaving the liquid below pristine. Our tests confirmed that this method is supremely effective, but it does have one huge disadvantage: It takes a lot of time. Do you know many cooks who have hours to spare—up to 24 hours for a large quantity of liquid—waiting for their stock to chill? Me neither. And what if you are defatting the drippings from a roast for gravy that's to be served along with the meat in just 10 minutes?

And so we turn to the fat separator. No matter what the specific design, fat separators work for two reasons. One, because fat and water do not mix—their incompatible molecular structures and electrical charges keep them apart—and two, because fat always rises above the liquid in the container—fat is less dense than water.

Five of the eight models we tested were essentially pitchers with the pouring spout set into their base, like the small watering cans used to reach houseplants in high spots. When the liquid settles in the container, you can pour it off, stopping just before the layer of fat floating on the liquid's surface reaches the opening for the spout.

While all of the pitcher-type separators worked well, one feature that proved especially important was capacity. In general, we like large separators—usually around four cups—best. Large models can be used with good effect to separate the fat from either small or large quantities of

liquid, whereas you could grow old working your way through a gallon of stock with a 1½- or 2-cup model. Large separators also have large mouths, which make for easier pouring when you're adding the stock to the separator. Because of its oblong shape, the Trudeau Gravy Separator had the widest mouth of all, a point in its favor. The Trudeau also had an integrated strainer, which is helpful when you're defatting pan drippings that are still mixed with chunks of aromatic vegetables, herb sprigs, or other flavorings. In terms of materials, the shock resistance of plastic is better

suited to this tool than glass. During testing, one of the separators slipped out of our hands (which had gotten greasy from the fat) and fell to the floor. Had it been the glass model, we would have had to run out to buy a replacement.

Fat-separating ladles work when dipped just below the surface layer of fat that has accumulated atop the slightly cooled liquid. A series of slot-shaped holes along one side of the ladle allow fat to drain into the bowl of the ladle so it can be discarded. This procedure is repeated until as much fat as possible has been removed.

Separation Anxiety All Over Again

Over the years, we have picked up several tips on how to remove surface fat from stocks, soups, and stews when no fat separator is on hand. We wondered if any of these homespun methods could hold its own when applied to a gallon of fatty broth. Eight tests later, we found that the most familiar method—skimming with a cooking spoon—did the best job. Methods are listed in order of preference, from best to worst. In the end, however, a good fat separator beats all of these homespun tips with ease. –Nina West

TOOL	RESULTS
Cooking Spoon METHOD: Allow liquid to settle for about 10 minutes and use a wide, shallow (one- to two-ounce) spoon to skim the surface.	TESTERS' COMMENTS: Tedious, but tried, true, and effective.
Zipper-Lock Bag METHOD: Fill a heavy-duty zipper-lock bag with liquid, allow fat to rise, snip a small hole in corner of bag, and allow liquid to flow into another container. Pinch bag before fat flows out.	TESTERS' COMMENTS: Worked very well, provided your reflexes are quick enough to stop the flow of liquid before the fat pours out. Make sure the liquid is cool enough to handle without burning yourself.
Bulb Baster METHOD: Plunge tip of baster into liquid beneath fat, draw liquid into baster, and deposit it in another container.	TESTERS' COMMENTS: Worked remarkably well, with little fat transferred to the new container.
Ladle METHOD: Allow the liquid to settle for about 10 minutes, then skim the surface.	TESTERS' COMMENTS: Works best if you transfer the fatty liquid to a very tall, narrow container, creating a deep layer of fat. In other containers, it's easy to skim the liquid along with the fat.
Ice Bath METHOD: Place a pot filled with fatty liquid in an ice bath. The fat should cling to the sides of the pot once the pot is cold. The congealed fat can then be scraped away with a spoon.	TESTERS' COMMENTS: We waited (and waited and waited) for the pot to cool enough for the fat to cling to the sides. This method finally worked, but it was much too time-consuming.
Paper Towel METHOD: Skim the fatty surface of the liquid with sheets of paper towel.	TESTERS' COMMENTS: Convenient, though slow and messy. Better for small amounts of fat. For big jobs, you could use nearly an entire roll.
Cold Lettuce Leaf METHOD: Skim the fatty surface of the liquid with a cold lettuce leaf; the fat should cling to it.	TESTERS' COMMENTS: Ultimately ineffective. The leaves wilt quickly, so a new one is required every few strokes. Works better on small amounts of fat.
Frozen Soda Bottle METHOD: Freeze water solid in liter- or quart-sized bottle, then use it to stir fatty liquid. The fat should cling to the bottle.	TESTERS' COMMENTS: Worked well for the first plunge, but much less so for subsequent plunges. The paradox is that if you rinse off the fat, the ice melts, yet if the fat is left on the bottle, it gets added back to the liquid in the next pass.

RATING FAT SEPARATORS

We tested eight fat separators and evaluated them according to the following criteria. If the design or capacity of a particular unit precluded it from a test, the result is listed as N/A. All of the separators were dishwasher-safe, and all emerged from the dishwasher clean and odor-free. Separators are listed in order of preference.

PRICE: Prices paid in Boston-area stores, in national mail-order catalogs, and on Web sites.

MATERIAL: Primary material from which the separator is made.

CAPACITY: Total amount the separator will hold and still operate properly.

PERFORMANCE: We simmered 1 gallon of canned low-sodium chicken broth with 10 ounces schmaltz (rendered chicken fat) for 30 minutes, allowed the mixture to cool for 15 minutes, and then used each separator to separate the fat from the liquid in two amounts (wherever applicable), 1 cup and 4 cups. Scores from these two tests were averaged to determine an overall performance rating.

HANDLE COMFORT: Tested with both bare hands and an oven mitt (fat separators are often used to defat very hot liquids, so many cooks protect their hands by wearing oven mitts). Secure, roomy, easily grasped handles were preferred.

EASE OF USE: Separators that were easy to pour liquid into, that poured liquid neatly and easily, and that had easy-to-read measurement markings were preferred.

TESTERS' COMMENTS: These comments augment the information on the chart with observations about the separators' design or performance in specific tests.

BEST FAT SEPARATOR

Trudeau Gravy Separator with Integrated Strainer, Model 099-1105
MATERIAL: Plastic/polycarbonate

PRICE: $9.99
CAPACITY: 4 cups
PERFORMANCE: ★★★
HANDLE COMFORT: ★★★
EASE OF USE: ★★★

TESTERS' COMMENTS

If it's possible to get excited about a fat separator, this is the one to inspire enthusiasm. Its wide, oblong shape makes it easy to pour into, the integrated strainer is a great feature for pan drippings (although it would be better with smaller holes), and an angled shield near the spout prevents spillovers. Reasonably priced, too.

RECOMMENDED

Pedrini Gravy Separator
MATERIAL: Plastic/polycarbonate

PRICE: $14.95
CAPACITY: 5 cups
PERFORMANCE: ★★★
HANDLE COMFORT: ★★★
EASE OF USE: ★★★

Extra-large capacity and a nicely integrated handle. Spout traps a tiny bit of fat at the tip, but not enough to affect the defatted liquid.

East Hampton Industries Souper Strain, No. 824
MATERIAL: Plastic/polycarbonate

PRICE: $10.99
CAPACITY: 4 cups
PERFORMANCE: ★★★
HANDLE COMFORT: ★★
EASE OF USE: ★★★

This is the basic design that most cookware, discount, and hardware stores carry. Does a good job removing fat and pours neatly. Because the handle is not attached at the bottom of the cup, as it is on similar models from competing brands, this model is marginally less stable when the cup is full.

OMI (Oil Mop, Inc.) The Original Fat Mop
MATERIAL: Nylon bristles/metal spine/plastic handle

PRICE: $4.99
CAPACITY: N/A
PERFORMANCE: N/A
HANDLE COMFORT: ★★★
EASE OF USE: ★★★

Defatting a large quantity of liquid was inefficient and tedious, but this tool works well on stews, sauces, and other chunky dishes. Does not clean up in the dishwasher as thoroughly as the others, but it's inexpensive enough to replace periodically without breaking the bank.

East Hampton Industries Gravy Strain, No. 823
MATERIAL: Plastic/polycarbonate

PRICE: $5.99
CAPACITY: 1½ cups
PERFORMANCE: ★★★
HANDLE COMFORT: ★★★
EASE OF USE: ★★★

Works as well as its big brother, but better suited to defatting drippings than a whole pot of stock because of its small capacity.

Catamount Glass 2-Cup Fat Separator/Strainer
MATERIAL: Heatproof laboratory glass

PRICE: $16.95
CAPACITY: 2¼ cups
PERFORMANCE: ★★★
HANDLE COMFORT: ★★★
EASE OF USE: ★★★

Measurements are printed in dark ink and are therefore much easier to read than those on all of the plastic models. Difficult to pour neatly when filled to capacity.

NOT RECOMMENDED

WMF Profi Plus 11-Inch Stainless Steel Fat Skimming Ladle
MATERIAL: Stainless steel

PRICE: $19.99
CAPACITY: N/A
PERFORMANCE: ★★★
HANDLE COMFORT: ★★★
EASE OF USE: ★

The reason we wouldn't recommend this unit is not that it's a particularly bad ladle-style skimmer. In fact, with considerable patience and steadiness, it works fine. And that's just it. Using a ladle requires considerable patience and steadiness, whereas using a pitcher-style separator does not.

East Hampton Industries Skim It Fat Separator, No. 826B
MATERIAL: Plastic/polycarbonate

PRICE: $4.99
CAPACITY: N/A
PERFORMANCE: ★
HANDLE COMFORT: ★★
EASE OF USE: ★

Because liquid is resistant to the broad, blunt base of this separator, it's difficult to dip into liquid with enough precision to control the flow of fat. In short, it's hard to use. Designed to work with large quantities of liquid, so it wouldn't work with drippings from a roast.

Our testers found this to be a tedious process requiring fine control of the ladle, which, when dipped too low, let in the broth along with the fat. A spout on one side of the ladle—much like that on the pitcher-type separators—is designed to pour off the liquid while trapping the fat, but you cannot see where the broth stops and the fat begins, as you can in a clear pitcher-style separator. Frankly, skimming the surface fat with a wide, shallow spoon is just as effective and less frustrating.

Surprisingly, the cheesiest tool in the group, the "As Seen on TV" Fat Mop, turned out to be pretty interesting. The mop head is made of plastic fibers that attract fat. As the packaging says, it is designed to defat stews, gravies, soups, chilis, and fried foods—items for which it would be impossible to use another kind of fat separator—as it sweeps across the surface to wick away fat. In our tests, it did in fact prove effective with chunky tomato sauce and pot-au-feu. Strictly speaking, however, the Fat Mop is not intended for use with large amounts of liquid, though we did manage to defat 4 cups of broth in more than 20 swipes.

If we could have just one fat separator in the kitchen, Trudeau's version of the common pitcher-type would be our choice. For another five bucks, though, the Fat Mop makes a useful supplement, especially if you have to remove fat from chunky stews and chilis. Between the two, neither the fat nor the process of separating it should be cause for anxiety.

KITCHEN NOTES

⇒ BY BRIDGET LANCASTER ⇐

The Great Caper

We think that capers, those pickled Mediterranean buds, are a great finishing touch for salads, pan sauces, and just about any pasta dish you can think of, especially when fried. Many recipes for fried capers recommend adding the capers directly to hot oil. But, as we recently discovered in the test kitchen, this method can

PRESSED
To remove moisture

FRIED
Until crisp and crunchy

be dangerous; the moisture-packed capers explode when they open and splatter hot oil everywhere (think of popping popcorn with the pan lid off and you'll get the picture).

After several tests, we found a couple of ways to minimize the potential for disaster. First was to remove moisture from the capers by pressing them between several layers of paper towels. Second was to start the capers in cold oil, then heat them gradually.

Here's how to fry enough capers to garnish 1 pound of pasta: Drain, rinse, and press 2 tablespoons of capers between several layers of paper towels to remove as much

liquid as possible. Add the pressed capers and 2 tablespoons of olive oil to an 8-inch skillet and turn the heat to medium-low. Cook until most of the capers have split open (a few will still pop) and are crisp, 3 to 5 minutes. Transfer the capers to dry paper towels to drain, and enjoy!

Temperature Adjustment

During the development of our pot-au-feu recipe, we found that our favorite instant-read thermometer, the Thermapen, was registering the temperature of boiling broth at 215 degrees. Some unexplained culinary phenomenon, perhaps? Nah, just a reminder that it was

time to calibrate the thermometer.

We contacted ThermoWorks (www.thermoworks.com), maker of the Thermapen, and a company representative faxed us calibrating instructions. After removing the back label, which covers the two calibration adjustment screws, we placed the tip of the probe in ice water (being careful not to let the probe tip touch the container) and adjusted the "Zero" screw (on the right) until the temperature read 32 degrees. Then we repeated the same test, this time using boiling water and adjusting the "Span" screw (on the left) until the thermometer read 212 degrees. (You'll

---

TESTING PRODUCTS: "Out, Damn'd Spot!"

Food-stained clothing is a sad reality in our test kitchen. We decided to get serious about laundry, so we purchased 16 stain removers from local supermarkets and put them to the test. These products fell into four categories:

Pretreaters are applied to the stained garment, which is then thrown into the wash. This group included Spray 'n Wash, Shout, Zout, Shout Ultra Gel, Shout Action Gel, Extra-Strength Spray 'n Wash, and Spray 'n Wash Stain Stick.

Laundry additives go right into the machine with the wash to boost the stain-removing power of the detergent used. Both products in this group were made by Spray 'n Wash, one a liquid additive and one a concentrated tablet referred to as Actionball.

Spot removers are applied to clothes, which are then rubbed to remove stains and washed. Those tested included Gonzo Stain Remover, Amodex Premium Spot Remover, and Didi Seven Ultra Super Concentrated Cleaner.

Oxygen-based powders are diluted with water to make a soaking solution for garments. Once the stains are gone, the clothes can be washed. This group included All Oxi-Active, Shout Oxy Power, Clorox Oxygen Action, and Oxi-Clean.

THE TESTS For our tests, we took plain 100 percent cotton T-shirts and dirtied them with the foods most infamous for leaving unrelenting stains: pureed blueberries, pureed beets, black coffee, red wine, ketchup and yellow mustard (to simulate a hot dog mishap), melted bittersweet chocolate, and chili (which also covered grease stains). Each cleaning product was applied according to the manufacturer's instructions for maximum stain removal.

All of the products removed the coffee, wine, ketchup, and beet stains, but only the spot removers and oxygen-based powders managed to completely remove the tougher stains left by chili, blueberries, chocolate, and mustard. T-shirts tested with the pretreaters and laundry additives came out of the wash with several distinct, if muted, stains.

Spot removers call for brushing or blotting the stain until it is gone, and although this method is the most labor-intensive (in some cases up to seven applications were necessary), even the toughest stains were gone before the garment went into the washing machine. If time is a luxury you can afford and scrubbing and blotting are not your thing, then the oxygen-based powders are the way to go. T-shirts treated with these cleaners—used as concentrated soaking solutions, as per the manufacturers' instructions—needed only a light rubbing to remove the toughest stains. Although the T-shirts did need to soak for up to three hours (with Oxi-Clean working in the shortest amount of time), the labor was mostly hands-off (sounds good to us).

OUR CONCLUSION If you can't part with that favorite blouse or pair of pants and you don't mind an investment of time but little elbow grease, use an oxygen-based powder.

chili   blueberries

coffee   mustard

beets   ketchup

chocolate   red wine

THE T-SHIRT & THE STAINS

PRETREATERS
These apply-and-wash products couldn't cut through the toughest stains.

LAUNDRY ADDITIVES
Not enough boosting power to remove all food stains.

SPOT REMOVERS
Although labor-intensive, these products worked well to remove the stains before the shirt was washed.

OXYGEN-BASED POWDERS
With very little work but considerable soaking time, these products removed the toughest food stains.

need to adjust for the fact that the boiling temperature of water drops 1 degree for every 500-foot increase in elevation above sea level.)

If you have a dial-face thermometer, the process is even simpler. Just immerse the thermometer in a slurry of ice water (boiling temperature calibration is not necessary), being careful not to touch the container and, using a pair of needle-nose pliers, adjust the screw on the underside of the dial face until it reads 32 degrees.

The Quest for Cheesecloth

Can't find cheesecloth at your local grocer to strain out those last bits of herbs and veggies from your broth or stock? Luckily, cheesecloth is a multiuse item, and we found it in many hardware, paint, fabric, and craft stores.

Still can't locate cheesecloth? Don't worry, an at-hand solution is to line a mesh strainer with at least three layers of plain, white paper towels (no prints, please) and pour the broth through carefully (and slowly).

Leave It to Cleaver

When making stock (see pages 16–17), we found that the best way to release maximum flavor from the bones is to hack them up with a meat cleaver. We asked five test cooks (with various hand sizes and arm strength ranging from meek to macho) to evaluate five meat (not vegetable) cleavers. Testers hacked chicken wings, breasts, legs, and thighs with each cleaver and rated them on comfort, balance, and performance.

We found two winners (see below). Two other models tested—

the Henckels Professional S 6-Inch Cleaver ($49.99) and the Wüsthof Trident 6-Inch Cleaver ($69.99)— featured squared-off handles that testers found uncomfortable, while the Forschner Victorinox 6-Inch Household Cleaver ($70.99) was deemed too heavy and its blade too dull.

(**Cook's Extra** gives you free additional information online. For the complete results of our cleaver tests, visit www.cooksillustrated.com and key in code 1043.)

Sun-Dried Tomato Taste Test

A recent taste test showed that not all oil-packed sun-dried tomatoes taste the same, at least straight from the jar. We tasted tomatoes from Harry's Bazaar, Pastene, Mezzetta, Bella San Luci, Mediterranean (organic), L'Esprit De Campagne, and Trader Joe's. Tasters thought that only the Trader Joe's tomatoes, which are packed in olive oil, garlic, herbs, spices, and sulfur dioxide (to retain color), had the right balance of flavors and sweetness. All other brands were thought to have an overpowering musty, herbal flavor.

TOP TOMATOES
After tasting seven brands, our panel named Trader Joe's sun-dried tomatoes the best choice.

Although Trader Joe's tomatoes taste best straight from the jar, we found that we could improve the flavor of the other brands by rinsing away excess herbs and spices. The rinsed tomatoes won't taste as good as our favorite brand, but they won't tasty musty, either.

Tale of Two Chickens

Many readers have written to us about the saltiness of the buttermilk brine for our Ultimate Crispy Fried Chicken (May/June 2001). After retesting the recipe a few times, we found it highly seasoned. Some tasters thought it was perfect, but others argued that it was a tad too salty. After some trial and error, we came up with two amendments to the original recipe that would reduce the salty flavor without compromising the moistness provided by brining.

First, we reduced the salt and sugar in the brine by half while keeping the liquid amount the same (3/4 cup kosher salt, 2 tablespoons sugar, 7 cups buttermilk). Second, we eliminated the white breast meat in the recipe by switching from a whole butchered chicken to four chicken leg quarters, cut into eight thigh and drumstick pieces. Because of its higher fat content, the dark meat in the chicken leg quarters tastes juicier than white meat.

No Wine-ing

Looking for ways to replace the alcohol—especially from wine and fortified wines—in your recipes? Then you have something in common with many readers, especially when it comes to pan sauces (such as those accompanying the pan-roasted chicken breasts in our March/April 2003 issue).

In responding to these requests, our first impulse was to replace wine or vermouth with an equal amount of broth, but upon testing we found that sauces prepared this way lacked acidity and balance. After several rounds of tests, we found four ingredients—dealcoholized white wine (Sutter Home Fre, for example), verjus (the unfermented juice of unripe wine grapes), lemon juice, and white wine vinegar—that could make up for the lack of acidity. Formulas for substitutions are summarized below. For ingredients added when the sauce is ready to serve, use the lower amount, taste, and then add more if greater acidity is desired.

Alcohol-Free Pan Sauces To replace 1/2 cup wine or vermouth, try:

Ingredient	When to Add
1/4 cup each DEALCOHOLIZED WINE and CHICKEN BROTH	Use to deglaze pan
2–4 tablespoons VERJUS	Just before serving
1/2–1 teaspoon LEMON JUICE	Just before serving
1/2–1 teaspoon WHITE WINE VINEGAR	Just before serving

Steaks Worth Their Salt

Some readers have wondered why we emphasize seasoning meat with salt before cooking. To prove our point, we grilled two T-bone steaks and pan-seared two strip steaks and two filets mignons according to recipes published in the magazine. In each case, we salted one steak before and one after cooking (but before resting) with the same amount of kosher salt (a test kitchen favorite for this purpose).

When tasted, the steaks seasoned with salt after being cooked had a salty bite that overshadowed the flavor of the meat. And because the salt never fully dissolved, there were uneven pockets of crunchy kosher salt on the meat's surface. The steaks salted prior to cooking, on the other hand, had a well-seasoned, beefy taste. Seasoning with salt prior to cooking allows the crystals to dissolve and ensures even seasoning and no salty pockets.

If you still want a saltier punch on your well-seasoned steak, sprinkle more kosher or coarse sea salt on at the table. But by salting before cooking, you ensure that the meat has a baseline of seasoning. –Compiled by Nina West

IF YOU HAVE A QUESTION about a recently published recipe, let us know. Send your inquiry, name, address, and daytime telephone number to Recipe Update, Cook's Illustrated, P.O. Box 470589, Brookline, MA 02447, or to recipeupdate@bcpress.com.

OUR FAVORITES

BEST CLEAVER: GLOBAL
➤ $106
Perfectly balanced, with a razor-sharp blade. Easily handled tasks that stymied other meat cleavers.

BEST BUY: LAMSONSHARP
➤ $40
Lightweight, with comfortable handle. Popular among testers with modest hand strength.

Most of the ingredients and materials necessary for the recipes in this issue are available at your local supermarket, gourmet store, or kitchen supply shop. The following are mail-order sources for particular items. Prices listed below were current at press time and do not include shipping or handling unless otherwise indicated. We suggest that you contact companies directly to confirm up-to-date prices and availability.

NONSTICK SHEET PAN

Contrary to our usual thinking about nonstick sheet pans, we liked the new one from Calphalon for our oven fries (page 21). This was our first encounter with a sheet pan that provides both a nonstick finish and the sort of heavy-duty construction that will resist warping in the intense heat needed to brown our fries. The baking sheet can be ordered for $27.95 from **Cooking.com (Guest Assistance, 2850 Ocean Park Boulevard, Suite 310, Santa Monica, CA 90405; 800-663-8810, www.cooking.com)**, item #181768.

SPECIALTY CITRUS

All of the citrus pictured on the back cover, from the relatively common Meyer lemon to the exotic citron known as Buddha's Hand, are available from **Specialty Produce (5245 Lovelock Street, San Diego, CA 92110; 619-295-1668; www.specialtyproduce.com)**. Prices fluctuate with the market, and availability is seasonal for most items. The good news is that the season for these fruits is now.

CLEAVERS

With its comfortable handle, manageable weight, and modest price ($40), the LamsonSharp 7¼-inch meat cleaver is a good choice when you want to hack up a chicken to make stock (see pages 16–17). You can order one directly from the manufacturer, **Lamson & Goodnow Mfg. Co. (45 Conway Street, P.O. Box 128, Shelburne Falls, MA 01370; 413-625-6331; www.lamsonsharp.com)**, item #33100 for a walnut handle or #39555 for ebony. For those who are not on a budget, however, the 6-inch Global meat cleaver is unmatched in sharpness and can complete most tasks in one shot. **A Cook's Wares (211 37th Street, Beaver Falls, PA 15010; 800-915-9788; www.cookswares.com)** sells the G-12 Global cleaver, item #4745, for $106.

ROTISSERIES

While we can't be enthusiastic about any of the countertop rotisseries tested on page 12, we found two that were acceptable: the George Foreman GR82B George Jr. Rotisserie (item #B00005B6Z3) and the Popeil Jr. Showtime Rotisserie and Barbecue (item #B000066BEQ). To order one without having to stay up late for the infomercials, try **Amazon.com**, which sells each brand for $99.99.

DIJON MUSTARD

Our tasting of Dijon mustards turned up two hard-to-find brands that we liked. Domestic newcomer **Haus Barhyte (P.O. Box 1499, Pendleton, OR 97801; 800-227-4983; www.mustardpeople.com)** offers a 9-ounce jar for $4.00. Delouis Fils, considered by many to be the quintessential Dijon mustard, is available from the **Mount Horeb Mustard Museum (P.O. Box 468, 100 West Main Street, Mount Horeb, WI 53572; 800-438-6878; www.mustardmuseum.com)**, which sells a 7-ounce jar, item #DLF100, for $4.75.

SALT PIG

The salt pig shown on page 3 makes it easy to measure salt when cooking. You can order it for $29.95 from **The Baker's Catalogue (P.O. Box 876, Norwich, VT 05055; 800-827-6836; www.kingarthurflour.com)**. Ask or search for the "salt piglet," item #6186.

"BEST BUY" KNIFE SET

The Forschner knives mentioned on page 2 are available at **CutleryAndMore.com (645 Lunt Avenue, Elk Grove, IL 60007; 800-650-9866; www.cutleryandmore.com)**: chef's knife, 8-inch blade, item #40520, $21.50; paring knife, 3¼-inch blade, item #40508, $4.25; serrated/bread knife, 10¼-inch blade, item #40040, $29.95.

LENTILS DU PUY

The earthy flavor and firm texture of lentils du Puy, or French green lentils, make them the lentil of choice for the hearty soup on page 15. If hard to come by, the lentils can be ordered from **Kalustyan's (123 Lexington Avenue, New York, NY 10016; 800-352-3451; www.kalustyans.com)**, item #200F01, in 1-pound bags for $4.99. To search online by keyword, type Lentilles Varde de Puy.

BUNDT PANS

Heft and handles are the strong points of NordicWare's Platinum 12-cup nonstick Bundt pan, available for $27.95 at **Cooking.com**, item #129177. A lighter-weight, more economical option at $11.99 is the Baker's Secret nonstick 9½ by 3⅜-inch pan. Contact **World Kitchen (www.worldkitchen.com)** for a list of stores that carry the Baker's Secret line, or call **888-246-2737** to locate a factory store near you.

FAT SEPARATORS

As noted on page 29, the task of defatting dishes such as tomato sauce and chili is made easy with Oil Mop's Original Fat Mop, item #8066, available for $4.99 from **Fante's Kitchen Ware Shop (1006 South Ninth Street, Philadelphia, PA 19147; 800-443-2683; www.fantes.com)**. To remove the fat in larger, more traditional applications, try the generously sized Trudeau Gravy Separator with Integrated Strainer, also from Fante's (item #8711, $9.99), our tool of choice for degreasing stock.

United States Postal Service
Statement of Ownership, Management, and Circulation

1. Publication Title	2. Publication Number	3. Filing Date
Cook's Illustrated	1 0 6 8 – 2 8 2 1	10/01/03

4. Issue Frequency	5. Number of Issues Published Annually	6. Annual Subscription Price
Bi-monthly	6 issues	$35.70

7. Complete Mailing Address of Known Office of Publication (Not printer) (Street, city, county, state, and ZIP+4)
Boston Common Press
17 Station Street, Brookline, MA 02445
Contact Person
Telephone 617-232-1000

8. Complete Mailing Address of Headquarters or General Business Office of Publisher (Not printer)
Same as Publisher.

9. Full Names and Complete Mailing Addresses of Publisher, Editor, and Managing Editor (Do not leave blank)
Publisher (Name and complete mailing address)
Christopher Kimball, Boston Common Press
17 Station Street, Brookline, MA 02445

Editor (Name and complete mailing address)
Same as Publisher.

Managing Editor (Name and complete mailing address)
Barbara Bourassa, Boston Common Press
17 Station Street, Brookline, MA 02445

10. Owner (Do not leave blank. If the publication is owned by a corporation, give the name and address of the corporation immediately followed by the names and addresses of all stockholders owning or holding 1 percent or more of the total amount of stock. If not owned by a corporation, give the names and addresses of the individual owners. If owned by a partnership or other unincorporated firm, give its name and address as well as those of each individual owner. If the publication is published by a nonprofit organization, give its name and address.)

Full Name	Complete Mailing Address
Boston Common Press	17 Station Street
Limited Partnership	Brookline, MA 02445
(Christopher Kimball)	

11. Known Bondholders, Mortgagees, and Other Security Holders Owning or Holding 1 Percent or More of Total Amount of Bonds, Mortgages, or Other Securities. If none, check box. ▶ ☐ None

Full Name	Complete Mailing Address
N/A	

12. Tax Status (For completion by nonprofit organizations authorized to mail at nonprofit rates) (Check one)
The purpose, function, and nonprofit status of this organization and the exempt status for federal income tax purposes:
☐ Has Not Changed During Preceding 12 Months
☐ Has Changed During Preceding 12 Months (Publisher must submit explanation of change with this statement)

PS Form 3526, October 1999
(See Instructions on Reverse)

13. Publication Title	14. Issue Date for Circulation Data Below
Cook's Illustrated	September/October 2003

15.	Extent and Nature of Circulation	Average No. Copies Each Issue During Preceding 12 Months	No. Copies of Single Issue Published Nearest to Filing Date
a.	Total Number of Copies (Net press run)	716,595	724,683
b. Paid and/or Requested Circulation	(1) Paid/Requested Outside-County Mail Subscriptions Stated on Form 3541. (Include advertiser's proof and exchange copies)	513,672	506,732
	(2) Paid In-County Subscriptions Stated on Form 3541 (Include advertiser's proof and exchange copies)	0	0
	(3) Sales Through Dealers and Carriers, Street Vendors, Counter Sales, and Other Non-USPS Paid Distribution	91,204	87,263
	(4) Other Classes Mailed Through the USPS	0	0
c.	Total Paid and/or Requested Circulation (Sum of 15b. (1), (2),(3),and (4)) ▶	604,876	593,995
d. Free Distribution by Mail (Samples, compliment ary, and other free)	(1) Outside-County as Stated on Form 3541	3,230	3,270
	(2) In-County as Stated on Form 3541	0	0
	(3) Other Classes Mailed Through the USPS	0	0
e.	Free Distribution Outside the Mail (Carriers or other means)	4,188	8,285
f.	Total Free Distribution (Sum of 15d. and 15e.) ▶	7,418	11,555
g.	Total Distribution (Sum of 15c. and 15f) ▶	612,294	605,550
h.	Copies not Distributed	104,302	119,133
i.	Total (Sum of 15g. and h.) ▶	716,596	724,683
j.	Percent Paid and/or Requested Circulation (15c. divided by 15g. times 100)	98.79%	98.09%

16. Publication of Statement of Ownership
☑ Publication required. Will be printed in the Jan/Feb 2004 issue of this publication. ☐ Publication not required.

17. Signature and Title of Editor, Publisher, Business Manager, or Owner
Christopher Kimball Editor; Publisher
Date 10/1/03

I certify that all information furnished on this form is true and complete. I understand that anyone who furnishes false or misleading information on this form or who omits material or information requested on the form may be subject to criminal sanctions (including fines and imprisonment) and/or civil sanctions (including civil penalties).

Instructions to Publishers

1. Complete and file one copy of this form with your postmaster annually on or before October 1. Keep a copy of the completed form for your records.
2. In cases where the stockholder or security holder is a trustee, include in items 10 and 11 the name of the person or corporation for whom the trustee is acting. Also include the names and addresses of individuals who are stockholders who own or hold 1 percent or more of the total amount of bonds, mortgages, or other securities of the publishing corporation. In item 11, if none, check the box. Use blank sheets if more space is required.
3. Be sure to furnish all circulation information called for in item 15. Free circulation must be shown in items 15d, e, and f.
4. Item 15h., Copies not Distributed, must include (1) newsstand copies originally stated on Form 3541, and returned to the publisher, (2) estimated returns from news agents, and (3), copies for office use, leftovers, spoiled, and all other copies not distributed.
5. If the publication had Periodicals authorization as a general or requester publication, this Statement of Ownership, Management, and Circulation must be published; it must be printed in any issue in October or, if the publication is not published during October, the first issue printed after October.
6. In item 16, indicate the date of the issue in which this Statement of Ownership will be published.
7. Item 17 must be signed.

Failure to file or publish a statement of ownership may lead to suspension of Periodicals authorization.

PS Form 3526, October 1999 (Reverse)

RECIPES
January & February 2004

Hearty Lentil Soup, 15

Garlic-Rosemary Roast Chicken, 11

Fish Meunière with Browned Butter and Lemon, 19

Pasta with Sun-Dried Tomatoes, Ricotta, and Peas, 13

Pot-au-Feu, 7

PHOTOGRAPHY: CARL TREMBLAY, STYLING: MARY JANE SAWYER

---

www.cooksillustrated.com

Get all 11 years of *Cook's Illustrated* and a Free Gift!
Join www.cooksillustrated.com today and gain access to 11 years' worth of recipes, equipment tests, and food tastings . . . anytime and from anywhere! Plus, as a *Cook's* subscriber, you're offered a 20% discount.

Free Gift: As a paid member, you'll get *The Essential Kitchen: 25 Kitchen Tools No Cook Should Be Without*. From the editors of *Cook's Illustrated*, this helpful online guide provides recommendations on the best cookware, tools, and gadgets for your kitchen. Simply type in the promotion code **CB41A** when signing up online.

Here are a few of the many things available at our site:
Best Recipes: Eleven years' worth of recipes developed in America's Test Kitchen.
Cookware Reviews: Every cookware review published since 1993, plus many reviews never seen in *Cook's*.
Ingredient Tastings: Eleven years' worth of taste tests, providing you with recommendations on which supermarket ingredients to buy.
Online Bookstore: Cookbooks from the editors of *Cook's*, plus much more.

Oven Fries, 21

PHOTOGRAPH: CARL TREMBLAY

AMERICA'S TEST KITCHEN
Join the millions of cooks who watch our show, *America's Test Kitchen*, on public television every week. For more information, including recipes from the show and a schedule of program times in your area, visit www.americastestkitchen.com.

Eggplant Parmesan, 9

Chocolate Sour Cream Bundt Cake, 23

Skillet Apple Brown Betty, 25

Kumquat

Sweet Lime

Meyer Lemon

Pomelo

Key Lime

Buddha's Hand

Melogold

Citron

EXOTIC CITRUS

COOK'S
ILLUSTRATED

Classic Brownies
Not Cakey, Not Fudgy, Just Right

Juicy Pork Chops
Start with a Cold Pan?

Spinach Lasagna
Presoak Noodles and Quick-Bake

Chicken and Rice
Indian Spices, Complex Flavors

Tasting Bittersweet Chocolates
Ghirardelli Wins, Hershey's Scores

Pan-Seared Shrimp

Rating Baking Pans
$9 Pan Beats $95 Model

Perfect Baklava
Pizza Provençal-Style
How to Buy Pork
Orange Salads
Extra-Crisp Waffles

www.cooksillustrated.com

$5.95 U.S./$6.95 CANADA

04>

0 74470 62805 7

CONTENTS

March & April 2004

www.cooksillustrated.com

HOME OF AMERICA'S TEST KITCHEN

Founder and Editor	Christopher Kimball
Executive Editor	Jack Bishop
Senior Editors	Adam Ried
	Dawn Yanagihara
Director of Editorial Operations	Barbara Bourassa
Editorial Manager, Books	Elizabeth Carduff
Art Director	Amy Klee
Test Kitchen Director	Erin McMurrer
Senior Editors, Books	Julia Collin Davison
	Lori Galvin-Frost
Senior Writer	Bridget Lancaster
Associate Editors	Matthew Card
	Rebecca Hays
Science Editor	John Olson
Web Editor	Keri Fisher
Copy Editor	India Koopman
Test Cooks	Erika Bruce
	Keith Dresser
	Sean Lawler
	Diane Unger-Mahoney
Assistant Test Cooks	Garth Clingingsmith
	Charles Kelsey
	Nina West
Assistant to the Publisher	Melissa Baldino
Kitchen Assistants	Laura Courtemanche
	Nadia Domeq
	Ena Gudiel
Contributing Editor	Elizabeth Germain
Consulting Editors	Shirley Corriher
	Jasper White
	Robert L. Wolke
Proofreader	Louise Gachet

Vice President Marketing	David Mack
Sales Director	Leslie Ray
Retail Sales Director	Jason Geller
Corporate Sponsorship Specialist	Laura Phillipps
Sales Representative	Shekinah Cohn
Marketing Assistant	Connie Forbes
Circulation Manager	Larisa Greiner
Products Director	Steven Browall
Direct Mail Director	Adam Perry
Customer Service Manager	Jacqueline Valerio
Customer Service Representative	Julie Gardner
E-Commerce Marketing Manager	Hugh Buchan

Vice President Operations and Technology	James McCormack
Production Manager	Jessica Lindheimer Quirk
Assistant Production Manager	Mary Connelly
Production Assistants	Ron Bilodeau
	Jennifer McCreary
Systems Administrator	Richard Cassidy
WebMaster	Aaron Shuman
Production Web Intern	Miles Benson

Chief Financial Officer	Sharyn Chabot
Controller	Mandy Shito
Office Manager	Elizabeth Wray
Receptionist	Henrietta Murray
Publicity	Deborah Broide

For list rental information, contact: ClientLogic, 1200 Harbor Blvd., 9th Floor, Weehawken, NJ 07087; 201-865-5800; fax 201-867-2450.
Editorial Office: 17 Station St., Brookline, MA 02445; 617-232-1000; fax 617-232-1572. Subscription inquiries, call 800-526-8442.
Postmaster: Send all new orders, subscription inquiries, and change of address notices to: Cook's Illustrated, P.O. Box 7446, Red Oak, IA 51591-0446.

PRINTED IN THE USA

STALKS AND SHOOTS Although many shoots and stalks are now available year-round, they are traditionally harbingers of spring. Asparagus is available in shades of green, white, or purple. Fiddlehead ferns are young, unfurled fern shoots, aptly named for their resemblance to the head of a violin. They have a chewy texture and a flavor somewhere between asparagus and green beans. Thriving in cooler climates, field-grown rhubarb has rosy red and bright green hues, whereas the hothouse types come in paler shades. The roots and leaves are poisonous and should not be eaten. The artichoke, the unopened bud of a thistle stalk, is best eaten when it has a deep green color and tightly closed leaves. Also a member of the thistle family, cardoon looks like oversize celery but has the flavor of a mild artichoke. It is best braised, boiled, or fried. Celery can range in color from white to green. Fennel can be eaten raw or cooked, in which case its mild licorice flavor becomes even milder. Lemon grass stalks are used like herb sprigs to infuse many Asian dishes with a mild lemon flavor.

COVER (*Eggs*): Elizabeth Brandon, BACK COVER (*Stalks and Shoots*): John Burgoyne

THANKSGIVING DAYS

The day before Thanksgiving, my 8-year-old son, Charlie, and I set out up the mountain with my Winchester 32 special (Charlie had his lever-action BB gun) and hiked up to the ledges, rocky outcroppings that give a hunter a commanding view of the woods below. The old logging trails stood out as if they had been marked by a road crew, and the shape of the ridges, knolls, and valleys rose up through the bare trees. After sitting a bit, we headed up over the backside of the mountain into a hollow, where we came upon paths littered with sign, plenty of tree scrapings, and my favorite old elm, with its smooth, sculpted trunk that splits into thirds and spirals up and away from the forest floor. An hour later, we ended up on a narrow ridge with the wind surging through the pines and a view down the other side through a stand of half-dead chestnuts, gnarled, moss-covered, and standing round-shouldered like overdressed old men in holiday vests. In the distance we could see the remains of Fred West's farm, the house having been destroyed by fire last summer, three chimneys blackened and standing bare, as if in a child's drawing.

The sun was sinking into long dirty fingers of clouds, and the two of us peered down into a wooded bowl, a hazy abyss of trees and rocks a sea of browns and grays, indistinct and smoky in twilight. Above, we looked up to the surface, patches of pale blue sky visible, where the sun was still strong, its warmth no longer reaching the depths. Winter was on its way, but Charlie's boyish enthusiasm for the hunt overwhelmed thoughts of a dark season.

The week before I had attended a family funeral in Baltimore. The relatives had gathered as if at a standing room–only Thanksgiving; a quiet chattiness descended on the room, which was overheated and decorated in a woody 1950s style, with a large bowl of wrapped peppermint candies by the door.

This half of my family is an odd bunch and fond of nick-names. The four sisters (my grandmother among them) were named Mick, Dick, Kid, and Shick; one of their daughters was called Snoozie (as a baby, she slept most of the day) and another Squee (now referred to, with more deference, as Dee). Kid's first husband, John Condit, firmly believed that he could build a moon rocket. In Florida back in the 1920s, he actually constructed one, charged admission, and then skipped town on the day of the launch. Kid (named after the Yellow Kid comic strip) was herself a character. She kept a monkey as a pet, raised pit bulls, and more or less terrorized the rest of the family. (With her last breath, she called the nurse over to the bed, pinched her hard on the thigh, and then expired.) Shick, who was commonly referred to as Aunt Charlotte, was an artist, making sculptures of boiled chicken bones and colored glass. On a visit to her house as a child, I opened a large bureau only to find a treasure trove of these medieval artifacts, each delicately wrapped in tissue.

In the reception room at the cemetery, the youngest among us were prim, quiet, and stiff; the older family members, being used to the fleeting nature of life, were rather enjoying themselves, soft laughter bubbling up through hushed reminiscences. There was a procession to the graveside and then a short service performed by a stout, hirsute nun, a bit unsteady on her feet, from a nearby church. The wind whipped the holy water and earth into the faces of those seated in the front row, stinging their eyes with a reminder of life's indignities. The cemetery was raw and cold, the sky gray; perfect weather for hunting, I thought. Photographs were taken of old men standing behind overdressed

Christopher Kimball

children, the two groups bound uncomfortably by ritual. A postfuneral lunch at a nearby country club offered snow crab soup, soft-shell crab club sandwiches, and stiff, well-seasoned bloody marys.

Back on the farm, around the Thanksgiving table, adults and children had gathered once again. The last piece of chocolate trifle had been scooped off the plate, and, with the apple, pecan, and pumpkin pies half-gone, silence descended and the table was as quiet as the woods. Five-year-old Emily was folded up in her Mom's lap. Our teenage girls were temporarily sated from the pleasures of dessert. Parents and guests were happy to just sit back and watch the fire.

Now that I am decidedly closer to death than birth, I am often surrounded by the young and the old, celebrating beginnings and endings. Winter comes, the dead are buried, the young grow up, and we meet again in familiar places. These days, I seem to focus on the food and the fire rather than on meanings. Horace, the Roman philosopher-poet, was given a farm upon retirement, and he was quoted as saying, "Now I have nothing left to pray for." I am quite content to live on the edge of darkness, with my son by my side in the twilight or seated awkwardly at funerals, hugged by a cold, wet wind. Those lucky to have lived long enough finally see only what is before them. In the woods, we look for signs of prey, not deliverance. At a funeral, we see friends remembered, not forgotten.

In this life, on this day, I see a table well stocked with children and pie. I start to think that Horace and I have a lot in common. On a farm, on the far side of need, we have finally found nothing left to pray for.

FOR INQUIRIES, ORDERS, OR MORE INFORMATION:

www.cooksillustrated.com

At www.cooksillustrated.com you can order books and subscriptions, sign up for our free e-newsletter, or check the status of your subscription. Subscribe to the Web site and you'll have access to 11 years of Cook's recipes, cookware tests, ingredient testings, and more.

COOKBOOKS

We sell more than 40 cookbooks by the editors of Cook's Illustrated. To order, visit our bookstore at www.cooksillustrated.com or call 800-611-0759 or 515-246-6911 from outside the U.S.

COOK'S ILLUSTRATED Magazine

Cook's Illustrated magazine (ISSN 1068-2821), number 67, is published bimonthly by Boston Common Press Limited Partnership, 17 Station Street, Brookline, MA 02445. Copyright 2004 Boston Common Press Limited Partnership. Periodicals postage paid at Boston, Mass., and additional mailing offices, USPS #012487. POSTMASTER: Send address changes to Cook's Illustrated, P.O. Box 7446, Red Oak, IA 51591-0446. For subscription and gift subscription orders, subscription inquiries, or change-of-address notices, call 800-526-8442 in the U.S. or 515-247-7571 from outside the U.S., or write us at Cook's Illustrated, P.O. Box 7446, Red Oak, IA 51591-0446.

Measuring Greens

Recipes often call for 8 or 10 cups (or a volume measurement) of salad greens, but greens are usually sold by weight or by the head. How do I make the conversion from weight or heads to cups?

BILL CONKLIN
PORT TOWNSEND, WASH.

➤ Hoping that we could find a simple formula for converting from weight to volume, we purchased baby spinach, mesclun, and a couple of heads of red leaf lettuce. Back in the test kitchen, we happily found that in each case 1 ounce of greens (we tore the lettuce leaves into bite-size pieces so they could be measured) equaled about 1 cup lightly packed. While there's no waste when buying baby spinach or mesclun, figure on losing about 20 percent per head of lettuce after coring and cleaning. If you want 10 cups of cleaned, torn lettuce leaves, buy a head that weighs 12 ounces. We generally find that about 2 ounces (or 2 cups) of greens makes for a single serving.

All–Purpose Ramekins

I never seem to have enough of the right-size ramekins for whatever individual-type dessert I'm making. I don't want to fill my cabinets with a dozen of every size. As it is, I'm overrun! Does anyone know what the most commonly used size is? Is it better to go bigger and fill less when necessary? Please help before I buy again!

JOANNE FORMISANO
MORGANVILLE, N.J.

➤ If you want to purchase one set of ramekins and one set only, we have the following advice. As for size, go (slightly) large rather than small; a size between 6 and 8 ounces (but no bigger) should accommodate recipes calling for 4-ounce ramekins, but 4-ounce ramekins will not accommodate larger recipes. For material, select sturdy, high-fired porcelain over Pyrex glass custard cups, which are neither broilersafe nor the most attractive container for an elegantly executed crème brûlée. For shape, the most practical choice is round. Although we like shallow oval ramekins for our November/December 2001 crème brûlée recipe because they provide a high ratio of sugary burnt crust to custard, a round vessel with straight sides is necessary if you want to use ramekins for individual soufflés; soufflés will rise successfully only if they have the straight sides of a vessel to climb. Also with regard to shape, avoid overly deep ramekins with a narrow circumference. Ramekins ranging from 6 to 8

ounces should measure 3 to 4 inches across. You can determine the volume of any ramekins you have at home by measuring the amount of water they will hold when filled to the rim.

Leave the Stirring to Us

What do you know about a gadget called the StirChef? It supposedly saves you time by stirring the pot for you—a replacement for the personal chef, perhaps?

MARGARET MOREY
PORTLAND, MAINE

HANDS-FREE STIRRING
Can the StirChef take the place of a real cook with two hands? Can it make decent risotto?

➤ For $30, the StirChef buys you the freedom to handle other tasks while it stirs food on the stovetop. Of the more than a dozen types of food the StirChef is supposed to be able to stir, we tried three: risotto, which requires a long period of constant stirring; chili, which needs intermittent stirring; and chocolate pudding, which calls for a brief but steady stretch of stirring.

The StirChef comes with a cylindrical motor run on four AA batteries (guaranteed to hold up for three to four hours of constant stirring), three different-sized stirring paddles (to fit saucepans 6 to 8½ inches wide, or about 1½ to 4½ quarts), and a stainless steel shaft that connects any of the paddles to the motor. The motor also has three arms to stabilize it; they stretch as needed to fit the size of the pan. Once we figured out how to put all of these pieces together (and which end was up—no easy task), we started cooking.

The most annoying thing about the StirChef is that once you set it up in the pot, you can't remove it until you finish cooking (try and you'll burn your hands). That also means that if you want to add ingredients to the pot during cooking, you have to maneuver around the StirChef. Thus for the risotto, we had to add butter, onion, and, most inconveniently, a cup of rice through the rather small spaces between the arms

grabbing the sides of the pot. This requirement became even more inconvenient when we had to ease in a couple of cans of beans and tomatoes and a pound of ground beef when making chili. (We made only half a recipe because that was all that would fit in a 4-quart saucepan. This points up another limitation imposed by the StirChef.) Finally, the StirChef also makes it impossible to cover the pot because the motor sticks up above the rim (no matter the size of the pot used). This was a problem when making our chili recipe, which calls for one hour of cooking covered and one hour uncovered.

Yes, the StirChef did deliver creamy risotto (with no scorching), evenly cooked chili (with very, very minor scorching), and serviceable chocolate pudding (no curdling, but the texture was not completely smooth). No, we still don't recommend it. The idea of a tool that will do the stirring for you sounds like such a convenience, but, in practice, it's not. In fact, given all of its limitations, it's more of an inconvenience, and who wants to spend $30 on that?

Reusing Oil for Frying

I have tried reusing cooking oil for deep-frying and have found that the second time I use the oil there are tiny little particles in it that coat the food and darken it; this seems to affect appearance and taste to a degree. Is it not possible to reuse oil, or can it be reused, and, if so, how does one filter out the tiniest of these particles? I hate to throw away all of that oil, which seems perfectly good other than the suspended particles.

CHARMAINE MCCRYSTAL
REDWOOD CITY, CALIF.

➤ The test kitchen doesn't like the idea of wasting seemingly good, if slightly used, oil, either, and generally filters out food particles with a fine-mesh strainer. For very fine particles, the strainer can be lined with two or three layers of cheesecloth. A strainer lined with a paper coffee filter works, too. Once the oil has been filtered, the test kitchen stores it in the refrigerator and generally finds that the oil is good for three or four uses (with filtration after each use). Of course, the kitchen goes through stored oil more quickly than most home cooks and so ends up keeping it for only three or four months. One more point: While you can reuse oil that has been used to fry potatoes or doughnuts or any other bakery product, do not reuse oil used to fry protein, such as fish or chicken, because of the off flavors these foods impart to the oil.

Understanding Wild Rice

In "Wild about Rice" in Kitchen Notes (November/December 2002), you say that calling wild rice a rice isn't correct because wild rice is an aquatic grass. Well, rice, the domesticated kind that more than half the world eats, is also an aquatic grass. Both are in the grass family, as are almost all of the grains that have been domesticated and are eaten around the world—wheat, corn, barley, rye, and oats.

KAREN BOSWORTH
JUNEAU, ALASKA

➤ The notion that wild rice and domestic rice are altogether different creatures is a common one, so we can thank you and an expert on the subject, Raymie Porter, for setting us all straight. According to Porter, an associate at an agricultural research center at the University of Minnesota, where a great deal of research has been done on the official state grain—wild rice—both white rice and wild rice are aquatic (each grows in water, be it in a lake or a cultivated paddy) and both are grasses (as are wheat, corn, barley, rye, oats, and all other cereal grains). The wild rice of the Great Lakes Region is called *Zizania palustris* (not *Zizania aquatica*, as is often presumed), and white rice is called *Oryza sativa*. Recent research shows that these two grains have a lot more in common with each other than most people—scientists and cooks included—ever thought.

A New Zest Trap

In the Kitchen Notes section of your May/June 2003 issue, you had an update on Microplane rasp-style graters. Did you know that you can also purchase a "zester holder"? I have one, and it does an excellent job catching all of the zest.

DEWAYNE BAXTER
JACKSON, MICH.

➤ We tried the zester holder (see photo below), which slides easily and fits snugly under the 12-inch, handle-free model of the Microplane rasp-style grater. It does in fact do a good job of capturing every single shred of citrus zest or grated hard cheese and then neatly transferring it to a bowl, and it costs only $4.95. So it works, and we like it.

We've also found, however, that a metal bench scraper works well to scoop zest or grated cheese off the counter and into the bowl, and the bench scraper, unlike the zester

NEATER ZESTING
The zester holder keeps grated cheese and citrus zest off the counter.

This odd gripper is supposed to make slicing an onion easier, but it doesn't.

holder, serves other purposes. The one advantage of the zester holder is that neither zest nor cheese ever touches the counter in the first place. Considering this convenience and the holder's modest price, we consider it to be a "nice-to-have," but not a "must-have," tool.

No Scrubbing, No Soaking–Not Exactly

I tried that new cleaner—Dawn Power Dissolver—on a couple of nasty pans and had good results. I would love to know what you think of it.

CONNIE WU
BOSTON, MASS.

➤ Procter & Gamble makes the claim that its product Dawn Power Dissolver does such a good job of cutting through all sorts of grease and tough, baked-on grime that you'll never have to soak or scrub a dirty pot or pan again. Just spritz on some Dawn Power Dissolver, wait 15 to 30 minutes depending on the toughness of the job, wipe with a sponge, and rinse. We tried this technique with stainless steel pots in which we'd scorched jam and *fond* (drippings from burnt meat); various cookware (metal cookie sheets, a Pyrex baking pan, fry pans, a broiler pan) stained from previous use; and a stovetop in the home of a

colleague who hadn't cleaned it for months.

We found that the "no soaking, no scrubbing" principle applied in the cases of the burnt fond and the easier-to-clean surface grease on the stovetop. In most other cases, we found Dawn Power Dissolver to be effective only if we scrubbed, and, in a couple of cases (an old cookie sheet, the broiler pan, the worst of the stains on the stovetop), more than one application was required. (A note in small type on the back label does say that for the toughest jobs some scrubbing and a couple of applications may be necessary.) The product was not successful in removing the scorched jam.

In our tests, Dawn Power Dissolver excelled at cutting through grease, and, as far as we know, it is unique in its ability to remove old brown stains from Pyrex. Our cleansers of choice for tough jobs, Cameo and Bar Keeper's Friend, aren't terribly effective grease cutters, and in our tests did not remove staining from Pyrex. (Also, like the Dawn cleaner, they were not much help with scorched jam.) And they require much more scrubbing to clean up an old broiler pan. Still, these products do remove fond and brown stains from most cookware with a modicum of scrubbing, they don't require a 15-minute soak, and they are cheaper than Dawn Power Dissolver: A 12.8-ounce spray bottle costs $2.79; we went through more than half of the bottle for the above tests.

Would we add Dawn Power Dissolver to our battery of cleaning aids? Yes. But we would reserve it for use on problems such as stained Pyrex, broiler pans, and stovetops, where there isn't a cheaper alternative that's equally effective.

Quick Tips

COMPILED BY REBECCA HAYS AND NINA WEST

Kitchen Twine Stand-In

Finding himself in need of kitchen twine but with none at hand, Norman Lamberg of Arlington, Va., came up with a substitute. He now ties meat, poultry, and bouquet garni with unflavored, unwaxed dental floss when kitchen twine is unavailable.

Crushing Peppercorns

While many cooks use the bottom of a small heavy skillet to crush peppercorns, Katherine Toy of San Francisco, Calif., favors a Pyrex measuring cup. The cup is heavy enough to crush the peppercorns, and its clear glass bottom allows her to gauge her progress as she works.

Reading Kitchen Scales

Bulky containers, large roasts, and the like can obscure the display on a digital scale. Lief Erikson of Minneapolis, Minn., found an ingenious way around the problem.

1. Steady a lightweight cake stand on the scale, and set the tare at zero.
2. The cake stand, which is wide enough to accommodate large pans and big cuts of meat, elevates items so that the display is visible.

Packing Dishes

Cathy Bush of Virginia Beach, Va., wraps dishes in plastic before boxing them for moving. Unlike newspaper, which can stain, plastic wrap keeps the dishes clean. Crumpled newspaper or bubble wrap can be used to pad the box and keep plastic-wrapped dishes and glassware safe.

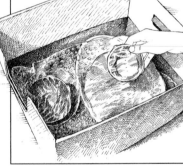

Offset Spatula Substitute

Unwilling to pay premium kitchenware store prices for a large offset icing spatula, Justin Bruce of Arcata, Calif., went shopping for affordable options at a hardware store. He bought a large offset palette knife with a flexible blade, which is normally used for mixing small amounts of paint or Spackle. The knife works almost as well as an icing spatula, and it costs only one quarter to one half as much. Palette knives can also be purchased at art supply stores.

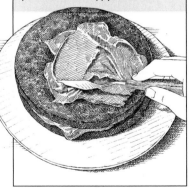

Heating Milk for Coffee

Jessica Joy Gadeken of Evanston, Ill., likes her coffee with milk, but she also likes it piping hot. Instead of pouring cold milk into her cup for a tepid drink, she does the following.

1. Measure the desired amount of milk into the empty carafe of an electric coffee maker before brewing.
2. As the hot coffee drips in, the warming plate of the coffee maker heats the milk, resulting in a pot of steaming hot coffee with milk.

Reviving Stale Chips

Self-described potato chip addicts, Valerie Dar of Westfield, Mass., and Craig Dill of Albuquerque, N.M., hate to throw away leftover chips, even if they've gone stale. They found that microwaving stale potato or tortilla chips restores crispness beautifully. Spread 2 cups of chips on a Pyrex pie plate and microwave on high for 1 minute. Place the hot chips on a double layer of paper towels and allow them to come to room temperature before serving.

Send Us Your Tip We will provide a complimentary one-year subscription for each tip we print. Send your tip, name, address, and telephone number to Quick Tips, Cook's Illustrated, P.O. Box 470589, Brookline, MA 02447, or visit www.cooksillustrated.com.

Homemade Flavored Coffee

Sandy Hyman of Denver, Colo., appreciates the taste of store-bought flavored coffee but has developed a creative way to make her own specialty brews at home.

For 10 cups of coffee, place ½ teaspoon of ground cinnamon, ⅛ to ¼ teaspoon cardamom, or ½ teaspoon allspice in the filter of a drip-style coffee maker along with the ground coffee. Brew the coffee as you normally would and enjoy a subtly scented drink.

Disposal Freshener

Rather than discarding the remnants of zested citrus peels, Patricia Fry of Wolfeboro, N.H., grinds leftover pieces of lemon, lime, orange, and grapefruit rind in her kitchen sink disposal. The strong scent of the fruit helps to mask unpleasant odors that sometimes collect in the disposal.

Cleaning Cheese Graters

Graters coated with the sticky residue from soft cheeses can be a chore to clean. Shirley Eisenson of Golden, Colo., found an easy way to handle this task.

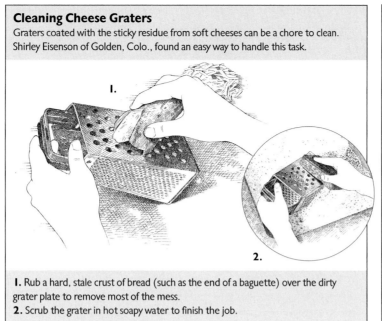

1. Rub a hard, stale crust of bread (such as the end of a baguette) over the dirty grater plate to remove most of the mess.
2. Scrub the grater in hot soapy water to finish the job.

Shaping Patties

Knowing that crab cakes must be uniformly shaped if they are to cook evenly, Elma Miller of Burlington, Ontario, Canada, came up with a way to shape them, as well as hamburgers and other patties, with a simple item she always has on hand.

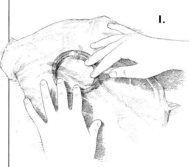 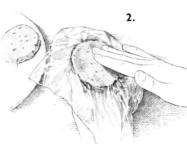

1. Line a small, two-piece Mason jar lid with plastic wrap.
2. Press enough fish, crab, or potato cake mixture into the lid to fill it completely and evenly.
3. Remove the patty by gently pushing the lid up from the bottom.

Instant Olive Paste

When A. Shirley Gudlink of Matteson, Ill., needs a few spoonfuls of very finely minced olives, capers, or sun-dried tomatoes, she pulls out a garlic press. She places two or three pitted olives, a teaspoonful of capers, or two oil-packed, sun-dried tomatoes in the hopper of a garlic press and squeezes. The pastes can be used to flavor salad dressings, dips, and sauces or be used as a pasta topping or sandwich spread.

Easy Ground Spices

When a recipe calls for a small amount of freshly ground whole spices, such as cumin or coriander seed, Chris Caldes of Golden, Colo., reaches not for an electric spice grinder but for an empty pepper mill designated for spices. Chris drops the whole spices into the hopper of a clean pepper mill, sets the mill to the desired level of coarseness, and starts grinding.

Handy Cake Tester

An avid baker, Betsy Regan of Branford, Conn., hangs a small, clean, unused straw whisk broom near her oven. When she needs to test a cake for doneness, she breaks off a straw and inserts it into the cake.

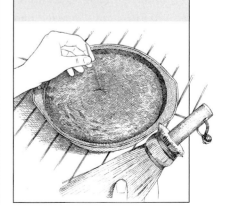

Resurrecting Raised Waffles

Yeasted waffles seem old-fashioned, and they require an ounce of planning,
but they are crisper, tastier, and more convenient to prepare than regular waffles.

≥ BY KERI FISHER WITH GARTH CLINGINGSMITH ≤

Raised waffles are barely on the current culinary radar, and that's a shame. Instead of being leavened with baking powder or baking soda, raised waffles rely primarily on yeast, which yields breakfast fare with a unique texture and flavor. Raised waffles are much more interesting than basic waffles; they are at once creamy and airy, tangy and salty, refined and complex.

The concept is simple enough. Most of the ingredients (flour, salt, sugar, yeast, milk, melted butter, and vanilla) are combined the night before and left to rise on the counter. The next day, eggs and baking soda are added and the batter is baked off. In fact, yeasted waffles involve less work than traditional waffles when it comes time to make them in the morning. But as we soon found out, many of the old recipes still in circulation are not reliable.

Serve these delicate, airy waffles with room-temperature syrup. Hot syrup quickly soaks into the waffles and softens their texture.

The Basics

Most raised waffle recipes call for the batter to be left out at room temperature overnight to rise. A warm kitchen provides a fertile field in which the yeast can feed. During my initial tests, however, I discovered that these recipes had too small a window of time before tangy turned downright sour. Batter left to rise unrefrigerated overnight (for me, from 5 o'clock in the afternoon—the end of the work day—until 9 o'clock the next morning) rose and fell, leaving behind a thin, watery batter that yielded an unpleasantly sharp-tasting waffle. A more flexible option, I discovered, was to leave the batter to rise—more slowly—in the refrigerator. Now I could prepare the batter before dinner and let it sit safely overnight. This simple change made the rest of my testing go much more smoothly.

Because most home cooks now use instant (rapid-rise) yeast, which does not require proofing, this was my leavener of choice. The question was, how much. A full packet of yeast (2¼ teaspoons) yielded an overly fluffy, insubstantial waffle; the large amount of yeast was producing a glut of gas. Waffles made with a scant 1 teaspoon of yeast were too bland, so I settled on 1½ teaspoons, which

imparted a pleasant tangy flavor and a texture halfway between airy and earthbound.

Choosing the right flour was confusing because raised waffles are part bread (think yeast bread) and part cake (think griddle cakes). Tests quickly determined that waffles made with bread flour were bready, tough, and chewy. Cake flour produced a sour, thin waffle. All-purpose flour lived up to its name and was the flour of choice, providing a solid base for both good flavor and good texture.

Tasters overwhelmingly preferred waffles made with milk to those made with heavy cream or buttermilk. The batter made with cream was too heavy for the leavening power of the yeast, and the resulting waffles were dense. The waffles made with buttermilk, on the other hand, were thought to taste "like cheese" (the yeast provides more than enough flavor), so I crossed it off my list, along with sour cream and yogurt. Too much milk made the waffles delicate;

the right amount was 1¾ cups. Whole, reduced-fat, and skim milk all yielded similar results, a big surprise until I recalled that I had already added a stick of melted butter; the total fat content of the batter wasn't changed much by the type of milk used. (I had tested 2 and 4 tablespoons of butter, but tasters preferred the extra-crisp exterior and rich flavor provided by a full stick.)

Just 1 teaspoon of vanilla added depth of flavor, and a full teaspoon of salt complemented the waffle's tangy flavor. A tablespoon of sugar gave the waffles a sweetness that wasn't cloying.

Thinking Ahead

At this point, my working recipe called for only two ingredients to be added in the morning: eggs and baking soda. Wondering if the eggs could be mixed in the night before, I prepared a batch and found that these waffles had the same great texture and flavor as a batch made with eggs added at the last minute. Best of all, adding the eggs at the outset made for even less last-minute work than was called for in the old-fashioned recipes. (Recipes that call for leaving the batter on the counter overnight add the eggs in the morning for safety reasons. Because I was letting the batter rise in the refrigerator, I could safely add the eggs at the outset.)

The next question concerned the baking soda called for in some recipes. Did these waffles really need it? Tests proved that waffles made with and without baking soda were virtually indistinguishable. Why, then, do most recipes call for it? Because batters left at warm room temperature for too long are usually batters that contain dead yeast in the morning (as I found out in an early test). The baking soda, then, is a fail-safe ingredient, one that ensures *raised* waffles. Because my recipe has

Yeasted versus Regular Waffles

LEAVENED WITH YEAST
Crispy and dark.

CHEMICALLY LEAVENED
Chewy and pale.

Why bother with yeasted waffles? Two reasons: The yeast gives the waffles a tangy flavor, and it makes them especially light, airy, and crisp (left). Typical waffles, made with baking powder or baking soda, are more dense and chewy and don't brown as much (right).

Fermentation is arguably the oldest of cooking techniques. Even the early hunters and gatherers must have noticed that meat and berries tasted and smelled quite different a few days after collection. Louis Pasteur made the seminal discovery that the changes in food over time often result from the metabolic activity of microbes; Pasteur was observing the action of yeast, which converts sugars to ethyl alcohol and releases carbon dioxide gas as a byproduct.

In our waffle recipe, yeast plays two roles, providing leavening and flavor. Initial tests convinced us that leaving the yeasted batter out all night at room temperature yielded an exhausted, sour-tasting batter. Curious to see how much faster yeast respiration occurred at room temperature than in the 40-degree environment of the refrigerator, I fashioned a simple respirometer using a test tube and a balloon. As the yeast breaks down sugars into carbon dioxide, gas becomes trapped in the balloon, causing it to inflate.

Within a short period of time (three hours), the room-temperature batter had produced enough carbon dioxide to inflate the balloon, indicating healthy yeast activity. But after 18 hours, the batter was spent and no longer produced carbon dioxide. The refrigerated batter produced carbon dioxide at a very slow but steady rate—which is good news for the cook. Rather than having to closely monitor a waffle batter left at room temperature, we refrigerate ours, thereby affording ourselves one of the greatest luxuries of all: sleeping in.
–John Olson, Science Editor

ON THE COUNTER		IN THE REFRIGERATOR	
After 3 hours	**After 18 hours**	**After 3 hours**	**After 18 hours**
The batter quickly produces enough carbon dioxide to fill the balloon.	Yeast cells have died and the batter has collapsed and separated.	The batter produces a little carbon dioxide to partially fill the balloon.	The batter continues to produce carbon dioxide at a steady rate.

the batter rise in the controlled environment of the refrigerator, the yeast is not given the chance to die off. (See "The Effects of Temperature on Yeast," above.) In dozens of tests, the yeast still had plenty of leavening power the next morning, making the baking soda redundant.

Now there was nothing to add in the morning except syrup. I had discovered that raised waffles not only taste better than the traditional variety but that a tiny bit of advance planning made them easier to prepare at breakfast time as well.

YEASTED WAFFLES
MAKES ABOUT SEVEN 7-INCH ROUND OR FOUR 9-INCH SQUARE WAFFLES

The batter must be made 12 to 24 hours in advance. We prefer the texture of the waffles made in a classic waffle iron, but a Belgian waffle iron will work, though it will make fewer waffles. The waffles are best served fresh from the iron but can be held in an oven until all of the batter is used. As you make the waffles, place them on a wire rack set above a baking sheet, cover them with a clean kitchen towel, and place the baking sheet in a 200-degree oven. When the final waffle is in the iron, remove the towel to allow the waffles to crisp for a few minutes. These waffles are quite rich; buttering them before eating is not compulsory and, to some, may even be superfluous.

1 3/4 cups whole, low-fat, or skim milk
8 tablespoons unsalted butter, cut into 8 pieces
2 cups (10 ounces) unbleached all-purpose flour
1 tablespoon sugar
1 teaspoon salt
1 1/2 teaspoons instant yeast
2 large eggs
1 teaspoon vanilla extract

1. Heat milk and butter in small saucepan over medium-low heat until butter is melted, 3 to 5 minutes. Cool milk/butter mixture until warm to touch. Meanwhile, whisk flour, sugar, salt, and yeast in large bowl to combine. Gradually whisk warm milk/butter mixture into flour mixture; continue to whisk until batter is smooth. In small bowl, whisk eggs and vanilla until combined, then add egg mixture to batter and whisk until incorporated. Scrape down sides of bowl with rubber spatula, cover bowl with plastic wrap, and refrigerate at least 12 and up to 24 hours.

2. Following manufacturer's instructions, heat waffle iron; remove waffle batter from refrigerator when waffle iron is hot (batter will be foamy and doubled in size). Whisk batter to recombine (batter will deflate). Bake waffles according to manufacturer's instructions (use about 1/2 cup for 7-inch round iron and about 1 cup for 9-inch square iron). Serve waffles immediately or hold in low temperature oven (see note).

Waffle Irons

Waffle irons range in price from less than $20 to almost $100. Is there as wide a range in quality? To find out, we gathered eight classic (not Belgian) models. There were two types of iron: The first group, large and square, yielded huge perforated waffles that can be torn into four smaller squares for individual servings; the second yielded a much smaller, round waffle that serves one.

All of the models tested featured a sensor that lit or dimmed to indicate whether the waffle was ready. All but two models had adjustable temperatures, letting you choose how dark you want your waffles. The two unadjustable models—the Hamilton Beach/Proctor Silex Waffle Baker, priced at $16.99, and the Toastmaster Cool-Touch Waffle Baker, priced at $19.99—produced insipid waffles. Neither model is recommended.

Our favorite irons were those that produced waffles with good height and dark, even browning. Topping the list were two VillaWare models (Uno Series Classic Waffler 4-Square, $89.95, and Classic Round, $59.95); the Cuisinart Classic Waffle Maker, $29.95; and the Black and Decker Grill and Waffle Baker, $56.99. The VillaWare models featured not only a ready light but also a ready bell.

A more meaningful feature on which to base your choice is size. The VillaWare Classic Round and Cuisinart irons are fine if you don't mind making one small waffle at a time. In the end, we preferred the convenience of the VillaWare 4-Square and the Black and Decker Grill and Waffle Baker, which cook four individual waffles at once. While the VillaWare produced a marginally better waffle (which was slightly darker and more evenly colored), the Black and Decker costs $30 less and also features reversible griddle plates. –K.F.

BEST PERFORMANCE
VILLAWARE Uno Series
Classic Waffler 4-Square,
$89.95
➤ Makes the best waffles, and the iron chimes when waffles are done, but note the price tag.

BEST VALUE
BLACK AND DECKER Grill and Waffle Baker, $56.99
➤ Makes big, beautiful waffles and also doubles as a griddle.

WORST PERFORMANCE
PROCTOR SILEX Waffle Iron, $16.99
➤ No way to adjust thermostat, and waffles are pale and very flat.

Chicken and Rice, Indian-Style

Chicken biryani is a complicated (and often greasy) classic Indian dish. Chicken and rice is a plain and simple American one-pot meal. Could I find a happy medium?

⋟ BY MATTHEW CARD ⋞

Chicken biryani has about as much in common with American-style chicken and rice as naan does with Wonder bread. They both share the same major ingredients but diverge widely from there. In biryani, long-grain basmati rice takes center stage, enriched with butter, saffron, and a variety of fresh herbs and pungent spices. Pieces of tender chicken and browned onions are layered with the rice and baked until the flavors have mingled. This is India in a pot, a far cry from everyday chicken and rice.

But it comes at a stiff price. Traditional biryani recipes are long in both ingredients and labor. The chicken is rubbed with spices and marinated before being browned; the rice is soaked, blanched, and mixed with a complex *masala,* or blend, of innumerable spices; the onions are deep-fried; and everything is finally layered—rice, onions, chicken, repeat—into a cooking vessel and baked or steamed until the flavors have blended. In addition, most biryani recipes I tested were made greasy by the deep-fried onions and had overcooked the rice by the time the chicken was done. I set out to find a middle path between the extremes of dull simplicity and epicurean complexity.

Getting Started

I prepared a few classic biryani recipes to better acquaint myself with the dish, a task that required a full day in the test kitchen and produced a huge pile of dirty dishes. I made three time-saving discoveries. First, I learned that I could skip the step of marinating the chicken (too much time, too little flavor enhancement). Second, I found I could prepare the whole recipe on the stovetop, eliminating the need for an oven. Third, it was possible to cook the onions and the chicken in the same large skillet, saving a pan. The streamlined recipe, although still not a 30-minute supper, now consisted of cooking the onions, browning the chicken, parboiling the rice, and then simmering/steaming the layered biryani until done.

The best-tasting biryani from my recipe tests was made with two abundant layers of deep-fried onions, but they inevitably turned the dish greasy. Onions sautéed in a tablespoon of fat (oil or butter) failed to brown in a similar fashion. More fat

Chicken and rice gets a makeover with Indian ingredients and European cooking techniques. A yogurt sauce tames the heat of the spices.

was clearly necessary, but how much could I add without turning the dish greasy? I started with ½ cup of fat for two sliced onions and reduced it 1 tablespoon at a time. In the end, 3 tablespoons proved sufficient. Butter prevailed over oil, adding more flavor and color.

Chicken and Spices

Tasters preferred dark meat chicken—it was more flavorful and juicy than white meat, which ended up dry. Bone-in thighs are the test kitchen favorite because they are so meaty. Having already eliminated marinating, I followed test kitchen protocol for braising chicken pieces. (Biryani is, in essence, a braise because it uses moist, low heat for cooking.) To eke out as much flavor as I could, I browned the chicken deeply, with the skin on for protection. Before layering the pieces with the rice, I stripped the skin. With this last step, the greasiness issue was finally put to rest.

Biryani's subtle, delicate flavor and aroma are largely derived from the masala of whole spices blended into the rice. (Ground spices—I tested

these as well—tasted raw.) Cardamom and cinnamon are essential, but too much of either easily overwhelmed other flavors. Tasters quickly ruled out nutmeg and cloves as overpowering. Coriander, too, was excluded—but it was for being too mild. In the end, tasters approved of cardamom, cinnamon, cumin seed, and fresh ginger sliced into coins. Sweet, earthy, sharp, and musky, the spices paired well together. Lightly smashing the cardamom and ginger with a chef's knife intensified their flavor.

Before serving, I diligently fished out the spices from the rice as tasters strongly objected to unexpectedly biting down on whole cardamom pods, but this nitpicky task grew tiresome. I began thinking of ways to isolate the spices. In French cooking, herbs and spices are often bundled together in cheesecloth and added to soups. The liquid flows through the permeable bundle, and the soup is flavored. I decided to try a little fusion cooking and give the bundle idea a whirl. I tied the spices together and added the bundle to the layered biryani before steaming, but that accomplished little. In the end, an even easier solution delivered big flavor. I simply simmered the bundle in the water used to parboil the rice. I also found that adding a portion of this flavored liquid to the layered biryani—sort of like adding pasta cooking water to a pasta dish—further intensified the spice flavor. Now I had included both French and Italian technique in streamlining a classic Indian dish.

The Final Touches

Saffron is mixed with the rice as both a coloring and flavoring agent. Any more than a pinch turned the rice Day-Glo orange and made it taste medicinal. Tasters demanded a fair amount of garlic and jalapeño, as well as some seeds from the chiles for additional fire. A little sweetness from currants (or raisins, in a pinch) helped to temper the heat and accent the warm spices. Cilantro and mint, both standard biryani ingredients, found favor with tasters.

Now I had a two-pot chicken and rice with plenty of personality that had been made without the fussy techniques of an "authentic" chicken biryani. This is the essence of good

American home cooking: Take the best parts of a foreign cuisine and adapt them to their new home. I had a renewed appreciation of the term "melting pot."

CHICKEN BIRYANI
SERVES 4

This recipe requires a 3½- to 4-quart saucepan about 8 inches in diameter. Do not use a large, wide Dutch oven, as it will adversely affect both the layering of the dish and the final cooking times. Begin simmering the spices in the water prior to preparing the remaining ingredients; the more time the spices have to infuse the water (up to half an hour), the more flavor they will give to the rice. Biryani is traditionally served with a cooling yogurt sauce; ideally, you should make it before starting the biryani to allow the flavors in the sauce to meld.

10	cardamom pods, preferably green, smashed with chef's knife
1	cinnamon stick
1	piece fresh ginger (about 2 inches), cut into ½-inch-thick coins and smashed with chef's knife
½	teaspoon cumin seed
3	quarts water
	Salt
4	bone-in, skin-on chicken thighs (about 1½ pounds), trimmed of excess skin and fat and patted dry with paper towels
	Ground black pepper
3	tablespoons unsalted butter
2	medium onions, sliced thin (about 4 cups)
2	medium jalapeño chiles, one seeded and chopped fine, the other chopped fine with seeds
4	medium garlic cloves, minced or pressed through garlic press (about 1½ tablespoons)
1¼	cups basmati rice
½	teaspoon saffron threads, lightly crumbled
¼	cup dried currants or raisins
2	tablespoons chopped fresh cilantro leaves
2	tablespoons chopped fresh mint leaves
	Yogurt Sauce (recipe follows)

1. Wrap cardamom pods, cinnamon stick, ginger, and cumin seed in small piece of cheesecloth and secure with kitchen twine. In 3½- to 4-quart heavy-bottomed saucepan about 8 inches in diameter, bring water, spice bundle, and 1½ teaspoons salt to boil over medium-high heat; reduce to medium and simmer, partially covered, until spices have infused water, at least 15 minutes (but no longer than 30 minutes).

2. Meanwhile, season both sides of chicken thighs with salt and pepper and set aside. Heat butter in 12-inch nonstick skillet over medium-high heat until foaming subsides; add onions and cook, stirring frequently, until soft and dark brown about edges, 10 to 12 minutes. Add jalapeños and garlic and cook, stirring frequently,

until fragrant, about 2 minutes. Transfer onion mixture to bowl, season lightly with salt, and set aside. Wipe out skillet with paper towels, return heat to medium-high, and place chicken thighs skin-side down in skillet; cook, without moving chicken, until well browned, about 5 minutes. Flip chicken and brown second side, 4 to 5 minutes longer; transfer chicken to plate and remove and discard skin. Tent with foil to keep warm.

3. If necessary, return spice-infused water to boil over high heat; stir in rice and cook 5 minutes, stirring occasionally. Drain rice through fine-mesh strainer, reserving ¾ cup cooking liquid; discard spice bundle. Transfer rice to medium bowl; stir in saffron and currants (rice will turn splotchy yellow). Spread half of rice evenly in bottom of now-empty saucepan using rubber spatula. Scatter half of onion mixture over rice, then place chicken thighs, skinned-side up, on top of onions; add any accumulated chicken juices. Evenly sprinkle with cilantro and mint, scatter remaining onions over herbs, then cover with remaining rice; pour reserved cooking liquid evenly over rice.

4. Cover saucepan and cook over medium-low heat until rice is tender and chicken is cooked through, about 30 minutes (if large amount of steam is escaping from pot, reduce heat to low).

The Layered Look

Layering the ingredients into a saucepan is the secret to the mingling of flavors in chicken biryani. Here's the assembly method that works best: Return half of the parboiled rice to the saucepan, top with half the onions, followed by the chicken pieces, the rest of the onions, and then the rest of the rice. Moisten everything with the spice-infused cooking liquid from the rice, cover, and steam over medium-low heat until the chicken is done and the rice is tender.

Run heatproof rubber spatula around inside rim of saucepan to loosen any affixed rice; using large serving spoon, spoon biryani into individual bowls, scooping from bottom of pot and serving 1 chicken thigh per person.

YOGURT SAUCE
MAKES ABOUT 1¼ CUPS

1	cup whole milk or low-fat plain yogurt
1	medium garlic clove, minced or pressed through garlic press (about 1 teaspoon)
2	tablespoons minced fresh cilantro leaves
2	tablespoons minced fresh mint leaves
	Salt and ground black pepper

Combine first four ingredients in small bowl; season to taste with salt and pepper. Let stand at least 30 minutes to blend flavors.

TASTING: **Basmati Rice—Buy American?**

Basmati is a variety of very long-grain rice most commonly grown in northern India and Pakistan. It is aged for a minimum of a year, though often much longer, before being packaged. Aging dehydrates the rice, which translates into grains that, once cooked, expand greatly—more so than any other long-grain rice.

Several American rice growers now sell their own basmati. Unfortunately, the two products we tasted couldn't compare with the real thing. Their flavor was not nearly as aromatic as Indian-grown basmati, and the cooked grains were soft and stubby. I later learned that American-grown basmati is not aged and hence doesn't expand as much as Indian-grown rice. Luckily, Indian rice is widely available in most supermarkets and costs about the same as domestic. Make sure that the label indicates that the rice has been aged; otherwise your biryani might be uncharacteristically mushy. —M.C.

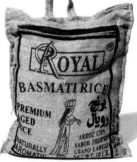

CALIFORNIA DREAMIN'
This California rice lacked the aroma and flavor of the Indian original, and tasters found the cooked grains "mushy" and broken.

TROUBLE IN TEXAS
Comments on this rice were nearly identical to those about the California rice, including "gummy," "soft," and "chewed-up looking."

THE ORIGINAL AND BEST
Tasters' comments on Indian-grown, aged rice included "great texture," "great grain separation," "something to chew on," and "toasty."

Juicy Weeknight Pork Chops

Dry, tough pork chops are the reality. My dream was juicy, tender pork chops in 20 minutes.

⇒ BY BRIDGET LANCASTER ⇐

There are two kinds of pork chops: the double-thick chops—with dark, caramelized exteriors and juicy, succulent interiors—that are great when I have the time to brine, rub, sear, roast, or grill, and the run-of-the-mill chops that I grab in haste at the supermarket and throw into a skillet at home, hoping for the best. Hope flies out the window, however, when I sink my teeth into a chop that's dry as leather and tough as nails. Then there's nothing to do but open a jar of applesauce and cover the chop with it, using it like a sheet at a crime scene.

But with all its many flaws, this basic pork chop has one major benefit: time. From beginning to end, it's only minutes away from the table (just enough time to open the applesauce). Sure, I'd like a juicier, more tender chop, but at what cost? Would I need to succumb to the temptation of brining or grilling? Or could I find a simple way to create the elusive juicy pork chop and get it on the table in 20 minutes?

Choosing the Chops

Boneless chops cooked up much drier than bone-in and were eliminated from contention. Also rejected were superthin chops (about ¼ inch thick), which dried out in the course of being walked through a hot kitchen. Thick, 1-inch (or more) chops, which were less apt to dry out, necessitated the use of the stovetop and the oven, the former to brown the chops and the latter to cook them through without burning the exterior. This just wasn't quick enough to meet my 20-minute goal. The right thickness was ½ inch to ¾ inch—thin enough to keep the cooking on the stovetop and thick enough to give the chops a fighting chance for a juicy interior.

The next decision was which cut to buy: blade chop, center-cut chop, or rib chop (see page 17 for more information). Rib chops fared best; center-cut were a close second.

Recipe Review

Pork chop recipes use one of three basic approaches. In the first, the chops are seared over high heat and then cooked uncovered over medium-low. The second method also starts the chops on high heat, then adds stock or water and covers the pan before reducing the heat. The third method again sears the chops over high heat but covers the pan without adding any liquid beforehand. The worst of the lot was leaving the

An unusual method, which starts by placing the chops in a cold pan, produces juicy chops without any fussing.

pan uncovered, which produced unevenly cooked chops. Adding liquid and then covering the pan was not much better. After 15 minutes (about the same cooking time the other two methods required), the chops were still tough. The last method, which seared the pork chops over high heat and covered the pan without first adding liquid, showed the most promise. Although still miles away from my dream of juicy, tender pork chops, I didn't need a gallon of water or the jaw strength of a bear to get them down.

Using the high-heat, covered-pan cooking method, I uncovered a few secrets of pork chop cookery. First, chops should not be cooked to an internal temperature much higher than 140 degrees—cooking them beyond this point results in tough, dry chops. I also found that when I reduced the searing time from three minutes per side to one minute per side, the chops were more moist, albeit not juicy. In fact, I needed only to look in the pan to see the enormous amount of juices that had been released. If the juices were in the pan, they weren't in the chops.

As I thought out loud (aka complained) to my colleagues, one raised an interesting query: Was the high heat causing the problem? Although we usually sear pork roasts and thick chops over high heat to develop flavor, perhaps these thinner chops were too quick to dry out in a hot pan. I raced back to the stove and heated the pan over a more modest medium heat before adding the chops. After a few minutes, I covered the chops and cooked them over medium-low. When I uncovered the chops, voilà—I found a large reduction in the amount of pan juices. I cut into what appeared to be a pretty tender chop and happily found the juices right where they belonged, inside the meat. Progress!

Perhaps pushing my luck, I wondered what would happen if the pork chops were introduced to heat at an even slower pace. If medium heat was good, what about—you guessed it—no heat? Although it seemed strange, I placed the next batch of chops in a cold pan and then turned the heat to medium. After the chops had cooked for a few minutes on each side, I covered them

STEP-BY-STEP | COOKING THE CHOPS

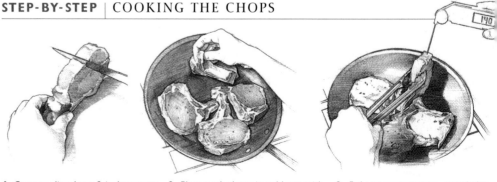

1. Cut two slits about 2 inches apart through fat and connective tissue.

2. Place pork chops in cold pan with bony ribs facing center.

3. Rely on temperature, not timing, to judge when chops are done.

SCIENCE: Why Pork Chops Don't Like High Heat

Curious about the unconventional cold-pan method of cooking chops in our recipe, I decided to investigate the effect of heat on pork. What I discovered was that the secret to juicy pork resided in the structure of its muscle proteins.

Proteins are long chains of linked amino acids that fold into a huge variety of three-dimensional shapes. Folded muscle protein also holds and immobilizes a considerable amount of water in an ordered fashion. When things heat up, this organized state of affairs is thrown into disarray as the proteins unfold. Thermal analysis of pork has shown that there are three approximate temperatures at which groups of pork proteins come undone: 126 degrees, 144 degrees, and 168 degrees. As each of these temperatures is reached, more water is freed from the proteins. Meat proteins also tend to compact as they cook, squeezing out the freed-up water.

All cooks focus on the temperature reached at the middle of a piece of meat to determine doneness, but this may be too myopic. The means by which the middle gets to that temperature is at least as important. High-heat cooking methods, such as searing, guarantee that the outer layer of meat will be well browned before the inside is just done. By keeping the heat level low, water loss on the outside of the chop is minimized, and more of the juice that is bound inside the meat remains there. And so the secret to juicy pork chops is revealed: Slow cooking over low heat is best. –John Olson, Science Editor

The top photo shows the dramatic effects of high-heat cooking on what had been a perfect cube of pork. The bottom of the cube, which was in direct contact with the hot pan, contracted significantly. The contraction of the meat fibers leads to significant moisture loss—in the case of four pork chops, about 5 tablespoons by the time they reached the proper internal temperature. The bottom photo shows that over low heat there is far less contraction of the meat fibers. In our tests, by the time the four chops reached the proper internal temperature, they had shed not even 1 tablespoon of liquid.

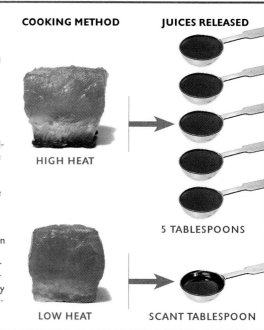

COOKING METHOD   **JUICES RELEASED**

HIGH HEAT

5 TABLESPOONS

LOW HEAT

SCANT TABLESPOON

---

and cooked them through over low heat while uttering a silent prayer. My hopes ran high when I noticed that there were barely any pan juices in the skillet. I plated a chop, bit down, and was met with the juiciest and most tender chop yet.

The only drawback was color—or lack thereof. These pork chops were as blond as the ubiquitous bombshell. Using a little sugar in addition to salt and pepper to season them went a long way toward helping to color the chops. I also found that instead of splitting the browning time and the sugar evenly between the two sides of a chop, it was better to sugar one side and let it develop a more substantial color.

Although starting meat in a cold pan seemed a little odd—if not downright weird—it made quick-cooking a weeknight pork chop almost foolproof. Would these pork chops win any beauty contest? I doubted it. But from now on I could serve my applesauce on the side.

EASY PORK CHOPS
SERVES 4

In this recipe, "natural" pork chops—not "enhanced"—work best; the liquid injected into enhanced pork inhibits browning. (For more information on enhanced pork, see page 16.) Electric burners are slower to heat than gas burners, so, if

using one, begin heating the burner before seasoning the chops. When cooking the first side of the chops, use color as an indicator of when to flip them; to determine doneness, use an instant-read thermometer—do not go solely by cooking times. Serve these simple pork chops with chutney or applesauce, or try one of the variations.

> 4   bone-in pork rib or center-cut chops, about 7 ounces each and ½ to ¾ inch thick, patted dry with paper towels and prepared according to illustration 1 on page 10
> 1   teaspoon vegetable oil
>   Salt and ground black pepper
> ½   teaspoon sugar

1. If using electric stove, turn burner to medium heat. Rub both sides of each chop with ⅛ teaspoon oil and sprinkle with salt and pepper. Sprinkle one side of each chop evenly with ⅛ teaspoon sugar, avoiding the bone.

2. Place chops, sugared-side down, in 12-inch nonstick skillet, positioning chops according to illustration 2 on page 10. Using hands, press meat of each chop into pan. Set skillet with chops over medium heat; cook until lightly browned, 4 to 9 minutes (chops should be sizzling after 2 minutes; if not, see box at left). Using tongs, flip chops, positioning them in same manner. Cover skillet, reduce heat to low, and cook until center of each chop registers 140 degrees on instant-read thermometer, 3 to 6 minutes (begin checking temperature—as shown in illustration 3—after 2 minutes); chops will barely brown on second side. Transfer chops to platter, tent with foil, and let rest 5 minutes; do not discard liquid in skillet.

3. Add any juices accumulated on platter to skillet. Set skillet over high heat and simmer vigorously until reduced to about 3 tablespoons, 30 seconds to 90 seconds; adjust seasonings with salt

and pepper to taste. Off heat, return pork chops to skillet, turning chops to coat with reduced juices. Serve chops immediately, browned-side up, pouring any remaining juices over.

PORK CHOPS WITH MUSTARD-SAGE SAUCE

Follow recipe for Easy Pork Chops; after transferring chops to platter, pour liquid in skillet into small bowl. While chops are resting, add 1 teaspoon vegetable oil and 1 medium garlic clove, minced, to now-empty skillet; set skillet over medium heat and cook until fragrant, about 30 seconds. Add ¼ cup low-sodium chicken broth; increase heat to high and simmer until reduced to about 2 tablespoons, about 3 minutes. Add pork chop juices to skillet. Off heat, whisk in 1 tablespoon Dijon mustard and 3 tablespoons unsalted butter until combined. Stir in 1 teaspoon minced fresh sage leaves and adjust seasonings with salt and pepper; spoon sauce over chops and serve immediately.

PORK CHOPS WITH BRANDY AND PRUNES

Cover ⅓ cup chopped pitted prunes with ¼ cup brandy and let stand. Follow recipe for Easy Pork Chops; after transferring chops to platter, pour liquid in skillet into small bowl. While chops are resting, add 1 teaspoon vegetable oil and 1 medium shallot, minced, to now-empty skillet; set skillet over medium heat and cook, stirring occasionally, until shallots have softened, about 2 minutes. Off heat, add brandy and prunes; set skillet over medium-high heat and cook until brandy is reduced to about 2 tablespoons, about 3 minutes. Add pork chops' juices to skillet. Off heat, whisk in 2 teaspoons minced fresh thyme leaves and 3 tablespoons butter until combined. Adjust seasonings with salt and pepper; spoon sauce over chops and serve immediately.

How to Pan-Sear Shrimp

We wanted shrimp that were well caramelized but still moist, briny, and tender.

≽ BY KEITH DRESSER ≼

Pan-searing is the easiest way to cook shrimp—if you know a few secrets.

Having prepared literally tons of shrimp in my lifetime as both a chef and a home cook, I have found that pan-searing produces the ultimate combination of a well-caramelized exterior and a moist, tender interior. If executed properly, this cooking method also preserves the shrimp's plumpness and trademark briny sweetness.

That being said, a good recipe for pan-seared shrimp is hard to find. Of the handful of recipes I uncovered, the majority resulted in shrimp that were variously dry, flavorless, pale, tough, or gummy—hardly appetizing. It was time to start some serious testing.

I quickly uncovered a few basic rules. First, tasters unanimously favored shrimp that were peeled before being cooked. Peeled shrimp are easier to eat, and unpeeled shrimp fail to pick up the delicious caramelized flavor that pan-searing provides. Second, the shrimp were best cooked in a 12-inch skillet; its large surface area kept the shrimp from overcrowding the pan and steaming—a surefire way to prevent caramelization. Third, oil was the ideal cooking medium, favored over both a dry pan (which made the shrimp leathery and metallic tasting) and butter (which tended to burn).

Because the test kitchen likes to brine shrimp before grilling them, I assumed that a successful recipe for pan-seared shrimp would include brining. Although brining did enhance their moistness and texture, the shrimp released just enough moisture to inhibit caramelization.

Although I rejected brining as a flavor enhancer, my brining tests yielded an unexpected benefit. I had been adding sugar to the brining solution with the hope of improving the shrimp's browning characteristics. While the sugar did not promote browning in the brined shrimp, it did accentuate their natural sweetness and nicely set off their inherent sea-saltiness. Capitalizing on this serendipitous discovery, I added a pinch of sugar to some unbrined shrimp along with the requisite salt and pepper. This did indeed boost the flavor, as I had expected, and, absent the water from the brine, the sugar also encouraged browning.

Even in a 12-inch skillet, 1½ pounds of shrimp must be cooked in two batches or it will steam instead of searing. The trick was to develop a technique that neither overcooked the shrimp nor let half of them turn cold while the other half finished cooking. To prevent overcooking, I tried searing the shrimp on one side, removing the pan from the flame, and then allowing the residual heat to finish cooking the other side of the shrimp. This worked like a charm. Better yet, the residual heat from the pan also solved the cold shrimp problem. As soon as the second batch finished cooking (the first batch was now near room temperature), I tossed the first batch back into the pan, covered it, and let residual heat work its magic once again. After about a minute, all of the shrimp were both perfectly cooked and piping hot. Now all I needed were a few ideas for some quick sauces.

I tested sauces made from assertive ingredients such as garlic, ginger, and chipotle chile mixed with plenty of acidity as a foil for the shrimp's richness. The most successful of these sauces were those that clung to the shrimp like a glaze. All of them could easily be made ahead of time and quickly tossed with the shrimp during the last stage of cooking, once the pan was removed from the heat.

PAN-SEARED SHRIMP
SERVES 4

The cooking times below are for 21/25 shrimp (that is, the size of the shrimp is such that there are 21 to 25 in 1 pound). If 21/25 shrimp are not available, adjust cooking times slightly. Either a nonstick or traditional skillet will work for this recipe, but a nonstick will simplify cleanup. For a guide to buying supermarket shrimp, see Kitchen Notes, page 30.

2	tablespoons vegetable oil
1½	pounds 21/25 shrimp, peeled and deveined
¼	teaspoon salt
¼	teaspoon ground black pepper
⅛	teaspoon sugar

Heat 1 tablespoon oil in 12-inch skillet over high heat until smoking. Meanwhile, toss shrimp, salt, pepper, and sugar in medium bowl. Add half of shrimp to pan in single layer and cook until spotty brown and edges turn pink, about 1 minute. Remove pan from heat; using tongs, flip each shrimp and let stand until all but very center is opaque, about 30 seconds. Transfer shrimp to large plate. Repeat with remaining tablespoon oil and shrimp; after second batch has stood off heat, return first batch to skillet and toss to combine. Cover skillet and let stand until shrimp are cooked through, 1 to 2 minutes. Serve immediately.

PAN-SEARED SHRIMP WITH
GARLIC-LEMON BUTTER

Beat 3 tablespoons softened unsalted butter with fork in small bowl until light and fluffy. Stir in 1 medium garlic clove, minced, 1 tablespoon lemon juice, 2 tablespoons chopped parsley, and ⅛ teaspoon salt until combined. Follow recipe for Pan-Seared Shrimp, adding flavored butter when returning first batch of shrimp to skillet. Serve with lemon wedges, if desired.

PAN-SEARED SHRIMP WITH
GINGER-HOISIN GLAZE

Stir together 2 tablespoons hoisin sauce, 1 tablespoon rice vinegar, 1½ teaspoons soy sauce, 2 teaspoons grated fresh ginger, 2 teaspoons water, and 2 scallions, sliced thin, in small bowl. Follow recipe for Pan-Seared Shrimp, substituting an equal amount red pepper flakes for black pepper and adding hoisin mixture when returning first batch of shrimp to skillet.

PAN-SEARED SHRIMP WITH
CHIPOTLE-LIME GLAZE

Stir together 1 chipotle chile in adobo, minced, 2 teaspoons adobo sauce, 4 teaspoons brown sugar, 2 tablespoons lime juice, and 2 tablespoons chopped cilantro in small bowl. Follow recipe for Pan-Seared Shrimp, adding chipotle mixture when returning first batch of shrimp to skillet.

Provençal Pizza

Pissaladière, the classic olive, anchovy, and onion pizza from Provence, is easy enough to prepare, but each ingredient must be handled just so.

⇒ BY JULIA COLLIN DAVISON ⇐

Pissaladière is Provençal street food, a fragrant, pizzalike tart prized for its contrast of salty black olives and anchovies against a backdrop of sweet caramelized onions and thyme. Supporting this rough and rustic flavor combination is a wheaty crust with a texture that is part chewy pizza and part crisp cracker. Commonly eaten as an appetizer or even a light supper alongside a salad, this classic French favorite is still something of a foreigner to most Americans—darkly handsome, but a bit difficult to understand.

I had to start with a series of "get acquainted" tests to fully comprehend the range of possibilities. Most recipes produced a crust in the style of a pizza, others called for savory pie dough fit into a fluted tart pan, and I even found a few that used squares of store-bought puff pastry. All of them called for caramelized onions, black olives, thyme, and anchovies, but additional sources of flavor, such as Parmesan, sun-dried tomatoes, basil, and oregano, were not uncommon. As for the basic flavor ingredients, almost all of the caramelized onions were underdone, while the bullish flavor of anchovies overran the olives and thyme. Anchovies, I thought, should not rule but rather act as a counterpoint to the sweet onions, briny olives, and fragrant thyme.

As for the crust, the test kitchen quickly eliminated puff pastry and pie dough. Unfortunately, the more authentic pizzalike crusts weren't very good, either. Textures were too short (think shortbread) and crackery or overly soft and doughy. Like me, tasters thought that good pissaladière should have a dual-textured crust that is crisp on the outside (like a cracker) and chewy on the inside.

This pizza captures the flavors of Provence—caramelized onions, black olives, anchovies, and fresh thyme—in every bite.

The Crust

Although pizza crusts aren't exactly right for pissaladière, I whipped up three different *Cook's* pizza crusts to see if any could be used as a jumping-off point. The thin crust wasn't sturdy enough and the deep-dish was much too doughy, but the traditional crust was the right thickness (about ½ inch) and had about the right flavor. Knowing that I wanted it to be chewier, with a more crackerlike exterior, I took a closer look at each of its four major ingredients—bread flour, oil, water, and yeast—to see where I could make adjustments.

I replaced various amounts of bread flour with all-purpose but made zero headway. Bread flour has more protein than all-purpose, and that translates into a more substantial chew. Testing amounts of olive oil ranging from none at all up to 6 tablespoons, I again found that the original recipe (which called for 1 tablespoon) produced the best balance of crisp to tender without causing the dough to be brittle (a problem when the amount of oil dropped below 1 tablespoon) or greasy (a problem when the amount of oil exceeded 1 tablespoon).

Next on my list of ingredients to tinker with was water. The original recipe called for ¾ cup of water to 2 cups of flour. Less water made the crust drier (no surprise) and tougher. More water made the dough chewier, but I soon learned that there was such a thing as too chewy. When I increased the water to 1¼ cups, the crust baked up with huge holes and was as chewy as bubble gum. The crust made with 1 cup of water proved to be a happy medium—chewier than the original pizza crust but not over the top.

When I varied the amount of yeast, the flavor changed (as did the rising time), but not the texture. Less yeast and an overnight rise—a common flavor-enhancing technique—did produce a crust with a slightly more complex flavor, but it was awfully hard to detect once it came up against the onions, olives, and anchovies. One teaspoon of yeast pumped the dough through the first rise in a convenient 75 minutes (give or take 15 minutes, depending on the humidity and the

Understanding the Dough

We found that the same basic ingredients—flour, water, yeast, salt, and oil—can yield doughs that bake up quite differently, depending on the ratio of ingredients as well as the shaping technique and baking temperature. Here are the characteristics and differences of four of our dough recipes.

FOCACCIA DOUGH
Focaccia is made with a lot of olive oil and is baked in a pan in a moderate oven. As a result, it bakes up thick, chewy, and very soft.

THIN-CRUST PIZZA DOUGH
This dough is rolled with a pin until very thin and baked directly on a heated stone in a superhot oven. It bakes up crisp and brittle.

DEEP-DISH DOUGH
This dough is baked in a pan set on a preheated stone. (Adding olive oil to the pan ensures a crisp bottom.) However, because the dough is so thick, the top and interior are fairly soft.

PISSALADIÈRE DOUGH
This recipe combines attributes of all the other doughs. A moderate amount of olive oil is rubbed into the exterior to crisp the crust, and, because the dough is not stretched thin, the interior remains chewy.

kitchen temperature), during which there was ample time to prep and caramelize the onions.

Doughs made in a standing mixer, a food processor, and by hand showed substantial differences, and, surprisingly, tasters preferred the method most professional bakers would scoff at. Doughs made by hand and in the mixer were tough and snappy after being baked, requiring a full set of well-rooted molars. To achieve the best texture, this dough apparently would accept only minimal handling. I knew that bread dough could be kneaded in a food processor in a two-step process. Step 1 is to whiz the ingredients for a mere 15 seconds until they come together; step 2 is to wait for two minutes and then knead the dough in the food processor an additional 30 seconds. It turned out that the secret to perfect pissaladière dough was to complete step 1 and simply ignore step 2! This crust was a winner, unanimously favored for its crackerlike exterior and decently chewy crumb. (I eventually figured out how to make the dough by hand and in a standing mixer, but the process for both was more time-consuming and difficult, and the timing and results were never as consistent.) The best part of the food processor technique is that it's foolproof. You know that the dough has been processed properly when it comes together in a ball. Nothing could be simpler.

Dough pressed onto a rimmed baking sheet didn't brown nearly as well as a free-form oval baked directly on a preheated baking stone at 500 degrees. Pressing the dough out on parchment paper made for an easy transfer to the oven. Tasters also preferred the rustic texture of dough that was pressed out by hand as opposed to the uniform consistency of dough flattened by a rolling pin.

A key problem with this recipe is the stickiness of the dough. I had been using plenty of flour when shaping the dough, until, on a whim, I tried oil instead. Good idea. Not only was it a snap to shape the dough on the parchment, but the extra oil pressed into the bottom of the crust made it even crisper. Brushing the dough with yet more olive oil before adding the toppings further ensured a crackerlike exterior, officially turning this crust from pizza to pissaladière.

The Flavors

Most recipes for caramelized onions subscribe to one of two methods—low and slow or fast and furious—yet neither works. Low and slow dries out the onions before they have a chance to get dark, while fast and furious leaves the onions crunchy and burnt tasting. Taking a cue from our story on caramelizing onions in the January/February 2002 issue of the magazine, I used a combination of high and low heat, starting the onions on high to release their juices and soften them, then turning the heat to medium-low to let the juices caramelize.

A nonstick skillet works best for caramelizing onions. The low sides of a skillet (as opposed to the high sides of a Dutch oven) allow the steam to evaporate rather than interfere with browning, while the nonstick surface ensures that the caramelization sticks to the onions, not the pan. I was having problems sprinkling the cooked onions over the pizza, as they tended to clump. The solution? I stirred in just a bit of water once I removed the onions from the heat.

Whereas most recipes call for whole black olives, I found that they roll around and occasionally fall off the crust. In addition, the intense heat of the oven dries them to a leathery texture. A better method was to chop the olives coarsely and layer them underneath the onions, where they are protected from overcooking. This same trick also worked with the leaves of fresh thyme.

It's traditional to arrange anchovies across the

top of a pissaladière in a crosshatched pattern. This was too much anchovy for the test kitchen staff, so I focused on how to incorporate their strong flavor without offending anyone. As with the olives, I found it best to chop and spread them underneath the onions. Just four anchovies per tart was perfect, and rinsing them first made sure they weren't too salty or fishy. (Still, several fish lovers missed the crosshatching, so I included it as an option.) The only untraditional flavors that passed our relatively strict code of authenticity were fennel seeds and freshly minced parsley, and both are optional. Now I can invite this relative stranger to dinner and expect to understand every word he says.

PISSALADIÈRE
MAKES 2 TARTS, SERVING 8 TO 10 AS A FIRST COURSE

Instant yeast is almost always sold under a marketing name; look for "rapid rise," "perfect rise," or "quick rise." If your food processor includes a plastic dough blade attachment, use it; its short blades and dull edges make kneading easier on the motor. If not, the regular metal blade works almost as well. For best flavor, use high-quality oil-packed anchovies; in a recent tasting, Ortiz were our favorite. The dough in this recipe rises for 1 to 1½ hours. If a longer or overnight rise is more convenient, make the dough with ½ teaspoon of instant yeast and let it rise in the refrigerator for 16 to 24 hours. The caramelized onions can also be made a day ahead and refrigerated. To prebake and freeze crusts for pissaladière, see Kitchen Notes, page 30.

Dough
- 2 cups (11 ounces) bread flour, plus extra for dusting work surface
- 1 teaspoon instant yeast
- 1 teaspoon salt
- 1 tablespoon olive oil, plus additional oil for brushing dough and greasing hands
- 1 cup (8 ounces) warm water (about 110 degrees)

Caramelized Onions
- 2 tablespoons olive oil
- 2 pounds yellow onions, sliced ¼ inch thick
- ½ teaspoon salt
- 1 teaspoon brown sugar
- 1 tablespoon water

Olives, Anchovies, and Garnishes
- Olive oil
- ½ teaspoon ground black pepper
- ½ cup niçoise olives, pitted and chopped coarse
- 8 anchovy fillets, rinsed, patted dry, and chopped coarse (about 2 tablespoons), plus 12 fillets, rinsed and patted dry for (optional) garnish
- 2 teaspoons minced fresh thyme leaves
- 1 teaspoon fennel seeds (optional)

- 1 tablespoon minced fresh parsley leaves (optional)

1. **FOR THE DOUGH:** In workbowl of food processor fitted with plastic dough blade (see note), pulse flour, yeast, and salt to combine, about five 1-second pulses. With machine running, slowly add oil, then water, through feed tube; continue to process until dough forms ball, about 15 seconds. Generously dust work surface with flour; using floured hands, transfer dough to work surface and knead lightly, shaping dough into ball. Lightly oil 1-quart measuring cup or small bowl, place dough in measuring cup (see photo, page 31), cover tightly with plastic wrap, and set aside in draft-free spot until doubled in volume, 1 to 1½ hours.

2. **FOR THE CARAMELIZED ONIONS:** While dough is rising, heat oil in 12-inch nonstick skillet over high heat until shimmering but not smoking; stir in onions, salt, and brown sugar and cook, stirring frequently, until moisture released by onions has evaporated and onions begin to brown, about 10 minutes. Reduce heat to medium-low and cook, stirring frequently, until onions have softened and are medium golden brown, about 20 minutes longer. Off heat, stir in water; transfer to bowl and set aside. Adjust oven rack to lowest position, set baking stone on rack, and heat oven to 500 degrees.

3. **TO SHAPE, TOP, AND BAKE THE DOUGH:** When dough has doubled, remove from measuring cup and divide into 2 equal pieces using dough scraper. Working with one piece at a time, form each piece into rough ball by gently pulling edges of dough together and pinching to seal (see illustration 1 below). With floured hands, turn dough ball seam-side down. Cupping dough with both hands, gently push dough in circular motion to

form taut ball (illustration 2). Repeat with second piece. Brush each lightly with oil, cover with plastic wrap, and let rest 10 minutes. Meanwhile, cut two 20-inch lengths parchment paper and set aside.

4. Coat fingers and palms of hands generously with oil. Using dough scraper, loosen 1 piece of dough from work surface. With well-oiled hands, hold dough aloft and gently stretch to 12-inch length (illustration 3). Place on parchment sheet and gently dimple surface of dough with fingertips (illustration 4). Using oiled palms, push and flatten dough into 14 by 8-inch oval (illustration 5). Brush dough with oil and sprinkle with ¼ teaspoon pepper. Leaving ½-inch border around edge, sprinkle ¼ cup olives, 1 tablespoon chopped anchovies, and 1 teaspoon thyme evenly over dough, then evenly scatter with half of onions (illustration 6). Arrange 6 whole anchovy fillets, if using, on tart and sprinkle with fennel seeds, if using. Slip parchment with tart onto pizza peel (or inverted rimless baking sheet), then slide onto hot baking stone. Bake until deep golden brown, 13 to 15 minutes. While first tart bakes, shape and top second tart.

5. Remove tart from oven with peel or pull parchment onto baking sheet; transfer tart to cutting board and slide parchment out from under tart. Cool 5 minutes; sprinkle with 1½ teaspoons parsley, if using. Cut tart in half lengthwise, then cut crosswise to form 8 pieces; serve immediately. While first tart cools, bake second tart.

> **COOK'S EXTRA** gives you free additional information online. For the full results of our olive tasting, visit www.cooksillustrated.com and key in code 2041. For the full results of our pizza cutter testing, key in code 2042. This information will be available until April 15, after which it will be available to site subscribers only.

STEP-BY-STEP | SHAPING PISSALADIÈRE

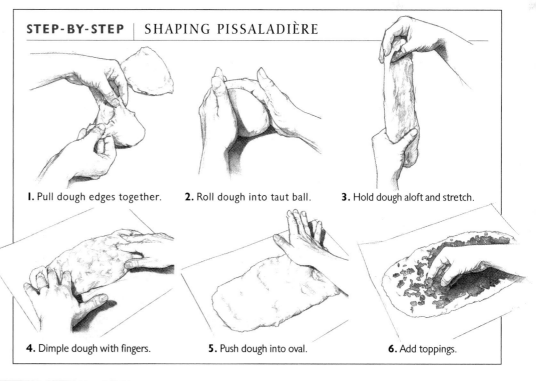

1. Pull dough edges together.　**2.** Roll dough into taut ball.　**3.** Hold dough aloft and stretch.

4. Dimple dough with fingers.　**5.** Push dough into oval.　**6.** Add toppings.

A Guide to Buying Fresh Pork

Here's everything you need to know about cooking today's lean pork, including identifying the best cuts and choosing the proper cooking method. BY REBECCA HAYS

The Thinning of the American Pig

In 1985, amid growing concerns about saturated fat in the American diet, Congress created the National Pork Board with the goal of helping producers provide consumers with the leaner meat they desired. Working with the board, producers developed new breeding techniques and feeding systems aimed at slimming down pigs. As a result, pigs are now much leaner and more heavily muscled than they were 20 years ago, with an average of 31 percent less fat. This is good news for our waistlines, but much of the meaty flavor, moisture, and tenderness disappeared along with the fat, causing some cuts of fresh pork to taste like diet food. For this reason, choosing the right cut and the right cooking method make a big difference when preparing today's pork.

TASTING: Enhanced or Unenhanced Pork?

Because modern pork is remarkably lean and therefore somewhat bland and prone to dryness if overcooked, a product called enhanced pork has overtaken the market. Enhanced pork is injected with a solution of water, salt, sodium phosphates, sodium lactate, potassium lactate, sodium diacetate, and varying flavor agents to bolster flavor and juiciness, with the total amount of enhancing ingredients adding 7 percent to 15 percent extra weight. The Pork Board claims that the purpose of enhancement is not to improve inferior meat but to boost the overall quality of the product. Pork containing additives must be so labeled, with a list of the ingredients.

After several taste tests, we have concluded that while enhanced pork is indeed juicier and more tender than unenhanced pork, the latter has more genuine pork flavor. Some tasters picked up unappealing artificial, salty flavors in enhanced pork. Enhanced pork can also leach juices that, once reduced, will result in overly salty pan sauces. If you want to add moisture and flavor to a dry cut, buy unenhanced pork and brine it at home (that is, soak the meat in a saltwater solution).

TASTING: Modern versus Old-Fashioned Pork

We purchased center-cut pork chops from New York farmers who raise heritage breeds the old-fashioned way (the animals roam free and are fed wholesome, natural diets) and tasted them alongside supermarket chops. Tasters had an interesting response to the farm-raised pork, noting that while it was juicy, with significantly more fat than the supermarket chops, it also had unusual "mineral" and "iron" flavors. Some tasters also found that the extra fat in the old-fashioned pork left behind an unpleasant coating in their mouths. Surprisingly, most tasters favored the more familiar supermarket meat. A few tasters thought that the old-fashioned pork was delicious but definitely an acquired taste.

We wondered just how fatty this old-fashioned pork was and so sent a sample pork butt to a food laboratory to be ground and analyzed for fat content. For comparison, we also sent a supermarket sample of the same cut. As we expected, the old-fashioned pork butt had significantly more fat—50 percent more—than the supermarket butt. Old-fashioned pork chops had 210 percent more fat than the supermarket samples, but this sky-high fat level was probably due to differences in the way the two kinds of pork were trimmed; supermarkets tend to remove most external fat; pork farmers who raise heritage breeds do not.

Primal Cuts

The term "primal cuts" refers to the basic cuts made to an animal when it is initially butchered. Butchers turn primal cuts into the chops, roasts, and other cuts sold at the retail level. Retail cuts from the same primal cut generally share similar traits, so when shopping it helps to understand the characteristics of the five primal cuts of pork.

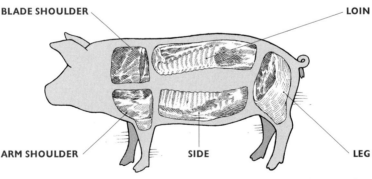

BLADE SHOULDER   **LOIN**

ARM SHOULDER   **SIDE**   **LEG**

BLADE SHOULDER Cuts from the upper portion of the well-exercised front legs of the pig tend to be tough, with a fair amount of fat. Shoulder cuts require long, slow cooking to become fork-tender.

ARM SHOULDER The economical arm, or picnic shoulder, has characteristics similar to the blade shoulder. Shoulder hocks (used primarily as a flavoring agent in soups, slow-cooked greens, and stews) also come from this part of the pig, whereas ham hocks come from the hind legs of the animal.

LOIN Butchers divide this area between the shoulder and the leg into some of the most popular cuts of pork, including pork chops, tenderloin, roasts, and ribs. Because the loin area is so lean, these cuts are prone to dryness.

SIDE The side, or belly, of the pig is the fattiest part, home to spareribs and bacon.

LEG The leg is sometimes referred to as the ham. Ham can be wet- or dry-cured or sold fresh, as a roast. Our favorite cured hams are sold bone-in and spiral-sliced.

Retail Cuts

We tested 15 common cuts of fresh pork in the test kitchen to determine our favorites and find the best ways to cook them. We rated the cuts for flavor (★★★★ being the best) and cost per pound ($$$$ being the most expensive). We'd like to thank John Dewar, owner of John Dewar & Co. Quality Meats in Newton, Mass., and Ceci Snyder of the National Pork Board for sharing their expertise with us.

BLADE SHOULDER

Pork Butt
Alternate Names: Boston Shoulder, Pork Butt Roast, Boston-Style Butt
FLAVOR ★★★★
COST $$
BEST WAYS TO COOK Barbecue, Braise, Roast

This flavorful cut, which is often used for pulled pork, has enough fat to stay moist and succulent during long, slow cooking. It is often sold boneless and wrapped in netting, as pictured above.

ARM SHOULDER

Shoulder Arm Picnic
Alternate Names: Picnic Shoulder, Fresh Picnic, Picnic Roast
FLAVOR ★★★★
COST $
BEST WAYS TO COOK Barbecue, Braise, Roast

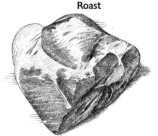

This affordable cut contains its fair share of fat and rind, but the meat has potent pork flavor and becomes meltingly tender with cooking. Picnic roasts are sometimes sold skinless and boneless.

LOIN

Blade Roast
Alternate Names (Bone-In Cuts):
Pork 7-Rib Roast, Pork 5-Rib Roast,
Pork Loin Rib End, Rib-End Roast
FLAVOR ★★★
COST $$
BEST WAY TO COOK Braise

The part of the loin closest to the shoulder, the bone-in blade roast can be difficult to carve because of its many separate muscles and fatty pockets. We prefer the boneless version of this roast.

Center Rib Roast
Alternate Names: Rack of Pork,
Pork Loin Rib Half, Center-Cut Roast
FLAVOR ★★★
COST $$$
BEST WAY TO COOK Roast

Often referred to as the pork equivalent to prime rib, this mild, fairly lean roast consists of a single muscle with a protective fat cap. It may be cut with anywhere from 5 to 8 ribs.

Center Loin Roast
Alternate Names: Center Cut,
Loin Roast Center Cut, Pork Roast
FLAVOR ★★★
COST $$$
BEST WAY TO COOK Roast

This popular roast is juicy, tender, and evenly shaped, with somewhat less fat than the center rib roast. As pictured,

this roast is sometimes sold with the tenderloin attached.

Sirloin Roast
Alternate Name: None
FLAVOR No stars
COST $$$
BEST WAY TO COOK Not recommended

This sinuous cut with a good amount of connective tissue is difficult to cook evenly and to carve.

Tenderloin
Alternate Name: None
FLAVOR ★★
COST $$$
BEST WAYS TO COOK Roast, Sauté, Grill, Stir-Fry

Lean, delicate, boneless tenderloin has little marbling, cooks very quickly, and can dry out faster than fattier cuts.

Baby Back Ribs
Alternate Names: Loin Back Ribs, Riblets
FLAVOR ★★★★
COST $$$$
BEST WAY TO COOK Barbecue

These ribs, cut with 11 to 13 bones, come from the upper end of the rib cage closest to the backbone. They are lean, tender, and smaller than other ribs. Choose meatier racks, preferably those weighing more than 1¾ pounds.

Country-Style Ribs
Alternate Name: Country Ribs
FLAVOR ★★★★
COST $$$
BEST WAYS TO COOK Barbecue, Braise

These meaty, tender ribs are cut from the upper side of the rib cage from the fatty blade end of the loin. Butchers

usually cut them into individual ribs and package several together.

Blade Chops
Alternate Name: Pork Chop End Cuts
FLAVOR ★★★
COST $$$
BEST WAY TO COOK Not recommended

Cut from the shoulder end of the loin, these chops can be difficult to find at the market. They are fatty and tough, despite good flavor and juiciness.

Rib Chops
Alternate Names: Rib Cut Chops,
Pork Chops End Cut
FLAVOR ★★★★
COST $$$
BEST WAYS TO COOK Pan-Sear and Roast, Grill, Braise, Sauté

Our favorite chops are cut from the rib section of the loin. They have a relatively high fat content, rendering them flavorful and unlikely to dry out during cooking. Rib chops can be distinguished by the section of rib bone running along one side.

Center-Cut Chops
Alternate Names: Top Loin Chops,
Loin Chops
FLAVOR ★★★
COST $$$$
BEST WAYS TO COOK Pan-Sear and Roast, Grill, Braise, Sauté

Identify these chops by the bone that divides the loin meat from the tenderloin muscle, as in a T-bone steak. The lean tenderloin section cooks more quickly than the loin section, making these chops a challenge to

cook. They are sometimes available boneless and may then be referred to as America's cut.

Sirloin Chops
Alternate Name: Sirloin Steaks
FLAVOR No stars
COST $$$
BEST WAY TO COOK Not recommended

These chops, cut from the sirloin, or hip, end of the pig, are tough, dry, and tasteless. The chops contain tenderloin and loin meat, plus a slice of hip bone.

SIDE

Spareribs
Alternate Name: St. Louis–Style Ribs
FLAVOR ★★★
COST $$$$
BEST WAYS TO COOK Barbecue, Braise

These fatty, succulent ribs are cut from the underbelly, or lower rib cage. A full rack contains 13 ribs and weighs about 3 pounds. St. Louis–style ribs are prepared by removing the brisket (shown on the left side of this illustration) so that the rack is more rectangular.

LEG

Fresh Ham
Alternate Name: Fresh Leg
FLAVOR ★★★★
COST $$
BEST WAY TO COOK Roast

Fresh ham is not cured. We prefer the shank end (shown here) over the rounded sirloin (butt) end because it is easier to carve.

Better, Easier Spinach Lasagna

We dump the mozzarella, add cottage cheese, and soak no-boil noodles in hot tap water. Is this any way to treat a northern Italian classic?

≥ BY REBECCA HAYS ≤

In northern Italy, where traditional spinach lasagna has its roots, cooks keep things simple, combining layers of homemade pasta, fresh spinach, béchamel (white sauce), and cheese. Given its delicate flavors and straightforward ingredient list, it makes an ideal entrée for informal dinner parties. Yet the Americanized recipes I've encountered invariably fail.

The problem (but not the solution) is simple enough. Most American cookbook authors call for convenient no-boil (also called oven-ready) noodles, whereas traditional Italian recipes use homemade fresh pasta. Lasagna made with fresh pasta, which cooks in an instant, requires only a brief stay in the oven to give the separate layers a chance to bind. No-boil noodles are a different story. No matter what the brand, the instructions on the back of the box—which I confirmed in the test kitchen—insist on at least 50 minutes of baking. This long stint in the oven robs the spinach of its vibrancy, rendering it greenish-gray and lifeless. The other complication is that béchamel—made with only milk, flour, and butter and serving as the necessary glue that holds the layers together—usually exhibits little more flavor than a squirt of Elmer's.

Getting the Spinach and Sauce Right

I knew I could rescue the spinach from ruin by shortening the baking time of the lasagna. As an interim solution, I used conventional lasagna noodles, cooked al dente, so that I could prepare test batches with 20-minute baking times. I dismissed frozen spinach because tasters consistently gave it low marks during preliminary tests. As for fresh spinach, two types are available at the market: tender baby leaves and the mature, crinkly variety. Though I generally favor the former, for this application, the heartier crinkly spinach proved ideal; baby spinach was too fragile to withstand the punishing heat of the oven. I then made four lasagnas, preparing the crinkly spinach differently for each.

We've taken a traditional Italian recipe and made it simpler and more flavorful.

Sautéed spinach took on a muddy flavor and baked up slimy. Finely chopped raw spinach retained a brilliant green color after baking but tasted grassy and underdone. Raw spinach that I wilted in the hot béchamel sauce didn't work; it took on an unappealingly wet texture. Blanching (dunking in boiling salted water, then shocking in an ice water bath) was the solution, as it allowed the spinach to retain its verdant color and pure flavor. I wrapped the spinach in a kitchen towel and forcefully wrung out excess liquid to guard against soggy lasagna.

Béchamel is a classic milk sauce thickened with a roux (see "Béchamel 101," page 19). Because the sauce thickens considerably in the oven (as the noodles leach starch), I needed a béchamel on the lighter side, finally settling on 5 tablespoons butter, ¼ cup flour, and 3½ cups milk. Then I needed to add some flavor. A lone bay leaf plus seasoning with salt and pepper did little. Replacing part of the milk with chicken stock wasn't the answer—the resulting sauce was watery and salty. Lemon juice and lemon zest were rejected as well, judged by tasters

as too acidic. I regrouped and sautéed a cup of minced shallots (they're sweeter and less harsh than onions) and plenty of garlic in butter before whisking in the flour for the roux. To infuse the sauce with even more flavor, I added two potent bay leaves (kept fresh in the freezer, as is our custom in the test kitchen) and freshly grated nutmeg and then finished by stirring in some grated Parmesan cheese. Sprinklings of salt and pepper were the only other refinements I needed for a luxurious sauce that would complement, but not obliterate, the flavor of the spinach.

The Cheese and the Noodles

Most recipes for spinach lasagna call for both ricotta and mozzarella, but I wanted to try other options as well. Whole milk ricotta was declared slightly heavy and grainy by my tasters. When I covertly added scoops of cottage cheese (pureed with an egg to smooth out its curds), not one taster could identify the mystery ingredient. Although heretical to any "real" northern Italian cook, it provided a pleasing tang and extra creaminess without the distinct, somewhat dry layer created by the ricotta. Finally, I tried replacing bland mozzarella with fontina, a creamy, semifirm Italian cheese with buttery, nutty tones. Its complex flavor was a welcome addition, and it also melts beautifully.

With approximately 40 lasagnas under my belt, I'd grown tired of the slick, cooked conventional noodles draped over every colander and bowl in the kitchen. I was determined to find a way to use no-boil noodles, despite my misgivings about their lengthy baking time. I covered a lasagna made with no-boil noodles with aluminum foil to trap the heat and cranked up the dial on the oven, but the lasagna still took too long to cook—the spinach was overdone while the noodles remained chewy. Next, I parcooked no-boil noodles by soaking them in boiling water and met with some success, although it seemed ridiculous to be boiling water for no-boil noodles. The simpler solution—and the key to this recipe—was to soak the noodles in hot tap water for just 5 minutes. After only 20 minutes in a 425-degree oven, the noodles were perfectly cooked and, just as important, the spinach had maintained its vitality. The only cooking left to do involved a quick trip to

Béchamel 101

Béchamel is a simple white sauce made with flour and butter (the roux) and milk. Béchamel is the base for a number of creamy dishes, including gratins, macaroni and cheese, and creamed spinach. For a proper béchamel, the flour must be adequately cooked to eliminate its raw taste and the milk slowly whisked in to prevent lumps.

1. Melt butter until foaming, then whisk in flour to make a white roux. Cook roux for 1½ to 2 minutes to eliminate any raw, floury flavor, but do not brown.

2. Whisking constantly, slowly add milk to roux. (There's no need to scald milk, as most recipes direct; see Kitchen Notes, page 30, for more information.)

3. Bring sauce to low boil, whisking often, and let simmer about 10 minutes. Finished sauce should be glossy, with consistency of heavy cream.

A five-minute soak in hot tap water dramatically reduces the baking time for the no-boil noodles, allowing the spinach to remain fresh looking and tasting. We tested five brands of no-boil noodles in our spinach lasagna recipe and found them all to be adequate. We did, however, notice differences in various brands. Our favorite, Barilla, consists of very thin noodles that resemble fresh pasta; it is available in supermarkets nationwide.

---

the broiler to brown the cheese.

And now I had 10 minutes (lasagna needs to rest before being served) to wonder whether this spinach lasagna was as good as a classic, full-flavored meat lasagna. As a dozen test cooks eagerly lined up for this final tasting, I think I knew the answer.

SPINACH LASAGNA
SERVES 6 TO 8

Be sure to use Italian fontina rather than bland and rubbery Danish or American fontina; if it is not available, substitute whole milk mozzarella. To make the cheese easier to shred, freeze it for 30 minutes to firm it up. If fresh nutmeg is unavailable, use only ½ teaspoon ground nutmeg. Because the lasagna is broiled at the end of cooking to brown the surface, make sure to use a baking dish that is broilersafe.

Spinach
- 1 tablespoon salt
- 2 bags (10 ounces each) curly spinach, stemmed and rinsed

Béchamel
- 5 tablespoons unsalted butter, plus 1 tablespoon for baking dish
- 5 large shallots, minced (about 1 cup)
- 4 medium garlic cloves, minced or pressed through garlic press (generous 1 tablespoon)
- ¼ cup all-purpose flour
- 3½ cups whole milk
- 2 bay leaves
- ¾ teaspoon freshly grated nutmeg
- ½ teaspoon salt
- ¼ teaspoon ground black pepper
- 1 ounce finely grated Parmesan cheese (about ½ cup)

Cheeses and Pasta
- 8 ounces whole milk cottage cheese
- 1 large egg
- ¼ teaspoon salt
- 12 no-boil lasagna noodles from 1 box
- 2 ounces finely grated Parmesan cheese (about 1 cup)
- 8 ounces Italian fontina, shredded (about 2 cups)

1. **FOR THE SPINACH:** Fill large bowl with ice water. Bring 4 quarts water to boil in large Dutch oven or stockpot over high heat; add salt and spinach, stirring until spinach is just wilted, about 5 seconds. Using skimmer or fine-mesh strainer, transfer spinach to ice water and let stand until completely cool, about 1 minute, then drain spinach and transfer to clean kitchen towel. Wrap towel tightly around spinach to form ball and wring until dry (see illustration, below). Chop spinach medium and set aside.

2. **FOR THE BÉCHAMEL:** Melt 5 tablespoons butter until foaming in medium saucepan over medium heat; add shallots and garlic and cook, stirring frequently, until translucent, about 4 minutes. Add flour and cook, stirring constantly, for about 1½ minutes; do not brown. Gradually whisk in milk. Bring mixture to boil over medium-high heat, whisk in bay leaves, nutmeg, salt, and pepper; reduce heat to low and simmer 10 minutes, whisking occasionally. Whisk in Parmesan and discard bay leaves. Transfer sauce to bowl, press plastic wrap directly against surface, and set aside.

3. **FOR THE CHEESES, PASTA, AND ASSEMBLY:** Blend cottage cheese, egg, and salt in food processor or blender until very smooth, about 30 seconds. Transfer to bowl and set aside. Adjust oven rack to middle position and heat oven to 425 degrees. Place noodles in 13 by 9-inch broilersafe baking dish and cover with

hot tap water; let soak 5 minutes, agitating noodles occasionally to prevent sticking. Remove noodles from water and place in single layer on kitchen towel. Wipe baking dish dry and coat with remaining 1 tablespoon butter. Use rubber spatula to distribute ½ cup béchamel in bottom of baking dish; position 3 noodles on top of sauce. Stir spinach into remaining béchamel in bowl, mixing well to break up clumps of spinach (you should have about 4 cups spinach/ béchamel mixture). Spread 1 cup spinach mixture evenly over noodles, sprinkle evenly with Parmesan, and top with 3 more noodles. Spread 1 cup spinach mixture evenly over noodles, sprinkle evenly with 1 cup fontina, and top with 3 more noodles. Spread 1 cup spinach mixture evenly over noodles, followed by cottage cheese mixture. Finish with 3 noodles, remaining cup spinach mixture, and remaining cup fontina. Lightly spray large sheet foil with nonstick cooking spray and cover lasagna. Bake until bubbling, about 20 minutes, then remove foil. Remove lasagna and adjust oven rack to uppermost position (about 6 inches from heating element) and heat broiler. Broil lasagna until cheese is spotty brown, 4 to 6 minutes. Cool 10 minutes, then cut into pieces and serve.

Squeezing the Spinach

If excess water is not removed from the blanched spinach, the lasagna will be watery. After blanching, shocking, and draining the spinach, wrap it in a clean kitchen towel and wring the towel to expel as much water as possible. When you're done, the spinach will form a dry ball.

Better Orange Salads

Slice the oranges into small pieces, and use lime juice to make a bold-flavored dressing.

≥ BY ERIN MCMURRER ≤

With their sweet juice, oranges can turn a simple salad into something special. Unfortunately, they often sink to the bottom of the bowl. And when you try to remix the salad, the greens bruise and the oranges fall apart. In addition, their abundant juice dilutes the dressing.

I started my testing by trying to determine the best way to cut the oranges so that they would retain their shape. The winning method turned out to be cutting the oranges pole to pole, removing the center pith, cutting each half in thirds (pole to pole), and then finishing with ¼-inch slices cut crosswise.

For the dressing, my first thought was to make a quick vinaigrette, using the juice from the oranges along with the standard ingredients of mustard, oil, salt, and pepper, but the result was too sweet. More acidity was needed, and the addition of lime juice, rather than lemon juice, did the trick. But when I tasted the dressing on the salad, I found it had became diluted. What to do? Make a bold vinaigrette using only lime juice—no orange juice, as the oranges would release some juice into the dressing no matter what. I did find, though, that letting the cut oranges sit in a fine-mesh strainer while I prepared the other ingredients relieved them of excess juice.

For the salad ingredients, I found that small amounts of greens (or no greens at all) worked best, keeping the oranges in the forefront. As for the oranges falling to the bottom of the bowl while the salad is tossed, my advice is, don't try to fight gravity. Toss the salad as little as possible and then plate individual portions, evenly distributing the oranges and other weightier ingredients that remain at the bottom of the bowl.

ORANGE, AVOCADO, AND WATERCRESS SALAD WITH GINGER-LIME VINAIGRETTE
SERVES 4

- 1½ cups prepared oranges (see illustrations) from 3 medium oranges
- 1 teaspoon grated fresh ginger
- ¼ teaspoon Dijon mustard
- 1 tablespoon juice from 1 lime
  Pinch cayenne
- 1 tablespoon finely chopped fresh mint leaves
  Salt
- 3 tablespoons vegetable oil
- ¼ small red onion, sliced very thin (about ¼ cup)
- 1 medium avocado, ripe but firm

- 1 small bunch watercress, stemmed and cut into 2-inch pieces (about 2½ cups)

1. Place orange pieces in nonreactive mesh strainer set over bowl; let stand to drain excess juice. Meanwhile, whisk ginger, mustard, lime juice, cayenne, mint, and ⅛ teaspoon salt in large bowl until combined. Whisking constantly, gradually add oil. Toss onion in dressing and set aside.

2. Halve and pit avocado; cut each half lengthwise to form quarters. Using paring knife, slice flesh of each quarter (do not cut through skin) lengthwise into fifths. Using soup spoon, carefully scoop flesh out of skin and fan slices from each quarter onto individual plates; season avocado lightly with salt.

3. Add oranges to bowl with onions; toss to coat. Add watercress and toss gently. Divide watercress among individual plates, mounding it in center; place portion of orange pieces and onions on top of watercress. Drizzle any dressing in bowl over avocado; serve immediately.

ORANGE-JÍCAMA SALAD WITH SWEET AND SPICY PEPPERS
SERVES 4

- 1½ cups prepared oranges (see illustrations) from 3 medium oranges
- 3 tablespoons juice from 2 to 3 limes
- ¼ teaspoon Dijon mustard
- ½ teaspoon ground cumin, toasted in small dry skillet until fragrant, about 30 seconds
  Salt
- 4 tablespoons vegetable oil
- 1 medium jícama (about 1 pound), peeled and cut into 2-inch-long matchsticks (about 4 cups)
- 1 medium red bell pepper, seeded and cut into ⅛-inch-wide strips (about 1½ cups)
- 2 medium jalapeños, quartered lengthwise, seeded, then cut crosswise into ⅛-inch-thick slices

- ½ cup fresh cilantro leaves, chopped coarse
- 3 medium scallions, green parts sliced thin on bias

1. Place orange pieces in nonreactive mesh strainer set over bowl; let stand to drain excess juice. Meanwhile, whisk lime juice, mustard, cumin, and ¼ teaspoon salt in large bowl until combined. Whisking constantly, gradually add oil.

2. Toss jícama and red bell pepper with ⅛ teaspoon salt in medium bowl until combined. Add jícama mixture, oranges, jalapeños, cilantro, and scallions to bowl with dressing and toss well to combine. Divide among individual plates, drizzle with any dressing in bowl, and serve immediately.

ORANGE AND RADISH SALAD WITH ARUGULA
SERVES 4

- 1½ cups prepared oranges (see illustrations) from 3 medium oranges
- 5 teaspoons juice from 1 to 2 limes
- ¼ teaspoon Dijon mustard
- ½ teaspoon ground coriander, toasted in small dry skillet until fragrant, about 30 seconds
- ⅛ teaspoon salt
  Ground black pepper
- 3 tablespoons vegetable oil
- 5 radishes, quartered lengthwise and cut crosswise into ⅛-inch-thick slices (about 1⅓ cups)
- 4 ounces baby arugula (about 4 cups)

1. Place orange pieces in nonreactive mesh strainer set over bowl; let stand to drain excess juice. Meanwhile, whisk lime juice, mustard, coriander, salt, and pepper to taste in large bowl until combined. Whisking constantly, gradually add oil.

2. Add oranges, radishes, and arugula to bowl and toss gently to combine. Divide arugula among individual plates, place a portion of oranges and radishes over arugula, and drizzle with any dressing in bowl; serve immediately.

STEP-BY-STEP | CUTTING ORANGES

1. Cut thin slice from top and bottom, stand on end, and slice away rind and white pith.

2. Cut in half from end to end, remove stringy pith, cut each half into three wedges, and cut crosswise into ¼-inch pieces.

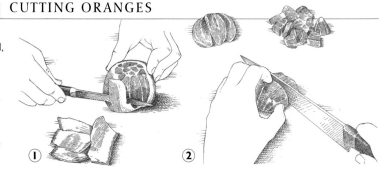

Perfecting Baklava

Part pastry, part confection, baklava is often subject to the foibles of both: too soggy and too sweet. We made more than three dozen batches to uncover its secrets.

⋛ BY DAWN YANAGIHARA ⋜

Baklava is a cross-cultural sweetmeat phenomenon. It is commonly regarded as a Greek pastry but accepted as Turkish in origin, and its ancient progenitors are said to be Assyrian. Yet the question remains unanswered as to why, in this country, in this modern age, baklava, so lavish with butter, sugar, and nuts, is so often a lamentable experience. Sad, soggy, punishingly sweet, and utterly lifeless specimens are ubiquitous. Extremely rare are crisp, flaky, buttery lozenges, light yet rich, filled with fragrant nuts and spices, and sweetened just assertively enough to pair perfectly with a Turkish coffee.

Baklava comes in numerous forms, from cigar-shaped rolls to turbanlike nests. The American notion of baklava is a multilayered diamond-shaped pastry, and so that was the shape I decided to pursue. I opted to develop a Greek-style baklava, also sweetened in part by honey and flavored with spices such as cinnamon and cloves. A Turkish or Middle Eastern baklava—scented with cardamom and rose or orange-flower water and less familiar to the American palate—I decided to leave to a variation.

Over the course of three days, I plodded through six representative recipes to a disappointing end. Though the ground rules for all of the recipes were the same—buttered phyllo sheets are layered into a baking dish with nuts, the assemblage baked and then soaked in sugar syrup—the outcomes were vastly different. Whereas one was awash in a thin, watery syrup, another was dry, its viscous, chewy syrup offering no relief. Yet another was overspiced, one lacked cohesiveness, and the worst had a moist, pasty nut filling that made the baklava heavy and soggy. The sixth was remarkable in that there was nothing egregiously wrong with it, but its filling was meager and lacked flavor, its stature was slight, and it was highly oversweetened. I had work to do.

Phyllo Facts

Prepared phyllo (homemade phyllo was out of the question) is sold boxed in the supermarket freezer section and, when halved crosswise, the phyllo sheets conveniently yield perfectly sized pieces for a straight-sided 13 by 9-inch baking pan. I quickly learned that packages caked with ice are almost

Baklava is a labor of love, but if you follow some precautions you can rest assured that this dessert will turn out crisp, flaky, and lightly sweetened.

sure to contain phyllo that is cracked and brittle, so avoid such boxes. It is no surprise that phyllo needs to be fully defrosted before use. Storing it overnight in the refrigerator requires forethought but is a good method, as is a four- to five-hour thaw on the countertop. Do not be fooled, as I was, by phyllo that has been sitting at room temperature for only an hour; still in its plastic sleeve (but out of the box), the roll felt pliant and thawed, but its core was still frozen. An attempt to use only partially defrosted phyllo resulted in frustration. Unfolding caused multiple large cracks and tears, rendering the sheets unusable.

Phyllo has a reputation for being difficult to work with in its uncooked state. Indeed, the paper-thin sheets are quick to dry out and become brittle. Despite recipes' advice to use one or another protective covering, I found that during baklava assembly the phyllo was best kept under a sheet of plastic wrap, then covered with a damp kitchen towel as added insurance.

Using a pound of very finely chopped nuts (about 4 cups), a full 1-pound box of phyllo (some recipes called for only ½ or ¾ pound),

and a 13 by 9-inch baking pan, I started building the baklava. Pieces of baklava with only one thick, central layer of nuts tended to split in two (they lacked cohesion). With the nuts divided into two layers separated by several sheets of phyllo, the pieces held together better, but the baklava composed of three relatively thin nut layers (I reduced the nuts by 4 ounces) between four sections of phyllo had the superior structure. My final recipe called for eight to 10 phyllo sheets in the bottom; three nut layers, each separated by six sheets; and another eight to 10 phyllo sheets to cover. This required nearly the entire pound of phyllo.

Nuts, Spices, and Butter

I immediately dismissed pecans as too sweet and too American. Hazelnuts need to be husked and were not well liked by tasters. Most everyone also objected to an all-walnut filling (too harsh and bitter) or an all-almond filling (rather nondescript). Eight ounces of almonds and 4 ounces of walnuts (chopped very finely in a food processor—indeed, nearly ground) was a good blend. Pistachios are also a common baklava filling, and when I tried them they were a smash, but they are better suited to a baklava with Turkish or Middle Eastern flavors. Toasting the nuts was unnecessary, if not a misstep, because the nuts cook thoroughly in the time it takes to bake the baklava. I tried various spice combinations, and the winner consisted of 1¼ teaspoons warm, familiar ground cinnamon and ¼ teaspoon deep, rich ground cloves.

Must the butter be clarified, as many recipes suggested? (To learn more about clarified butter, see "Clarifying the Situation," page 22.) The surface of the baklava made with whole butter was splotchy brown, while that made with clarified butter colored uniformly. It also had a cleaner, sweeter flavor. And because the water had been extracted from the clarified butter, the phyllo layers were slightly flakier and crisper.

I tried, as one recipe suggested, to butter every other sheet of phyllo, but this resulted in a dry baklava that was chalky and gritty. Clearly, every sheet needed a coating of butter. Some recipes advocated dousing the assembled baklava with a generous amount (a half cup or more) of melted butter, a step that I found absurdly excessive. Yet

SCIENCE: Clarifying the Situation

Butter has a lot of fat, but it also contains—in small amounts—proteins, carbohydrates, and minerals (the milk solids), as well as water, all of which are distributed throughout the fat in an emulsion. Usually these residual ingredients are welcome flavor bonuses, but in certain rare applications, such as baklava, these extras become more nuisance than nuance and should be removed in a process called clarifying.

To clarify butter, butter is heated to break the emulsion, which causes its different components to separate according to density and chemical predisposition. White foam collects at the top; this consists of air that has been encapsulated by milk solids. Directly below the foam lies the butterfat; by law, the fat must make up 80 percent of the total content of the butter. Underneath the fat lies a thin layer that includes proteins and phospholipids. Finally, at the bottom lies the aqueous layer; this is predominantly water along with some dissolved material.

The simplest method of clarifying butter is to cut it into 1-inch chunks, then melt it in a small saucepan over medium-low heat, which takes about 10 minutes. Once taken off the heat, the butter is allowed to settle for 10 minutes and is then skimmed with a soup spoon (see illustrations below) to clarify it.

Butter can also be clarified using a microwave oven. Start by cutting the butter into 1-inch chunks, then place it in a microwave-safe bowl covered with plastic in the microwave at 50 percent power for about five minutes. Let the butter settle for 10 minutes, then skim off and discard the foam on the surface. Let the butter cool to room temperature, then cover it with plastic wrap and refrigerate until the fat solidifies, which takes at least four hours. The solidified butter can then be popped out of the bowl (where the water and solids will remain) and its damp bottom dried with paper towels. —D.Y. with John Olson, Science Editor

CLARIFYING BUTTER

1. Let melted butter settle for 10 minutes. With soup spoon, carefully skim off foam from surface.

2. Spoon butterfat into small cup, tipping saucepan gently and only when it becomes necessary.

3. Make sure to leave water and milk solids behind in saucepan so they can be discarded.

it turned out that this step was indeed essential to help prevent (though not eliminate) the curling of the uppermost phyllo sheets during baking. I, however, opted for a more modest 4 tablespoons of butter.

After assembly but before baking, the baklava must be cut into the familiar diamond-shaped pieces. Merely scoring the layers, as some recipes suggest, was a waste of time; the baklava needs to be fully cut. A serrated knife or a bread knife, used with a gentle sawing motion, made the easiest and cleanest cuts, but even with a good knife, this step does take a bit of patience (and perseverance).

A low 300-degree oven and a slow 75- to 90-minute baking time proved best. The top and bottom phyllo layers colored evenly, and the nuts became golden and fragrant. Even with shorter baking times, higher temperatures tended to overdarken both the bottom pastry layer and the nuts.

Except for a few tablespoons of sugar mixed into the nut filling, the sugar in baklava is introduced after baking in the form of a syrup. The syrup is absorbed by the bottom layers of pastry and nuts, which become moist and cohesive.

Honey is an essential ingredient in a Greek-style baklava, but tasters found its flavor to be cloying and overpowering when used in large quantities. One-third of a cup of a mild-flavored honey such as orange blossom was the ideal amount; 1¼ cups of granulated sugar supplemented the sweetness.

Why Clarified Butter Matters

MADE WITH WHOLE BUTTER
Overbrowned in spots.

MADE WITH CLARIFIED BUTTER
Evenly browned.

The milk solids in whole butter will burn during baking, causing dark spots and uneven browning. Clarified butter has no milk solids, so the phyllo colors uniformly.

The amount of water in the syrup determines its viscosity, a key factor in the moistness and crispness of the pastry. If the syrup is too thin and watery, the pastry becomes wet and soggy. If the syrup is too thick, the baklava resists absorption and the bottom layers are sticky and heavy. Three-quarters of a cup of water was the right amount, combined with 1 tablespoon of lemon juice to spruce up flavors.

Taking full advantage of the fact that the syrup must be heated to dissolve the sugar, I tried infusing it with a few spices, a step common to most recipes. A few strips of lemon zest, a cinnamon stick, several cloves, and a pinch of salt were all welcome additions. They added a full, soft flavor and a rich, heady fragrance.

Finally, I needed to determine how to introduce the syrup to the baklava. Some recipes assert that for best absorption, room-temperature syrup must be poured over hot baklava as it emerges from the oven. Others take the opposing stance—that the baklava must be room temperature and the syrup hot. I baked four baklava to test all of the permutations: cool-hot, hot-cool, hot-hot, and cool-cool. Hot baklava joined by cool syrup clearly gave the individual pieces superior cohesion, moistness, and texture. When pouring the syrup over the baklava, I poured the majority into the cuts so as not to soften the top layers of crisped pastry. When down to only a couple tablespoons, I lightly drizzled the syrup over the entire surface, which gave the baklava a glistening sheen and a tackiness to which a nut garnish could adhere.

As if the process of making perfect baklava weren't arduous enough, it really should not be consumed the same day, not even as a reward for having expended the effort. If left to stand overnight, the flavors meld and mellow and the texture becomes more unified. But take consolation in the thought that it holds for upward of a week (so long as humidity doesn't ruin its crispness) and that its lavishness allows for it to be consumed only one piece at a time.

BAKLAVA
MAKES 32 TO 40 PIECES

A straight-sided traditional (not nonstick) metal baking pan works best for making baklava; the straight sides ensure that the pieces will have nicely shaped edges, and the surface of a traditional pan will not be marred by the knife during cutting, as would a nonstick surface. If you don't have this type of pan, a glass baking dish will work. Make sure that the phyllo is fully thawed before use; leave it in the refrigerator overnight or on the countertop for four to five hours. When assembling, use the nicest, most intact phyllo sheets for the bottom and top layers; use sheets with tears or ones that are smaller than the size of the pan in the middle layers, where their imperfections will go unnoticed. If, after assembly, you have remaining clarified butter, store it in an airtight container in the refrigerator; it can be used for sautéing.

Sugar Syrup
1¼ cups sugar
¾ cup water
⅓ cup honey
1 tablespoon juice from 1 lemon plus 3 strips zest removed in large strips with vegetable peeler
1 cinnamon stick
5 whole cloves
⅛ teaspoon salt

Nut Filling
8 ounces blanched slivered almonds
4 ounces walnuts
1¼ teaspoons ground cinnamon
¼ teaspoon ground cloves
2 tablespoons sugar
⅛ teaspoon salt

Pastry and Butter
1½ cups (3 sticks) unsalted butter, clarified (see box on page 22 for instructions), melted and cooled slightly (about 1 cup)
1 pound frozen phyllo, thawed (see note)

1. **FOR THE SUGAR SYRUP:** Combine syrup ingredients in small saucepan and bring to full boil over medium-high heat, stirring occasionally to ensure that sugar dissolves. Transfer to 2-cup measuring cup and set aside to cool while making and baking baklava; when syrup is cool, discard spices and lemon zest. (Cooled syrup can be refrigerated in airtight container up to 4 days.)

2. **FOR THE NUT FILLING:** Pulse almonds in food processor until very finely chopped, about twenty 1-second pulses; transfer to medium bowl. Pulse walnuts in food processor until very finely chopped, about fifteen 1-second pulses; transfer to bowl with almonds and toss to combine. Measure out 1 tablespoon nuts and set aside for garnish. Add cinnamon, cloves, sugar, and salt; toss well to combine.

3. **TO ASSEMBLE AND BAKE:** Brush 13 by 9-inch traditional (not nonstick) baking pan with butter. Adjust oven rack to lower-middle position and heat oven to 300 degrees. Unwrap and unfold phyllo on large cutting board; carefully smooth with hands to flatten. Following illustration 1, right, and using baking pan as guide, cut sheets crosswise with chef's knife, yielding two roughly evenly sized stacks of phyllo (one may be narrower than other). Cover with plastic wrap, then damp kitchen towel to prevent drying.

4. Following illustration 3, place one phyllo sheet (from wider stack) in bottom of baking pan and brush until completely coated with butter. Repeat with 7 more phyllo sheets (from wider stack), brushing each with butter.

5. Following illustration 4, evenly distribute

about 1 cup nuts over phyllo. Cover nuts with phyllo sheet (from narrower stack) and dab with butter (phyllo will slip if butter is brushed on). Repeat with 5 more phyllo sheets (from narrower stack), staggering sheets slightly if necessary to cover nuts, and brushing each with butter. Repeat layering with additional 1 cup nuts, 6 sheets phyllo, and remaining 1 cup nuts. Finish with 8 to 10 sheets phyllo (from wider stack), using nicest and most intact sheets for uppermost layers and brushing each except final sheet with butter. Following illustration 6, use palms of hands to compress layers, working from center outward to press out any air pockets. Spoon 4 tablespoons butter on top layer and brush to cover all surfaces. Following illustration 7, use bread knife or other serrated knife with pointed tip in gentle sawing motion to cut baklava into diamonds, rotating pan as necessary to complete cuts. (Cut on bias into eighths on both diagonals.)

6. Bake until golden and crisped, about 1½ hours, rotating baking pan halfway through baking. Immediately after removing baklava from oven, pour cooled syrup over cut lines until about

2 tablespoons remain (syrup will sizzle when it hits hot pan); drizzle remaining syrup over surface. Garnish center of each piece with pinch of reserved ground nuts. Cool to room temperature on wire rack, about 3 hours, then cover with foil and let stand at least 8 hours before serving. (Once cooled, baklava can be served, but flavor and texture improve if left to stand at least 8 hours. Baklava can be wrapped tightly in foil and kept at room temperature up to 10 days.)

PISTACHIO BAKLAVA WITH CARDAMOM AND ROSE WATER

Follow the recipe for Baklava, making the following changes:

1. In sugar syrup, increase sugar to 1¾ cups; omit honey, lemon zest, and cinnamon; substitute 10 black peppercorns for cloves; and stir in 1 tablespoon rose water after discarding peppercorns.

2. In nut filling, substitute 12 ounces raw shelled pistachios for almonds and walnuts and 1 teaspoon ground cardamom for cinnamon and cloves.

STEP-BY-STEP | ASSEMBLING BAKLAVA

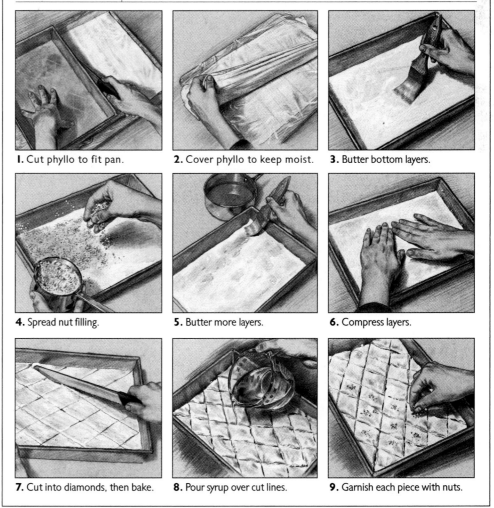

1. Cut phyllo to fit pan.
2. Cover phyllo to keep moist.
3. Butter bottom layers.
4. Spread nut filling.
5. Butter more layers.
6. Compress layers.
7. Cut into diamonds, then bake.
8. Pour syrup over cut lines.
9. Garnish each piece with nuts.

The Best Classic Brownies

Whatever happened to the chewy, not over-the-top, yet chocolatey brownie?

≳ BY ERIKA BRUCE ≲

These days, if you go to a bakery and order a brownie, chances are you'll end up with a heavy chunk of pure confection. While there's no denying that such brownies are sumptuous, they are also most often overwhelming. More candy than cake, such brownies are fine as infrequent treats, but many of us can look back to a time when the brownie was a much simpler affair, more chocolate bar than chocolate truffle, more bake sale than upscale café.

My initial recipe testing was not a success. Either pale and dry or cloyingly sweet, all of the brownies I baked lacked substantial chocolate flavor. I wanted an old-fashioned brownie, but I also wanted serious chocolate flavor. I wanted brownies I enjoyed in my youth—Mom's brownies—but altered to cater to my adult tastes.

Before I embarked on a long course of testing, however, there was one thing about all of these recipes that I knew I wanted to change: their size. The recipes called for baking the brownies in skimpy 8-inch-square pans. I wanted big brownies, and a lot of them, so a 13 by 9-inch baking pan was the size of choice. I then constructed a master recipe that contained 4 ounces of unsweetened chocolate, 2 sticks of butter, 2 cups of sugar, 4 eggs, and 1¼ cups of all-purpose flour.

Flour, Leavener, Sugar

My working recipe yielded brownies that were dense and a bit greasy. Cutting back on the butter seemed like an obvious way to make them less greasy. Going from 2 sticks to 1½ sticks did the trick, but it also produced an unintended side effect—an unpleasantly gritty texture. I suspected that the source of the problem might be in the starch in the recipe, not just from the all-purpose flour I'd been using but from the chocolate, which also contains starch. Not wanting to alter the amount of chocolate (my brownies needed more chocolate flavor, not less), I decreased the flour. The brownies were still too gritty. Next I tried substituting the whole amount of all-purpose

When stirred into brownie batter, nuts steam in the oven and become soggy. Sprinkling the nuts over the batter helps to keep them crunchy.

flour with cake flour. This solved the problem, producing nicely tender brownies. (Cake flour is milled from softer wheat than all-purpose flour and contributes less protein, or gluten, to a recipe. The result is a finer-textured product, which, in the case of these brownies, was preferred.) Here was my first big revelation: Cake flour makes tender brownies with a delicate chew.

Though tender, the brownies were still too compact. I thought an extra egg might provide more structure, but it made the brownies too cakey. Maybe baking powder would lighten the crumb. Well, too much baking powder produced a dry and cakey brownie, but a modest ¾ teaspoon was just right. The texture of the brownies was now nearly perfect, right in the middle between cakey and fudgy.

Sugar was the next ingredient subject to scrutiny. Both light and dark brown sugars created a moister, slightly wetter brownie, and tasters found the flavor of these sugars to be a distraction from the chocolate. Granulated sugar was the best choice. Tasters felt that my working recipe could use a bit more than the original 2 cups, so I added another ¼ cup and everyone was happy.

Pumping Up Chocolate Flavor

My brownies now had the right texture—neither fudgy nor cakey, with a tender chew—but the flavor was a bit insipid. Although I didn't want the decadent texture of fudgy brownies, I did appreciate their assertive chocolate flavor. Often, these recipes call for a mix of different chocolates, and they sometimes even add cocoa powder. In search of a similar chocolate intensity, I added a little high-quality bittersweet chocolate to the unsweetened chocolate in my working recipe. These brownies were too sweet, too greasy, and too heavy. When I cut back on the sugar, the brownies were less sweet, but they remained heavy and soggy. In addition, tasters felt that the flavor was more reminiscent of milk chocolate (that is, very mild) than bittersweet chocolate. When I used considerably more bittersweet chocolate, the flavor was more intense but the texture now decidedly confection-like. Ounce for ounce, unsweetened chocolate has more chocolate flavor than bittersweet or semisweet chocolate (which are one-third to one-half sugar). To get enough flavor from the these chocolates, you have to use a lot, and that made the brownies fudgy and rich—exactly what I did not want for my recipe.

In small amounts, cocoa did nothing to pump up the chocolate flavor. Using ¼ cup cocoa in place of an equal amount of flour helped some (at least according to a few tasters), but now the texture was dense and pasty. I realized that for the cocoa to do its work, I would have to remove so much flour that the brownies would lose their structure and chew. I crossed cocoa off my list.

I now tried the simplest idea yet—increasing the amount of unsweetened chocolate in my working recipe. Using 6 ounces (rather than 4 ounces) of unsweetened chocolate gave me the desired flavor—not too sweet, with profound chocolate notes. Although I had performed a lot of unnecessary tests, I now realized why Mom's recipe usually called for unsweetened chocolate. I just needed to use more to make my recipe taste better than Mom's.

Mixing Method and Bake-Off

Many recipes call for creaming the butter (beating it until light-textured), but my tests showed that this produced a light, dry texture. Much to

Seemingly minor changes in brownie recipes can yield quite different results.

TOO CAKEY	TOO FUDGY	JUST RIGHT
This recipe called for creaming the butter and sugar and for lots of baking powder, yielding brownies with a fluffy, cakey texture.	This recipe called for a lot of chocolate and no baking powder and produced a confection-like brownie that was extremely rich and dense.	With a moderate amount of chocolate and a little baking powder, our brownie has good flavor and a moist texture that is neither cakey nor fudgy.

my delight, the easiest method worked best: Melt the chocolate and butter, add the sugar, eggs, and vanilla, and then fold in the flour.

As simple as they are to mix up, these brownies need to be baked just right to guarantee the perfect texture. An even temperature of 325 degrees baked them through without drying the edges—a problem when the oven temperature was higher. Close attention near the end of the baking time proved beneficial as well. Underbaking by just a couple of minutes resulted in a gummy (undercooked) center, and overbaking quickly dried them out. Because home ovens are notoriously fickle and poorly calibrated, the baking times in this recipe should be used only as a general guide.

When I mixed nuts into the batter before baking the brownies, they steamed and became soft. Sprinkling the nuts on top just before baking kept the nuts dry and crunchy; toasting them first made them even crunchier while also enhancing their flavor.

Looking back over my test results, I realized that I had not reinvented the wheel but simply made small adjustments to a classic recipe. That being said, these minor changes greatly improved the brownies' taste and texture. I think Mom would be proud to bring them to the next bake sale or potluck supper.

CLASSIC BROWNIES
MAKES TWENTY-FOUR 2-INCH-SQUARE BROWNIES

Be sure to test for doneness before removing the brownies from the oven. If underbaked (the toothpick has batter clinging to it), the texture of the brownies will be dense and gummy; if overbaked (the toothpick comes out completely clean), the brownies will be dry and cakey.

1	cup (4 ounces) pecans or walnuts, chopped medium (optional)
1¼	cups (5 ounces) cake flour
½	teaspoon salt
¾	teaspoon baking powder
6	ounces unsweetened chocolate, chopped fine

12	tablespoons (1½ sticks) unsalted butter, cut into six 1-inch pieces
2¼	cups (15¾ ounces) sugar
4	large eggs
1	tablespoon vanilla extract

1. Adjust oven rack to middle position; heat oven to 325 degrees. Cut 18-inch length foil and fold lengthwise to 8-inch width. Fit foil into length of 13 by 9-inch baking dish, pushing it into corners and up sides of pan; allow excess to overhang pan edges. Cut 14-inch length foil and, if using extra-wide foil, fold lengthwise to 12-inch width; fit into width of baking pan in same manner, perpendicular to first sheet. Spray foil-lined pan with nonstick cooking spray.

2. If using nuts, spread nuts evenly on rimmed baking sheet and toast in oven until fragrant, 5 to 8 minutes. Set aside to cool.

3. Whisk to combine flour, salt, and baking powder in medium bowl; set aside.

4. Melt chocolate and butter in large heatproof bowl set over saucepan of almost-simmering water, stirring occasionally, until smooth. (Alternatively, in microwave, heat butter and chocolate in large microwave-safe bowl on high for 45 seconds, then stir and heat for 30 seconds more. Stir again, and, if necessary, repeat in 15-second increments; do not let chocolate burn.) When chocolate mixture is completely smooth, remove bowl from saucepan and gradually whisk in sugar. Add eggs one at time, whisking after each addition until thoroughly combined. Whisk in vanilla. Add flour mixture in three additions, folding with rubber spatula until batter is completely smooth and homogeneous.

5. Transfer batter to prepared pan; using spatula, spread batter into corners of pan and smooth surface. Sprinkle toasted nuts (if using) evenly over batter and bake until toothpick or wooden skewer inserted into center of brownies comes out with few moist crumbs attached, 30 to 35 minutes. Cool on wire rack to room temperature, about 2 hours, then remove brownies from pan by lifting foil overhang. Cut brownies into 2-inch squares and serve. (Store leftovers in airtight container at room temperature up to 3 days.)

Just What Is Dark Chocolate, Anyway?

A tasting of nine "dark" chocolates revealed an industry with little regulation and two widely available (and inexpensive) brands that beat out the pricier competition.

⋗ BY ERIKA BRUCE AND ADAM RIED ⋖

Dark chocolate sounds simple enough, doesn't it? In reality, though, dark chocolate is anything but simple. Located somewhere between milk chocolate and unsweetened chocolate, dark chocolates are made mostly from two basic ingredients: chocolate liquor (also called cocoa mass or abbreviated to just cocoa on labels; it is the result of grinding roasted cacao beans) and sugar. Although the term "dark" has no official meaning, it generally refers to chocolates labeled sweet, semisweet, or bittersweet. The only regulation from the U.S. Food and Drug Administration (FDA) that concerns these dark chocolates is that they must contain at least 35 percent chocolate liquor, although most contain more than 55 percent and on rare occasions go as high as 99 percent. The rest consists of sugar and, depending on the manufacturer, emulsifiers, flavorings, extra cocoa butter (for fluidity and smoothness; some cocoa butter exists naturally in the chocolate liquor), and milk fat (if present, in small amounts only).

To complicate matters, many companies sell more than one line of dark chocolate, the difference being in their percentage of chocolate liquor. The consumer is readily stymied by the fact that these percentages are not always printed on the label. As a result, many labels offer little reliable indication of what the chocolate inside tastes like, leaving us all, as it were, in the dark.

Hoping to make some sense of this confusing array of dark chocolate choices, we organized a tasting. We included nine samples chosen to mirror the widely divergent choices that every consumer faces, tasting each chocolate raw, in chocolate sauce, and in flourless chocolate cake.

Chocolate Primer

All chocolate begins as cacao beans, which are the seeds of large pods that grow on cacao trees in equatorial regions. The beans are fermented, dried, and roasted to develop the telltale chocolate flavor, which can be altered depending on the roasting time and temperature. The meats of the roasted beans, called nibs, are then ground into a paste called chocolate liquor, which consists of cocoa butter, a natural fat, and cocoa solids (but no alcohol, the word "liquor" notwithstanding).

For chocolate liquor to become the dark chocolate we nibble and cook with, it is processed with the additional ingredients listed above, the primary additive being sugar. (If a dark chocolate is 62 percent chocolate liquor, for example, most of what remains—35 percent to 38 percent—will be sugar.) Companies guard their formulas carefully and, in our experience, are steadfast in their refusal to divulge specific information about them. To get some help, we turned to noted chocolate technologist, researcher, and industry expert Terry Richardson of Richardson Researches in Oakland, Calif. Richardson explained that companies sometimes add cocoa butter to improve flow properties, especially when the percentage of chocolate liquor is on the low side. The other ingredients—an emulsifier, flavoring, and, in some cases, milk fat—are part of each manufacturer's proprietary formula.

Prepared to assess the various chocolates in the tasting as we would fine wines (the flavor descriptors typically used to describe chocolate include fruit, apple, smoke, tobacco, cherry, raspberry, and tannin), we ended up judging them on a much simpler scale. We found, to our great surprise, that one factor had more influence on the success or failure of a chocolate than any other: sugar.

Sugar Rules

If sugar content is that important, we reasoned, it should be readily identifiable on labels. For that matter, we assumed, sugar content should be regulated. Wrong, on both counts. The government-mandated nutritional information printed on the back of the labels includes sugar by number of grams but not in percentage terms. Not even the terms "semisweet" and "bittersweet" are surefire indicators of a chocolate's sweetness. (Some brands of bittersweet contain more sugar than some brands of semisweet. Callebaut Dark Bittersweet, for example, contains more sugar then Scharffen Berger's semisweet.) The FDA draws no official distinction between the two.

To figure out total sugar content (a number that includes added sugar as well as sugars that occur naturally in the chocolate liquor), you must divide the number of sugar grams by the number of grams in the serving size (both listed on all labels) and then multiply by 100. Our top three finishers—Ghirardelli, Callebaut, and Hershey's—had sugar contents of 44 percent, 44 percent, and 49 percent, respectively.

The four high-cocoa (remember, that's chocolate liquor) chocolates tasted—the expensive brands revered by pastry chefs—had sugar contents that ranged from 28 percent to 35 percent, about 10 percent lower than the sweeter chocolates at the top of the ratings. While they did earn ardent support from a vocal minority of tasters, they ended up in the lower half of the ratings overall because most tasters were put off by their lack of sweetness and challenging flavor profiles.

If the really bitter dark chocolates did not score well in our tasting, what, then, is their appeal?

Testing the Sugar Theory

Curious to test our theory that more sugar makes a more popular dark chocolate, we invited 75 food editors from newspapers and magazines around the country to participate in a second dark chocolate tasting in our test kitchen. Included were two identical samples of the favorite from the first tasting—Ghirardelli Bittersweet (one served as the control to assess the accuracy of the tasters' results)—as well as two different samples of the brands Lindt, El Rey, Valrhona, and Scharffen Berger—one of each sample being 70 percent cocoa (chocolate liquor) and the other being a sweeter, lower-cocoa version of each of the four brands. Would the sweeter chocolates overtake their more bitter brethren when tasted in chocolate sauce, thus confirming our theory of "the more sugar the better?"

The sweeter Scharffen Berger prevailed over the more bitter version. In fact, it won this second tasting. In addition, dozens of professional food editors agreed with our selection of Ghirardelli Bittersweet as a winner: It came in second. The bitter and sweeter Valrhona chocolates tied in the ratings and, a bit to our surprise, the food editors preferred the more bitter, 70 percent cocoa versions of the Lindt and El Rey to those with less cocoa and more sugar.

Ghirardelli, then, emerged as a clear winner after being tasted by our staff at the magazine and 75 food editors. We also noted that tasters' perceptions of Scharffen Berger improved greatly when given the company's semisweet chocolate (with 62 percent cocoa) rather than its bittersweet chocolate (with 70 percent cocoa).
–Adam Ried

TASTING DARK CHOCOLATE

Twenty tasters sampled nine different dark chocolates in three formats: raw, in chocolate sauce, and baked into flourless chocolate cake. All of the samples fell under the broad category of "dark chocolate," which includes chocolates that are labeled "semisweet," "bittersweet," "mildly sweet," or "dark bitter" and that have identifiable percentages of chocolate liquor. We tried samples in different orders to eliminate palate fatigue, with one sample repeated twice as a control. The chocolates are categorized as "sweet" or "distinct and bitter" based on tasters' perceptions and the total sugar content, rounded to the nearest whole number. Within each category, the chocolates are listed in order of preference based on their combined scores from the three taste tests.

FAVORITE DARK CHOCOLATE
GHIRARDELLI Bittersweet Chocolate Premium Baking Bar, $2.29 for 4 ounces
➤ **44% sugar**

With its high percentage of sugar, this California chocolate was considered the most balanced—neither too bitter nor too sweet. Its smooth, creamy texture won points in the raw and sauce tests, while solid acidity and fruity flavor notes shone through in the cake despite its sweetness. Tasters noted both "flavor bursts" and a flavor range with comments such as "starts sweet and finishes bitter," which explains why this chocolate stood out.

SWEETER DARK CHOCOLATES

CALLEBAUT Dark "Bittersweet" Chocolate, 835, $42.95 for 11 pounds
➤ **44% sugar**

Sold for about $6 per pound at the supermarket in large, plastic-wrapped chunks labeled simply "Callebaut Bittersweet Chocolate," 835 is, in fact, one of seven dark chocolates available from that company. The merits of this Belgian chocolate were a creamy texture, gentle bitterness, and interesting nutty and tropical "coconut" notes. Other tasters picked up dairy flavors, calling it "sweet and milky."

HERSHEY'S Special Dark Mildly Sweet Chocolate, $1.59 for 7 ounces
➤ **49% sugar**

The sweetest sample and appreciated for it. Numerous tasters remarked on its "milky" qualities, and some even picked up a sweetness akin to bananas. A slight waxy texture was noted when sampled raw, but both the sauce and the cake were considered "very creamy and smooth." This chocolate was comforting and familiar to tasters.

BAKER'S Bittersweet Baking Chocolate Squares, $2.29 for 6 ounces
➤ **36% sugar**

True to its name, tasters preferred Baker's (made by Kraft) when cooked. Without much bitterness, "nutty," "roasty," and "coffee" flavor notes came through in the sauce and cake, but raw Baker's scored poorly because the texture was "gritty" and "chalky." Not for nibbling.

PERUGINA Bittersweet Chocolate, $1.99 for 3.5 ounces
➤ **36% sugar**

Made by Nestlé, the flavor profile of this chocolate was comparable with Hershey's. Giving it high ratings in the cake test, tasters considered Perugina "balanced," "subtle," and "not overwhelming." The "silky, creamy" texture was well received in all tests, but the flavor was too mild for some when eaten plain or in sauce, and a few tasters picked up "artificial" and "plastic" flavor notes.

DISTINCT AND BITTER DARK CHOCOLATES

LINDT Excellence Dark Chocolate, 70% Cocoa, $2.75 for 3.5 ounces
➤ **28% sugar**

Rated fairly smooth, complex, and creamy across the board, Lindt was better received raw than in sauce. In the cake, many tasters found it lacking in sweetness, complaining that it was "very bitter, like coffee" and that it "tastes strongly of unsweetened chocolate." The opposing camp proclaimed "lots of personality" and noted the flavors of "roasted nuts," "tobacco," and "burnt caramel."

EL REY Gran Saman Dark Chocolate Carenero Superior 70%, $2.95 for 2.8 ounces ➤ **35% sugar**

Considered aggressively bitter, this Venezuelan chocolate was also rated as one of the most complex. Tasters frequently repeated the adjectives "roasted," "nutty," and "smoky" and rarely used the word "sweet." The texture when tasted raw was characterized as "firm" and "crunchy," with hints of "chalkiness." Not a chocolate for the faint of heart.

VALRHONA Guanaja 70% Cacao Dark Bitter Chocolate, $3.50 for 2.6 ounces
➤ **35% sugar**

Earning consistently average scores in each test, this "very bitter and fruity" French chocolate had unique flavor characteristics. Tasters found "cherry," "wine," "raisins in port," and even a mild vegetal flavor akin to olive oil. The texture was described as dry and firm.

SCHARFFEN BERGER Bittersweet Pure Dark Chocolate, 70% Cacao, $8.95 for 9.7 ounces ➤ **33% sugar**

This complex Californian scored very high when eaten raw, with tasters noticing flavors from "acidic" to "cherry" and "earthy," but not sweet. It fared poorly, however, in the sauce and cake, in which it was considered "too bitter" and "astringent." Aside from a few who noted that the texture was "chalky" in the cake, most tasters praised the smooth texture of this chocolate.

Technical advisors from the Belgian chocolate company Barry Callebaut put it this way. "Sugar," they said, "interferes with the perception of chocolate flavor nuances in the product." The experts argue that high-cocoa chocolates have a more robust and nuanced flavor, and our tasters' comments supported this assertion.

In descriptions of the cake and the sauce made with these chocolates, the words "bitter," "sour," and "sharp" appeared again and again, but a few tasters picked up on distinct flavors they didn't notice in the sweeter chocolates. In the Lindt, people noticed coffee, tobacco, smoke, and tannin; in the El Rey it was a roasted quality, smoke, cherry, and fruit; the Valrhona evoked toast, raspberry, sour apple, and vegetable; and in Scharffen Berger it was cherry, wine, raisins, flowers, and fruit. These lower-sugar chocolates have flavor profiles that are more complex than those of our winners, but they are not necessarily more likable.

What, then, to buy? Unless you have a rarefied palate (at least when it comes to chocolate), you don't have to shell out a lot of money or search gourmet shops to find a winning brand. Our top three choices included the inexpensive and ubiquitous Hershey's Special Dark as well as the reasonably priced Ghirardelli Bittersweet.

What Makes a Better Baking Pan?

You can spend $9 or $95 on a baking pan. Does more money buy you better results?

⋝ BY ADAM RIED WITH GARTH CLINGINGSMITH ⋜

Here in cake-and-casserole-crazed America, the shallow, rectangular 13 by 9-inch baking dish is a kitchen workhorse. As you might expect, there is a huge variety of options from which to choose, many with new designs, materials, finish colors, and baking surface textures, all taking aim at the tried-and-true pans of old—Pyrex and stoneware. These "improvements," of course, come at a cost. Would our grandparents have spent nearly $100 on a baking pan? En route to determining the true value of these pans, we found ourselves knee-deep in cornbread, lasagna, raspberry squares, and gingerbread, all baked in each of 12 pans representing the major designs and materials, both old and new.

Tried-and-True—and New—Designs

Though no longer common, rough stoneware and earthenware pans have been around since the days of communal bread ovens in the village square. Ovensafe glass, represented by the Pyrex brand, came to market in 1915 and in the years since has become a standard kitchen item familiar to almost every home cook.

Pans made from both materials performed well in our tests, browning cornbread deeply and evenly. (We put a high value on the enhanced flavor and texture of deeply browned exterior surfaces. Pans that did not brown well were marked down.) Like a trusty cast-iron skillet, stoneware has a huge capacity to absorb and retain heat. The story is similar for glass. Although it heats up slowly, once glass is hot, it stays that way. In both cases, it's good news for fans of deeply browned crusts.

Our group included six pans with nonstick surfaces. All but the Wearever (which is also insulated—more on this later) browned cornbread deeply. Previous bakeware tests have shown—and the cornbread baked in this test confirmed—that when it comes to browning, a dark surface color is more important than the material of the pan. Dark-colored surfaces absorb heat in the oven; bright surfaces do, too, but they also reflect it.

The nonstick pans did, however, present a serious practical consideration. Many dishes baked in a 13 by 9-inch pan, including the lasagna we tested, are customarily cut and served right from the pan. With a nonstick pan that's a problem, because the use and care recommendations usually advise against cutting in the pan to protect the nonstick coating. Though not officially part of this test, some old, poorly cared for pieces of nonstick bakeware brought in from home by several editors were scarred, chipped, and rusted, proving that it pays to follow the manufacturer's guidelines in this respect. In our view, not being able to cut in a pan is a strike against it (in fact, it precluded the use of a nonstick pan for the baklava on page 21 of this very issue).

In the last couple of years, some manufacturers, including Doughmakers and Emerilware, have introduced heavy-gauge aluminum pans with textured baking surfaces that are supposed to increase airflow beneath the baked good to improve browning and release. Although pure aluminum is known to conduct heat efficiently, previous tests of bakeware have shown that this advantage is offset by its shiny surface, which reflects some of the oven's radiant heat. (The crusts of cornbread baked in these pans were on the light side.) Also, when you grease a textured pan, excess lubricant clings to the ridges, which in our tests caused the bottom of the gingerbread cake to turn soggy.

In addition to subpar browning, aluminum pans have another limitation. Manufacturers recommend against preparing acidic foods (such as tomato-based products) in them because acid and aluminum can react, causing off flavors.

The Rolls-Royce of the aluminum group was the All-Clad. Though it was solid as a rock, this wallet-wilting $95 pan didn't brown cornbread or raspberry squares as well as some of its darker competitors. Yes, it's nonreactive, and, yes, you can put it under the broiler and use metal utensils with it, but this pan just costs too much for us to recommend it over less expensive alternatives that performed better.

Another design innovation that has surfaced in recent years is insulated bakeware, which incorporates an air layer between two sheets of metal. Although this pan has a dark nonstick finish on the cooking surface, it did a lousy job of browning. Part of the problem was the reflective, shiny exterior surface of the pan. The pan's main selling point, its insulating air layer, was the second problem. We found that it also prevents baked goods from browning—not a good thing.

The newest and most unexpected design in our group was the Kaiser Backform Noblesse springform, which brings the removable sides of a classic round cheesecake pan to a 13 by 9-inch size. This unique pan had both pros and cons. Removal of baked goods intact couldn't have been easier, but the seal between the sides and bottom was not tight enough to prevent some lasagna juices from leaking out and burning in the oven.

Coming Full Circle

It turns out that our story ends almost right where it began, with Pyrex. This pan may not be perfect, but it did have five distinct advantages over the newcomers. First, it browned on a par with the dark-colored nonstick pans. Second, it is compatible with metal utensils. Third, it is nonreactive. Fourth, while it's no stunning beauty, most people we asked were perfectly willing to set it on a dining table at dinnertime, which allows it to pull double duty in sweet and savory baking. Last, it's inexpensive; only two other pans in the lineup cost less. The stoneware pan offers the same virtues but costs more. Of course, if your baking is usually of the sweet variety and you are willing to forgo cutting foods right in the pan, any of the recommended nonstick models will also serve you well.

We Like Brown Better

NICELY BROWNED AND VERY FLAVORFUL **SPOTTILY BROWNED AND LESS FLAVORFUL** **PALE AND DOWNRIGHT BLAND**

Cornbread baked in a dark nonstick pan (left) browned very well, as did cornbread baked in glass and stoneware pans. When we baked the same recipe in a light-colored metal pan, the browning was spotty (center). An insulated baking pan yielded cornbread that was much too light (right).

RATING 13 x 9-INCH PANS

We tested twelve 13 x 9-inch cake/baking pans in the test kitchen by baking four *Cook's Illustrated* recipes in each—cornbread, raspberry squares, gingerbread, and simple lasagna—and evaluated the pans according to the following criteria. Two brand new, freshly calibrated ovens were used for all tests, and all like food items were baked in the same oven—that is, one oven was used for all of the cornbread, one oven for all of the lasagna, and so on. For the cornbread and gingerbread, all pans were coated with 1 tablespoon butter; a buttered parchment paper sling was used for the raspberry squares; and the pans were not prepared or greased at all for lasagna. Performance differences between the pans that did well were minor enough to let us recommend any of them. Within the Recommended and Not Recommended categories, pans are listed in ascending order by price.

PRICE: Prices paid in Boston-area stores, in national mail-order catalogs, and on Web sites.
MATERIAL/FINISH: Material from which the pan is made and the color of the baking surface.
DISHWASHER-SAFE: Dishwasher-safe pans preferred.
PERFORMANCE: Pan scores on the cornbread, raspberry squares, gingerbread, and lasagna tests were averaged to determine an overall performance rating. Of the four tests, cornbread carried the most weight because it provided the clearest illustration of each pan's browning characteristics.
RESTRICTIONS: Warnings noted in a pan's use and care guide that might influence the decision to purchase, regardless of performance.
TESTERS' COMMENTS: Observations regarding the pan design, features, performance in specific tests, care, and cleaning.

FAVORITE PAN

TESTERS' COMMENTS

Pyrex Bakeware 13 x 9 Baking Dish
MATERIAL/FINISH: **Ovensafe glass/clear**
RESTRICTIONS: Breakable; no severe temperature changes, contact with flame or direct heat source (stovetop, broiler, or toaster oven), harsh cleansers, or scouring pads. Cool pan before submerging in water.

PRICE: **$8.95**
DISHWASHER-SAFE: **Yes**
PERFORMANCE: **★★★**

Produced deep and evenly golden brown cornbread and slightly dark edges on raspberry squares and gingerbread. The latter were by no means unacceptable, and the clear glass makes it easy to monitor browning.

RECOMMENDED PANS

Baker's Secret Non-Stick Oblong Cake Pan
MATERIAL/FINISH: **Tinned steel/medium-gray nonstick**
RESTRICTIONS: No metal utensils, steel wool, abrasive pads or cleansers, aerosol cooking spray, long-term food storage, direct contact with flame, or microwave.

PRICE: **$6.29**
DISHWASHER-SAFE: **Yes**
PERFORMANCE: **★★★**

Browns deeply and evenly, cleans up easily, and it's inexpensive. Not the sturdiest pan, but cheap enough to replace if need be.

Chicago Metallic Professional Bake N' Roast Pan
MATERIAL/FINISH: **Aluminized steel/medium-gray nonstick**
RESTRICTIONS: No metal utensils, cutting in pan, steel wool, abrasive pads or cleansers, or exposure to oven temperatures above 550 degrees.

PRICE: **$18.99**
DISHWASHER-SAFE: **Yes**
PERFORMANCE: **★★★**

Pan produced handsome dark golden brown cornbread and raspberry squares. Water collected in, then oozed out of, folded interior corner seams after washing and drying.

KitchenAid Sheet Cake Pan 13 x 9
MATERIAL/FINISH: **Carbon steel/black-brown nonstick**
RESTRICTIONS: No cutting in pan, steel wool, or abrasive pads or cleansers.

PRICE: **$24.99**
DISHWASHER-SAFE: **No**
PERFORMANCE: **★★★**

Oversized rims/handles make for especially easy handling. It is safe to use metal utensils, excluding knives, forks, and other pointed items.

Calphalon Commercial Nonstick Bakeware Rectangular Cake Pan
MATERIAL/FINISH: **Aluminized steel/dark-gray nonstick**
RESTRICTIONS: No metal utensils, steel wool, abrasive pads or cleansers.

PRICE: **$25.99**
DISHWASHER-SAFE: **No**
PERFORMANCE: **★★★**

Absence of rims or handles made it a bit tricky to grab with oven mitts. Items baked in this pan, however, were very deep golden brown and evenly cooked.

Kaiser Backform Noblesse Quadro 13 x 9 Springform Pan
MATERIAL/FINISH: **Chromium-plated steel/light-gray nonstick interior/dark-black nonstick exterior**
RESTRICTIONS: None listed.

PRICE: **$29.99**
DISHWASHER-SAFE: **No**
PERFORMANCE: **★★★**

Despite super-easy release owing to the springform design, we recommend this pan with a caveat: We wouldn't use it for dishes that might produce juices, for fear of leakage. Strictly for baking.

Pampered Chef Family Heritage Stoneware Rectangular Baker
MATERIAL/FINISH: **Unglazed stoneware/light matte beige**
RESTRICTIONS: Breakable; no sudden temperature changes, contact with flame or direct heat source, contact with soap, detergents, or cleansers of any kind. Cool pan before submerging in water. Requires initial seasoning.

PRICE: **$30.75**
DISHWASHER-SAFE: **No**
PERFORMANCE: **★★★**

The browning, especially on cornbread and gingerbread, was good, and it's OK to cut foods with a knife right in the pan. Did not retain food odors, as might be expected from unglazed ceramic.

NOT RECOMMENDED PANS

Wilton Performance Pan 13 x 9 x 2 Sheet
MATERIAL/FINISH: **Anodized aluminum/matte silver**
RESTRICTIONS: Not recommended for tomato-based recipes.

PRICE: **$7.69**
DISHWASHER-SAFE: **No**
PERFORMANCE: **★★**

Cooked raspberry squares less thoroughly than other pans and not as easy to clean as nonstick pans.

Doughmakers 13 x 9 Cake Pan
MATERIAL/FINISH: **Aluminum/shiny silver, textured "Pebble Pattern"**
RESTRICTIONS: No steel wool, abrasive pads or cleansers, aerosol cooking spray, high-acid foods, or long-term food storage.

PRICE: **$19.99**
DISHWASHER-SAFE: **No**
PERFORMANCE: **★★**

On the pro side, solidly constructed with generous handles. On the con side, the crust of the cornbread and the base of the raspberry squares were lighter than examples baked in darker nonstick pans.

Wearever CushionAir Covered Oblong Baking Pan
MATERIAL/FINISH: **Two sheets of aluminum with an air layer in between/medium-gray nonstick**
RESTRICTIONS: No soaking in water, dishwasher detergent tablets, steel wool, abrasive pads or cleansers, or knives or other sharp-pointed utensils.

PRICE: **$22.99**
DISHWASHER-SAFE: **Yes**
PERFORMANCE: **★**

Produced pale, spongy cornbread, raspberry bars ranging from pale to raw, and leaden, underbaked gingerbread. Additional baking time may have helped (as the use and care instructions state), but other pans performed better within prescribed baking times.

Emerilware 13 x 9 All Purpose Pan
MATERIAL/FINISH: **Aluminum/shiny silver, textured "Diamond Surface"**
RESTRICTIONS: No steel wool, abrasive pads or cleansers, detergents with chlorine, or aerosol cooking spray.

PRICE: **$24.99**
DISHWASHER-SAFE: **No**
PERFORMANCE: **★★**

As in the other textured-aluminum entrant, cornbread crusts and raspberry square bottoms were lighter than we prefer, and the bottom of the gingerbread was soggy.

All-Clad Rectangular Cake Pan 13 x 9, #9004
MATERIAL/FINISH: **Aluminum core with stainless steel exterior and light-gold, stick-resistant interior**
RESTRICTIONS: No steel wool, abrasive pads or cleansers, or cleansers with chlorine bleach.

PRICE: **$94.99**
DISHWASHER-SAFE: **Yes**
PERFORMANCE: **★★**

Browning of the cornbread crust and raspberry squares was acceptable but not stellar. Given the price, this pan should slice and butter your cornbread for you.

KITCHEN NOTES

⇒ BY BRIDGET LANCASTER ⇐

The Scalding Truth

Once upon a time, scalding milk—the practice of heating milk almost to the boiling point—was the only way to destroy potentially dangerous bacteria. Thanks to pasteurization, we don't have to worry about that anymore. But this begs the question: Is it still necessary to scald milk when making béchamel (white sauce) or pastry cream or when baking bread?

When it comes to the béchamel sauce for our Spinach Lasagna (page 18), the answer is no. We made two sauces, one with scalded milk and one with milk straight from the carton, and could discern no difference between them. Evidently, the only function served by scalding the milk for this recipe was to add an extra step (and another dirty pan).

As for pastry cream, scalding the milk turned out to be a matter of convenience, not necessity. Typically, the milk is scalded separately and gradually added to egg yolks, sugar, and cornstarch, then brought back over heat for about 30 seconds, during which time the

MADE WITH SCALDED AND SKIMMED MILK   **MADE WITH ROOM-TEMPERATURE MILK**

The effects of scalding are clear, at least in terms of bread making, with scalded milk yielding a taller loaf with a light crumb (left).

pastry cream thickens. Except for these last few seconds, the whole procedure is basically hands-off. To see if we could skip the scalding step, we added cold milk to the other ingredients in the saucepan (making sure that everything was well mixed) and cooked the mixture over medium heat while stirring constantly. After about seven minutes, we had perfectly good pastry cream. Without scalding, the process was more labor-intensive, but there also was one less bowl to wash.

Scalding milk is also used often in bread baking. According to the Oregon State University Food Resource Web site, scalding breaks down a constituent in milk that can weaken gluten, the protein in dough that gives bread its structure. That milk protein is removed when the skin that forms on the scalded milk is skimmed off and discarded. Thus a loaf made with unscalded milk will not rise to the level of a loaf made with scalded milk.

Always ones to question science, we decided to test this theory and baked up a few loaves of white sandwich bread. One was made with scalded and skimmed milk that was then cooled to room temperature, and one with milk that was simply heated to room temperature. We also included a third loaf made with scalded

milk that had not been skimmed to determine whether or not the milk protein in question had to be physically removed from the milk or was simply destroyed by the scalding process. There was no doubt that both scalding and skimming were required to remove the protein. The loaf made with the scalded and skimmed milk rose much higher, had a much more open crumb, and was more tender than the other two, which were nearly identical. We baked up four more loaves of each and had exactly the same results: The bread made with scalded and skimmed milk was superior every time. So if you're following a bread recipe that calls for scalded milk, the extra dirty pan you'll need is well worth it.

A Frozen Crust

Want a good frozen pizza? Make it yourself. We found that by parbaking our pissaladière crust (page 15) and then storing it in the freezer, we could pull out the makings for a hot, homemade pizza whenever we wanted. The process is simple. Make and shape the dough as directed in the recipe. Brush each crust liberally with olive oil and bake on a baking stone in a preheated 500-degree oven until the crust is just set, two or three minutes. Remove the crust from the oven, peel off the parchment, and place the crust on a cooling rack until completely cooled. Repeat with the remaining crust. Wrap the cooled crusts in plastic wrap and place in your freezer for

---

SHOPPING WITH THE TEST KITCHEN: Frozen Shrimp
Even the most basic market now sells several kinds of shrimp. We cooked more than 100 pounds to find out just what to look for (and avoid) at the supermarket.

FRESH OR FROZEN?
➤ Because nearly all shrimp are frozen at sea, you have no way of knowing when those "fresh" shrimp in the fish case were thawed (unless you are on very personal terms with your fishmonger). We found that the flavor and texture of thawed shrimp deteriorate after a few days, so you're better off buying frozen.

PEELED OR UNPEELED?
➤ If you think you can dodge some work by buying frozen shrimp that have been peeled, think again. Someone had to thaw those shrimp in order to remove their peel, and they can get pretty banged up when they are refrozen (compare the left and center photos).

CHECK THE "INGREDIENTS"
➤ Finally, check the ingredient list. Frozen shrimp are often treated or enhanced with additives such as sodium bisulfate, STP (sodium tripolyphosphate), or salt to prevent darkening (which occurs as the shrimp ages) or to counter "drip loss," the industry term referring to the amount of water in the shrimp that is lost as it thaws. We have found that treated shrimp have a strange translucency and an unpleasant texture and suggest that you avoid them (see right photo). Look for the bags of frozen shrimp that list "shrimp" as the only ingredient.

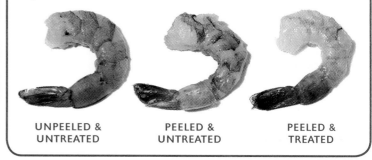

UNPEELED & UNTREATED   **PEELED & UNTREATED**   **PEELED & TREATED**

TEST KITCHEN TIP: Keep It Cold

OK, you've made the bread dough—now for the cleanup. But before you go and gum up your kitchen sponge or pot scrubber with dough remnants from the bottom of the mixing bowl (which, by the way, will never come out of the sponge), we suggest that you try the following, counterintuitive though it may be.

First, use **cold water**, not hot, to remove the dough residue from the bowl. Hot water will only make the dough stickier and harder to remove, while cold water helps to solidify it. Second, **use your hand**, not a scrubber, to remove the dough. Dough comes off very easily when you scrub it with your fingers. Once the dough has been cleared away, you can turn on the hot water, soap up your sponge, and rinse away.

TEST KITCHEN TIP: Double Duty

JUST MIXED   FULLY RISEN

A quart-sized liquid measuring cup is good for more than just holding liquid. We let the pissaladière dough (see page 13) rise in a measuring cup covered with plastic wrap.

---

up to two months. When you're ready to bake, preheat the oven (with the baking stone) again at 500 degrees for an hour (this gives you plenty of time to make the toppings). Top the crusts, and bake for 10 to 12 minutes.

A Blade for All Doughs?

We usually call for the metal food processor blade when making bread dough. In our recipe for Pissaladière (page 15), however, we prefer to use the plastic dough blade, finding that this duller blade has an easier time mixing the sturdy dough than the metal blade. (The arms of the plastic blade are shorter and do not span the full diameter of the workbowl, so the dough moves more freely.) We decided to put the dough blade up to a real challenge—namely, our Rustic Country Bread (January/February 1995), which, during its development, was responsible for the demise of many a food processor.

In the original recipe, which calls for the metal blade, this huge, wet mass of dough has to be processed in two batches. We wondered if the plastic blade would let us complete the processing in just one batch. No way! While the plastic blade fared much better than the metal blade, the vast amount of dough was still too much for it to handle at once. So we cut the next batch of dough in half and again used the plastic blade. This was a big improvement. When working the dough with the metal blade, our food processor danced across the counter and the motor housing of the machine became very hot. The plastic blade brought the dough together much more quickly and with only a bit of shimmying on the machine's part.

A touch to the motor housing revealed that it was warm—but not hot—making for a much happier machine.

The metal blade still plays a role in making dough. We found that the plastic blade can't cut butter into flour when making dough for pies or tarts. For these jobs, you need the sharp metal blade. But for wet bread dough, the plastic blade is now our first choice.

Ode to a Wonderful Cup

O, Wonder Cup . . . how did we ever get along without you? Composed of nothing more than a clear acrylic tube and a plunger-type insert, the Wonder Cup (see Resources, page 32) makes quick and clean work of measuring sticky ingredients (such as honey, shortening, and peanut butter) that cling to other measuring cups. The clear tube is marked with measurement increments in teaspoons, tablespoons, cups, fluid ounces, and even milliliters. Just pull the insert top down to the desired measurement, fill the container, then turn the cup upside down over a bowl and plunge out the ingredients. Every bit of the ingredient is removed from the cup with ease.

A WONDER WITH STICKY STUFF

RECIPE UPDATE: **READERS RESPOND**

Know Your Dough

Wet, sticky bread dough can be difficult to manipulate and can lead home cooks to wonder if they've made a mistake. We've come up with some guidelines to follow if you're working with one of our popular recipes in which the dough is on the sticky side, such as **Cinnamon Buns (May/June 2002)**, **Rustic Italian Loaf (January/February 2003)**, or **Ricotta Calzones (September/October 2003)**.

Using the correct type and brand of flour can make a big difference. Unless otherwise specified, our recipes call for unbleached all-purpose flour with about 10.5 percent protein, such as Gold Medal or Pillsbury. If you use a low-protein flour, such White Lily or Martha White, wet doughs will be downright soupy.

When rolling or kneading the dough, avoid the temptation to add more flour to make the dough easier to handle. Moisten your hands or, better yet, use a metal or plastic dough scraper to knead, fold, and roll moist doughs. Knead the dough in a large bowl to keep it corralled—and from sticking to the counter.

Beyond Margaritas

When we developed our recipe for **Fresh Margaritas (July/August 2000)**, we were—owing to the nature of the drink—obligated to pair the Citrus Mix (see recipe in chart) with tequila. But several readers wondered if this bracing citrus mix could be used in other drinks, both with and without alcohol. The answer is yes.

New Uses for Citrus Mix

CITRUS MIX RECIPE: 4 teaspoons each grated lemon and lime zest + 1/2 cup each lemon and lime juice + 1/2 cup sugar + pinch of salt

drink	citrus mix +	crushed ice +	liquid
LEMON/LIMEADE	1/4 cup	1/2 cup	1/2 cup water
SPARKLING LEMON/LIMEADE	1/4 cup	1/2 cup	1/2 cup soda water
VODKA/RUM/GIN COLLINS	1/4 cup	1/2 cup	1/4 cup liquor 1/4 cup soda water
CITRUS ICED TEA	1–2 tbsp	1/2 cup	1 cup iced tea

Really Red Meat

We wouldn't hesitate to send back a restaurant steak if the internal color weren't to our liking. But would you relent if you knew that color isn't always a good indicator of doneness? Such a paradox is reflected in our recipe for **Sirloin Steak Tips (May/June 2003)**. Readers noted that even when carefully cooked to temperature (135 degrees, or medium, being ideal in the recipe), rested, and then cut, the steak tips retained a bright red color in the very center.

We cooked six batches of steak tips to six different temperatures to observe the correlation between color and temperature. Between 125 and 140 degrees, there was very minimal change in the meat's internal color. After being rested and sliced for serving, the meat still had a bright red tinge in the very center. We began to see darker colors emerge only with steaks taken off the grill at 150 to 160 degrees.

Myoglobin gives meat its red color when raw. This protein remains relatively unchanged until the temperature of the meat reaches 140 degrees. Because the flap meat used in our steak tip recipe has an unusually high concentration of myoglobin, its color is more intense than that of steaks with less myoglobin. It's surprising and, to some, slightly off-putting, as we expect the temperature/color correlation to remain constant in all steaks. This is further proof that your instant-read thermometer should always be at the ready when you're trying to decide if the meat is done—temperature is almost always a better indicator than color alone.

–Complied by Nina West

IF YOU HAVE A QUESTION about a recently published recipe, let us know. Send your inquiry, name, address, and daytime telephone number to Recipe Update, Cook's Illustrated, P.O. Box 470589, Brookline, MA 02447, or to recipeupdate@bcpress.com.

RESOURCES

Most of the ingredients and materials necessary for the recipes in this issue are available at your local supermarket, gourmet store, or kitchen supply shop. The following are mail-order sources for particular items. Prices listed below were current at press time and do not include shipping or handling unless otherwise indicated. We suggest that you contact companies directly to confirm up-to-date prices and availability.

BASMATI RICE

Basmati roughly translates from Hindu into "the fragrant one." Unfortunately, most of the domestically grown basmati rice available in supermarkets is anything but fragrant. Imported, aged basmati rice, both nutty and aromatic, is the key ingredient in our rich, flavorful chicken biryani (page 9). Many better food markets offer a true aged Indian basmati. It is also available at **Kalustyan's (123 Lexington Avenue, New York, NY 10016; 800-352-3451; www.kalustyans.com)**, item #300B10, in 1- and 4-pound bags for $2.49 and $7.99, respectively. If ordering online, search for "Dehraduni" at Kalustyan's Web site.

PIZZA WHEEL

Oxo has produced the Hummer of the pizza-cutting world. This massive 4-inch wheel plows through deep-dish pizza as well as the pissaladière on page 15. **Sur La Table (1765 Sixth Avenue South, Seattle, WA 98134-0852; 800-243-0852; www.surlatable.com)** sells the Oxo Good Grips 4-Inch Pizza Wheel, item #209023, for $10.95.

WAFFLE IRONS

Of the eight waffle irons we tested for our yeasted waffles (page 7), two baked crisp, evenly browned waffles every time, and both made four waffles at once. If price is not an issue, the $89.95 VillaWare Classic Square does an exemplary job. It's available from **Williams-Sonoma (P.O. Box 7456, San Francisco, CA 94120-7456; 877-812-6235; www.williams-sonoma.com)**, item #90-3684271. For those on a tighter budget, Black & Decker offers the Grill & Wafflebaker for $56.99. It pulls double duty as a waffle maker and sandwich press–style griddle by way of interchangeable cooking plates. It is available from **Main St. Supply (101 N. Sutherland Avenue, Monroe, NC 28110; 800-624-8373; www.mainstsupply.com)**, item #55479.

BAKING PAN

Even with nonstick coatings, insulating air barriers, innovative surface textures, and price tags pushing triple digits, no baking pan could surpass the Pyrex 3-quart baking dish, which turned out fine results in every test (see page 28) and looks good enough to be brought to the table—all for less than $10. Pyrex products are available at many retailers and supermarkets or can be ordered from **Cooking.com (2850 Ocean Park Blvd., Suite 310, Santa Monica, CA 90405; 800-663-8810; www.cooking.com)**, where the 13 by 9 by 2-inch pan, item #159018, sells for $8.95.

RAMEKINS

Although we have a shelf-full of just about every size ramekin and soufflé dish known to the culinary world, the one we reach for more than any other is made by Apilco. With a capacity of just over 6 ounces, a 4-inch diameter, and a depth of 1⅞ inches, this enameled porcelain dish is about as all-purpose as a ramekin can get, whether used for baking crème brûlées and individual soufflés or organizing the ingredients for a stir fry (see page 2 for more information on ramekins). Safe in the oven, microwave, and dishwasher, the Apilco ramekin, item #APAP-S-2, is available from **Bridge Kitchenware (214 East 52nd Street, New York, NY 10022; 212-688-4220; www.bridgekitchenware.com)** for $9.00.

WONDER CUP

The Wonder Cup (tested on page 31) is designed to measure any ingredient but excels at gauging those items we all dread to measure. Molasses, honey, mayonnaise, peanut butter, shortening, and any other sticky, semisoft substance can be packed into the delineated, clear plastic tube and simply plunged out and scraped off. The Wonder Cup is available in 1-cup (item #1CMWC, $3.95) and 2-cup (item #2CMWC, $6.50) capacities from **The Posh Peddler (627 South Main Street, Sharon, MA 02067; 877-578-0088; www.theposhpeddler.com)**. At the Web site, click "Measuring Cups & Gadgets."

SKILLET LIDS

In the recipe for pork chops on page 11, a 12-inch skillet with a lid is essential. We make the recipe in our prized All-Clad 12-inch skillet, which is sold lidless. The good news is that a matching lid can be ordered from **Cutlery and More (645 Lunt Avenue, Elk Grove, IL 60007; 800-650-9866; www.cutleryandmore.com)**, item #3912, for $44.95.

All-Clad is not the only company that sells a skillet without a matching lid. Luckily, there is a very affordable way around this problem. Mirro makes a near-universal lid intended to fit any skillet, pot, or pan measuring between 8 and 12 inches in diameter. This lightweight aluminum disk is gradually recessed from a diameter of nearly 12½ inches to an innermost ring of 7 inches. On the downside, the lid's concave design does not allow for much headroom in a wide, shallow skillet such as the All-Clad, and in smaller skillets the skillet handle often keeps the lid from forming a tight seal. Still, at $7.99, this piece of equipment is a bargain, even if you never use it on anything but a 12-inch skillet. The Mirro Multi Purpose Lid, item #189888, is available from **Kitchen Etc. (32 Industrial Drive, Exeter, NH 03833; 800-232-4070; www.kitchenetc.com)**.

ZESTER HOLDER

Those cooks who want to get every last bit of citrus zest or Parmesan cheese in the bowl and not on the countertop may want to purchase the Zester Holder featured on page 3. It fits snugly over the 12-inch handle-free model of the Microplane rasp-style grater, our favorite tool for the job. The holder, item #27W02.11, is available for $4.95 from **Lee Valley Tools (P.O. Box 1780, Ogdensburg, NY 13669; 800-871-8158; www.leevalley.com)**. The grater and holder can be purchased as a set for $12.95.

DARK CHOCOLATE

Baker's and Hershey's Special Dark are available at most supermarkets nationwide. Ghirardelli Bittersweet Chocolate Premium Baking Bar (item #F3146) is available in 4-ounce bars for $2.29 from **Cooks Corner (P.O. Box 220, 836 S. 8th Street, Manitowoc, WI 54221-0220; 800-236-2433; www.cookscorner.com)** and at many better supermarkets. The remaining chocolates we tasted are available from the following sources. Perugina Bittersweet Chocolate bars weigh in at 3.5 ounces and are available for $1.99 at **Erika's Delicatessen (4547 28th Street S.E., Grand Rapids, MI 49512; 877-278-1993; www.erikasonlinestore.com)**. The remaining five chocolates can be ordered from **ChocolateSource.com (9 Crest Road, Wellesley, MA 02482; 800-214-4926; www.chocolatesource.com)**. Callebaut Dark "Bittersweet" Chocolate is a favorite in the pastry industry and is available only in wholesale quantities. An 11-pound block (item #835) costs $42.95 and should get you through a few holiday seasons. The other four chocolates can be ordered in quantities more reasonable for the home cook: Lindt Excellence Dark Chocolate 70%, item #L498014, four 3-ounce bars for $12.25; El Rey Gran Saman Dark Chocolate Carenero Superior 70%, item #ER444, six 2.8-ounce bars for $15.05; Valrhona Guanaja 70% Cacao Dark Bitter Chocolate, item #V2812, pack of four 2.62-ounce bars for $12.25; and 70% Scharffen Berger Cocoa Home-Chef Bars, item #SB300, one 10-ounce bar for $8.95.

RECIPES

March & April 2004

www.cooksillustrated.com

Get all 11 years of *Cook's Illustrated* magazine and a free gift!

Join www.cooksillustrated.com today and gain access to 11 years worth of recipes, equipment tests, and food tastings . . . any time and from anywhere! Plus, as a *Cook's Illustrated* subscriber, you're offered a 20% discount.

Free Gift: As a paid member, you'll also get *The Essential Kitchen: 25 Kitchen Tools No Cook Should Be Without*. This downloadable online guide produced by the editors of *Cook's Illustrated* provides recommendations on the best cookware, tools, and gadgets for your kitchen. Simply type in the promotion code **CB43A** when signing up online.

Here are a few of the many things available at our site:

Best Recipes: Eleven years worth of recipes developed in America's Test Kitchen.
Cookware Reviews: Every cookware review published since 1993, plus many reviews never seen in *Cook's*.
Ingredient Tastings: A decade of taste-test results, offering recommendations on everything from ketchup and mayonnaise to flour, yeast, and salt.
Online Bookstore: Cookbooks from the editors of *Cook's*, plus much more.

AMERICA'S TEST KITCHEN TV SHOW

Join the millions of home cooks who watch our TV show, *America's Test Kitchen*, on public television every week. For more information, including recipes and a schedule of program times in your area, visit www.americastestkitchen.com.

Spinach Lasagna, 19

Yeasted Waffles, 7

Chicken Biryani with Yogurt Sauce, 9

Pork Chops with Brandy and Prunes, 11

Pissaladière, 15

Orange, Avocado, and Watercress Salad with Ginger-Lime Vinaigrette, 20

Pan-Seared Shrimp with Garlic-Lemon Butter, 12

Pistachio Baklava with Cardamom and Rose Water, 23

Classic Brownies, 25

PHOTOGRAPHY: CARL TREMBLAY, STYLING: MARY JANE SAWYER

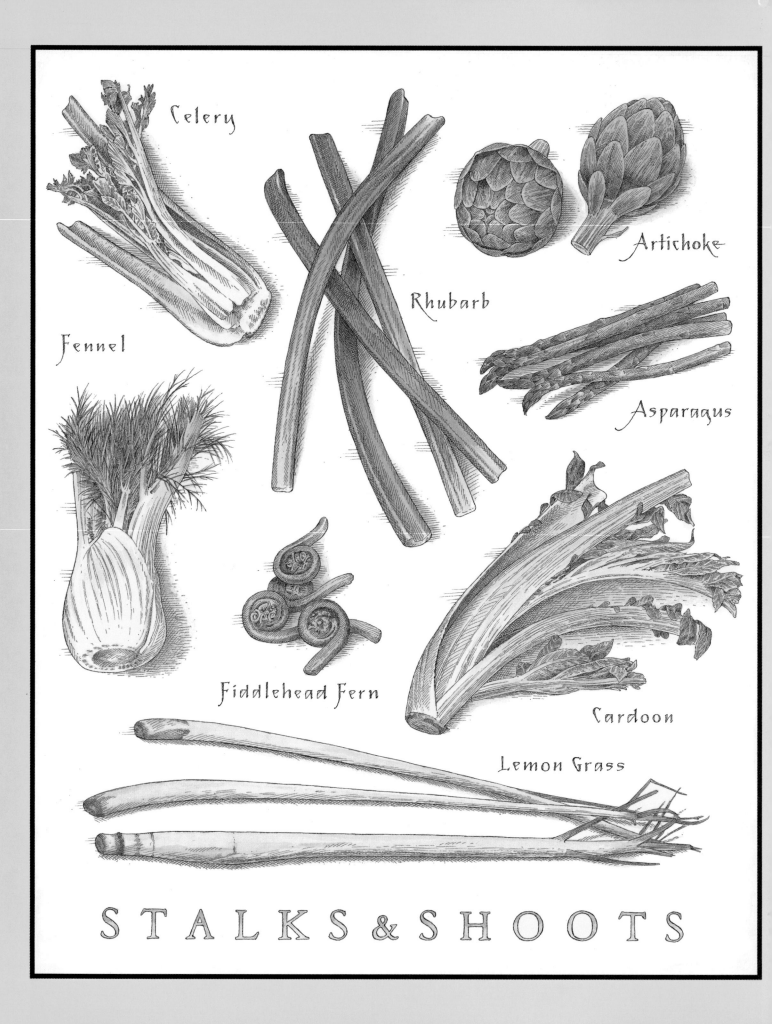

Celery

Fennel

Rhubarb

Artichoke

Asparagus

Fiddlehead Fern

Cardoon

Lemon Grass

S T A L K S & S H O O T S

COOK'S
ILLUSTRATED

www.cooksillustrated.com

$5.95 U.S./$6.95 CANADA

0   74470 62805   7

06>

CONTENTS

May & June 2004

COOK'S
ILLUSTRATED

www.cooksillustrated.com

HOME OF AMERICA'S TEST KITCHEN

Founder and Editor	Christopher Kimball
Executive Editor	Jack Bishop
Senior Editors	Adam Ried
	Dawn Yanagihara
Editorial Manager, Books	Elizabeth Carduff
Art Director	Amy Klee
Test Kitchen Director	Erin McMurrer
Senior Editors, Books	Julia Collin Davison
	Lori Galvin
Senior Writer	Bridget Lancaster
Managing Editor	Rebecca Hays
Associate Editors	Matthew Card
	Keith Dresser
Science Editor	John Olson
Web Editor	Keri Fisher
Copy Editor	India Koopman
Test Cooks	Erika Bruce
	Sean Lawler
	Diane Unger-Mahoney
Assistant Test Cooks	Garth Clingingsmith
	Charles Kelsey
	Nina West
Assistant to the Publisher	Melissa Baldino
Kitchen Assistants	Laura Courtemanche
	Nadia Domeq
	Ena Gudiel
Contributing Editor	Elizabeth Germain
Consulting Editors	Shirley Corriher
	Jasper White
	Robert L. Wolke
Proofreader	Jean Rogers

Vice President Marketing	David Mack
Sales Director	Leslie Ray
Retail Sales Director	Jason Geller
Corporate Sponsorship Specialist	Laura Phillipps
Sales Representative	Shekinah Cohn
Marketing Assistant	Connie Forbes
Circulation Manager	Larisa Greiner
Products Director	Steven Browall
Direct Mail Director	Adam Perry
Customer Service Manager	Jacqueline Valerio
Customer Service Representative	Julie Gardner
E-Commerce Marketing Manager	Hugh Buchan

Vice President Operations	James McCormack
Senior Production Manager	Jessica Lindheimer Quirk
Production Manager	Mary Connelly
Production Artist	Ron Bilodeau
Production Assistant	Jennifer McCreary
Systems Administrator	Richard Cassidy
WebMaster	Aaron Shuman

Chief Financial Officer	Sharyn Chabot
Controller	Mandy Shito
Office Manager	Elizabeth Wray
Receptionist	Henrietta Murray
Publicity	Deborah Broide

For list rental information, contact: ClientLogic, 1200 Harbor Blvd., 9th Floor, Weehawken, NJ 07087; 201-865-5800; fax 201-867-2450.
Editorial Office: 17 Station St., Brookline, MA 02445; 617-232-1000; fax 617-232-1572. Subscription inquiries, call 800-526-8442.
Postmaster: Send all new orders, subscription inquiries, and change of address notices to: Cook's Illustrated, P.O. Box 7446, Red Oak, IA 51591-0446.

MINT

MINT The most often used mints are spearmint and peppermint. The purple-tinged leaves of the latter have a more assertive flavor and are used to make tea, oils, and extracts. Spearmint, which has straight or curly light green to deep green leaves, has a milder flavor and fragrance and is commonly used in mint jellies and sauces; it's also the kind of fresh mint found in the supermarket. Apple and pineapple mint are closely related and have a similar taste, although pineapple mint's white-streaked, frilly leaves can be sweeter and fruitier than the subtly flavored, velvety leaves of the apple mint. Orange mint has mild citrus undertones and is used in the liqueur Chartreuse. Gold-flecked ginger mint has a fruity scent and a mildly spicy ginger flavor. Chocolate mint has a flavor that is faintly reminiscent of mint chocolate candy. Several other herbs, in the same family as the above mints but of a different genus, include the following: licorice, or Korean, mint; calamint, with mint-flavored leaves and flowers; and mountain, or wild, mint, which has a bold flavor. COVER (*Endive and Radicchio*): Elizabeth Brandon, BACK COVER (*Mint*): John Burgoyne

PRINTED IN THE USA

DEAR EMILY

Last Christmas, my oldest daughter, Whitney, purchased a doggy hat with earflaps for our youngest, 5-year-old Emily. It is pink and white with a big brown nose, eyes, and ears and has become her favorite piece of headgear. If you were to meet Emily on a cold winter day, however, you would be immediately struck by the fact that she takes this hat quite seriously, despite its cartoonlike appearance. She will entertain no lighthearted discussion about the fact that she appears to be wearing a dog on her head.

That, I suppose, is the essence of being 5 years old; reality is simply whatever you decide it ought to be. Saturday mornings, Emily will stride into my office and ask me to assume the role of husband to her wife, who then has to cook dinner on her bright yellow plastic kitchen set (the menu is limited to ersatz hamburgers, pizza, pickles, and cookies). Other times, she will dress up for the role of princess and I have to win her love. Of course, she understands that royalty is a tough business, so things usually do not go well for me, the prince. Princesses are, in Emily's view, not patient people.

Adrienne and I have four children, and Emily is our last. Being parents is nothing new for us and so we are less apt, perhaps, to treasure every cute drawing, every charming utterance. (That being said, Adrienne has collected a basement-full of childhood drawings, plaster handprints, class photos, and other childhood memorabilia.) Once the first (and second and third) blush of parenthood is gone, however, the true miracle of life remains. This notion is, admittedly, a bit tread-worn, but I defend the thought nonetheless. As when a scientist contemplates a remote corner of the universe, there is no percentage in being offhand and incurious. So before my last child grows up and leaves home, I want to offer this goodbye.

Dear Emily. You are about to forget many things. You will forget the icy spray of snow crystals as you sled with your mother down toward the horse pasture. You will no longer know how to whisper wet nothings in my ear and how to chase guinea hens around the yard. You will have forgotten the many goldfish won and then lost at the fireman's parade, the sound of fiddlers at the Ox Roast, and perhaps even the taste of the buttermilk biscuits I make for you on Saturday mornings. You will no longer be startled by your "Dragon Breath" on a cold winter's morning nor demand a Hug, Kiss, Tickle, and Taste from your mom when you get home from school. You may still remember *Bartholomew and the Oobleck* but have forgotten *Mr. Popper's Penguins, Arthur's Teacher Trouble,* and the windup alarm clock with the organ grinder and his monkey. And, of course, you will no longer talk like Elmer Fudd, telling us that you fell down and got a "bwues" or that the toilet's "pwogged." And, by the time you go off to college, we do hope that you are no longer sucking your thumb.

But perhaps it is what I am likely to forget that is more the issue. I won't remember that you used to call me "Dumb Pants" or that you usually ask for a scary story at bedtime but halfway through the telling often cry out, "Not that scary!" I will forget that, when told that all-beef hot dogs were no longer a lunch option owing to Mad Cow Disease, you thought for a moment, looked at your plate of insipid chicken salad, and then said calmly, "Well, I bet you haven't heard about Mad Chicken Disease!" I will also forget what my lap is really for, the sweet smell of childhood, and the spidery touch of tiny hands around my shoulders as you creep up from behind, standing on a chair.

Most of all, I will forget the push and pull of youth, when you venture out into the pond just a bit too far from shore, panic, and then frantically paddle back or when you taunt your older brother, Charlie, in order to liven up a dull evening and then end up in a shock of tears. Adults have no prescribed limits, there is nothing lurking on the edge of darkness, the woods have all been mapped. Yet on a cold winter's morning, your world can still be measured in inches from the wood cookstove while the rest of us pace off the universe in light-years. Your day is measured by the length of a crayon, the size of a lollipop, and the pieces of a puzzle.

You have shown us the importance of the inner eye, the one that sees a bear in a bush, a face in a fire, or a mountain in a cloud. There is no need to instruct a child, "To thine own self be true," yet it is the greatest struggle faced by those more traveled in years and adversity. You see the world through imagination; adults see it through opportunity.

These "airy nothings" of childhood—fairies and flying monkeys—can fade and be forgotten or, instead, as Shakespeare put it, "grow to something of great constancy, however strange and admirable." You have taught us that childhood is not like the passing mist after a summer rain but that we should learn to see a world "as new as foam and as old as the rock." Perhaps our best hope is to eat biscuits by the woodstove on cold mornings or to sled, your mother and I, down the hill toward the lower pasture with eyes wide open, blinded by fresh snow. And then, just before bed, we might peek into the mirror and see kings and queens, remembering that our love for you is limited only by your imagination.

FOR INQUIRIES, ORDERS, OR MORE INFORMATION:

www.cooksillustrated.com

At www.cooksillustrated.com, you can order books and subscriptions, sign up for our free e-newsletter, or check the status of your subscription. Subscribe to the Web site and you'll have access to 11 years of *Cook's* recipes, cookware tests, ingredient tastings, and more.

COOKBOOKS

We sell more than 40 cookbooks by the editors of *Cook's Illustrated*. To order, visit our bookstore at www.cooksillustrated.com or call 800-611-0759 or 515-246-6911 from outside the U.S.

COOK'S ILLUSTRATED Magazine

Cook's Illustrated magazine (ISSN 1068-2821), number 68, is published bimonthly by Boston Common Press Limited Partnership, 17 Station Street, Brookline, MA 02445. Copyright 2004 Boston Common Press Limited Partnership. Periodicals postage paid at Boston, Mass., and additional mailing offices, USPS #012487. POSTMASTER: Send address changes to Cook's Illustrated, P.O. Box 7446, Red Oak, IA 51591-0446. For subscription and gift subscription orders, subscription inquiries, or change-of-address notices, call 800-526-8442 in the U.S. or 515-247-7571 from outside the U.S., or write us at Cook's Illustrated, P.O. Box 7446, Red Oak, IA 51591-0446.

Pie Crust without Crisco?

I'm looking for pie pastry recipes that do not contain the hydrogenated (or trans) fats found in vegetable shortening (such as Crisco). While I understand that shortening is recommended in pie crusts for textural reasons, for health reasons, neither I nor my family wishes to consume it. Is it sufficient to replace it with butter?

KASEY SASSER
CHALMETTE, LA.

➤ In previous tests conducted when developing our recipe for American pie dough, which calls for 6 tablespoons of butter and 4 tablespoons of shortening, we found that you can substitute the same amount of butter for the shortening with good results. The flavor of an all-butter crust is better and its texture just a bit less tender than a crust made with both butter and shortening. A dough made with all butter can be more difficult to work with, however, because butter melts more readily than shortening. The shortening gives a less experienced baker more time to roll out the dough before it softens to the point of becoming unworkable. Make sure to chill an all-butter dough thoroughly.

Another alternative to standard shortening is a new product called Spectrum Organic Shortening. It is not mechanically hydrogenated and so contains no trans fats (now thought to be the least healthy of all fats) and, according to the manufacturer, can be substituted tablespoon for tablespoon for hydrogenated shortenings such as Crisco. Spectrum comes in a tub and is pure white, just like regular shortening, and its only ingredient is palm oil, which is naturally solid at room temperature. We substituted Spectrum for Crisco in our pie crust recipe and did detect a couple of differences, though each was subtle.

One difference that we noticed straight off is that Spectrum is a bit harder and less creamy at room temperature than Crisco. This "hardness" was evident when we rolled out the dough after having let it sit overnight in the refrigerator; it was certainly workable, but not as malleable as the dough made with Crisco. Letting the Spectrum dough sit out at room temperature to soften was helpful; like Crisco, Spectrum extends the "window of workability" for the dough.

There were also slight differences in the taste and texture of the baked crusts. Most tasters found the Spectrum crust sweeter and crisper than the Crisco crust. Do "sweeter" and "crisper" mean "better"? Here tasters diverged. Some preferred the crust made with Spectrum, but more than one favored the classically tender texture of the crust made with Crisco.

Taking taste, texture, and dough workability into account, neither all butter nor a Spectrum/butter combination produces exactly the same result as a Crisco/butter combination, but each produces a satisfactory result.

A Killer Oven Mitt

Have you seen the Orka? It's a silicone oven mitt that's supposed to be heat-resistant up to 500 degrees Fahrenheit. It certainly takes the charm out of oven mitts. . . . But does it work?

PATIENCE WHITTEN
BROOKLINE, MASS.

➤ The manufacturers claim that the Orka allows you to submerge your hand in boiling water or bubbling oil. We put it to those tests—after first trying a few uses that were a bit less, well, scary.

We used the Orka when grilling, grabbing the hot rack to add coals to the grill, and didn't feel a trace of heat. We used it to move hot pans out of the oven and off the stovetop, and we still didn't feel any heat. We used it instead of wadded paper towels to turn a large roast chicken—still no transfer of heat. Now we were starting to feel confident in this whale-shaped techno-mitt (see photo below) and prepared ourselves for the big tests: boiling water and peanut oil that was hot enough to fry chicken (about 350 degrees; even we were scared of a smoking pot of 500-degree oil). Millimeter by millimeter, an editor lowered her mitt-clad hand into a pot of just-boiled eggs. Did she feel the heat? Some, yes, but the mitt as well as her fingers were still intact. Results from submersion in hot oil were the same.

Do we recommend the Orka? Although it offers lots more protection from heat than you'd get with a traditional terrycloth or leather potholder or oven mitt, it has a big drawback: It's bulky and can be awkward, especially for cooks with small hands. In an attempt to retrieve a hard-cooked egg from the above-mentioned pot

ORKA MITT
This whale of a techno-mitt can take the heat, but it's also clumsy.

of boiling water, our editor ended up crushing it. We also found that wearing the mitt made our hands sweaty. Of the tasks we tested, we would use the Orka for only one: moving a hot grill rack. For the other tasks tested, we prefer a traditional mitt or potholder (or a slotted spoon). The $20 Orka is available at most kitchen stores. See Resources on page 32 for details.

Shattering Pyrex Revisited

Two readers had further questions about the safe use of Pyrex bakeware following the question raised in this section in the March/April 2003 issue by Penny Robie, who had a problem with a baking dish shattering when she placed it directly from the oven into a serving basket on the table.

I recently made your recipe for American Loaf Bread (May/June 1996). To create a crisp crust, the instructions suggest placing an empty loaf pan on the bottom rack of the oven during preheating (to 350 degrees), then filling it with boiling water when the bread is put in the oven. I use Pyrex loaf pans, and when I poured the boiling water in the hot pan, it popped loudly and cracked down the middle. Next time, I'll definitely use a metal pan to hold the hot water. But what happened?

ELLEN FORMAN
AUSTIN, TEXAS

I want to make your "Do Ahead Fresh-Baked Apple Pie" (November/December 1997). The recipe says to take the pie out of the freezer and put it directly into a preheated oven. I know you recommend Pyrex pie plates, but I would think that putting a frozen Pyrex pie plate in a preheated oven would break the dish. Should I thaw the pie or do exactly what the recipe states?

EILEEN MITTLEIDER
MARIETTA, GA.

➤ Pyrex is most vulnerable to cracking when it experiences a dramatic drop in temperature, especially if there is even a tiny, all-but-imperceptible crack in the glass. Why, then, would a hot loaf pan crack when hot water is poured into it? Although the water was boiling, it was still much cooler at 212 degrees than the pan, which had been preheating in a 350-degree oven. This sudden drop in temperature could easily cause the loaf pan to crack. A metal loaf pan is the way to go.

In the case of the do-ahead apple pie, in which a pie frozen in a Pyrex dish goes straight from the freezer to a preheated oven, a couple of factors are at work. For one, glass going from cold to hot is less vulnerable (though of course not invulnerable) to breaking. More important is the fact that the pie plate is going from cold to hot slowly. Unlike water, air delivers heat slowly, which is why you can briefly stick your hand in a hot oven without burning it. (You would never stick a bare hand in boiling water, even though the temperature of the water is so much lower than that of a 350-degree oven.) So it's safe to move a Pyrex pie plate directly from the freezer to a hot oven. And we do recommend baking pies in Pyrex plates because they do such a good job of browning the crust.

Our Policy on Salt for Brines
In your January/February 2004 issue, you say to brine the chicken for the Garlic-Rosemary Roast Chicken with ½ cup salt. Is that table or kosher salt? You usually indicate which to use.

LINDA JANOWITZ
SANTA CLARA, CALIF.

➤ Kosher salt is an ideal choice for brining because its large, airy crystals dissolve so quickly in water. Unfortunately, the two major brands of kosher salt—Morton's and Diamond Crystal—are not equally airy. Because the crystals in Morton's are a bit more compact, you need less of it cup for cup than you do of Diamond Crystal. One-quarter cup table salt is equivalent to ¼ cup plus 2 tablespoons of Morton's but ½ cup of Diamond Crystal. This difference makes precise recipe writing a challenge. Because there's no accounting for which brand of kosher salt a reader might use, we have decided to list table salt in our brining recipes. (Sorry, we should have been clearer in the Garlic-Rosemary Roast Chicken recipe.) To use kosher salt in this or any recipe, just apply one of the above conversions, depending on the brand you have on hand.

Best Pastry Blender
I know I'm old-fashioned, but I like to make pie dough by hand rather than in a food processor. I'm looking to replace an old pastry blender with a new one that's easier to use and clean. What do you recommend?

RICHARD HAROLD AINSWORTH
JOLIET, ILL.

➤ The food processor is our tool of choice for making pastry dough because it's so fast, easy, and effective. The next best thing is a pastry blender; cutting butter into flour with two knives is much more of a chore. A pastry blender

WHAT IS IT?

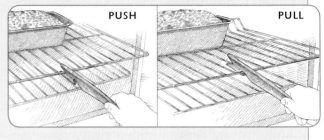

We found this for a dollar in a box of other unnamed kitchen tools in what some might call an antique shop (we'd say it's closer to a junk shop). Do you know what it's used for?

MR. AND MRS. ALFRED SCHLETTER
MIDDLE VILLAGE, N.Y.

NO MORE BURNT KNUCKLES
An oven rack adjustor keeps hands away from hot oven racks.

➤ In our July/August 1996 issue, we featured this item—an oven rack adjustor—as one of nine truly "Useful Kitchen Gadgets." Made of wood and measuring about 12 inches long by 1 inch wide, it's used to pull out an oven rack (use the notch carved a few inches down the side of the tool) to check on the doneness of whatever might be cooking and then to

PUSH / PULL

push the rack back in place (use the notch carved into the tip of the tool). The oven rack adjustor offers much better protection against burns than a potholder. It's available at craft and kitchen stores for as little as $4.

consists of a handle that you grip with a fist and a collection of curved wires or blades that loop from one end of the handle to the other (see the photos below). The basic question to ask when buying a pastry blender is: wires or blades? We purchased a couple of each type and used them to make pie dough. We preferred the stiffness of the blade-type cutters to the flexibility of the wire cutters. The rigid blades required less force to cut through the fat and did so more cleanly and quickly than the wire cutters. In addition, blades were easier to clean than wires. We also liked cutters with rubber handles; wood and steel handles are less comfortable and don't provide as good a grip. Our favorite, the Cuisena Dough Blender, costs $6.99. See page 32 for details.

WHICH IS THE BETTER PASTRY BLENDER?
The stiff blades of the blender on the left are more efficient than the flexible wires of the blender on the right.

Diluting Thickened Condiments
Regarding your suggestion on storage and use of oyster-flavored sauce in the January/February 2004 issue, I would like to suggest that water not be added to oyster sauce that has gotten too thick, except to the amount that will be immediately used. If you add water to the bottle that will again be returned to the refrigerator for storage, you may be adding contaminants—bacteria—from the water. At the same time, the water is diluting the salt (or sugar or acid) that

is the preservative. It's a double whammy of less preservative power and more possible contamination. If dilution is needed, remove the amount to be used from the bottle and dilute that.

MARY A. KEITH, PH.D., L.D.
HILLSBOROUGH COUNTY COOPERATIVE
EXTENSION SERVICE
SEFFNER, FLA.

➤ Thanks for the advice. Your suggestion could also be applied to other condiments that have thickened over time, including hoisin sauce and chili sauce.

The Elusive Key Lime
In the "Exotic Citrus" illustration on the back cover of your January/February 2004 issue, you show green Key limes. In my 25 years of visiting the Florida Keys, I learned from old-timers and restaurateurs that real Key limes are yellow (I've seen them), tiny (those pictured on the cover look the size of a typical supermarket, or Persian, lime), and very rare.

FRED HINDLEY
SOUTH LYON, MICH.

➤ The Key limes pictured on the back cover do, we now realize, look too green and too big to be Key limes. But they are not Persian limes. The limes were likely green and not yellow because they weren't ripe. Their larger-than-life size (their actual size was about the same as that of a walnut) is the choice of the artist, who's given some license when depicting size for the sake of the overall aesthetics of the cover. Almost all so-called Key limes sold in this country now come from Mexico. Florida Key limes are grown by a handful of home gardeners who generally don't sell their wares to supermarkets.

Quick Tips

⇒ COMPILED BY REBECCA HAYS AND NINA WEST ⇐

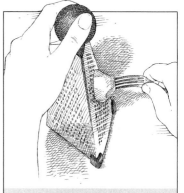

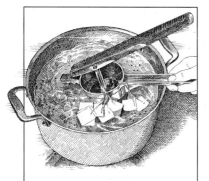

Making Large Batches of Tea

To brew a large batch of tea without the mess of fishing out hot tea bags, Jennifer Roap of Iron Bridge, Ontario, Canada, puts loose tea bags into a potato ricer and submerges the basket in a 3- to 4-quart pot of just-boiled water. Once the tea has reached full strength, she lifts the ricer out of the pot and discards the tea bags.

Easier Food Processor Cleanup

Some food processor lids have non-removable sliding feed tubes that don't get completely clean in the dishwasher because the pieces stick together. P.J. Hirabayashi of San Jose, Calif., found a way to solve the problem—with a chopstick. She pulls up the top portion of the lid and inserts a chopstick between the tube and the lid to separate the pieces. Soapy water can now flow through the pieces, and the entire lid emerges from the dishwasher perfectly clean.

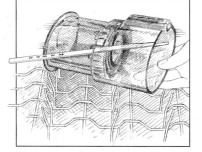

Paper Towel Substitute

Carole Nicolet of Bremerton, Wash., suggests an economical, earth-friendly way to conserve paper towels and recycle newspapers. When she needs several layers of paper towels to absorb water or grease, she spreads out a few layers of newspaper and tops them with a single layer of paper towels. The newspapers are wonderfully absorbent and much less expensive than paper towels.

Quick Homemade Funnel

To make a funnel for filling a pepper mill or adding spices to jars or a food processor feed tube, Stephanie Klauser of Madison, Wis., uses a paper cone-style coffee filter.

1. Cut off the bottom ¼ inch of the filter.
2. Fold the filter in half and separate the layers to create a funnel.
3. Insert the narrow end of the funnel into a pepper mill and add spices.

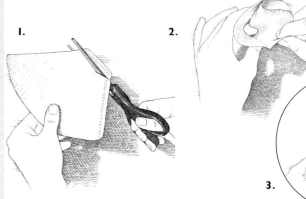

Homemade Microwave Popcorn

Instead of buying expensive (and sometimes unhealthy) microwave popcorn at the supermarket, Gloria Wong of Sunnyside, N.Y., and Alan and Sara Rimm-Kaufman of Earlysville, Va., have taken to making a homemade version.

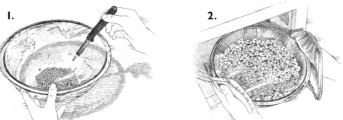

1. Place ¼ cup bulk popcorn in a 4-quart microwave-safe bowl with 1 teaspoon vegetable or olive oil. (For the calorie-conscious, good results can also be achieved without any oil.) Cover the bowl tightly with plastic wrap, poke a few holes in the surface, and place the bowl in the microwave. Depending on the power of your microwave, the popcorn will take between two and six minutes to pop. Check its progress frequently.
2. When the majority of the kernels have popped, use potholders to remove the bowl from the microwave and place it on a clean, dry surface—it will be extremely hot. Toss the popcorn with melted butter and salt, if desired.

Safer Ginger Grating

It can be hazardous to grate a small knob of fresh ginger, with your knuckles skimming dangerously close to the grater. To avoid scraping herself, E. Lyster of Cambridge, Mass., sticks a fork into the peeled piece of ginger and rubs it over the grater, using the fork as a handle.

Kitchen Twine Replacement

When she needs a short length of foodsafe string to tie a spice bag or secure a bunch of herbs and doesn't have any kitchen twine handy, Rachael Thompson of University Heights, Ohio, clips the string off of a tea bag. She finds that the string is the perfect size for such small tasks. If a longer length is required, two lengths of string can be tied together.

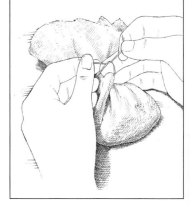

Send Us Your Tip We will provide a complimentary one-year subscription for each tip we print. Send your tip, name, and address to Quick Tips, Cook's Illustrated, P.O. Box 470589, Brookline, MA 02447, or to quicktips@bcpress.com.

Removing Tea Stains

After reading the tip in the January/February 2004 issue about cleaning tea-stained ceramics with a denture cleansing tablet, Diane Von Behren of Kenner, La., sent us her own stain removal method, which also removes coffee stains.

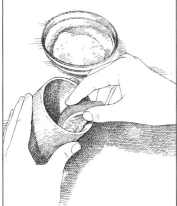

Cut a fresh lemon in quarters and use the fruit as a scrubber, gently squeezing its juice into a stained coffee mug or teapot. For extra cleaning power, first dip the lemon in kosher salt, which acts as an abrasive. Follow with a wash in hot soapy water.

Improvised Proofing Box

Stephanie Shultz of Yakima, Wash., a frequent baker who lives in a dry, desertlike climate, uses her dishwasher to create a humid, draft-free environment in which her bread dough can rise.

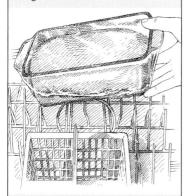

Turn on the dishwasher for about four minutes, or long enough for some warm water to fill the bottom. Place the dough to be proofed in a loaf pan or bowl, cover it with plastic wrap, set it on the bottom rack of the dishwasher, and close the door. Make sure to turn off the dishwasher; otherwise the water will start to flow again once you close the door.

Microwave-Toasted Nuts and Sesame Seeds

When Casandra Selberg of Corvallis, Ore., needs to toast nuts or sesame seeds and her stovetop and oven are unavailable, she uses the microwave.

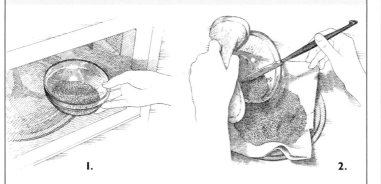

1.   2.

1. For fragrant, browned results, place ½ cup of sesame seeds or nuts in a microwave-safe bowl and microwave at full power for about two minutes, checking and stirring every 30 seconds, until the seeds or nuts are golden brown.
2. Spread the seeds or nuts on paper towels to cool and absorb oils. This technique works best for cashews, almonds, pine nuts, hazelnuts, and sesame seeds.

Neatly Wrapping Cupcakes

Cupcake aficionados know how messy frosted cupcakes can be when packed into a lunch bag or box, even when plastic wrap is used. Celeste Garber of Pittsburgh, Pa., offers this tip for preserving the luscious frosting. Cut the cupcake in half horizontally and flip the top half upside down so that the icing is in the middle, making a little layer cake. Wrap the cupcake (or piece of frosted sheet cake) in plastic wrap or a plastic bag, and the cupcake is good to go.

Transporting Fragile Pastries and Hors d'Oeuvres

When asked to bring dessert to a family party, A. McGrath of Madison, Wis., likes to prepare homemade bite-size tartlets. But the delicate tart shells, which break easily, were difficult to transport until she came up with the following idea. She now packs the tartlets in a cardboard egg carton that she has lined with plastic wrap.

Storing Vanilla Beans

Vanilla beans, expensive as they are, warrant proper storage when fresh to preserve their suppleness. To keep vanilla beans from drying out, Stephanie Perry Kipp of Anchorage, Alaska, stores them in a tall bottle (such as a clean caper bottle) filled with vanilla extract. The beans stay moist, full of flavor, and ready to use.

Keeping Track of Bakeware Sizes

With manufacturers' indications of size on baking pans being either illegible or nonexistent, Joan Grace of Bath, Maine, takes matters into her own hands and uses ovensafe metal paint (available at hardware stores) to mark pan bottoms, noting dimensions or capacity.

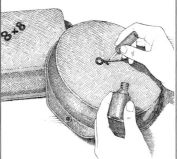

Shopping for Top-Rated Products

An avid *Cook's Illustrated* reader, Denise Amos of Crestwood, Ky., prefers to buy top-rated ingredients at the grocery store. To keep track of the best brands while shopping, she writes notes on index cards that she uses as category dividers in her coupon holder.

Easy Pureed Garlic

In addition to grating nutmeg, citrus, and hard cheese, a Microplane grater is an ideal tool for producing finely pureed garlic, shallot, or onion. For recipes such as Caesar salad or aioli, Bev Drake of Belmont, Calif., peels a clove of garlic and grates it on the Microplane before adding it to her recipe.

Quick Cheese Bread

Run-of-the-mill cheese bread is at once dry and greasy, with fleeting cheese flavor.
We were after something different: a rich, moist loaf topped with a bold, cheesy crust.

⇒ BY REBECCA HAYS ⇐

Cheese bread sounds like a great idea, a pairing of two of America's favorite foods. Unlike pizza, wherein bread dough is merely topped with cheese, a true cheese bread involves a more intimate relationship, going well beyond the quick blind date in which the two ingredients are merely thrown together and then heated. Good cheese bread displays a subtle balance of flavor and texture, neither party getting the upper hand. But most of the recipes I tested offered the worst of both worlds: dry bread and no cheese flavor.

The quickest (and easiest) recipe I came across was a chemically leavened bread that I mixed up in 10 minutes; the most difficult required a trip to a cheese shop plus a 48-hour time investment. Made with yeast, this bread was fantastic, and I will likely make it again when I have a spare weekend. But for most purposes, cheese bread ought to be quick.

I baked a half-dozen more quick recipes, but the results were, dare I say it, awful. The breads elicited comments from tasters such as "cardboardy," "tough," and "totally devoid of cheese flavor." My colleagues yearned for a moist, hearty bread with bits of cheese tossed throughout, plus a cheesy crust. My first step toward this end was to create a working recipe that consisted of 3 cups flour, 1 tablespoon baking powder, 6 tablespoons melted butter, 2 cups milk, and one egg. For the cheese, I chose shredded cheddar, the most frequently used type in my stack of recipes. My working recipe had lots of problems, but I could now methodically test every variable.

Constructing the Bread

In search of a moderately hearty crumb, I experimented with different flours, making one loaf with all-purpose, another with bread flour, and yet another with half bread and half all-purpose flour. A few tasters noticed that the breads made with all or part of the higher-protein bread flour were slightly rubbery, but the difference was not that dramatic. Still, all-purpose was clearly the best, and most convenient, choice.

For maximum flavor, this bread has cheese baked into the top and bottom crusts as well as the crumb.

Buttermilk is a common ingredient in quick breads, and it produced a decent loaf. Skim milk was too watery and produced a crumbly, dry loaf. The whole milk version was the best, though, with a creamier, cleaner, cheesier flavor.

I next tinkered with the amount of butter, which was preferred over oil for its flavor. Starting with 6 tablespoons, I worked my way down to a mere 3, putting an end to the slick hands and lips I'd been experiencing after eating a piece of bread. Less fat also pushed the bread away from the texture of a delicate cake and toward that of a hearty muffin. The single egg I'd been using turned out to be just right. When I once mistakenly omitted it, the loaf failed to rise properly and had little structure. Loaves made with more than one egg had a beautiful golden hue but tasted more like quiche than cheese bread.

So far so good, but I was falling short in the texture department. Because I wanted a rich loaf, similar to a good banana bread, I replaced a

portion of the milk in each of two breads with scoops of yogurt and sour cream, respectively. Given that this was cheese bread, it also seemed logical to try cottage cheese, cream cheese, goat cheese, and ricotta. In the end, most tasters chose the sour cream–based bread. It was rich and moist without being greasy, just what I'd been aiming for. The sour cream also added a nip of tartness to the bread, offsetting the richness of the cheese without overpowering it.

It was time to decide on the leavening: baking soda or baking powder. To do its job, baking soda needs an acidic ingredient (such as the lactic acid in sour cream), while baking powder is self-reliant, essentially composed of baking soda plus one or two acids. I made two breads, one with 1 tablespoon baking powder (this was a heavy batter that needed a decent amount of powder for proper leavening) and a second with ¾ teaspoon baking soda. (One teaspoon of baking powder contains ¼ teaspoon of baking soda.) Both breads rose into beautiful domed loaves, but the bread made with baking powder was preferred, possessing a more complex flavor.

Curious about these findings, I had the pH levels of the finished breads tested and discovered that the bread made with baking powder was quite acidic, with a pH of 5.8, whereas the bread made with baking soda was actually alkaline, with a pH of 8.3. The reason? The baking soda had neutralized the lactic acid in the sour cream, whereas the baking powder, which brings its own acid to the mix, had not. The acid was giving the bread more flavor.

Working in the Cheese

Test results showed that small chunks, not shreds, were best, as they melted into luscious, cheesy pockets. In terms of the cheese itself, I tested five supermarket offerings: extra-sharp cheddar, Muenster, Asiago, Gruyère, and Monterey Jack. Cheddar and Asiago were the leaders of the pack, with Muenster and Monterey Jack being too mild and Gruyère too pungent (although I liked this last cheese in a variation made with bacon). I quickly determined that excess cheese weighed down the bread, causing it to collapse into itself. With a modest 4 ounces of cheese, the bread had plenty of flavor but still rose to its full potential.

The final problem to solve concerned the top crust. I wanted rich flavor and color. The solution was a topping of shredded Parmesan. Nutty and salty, it was liked so much that some of the test cooks were scalping loaves when my back was turned. A colleague suggested that I coat the bottom of the pan with cheese as well, thus doubling the cheesy exterior. Her idea worked brilliantly. Now every bite was packed with flavor. The Parmesan also turned the crust a deep bronze color.

In the end, my cheese bread tasted like recipes that required considerable preparation time, but this recipe was oven-ready after just 15 minutes of hands-on work. In my opinion, that's time very well spent.

QUICK CHEESE BREAD
MAKES ONE 9 BY 5-INCH LOAF

If using Asiago, choose a mild supermarket cheese that yields to pressure when pressed. Aged Asiago that is as firm as Parmesan is too sharp and piquant for this bread. If, when testing the bread for doneness, the toothpick comes out with what looks like uncooked batter clinging to it, try again in a different—but still central—spot; if the toothpick hits a pocket of cheese, it may give a false indication. The texture of the bread improves as it cools, so resist the urge to slice the loaf while it is piping hot. Leftover cheese bread is excellent toasted; toast slices in a toaster oven or on a baking sheet in a 425-degree oven for 5 to 10 minutes, not in a conventional toaster, where bits of cheese may melt, burn, and make a mess.

3 ounces Parmesan cheese, shredded on large holes of box grater (about 1 cup)
3 cups (15 ounces) unbleached all-purpose flour
1 tablespoon baking powder
¼ teaspoon cayenne
1 teaspoon salt
⅛ teaspoon ground black pepper
4 ounces extra-sharp cheddar cheese, cut into ½-inch cubes, or mild Asiago, crumbled into ¼- to ½-inch pieces (about 1 cup)
1¼ cups whole milk
3 tablespoons unsalted butter, melted
1 large egg, beaten lightly
¾ cup sour cream

1. Adjust oven rack to middle position; heat oven to 350 degrees. Spray 5 by 9-inch loaf pan with nonstick cooking spray, then sprinkle ½ cup Parmesan evenly in bottom of pan.

2. In large bowl, whisk flour, baking powder, cayenne, salt, and pepper to combine. Using rubber spatula, mix in cheddar or Asiago, breaking up clumps, until cheese is coated with flour. In medium bowl, whisk together milk, melted butter, egg, and sour cream. Using rubber spatula, gently fold wet ingredients into dry ingredients until just combined (batter will be heavy and thick). Do not overmix. Scrape batter into prepared loaf pan; spread to sides of pan and level surface with rubber spatula. Sprinkle remaining ½ cup Parmesan evenly over surface.

3. Bake until deep golden brown and toothpick or skewer inserted in center of loaf comes out clean, 45 to 50 minutes. Cool in pan on wire rack 5 minutes; invert loaf from pan and continue to cool until warm, about 45 minutes. Cut into slices and serve.

QUICK CHEESE BREAD WITH BACON, ONION, AND GRUYÈRE

---

1. Cut 5 slices bacon (about 5 ounces) into ½-inch pieces and fry in medium nonstick skillet over medium heat, stirring occasionally, until browned and crisp, about 8 minutes. Using slotted spoon, transfer bacon to paper towel–lined plate and pour off all but 3 tablespoons bacon fat from skillet. Add ½ medium onion, minced (about ½ cup), to skillet and cook, stirring frequently, until softened, about 3 minutes; set skillet with onion aside.

2. Follow recipe for Quick Cheese Bread, substituting Gruyère for cheddar, adding bacon and onion to flour along with cheese, and omitting butter.

STEP-BY-STEP | MAKING CHEESE BREAD

1. Coat the bottom of greased loaf pan with Parmesan cheese to create flavorful crust.

2. Add cubed cheese to bowl with dry ingredients and mix well, breaking apart pieces that clump.

3. Whisk wet ingredients in second bowl. Pour into bowl with dry ingredients and fold until combined.

4. Scrape batter into prepared pan, sprinkle with remaining Parmesan, and bake.

TESTING EQUIPMENT:
Rotary Graters

The server at your local Italian restaurant uses a rotary grater to rain Parmesan over pasta at the table, but does this grater have a place at home? To find out, we tested eight models, grating Parmesan, cheddar, mozzarella, and even chocolate and including a variety of test cooks with different hand sizes and strengths.

Most of the handles were tiny and slippery, and even the most comfortable of the lot became painful after extended use. All but the Pedrini and KitchenAid struggled with mozzarella and cheddar; they were more successful because of their larger grating drums, which kept the cheese from sticking.

We concluded that a rotary grater is much too slow for use in the kitchen. None of the grater hoppers could accommodate more than one or two ounces of cheese at a time, and each grater gave us hand fatigue after just a few moments of use. Get out a box or rasp grater if you need grated cheese for a recipe.

All of this said, a rotary grater is nice for the table, in part because there's no risk of raking your knuckles across the grater plate—a common occurrence with a box or rasp grater. Be careful, though, when it's time to clean up. Many rotary graters take some finesse to disassemble, as you must touch the sharp grater drum to release the handle for cleaning. –R.H.

OUR FAVORITES

➤ **PEDRINI, $14.99**
An Italian-made grater with a large hopper, sharp grating teeth, and well-designed handle.

➤ **KITCHENAID, $19.99**
Large hopper, sharp grating teeth, and fairly comfortable grip. Not designed for lefties.

OTHER MODELS TESTED

➤ **CUISIPRO, $20.00**
This stainless steel grater was sturdy and fast but uncomfortable.

➤ **MICROPLANE, $16.95**
Turns out the fluffiest, finest shreds, but it was the slowest model tested.

➤ **OXO GOOD GRIPS, $14.99**
Likable rubberized handle, but the hopper is rather small. Not designed for lefties.

➤ **HOFFRITZ, $15.99**
Awkward design hurt testers' hands. Not designed for lefties.

➤ **NORPRO, $15.99**
This heavy-duty stainless steel grater quickly caused hand fatigue.

➤ **ZYLISS, $14.99**
Downgraded for its small handle, which becomes slippery with use.

Better Chef's Salad

Fast-food joints have given this retro supper salad a bad name (and a plastic fork).
Could we produce a substantial salad with supermarket staples?

⇒ BY SEAN LAWLER ⇐

Most chef's salad recipes read like loose guidelines for cleaning out the fridge: Toss whatever greens you have lying around with some aging cold cuts and serve with a sigh. The resulting piles of oily ham, characterless Swiss, and bland iceberg lettuce should not be eaten but taken as an object lesson, demonstrating that recipes, even for simple salads, need structure and discipline.

After all, a hearty green salad topped with boiled eggs, tomatoes, cold meats, and cheese is a more than presentable dinner for a warm summer night. Unfortunately, the versions we sampled in the test kitchen were far from classic in either taste or technique. Their ingredient lists were haphazard and vague, resulting in bland, muddled flavors, while the procedures were often fussy, time-consuming, and ultimately self-defeating. Why spend an hour julienning ingredients into stringy, unwieldy shapes? Why arrange them in an exacting pattern only to toss the salad into a jumbled mess, with the meat and cheese drowning in a pool of dressing at the bottom of the bowl?

Simple tricks—such as more vinegar in the dressing and thicker slices of meat and cheese—elevate a basic chef's salad.

Building a Better Salad

As the foundation, the greens would have to stand up to the strong flavors of the meat and cheese—and support their physical weight as well. Bland iceberg lettuce failed the first test, while tender field greens such as mesclun flunked the second. Other common mild greens, including romaine, Bibb, and red- and green-leaf lettuces, all held their shape under the weight of the other ingredients, but tasters preferred them mixed with the stronger flavors of spicy greens such as watercress or arugula. A 3:1 ratio of mild to spicy greens worked best.

Personal tastes varied when it came to types of meat and cheese, but tasters agreed on one thing: Thin, stringy strips were unappealing, especially when covered with oily dressing. I readily solved the thin-slice problem by ordering ¼-inch-thick slices at the deli counter. These were easy to stack and cut into 2-inch-long matchsticks, a convenient size for spearing with a fork.

Dressing the Salad

Many recipes suggested creamy Russian or ranch-style dressings, but tasters opposed them. Combined with the meat and cheese, these dressings made the salad far too rich. Vinaigrettes, on the other hand, could not hold their own against the other ingredients, even when livened up with shallot, garlic, and fresh herbs. Tasters declared salad after salad to be bland and oily. Our classic vinaigrette recipe calls for a 4:1 ratio of oil to vinegar, but I decided to balance the meat and cheese with a leaner, more acidic dressing. I reduced the ratio of oil to vinegar first to 3:1, then to 2:1, before tasters were satisfied.

From the way tasters scowled at piles of meat and cheese at the bottom of the salad bowl, I knew a traditional toss was out. The heavier ingredients fell right to the bottom. I discovered that I did not need to dress the meat and cheese. Other components— greens, radishes, cucumbers, tomatoes, and hard-cooked eggs—could be tossed individually or placed on the salad and then drizzled with vinaigrette. When placed in a wide serving bowl, with the meat and cheese piled on top, the salad could be served family-style but still accommodate individual (even vegetarian) preferences. Diners could serve themselves greens and vegetables from around the sides of the salad, then take whatever meat and cheese they desired from the center.

CHEF'S SALAD
SERVES 6 TO 8 AS A LIGHT MAIN DISH

At the deli counter, be sure to have the meats and cheeses sliced ¼ inch thick.

Vinaigrette
- 6 tablespoons extra-virgin olive oil
- 3 tablespoons red wine vinegar
- 2 teaspoons minced shallot
- 1 teaspoon minced garlic
- 1 teaspoon minced fresh thyme leaves
- ¼ teaspoon salt
- ⅛ teaspoon ground black pepper

That's One Tart Dressing

TRADITIONAL 4:1
RATIO FOR
GREEN SALAD

HIGH-ACID 2:1
RATIO FOR
CHEF'S SALAD

To make a traditional vinaigrette for a basic leafy salad, we use 4 parts oil to 1 part vinegar. Because chef's salad contains so many fatty ingredients, we found it necessary to alter this ratio, using just 2 parts oil to 1 part vinegar to create a high-acid dressing.

COOK'S EXTRA gives you free recipes online. Visit www.cooksillustrated.com and key in code 3041 for a recipe for hard-cooked eggs. For another variation on our chef's salad, key in code 3042. The recipes will be available until June 15, 2004.

Salad

- 1 medium cucumber, peeled, halved lengthwise, seeded, and sliced crosswise ¼ inch thick
- 2 medium heads leaf lettuce, washed, dried, and torn into bite-size pieces (about 3 quarts)
- 8 ounces arugula, washed, dried, and torn into bite-size pieces (about 1 quart)
- 6 ounces radishes, trimmed, halved, and sliced thin
  Salt and ground black pepper
- 1 pint cherry tomatoes, halved or quartered if large
- 3 large hard-cooked eggs, each cut into 4 wedges
- 8 ounces deli ham, sliced ¼ inch thick and cut into 2-inch-long matchsticks
- 8 ounces deli turkey, sliced ¼ inch thick and cut into 2-inch-long matchsticks
- 8 ounces sharp cheddar cheese, sliced ¼ inch thick and cut into 2-inch-long matchsticks
- 1 recipe Garlic Croutons (recipe follows)

1. **FOR THE VINAIGRETTE:** Whisk ingredients in medium bowl until combined. Add cucumber and toss; let stand 20 minutes.

2. **FOR THE SALAD:** Toss lettuce, arugula, and radishes in large, wide serving bowl. Add cucumbers and all but 1 tablespoon dressing and toss to combine. Season to taste with salt and pepper. Toss tomatoes in remaining dressing in bowl; arrange tomatoes around perimeter of greens. Arrange egg wedges in ring inside tomatoes and drizzle with any dressing in bowl. Arrange ham, turkey, and cheese over center of greens; sprinkle with croutons and serve immediately.

CHEF'S SALAD WITH FENNEL, ASIAGO, AND SALAMI
SERVES 6 TO 8 AS A LIGHT MAIN DISH

If water-packed artichoke hearts cannot be found, use marinated artichoke hearts, but rinse and drain them before use. For this salad, opt for a mild, soft Asiago cheese that crumbles easily; avoid aged Asiago that has a hard, dry texture.

Vinaigrette

- 6 tablespoons extra-virgin olive oil
- 3 tablespoons balsamic vinegar
- 1 teaspoon minced garlic
- ¼ teaspoon salt
- ⅛ teaspoon ground black pepper

Salad

- 2 heads romaine lettuce, washed, dried, and torn into bite-size pieces (about 3 quarts)
- 4 ounces watercress, washed, dried, and stemmed (about 1 quart)
- ½ cup flat-leaf parsley leaves
- 1 small fennel bulb, trimmed and sliced thin (about 2 cups)
  Salt and ground black pepper
- 1 jar (8 ounces) roasted red peppers, drained, peppers cut crosswise into ½-inch-wide strips

- 1 jar (7 ounces) artichoke hearts packed in water, drained, each heart halved (see note)
- 8 ounces hard salami, sliced ¼ inch thick and cut into 2-inch-long matchsticks
- 8 ounces deli turkey, preferably pepper-crusted, sliced ¼ inch thick and cut into 2-inch-long matchsticks
- 8 ounces mild Asiago cheese, crumbled (see note)
- ½ cup kalamata olives, pitted and chopped coarse
- 1 recipe Garlic Croutons (recipe follows)

1. **FOR THE VINAIGRETTE:** Whisk ingredients in medium bowl until combined.

2. **FOR THE SALAD:** Toss romaine, watercress, parsley, and fennel in large serving bowl. Add all but 1 tablespoon dressing and toss to combine.

Slice It Thick

Deli meat should be cut thick enough to prevent clumping in the bowl but trim enough to be easily incorporated into the salad. At the deli counter, ask for ham and turkey sliced ¼ inch thick. At home, cut the deli meats into matchstick pieces that measure ¼ inch thick and 2 inches long.

Season to taste with salt and pepper. Toss peppers and artichokes in remaining dressing, then arrange around perimeter of greens. Arrange salami, turkey, and cheese over center of greens; top with olives and croutons. Serve immediately.

GARLIC CROUTONS
MAKES ABOUT 1½ CUPS

- 1 large garlic clove, minced to paste or pressed through garlic press (about 1¼ teaspoons)
- ⅛ teaspoon salt
- 1½ tablespoons extra-virgin olive oil
- 6 slices (6 ounces) good-quality white sandwich bread, cut into ½-inch cubes (1½ cups)

Adjust oven rack to middle position and heat oven to 350 degrees. Combine garlic, salt, and oil in small bowl; let stand 20 minutes, then pour through fine-mesh strainer into medium bowl. Add bread cubes and toss to coat. Spread bread cubes in even layer on rimmed baking sheet and bake, stirring occasionally, until golden, about 15 minutes. Cool on baking sheet to room temperature. (Can be covered and stored at room temperature up to 24 hours.)

Oven-Barbecued Chicken

The idea—barbecued chicken straight from your oven—is a great one. Unfortunately, the real thing is dry and tough, with a tasteless, baked-on sauce. Could we save this recipe?

≥ BY ERIN MCMURRER WITH ADAM RIED ≤

When you hear the phrase "hospital food," what do you see in your mind's eye? That's right—plain baked chicken, the very portrait of bland institutional fare, a culinary yawn. The need to dress up this dull, workaday recipe probably inspired the idea of oven-barbecued chicken, which should, in theory at least, add sweet, tangy, spicy flavors to tender chicken by way of a rich, tomatoey sauce in the classic Kansas City style. In our experience, though, the idea remains just that—a theory. As expected, the five initial recipes we tried in the test kitchen delivered tough, rubbery, or unevenly cooked chicken in sauces ranging from pasty and candy-sweet to greasy, stale, thin, or commercial tasting.

Monumental as these problems seemed, we were inspired by the challenge. Surely this dish would be worthwhile if the chicken was juicy, tender, and evenly cooked and the sauce tasted fresh and multidimensional, clinging to the chicken in a thick, lightly caramelized coat.

Choosing and Prepping the Chicken
The recipes we scoured indicated that our chicken options were wide open, as they called for, variously, half chickens, quarter chickens, whole chickens cut into serving pieces, bone-in breasts, thighs, drumsticks, and wings, and even meat that was cooked, boned, shredded, and mixed with barbecue sauce, à la pulled pork. To methodically test each option, we cobbled together a basic baking procedure: Bake the chicken at 350 degrees until partially done, coat with barbecue sauce—a bottled brand from the supermarket for now—and continue baking until the chicken is cooked through, basting with the sauce several times along the way.

Success was elusive. The halved and quartered chickens cooked unevenly and were awkward to eat. Butchering a whole chicken was more work than we saw fit to do for an easy Tuesday-night supper. Of course, purchasing cut-up serving pieces eliminated the work, but time and time

A large skillet, a super easy homemade sauce, and an ingenious cooking method produce superior oven-barbecued chicken—in just half an hour.

again we found them to be sloppily butchered or even mismatched. Using a single cut of chicken, such as all breasts or thighs, helped with the evenness of cooking, at least, and we confirmed that tasters preferred the mild white meat of the breasts as a backdrop for the sauce. Shredding the cooked chicken to mix with the sauce was a messy, tedious process, so we settled on breasts as our best option.

One of the first problems to solve was the skin, which was consistently flabby, rubbery, and fatty. Any fat that rendered from the skin during cooking left the sauce not thick and clingy but greasy and loose, so it slid right off the skin. To cover our bases, we tried cooking the chicken skin-side down in a preheated pan, slashing the skin lightly to expose extra surface area and expedite rendering, and air-drying the chicken prior to cooking. In the end, we rejected all of these methods as either not successful enough or too fussy for a quick weeknight dinner.

The solution, we hoped, would be to jettison the skin entirely. We gave skinless, boneless breasts

a whirl and were delighted to find that they made for a dramatic improvement. The chewy skin became a nonissue, and we discovered an extra benefit in that both sides of the chicken meat were now coated with sauce.

Building Barbecue Flavor
We were next determined to achieve our goal of a fresh, lively sauce with a properly thick and sticky texture. Could we find it in a bottled sauce? Hoping for an easy out, we tried several types, from supermarket standards to fancy mail-order products. We had the best luck with Bull's-Eye, a sauce that won a blind tasting here at *Cook's* last year, but we still felt that a homemade sauce could lift this recipe from pretty good to great.

That certainly didn't mean that the sauce had to be complicated. We began with our own Simple Sweet and Tangy Barbecue Sauce, a quick-cooked number from the July/August 2000 issue. Although this sauce took about half an hour to prepare and required the use of a food processor and strainer, it did offer both fresh, balanced flavors and a thick, clingy texture.

Rather than building a new recipe from the ground up, we tried stripping this one down to make it even faster and simpler. After dozens of tests, we learned that ketchup, Worcestershire, mustard, molasses, chili powder, and cayenne were absolutely necessary, as were maple syrup and the tang of cider vinegar. We substituted grated onion for the onion juice in the original recipe and eliminated the hot pepper sauce, garlic, and liquid smoke. Only four minutes over medium heat were needed to blend the flavors, which became further concentrated when the sauce cooked again on the chicken.

We tried a few other flavoring tricks, including rubbing the chicken with a dry spice rub and marinating it overnight in the sauce before cooking it, but none was worth the effort. Brining was also a bust. The extra seasoning was superfluous in the face of the assertively flavored barbecue sauce, and the extra moisture in the meat from the brine tended to thin the sauce.

The Problem with Packaged Chicken Breasts

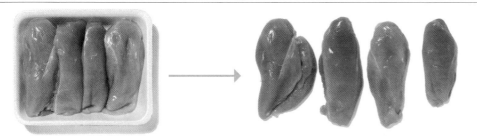

THESE BREASTS LOOK THE SAME . . . BUT OUT OF THE PACKAGE, THEY ARE QUITE DIFFERENT

Uniformly sized chicken breasts will cook more evenly than breasts of varying sizes. Unfortunately, it's difficult to discern size of individual breasts when they're squished into a supermarket package (see left photo). Once we removed the breasts from this package (see right photo) and weighed them, we discovered that one breast weighed 9 ounces, two weighed 6 ounces, and one weighed just 4½ ounces. To prepare oven-barbecued chicken, we recommend buying a family pack with at least six breasts and then freezing the largest and smallest breasts for future use in a stir-fry, where size won't matter.

Cooking BBQ Chicken without a Grill

In terms of cooking temperature and method, we tried dousing the chicken with sauce and then baking it as well as dredging the chicken in seasoned flour and pan-frying it before undertaking an intricate dance of baking and basting. Both approaches failed.

From there, we focused on oven mechanics, testing various oven rack positions, various combinations of low and high temperatures (from 325 to 500 degrees), and additions of sauce at various points during cooking. Alas, despite the moniker "oven-barbecued," none of these oven-based methods worked, although we did learn that lower oven temperatures cooked the irregularly shaped chicken breasts evenly and that higher temperatures helped to concentrate the sauce.

Standing in the kitchen, scratching our heads after the umpteenth test, we looked at the skillet of waiting barbecue sauce and an idea flashed. We remembered a method we had used to make maple-glazed pork roast in the March/April 2003 issue. It involved searing the roast in a skillet, reducing the glaze in the same skillet, and then finishing the roast in that already hot skillet in the oven. Would a similar technique help us to master our current challenge?

The first attempt showed promise, but it wasn't perfect because the exteriors of the breasts were dry from aggressive pan-searing. The solution was to sear the chicken breasts only very lightly, just until they began to color and develop a slightly rough surface to which the sauce could adhere. The chicken was then removed from the pan, the sauce made, the chicken added back and coated with sauce, and the pan slipped under the broiler. The results were good, but the heat of the broiler had dried out the chicken a bit. The solution was to start the skillet in a 325-degree oven and then finish it under the broiler. The chicken was now juicy and thickly coated with a perfectly concentrated sauce.

SWEET AND TANGY OVEN-BARBECUED CHICKEN
SERVES 4

Real maple syrup is preferable to imitation syrup, and "mild" or "original" molasses is preferable to darker, more bitter types. If you are content to use bottled sauce, we had the best luck with Bull's-Eye Original, winner of a blind tasting held last year. Use 1¾ cups of sauce and, in step 2, reduce the sauce cooking time from 4 minutes to 2 minutes.

Some notes on equipment: First, to grate the onion, use a Microplane grater or the fine holes of a box grater. Second, resist the temptation to use a nonstick skillet; most nonstick skillets are not broilersafe. Third, and most important, you should make this recipe only in an in-oven broiler; do not use a drawer-type broiler. Finally, be aware that broiling times may differ from one oven to another. For instance, in one editor's powerful professional-style oven, the chicken took just 4 minutes to reach 160 degrees, so we urge you to check the chicken for doneness after only 3 minutes of broiling. You may also have to lower the oven rack if your broiler runs very hot.

1	cup ketchup
2	tablespoons finely grated onion
2	tablespoons Worcestershire sauce
2	tablespoons Dijon mustard
3	tablespoons molasses
2	tablespoons maple syrup
3	tablespoons cider vinegar
1	teaspoon chili powder
¼	teaspoon cayenne
4	boneless, skinless chicken breasts, 6 to 7 ounces each (with tenderloins), patted dry with paper towels
	Salt and ground black pepper
1	tablespoon vegetable oil

1. Adjust oven rack to upper-middle position, about 5 inches from upper heating element; heat oven to 325 degrees. Whisk ketchup, onion, Worcestershire, mustard, molasses, maple syrup, vinegar, chili powder, and cayenne in small bowl; set aside. Season chicken with salt and pepper.

2. Heat oil in heavy-bottomed, nonreactive, 12-inch ovenproof skillet over high heat until beginning to smoke. Brown chicken skinned-side down until very light golden, 1 to 2 minutes; using tongs, turn chicken and brown until very light golden on second side, 1 to 2 minutes longer. Transfer chicken to plate and set aside. Discard fat in skillet; off heat, add sauce mixture and, using a wooden spoon, scrape up browned bits on bottom of skillet. Simmer sauce over medium heat, stirring frequently with heatproof spatula, until sauce is thick and glossy, and spatula leaves clear trail in sauce, about 4 minutes. Off heat, return chicken to skillet, and turn to coat thickly with sauce; set chicken pieces skinned-side up and spoon extra sauce over each piece to create thick coating. Place skillet in oven and cook until thickest parts of chicken breasts register 130 degrees on instant-read thermometer, 10 to 14 minutes. Set oven to broil and continue to cook until thickest parts of chicken breasts register 160 degrees, 5 to 10 minutes longer. Transfer chicken to platter and let rest 5 minutes. Meanwhile, whisk to combine sauce in skillet and transfer to small bowl. Serve chicken, passing extra sauce separately.

Oven-Barbecued Chicken, Reinvented in a Skillet

1. Lightly brown chicken, transfer pieces to plate, and pour off fat from skillet.

2. Add sauce ingredients to empty pan and cook until heatproof spatula leaves clear trail.

3. Return chicken to skillet, turn to coat with sauce, then spoon more sauce over each piece.

4. Bake chicken and sauce in skillet, broil to caramelize sauce, and then serve.

Foolproof Brown Rice

Forget the instructions on the back of the bag, unless you want scorched or mushy rice.

⇒ BY REBECCA HAYS ⇐

Most cooks I know shun brown rice, classifying it as wholesome yet unappealing sustenance for penniless vegetarians, practitioners of macrobiotics, and the like. But I'm not sure why. I find it ultimately satisfying, with a nutty, gutsy flavor and more textural personality—slightly sticky and just a bit chewy—than white rice. An ideal version should be easy to come by: Just throw rice and water in a pot and set the timer, right? Yet cooks who have attempted to prepare brown rice know it isn't so simple. My habit, born of impatience, is to crank up the flame in an effort to hurry along the slow-cooking grains (brown rice takes roughly twice as long to cook as white), which inevitably leads to a burnt pot and crunchy rice. Adding plenty of water isn't the remedy; excess liquid swells the rice into a gelatinous mass.

I pulled out an expensive, heavy-bottomed pot with a tight-fitting lid (many recipes caution against using inadequate cookware), fiddled with the traditional absorption method (cooking the rice with just enough water), and eventually landed on a workable recipe. Yet when I tested the recipe with less than ideal equipment—namely, a flimsy pan with an ill-fitting lid—I was back to burnt, undercooked rice. With the very best pot and a top-notch stove, it is possible to cook brown rice properly, but I wanted a surefire method that would work no matter the cook, no matter the equipment.

I wondered if the microwave might work well in this instance, given that it cooks food indirectly, without a burner. Sadly, it delivered inconsistent results, with one batch turning brittle and another, prepared in a different microwave, too sticky. A rice cooker yielded faultless brown rice on the first try, but many Americans don't own one.

I set out to construct a homemade cooker that would approximate the controlled, indirect heat of a rice cooker—and so began to consider the merits of cooking the rice in the oven. I'd have more precise temperature control, and I hoped that the oven's encircling heat would eliminate the risk of scorching. My first try yielded extremely promising results: With the pan tightly covered with aluminum foil, the rice steamed to near-perfection. Fine-tuning the amount of water, I settled on a ratio similar to that used for our white rice recipe: 2⅓ cups of water to 1½ cups of rice, falling well short of the 2:1 water-to-rice ratio advised by most rice producers and nearly every recipe I consulted. Perhaps that is why so much brown rice turns out sodden and overcooked.

My next task was to spruce up the recipe by bringing out the nutty flavor of the otherwise plain grains. Toasting the rice dry in the oven imparted a slight off flavor. When I sautéed the rice in fat before baking, the grains frayed slightly; tasters preferred rice made by adding fat to the cooking water. A small amount (2 teaspoons) of either butter or oil adds mild flavor while keeping the rice fluffy.

To reduce what was a long baking time of 90 minutes at 350 degrees, I tried starting with boiling water instead of cold tap water and raising the oven to 375 degrees. These steps reduced the baking time to a reasonable one hour. (A hotter oven caused some of the fragile grains to explode.)

No more scorched or mushy brown rice for me, and no more worrying about finding just the right pan or adjusting the stovetop to produce just the right level of heat. Now I can serve good brown rice anytime, even to a meat lover.

FOOLPROOF OVEN-BAKED BROWN RICE
SERVES 4 TO 6

To minimize any loss of water through evaporation, cover the saucepan and use the water as soon as it reaches a boil. An 8-inch ceramic baking dish with a lid may be used instead of the baking dish and foil. To double the recipe, use a 13 by 9-inch baking dish; the baking time need not be increased.

1½ cups long-, medium-, or short-grain brown rice
2⅓ cups water
2 teaspoons unsalted butter or vegetable oil
½ teaspoon salt

1. Adjust oven rack to middle position; heat oven to 375 degrees. Spread rice in 8-inch-square glass baking dish.

2. Bring water and butter or oil to boil, covered, in medium saucepan over high heat; once boiling, immediately stir in salt and pour water over rice. Cover baking dish tightly with doubled layer of foil. Bake rice 1 hour, until tender.

3. Remove baking dish from oven and uncover. Fluff rice with dinner fork, then cover dish with clean kitchen towel; let rice stand 5 minutes. Uncover and let rice stand 5 minutes longer; serve immediately.

BROWN RICE WITH PARMESAN, LEMON, AND HERBS

1. Heat 2 tablespoons unsalted butter in medium nonstick skillet over medium heat until foaming; add 1 small onion, minced, and cook until translucent, about 3 minutes. Set onion aside.

2. Follow recipe for Foolproof Oven-Baked Brown Rice, substituting chicken broth for water, omitting butter or oil, reducing salt to ⅛ teaspoon, and stirring onion mixture into rice after adding broth. Cover and bake as directed. After removing foil, stir in ⅛ teaspoon ground black pepper, ¼ cup minced fresh parsley, ¼ cup chopped fresh basil, ½ cup grated Parmesan, 1 teaspoon grated lemon zest, and ½ teaspoon lemon juice. Cover with clean kitchen towel and continue with recipe.

COOK'S EXTRA gives you free recipes online. For two more variations on our brown rice recipe, visit www.cooksillustrated.com and key in code 3043. These recipes will be available until June 15, 2004.

Getting the Texture Right

PROBLEM:
WET & SOUPY

PROBLEM:
BURNT & CRUNCHY

PERFECT:
FLUFFY & CHEWY

We found that following the directions on the back of the bag usually results in wet, porridgelike rice (left). Many recipes call for too much heat, and, unless you use a very heavy pot, the rice will scorch (center). By using less water than is typical and taking advantage of the even heat of the oven, you can turn out perfectly cooked brown rice every time (right).

Rescuing Steak Diane

Reduced to the level of bad dinner theater, this legendary tableside showpiece was in need of a revival. Could we give this tired classic a new life at home?

⋑ BY DIANE UNGER-MAHONEY ⋐

Why would anyone want to make steak Diane—a pan-seared steak demanding a rich sauce based on an all-day veal stock reduction—at home? Fifty years ago, it was a hot menu item at fancy restaurants, prepared tableside, and it included a burst of pyrotechnics supplied by a match and some cognac. To rescue this outdated piece of culinary showmanship, I needed some motivation, and I found it when I considered the everyday skillet steak. Transforming this simple recipe into a Saturday night special, more black tie than blue jeans, would, I hoped, be worth the effort.

After reviewing 27 recipes and testing five, however, my enthusiasm quickly waned. Recipes were consistent in requiring a sauce based on a labor-intensive veal stock reduction, an abundance of butter and cream, and varying amounts of shallot, mustard, and Worcestershire sauce. They varied widely when it came to what cut of steak to use (sirloin shell, rib eye, strip, or tenderloin), how to prepare it (paper-thin or as thick as it comes), and how to cook it (some were lightly browned, some deeply caramelized, others practically stewed in butter). My goal, I then decided, would be to develop a recipe for a quick stock, to slim down the sauce, and to determine the best cut of steak and a foolproof method for cooking it. In the end, I hoped to sit down to a dinner of tender, perfectly cooked steak napped in a deeply satisfying pan sauce—having done it all in less than an hour.

Finding a Stand-In for Veal Stock
The cornerstone of the sauce for this dish is veal stock, which imparts a silky texture and deep flavor. Because homemade veal stock—a staple in any half-decent restaurant—was out of the question, I had to come up with a good stunt double that could be made in less than an hour. (See page 14 for tips on buying veal stock.) I started my testing by browning onions, carrots, and garlic to develop flavor and then deglazing the pan with red wine. Because prior tastings in the test kitchen had revealed that canned beef broth on its own tastes tinny and watery, I tried equal parts beef and chicken broths

Flambéing the cognac is a key step in developing a restaurant-quality sauce for steak Diane.

(both low sodium) and reduced the mixture by half. The result? The color of this concoction was murky, its consistency watery, and its flavor lacking. Progress, it seemed, would be slow.

I revisited some tried-and-true French cookbooks and was reminded that veal stocks typically contain tomato in some form. I wondered what would happen if I sautéed tomato paste in oil before adding the vegetables to the pan. The tomato paste lost its neon color and turned a deep reddish-brown, and when the vegetables were added it coated them with rich flavor. The only problem was that the paste began to burn before the vegetables were fully browned. The solution that came to mind was water.

I added 2 tablespoons to the pan just as the paste was about to burn and then scraped the browned bits from the pan bottom. I let the deep red liquid reduce almost to the point of no return and then added another 2 tablespoons of water. The flavors intensified each time, giving me the

richest "roasted" flavor possible. To enhance the meaty flavor, I cut back on the chicken broth, doubled the beef broth, and added red wine, fresh thyme, bay leaf, and a hefty amount of black peppercorns. Then I let that mixture reduce for 35 minutes. I had now distilled 54 ounces of watery liquid to 10 ounces of concentrated stock, and the results were worth the wait: The flavor was dead on. But I wasn't done yet, as the sauce was still thin.

To thicken the sauce I experimented with cornstarch, arrowroot, gelatin, and flour. Cornstarch and arrowroot gave the sauce the gluey substance of bad takeout Chinese food. Gelatin turned it into something resembling beef Jell-O. It turned out that a small amount of flour, sprinkled over the browned vegetables, added the perfect viscosity without masking flavors. I now had an intensely flavored foundation with a consistency similar to serious veal stock reductions. Not as good as the real thing, to be sure, but outstanding considering the modest investment in time.

Getting to the Meat
Of the four cuts of meat I had cooked for my first tests, I ruled out sirloin shell for its toughness and rib eye for the mass of trimmings that ended up in the garbage. Both tenderloin and strip steaks were well liked, but tasters preferred the flavorful strip to the somewhat boring tenderloin. I wanted to be able to cook four steaks quickly, so I trimmed them of excess fat and tested a range of thicknesses, from ⅛ inch to 1 inch. The deciding factor turned out to be the diameter of the bottom of my 12-inch skillet (I was using a traditional skillet with flared

BUYING: **Shopping for Strip Steaks**

Watch out for steaks from the sirloin end of the strip, which may have a thick line of gristle in the center.

Preparing the Steaks

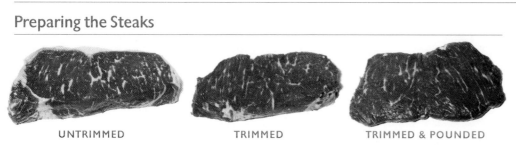

UNTRIMMED   TRIMMED   TRIMMED & POUNDED

The steak on the left has not been trimmed. To keep the sauce from becoming too fatty, trim all visible fat from the perimeter of the steak, as has been done with the steak in the middle. To ensure even cooking, use a meat pounder or mallet to pound the steak to an even ½-inch thickness, as in the steak on the right.

sides, meaning that the measure across the top was greater than across the bottom), which let me cook two 4½-inch-wide steaks at a time. This meant that I could pound each of the steaks to a half-inch thickness. Unfortunately, the steaks were not browning as evenly as I had hoped. I discovered that weighting them with a heavy-bottomed skillet or Dutch oven as they cooked on the second side gave me the color I was looking for and added more fond, or flavorful browned bits, to the pan bottom.

Finishing the Sauce with a Flourish

With the steaks cooked, it was time to take my faux veal stock and create a sauce. Because the sauce base included red wine, I tested Madeira, sherry, white wine, and brandy. Madeira and sherry were too sweet, and white wine made the sauce too acidic. Brandy was the winner, so I went on to taste cognac and Armagnac, both straight up and in the sauce. Armagnac had a bitter aftertaste, so I settled on cognac.

I had now reached the denouement of recipe development for steak Diane: It was time to introduce the flambé. Once I finished cooking the

steaks and removed them from the pan, I added minced shallot and 6 tablespoons of cognac and tipped my pan toward the gas burner. The flames shot up into the ventilation system. I cut back to 4 tablespoons of cognac, allowed the alcohol vapors to evaporate slightly, and then tipped my pan toward the flame. This time I got what I wanted: a nice flambé, with no need for the fire extinguisher. But I wondered, was the flambé crucial to the flavor of the dish, or was it just for show? To answer this question, I conducted a head-to-head blind tasting of two sauces, one flamed, one unflamed. The clear winner was the flambéed sauce, which was more balanced and slightly sweeter. The question now was, why? A bit of scientific examination was in order. (To see what we found out, read "Is a Flambé Just for Show?" on page 15.)

Once the cognac had been flamed and the browned bits scraped from the skillet, I added the faux veal stock I had prepared earlier and focused on the final seasonings. Dijon mustard was well received, but tasters took issue with the quantity of Worcestershire sauce used in most recipes, so I reduced it to a mere teaspoon. After sampling sauces finished with cream, butter, and a combination

of the two, I realized that while cream may add body to a pan sauce with a thin base, it was diluting the flavors of my base. A simple finish with butter added luster and sheen.

Finally, I plated the steaks individually and spooned just enough of the sauce over the center of each to moisten them, not to drown them. A colorful sprinkling of fresh chives, and my skillet steak was ready for formal wear.

SAUCE BASE FOR STEAK DIANE
MAKES 1¼ CUPS

This recipe yields a sauce base that is an excellent facsimile of a demi-glace, a very labor-intensive and time-consuming classic French sauce base. Because the sauce base is very concentrated, make sure to use low-sodium chicken and beef broths; otherwise, the base may be unpalatably salty. The sauce base can be made ahead and refrigerated for up to three days.

2	tablespoons vegetable oil
4	teaspoons tomato paste
2	small onions, chopped medium (about 1⅓ cups)
1	medium carrot, chopped medium (about ½ cup)
4	medium garlic cloves, peeled
¼	cup water
4	teaspoons all-purpose flour
1½	cups dry red wine
3½	cups low-sodium beef broth
1¾	cups low-sodium chicken broth
2	teaspoons black peppercorns
8	sprigs fresh thyme
2	bay leaves

1. Heat oil and tomato paste in Dutch oven over medium-high heat; cook, stirring constantly,

---

TASTING: **Veal Stock**

Real restaurant-quality veal stock takes hours of roasting and simmering, all of which results in a highly reduced stock referred to as either a demi-glace or glace de viande. (Strictly speaking, a demi-glace is a reduced brown sauce, whereas a glace de viande is simply a meat stock that has been reduced to a thick syrup.) We tested four demi-glace products and three that were labeled "glace de viande." The demi-glace offerings were universally disliked by tasters. Typical comments were "no meat

flavor" and "vegetal and sour." The demi-glaces also had ingredient lists that were as long (and confusing) as a four-star chef recipe. The glace de viande products (also called glace de veau) were far superior, no doubt because they contained recognizable ingredients. Our favorites were Provimi and CulinArte' Bonewerks. Both companies offer frozen 1-pound envelopes for about $14 each. See Resources on page 32 for details. –D.M.

OUR TWO FAVORITES

PROVIMI Glace de Veau
"Sweet and meaty" and "balanced."

CULINARTE' Bonewerks Glace de Veau
"Strong meaty flavor" and "herbaceous."

THE REST OF THE PACK

MORE THAN GOURMET Glace de Viande
"Way too salty" and "artificially sweet."

AROMONT Demi-Glace
"Gluey," "salty," and "tastes burned."

WILLIAMS-SONOMA Veal Demi-Glace
"Thin and vinegary," "metallic," and "chickeny."

CULINARTE' Bonewerks Demi-Glace
"Butterscotch flavor" and "weak meat flavor."

MORE THAN GOURMET Demi-Glace
"Sour," "vegetal," and "yeasty."

until paste begins to brown, about 3 minutes. Add onions, carrot, and garlic; cook, stirring frequently, until mixture is reddish brown, about 2 minutes. Add 2 tablespoons water and continue to cook, stirring constantly, until mixture is well browned, about 3 minutes, adding remaining water when needed to prevent scorching. Add flour and cook, stirring constantly, 1 minute. Add wine and, using a heatproof rubber spatula, scrape up browned bits on bottom and sides of pot; bring to boil, stirring occasionally (mixture will thicken slightly). Add beef and chicken broths, peppercorns, thyme, and bay; bring to boil and cook, uncovered, occasionally scraping bottom and sides of pot with spatula, until reduced to 2½ cups, 35 to 40 minutes.

2. Strain mixture through fine-mesh strainer, pressing on solids to extract as much liquid as possible; you should have about 1¼ cups.

STEAK DIANE
SERVES 4

If you prefer not to make the sauce base, mix ½ cup glace de viande (see the veal stock tasting on page 14) with ¾ cup water and ¼ cup red wine and use this mixture in place of the base in step 2. For this recipe, use a traditional skillet. The steaks leave behind more fond (browned bits) than they do in a nonstick skillet, and more fond means a richer, more flavorful sauce. A superb embellishment for Steak Diane is a drizzle of white truffle oil just before serving. If you do not wish to flambé, simmer the cognac in step 2 for 10 to 15 seconds for a slightly less sweet flavor profile.

Steaks
- 2 tablespoons vegetable oil
- 4 strip steaks (about 12 ounces each), trimmed of all excess fat and pounded to even ½-inch thickness (see photos on page 14)
     Salt and ground black pepper

Sauce
- 1 tablespoon vegetable oil
- 1 small shallot, minced (about 2 tablespoons)
- ¼ cup cognac
- 1 recipe Sauce Base for steak Diane (see note)
- 2 teaspoons Dijon mustard
- 2 tablespoons cold unsalted butter
- 1 teaspoon Worcestershire sauce
- 2 tablespoons minced fresh chives

1. **FOR THE STEAKS:** Heat 1 tablespoon oil in 12-inch heavy-bottomed skillet over medium-high heat until smoking. Meanwhile, season steaks with salt and pepper. Place 2 steaks in skillet and cook until well browned, about 1½ minutes. Following illustrations at right, flip steaks and weight with heavy-bottomed pan; continue to cook until well browned on second side, about 1½ minutes longer. Transfer steaks to large

platter and tent with foil. Add 1 tablespoon oil to now-empty skillet and repeat with remaining steaks; transfer second batch of steaks to platter.

2. **FOR THE SAUCE:** Off heat, add 1 tablespoon oil and shallots to now-empty skillet; using skillet's residual heat, cook, stirring frequently, until shallots are slightly softened and browned, about 45 seconds. Add cognac; let stand until cognac warms slightly, about 10 seconds, then set skillet over high heat. Using chimney match, ignite cognac; shake skillet until flames subside,

then simmer cognac until reduced to about 1 tablespoon, about 10 seconds. Add sauce base and mustard; simmer until slightly thickened and reduced to 1 cup, 2 to 3 minutes. Whisk in butter; off heat, add Worcestershire sauce, any accumulated juices from steaks, and 1 tablespoon chives. Adjust seasoning with salt and pepper.

3. Set steaks on individual dinner plates, spoon 2 tablespoons sauce over each steak, sprinkle with chives, and serve immediately, passing remaining sauce separately.

FLAME

IGNITION SOURCE

ALCOHOL VAPORS

COGNAC PAN SAUCE

HEAT SOURCE

STEP-BY-STEP | BROWNING THE STEAKS

The following method yields well-browned steaks. It also leaves behind, over the entire surface of the pan, lots of crusty browned bits, or fond, which make for a richly flavored sauce.

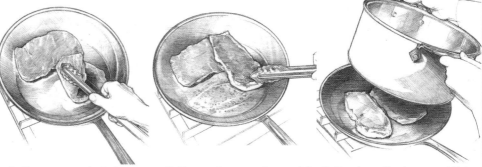

1. Place two steaks in hot pan, side by side, and cook until well browned.

2. Turn steaks over and rotate 90 degrees to ensure that entire pan surface will be covered with fond.

3. Place heavy Dutch oven or skillet on top of steaks and continue cooking until well browned.

Mastering the Art of Sauté

From proper pans and equipment to perfect technique, we take the guesswork out of this often confusing cooking method. BY MATTHEW CARD

Sauté is a vaguely defined cooking method in which vegetables, thin pieces of meat or fish, or shellfish are cooked over moderately high heat with a minimum of fat. It's a building block in some recipes—think vegetables for a soup or sauce—but makes for a finished dish in others—sautéed cutlets or a vegetable sauté. Most cooks understand the technique in theory but fail in practice. Follow the tips and techniques below for crisp, tender vegetables and browned, juicy cutlets.

EQUIPMENT

Cookware: Pans designed for sautéing come in two distinct styles: straight sided and sloped sided. Through testing, we have found that straight sides inhibit moisture evaporation, allowing foods to "stew." Sloped-sided pans allow for quicker evaporation and facilitate the sauté "snap," that flick of the wrist that sends food up and over itself in a smooth arc and evenly redistributes it in the pan (see "The Sauté Snap" at the bottom of page 17).

Depending on the manufacturer, a sloped-sided pan may be called everything from omelette pan to a skillet to a fry pan. For the sake of standardization, we refer to any sloped-sided shallow pan as a skillet. For a list of our favorite skillets—traditional, nonstick, and best buys—check out Resources (on page 32).

Ill-Suited for Sautéing
Straight-sided pans inhibit evaporation and don't facilitate the sauté "snap." They are best used for pan-frying and shallow braising.

Perfect for Sautéing
Sloped sides allow for quick evaporation of moisture—preventing foods from stewing in exuded juices—and for a smooth "snap."

Measuring a Skillet
The industry may not agree on what to call a slope-sided pan, but there is agreement on sizing conventions. All skillets are measured outer lip to outer lip.

Traditional vs. Nonstick Skillets: When to Use Which for What?

Traditional or nonstick? It's a question we often ask ourselves in the test kitchen. Nonstick skillets facilitate cleanup and minimize the need for lubricating fat—definite bonuses—but what is the downside? A dirty four-letter word: *fond*. Nonstick coatings inhibit the buildup of those crusty stuck-on bits that, when deglazed with a splash of liquid, dissolve and add deep flavor and color to pan sauces. We tasted our Steak Diane sauce (page 13) prepared in both traditional and nonstick skillets and found the latter version downright anemic in terms of flavor and color.

SAUTÉED DISHES BEST PREPARED IN A TRADITIONAL SKILLET:
- **Steak**
- **Chops:** pork, lamb, or veal
- **Cutlets with pan sauce:** chicken, turkey, or pork

SAUTÉED DISHES BEST PREPARED IN A NONSTICK SKILLET:
- **Cutlets without pan sauce:** chicken, turkey, or pork
- **Seafood:** fish steaks or fillets, scallops, or shrimp

The Right Tools: To maneuver food in a skillet as it sautés, you need the following tools. See page 32 for more information on our recommended models.

TONGS   RUBBER SPATULA   FISH SPATULA

Tongs are a heatproof extension of your hand and are invaluable whether moving cutlets or stirring vegetables (when closed, they work like a spoon or spatula). After testing a variety of brands and styles, we found models from Oxo and Edlund to be our favorites because they opened wide, had a firm yet comfortable spring tension, and had scalloped—not serrated—tips that gripped securely without damaging food. Medium-length (12-inch) tongs are the most versatile size.

Heatproof rubber spatulas will do all of the work of wooden spoons but also do a much better job of scraping up stuck-on bits of food. After testing 10 popular brands (through baking tasks, general scraping chores, and an abuse test), we found Rubbermaid's High Heat Scraper to be the best of the bunch.

Fish spatulas maneuver delicate foods with ease. Matfer's Slotted Pelton Fish Spatula was our favorite in a recent test. For the full results of the test, visit **Cook's Extra** at www.cooksillustrated.com and key in code 3044. This information will be available until June 15, 2004.

OIL

Best Choice: After sautéing chicken in a variety of different oils, from $48 per liter extra-virgin olive oil to cheap canola oil, we found flavor differences to be virtually imperceptible. That said, we avoid unrefined oils such as extra-virgin olive oil because they have a low smoke point and are thus an inaccurate guide to the skillet's temperature. Butter, too, burns fairly easily unless mixed with oil.

For sautéing, a vegetable-based oil—soy, corn, peanut (not roasted peanut oil, however), olive (not extra-virgin), or canola—is the best choice.

Heat until Shimmering: With proper temperature critical to a successful sauté, how do you gauge when the skillet is hot enough? We've tried a long list of eccentric tests—from water droplets skittering about to crumbs browning—and found the only definitive answer resided in oil temperature. We heat the skillet over medium-high heat with a minimum of oil (as sautéing dictates); as soon as the oil is shimmering, the pan is ready to go.

ILLUSTRATION: JOHN BURGOYNE

SAUTÉ TROUBLESHOOTING

Over the years, we've found that the following problems are most likely to cause poor results when sautéing.

Warped Skillet: It's nearly impossible to brown cutlets evenly in a skillet with an uneven, warped bottom. If you are unsure of your skillet's evenness, rest the pan on a flat surface. Does it rock to and fro? Does water pool in a particular spot? Adding extra oil to the skillet will help "level" the pan and can improve browning, but it's no guarantee. Warped pans, however, are fine for sautéing vegetables because they are moved frequently.

Uneven Heating: Make sure your pan is properly sized to the burner and vice versa. If the skillet is too big for the burner, only the center will fully heat; if it's too small, the pan may become excessively hot.

Thin Pans: Thin, inexpensive pans heat and cool more rapidly than thicker, heavy-bottomed pans and thus demand more attention. Gauge the browning speed and adjust the burner temperature accordingly.

FOOD PREPARATION
Proper equipment and temperature are half the battle; preparation and technique make up the rest. For the best results, follow these tips.

Cutlets: To ensure even cooking, limit splatter, and promote a crisp crust, make sure meat and fish are thoroughly blotted dry between paper towels and any excess coating (flour or breading) is shaken free.

Vegetables: For uniform cooking, vegetables must be cut to the same size; large pieces will remain crunchy and taste vegetal; small bits will overcook and lose flavor.

VOLUME
Avoid overcrowding the pan, which will cause food to steam and thereby affect flavor, color, and texture. Choose the right pan size and don't add more food than will fit comfortably.

The Dangers of Overcrowding: Place only as many cutlets as will fit into the skillet without touching and without crawling up the sides of the skillet; otherwise, the cutlets may expel juices (and steam), fuse together, and/or cook unevenly. Three chicken cutlets fit perfectly into a 10-inch skillet (as shown) with space on all sides, but jam a fourth cutlet into the same pan and there is a good deal of overlap.

SAUTÉ TIPS

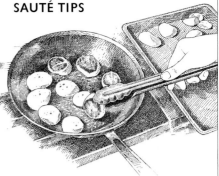

Even Cooking of Multiple Items: When sautéing more than a few items, as with scallops, it's easy to forget which items went into the pan first. To keep track, we position the items in a clockwise circular pattern, starting at 12 o'clock and working our way around. When it's time to begin flipping them, start once again at 12 o'clock and work your way around. Items should come out of the pan in the same order in which they went into the pan.

Stuck-On Foods: If cutlets fuse to the skillet, try this tip for freeing them. Dip a flexible spatula into cold water and slide the inverted spatula blade underneath the cutlet. The cool, wet spatula blade breaks the bond between skillet and meat.

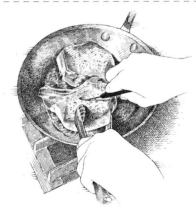

Determining Doneness of Cutlets, Chops, and Steaks: An instant-read thermometer delivers the most accurate reading of doneness, but the "nick-and-peek" method also works in a pinch. When you think the food is nearing doneness, make a small nick halfway through the meat with a paring knife. If there is a bone, nick next to the bone for an accurate reading (the area along the bone takes the longest to cook).

THE SAUTÉ SNAP
Tongs and a spatula will get you only so far; flipping the food with a quick snap of the wrist evenly redistributes foodstuffs with just one smooth motion. Food that was on the bottom of the pan is replaced by that sitting on top and vice versa. The "snap" takes some practice—something we recommend first trying outdoors with some dried beans or rice, not the night's dinner. This technique should be employed with an absolute minimum amount of oil; otherwise, hot oil may splatter.

I. Securely grasp the skillet handle with your thumb positioned on top, pointing toward the skillet. If the skillet is heavy, use both hands.

2. With a fluid motion, snap the pan forward and then jerk it toward you, which will send the food sliding forward and up.

3. Tip the back of the pan (that is closest to you) slightly forward, as if to receive the food. Repeat as necessary to disperse food evenly.

Family-Style Macaroni and Cheese

Neither dull nor excessively rich, macaroni and cheese should please a multitude of palates. Could we find a simple way to make this dish appealing to adults and kids alike?

⇒ BY BRIDGET LANCASTER ⇐

With the possible exception of meatloaf and fried chicken, few dishes are as personal as macaroni and cheese. Baked or stovetop, custard based or little more than white sauce and pasta, with or without toasted bread crumbs, there must be a million recipes out there, surely enough to satisfy nearly everyone. Unfortunately, no one of these recipes can satisfy everyone at the same time. Sure, the kids would be fine with the contents of the blue box brand, but for me this ready-mix mac and cheese lost its appeal soon after I learned how to boil water. Conversely, decadent recipes replete with cream, eggs, and a who's-who list of pungent cheeses are decidedly adults-only; just try to serve them to the kids and you'll get upturned noses and pushed-back plates.

To get my bearings, I scoured the aforementioned million recipes (or at least 40), starting with our own recipe, published in January/February 1997. A custard-style macaroni and cheese, this recipe uses eggs and evaporated milk (as opposed to the more traditional whole milk) to prevent the custard from curdling (a common occurrence in recipes with eggs). Although a long-standing test kitchen favorite, this dish is incredibly rich. I wanted something simpler—but, as my next test revealed, not too simple. When I layered cooked pasta and cheese into a casserole dish, poured milk over the lot, and put the dish in the oven, the fat from the cheese separated and the result was a greasy mess. I concluded that the cheese needed some sort of binder—either eggs or flour.

Béchamel Basics

I was now left with the path chosen by the vast majority of recipe writers: béchamel sauce. Béchamel is a white sauce made by cooking flour and butter to form a light roux. Milk is gradually whisked in, and the béchamel is cooked until it thickens. Combined with cheese and partially cooked noodles, the mix is then poured into a casserole dish and baked.

Traditional recipes incorporate the cheese into the béchamel before stirring in parcooked pasta and then bake the dish until the sauce is bubbling hot and thick. It sure sounds easy. But no matter

Great macaroni and cheese doesn't have to be difficult, and it doesn't require fancy cheeses.

how much attention I paid, I just couldn't pull a great baked macaroni and cheese out of the oven. Sometimes the pasta was overcooked—a result of just one minute too many of boiling on the stovetop. Even worse were the batches made with undercooked noodles. I tried to remedy these by keeping the dishes in the oven longer (anywhere from 20 to 30 minutes), but after a while the bubbling cheese began to separate and the dishes took on an oily, grainy feel.

Frustrated, I pushed aside the idea of using the oven and started working solely on the stovetop. Maybe I could better prevent the overcooking (and undercooking) of the pasta.

I made the next batch of sauce and boiled my pasta on the side. I cooked the pasta until it was a few minutes shy of being done, tossed it in with the sauce and cheese, and simmered it until the pasta was tender, which took a good 10 minutes. To my dismay, this batch had begun to separate, just like my oven-baked experiments, and the parcooked pasta released its starch into the sauce, giving it a gritty feel. Next I cooked the pasta until very tender and quickly mixed it with the

cheese and sauce. This time tasters thought that the noodles needed more time to absorb the sauce. I needed to cook the pasta less at the outset. Boiled until just past al dente, the noodles still had enough structure to stand up to the heat of the sauce for a few minutes without turning mushy, and the cheese sauce filled every nook and cranny.

Foray into Mornay

I next decided to work on the correct proportions of butter to flour to milk, reasoning that the winning combination would provide the desired silky sauce. Béchamel recipes that used more butter than flour lacked cohesion. Those using equal parts butter and flour seemed heavy and dull. I had much better luck using slightly more flour than butter (6 tablespoons to 5 tablespoons, respectively). Just this little change cut enough of the richness that I was trying to avoid, and, when I added 5 cups of whole milk, there was a plentitude of sauce with which to smother the noodles.

Technically speaking, as soon as I added cheese to my white sauce, it turned from béchamel to Mornay. I knew that choosing the right cheese would affect not only the flavor of the dish but also its texture. Indeed, an unpleasant grainy feel was introduced by hard cheeses such as Parmesan, Gruyère, and some aged cheddars, to say nothing of their overly distinct flavor. On the other hand, incredibly mild, soft cheeses such as mascarpone and ricotta contributed no flavor, and their creamy texture pushed the macaroni and cheese right back into sickly territory. What worked best were two cheeses: sharp cheddar for flavor and Monterey Jack for creaminess. For a more detailed explanation of these choices, see "Two Cheeses Are Better Than One" on page 19.

How much cheese to use? Many recipes called for twice as much cheese as pasta (I was using 1 pound of pasta). The result was a sticky, stringy macaroni and cheese that was off the charts in terms of richness. More frugal recipes seemed designed around an impending cheese shortage, using merely ½ pound of cheese to a pound of pasta. The result was more macaroni and milk than macaroni and cheese. I found that 1 pound of cheese was the perfect amount for 1 pound of pasta—just the right texture and flavor, and easy to remember, too.

Back in the Oven

I was done, right? Wrong. Many of my tasters wanted at least the option of adding a toasty, golden topping of bread crumbs—a flashback to the baked versions. To keep to my stovetop commitment, I tossed homemade bread crumbs with melted butter and toasted them on the stovetop, then portioned them out over individual servings in generous amounts. But these crumbs seemed more like an afterthought than part of the dish. I wasn't about to go back to baking the macaroni and cheese, but I wondered if instead I could use the broiler for a quick blast of heat. I placed fresh buttered bread crumbs atop my next batch of macaroni and cheese and placed it under the broiler. This was it. The broiler concentrated the heat right on the bread crumbs, turning them a deep, golden brown. Better still, the process took only a few minutes—yet it was just enough time to let the bottom of the crumbs sink into the cheese sauce and seem baked right in.

Finally, I had a macaroni and cheese that more than passed muster, at least with my test kitchen colleagues. But would it please my toughest critics, the kids? I made one more batch at home, passed it around the table, and held my breath. With comments like "Yum," "Oooh," and "Not bad, Mrs. Lancaster," I was victorious. Of course, one young taster asked, "How come it's not orange?" I guess you can't please absolutely everyone.

CLASSIC MACARONI AND CHEESE
SERVES 6 TO 8 AS A MAIN COURSE OR
10 TO 12 AS A SIDE DISH

It's crucial to cook the pasta until tender—just past the "al dente" stage. In fact, overcooking is better than undercooking the pasta. Whole, low-fat, and skim milk all work well in this recipe. The recipe can be halved and baked in an 8-inch-square, broiler-safe baking dish. If desired, offer celery salt or hot sauce (such as Tabasco) for sprinkling at the table.

Bread Crumb Topping
- 6 slices (about 6 ounces) good-quality white sandwich bread, torn into rough pieces
- 3 tablespoons cold unsalted butter, cut into 6 pieces

Pasta and Cheese
- 1 pound elbow macaroni
- 1 tablespoon plus 1 teaspoon salt
- 5 tablespoons unsalted butter
- 6 tablespoons all-purpose flour
- 1½ teaspoons powdered mustard
- ¼ teaspoon cayenne (optional)
- 5 cups milk (see note)
- 8 ounces Monterey Jack cheese, shredded (2 cups)
- 8 ounces sharp cheddar cheese, shredded (2 cups)

1. **FOR THE BREAD CRUMBS:** Pulse bread and butter in food processor until crumbs are no

larger than ⅛ inch, ten to fifteen 1-second pulses. Set aside.

2. **FOR THE PASTA AND CHEESE:** Adjust oven rack to lower-middle position and heat broiler. Bring 4 quarts water to boil in Dutch oven over high heat. Add macaroni and 1 tablespoon salt; cook until pasta is tender. Drain pasta and set aside in colander.

3. In now-empty Dutch oven, heat butter over medium-high heat until foaming. Add flour, mustard, and cayenne (if using) and whisk well to combine. Continue whisking until mixture becomes fragrant and deepens in color, about 1 minute. Gradually whisk in milk; bring mixture to boil, whisking constantly (mixture must reach full boil to fully thicken). Reduce heat to medium and simmer, whisking occasionally, until thickened to consistency of heavy cream, about 5 minutes. Off heat, whisk in cheeses and 1 teaspoon salt until cheeses are fully melted. Add pasta and cook over medium-low heat, stirring constantly, until mixture is steaming and heated through, about 6 minutes.

4. Transfer mixture to broiler-safe 9 by 13-inch baking dish and sprinkle evenly with bread crumbs.

Broil until crumbs are deep golden brown, 3 to 5 minutes, rotating pan if necessary for even browning. Cool about 5 minutes, then serve.

MACARONI AND CHEESE WITH HAM AND PEAS

Cut 8 ounces baked deli ham, sliced ¼ inch thick, into 1-inch squares. Follow recipe for Classic Macaroni and Cheese, adding ham and 1 cup frozen peas to cheese sauce along with pasta.

MACARONI AND CHEESE WITH KIELBASA AND MUSTARD

Cut 8 ounces smoked kielbasa lengthwise into quarters, then cut each quarter crosswise into ½-inch slices. Follow recipe for Classic Macaroni and Cheese; in step 3, add 1 medium onion, chopped fine, to foaming butter and cook, stirring occasionally, until onion begins to brown, about 6 minutes. Add flour to onion and continue with recipe, reducing salt in sauce to ½ teaspoon and adding kielbasa and 4 teaspoons whole-grain Dijon mustard to cheese sauce along with pasta.

RECIPE TESTING: **Some Failed Experiments**

OILY AND SEPARATED   **CURDLED AND CLUMPY**   **RICH AND CLOYING**

Some early tests revealed common problems with macaroni and cheese. When we layered the noodles, milk, and cheese (without first cooking them) in the pan, the fat separated from the cheese and the macaroni and cheese was oily (left). When we added eggs to the recipe, they curdled and produced a lumpy sauce (center). An overabundance of cheese made the macaroni so rich you could eat only two or three spoonfuls (right).

The Problem with Chicken Stir-Fries

Tired of dry, stringy chicken in your stir-fry? We have the solution.

⇉ BY KERI FISHER ⇇

The most common, and probably most appealing, stir-fry is made with chicken. Sounds easy, right? Well, it turns out that a good chicken stir-fry is more difficult to prepare than a beef or pork stir-fry because chicken, which has less fat, inevitably becomes dry and stringy when cooked over high heat. I was after a stir-fry that featured tender, juicy, bite-size pieces of chicken paired with just the right combination of vegetables in a simple yet complex-flavored sauce. And because this was a stir-fry, it had to be fairly quick.

In the past, we've used a marinade to impart flavor to meat destined for stir-fries. Chicken was no exception. Tossing the pieces of chicken into a simple soy-sherry mixture for 10 minutes before cooking added much-needed flavor, but it did nothing to improve the texture of the meat.

The obvious solution to dry chicken was brining, our favorite method of adding moisture to poultry. A test of brined boneless breasts (preferred over thighs) did in fact confirm that this method solved the problem of dry chicken. However, a half hour or more of brining time followed by 10 minutes of marinating was out of the question for a quick mid-week stir-fry. It seemed redundant to soak the chicken first in one salty solution (brine) and then another (marinade), so I decided to combine the two, using the soy sauce to provide the high salt level in my brine. This turned out to be a key secret of a great chicken stir-fry. Now I was turning out highly flavored, juicy pieces of chicken—most of the time. Given the finicky nature of high-heat cooking, some batches of chicken still occasionally turned out tough because of overcooking.

The Velvet Glove

I next turned to a traditional Chinese technique called velveting, which involves coating chicken pieces in a thin cornstarch and egg white or oil mixture, then parcooking in moderately heated oil. The coating holds precious moisture inside; that extra juiciness makes the chicken seem more tender. Cornstarch mixed with egg white yielded a cakey coating; tasters preferred the more subtle coating provided by cornstarch mixed with oil. This velveted chicken was supple, but it was also pale, and, again, this method seemed far too involved for a quick weeknight dinner.

A sprinkle of sesame seeds is the finishing touch for a stir-fry featuring a hybrid brining/marinating method that adds flavor and moisture to lean chicken.

I wondered if the same method—coating in a cornstarch mixture—would work if I eliminated the parcooking step. It did. This chicken was not only juicy and tender, but it also developed an attractive golden brown coating. Best of all, the entire process took less than five minutes. The only problem was that the coating, which was more of an invisible barrier than a crust, became bloated and slimy when cooked in the sauce.

Our science editor explained that the cornstarch was absorbing liquid from the sauce, causing the slippery finish. He suggested cutting the cornstarch with flour, which created a negligible coating—not too thick, not too slimy—that still managed to keep juices inside the chicken. Substituting sesame oil for peanut oil added a rich depth of flavor.

After trying everything from pounded to cubed chicken, tasters voted for simple flat ¼-inch slices, which were all the more easy to cut after freezing the breasts for 20 minutes. These wide, flat slices of chicken browned easily. I cooked them in two batches, first browning one side, then turning them over to quickly brown the second side rather than constantly stirring (or "stir"-frying) as so many other recipes suggest. Although choosing not to stir-fry seemed counterintuitive, I found that the constant motion of that method detracted from the browning of the chicken.

The Finish

As for the vegetables in my master recipe, a combination of bok choy and red bell pepper worked well with the chicken. Other flavor combinations worked well as variations, including a pairing of green beans and shiitake mushrooms. For the sauce, the test kitchen has found that chicken broth, rather than soy sauce, makes the best base because it is not overpowering. Hoisin and oyster sauce work nicely as flavoring ingredients. We have also tested the addition of cornstarch to help the sauce coat the meat and vegetables and have found that a small amount is necessary. Otherwise, the sauce is too thin and does not adhere properly.

RECIPE KEY: Choosing the Right Pan

THE BEST CHOICE: NONSTICK SKILLET

A MEDIOCRE CHOICE: FLAT-BOTTOMED WOK

A BAD CHOICE: TRADITIONAL SKILLET

THE WORST CHOICE: SMALL SKILLET

When stir-frying, a 12-inch nonstick skillet is large enough to accommodate food without any steaming or sticking. A flat-bottomed wok is better than a regular curved wok but still has less surface area in contact with the stovetop than the completely flat-bottomed skillet. The batter on the chicken sticks and burns in a conventional 12-inch skillet. A 10-inch skillet is so small that food steams as it cooks.

The basic stir-fry method was developed several years ago in the test kitchen. After the protein (in this case, the chicken) is cooked and removed from the pan, the vegetables are stir-fried in batches, garlic and ginger (the classic stir-fry combination) are quickly cooked in the center of the pan, and then the protein is returned to the pan along with the sauce. This final mixture is cooked over medium heat for 30 seconds to finish.

In the end, a great chicken stir-fry doesn't really take more time to prepare than a bad one. It does, however, require more attention to detail and knowledge of a few quick tricks.

MARINATED VELVETED CHICKEN FOR STIR-FRY

To make the chicken easier to slice, freeze it for 20 minutes, until it is firm but not frozen. Prepare the stir-fry ingredients while the chicken marinates.

¼ cup soy sauce
¼ cup dry sherry
1 cup water
1 pound boneless, skinless chicken breasts, trimmed of excess fat and prepared according to illustrations 1 through 3, above
2 tablespoons Asian sesame oil
1 tablespoon cornstarch
1 tablespoon all-purpose flour

1. Combine soy sauce, sherry, and water in medium bowl; add chicken and stir to break up clumps. Cover with plastic wrap and refrigerate for at least 20 minutes or up to 1 hour.

2. Mix sesame oil, cornstarch, and flour in medium bowl until smooth. Drain chicken in strainer; press out excess liquid. Toss chicken in cornstarch/flour mixture until evenly coated. Use immediately in one of following recipes.

GINGERY STIR-FRIED CHICKEN AND BOK CHOY
SERVES 4 AS A MAIN DISH WITH RICE

¼ cup low-sodium chicken broth
2 tablespoons dry sherry
1 tablespoon soy sauce
1 tablespoon oyster-flavored sauce
½ teaspoon Asian sesame oil
1 teaspoon cornstarch
1 teaspoon sugar
¼ teaspoon red pepper flakes
4 teaspoons minced fresh ginger (from 1½-inch piece)
1 medium garlic clove, minced or pressed through garlic press (about 1 teaspoon)
 Peanut or vegetable oil
1 recipe Marinated Velveted Chicken for Stir-Fry
1 small head bok choy (about 1 pound), stalks and greens separated, stalks cut on bias into ¼-inch slices and greens cut into ½-inch strips
1 small red bell pepper, cut into ¼-inch strips

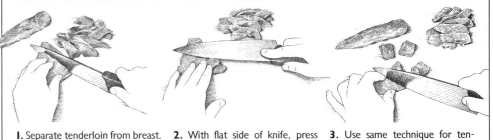

1. Separate tenderloin from breast. Starting at thick end, cut into ¼-inch slices. Stop slicing when you reach tapered triangle end.

2. With flat side of knife, press each slice to an even ¼ inch thickness and then cut slices into 1-inch squares.

3. Use same technique for tenderloin, flattening it with side of knife and then cutting into 1-inch pieces.

1. Whisk broth, sherry, soy, oyster-flavored sauce, sesame oil, cornstarch, sugar, pepper flakes, and 2 teaspoons ginger in small bowl; set aside. Combine remaining 2 teaspoons ginger, garlic, and 1 teaspoon peanut oil in small bowl; set aside.

2. Heat 2 teaspoons peanut oil in 12-inch non-stick skillet over high heat until smoking; add half of chicken to skillet in flat, even layer. Cook, without stirring, but gently separating pieces, until golden brown on first side, about 1 minute; turn chicken pieces and cook until lightly browned on second side, about 30 seconds. Transfer chicken to clean bowl. Repeat with additional 2 teaspoons peanut oil and remaining chicken.

3. Add 1 tablespoon peanut oil to now-empty skillet; heat until just smoking. Add bok choy stalks and red bell pepper; stir-fry until beginning to brown, about 1 minute. Push vegetables to sides of skillet to clear center; add garlic/ginger mixture to clearing and cook, mashing mixture with spoon, until fragrant, 15 to 20 seconds, then stir mixture into stalks and continue to cook until stalks are tender-crisp, about 30 seconds longer. Stir in bok choy greens and cook until beginning to wilt, about 30 seconds; return chicken to skillet. Whisk sauce to recombine, then add to skillet; reduce heat to medium and cook, stirring constantly, until sauce is thickened and chicken is cooked through, about 30 seconds. Transfer to serving platter and serve immediately.

SPICY STIR-FRIED SESAME CHICKEN WITH GREEN BEANS AND SHIITAKE MUSHROOMS
SERVES 4 AS A MAIN DISH WITH RICE

½ cup low-sodium chicken broth
3 tablespoons soy sauce
2 tablespoons dry sherry
1 tablespoon plus 1 teaspoon Asian chili sauce
1 tablespoon plus 1 teaspoon sugar
1 teaspoon cornstarch
1 tablespoon white sesame seeds, toasted in small dry skillet until golden, about 4 minutes
2 teaspoons Asian sesame oil
3 medium garlic cloves, minced or pressed through garlic press (about 1 tablespoon)
1 teaspoon minced fresh ginger

 Peanut or vegetable oil
1 recipe Marinated Velveted Chicken for Stir-Fry with 1 tablespoon white sesame seeds added to flour mixture
1 pound green beans, cut on bias into 1-inch pieces
8 ounces shiitake mushrooms, stems removed, caps sliced ⅛ inch thick

1. Whisk chicken broth, soy, sherry, chili sauce, sugar, cornstarch, 2 teaspoons sesame seeds, 1 teaspoon sesame oil, and 1 teaspoon garlic in small bowl to combine; set aside. Combine remaining 2 teaspoons garlic, ginger, and 1 teaspoon peanut oil in small bowl; set aside.

2. Heat 2 teaspoons peanut oil in 12-inch non-stick skillet over high heat until smoking; add half of chicken to skillet in flat, even layer. Cook, without stirring, but gently separating pieces, until golden brown on first side, about 1 minute; turn chicken pieces and cook until lightly browned on second side, about 30 seconds. Transfer chicken to clean bowl. Repeat with additional 2 teaspoons peanut oil and remaining chicken.

3. Add 1 tablespoon peanut oil to now-empty skillet; heat until just smoking. Add green beans and cook, stirring occasionally, 1 minute; add mushrooms and stir-fry until mushrooms are lightly browned, about 3 minutes. Push vegetables to sides of skillet to clear center; add garlic and ginger to clearing and cook, mashing mixture with spoon, until fragrant, 30 to 45 seconds; stir mixture into beans and mushrooms. Continue to stir-fry until beans are tender-crisp, about 30 seconds longer; return chicken to skillet. Whisk sauce to recombine, then add to skillet; reduce heat to medium and cook, stirring constantly, until sauce is thickened and chicken is cooked through, about 30 seconds. Transfer to serving platter, drizzle with remaining teaspoon sesame oil, and sprinkle with remaining teaspoon sesame seeds. Serve immediately.

COOK'S EXTRA gives you free recipes online. For our Sweet, Sour, and Spicy Stir-Fried Orange Chicken and Broccoli with Cashews, visit www.cooksillustrated.com and key in code 3045. This recipe will be available until June 15, 2004.

Extra-Fruity Fruit Sherbet

Unlike ice cream, store-bought sherbet is usually third-rate. If you want a really good fruit sherbet, do you have to make it yourself? Yes.

≽ BY ERIKA BRUCE ≼

Frozen sherbet is an American invention of pure refreshment, the perfect foil to summer's heat. But quintessential (or even pretty good) sherbet can be hard to find. The standard triple-flavored packages of rainbow sherbet sold in the supermarket have only one redeeming quality: They are cold. A quick tasting in the test kitchen reminded us of just how bad these commercial sherbets can be. Why was orange sherbet the color of a neon light? Why did lime sherbet smell like furniture polish? And why was raspberry sherbet so saccharine that the only detectable flavor was not fruity but sweet, very sweet?

The perfect sherbet is a cross between sorbet and ice cream, containing fruit, sugar, and dairy but no egg yolks. Like its foreign cousin, sorbet, sherbet should taste vibrant and fresh. In the case of sherbet, however, its assertive flavor is tempered by the creamy addition of dairy. Ideally, it is as smooth as ice cream but devoid of ice cream's richness and weight.

The Texture Tests

To hammer out a basic recipe, I decided to start with orange sherbet and used the simplest of ingredients: orange juice, sugar syrup made from equal parts sugar and water boiled together (known, appropriately, as simple syrup), and half-and-half. From the recipe tests, I knew that the freezing method made a difference, so I tried making sherbet with and without an ice cream maker. The latter, in which ingredients were mixed, poured into a container, and frozen, was noticeably more icy and grainy than the former. There was simply no competing with the smooth, even-textured sherbet produced by the slow freezing and consistent churning of an ice cream machine.

As with sorbet, the texture of sherbet hinges on the concentration of sugar in the recipe (see "The Role of Sugar in Frozen Desserts" on page 23). But even when I used twice as much sugar syrup as orange juice, I could not get the smooth texture I was looking for. The proportion of water to sugar was still too high. To reduce the water content, I eliminated the sugar syrup entirely and dissolved the granulated sugar directly in the

A simple recipe solves the riddle of icy, insipid sherbet. Ours is creamy, smooth, and bursting with fruit flavor.

juice. Now I had better texture, improved flavor, and a simpler recipe.

Next I tested dairy, making the sherbet with heavy cream, half-and-half, whole milk, skim milk, evaporated milk, condensed milk, buttermilk, sour cream, soy milk, and yogurt. While whole milk alone did not yield a bad product, it was more like a sorbet. Increasing the milk merely resulted in an icy, diluted product. Half-and-half produced a creamier flavor, but the texture was still too icy. I finally settled on heavy cream—a modest ⅔ cup. Other dairy choices either clouded the flavor or failed to improve the texture.

A common technique in sherbet making is the addition of whipped egg whites, either raw or in the fashion of an Italian meringue, in which the whites are beaten with boiling sugar syrup. To my surprise, neither did anything to improve texture. In fact, they made the sherbet more icy, a result I attributed to the water added by means of the egg whites. Adding gelatin, which is often used to stabilize sorbets and sherbets, was labor-intensive; what's more, it did little to improve the texture. Happy to discard it, I tried corn syrup, a much simpler ingredient that is often used to soften frozen goods. Again, no luck. The sherbet made

without corn syrup had a brighter flavor and a smoother texture. The only effective addition to the mix was alcohol. Triple Sec or vodka in the amount of 2 teaspoons created a smoother, more refined texture, with no off flavors.

Although I had made a lot of progress, the sherbet remained heavier than I liked. Then I realized that I could whip the heavy cream before mixing it with the other ingredients. I held my breath as tasters sampled sherbet made with whipped cream. To my delight, every taster preferred its lighter, smoother texture. Interestingly, these textural differences were more apparent when the sherbet had softened slightly after removal from the freezer. From this I discovered that sherbet has an optimal serving temperature of between 12 and 15 degrees. Its smooth, creamy texture is compromised when served too cold.

The End of the Rainbow

My last tests were about flavor. Many recipes add orange zest, but tasters found that the bits of zest interfered with the otherwise smooth texture. Straining out the zest removed most of its flavor. After trying many methods (using large amounts of zest, leaving the zest in the juice overnight, and macerating the oranges, rind and all, with the sugar), I finally came upon the right one. Processing a tablespoon of zest with the sugar in a food processor released its essential oils and resulted in the perfect orange flavor—intense without being harsh. The second step was to add the juice to the food processor and to then strain out any unwanted pieces of zest. To brighten the orange flavor, I tested various amounts of lemon juice and found 3 tablespoons to be just right. Finally, I added ⅛ teaspoon of salt, which heightened both flavor and sweetness.

With the recipe for orange sherbet nailed down, it was time for me to try lime and raspberry. Because lime juice is more acidic than orange juice, I had to add water to dilute it and

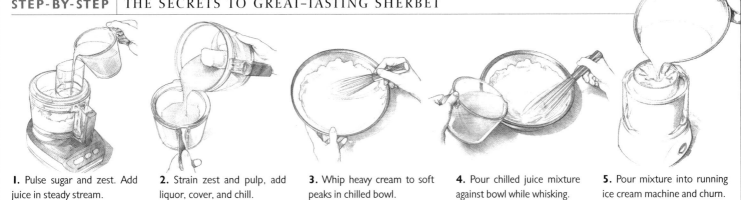

1. Pulse sugar and zest. Add juice in steady stream.

2. Strain zest and pulp, add liquor, cover, and chill.

3. Whip heavy cream to soft peaks in chilled bowl.

4. Pour chilled juice mixture against bowl while whisking.

5. Pour mixture into running ice cream machine and churn.

more sugar to balance its tartness. And because lime is not everyone's favorite, I tried substituting lemon for lime. This variation was also a success, although the flavors were notably more delicate and floral. For my last variation, I found that gently cooking raspberries with a little water and all of the sugar served to break down the berries and release their juices. Passing the mixture through a sieve eliminated the seeds.

FRESH ORANGE SHERBET
MAKES ABOUT 1 QUART

If using a canister-style ice cream machine, freeze the canister for at least 12 hours or, preferably, overnight. If the canister is not thoroughly frozen, the sherbet will not freeze beyond a slushy consistency. For the freshest, purest orange flavor, use freshly squeezed unpasteurized orange juice (either store-bought or juiced at home). Pasteurized fresh-squeezed juice makes an acceptable though noticeably less fresh-tasting sherbet. Do not use juice made from concentrate, which has a cooked and decidedly unfresh flavor.

1	tablespoon grated zest from 1 to 2 oranges
1	cup (7 ounces) sugar
⅛	teaspoon salt
2	cups orange juice, preferably unpasteurized fresh-squeezed (see note)
3	tablespoons juice from 1 to 2 lemons
2	teaspoons Triple Sec or vodka
⅔	cup heavy cream

1. Process zest, sugar, and salt in food processor until damp, ten to fifteen 1-second pulses. With machine running, add orange juice and lemon juice in slow, steady stream; continue to process until sugar is fully dissolved, about 1 minute. Strain mixture through nonreactive fine-mesh strainer into medium bowl; stir in Triple Sec, then cover with plastic wrap and chill in freezer until very cold, about 40 degrees, 30 to 60 minutes. (Alternatively, set bowl over larger bowl containing ice water.) Do not let mixture freeze.

2. When mixture is cold, using whisk, whip cream in medium bowl until soft peaks form.

Whisking constantly, add juice mixture in steady stream, pouring against edge of bowl. Immediately start ice cream machine and add juice/cream mixture to canister; churn until sherbet has texture of soft-serve ice cream, 25 to 30 minutes.

3. Remove canister from machine and transfer sherbet to storage container; press plastic wrap directly against surface of sherbet and freeze until firm, at least 3 hours. (Can be wrapped well in plastic wrap and frozen for up to one week.) To serve, let sherbet stand at room temperature until slightly softened and instant-read thermometer inserted into sherbet registers 12 to 15 degrees.

FRESH LIME SHERBET

Be sure to use freshly squeezed (not bottled) lime juice. For lemon sherbet, substitute lemon juice and zest for the lime juice and zest.

Follow recipe for Fresh Orange Sherbet, making these changes: Substitute lime zest for orange zest, increase sugar to 1 cup plus 2 tablespoons, and substitute ⅔ cup lime juice combined with 1½ cups water for orange and lemon juices.

FRESH RASPBERRY SHERBET

In-season fresh raspberries have the best flavor, but when they are not in season, frozen raspberries are a better option. Substitute a 12-ounce bag of frozen raspberries for fresh.

In medium nonreactive saucepan, cook 3 cups fresh raspberries, ¾ cup water, 1 cup sugar, and ⅛ teaspoon salt over medium heat, stirring occasionally, until mixture just begins to simmer, about 7 minutes. Pass mixture through fine-mesh strainer into medium bowl, pressing on solids to extract as much liquid as possible. Add 3 tablespoons lemon juice and 2 teaspoons Triple Sec or vodka; cover with plastic wrap and chill in freezer until very cold, about 40 degrees. Do not let mixture freeze. Follow recipe for Fresh Orange Sherbet from step 2, substituting raspberry mixture for orange mixture.

SCIENCE: **The Role of Sugar in Frozen Desserts**

A microscopic view of sherbet would reveal small grains of ice lubricated with syrup, fat, and bubbles of air. The simple churning of an ice cream machine can add lots of air. The other piece of the chemical puzzle—the transformation of the sherbet from liquid to solid—is more complicated. Sugar, it turns out, is the mediating factor between the two.

Water freezes at 32 degrees, but the addition of sugar makes it harder for water molecules to form ice crystals and thus lowers the freezing temperature of the mixture. The higher the sugar concentration (that is, the more sugar there is in proportion to water), the greater this effect will be. As the temperature of the sherbet mixture drops below 32 degrees, some water starts to freeze into solid ice crystals, but the remaining water and sugar, which are in syrup form, remain unfrozen. As more water freezes, the sugar concentration in the remaining syrup increases, making it less and less likely to freeze.

Unfrozen, highly concentrated sugar syrup allows the sherbet to be scooped straight from the freezer, as seen in the bottom photo. (Without the sugar, the sherbet would be as hard as ice, as seen in the top photo.) Sugar also reduces the size of the ice crystals, physically interfering with their growth. Smaller ice crystals translate into a less grainy texture. Sugar, then, not only makes sherbet sweet but also makes it smooth and scoopable. –John Olson, Science Editor

NO SUGAR ADDED:
Hard and Icy

1 CUP SUGAR ADDED:
Somewhat Softer

2 CUPS SUGAR ADDED:
Smooth and Creamy

Putting the "Coconut" in Cream Pie

Most coconut cream pies are no more than coconut-dusted vanilla cream pies. Others use artificial flavoring and taste like suntan lotion. We wanted honest coconut flavor.

> BY DAWN YANAGIHARA <

I can pass up any pie, except coconut cream pie. Yet the first bite almost always disappoints, as I am quickly reminded that most recipes for this diner dessert are nothing more than a redecorated vanilla cream pie. A handful of coconut shreds stirred into the filling or sprinkled on the whipped cream might be enough to give it a new name, but certainly not to give it flavor. Then there's the crust—soft and soggy—and the miserable texture of the filling—rubbery, resilient, and starchy. The essence of a great coconut cream pie ought to be the exotic and elusive flavor of tropical coconut rather than a thinly disguised vanilla custard.

After testing a handful of recipes, it became clear that when it came to the crust, a toasty, sweet, sandy, and crisp crumb crust was a better match for the filling than the common and more labor-intensive pastry crust, whose plain-Jane personality tended to both disappear into the filling and turn sodden to boot. Beyond the obvious and reliable graham crackers, I also considered Oreos, whose bitter flavor (good for chocolate cream pie) was too forceful. The same was true of the overpowering artificial vanilla effluvium of Nilla wafers. I also tried Pepperidge Farm Bordeaux cookies, Nabisco Social Tea Biscuits, and animal crackers. The very innocuous and not-too-sweet animal crackers made the favorite crust, one with a delicate, cookielike texture that did not overshadow the coconut filling. For added flavor, I also ground a couple tablespoons of shredded coconut in the food processor along with the crackers.

A Shred of Flavor
For the filling, the working recipe that I had put together hardly differed from many others. It consisted of whole milk, cornstarch, egg yolks, sugar, butter, sweetened shredded coconut, and vanilla, and it was made on the stovetop in the manner of a pastry cream or homemade pudding.

I was optimistic that the obvious thing to try—substituting coconut milk for whole milk—would be an easy way to enhance flavor. When I tried this, though, the filling was so fat-laden that an oil slick surfaced during cooking. I chilled the pie anyway. Once cold, the flavor was superb, but the fat was perceptible as tiny globules that were unacceptably

Pastry cream flavored with both coconut milk and unsweetened coconut is the key to a pie with great taste and texture.

granular and waxy. I then tried "light" coconut milk, which, according to the label, has about 60 percent less fat than regular coconut milk. But as testing bore out, with fat went flavor.

Next I mixed 1¾ cups of coconut milk (the amount in one can) with 1 cup of various dairy products: half-and-half, whole milk, low-fat milk, and skim milk. The coconut milk/whole milk

version was the favorite; the half-and-half was too rich and the others too lean. The filling now had more coconut flavor, but still not enough. I tried sweet, thick cream of coconut—think piña colada—but no matter how little I used, its unctuous, slightly slimy, and slippery texture was detectable.

Coconut extract was rejected. Its flavor was artificial and its aroma reminiscent of sunbathers on Waikiki beach. I then reconsidered the sweetened coconut shreds I had been using, since they provided a uniquely hirsute look without enhancing flavor. When I made pies pitting them against unsweetened shredded coconut, there was no contest. One-half cup of unsweetened coconut was far superior to its saccharine counterpart, and the flavor was better, too. I took to cooking the coconut in the filling instead of stirring it in at the end; this way, the shreds had the opportunity to soften slightly in the hot milk.

Through Thick and Thin
The common thickeners for cream pie fillings are flour and cornstarch. In addition, I tested arrowroot. Flour was a loser. It made a filling with a heavy, starchy feel and a flavor to match. The arrowroot and cornstarch fillings were similar. Both were clean-tasting and nicely set, but whereas the cornstarch filling was lilting and creamy, the honorable-mention arrowroot filling was slightly bouncy and gelatin-like. All tasters agreed that ¼ cup of cornstarch was needed to make the pie sliceable; more simply made the filling unpleasantly stiff and pasty.

Searching for Real Coconut Flavor

| SWEETENED COCONUT | UNSWEETENED COCONUT | CREAM OF COCONUT | COCONUT MILK |

Shredded coconut is sold both sweetened and unsweetened. For coconut cream pie, we prefer the latter because it has more coconut flavor, better texture, and does not add more sweetness. Cream of coconut may work in a piña colada, but we found that it gave our pie filling a slimy texture. Coconut milk has a solid coconut flavor and won't harm the texture of the pie as long as you cut it with some whole milk.

Starch, however, is not the only thickener at work in a cream pie. Eggs serve the purpose as well, but to a lesser extent. Eggs' more important function is to give the filling richness of flavor and texture. Fillings with whole eggs turned out to be inferior; they were insubstantial in flavor and had a faintly gluey and pasty feel. Success lay in the fat- and protein-rich yolks. A five-yolk filling was supremely lush and luxurious; six was too much of a good thing (in a word, "eggy").

The filling, poured hot into the baked and cooled pie shell, had only to chill before it met its pouf of whipped cream. I decided on a generous endowment of whipped cream, sweetened with a little sugar and flavored with a touch of vanilla. After topping the pie, I dusted it with toasted coconut shreds. At long last, I had made a coconut cream pie with good, honest flavor, great texture, and a crisp coconut-flavored crust.

COCONUT CREAM PIE
MAKES ONE 9-INCH PIE, SERVING 8 TO 10

Light coconut milk lacks rich coconut flavor, so skip it in favor of regular coconut milk.

Crust
- 6 ounces animal crackers
- 2 tablespoons unsweetened shredded coconut
- 1 tablespoon sugar
- 4 tablespoons unsalted butter, melted and cooled

Filling
- 1 can (14 ounces) coconut milk
- 1 cup whole milk
- ½ cup unsweetened shredded coconut
- ½ cup plus 1 tablespoon sugar
- ⅜ teaspoon salt
- 5 large egg yolks
- ¼ cup cornstarch
- 2 tablespoons unsalted butter, cut into 2 pieces
- 1 teaspoon vanilla extract

Whipped Cream and Garnish
- 1½ cups cold heavy cream
- 2 tablespoons sugar
- ½ teaspoon vanilla extract
- 1 tablespoon unsweetened shredded coconut, toasted in small dry skillet until golden brown

1. **FOR THE CRUST:** Adjust oven rack to lower-middle position and heat oven to 325 degrees. In food processor, pulse animal crackers, coconut, and sugar to fine crumbs, eighteen to twenty 1-second pulses; then process until powdery, about 5 seconds. Transfer crumbs to medium bowl and add butter; stir to combine until crumbs are evenly moistened. Empty crumbs into 9-inch glass pie plate; using bottom of ramekin or ½ cup dry measuring cup, press crumbs evenly into bottom and up sides of pie plate. Bake until fragrant and medium brown, about 15 minutes, rotating pie shell halfway through baking time. Set on wire rack and cool to room temperature, about 30 minutes.

2. **FOR THE FILLING:** Bring coconut milk, whole milk, shredded coconut, ½ cup sugar, and salt to simmer over medium-high heat, stirring occasionally to ensure that sugar dissolves. Following illustrations 1 through 6, whisk yolks, cornstarch, and remaining 1 tablespoon sugar in medium bowl until thoroughly combined. Whisking constantly, gradually ladle about 1 cup hot milk mixture over yolk mixture; whisk well to combine. Whisking constantly, gradually add remaining milk mixture to yolk mixture in 3 or 4 additions; whisk well to combine. Return mixture to saucepan and cook until thickened and mixture reaches boil, whisking constantly, about 1 minute; filling must boil in order to fully thicken. (To determine whether filling has reached boil, stop whisking; large bubbles should quickly burst on surface.) Off heat, whisk in butter and vanilla until butter is fully incorporated. Pour hot filling into cooled pie shell and smooth surface with rubber spatula; press plastic wrap directly against surface of filling and refrigerate until firm, at least 3 hours and up to 12 hours.

3. **FOR THE WHIPPED CREAM:** Just before serving, beat cream, sugar, and vanilla with electric mixer until soft peaks form, 1½ to 2 minutes. Top pie with whipped cream (see tip on page 31) and then sprinkle with coconut. Cut pie into wedges and serve.

LIME-COCONUT CREAM PIE

Follow recipe for Coconut Cream Pie, adding 1½ teaspoons grated lime zest to filling along with vanilla and butter in step 2.

BANANA-CARAMEL COCONUT CREAM PIE WITH DARK RUM

This variation is a test kitchen favorite. You may be left with ⅓ cup or so of filling that will not fit into the crust because of the caramel and banana.

1. Follow recipe for Coconut Cream Pie through step 1 to make crust; while crust cools, bring ½ cup sugar and 3 tablespoons water to boil over high heat in small heavy-bottomed saucepan. Cook until dark amber, 5 to 8 minutes, occasionally swirling pan once sugar begins to color. Off heat, add 3 tablespoons heavy cream (caramel will bubble vigorously) and pinch salt; whisk to combine. Whisk in 2 tablespoons unsalted butter. Pour caramel into pie shell, tilting pie plate to coat evenly; set aside to cool.

2. When caramel is cool, peel 2 slightly under-ripe medium bananas (5 to 6 ounces each); slice each crosswise into ⅜-inch-thick rounds. Arrange slices in single layer on top of caramel; set aside.

3. Continue with recipe from step 2, adding 2 teaspoons dark rum to filling along with vanilla and butter in step 2.

STEP-BY-STEP | PASTRY CREAM 101

Pastry cream is the filling for most any cream pie as well as many tarts and other desserts. Pastry cream is not hard to prepare, but it does require attention to detail.

1. After heating milk and most of sugar, whisk egg yolks, cornstarch, and remaining sugar together.

2. Temper yolks by gradually pouring/ladling hot milk mixture over yolks while whisking constantly.

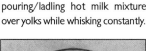

3. Add remaining hot milk to yolk mixture in 3 or 4 batches, whisking constantly until combined.

4. Pour mixture back into saucepan and cook, whisking constantly, until thickened.

5. Off heat, whisk in vanilla extract and butter until butter is melted and fully incorporated.

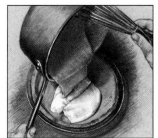

6. Pour hot filling into cooled pie shell and chill until firm.

Bringing Home the (Best) Bacon

Does it matter which brand of supermarket bacon you buy? Absolutely. Should you pay 250 percent more for premium, gourmet bacons? We'll let you decide.

≥ BY ERIKA BRUCE AND ADAM RIED ≤

Food enthusiasts and the media have made a fracas lately over the fact that retail bacon sales in America have risen sharply, nearly 50 percent over the last couple of years. In fact, in 2003, Americans spent more than $2 billion on bacon, according to Chicago market research firm Information Resources. Unfortunately, much of the media attention has been focused solely on expensive, artisan-produced specialty bacon rather than on the mass-produced brands that most home cooks buy at supermarkets and warehouse clubs. For us, then, the questions were: How would 10 popular national brands stack up in a side-by-side blind tasting, and how would they compare with a half-dozen brands of expensive, premium bacon?

Bacon Primer

We focused our tasting on the lowest common denominator—plain, regular-cut bacon—leaving aside center cut, thick and thin cut, flavored, specialty wood smoked, low salt, reduced fat, precooked, and microwave-ready. We did, however, include one nitrite-free "natural" sample because it is popular at our local natural foods market.

All bacon, with the exception of turkey- and tofu-based products, is made from pork belly. One fresh belly can weigh from 10 pounds to 25 pounds, though most fall between 12 and 18 pounds. The spare ribs are removed from the belly's interior, the skin is taken off the exterior, and the remaining slab is trimmed for further processing into bacon.

The next step is curing, which is generally done in one of two ways. Many small producers of artisan (aka smokehouse or premium) bacon choose to dry-cure by rubbing the slab with a dry mixture of seasonings (which always includes salt and sugar). Large producers usually inject the slabs with a liquid brine containing salt, sugar, and sometimes liquid smoke for flavor; sodium phosphate for moisture retention during processing and cooking; sodium ascorbate or sodium erythorbate to accelerate the curing process and promote color retention; and a curing salt that includes sodium nitrite to stave off bacteria and set flavor and color characteristics. (Are you still hungry for supermarket bacon?) Once the cure has been applied or injected, the slabs are hung. If a dry cure has been applied, this process could stretch up to one week. Curing with an injected brine can be completed in a mere one to three hours and so is quite cost-efficient.

The final step is thermal processing—which can take as few as four to five hours or as many as 24, depending on the processor. During thermal processing, the cured pork bellies are smoked and partially cooked to an internal temperature of roughly 130 degrees Fahrenheit, after which they finally merit the term *bacon*. The bacon is chilled to approximately 24 degrees, pressed to square it off for uniform slicing, sliced to the processor's specifications, and packaged. A package of regular-cut bacon usually contains between eighteen and twenty-two 1/16-inch-thick slices per pound, whereas a package of thick-cut bacon, sometimes called country style, contains twelve to sixteen 1/8-inch-thick slices per pound.

Picking Favorites

One product, the nitrite-free Applegate Farms Sunday Bacon, took tasters by surprise. Complaints arose about its unexpectedly pale color and particularly mild flavor, which led to a rating of "not recommended." A little knowledge of nitrites explains these characteristics. Sodium nitrite helps fix the red shade of the meat from its raw state by combining with the pigment myoglobin. According to Jay Wenther, director of science and technology for the American Association of Meat Processors, nitrites also contribute to bacon's characteristic cured flavor. "Nitrite-free bacon will both look and taste different from traditional bacon," he said. It makes sense, then, that Applegate Farms neither looked nor tasted the way most tasters expected. Having conducted hundreds of blind tastings over the years, our test kitchen has found that most folks prefer the familiar to the unfamiliar. Although Applegate received positive ratings from a couple of tasters, for most of us, nitrite-free bacon is clearly an acquired taste.

Tasters liked the nine other brands well enough to recommend them all. (Bad bacon is something of an oxymoron.) The highest rated product among them was Farmland, which tasters picked out as particularly meaty, full flavored, and smoky. Furthermore, neither of the two other prominent flavors in this top-rated bacon—salt and sweet—dominated, and tasters appreciated the balance.

We wondered why our tasters rated Farmland as the meatiest bacon in the pack (Oscar Mayer was rated as the least meaty). Our cadre of experts pointed out that because pork bellies are a natural product, there is no way to guarantee a perfectly consistent ratio of meat to fat from pound to pound to pound of bacon. A simple check of many packages of the same brands of bacon confirmed that fact—differences were obvious.

To get an accurate measure of the relative meatiness of our winning brand, Farmland, and to see how it stacked up against the least meaty brand in the group, Oscar Mayer, we sent both samples to our local food laboratory. The lab ground 3 pounds of each brand and then analyzed them for protein (lean), fat, and moisture. Sure enough, the lab confirmed our tasters' observations. Farmland had 15 percent more protein and almost 17 percent less fat than Oscar Mayer.

Smoky flavor, which is a defining characteristic of bacon, was another important factor in Farmland's success. Tasters appreciated assertive smoke, and Farmland was ranked the smokiest sample of all, scoring an 8 on the smokiness scale of 1 to 10. Processors can give bacon smoky flavor in one (or both) of two ways: adding liquid smoke flavoring to the liquid brine or applying real smoke during thermal processing (the thermal processing "unit" is also sometimes referred to as the smokehouse). Farmland uses the "real smoke" method.

Bringing Home the Bacon

What did we learn from this tasting? First, bacon, like wine, is an agricultural product and therefore subject to variation from hog to hog and from cut to cut. Would we tally exactly the same results six months from now if we tested the same brands? The only way to find out would be to conduct a follow-up tasting—which we'll do next year and report our findings. Second, the ratio of protein to fat as well as the smokiness factor are key to success. Farmland scored well in both categories. Finally, a good balance of salt and sugar is important. Texture, however, is a matter that is largely under the control of the home cook and therefore hard to judge based on brand. If you think you'll be happy with a good mass-market bacon, pick Farmland. If you prefer premium bacon, as we did overall, read "Tasting Premium Bacons" on page 27.

TASTING SUPERMARKET BACONS

Twenty-four tasters sampled 10 different nationally available supermarket bacons, labeled "regular sliced" and "hardwood smoked" or "hickory smoked." The bacon was oven-fried per *Cook's* recipe to the same degree of doneness (based on the browning of the meat). (To get our oven-fried bacon recipe online, visit www.cooksillustrated.com and go to **Cook's Extra,** then key in code 3047.

The recipe will be available until June 15, 2004.) Different tasters tried samples in different orders to eliminate the effects of palate fatigue, and one sample was repeated twice as a control. Tasters rated the bacon on a 10-point scale and judged saltiness, sweetness, smokiness, and meatiness. Bacons are listed in order of preference based on overall numerical score.

RECOMMENDED

FARMLAND Hickory Smoked Bacon
➤ **$3.99/pound**

This "very meaty," "full-flavored" bacon led the pack. Tasters gave high marks for its favorable balance of saltiness and sweetness, "good smoke flavor," and "crispy yet hearty" texture.

BOAR'S HEAD Brand Naturally Smoked Sliced Bacon
➤ **$3.99/pound**

Both flavor and texture were repeatedly described as "meaty." Tasters appreciated the "good balance" of flavors and the thick slices, which some claimed were "more like ham than bacon."

HORMEL Black Label Bacon, Original
➤ **$2.99/pound**

Comments focused largely on the "hearty, balanced flavor," with a meatiness (second only to Farmland) that some likened to Serrano ham and prosciutto. A couple of tasters noted "sweet," "maplelike" flavors.

ARMOUR Original Premium Bacon, Hickory Smoked
➤ **$3.99/pound**

For many, "too much sweetness" overshadowed what some characterized as a "nice smoky flavor." An especially low salt score, which may explain comments such as "quite bland."

SMITHFIELD Premium Bacon, Naturally Hickory Smoked
➤ **$3.99/pound**

While many tasters appreciated the smokiness of this sample, some objected to it, with comments such as "chemical," "fake smoke flavor," and "like eating a campfire."

OSCAR MAYER Naturally Hardwood Smoked Bacon
➤ **$4.99/pound**

Nearly as expensive as some premium bacons, yet slices were considered so thin that they "disintegrate on your tongue." Did find fans for its "good saltiness" and "nice full flavor," but others found it lacking in meatiness, yawning, "plain Jane."

JOHN MORRELL Hardwood Smoked Bacon
➤ **$3.99/pound**

Tipped the scales in perceived fat and considered not terribly meaty. Many tasters noted a favorable balance of salt and sugar, but others felt it was "too rich," "greasy," and "fatty."

PLUMROSE Premium Bacon, Old-Fashioned Hardwood Smoked
➤ **$3.99/pound**

According to the label, this bacon had less sugar than most others. Salt fanciers thought it had "great flavor," but others found it "too salty." The slices were also too thin for many tasters.

JONES Country Carved, Hickory Smoked Sliced Bacon
➤ **$4.49/pound**

What some tasters considered "balanced" and "very mild" struck others as bland, with comments such as "not very assertive." Thin slices cooked up "very crispy" to some and "dry" to others.

NOT RECOMMENDED

APPLEGATE FARMS Applewood Smoked Sunday Bacon
➤ **$2.99/8 ounces**

The only bacon in the tasting without nitrites, Applegate's "gray-green" color set it back. Though this "mild," "meaty" bacon did "taste like pork," the flavor couldn't compensate for the "muddy" color and "heavy smoke."

Tasting Premium Bacons

Like cheese and chocolate, bacon is available in gourmet varieties. To find out if such bacon really tastes better than our supermarket favorite, Farmland, we cooked up six popular smokehouse brands. Although every premium bacon outscored Farmland, in some cases the differences in scores were minimal. Several premium bacons had strong flavor characteristics, erring on the side of salty or smoky or sweet, which overwhelmed tasters who were looking for meaty flavor and balance, just as they had with the supermarket brands. That said, the top finisher, Niman Ranch, was a hands-down winner over Farmland. So premium bacons are better than the best supermarket bacon. But they're also much more expensive—up to 250 percent more—so shop carefully to match the character of the bacon with your preferences. – E.B. and A.R.

HIGHLY RECOMMENDED

NIMAN RANCH Dry Cured Center Cut Bacon, OAKLAND, CALIF.
➤ **$8.00/12 ounces**

Hearty, rich, balanced, and smoky. One taster said, "Yum . . . what bacon should be."

RECOMMENDED

NEW BRAUNFELS Smokehouse Comal Country-Smoked Sliced Bacon, NEW BRAUNFELS, TEXAS
➤ **$8.25/pound**

Deemed overly smoky by many tasters, though one said, "Has all the right elements. I could eat a lot of this one."

BURGERS' Smokehouse Sliced Country Bacon, Sugar Cured & Hickory Smoked, CALIFORNIA, MO.
➤ **$18.95/2 pounds**

Characterized by many as too salty and lacking in deep meaty flavor.

NODINE'S Smokehouse Apple Bacon, TORRINGTON, CONN.
➤ **$5.50/pound**

Over and over, tasters commented on its sweetness, using adjectives such as "caramelized," "candy-sweet," and "mapley."

NUESKE'S Smoked Bacon, WITTENBERG, WIS.
➤ **$19.95/2 pounds**

Nearly every taster zeroed in on its strong smoky character, with comments such as "whoa, smoky!" "crazy-smoky," "carbon-like," and "tastes like a campfire."

EDWARDS Virginia Bacon, Hickory-Smoked, Country Style, Dry Cured, SURRY, VA.
➤ **$4.00/12 ounces**

"Too salty," "way salty," "very salty," "overpowering salt," "salty like Ruffles potato chips." Get the picture?

Grinding Spices at Home

Is it worth the trouble? Yes. And it's no trouble at all if you choose the right grinder.

⇒ BY ADAM RIED ⇐

A few years ago, I spent some time on the championship chili cookoff circuit, where most competitors summarily dismiss packaged chili powder in favor of grinding their own dried chiles. I tested the matter thoroughly and found that grinding fresh, toasted chiles does indeed give chili con carne a noticeable depth and complexity of flavor. Having little doubt that fresh-ground spices also improve other dishes, I recently conducted two tests to prove my point. I baked plain pound cakes flavored with cardamom and simmered savory chutneys flavored with cumin, coriander, and cardamom, blind-tasting samples prepared with freshly ground and preground supermarket spices side by side. The fresh-ground spices won a decisive victory for their superior aroma, vibrancy, and roundness of flavor.

The test kitchen standard for grinding spices is an inexpensive blade-type electric coffee grinder (which we use for spices only, reserving a separate unit to grind coffee), but we had never put it up against other devices designed specifically for the task. Could we be missing out on something? To determine the answer to that question, I gathered 13 devices in three basic designs—dedicated spice grinders that are similar to pepper mills, old-fashioned mortars and pestles (and variations), and electric coffee grinders (choosing the models recommended in our November/December 2001 rating)—and used them to reduce mountains of cardamom seeds, toasted whole cumin and coriander seeds, and chipotle chiles to fine powders. I was looking for a grinder that would produce the most delicate, uniform powder and that was easy to both use and clean.

Grinding Three Ways

First up were the dedicated spice grinders. Like pepper mills, they are torsion-operated, meaning that you twist one part of the device (a glass or plastic jar loaded with spices) while holding a second part steady (a grinder housing screwed to the jar). The grinding mechanism consists of a rotating, grooved "male" head that fits into a stationary, grooved "female" ring. Wider grooves where the two meet break the seeds and feed the pieces down into finer grooves that grind them.

Many manufacturers tout grinding mechanisms made of ceramic, which is said to be superhard and corrosion-resistant. Despite these alleged advantages, I found that these models clogged easily with spice residue, essentially stopping the output of ground spices. The same was true for steel mechanisms. To keep things moving, I found myself repeatedly dismantling the units to clear their grooves with the fine tip of a bamboo skewer. This routine got very irritating very fast.

That, added to the exhausting, frustrating, endless twisting required to wrest ground spices from these units, made testing six of them consecutively seem like an act of masochism. Not that I couldn't use a little extra exercise, but who wants a grueling upper body workout when trying to grind a teaspoon of cumin?

It would be a different story if their output was strong and consistent, but I found that even the best of them, the Genius and the Emsa, frequently became clogged, especially when grinding oily spices. On the whole, I'd skip torsion-operated grinders altogether.

Next up were three versions of the age-old mortar and pestle, including a Japanese suribachi with a textured grinding surface to help break down the contents. As a group, these were no more effective than the torsion-operated grinders. To me, the action required to work a mortar and pestle was less stressful than the repetitive motion required to work the torsion-operated grinders, but it was still too much effort considering the disappointing piles of bruised, mangled seeds that I produced.

Last up were the electric coffee grinders, which were, in short, like breaths of fresh air. The only physical exertion required to use them was pressing a button. No stress, strain, or sore forearms, and they produced consistently good results on all of the test spices. And it only got better: The coffee grinders were easy to brush or wipe clean (just mind the blade!), easy to control for texture of grind, and no more expensive than the manual grinders and mortars and pestles.

The Spin on Coffee Grinders

So the coffee grinders reigned supreme. End of story, right? Not so fast. We ground on to compare the four models' performance grinding spices in three amounts: small (1 teaspoon), medium (1 tablespoon), and large (¼ cup).

In contrast with the manual grinders' tales of woe, the four blade-type electric grinders—by Capresso, Krups, Mr. Coffee, and Braun—whizzed through the tests with flying colors, producing fine powders from each amount of each spice. Along the way, though, I noted that I had to grind for a full minute or more (in short bursts, and shaking the grinder occasionally to even out the grind) to achieve a sufficiently fine particle size. Only the lone burr mill, which worked like a motorized pepper grinder, failed to grind the spices finely enough, even when adjusted to its finest setting. (I therefore omitted it from the chart on page 29.)

The lengthy grinding time required by the blade grinders was a concern, though. When I tested these grinders with coffee beans back in 2001, coffee industry experts reported that the blades, which spin at 14,000 to 20,000 RPM, can overheat the coffee as it's ground, degrading its flavor. Although tasters were unable to detect any deterioration in the coffee's flavor as a result, it takes more time to grind spices than it does to grind coffee beans, so I was worried—even though many cooks gently toast spices to bring out their flavor. Donna Tainter, director of quality, research, and development for Tone Brothers Spices in Ankeny, Iowa, explained that as with coffee, too much heat will evaporate, or "flash off," the volatile oils that give spices their flavor. "For large commercial grinders, which grind thousands of pounds of spices per lot," she said, "accumulated heat from the grinders can cause a significant threat to flavor." Commercial grinders, however, have processes to limit heat buildup during grinding (for instance, Tone's cools some spices with liquid nitrogen in a process called cryogenic grinding). Would overheating from the spinning blade of an electric grinder pose a problem for home cooks?

To find out, I returned to the cardamom cake and chutney, this time making one batch of each with whole spices that I ground manually in a torsion-operated grinder and another batch with whole spices ground in an electric coffee grinder. There were very subtle differences, but both types of grinder produced cake and chutney superior to those made with commercially ground spices. I concluded that there's no need to worry about overheating spices in an electric grinder.

While complex or ethnic dishes such as chilis, curries, and barbecues are natural candidates for fresh-ground spices, simple savories and sweets also benefit from the extra measure of flavor provided when you toast and grind your own fresh, whole spices. And there's no need to pump up your biceps along the way, provided you bypass the manual grinders and stick to an electric coffee grinder. In my book, it's the only way to go.

RATING SPICE GRINDERS

We tested 13 devices, including dedicated spice grinders, mortars and pestles, and blade-type coffee grinders—all referred to as *grinders* from here on. We fine-ground whole spices of varying hardness, density, shape, and oil content—cumin, coriander, cardamom, and chipotle chiles (torn into rough ¼-inch pieces)—in each and evaluated them according to the following criteria. Grinders are grouped by type and listed in order of preference within their type.

PRICE:
Prices paid in Boston-area stores, national mail-order catalogs, and on the Web.

EASE OF USE:
This rating was relative. All of the electric coffee grinders were equally—and very—easy to use. While none of the torsion-operated grinders were a joy to use, some were much more laborious than others. On the whole, however, neither torsion-operated manual grinders nor mortars and pestles were nearly as easy to use as the electric grinders, and the ratings reflect that fact.

QUALITY OF FINE GRIND:
Our most important test, based on the composite of performance scores earned for fine-grinding each of the test spices (in amounts of 1 tablespoon for torsion grinders and mortars and pestles and amounts of 1 teaspoon, 1 tablespoon, and ¼ cup for electric coffee grinders). We preferred grinders that produced the highest percentage of uniformly powdery particles fine enough to pass through a 40-mesh laboratory screen, but we did not necessarily mark down a grinder when only a small percentage of particles was left in the screen. If, on visual and tactile inspection, the fine-ground spices were judged exceptionally coarse or uneven, the grinder was marked down.

TESTERS' COMMENTS:
Additional observations about the devices' design, use, cleaning, or performance in specific tests.

RATINGS
GOOD: ★★★
FAIR: ★★
POOR: ★

KRUPS **BRAUN** **MR. COFFEE** **CAPRESSO**

RECOMMENDED: ELECTRIC COFFEE GRINDERS — TESTERS' COMMENTS

Krups Fast-Touch Coffee Mill, Model 203 PRICE: **$19.95**	EASE OF USE: ★★★ FINE GRIND: ★★★	Exceptionally fine grind of all spices, leaving very little in lab screen. Even material left in lab screen was fine enough to use.
Braun Aromatic Coffee Grinder, Model KSM 2B PRICE: **$14.99**	EASE OF USE: ★★★ FINE GRIND: ★★★	Fine and even grind in small and medium amounts. Also did impressive job grinding large amount of each spice.
Mr. Coffee Coffee Grinder, Model IDS55 PRICE: **$14.99**	EASE OF USE: ★★★ FINE GRIND: ★★★	All-around good performer that required bit of extra grinding to break down small amount of chipotle. Especially good value.
Capresso Cool Grind PRICE: **$19.99**	EASE OF USE: ★★★ FINE GRIND: ★★★	Required bit of extra grinding time to fully process large amounts of cumin and coriander.

GENIUS **EMSA** **WMF** **OXO** **SPICE ESSENTIALS** **WILLIAM BOUNDS**

NOT RECOMMENDED: TORSION-OPERATED MANUAL GRINDERS

Genius Spice Grinder Set (with four glass jars) PRICE: **$34.99**	EASE OF USE: ★ FINE GRIND: ★★★	Did better job than all other grinders of its kind, but output was slow compared with that of electric grinders. Relatively comfortable grip.
Emsa Würzmühle Spice Mill with Ceramic Grinders PRICE: **$18.50**	EASE OF USE: ★ FINE GRIND: ★★★	One of few grinders of its type that processed chiles, albeit slowly. Tester with large hands found this narrow model uncomfortable.
WMF Gewürzmühle Ceramill Glass Spice Mill PRICE: **$20.00**	EASE OF USE: ★ FINE GRIND: ★★★	Relatively easy to open, fill, and twist. Good job on cardamom but choked on chiles.
Oxo Grind It Spice Grinder PRICE: **$14.99**	EASE OF USE: ★ FINE GRIND: ★★★	Good grind quality, but too easy to accidentally pop grinder housing off jar while grinding, which sent seeds flying in every direction.
Spice Essentials Grinder with Ceramic Mechanism PRICE: **$27.95**	EASE OF USE: ★ FINE GRIND: ★★★	Chiles brought it to a grinding halt. Though not difficult to dismantle, cleaning was a chore.
William Bounds Spice Mill PRICE: **$14.95**	EASE OF USE: ★ FINE GRIND: ★	Crank so hard to turn that testers feared onset of carpal tunnel syndrome and tennis elbow! Output was meager.

MORTAR & PESTLE **SURIBACHI** **CREATIVE HOME**

NOT RECOMMENDED: MORTARS AND PESTLES

Mortar & Pestle, Marble PRICE: **$8.99**	EASE OF USE: ★ FINE GRIND: ★★	Good job on cardamom and chiles but did not produce satisfactory grind of cumin or coriander, even after working them for 30 minutes.
Suribachi PRICE: **$16.00**	EASE OF USE: ★ FINE GRIND: ★	Holy flying cardamom! And cumin! Broke down chiles completely but was not successful with cumin, coriander, or cardamom.
Creative Home Marble Spice Grinder PRICE: **$11.99**	EASE OF USE: ★ FINE GRIND: ★	Holy hand strain! Stubby pestle was uncomfortable, especially since you must bear down with considerable pressure to grind anything.

KITCHEN NOTES

⇒ BY BRIDGET LANCASTER ⇐

Keeping Your Cool

Have you checked your freezer's temperature lately? Maybe you should. When we asked staff members to test our fruit sherbet recipes (page 23) at home, several had trouble getting sherbets to firm up, even after hours of extra freezing time. Suspecting that "warm" freezers were to blame, we sent 10 staffers home with freezer thermometers (see page 32).

According to food safety standards, a freezer should register 0 degrees Fahrenheit or lower. Although about two-thirds of the freezers we tested hit this mark, a few tested as high as 7 and 10 degrees. (Freezer compartments located side by side with the refrigerator compartment were colder than those located above or below the refrigerator compartment.) A temperature of 10 degrees is warm enough to affect the sherbet recipe and quite possibly warm enough to affect the safety and quality of other foods.

If lowering the freezer thermostat (which should always be set to the lowest temperature) doesn't bring the temperature closer to zero, does that mean it's time to retire old frosty to the junkyard? Not necessarily. Working with our warmest freezer (the top unit of a small, not-so-new refrigerator), we found a few ways to cool things down.

We found that reducing the number of items stored there helped to lower the temperature. Shelves also help. Many freezer compartments located on the top of the refrigerator don't have shelves. If food packages are stacked one on top of the other, there's little chance for the cold air to circulate and ensure a thorough freeze. We found that inexpensive wire cabinet shelving placed in the freezer made it possible for us to keep our foods separate, easily identifiable, and well frozen. Finally, it's very important to keep foods away from the vent in the back wall of the freezer; this allows the cold air to circulate more efficiently. With all of these tricks, our once-faulty freezer cooled down to a perfectly cold 1 degree. Now that's cool.

Freezing Cheese Bread

Although the recipe title *Quick Cheese Bread* (see page 7) is no misnomer (the batter is in the pan in 15 minutes), when you add time for baking and cooling, the recipe does require a total of two hours. Luckily, like many of our other bread recipes, a baked loaf of cheese bread freezes beautifully, meaning a warm loaf need be only minutes away.

To freeze the bread, wrap the cooled loaf tightly with a double layer of aluminum foil and place in the freezer; it will keep for up to three months. When you're ready to serve the bread, place the frozen, wrapped loaf on the middle rack of a preheated 375-degree oven and heat for eight to 10 minutes, until the loaf yields under gentle pressure. Remove the foil and return the unwrapped bread to the oven for five minutes to crisp the exterior. Take the bread out of the oven and let cool on a rack for 15 minutes to make slicing easier. Enjoy.

A Tip for the Topping

When it comes to cream pie toppings, some border on architectural masterpieces, while others (more frequently) look like the whipped cream was applied by a small dump truck. In the test kitchen, we've

Use the tip of an icing spatula to create an attractive whipped cream topping for pies.

SHOPPING WITH THE TEST KITCHEN: A Better Butter?

Several new butter products have shown up at the supermarket recently, and two, in particular, both from Land O' Lakes, got our attention. The first is Land O' Lakes Ultra Creamy Butter. With a butterfat content of nearly 83 percent (up from 80 percent in the company's "regular" butter) and a price tag of $2.89 for 8 ounces (more than twice the price of the regular butter), this product is designed to compete with boutique butters such as Plugrá and Celles Sur Belle. The second product of interest is Land O' Lakes Soft Baking Butter with Canola Oil. The name says it all. Land O' Lakes has added canola oil to this butter to bring it to a soft, baking-ready texture straight from the fridge—a possible boon to spur-of-the-moment bakers.

To test these new products, we used them, along with regular Land O' Lakes Unsalted Sweet Butter, in three applications: sugar cookies, yellow cake, and buttercream frosting. We also tasted the butters plain. It should be noted that the Soft Baking Butter with Canola Oil comes only in a salted version. We chose the unsalted versions of the other two butters because unsalted is the standard in the test kitchen. We adjusted salt levels in the recipes as necessary.

When it came to the sugar cookies and the yellow cake, we were hard-pressed to tell the difference between the Ultra Creamy Butter and the regular butter. The butter with canola oil, on the other hand, was a world apart. Sure, it was easy to pull this "butter" right from the fridge and cream it without

ULTRA CREAMY BUTTER
The extra fat is often worth the extra money.

SOFT BAKING BUTTER:
Adding canola oil to butter is not a good idea.

having to wait for it to soften, but it produced cookies and cakes with a distinctly greasy feel. In addition, the cookies made with the Soft Baking Butter spread more in the oven than did the cookies made with the other butters.

As for the buttercream test, the Ultra Creamy Butter was the clear winner, making for frosting that was incredibly fluffy and rich tasting at the same time. The regular butter made a very good buttercream with a straightforward sweet and buttery taste, but it was not nearly as decadent. Tasters found the buttercream made with Soft Baking Butter to be "slick" and "slippery," and described the flavor as "fake."

Last, but certainly not least, a good butter should taste great right out of the box. Here the incredibly buttery and sweet Ultra Creamy Butter easily ascended to the top slot. Not far behind was the regular butter. Although more muted in flavor, it still is a great choice for buttering toast. Unsurprisingly, the soft baking butter came in dead last. The pure flavor of the butter was gone, replaced by an overtone of "margarine."

If you plan to use your butter straight up or in a recipe where its richness and flavor will be noticeable (such as in buttercream frosting), you may want to pay for the premium product from Land O' Lakes. But when it comes to baking and recipes where the flavor of the butter will be diluted, there's no need to shell out the extra dough—regular butter works just fine. As for canola oil—let's leave it out of the butter and keep it in the sauté pan, where it belongs.

TEST KITCHEN TIP: Managing Your Cutting Boards

From Oven-Barbecued Chicken (page 10) to chicken stir-fries (page 20), we cut up a lot of poultry in developing the recipes for this issue. And with the preparation of chicken (or any meat, for that matter) comes the issue of cross-contamination and how to avoid it.

In addition to washing and regularly sanitizing cutting boards, the test kitchen minimizes the risk of cross-contamination by means of a designated-use system. We reserve white boards for preparation of all raw meat, poultry, and seafood and blue boards for fruits, vegetables, and ingredients like nuts and chocolate. And, to keep odoriferous ingredients such as garlic, onions, and shallots from "contaminating" other foods with their odors, we reserve a green board for them. Nowadays, many kitchen supply stores carry acrylic cutting boards in many colors (see Resources, page 32), making it easy to set up a designated-use system of your own. To keep boards as clean as possible, make sure to buy a size that will fit in your dishwasher.

RAW MEAT:
WHITE BOARD

PRODUCE:
BLUE BOARD

STINKY STUFF:
GREEN BOARD

---

seen them all. Hundreds of cream pies later, we can recommend a simple way to present a handsome cream pie—one that doesn't look like it was made by an overeager 4-year-old.

Here's how: Use a large rubber spatula or spoon to mound the whipped cream in the center of the pie. Then, using an offset spatula, spread the whipped cream to the very edges of the pie, thereby creating a tall, evenly sloped mound of cream. Finally, use the tip of a metal offset spatula to gently create swirls and peaks.

Do Water and Rice Mix?

The question of whether rice should be soaked prior to cooking is often up for debate in our test kitchen. During the testing of our brown rice recipe (page 12), we decided to put this one to rest—once and for all. Some recipes call for soaking brown rice for three hours, so that's just what we did. We pitted the soaked rice against rice that was not soaked,

NO SOAKING, PLEASE
We tried soaking brown rice before cooking it and were not happy with the results (right). Soaking makes both white rice and brown rice bloated and mushy.

using both to make our recipe, slightly reducing the water in the recipe for the soaked batch. What did we find? To be frank, soaking was a waste of time. The rice was overcooked, and the grains tended to "blow out."

This result led us to test the wisdom of soaking other types of rice. And when we cooked up batches of long-grain white rice and basmati rice that had been soaked, we produced nearly identical results: bloated, overly tender rice.

Does that mean that there's no place for water in the world of rice preparation? Not necessarily. We found that the extra step of rinsing long-grain white or basmati rice in several changes of water was indispensable for a pilaf with distinct, separate grains. Rinsing washes away starches on these grains and doesn't cause the problems associated with soaking. What about rinsing brown rice? Our tests showed no benefit (or harm). Because the bran is still intact, brown rice doesn't have starch on its exterior. So rinsing doesn't accomplish anything—except for wasting time and water.

RECIPE UPDATE: READERS RESPOND

Lemon Curd

We're prone to adding a hit of fresh acid, such as citrus or vinegar, toward the end of the cooking process to brighten up a dish's flavor, and several readers wondered why we didn't follow this practice for the lemon curd topping on our **Lemon Cheesecake (May/June 2003)**.

As we learned when we made three batches of lemon curd with various combinations of lemon juice, adding an acid to brighten the flavor of a sauce for roast chicken is a lot simpler than adding it to a custard. The original recipe starts by heating 1/3 cup of fresh lemon juice with the eggs and sugar. This curd was pleasingly citrusy and had a silky consistency. For the second curd, we subtracted I tablespoon of juice from the initial 1/3 cup and added it at the end of cooking. This curd was grainy and overly thick. The third curd, to which we added an extra tablespoon of lemon juice at the end of the cooking, had the brightest flavor of the three but was unacceptably thin.

For the best balance of flavor and texture, lemon curd needs enough acid (or lemon juice) up front to help set the protein gel. Adding more acid once the curd is cooked makes the curd runny.

Molasses Cookies

If it hadn't happened to us in the test kitchen, we wouldn't have believed it when some readers reported that our **Molasses Cookies (January/February 2002)** resisted spreading in the oven and were overly thick and dense. We revisited this recipe and came up with a few tips that will help to ensure perfect results.

The first may seem obvious, but it's worth stating: Use of the wrong leavener—baking powder instead of baking soda—will produce mounded, rocklike cookies that resist spreading.

It's also important to make sure that your butter is at the proper temperature for creaming (65 to 67 degrees) and that you cream the butter and sugars for a full three minutes in an electric mixer at medium-high speed. When done properly, creaming creates air pockets that will help the cookies expand in the oven. If you undercream, the cookies will be thicker and cakier.

Finally, leaving just a tablespoon or two of sticky molasses behind in the

MADE WITH BAKING POWDER
Cookie is too thick and dense.

MADE WITH BAKING SODA
Cookie is chewy, puffed, and lined with attractive fissures.

measuring cup will result in a dry dough that won't spread properly. Measure the molasses on a scale (1/2 cup in a liquid measure should weigh 6 ounces) and scrape out the container thoroughly with a spatula.

Low-Fat Pastry Cream

Can you make low-fat pastry cream? The answer became very clear when we made three versions of the pastry cream from our recipe for **Classic Fresh Fruit Tart (July/August 2001)**. We compared the original recipe (made with half-and-half) with a second version made with whole milk and a third made with fat-free half-and-half (nonfat milk with ingredients such as corn syrup and carrageenan added to give it body).

We liked the version made with whole milk almost as much as the original. The original was richer, with a more luxurious texture, but the difference was subtle. The pastry cream made with fat-free half-and-half, however, was terrible. Its lean flavor and watery texture were a far cry from both the whole milk and regular half-and-half versions. If you need a substitute for half-and-half, reach for whole milk—some fat is better than no fat at all. –Compiled by Nina West

IF YOU HAVE A QUESTION about a recently published recipe, let us know. Send your inquiry, name, address, and daytime telephone number to Recipe Update, Cook's Illustrated, P.O. Box 470589, Brookline, MA 02447, or to recipeupdate@bcpress.com.

RESOURCES

Most of the ingredients and materials necessary for the recipes in this issue are available at your local supermarket, gourmet store, or kitchen supply shop. The following are mail-order sources for particular items. Prices listed below were current at press time and do not include shipping or handling unless otherwise indicated. We suggest that you contact companies directly to confirm up-to-date prices and availability.

ROTARY CHEESE GRATERS

Of the eight models we tested (see page 7) we can recommend only two. The Pedrini Rotary Grater did not clog when loaded with cheese and comes with three interchangeable drums. It is available from **TableTools.com (85 Furniture Row, Milford, CT 06460; 888-211-6603; www.tabletools.com)** for $14.95, item #29072. We also liked the KitchenAid Rotary Grater, item #913996 from **KitchenEtc (32 Industrial Drive, Exeter, NH 03833; 800-232-4070; www.kitchenetc.com)**. It is available in a wide range of colors and costs $19.99. This grater is suitable only for right-handed cooks.

SPATULAS AND TONGS

A flexible spatula, often referred to as a fish spatula or pelton, is perfect for getting under thin, delicate fillets. The Matfer 12-Inch Pelton was the least expensive spatula we tested while working on "Mastering the Art of Sauté" (see page 16), and it possessed the most aggressive ergonomic curve, making it our top choice. **CutleryAndMore.com (645 Lunt Avenue, Elk Grove Village, IL 60007; 800-650-9866, www.cutleryandmore.com)** sells the spatula, item #112420C, for $6.50.

If you are left-handed, the **LamsonSharp (800-872-6564; www.lamsonsharp.com)** 3-Inch by 6-Inch Chef's Turner LH, item #52865, is a better option—though a lot more expensive at $30.

Rubbermaid's 13½-Inch High Heat Spatula reigns as our winning rubber spatula and is a test kitchen favorite. **KitchenEtc** sells the spatula, item #439582, for $11.99.

Spring-loaded, locking tongs are an extremely useful tool for sautéing and many other tasks. We recommend two models. The Edlund Stainless Steel 12-Inch Scalloped Tongs, item #149187, are available from **Sur La Table (1938 Occidental Avenue South, Seattle, WA 98134; 800-243-0852; www.surlatable.com)** for $8.95. **Kitchen Etc.** sells the Oxo Good Grips 12-Inch Stainless Steel Tongs, item #470564, for $8.99.

SKILLETS

The All-Clad 12-Inch Stainless Omelette Pan is a workhorse in the test kitchen and perfectly suited to cooking Steak Diane (page 15). The pan, item #1009064, is available for $124.95 from Cooking.com (2850 Ocean Park Boulevard, Suite 310, Santa Monica, CA 90405; 800-663-8810; www.cooking.com). The only other pan we reach for as often is the 12-Inch Stainless Nonstick Omelette Pan from All-Clad, which is the perfect choice for a chicken stir-fry (page 21). This pan, item #1009106, is also sold at **Cooking.com**, where it sells for $139.95. For the budget-minded cook, there are two more reasonably priced options that rival our favorites, both of which are available at **Cooking.com**: the Calphalon Tri-Ply Omelette Pan, item #2019851, which costs $79.95, and our frugal nonstick option, the Farberware Millennium 18/10 Stainless Steel 12-Inch Nonstick Skillet, item #194802, which costs $29.99.

ICE CREAM CANISTERS

In developing the sherbet recipes on page 23, we found it extremely useful to have an extra canister for our ice cream maker on hand. If you can spare the freezer space, two canisters let you make two batches (in different flavors, if you like) on the same day instead of having to wait overnight for one canister to refreeze. Single canisters—including those for our two favorite ice cream makers—can be found at **Culinary Parts Unlimited (80 Berry Drive, Pacheco, CA 94553; 866-PART-HELP; www.culinaryparts.com)**. A canister for the Cuisinart ICE-20 Ice Cream Maker, item #CUICE-RFB, costs $29.99; a canister for the Krups 358 Ice Cream Maker, item #KR0907778, costs $35.99.

PASTRY BLENDER

In testing both wire-type and blade-type pastry blenders (see page 3), we ended up preferring the sturdier blade type—in particular, the Cuisena Dough Blender. It is available for $6.99 from **Cooks Corner (P.O. Box 220, 836 South 8th Street, Manitowoc, WI 54221-0220; 800-236-2433; www.cookscorner.com)**, item #81918.

OVEN MITT

The Orka Silicone Oven Mitt, reviewed on page 2, offers unsurpassed protection from heat but can be awkward. We found it most useful for moving hot grill racks when adding coals to the fire. The mitt is available for $19.99 at **KitchenEtc**, item #902544.

VEAL STOCK

For traditionalists who may pine for the unctuous richness of the real thing, veal stock can now be mail-ordered. **Provimi Veal Corporation's (W2103 County Road VV, Seymour, WI 54165; 800-833-**8325; www.provimi-veal.com)** Glace de Veau can be purchased directly or through a vendor listed on the company Web site. **Preferred Meats (P.O. Box 883122, San Francisco, CA 94188-3122; 800-397-6328; www.preferredmeats.com)** carries the CulinArte' Bonewerks Glace de Veau, item #14102-1P. It is available frozen, in 1-pound pouches, for $14.

FREEZER THERMOMETER

The optimal temperature for freezing our fruit sherbets (page 23) and other frozen desserts is 0 degrees Fahrenheit. To see if your freezer is chilly enough, try Taylor's Thermometer Freeze Guide 5925, which can be hung on a freezer shelf. You can order the thermometer, item #8524, for $6.99 from **Kitchen Kapers (385 West Lancaster Avenue, Wayne, PA 19087; 800-455-5567; www.kitchenkapers.com)**.

MAIL-ORDER BACON

Niman Ranch (1025 East 12th Street, Oakland, CA 94606; 510-808-0340) offers premium bacon that was superior to all other contenders in our bacon tasting (page 27). A 12-ounce package of this center-cut bacon smoked with apple wood costs $8. Many gourmet markets also carry Niman Ranch products. To find such a market near you, go to the Niman Ranch Web site **(www.nimanranch.com)**.

COLORED CUTTING BOARDS

To avoid cross-contaminating food in the test kitchen, we color-code our cutting boards, designating a particular color for a particular food group that is best kept to itself. KatchAll produces dishwasher-safe boards in four colors: white, green, red, and yellow; and a range of sizes. We recommend purchasing the largest board possible (that is, the largest that will fit in your dishwasher). The boards range in size from 12 by 10 inches ($10.95) up to 20 by 16 inches ($24.95) at **Cooking.com**. Search for "KatchAll" to view all of the options.

SPICE GRINDERS

All four of the electric, blade-type coffee mills we pressed into service as spice grinders (see page 28) produced excellent results. Considering the affordability of each one of the models, we suggest that you buy two: one for coffee and a second for spices. **Amazon.com** sells all four mills. The Krups Fast-Touch, item B0000Y6AKK, costs $19.95; the Braun Aromatic, item B00005IX9N, and the Mr. Coffee, item B00005OTXN, cost $14.99 each; and the Capresso Cool Grind, item B00004SU20, costs $19.99.

RECIPES
May & June 2004

Classic Macaroni and Cheese, 19

Steak Diane, 15

Spicy Stir-Fried Sesame Chicken with Green Beans and Shiitake Mushrooms, 21

Quick Cheese Bread, 7

www.cooksillustrated.com

Get all 11 years of *Cook's Illustrated* magazine and a free gift!

Join www.cooksillustrated.com today and gain access to 11 years' worth of recipes, equipment tests, and food tastings. . . at any time and from anywhere! Plus, as a *Cook's Illustrated* subscriber, you're offered a 20% discount.

Free Gift: As a paid member, you'll also get *The Essential Kitchen: 25 Kitchen Tools No Cook Should Be Without*. This downloadable online guide produced by the editors of *Cook's Illustrated* provides recommendations on the best cookware, tools, and gadgets for your kitchen. Simply type in the promotion code **CB45A** when signing up online.

Here are a few of the many things available at our site:

Best Recipes: Eleven years' worth of recipes developed in America's Test Kitchen.
Cookware Reviews: Every cookware review published since 1993, plus many reviews never seen in *Cook's*.
Ingredient Tastings: A decade of taste-test results, offering recommendations on everything from ketchup and mayonnaise to flour, yeast, and salt.
Online Bookstore: Cookbooks from the editors of *Cook's*, plus much more.

Fresh Lime, Raspberry, and Orange Sherbet, 23

Oven-Baked Brown Rice with Parmesan, Lemon, and Herbs, 12

Sweet and Tangy Oven-Barbecued Chicken, 11

AMERICA'S TEST KITCHEN TV SHOW
Join the millions of home cooks who watch our TV show, *America's Test Kitchen*, on public television every week. For more information, including recipes and a schedule of program times in your area, visit www.americastestkitchen.com.

Chef's Salad with Fennel, Asiago, and Salami, 9

Coconut Cream Pie, 25

PHOTOGRAPHY: CARL TREMBLAY (EXCEPT OVEN-BARBECUED CHICKEN: DANIEL J. VAN ACKERE), STYLING: MARY JANE SAWYER

Ginger

Pineapple

Orange

Mountain

Licorice

Chocolate

Peppermint

Apple

Spearmint

Calamint

MINT

NUMBER SIXTY-NINE

JULY & AUGUST 2004

COOK'S
ILLUSTRATED

Texas Beef Ribs
Real BBQ Flavor at Home

Rating
Japanese Knives

Tall, Fluffy Biscuits
Drop Them, Bake Them

Tasting Bottled Waters
Save Money and Drink Tap?

Easy Fruit Tart
Better Than Pie

Grilling Illustrated
Essential Tips and Techniques

Glazed Salmon
No Sticking, Big Flavor

Peach Cobbler

Spice Rubs for Steak

American Potato Salad

Thai Grilled Chicken

Best Tomato Salsa

www.cooksillustrated.com

$5.95 U.S./$6.95 CANADA

CONTENTS

July & August 2004

www.cooksillustrated.com

HOME OF AMERICA'S TEST KITCHEN

Founder and Editor Christopher Kimball
Executive Editor Jack Bishop
Senior Editors Maryellen Driscoll
Dawn Yanagihara
Editorial Manager, Books Elizabeth Carduff
Art Director Amy Klee
Test Kitchen Director Erin McMurrer
Senior Editors, Books Julia Collin Davison
Lori Galvin
Senior Writer Bridget Lancaster
Managing Editor Rebecca Hays
Associate Editors Matthew Card
Keith Dresser
Science Editor John Olson
Web Editor Keri Fisher
Copy Editor India Koopman
Test Cooks Stephanie Alleyne
Erika Bruce
Sean Lawler
Jeremy Sauer
Diane Unger-Mahoney
Assistant Test Cooks Garth Clingingsmith
Charles Kelsey
Nina West
Assistant to the Publisher Melissa Baldino
Kitchen Assistants Nadia Domeq
Maria Elena
Ena Gudiel
Contributing Editor Elizabeth Germain
Consulting Editors Shirley Corriher
Jasper White
Robert L. Wolke
Proofreader Jean Rogers

Vice President Marketing David Mack
Sales Director Leslie Ray
Retail Sales Director Jason Geller
Corporate Sponsorship Specialist Laura Phillipps
Sales Representative Shekinah Cohn
Marketing Assistant Connie Forbes
Circulation Director Bill Tine
Circulation Manager Larisa Greiner
Products Director Steven Browall
Direct Mail Director Adam Perry
Customer Service Manager Jacqueline Valerio
Customer Service Representative Julie Gardner
E-Commerce Marketing Manager Hugh Buchan

Vice President Operations James McCormack
Senior Production Manager Jessica Lindheimer Quirk
Production Manager Mary Connelly
Book Production Specialist Ron Bilodeau
Production Assistants Jennifer McCreary
Jennifer Power
Christian Steinmetz
Systems Administrator Richard Cassidy
WebMaster Aaron Shuman
Production Web Interns Ariana Berns
Lauren Feinberg

Chief Financial Officer Sharyn Chabot
Controller Mandy Shito
Office Manager Elizabeth Wray
Receptionist Henrietta Murray
Publicity Deborah Broide

For list rental information, contact: ClientLogic, 1200 Harbor Blvd., 9th Floor, Weehawken, NJ 07087; 201-865-5800; fax 201-867-2450.
Editorial Office: 17 Station St., Brookline, MA 02445; 617-232-1000; fax 617-232-1572. Subscription inquiries, call 800-526-8442.
Postmaster: Send all new orders, subscription inquiries, and change of address notices to: Cook's Illustrated, P.O. Box 7446, Red Oak, IA 51591-0446.

PRINTED IN THE USA

GRAPES

TABLE GRAPES There are dozens of varieties of table grapes, ranging in color from pale green to blue-black and coming in many different shapes and sizes. Perlette grapes, named for their pearl-like shape, arrive early, during spring. Italian Muscat grapes, used primarily for making dessert wines, have a honey-sweet flavor that also suits them perfectly for eating out of hand. Widely available Thompson Seedless grapes are recognized for their oblong shape and light green color. Similarly crisp and sweet, Flame Seedless grapes are a cross between Thompson Seedless and several other varieties. Another red-hued grape, the Crimson Seedless, has a more elongated shape and sweet-tart flavor. Impressive in size, seeded Red Globes can grow as large as small plums. At the other end of the size spectrum are the diminutive champagne, or Black Corinth, grapes, better known when dried as currants. Dark purple Black Marroo are seedless, firm, and juicy. Autumn Royals, which share the Marroos' oval shape, have a blue-black skin enclosing pale green flesh. More rounded Ribier grapes are seeded and have a mild flavor. Concord grapes are known for their sweet flesh and tart skins.   COVER (*Beets*): Elizabeth Brandon, BACK COVER (*Table Grapes*): John Burgoyne

HEAR THE GOOD NEWS

In our small Vermont town, there are many ways of getting news. You can sit at the "round table" at the Wayside Country Store before dawn and discuss everything from local DWI citations to the United Nations. Or you can meet on the road, two pickups stopped in opposite directions, the drivers lazily discussing the flatlander who likes to garden stark naked. Or perhaps a neighbor will just stop by while you're boiling sap, mucking a stall, feeding the pigs, or washing dishes. If it's close to high noon, you offer a beer; coffee is only for the early morning hours. One of our neighbors, John, used to ask for a cup of tea to which I often added a healthy shot of something made in the Scottish highlands. And of course there is coffee hour after church, the conversation often turning on the prospects for haying given the variable weather. The telephone is never used for social reasons. Old-time Vermonters will almost never answer it, and, when they do, they speak in words of one syllable until they can prematurely end the conversation with a "See you then," followed by a click and the inevitable dial tone.

Of course, there is also the *News Guide,* the free weekly newspaper. Announcements appear about the Square and Round Dance to benefit the Interfaith Council, the Easter Basket Raffle at the St. James Church, the local school bottle drive, and even the First Annual Woodchuck Festival, which features the Extreme Woodchuck Rescue Challenge. This spring, there was a close competition in the Wood-Chucking Contest (the winner tossed a log 20 feet, 6 inches), and the grand finale was the Woodchuck Ball, an event that includes a Woodchuck King and Queen.

The *News Guide* also contains a whole page of AA meetings followed by notices for support groups, wellness clinics, selectmen and planning committees, and notices about bridge and bingo. And if you look closely, you might come across a Pitch Card Party planned for the Grange Hall or an Embroidery Guild of America meeting at Trinity Church. The classified ads give you the opportunity to earn $5 for every envelope stuffed (Guaranteed!), to become a well driller helper, or, only if you are honest, to assemble refrigerator magnets. (Dishonest magnet assemblers need not apply.)

This is not to poke fun at country life—quite the opposite. I'd rather attend a wild game dinner, go to the Easter Egg Hunt sponsored by the fire department, or go see *Mr. Smith Goes to Washington* Saturday night at the town library than make the trip to see the latest off-Broadway entertainment. I guess that's because Vermonters feel that they shouldn't have to pay for their fun. Gossip is fun. Hard work is fun. Hunting and fishing are fun. A square dance is fun. The summer fireman's carnival is fun. And Old Home Day, held at the Methodist Church in early August, is fun (but the minister does pass the collection plate after reading out the shortfall in this year's fund-raising efforts).

It is also true that bad news travels faster than good news. When Sonny Skidmore had a stroke, Charlie Bentley got run over by a tractor, Fred DePeyster had a heart attack, or when our good friend John died suddenly on a Friday night, the whole town heard the news instantly. That's because the rescue squad is made up of neighbors. Of course, if you do any work on your house, the town assessors show up pretty quick to take a walk through, adding up the numbers in their heads.

On Sundays, down at the Methodist Church, we hear the good news that Christ died for our sins. Of course, in a small town, the worst sin is not being useful. I remember Russell Bain, who eventually ended up at the nursing home because he had a hard time walking. But he still wanted to be useful, so on Sundays Susie and Valerie picked him up and drove him back to town, where he was strapped with extra seat belts onto a riding

Christopher Kimball

mower. His memory wasn't too good either, so they put a photo of him on the mower next to his bed. That always cheered him up, that photo. He could see himself being useful.

In the summer, on the farm, we tell our kids that they have to fetch the eggs, feed the pigs, groom the horses, pick the berries, dig the potatoes, shuck the corn, and help with dinner. This is our salvation, hard work. Show up at Old Home Day with a plate or two of brownies and you are forgiven. Help stack a few cords of wood for a neighbor and you are pretty certain of seeing the gates of heaven. It's a simple rule to live by.

Last weekend, I baked two loaves of anadama bread and brought one over to Charlie Bentley. He was cooking a bachelor's dinner in a cast-iron skillet so I didn't stay long. When I walked in, he turned off the heat, and the sizzle of the meat started to quiet as we talked. I used to hay and milk with him as a kid and got paid 75 cents an hour. I wasn't much help—I walked like a circus clown with a bum leg when I tried to carry a heavy milking pail to the cooler—but I tried. Here I was 45 years later, guilty of most sins I can think of, still trying to be useful in spite of it.

All in all, most people would agree that cooks are pretty useful people. You'd have to ask our minister if forgiveness can be had for a loaf of bread, but I'd be willing to bet on it. This Easter, our 14-year-old, Caroline, surprised us by baking a cake: white on white, with "Happy Easter" written in pale blue and pink. When she whacked her younger brother, Charlie, after dinner, we forgave her. It was the lingering taste of the cake and a good cup of coffee that induced divine intervention. And if my anadama bread doesn't make me worthy of salvation, at least I baked an extra loaf for myself, just in case. As I have often told our four kids, a good cook always thinks ahead.

FOR INQUIRIES, ORDERS, OR MORE INFORMATION:

www.cooksillustrated.com

At www.cooksillustrated.com, you can order books and subscriptions, sign up for our free e-newsletter, or check the status of your subscription. Subscribe to the Web site and you'll have access to 11 years of *Cook's* recipes, cookware tests, ingredient tastings, and more.

COOKBOOKS

We sell more than 40 cookbooks by the editors of *Cook's Illustrated.* To order, visit our bookstore at www.cooksillustrated.com or call 800-611-0759 or 515-246-6911 from outside the U.S.

COOK'S ILLUSTRATED Magazine

Cook's Illustrated magazine (ISSN 1068-2821), number 69, is published bimonthly by Boston Common Press Limited Partnership, 17 Station Street, Brookline, MA 02445. Copyright 2004 Boston Common Press Limited Partnership. Periodicals postage paid at Boston, Mass., and additional mailing offices, USPS #012487. POSTMASTER: Send address changes to Cook's Illustrated, P.O. Box 7446, Red Oak, IA 51591-0446. For subscription and gift subscription orders, subscription inquiries, or change-of-address notices, call 800-526-8442 in the U.S. or 515-247-7571 from outside the U.S., or write us at Cook's Illustrated, P.O. Box 7446, Red Oak, IA 51591-0446.

Certified Angus Beef

When buying steak I gravitate toward Certified Angus Beef. It just seems to look better than the generic steaks. Is it really better? And what does "Certified Angus Beef" mean anyway?

MARK DEJON
MOULTONBOROUGH, N.H.

➤ Angus is a breed of beef cattle. Certified Angus Beef (CAB) is the oldest and largest of a growing number of so-called branding programs approved by the U.S. Department of Agriculture (USDA) and intended to signal "quality" to the consumer in much the same way that a brand of laundry detergent or toothpaste does. CAB is drawn from what the USDA identifies as the top two grades of beef, prime and choice, and the CAB program accepts only the top third of choice-grade beef. A key component of the USDA's grading system and the CAB program's selection criteria is the degree of marbling in the meat. Good marbling means that a fine network of fat (as opposed to big chunks) runs through the entire cut; the more and the finer the marbling, the more flavorful, tender, and juicy the meat once cooked.

The logo for Certified Angus Beef is intended to telegraph "quality" to the consumer when shopping for meat. Can it be trusted?

To see if we could differentiate CAB from other supermarket choices, we purchased 16 rib-eye steaks, including four CAB steaks ($11.99 per pound), eight "store label" steaks (four each from Stop & Shop, $10.99 per pound, and Shaw's, $9.49 per pound), and four steaks from another certified brand now appearing in many supermarkets, Swift Premium Classic ($11.49 per pound). The latter brand guarantees beef selected from the upper two thirds of the choice grade.

WELL MARBLED   **POORLY MARBLED**

The steak at left has plenty of marbling (an abundance of thin white lines of fat). It will be far tastier than the steak on the right, which has little marbling.

Tasters did detect differences in the steaks, but they were subtle, especially among the top three contestants. More than half of the tasters preferred the CAB steaks for their beefier flavor and relative juiciness; the next most popular choice was the Swift steak, followed by Stop & Shop. The Shaw's steaks were far less palatable.

Based on our sample, then, the CAB and Swift brands are an easy way to keep not-so-good steaks out of your shopping cart. But a smart shopper would also rely on careful visual inspection. The low-rated Shaw's steaks showed little marbling and were also the dullest in color. All three of the other steak types demonstrated good and very similar degrees of marbling, and all were a vivid shade of red. Our advice is simple—buy well-marbled steaks, which may be branded or not.

One more suggestion: If you merely see the word "Angus" on a label—as we did on the steak from Shaw's—don't assume that it tells you anything about the quality of the meat. Only the phrase "Certified Angus Beef" indicates that the meat has met that brand's quality standards.

Keeping Greens Fresh

How does Dole keep its prebagged greens from turning brown? Can I use a similar method to keep loose heads of lettuce from turning brown?

SCOTT HAMILTON
ANKENY, IOWA

➤ Producers of bagged lettuces and greens may employ one or more techniques to prevent browning. The most common is to pump nitrogen into the bags, the idea being to displace oxygen, which, when coupled with bruising of the produce, causes browning. Pumping the bags with nitrogen also creates a cushion of air around the contents that helps to prevent bruising during transport. As claimed on the packaging, most producers triple-wash the greens. Some add citric acid to the water to retard browning and chlorine to stave off decay. (It's not evident on the label which producers use these additives.) Finally, some producers use perforated bags that allow gases (such as oxygen) released by the greens to escape.

None of the above techniques is practical for the home cook. There are, however, two products now in the produce aisles of some supermarkets that claim to slow the aging process of greens as well as fruits and other vegetables. One is Evert-Fresh Green Bags, green plastic bags used to store produce; the other is ExtraLife, green plastic disks that are tossed in the crisper drawer. Both products make use of a mineral

called zeolite that neutralizes ethylene, the ripening gas emitted from most fruits and vegetables. In the crisper drawer, ethylene builds up such that it speeds the demise of produce.

To test the effectiveness of these products, we refrigerated red leaf lettuce, green beans, cucumbers, and cantaloupes according to the products' instructions. A third set of produce was stored without any life-extending product.

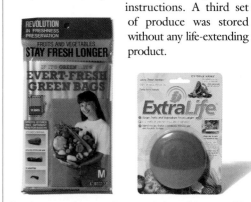

Do these products really extend the refrigerator life of fruits and vegetables?

The ExtraLife disks ($3.98 for one, which is to last for three months) were a complete waste of money, doing nothing to extend the life of the fruit or the vegetables. The Evert-Fresh bags ($3.98 for 10) seemed to have no effect on the melon or the cucumber but did buy the lettuce and the beans a couple of extra days. To our minds, though, this isn't much. In kitchen tests on storing greens, we've found that a loose head of lettuce is best thoroughly patted dry with paper towels (to remove excess moisture) and then transferred to a zipper-lock bag. It should stay fresh for several days.

Clouds in My . . . Tea?

What can be done about cloudy iced tea?

JENNIFER HIGGINS
WINCHESTER, MASS.

➤ According to Joe Simrany, president of the Tea Association of the U.S.A., certain kinds of tea are more likely to cloud (or "cream"—the term used by experts) than others. Assam teas from India are particularly susceptible. These teas are abundant in compounds called theoflavins and theorubigins, which combine with the calcium and/or magnesium in tap water to form salts that won't dissolve in cold water. As hot tea cools, the minerals in the water and the compounds in the tea clump, giving the tea a murky appearance.

We bought some Assam tea and made iced tea with it. Sure enough, upon adding ice to the hot

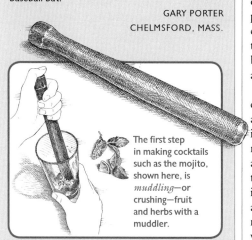
brewed tea, it "creamed," turning the color of toffee or dark butterscotch. Simrany told us that in general, full-bodied teas, such as Assams, that are found in specialty stores are more susceptible to creaming than supermarket varieties, which are now blended so that they can be used to make either hot or (clear) iced tea. Water with a high mineral content can also be the cause of murky tea, as we found when making tea with Evian water (see Kitchen Notes, page 30).

Stabilizing Whipped Cream

How far ahead can I whip cream, and what is the best stabilizer to use?

KAREN CRUSCO
CAMBRIDGE, MASS.

➤ In test results published in the September/October 1997 issue, we found that whipped cream could be kept for up to two days when refrigerated in a fine-mesh strainer over a bowl or when powdered milk was added (1 tablespoon per cup) before beating. Since then readers have come up with a few more suggestions: beating the cream to stiff peaks rather than soft peaks, beating in a melted marshmallow, and beating in a powdered product called Oetker's Whip It.

We found that cream beaten to stiff peaks did keep better than cream beaten to soft peaks, and better still if you held the whipped cream in a strainer. Much as we were rooting for the marshmallow, it turned out to be a bust. As soon as we quickly scraped a marshmallow melted in the microwave into the cold cream, it turned into a hard little rock. The Whip It performed as advertised, holding the whipped cream in the refrigerator for two days with little weeping. This whipped cream did, however, have a slightly tinny taste. Its texture was not as billowy, and it looked almost shiny—like a semigloss paint.

Considering the results of these and past tests, we find that the best and easiest method of storing whipped cream is to whip it to stiff peaks and then hold it in a strainer over a bowl or measuring cup. If you have powdered milk on hand, you can instead beat a tablespoon of it into a cup of heavy cream and just keep the whipped cream in a bowl. Either way, it's a good idea to cover the whipped cream with plastic wrap to keep it from absorbing odors in the refrigerator.

To Reserve Pasta Water or Not

My wife and I use a lot of your pasta recipes, but we are often unsure of whether we should reserve pasta water or not. Is there an easy way to know when we should reserve it?

DOUGLAS GREEN
PORTLAND, ORE.

➤ Oil-based sauces don't have the benefit of liquidy ingredients and can be dry. Rather than adding more oil, which could make the dish greasy, it's better to add moisture with the pasta cooking water, which, because it has been seasoned with salt and contains some starch from the pasta, will give the dish more flavor and body than plain water. Thick sauces, pestos in particular, often benefit from being thinned with pasta cooking water. So, too, can slow-simmered, heavily reduced tomato sauces.

When don't you need to reserve pasta cooking water? Quick sauces made from canned or fresh tomatoes often have the problem of being too watery, not too dry. Cream sauces also generally don't require additional moisture.

If a recipe does not direct you to save pasta water but you think it might be needed, it's a good idea to reserve about ½ cup. In the test kitchen, we put a liquid measuring cup in the colander that will be used to drain the pasta. The measuring cup reminds us to reserve some cooking water before draining the pasta.

Resting Cooked Meat

Everyone knows that you are supposed to let meat "rest, covered," after removing it from the heat. But when do you remove it (when it's reached the desired temperature or earlier) and how long should it rest? Does it change by type of meat?

HELENA SAGARO
RALEIGH, N.C.

➤ "Resting" cooked meat is a good practice, as it allows the juices within, which are driven to the center during cooking, to redistribute themselves. In an effect called carryover cooking, the cut of meat in question will continue to rise in temperature as it rests, usually from 5 to 15 degrees, depending on its size and the temperature at which it was cooked. (The larger or thicker the cut and the higher the cooking temperature, the more the temperature of the meat will rise during resting.) This means that meat should be taken off the heat before it reaches the desired internal temperature. Steaks and thin chops can be expected to rise about 5 degrees from carryover cooking and should rest for about 5 minutes; thick chops and small roasts will rise 5 to 10 degrees and should rest for 10 to 15 minutes; large roasts will rise from 10 to 15 degrees and should rest from 15 to 30 minutes. These numbers assume a relatively high cooking temperature, either on the grill or in the oven. If roasting or barbecuing meat at a low temperature (300 degrees or below), expect less carryover cooking.

More Information on Splenda

➤ In researching the sugar substitute Splenda for this section of the January/February 2004 issue of the magazine, we were surprised to learn that a product approved by the U.S. Food and Drug Administration as "no calorie" really did contain calories (about 4 per teaspoon—still fewer than sugar at 16 calories per teaspoon). Since then, we have learned that not only Splenda but all so-called no-calorie sugar substitutes have some calories, added by bulking agents that are used to make these products measure more like sugar.

Baking Illustrated Correction

➤ In our latest cookbook there is an error in the recipe for Basic Pie Dough on page 181. The amount of shortening should be ½ cup, not 1 cup, as is printed. We apologize for this error.

Transporting Frozen Groceries

During grocery shopping trips, Stewart Kume of Belmont, Calif., inevitably thinks of additional errands to run or ends up getting stuck in traffic. To eliminate the need to rush home from the market, he stores a Styrofoam cooler in the trunk of his car for holding perishable groceries. The cooler keeps ice cream and other frozen foods from melting and prevents fragile items like eggs from rolling around and breaking.

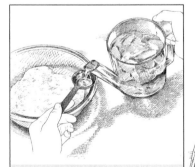

No-Fuss Ice Water

When making pie pastry or any recipe requiring ice water, Vivienne Shen of Southington, Conn., puts ice cubes and water into a fat separator. She can then measure out the water she needs through the spout, leaving the ice behind.

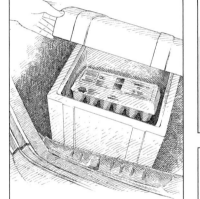

Freezing Fresh Herbs

When Andrea Killiard of Windham, Maine, buys a bunch of parsley, she often ends up using just a small fraction, only to watch the rest go bad. Then she figured out a good way to keep leftover parsley fresh—indefinitely. Her method also works with sage, rosemary, and thyme.

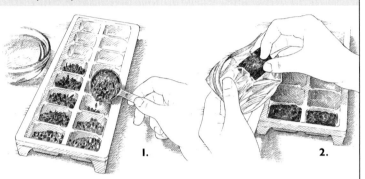

I. Chop leftover fresh herbs by hand or in the food processor, transfer by the spoonful into ice cube trays, and top with water to cover. For a standard ice cube tray, place 2 tablespoons chopped herbs and approximately 1 tablespoon water in each cube.
2. Once the cubes are frozen, transfer them to a zipper-lock plastic bag and seal. Store until you want to add them to sauces, soups, or stews.

Soak-Ahead Wood Chunks

Barbecue aficionado Kalle Willoughby of Zillah, Wash., likes to smoke ribs over wood chunks, but she doesn't like having to plan to soak the chunks an hour ahead of time. Here's what she recommends to make sure soaked wood chunks are always at the ready when starting up the grill:

I. Soak as many chunks as you like at the same time. Drain the chunks, seal them in a zipper-lock bag, and store them in the freezer.
2. When ready to grill, place the frozen chunks on the grill. They defrost quickly and impart as much flavor as freshly soaked chunks.

Adding Sugar to Iced Tea

Not one to enjoy undissolved granules of sugar in his iced tea, Matthew Beder of Andover, Mass., solves the problem by keeping a jar of sugar syrup, known as simple syrup, in the refrigerator.

To make the syrup, combine 1 cup water and 1 cup granulated sugar in a small saucepan. Set the pan over medium heat and whisk frequently, until the sugar dissolves completely. Simmer for 4 minutes, remove from the heat, and cool. For more flavor, simmer one of the following ingredients with the water and sugar:

- ½ scraped fresh vanilla bean and seeds for Vanilla Simple Syrup.
- 3 tablespoons packed mint leaves for Mint Simple Syrup.
- 3 ounces fresh berries (raspberries, blackberries, or blueberries) for Berry Simple Syrup.
- 2-inch piece of ginger cut into 4 coins for Ginger Simple Syrup.
- 2 teaspoons grated citrus zest (lemon, lime, or orange) for Citrus Simple Syrup.

Strain the flavorings out of the syrup once it cools.

Flavoring Summer Drinks

Laurie Parelengas of Granby, Mass., creates inventive summer drinks by stirring scoops of frozen juice concentrate into pitchers of iced tea to taste. Lemonade, limeade, and orange juice concentrates are the best choices.

Easier Way to Frost a Cake

Frosting a cake is made much easier when it can be elevated on a cake stand. For those infrequent bakers who may not own a cake stand, Deb Leno of Peabody, Mass., has come up with a workable substitute.

Place the cake on a cardboard round, then on an overturned 12-inch pizza pan or similarly sized baking sheet. Set the pizza pan on an upside-down, flat-bottomed metal bowl. The bowl provides height, and the pizza pan can be rotated as needed to ice the cake.

Foolproof Grill Lighting

A chimney starter is practically foolproof, but just to make absolutely sure that it will get the job done on a cold or windy day, Jon Puckett of Cypress, Texas, recommends the following trick.

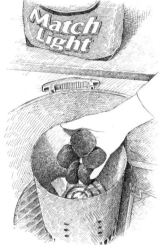

Place four or five briquettes of self-starting charcoal at the bottom of the chimney, then fill the balance with hardwood charcoal. By using just a handful of self-starting briquettes, you're guaranteed both a quick start and food without the acrid taste that comes from using self-starting charcoal exclusively.

Makeshift Grill Basket for Fish

Roxanne Wueste of Fort Worth, Texas, knows that a grill basket can cut down on the hassles of cooking delicate fish fillets outdoors. Here's how she assembles a basket with equipment most cooks already have on hand:

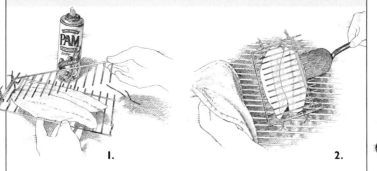

1. Oil and season the fish and place it on a small oiled cooling rack. Place another oiled cooling rack on top of the fish and fasten the racks securely together on each side with bendable wire or wire twist-ties.
2. To flip the basket, use a spatula in one hand to lift the basket and use your other, oven mitt–clad hand to turn it over.

Cheap Grill Brush Alternative

George Deindorfer of Virginia Beach, Va., discovered a frugal alternative to a grill brush at a hardware store. A welder brush, which can be purchased for a mere $2, has a long wooden handle attached to a wire brush, just like those grill brushes that cost 10 times as much. Its long wires and narrow design allow for deep scrubbing between the bars on a grill grate.

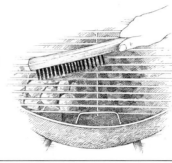

Homemade Cherry Pitters

Half the battle of making a fresh sour cherry pie is pitting the cherries efficiently, with minimal bruising of their delicate flesh.

1A. Billie Gold of New York, N.Y., recommends using a paper clip to pit cherries. Unfold one bend of a clean, large metal paper clip to create an elongated *S*-shape.
1B. Holding the cherry in one hand, stick one end of the *S* into the stem end of the cherry, hook it around the pit, and flick the pit out. Billie finds this method is faster and more effective than the commercial cherry and olive pitters she has tried.
2A. Charlie Raiser of Kirkwood, Mo., takes a different approach. Drive three clean stainless steel nails close together through a piece of clean, thin scrap wood to form a "basket."
2B. Gently push the cherry down onto the sharp tips of the nails to extract the pit. Entry and exit "wounds" are minimal.

1A.

1B.

2A.

2B.

Picnic Containers

Frances Rahaim of Montague, Mass., always has an abundance of empty plastic 35 mm film canisters. After giving them a quick cleanup, she uses them as receptacles for picnic condiments— salt and pepper, salad dressings, mustard, and so on.

Peeling Tomatoes

Once you blanch and shock tomatoes or stone fruits, a knife can still sometimes fail to remove the skin effectively. When her paring knife fails her, Jen Pantalokos of Barrington, N.H., places stubborn fruits in a kitchen towel and rubs lightly.

Sandwiches for Picnics

M.A. and Mal King of Stoughton, Mass., often head to the beach or the park for picnics. Instead of wrapping sandwiches individually, they stack prepared, unwrapped sandwiches in the bread bag they've emptied to make the sandwiches. They even recycle the original tab to seal the bag shut.

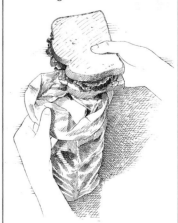

Mile-High Biscuits

Tall, fluffy, and tangy, drop biscuits are the holy grail of biscuit making, but they require just the right mix of ingredients and technique.

> BY ELIZABETH GERMAIN <

I tasted heaven at age 9 at a pit stop in Georgia when I sank my teeth into a piping hot, unusual-looking biscuit. Each rustic roll had a crisp, golden brown top that sat high above an extra-fluffy, moist, and tender crumb. The biscuits varied in height, but even the shortest towered above any I had seen up North. The biscuits had a rich and tangy flavor, and I slathered them with butter just because I could. Fast-forward almost four decades and I was still in search of a recipe that would equal the memory of those truly extraordinary biscuits.

I started my search with a thick folder of recipes and then prepared a half-dozen traditional "roll and cut" recipes—trying different flours, fats, mixing methods, and oven temperatures—and concluded that this common approach to biscuit making results in flaky, but not particularly fluffy, biscuits. I made another half-dozen recipes, this time exploring unusual approaches and different methods of shaping, and began thinking a drop biscuit might be the answer. My hunch was confirmed when I prepared Shirley Corriher's Touch-of-Grace Biscuits from her book *Cookwise* (Morrow, 1997). Finally, I tasted a biscuit that reminded me of that summer day in Georgia.

What sets Corriher's recipe apart from all of the others is the amount of buttermilk used: twice as much for the same volume of flour. The wet dough is then hand-shaped into round balls that are coated with flour and dropped into a cake pan. Once all of the biscuits have been fitted snugly in the pan, the tops are brushed with butter. A very wet and sticky dough, baked in a very hot oven, was this biscuit's secret to a fluffy high rise.

Flour, Fat, and Buttermilk

With this basic approach in mind, I began a new round of tests by comparing cake flour, all-purpose flour, and a 50-50 mix of cake and all-purpose. Cake flour, which is lower in protein than all-purpose, is known for yielding a more tender crumb. Tasters were surprised to discover that they preferred the batch made entirely with all-purpose flour. These biscuits had more flavor, the crust was crispier, and the crumb was moist and light without being cakey or gummy.

An unusual recipe yields the fluffiest-ever biscuits, with a mile-high rise, a tender crumb, and a crisp top.

I tried lard, vegetable shortening, and butter both separately and in combination. The biscuits made with lard or shortening were bland compared with the rich flavor of the all-butter biscuits. A few more tests showed that the best way to add the butter to the dough was to combine it—chilled straight from the refrigerator—with the dry ingredients in a food processor.

As for the liquid, I stuck with buttermilk, which was key to Corriher's recipe. Low-fat buttermilk produced biscuits richer in flavor and texture than nonfat, but tasters raved about both batches. Substituting either powdered buttermilk or clabbered milk (made with whole milk and white vinegar or lemon juice) proved disappointing, however. The dough lacked structure, and the exceptional rise was lost. When I tested various ways of adding the buttermilk to the dough, the food processor failed; its powerful stirring turned the dough into an elastic ball that baked up into rubbery biscuits. Instead, I dumped the flour/fat mixture into a bowl and quickly (and gently) stirred in the

buttermilk. Now the dough was airy looking, with a texture akin to that of whipped cottage cheese. The resulting biscuits were fluffy and moist, but they were still not quite as high as I wanted.

Rise and Shine

Knowing that steam was an important contributor to the high rise of the biscuits (moisture in the dough converts to steam in the oven, causing the biscuits to swell), I experimented with oven temperature. I had been baking them in an oven heated to 475 degrees; now I tried 500 degrees. The rise improved, but the tops browned too quickly. I then prepared a few more batches, starting the oven at 500 degrees and then lowering it for the remainder of the cooking time. Five minutes at 500 degrees followed by 15 minutes at 450 degrees maximized the rise from the steam. At this point, I had already made 60 batches of biscuits, but I couldn't help wondering if I could gain even more height by adjusting the chemical leaveners.

My starting point (a ratio common to other recipes) was ⅛ teaspoon baking soda to 1½ teaspoons baking powder. Time after time, I methodically increased the amount of one of the leaveners, always holding the other steady. The rise continued to improve, but I encountered a series of problems—yellow, dry, and metallic-tasting biscuits among them. Finally, with the help of *Cook's* science editor, I ended up with hefty amounts of both baking soda (½ teaspoon) and baking powder (1 tablespoon). A very hot, two-temperature oven and plenty of leavener produced biscuits that rose over the top of the cake pan, some measuring more than 2 inches high!

Drop, Dust, Shape, Brush

Up until now I had been shaping the incredibly wet and sticky dough into biscuits according to Corriher's recommended technique. With floured hands, I'd scoop up a biscuit-size lump of wet dough, dust it with flour, shape it into a round, and place it in a 9-inch nonstick cake pan. Once all of the biscuits were packed into the pan, I brushed the tops with melted butter. Could I omit any of these steps to simplify and speed up the process? More than a dozen tests later, I decided that each step was essential but that an assembly-line approach—in which I used a greased measuring cup to scoop the dough and a baking sheet to hold the flour and the shaped biscuits—saved time and reduced the mess.

Most biscuits are best hot from the oven, but mine were a bit gluey and damp in the middle. I learned that waiting a few minutes—as hard as that was—solved the problem by allowing some of the steam to escape from these high-moisture biscuits. By the end of testing, I had worked my way through more than a hundred batches (that's at least 1,200 individual biscuits), but now I can taste heaven anytime I want.

TALL AND FLUFFY BUTTERMILK BISCUITS
MAKES 12 BISCUITS

We prefer to use low-fat buttermilk in these biscuits, but nonfat buttermilk will work as well (though the biscuits will be a little lighter in texture and flavor). For the highest rise, use a double-acting baking powder, such as Calumet, Clabber Girl, or Davis (for more information on baking powders, see Kitchen Notes, page 31). Store leftover biscuits in an airtight zipper-lock bag. Reheat by placing them on a baking sheet in a 475-degree oven for 5 to 7 minutes.

Nonstick cooking spray

Dough
- 2 cups (10 ounces) unbleached all-purpose flour
- 1 tablespoon double-acting baking powder
- 1 tablespoon sugar
- 1 teaspoon salt
- ½ teaspoon baking soda
- 4 tablespoons cold unsalted butter, cut into ¼-inch cubes
- 1½ cups cold buttermilk, preferably low-fat

To Form and Finish Biscuits
- 1 cup (5 ounces) unbleached all-purpose flour, distributed in rimmed baking sheet
- 2 tablespoons unsalted butter, melted

1. Adjust oven rack to middle position and heat oven to 500 degrees. Spray 9-inch round cake pan with nonstick cooking spray; set aside. Generously spray inside and outside of ¼ cup dry measure with nonstick cooking spray.

2. **FOR THE DOUGH:** In food processor, pulse flour, baking powder, sugar, salt, and baking soda to combine, about six 1-second pulses. Scatter butter cubes evenly over dry ingredients; pulse until mixture resembles pebbly, coarse cornmeal, eight to ten 1-second pulses. Transfer mixture to medium bowl. Add buttermilk to dry ingredients and stir with rubber spatula until just incorporated (dough will be very wet and slightly lumpy).

3. **TO FORM AND BAKE BISCUITS:** Using ¼ cup dry measure and working quickly, scoop level amount of dough; drop dough from measuring

1. Using greased ¼-cup measure, scoop 12 level portions of dough onto floured baking sheet. Lightly dust top of each biscuit with flour.

2. With floured hands, gently pick up piece of dough, coating outside with flour, shaping it into ball, and shaking off excess flour.

3. Place 9 biscuits snugly around perimeter of cake pan, then arrange last 3 in center.

SCIENCE: **What Makes Biscuits Rise?**

Our biscuit recipe contains both baking soda and baking powder. Both leaveners, when activated, create carbon dioxide that provides lift. Baking soda, or sodium bicarbonate, has been used to leaven baked goods for almost 200 years. Its action is based on simple chemistry. In the presence of liquid acid, sodium is replaced by a hydrogen ion to form carbonic acid. Carbonic acid then breaks down into water and carbon dioxide. The part of the formula that is the hardest to figure out is how much soda and how much acid to add. Our acid was buttermilk, and we could not change the amount by much without changing the moisture content and flavor of the biscuits. When we used just ⅛ teaspoon soda (as suggested in many recipes), we ended up with a heavy dough. The minimum amount required for a light, spongy dough was ½ teaspoon.

Soda, unfortunately, has a few limitations. Because it acts instantly once mixed with acid, it loses power in the oven. To give our biscuits perfect oven rise, we had to turn to baking powder. Baking powder works on the same principle as baking soda—in fact, its active ingredient is baking soda—but baking powder also contains an acid, often two. Double-acting baking powder, the two-acid variety, is the perfect tool for biscuits because it contains a quick-acting acid, usually monocalcium phosphate, along with an acid that requires heat to dissolve, often sodium aluminum sulfate. This means that some of the acid is unavailable until the biscuits hit the oven.

Why then, you might ask, didn't we simply use baking powder alone? We tried making the biscuits without baking soda, and this attempt failed. Five teaspoons of baking powder were required to lift the biscuits. With so much baking powder, the dough dried out (baking powder contains cornstarch, which absorbed liquid in the batter) and picked up unpleasant metallic and mineral flavors. –John Olson, Science Editor

ALL BAKING SODA

ALL BAKING POWDER

JUST ENOUGH SODA & POWDER

Leaveners have a dramatic effect on the appearance, texture, and flavor of biscuits. Biscuits made with baking soda alone (left) did not rise fully (especially those in the middle of the pan), turned dark brown, and tasted bitter. Biscuits made with baking powder alone (middle) were dry and metallic tasting. Biscuits made with both baking soda and powder (right) were tall and fluffy and tasted the best.

cup into flour on baking sheet (if dough sticks to cup, use small spoon to pull it free). Repeat with remaining dough, forming 12 evenly sized mounds. Dust tops of each piece of dough with flour from baking sheet. With floured hands, gently pick up piece of dough and coat with flour; gently shape dough into rough ball, shake off excess flour, and place in prepared cake pan. Repeat with remaining dough, arranging 9

rounds around perimeter of cake pan and 3 in center. Brush rounds with hot melted butter, taking care not to flatten them. Bake 5 minutes, then reduce oven temperature to 450 degrees; continue to bake until biscuits are deep golden brown, about 15 minutes longer. Cool in pan 2 minutes, then invert biscuits from pan onto clean kitchen towel; turn biscuits right-side up and break apart. Cool 5 minutes longer and serve.

Introducing Thai-Style Grilled Chicken

Gai yang is popular Thai street food. Could we capture its complex flavors and adapt this dish for the American kitchen?

≥ BY KERI FISHER ≤

Thai grilled chicken, or *gai yang*, is classic street food. This herb- and spice-rubbed chicken is served in small pieces and eaten as finger food, along with a sweet and spicy dipping sauce. Thai flavors are wonderfully aromatic and complex, a refreshing change of pace from the typical barbecue. But is it possible to bring the flavors of Thailand into the American kitchen (or backyard) without using an ingredient list as long as your arm and making several trips to Asian specialty stores?

An initial sampling of recipes made me wonder if this dish ought to remain as indigenous street food. Among the hard-to-find ingredients were cilantro root and lemon grass, and there was a profusion of odd mixtures, including an unlikely marriage of peanut butter and brown sugar. In the end, the simplest version won out: a rub made only with cilantro, black pepper, lime juice, and garlic. I would use this as my working recipe.

Because tasters preferred white meat, I decided to go with bone-in breasts. Brined chicken was vastly preferred to unbrined, and tasters liked the addition of sugar along with salt, which complemented the sweetness of the sauce. I settled on ½ cup of each in 2 quarts of water.

At the table, spoon an intensely flavored sauce—made in minutes with supermarket ingredients—over the herb- and spice-rubbed grilled chicken.

Rubbing In Flavor

Tasters liked my working rub recipe, but they wanted more complexity of flavor. My first step was to reduce the amount of cilantro, as it had been overpowering the other ingredients. Curry powder made the chicken taste too much like Indian food, and coconut milk turned the chicken milky and soggy, with flabby skin. The earthy flavor of coriander was welcome, and fresh ginger

worked well in balance with the garlic. Tasters praised this blend as more complex and flavorful but still lacking bite, so I added more garlic.

The skin on the chicken was now crisp and flavorful, but not much rub was getting through to the meat. Coworkers offered suggestions ranging from slicing pockets in the meat and stuffing them with the rub to butterflying the breast and placing the rub inside. In the end, the best alternative proved to be the easiest: I took some of the rub

and placed it in a thick layer under the skin as well as on top of it. Now it was not only the crisp skin that was flavorful but the moist flesh beneath as well.

Most recipes call for grilling the chicken over a single-level fire, but this resulted in a charred exterior and an uncooked interior. I tried a two-level fire (one side of the grill holds all of the coals; the other side is empty) and, voilà, partial success! I first browned the chicken directly over the coals and then moved it to the cool side of the grill to finish cooking. This was a big improvement, but the chicken still wasn't cooking through to the middle. Covering the grill—to make it more like an oven—was an obvious solution, but better yet was using a disposable foil pan, which creates a "mini" oven. (Charcoal grill covers are home to deposits of smoke, ash, and debris that lend "off" flavors to foods.)

It's All about the Sauce

The true Thai flavors of this dish come through in the sauce, a classic combination of sweet and spicy. Most recipes suffered from the extremes. In my working recipe, I had tried to create a balance of flavors: 2 teaspoons of hot red pepper flakes, ⅓ cup of sugar, ¼ cup of lime juice, ¼ cup of white vinegar, and 3 tablespoons of fish sauce. But

---

COOK'S EXTRA gives you free information online. For the complete results of our fish sauce tasting (at right) and our portable gas grill tests (page 9), go to www.cooksillustrated.com and key in code 4041 for the tasting and code 4042 for the equipment test. This information will be available until August 15, 2004.

TASTING: **Fish Sauce**

Fish sauce is a potent Asian condiment based on the liquid from salted, fermented fish—and smells as such. It has a very concentrated flavor and, like anchovy paste, when used in appropriately small amounts, lends foods a salty complexity that is impossible to replicate. I gathered six brands from the local supermarket, natural foods store, and Asian market. Tasters had the option of tasting the fish sauce straight up (which few could stomach) or in a modified version of the Thai grilled chicken dipping sauce.

Our most interesting finding was that color correlates with flavor; the lighter the sauce, the lighter the flavor. That said, all six brands are recommended. There was in fact only one point (out of 10) separating all six sauces. With such a limited ingredient list—most brands contained some combination of fish extract, water, salt, and sugar—it makes sense that the differences in the sauces were nominal. And because fish sauce is used in such small amounts, minute flavor differences get lost among the other flavors of a dish. Our advice: Purchase whatever is available. —K.F.

This widely available sauce is just fine.

tasters found even this sauce to be overwhelmingly sweet and spicy.

Reducing the hot red pepper flakes was a step in the right direction, as it allowed the other flavors to come through. Everyone liked garlic, but not too much; there was already a lot of garlic on the chicken. A decrease in the amount of fish sauce was welcomed, reducing the fishy flavor of the sauce but not its salty complexity. I found it best to mix the sauce right after the chicken goes into the brine, which gives the flavors time to meld.

Traditionally, gai yang is cut into small pieces and eaten as finger food. But my version was just as good (and a whole lot neater) when served whole with a knife and fork. Was this an Americanized dish? Yes. But its flavors were true to its Thai roots, and its ingredients could be found in most grocery stores.

THAI-STYLE GRILLED CHICKEN WITH SPICY SWEET AND SOUR DIPPING SAUCE
SERVES 4

For even cooking, the chicken breasts should be of comparable size. The best way to ensure this is to buy whole breasts and split them yourself (for instructions, see Kitchen Notes, page 30). If you prefer to skip this step, try to purchase split bone-in, skin-on breasts that weigh about 12 ounces each. If using a charcoal grill, you will need a disposable aluminum roasting pan to cover the chicken (the lid on a charcoal grill can give the chicken resinous "off" flavors). Some of the rub is inevitably lost to the grill, but the chicken will still be flavorful.

Chicken and Brine
- ½ cup sugar
- ½ cup table salt
- 4 split bone-in, skin-on chicken breasts, about 12 ounces each (see note)

Dipping Sauce
- 1 teaspoon red pepper flakes
- 3 small garlic cloves, minced or pressed through garlic press (1½ teaspoons)
- ¼ cup distilled white vinegar
- ¼ cup juice from 2 to 3 limes
- 2 tablespoons fish sauce
- ⅓ cup sugar

Rub
- 12 medium garlic cloves, minced or pressed through garlic press (¼ cup)
- 1 piece (about 2 inches) fresh ginger, minced (about 2 tablespoons)
- 2 tablespoons ground black pepper
- 2 tablespoons ground coriander
- ⅔ cup chopped fresh cilantro leaves
- ¼ cup juice from 2 to 3 limes
- 2 tablespoons vegetable oil, plus more for grill grate

1. TO BRINE THE CHICKEN: Dissolve sugar and salt in 2 quarts cold water in large container or bowl; submerge chicken in brine and refrigerate at least 30 minutes but not longer than 1 hour. Rinse chicken under cool running water and pat dry with paper towels.

2. FOR THE DIPPING SAUCE: Whisk ingredients in small bowl until sugar dissolves. Let stand 1 hour at room temperature to allow flavors to meld.

3. TO MAKE AND APPLY THE RUB: Combine all rub ingredients in small bowl; work mixture with fingers to thoroughly combine. Slide fingers between skin and meat to loosen skin, taking care not to detach skin. Rub about 2 tablespoons mixture under skin. Thoroughly rub even layer of mixture onto all exterior surfaces, including bottom and sides. Repeat with remaining chicken pieces. Place chicken in medium bowl, cover with plastic wrap, and refrigerate while preparing grill.

4. TO GRILL THE CHICKEN: Using chimney starter, ignite about 6 quarts (1 large chimney, or 2½ pounds) charcoal briquettes and burn until covered with thin coating of light gray ash, about 15 minutes. Empty coals into grill; build two-level fire by arranging all coals in even layer in one half of grill. Position grill grate over coals, cover grill, and heat until grate is hot, about 5 minutes (grill should be medium-hot; you can hold your hand 5 inches above grill grate for 4 seconds); scrape grill grate clean with grill brush. Using long-handled grill tongs, dip wad of paper towels in vegetable oil and wipe grill grate. Place chicken, skin-side down, on hotter side of grill; cook until browned, about 3 minutes. Using tongs, flip chicken breasts and cook until browned on second side, about 3 minutes longer. Move chicken skin-side up to cool side of grill and cover with disposable aluminum roasting pan; continue to cook until instant-read thermometer inserted into thickest part of breast (not touching bone) registers 160 degrees, 10 to 15 minutes longer. Transfer chicken to platter; let rest 10 minutes. Serve, passing sauce separately.

THAI-STYLE GRILLED CHICKEN ON A GAS GRILL

1. Follow recipe for Thai-Style Grilled Chicken through step 3.

2. Turn all burners on gas grill to high, close lid, and heat until grill is very hot, about 15 minutes. Scrape grill grate clean with grill brush; using long-handled grill tongs, lightly dip wad of paper towels in vegetable oil and wipe grill grate. Turn all but 1 burner to low. Place chicken, skin-side down, on hotter side of grill; cook until browned, 4 to 5 minutes. Using tongs, flip chicken breasts and cook until browned on second side, 4 to 5 minutes longer. Move chicken skin-side up to cool side of grill and close lid; cook until instant-read thermometer inserted into thickest part of breast (not touching bone) registers 160 degrees, 12 to 15 minutes. Transfer chicken to serving platter; let rest 10 minutes. Serve, passing sauce separately.

American Potato Salad

Is there anything new to say about making this summertime classic? To find out, we tried an unlikely potato and an old-fashioned ingredient.

⋗ BY REBECCA HAYS ⋖

Potato salad hardly requires a recipe. After all, the main elements—potatoes, mayonnaise, and seasonings—are about as basic as they come. It's tempting to adopt a devil-may-care attitude, tossing boiled potatoes with a dollop of this and a squirt of that. But I can always tell when potato salad has been improvised, because the flavor is out of whack—too sweet or too acidic, underseasoned or overseasoned.

Yet when I carefully tested five different recipes here in the test kitchen, not one escaped serious critique. Some of the salads were hopelessly bland, others were too tart from an excess of vinegar, and one, with ⅓ cup sugar in the dressing, was practically inedible. These results inspired me to create my own recipe, but I didn't want to reinvent the wheel. My goal was simply to nail down a good, solid formula for this summer side dish. I was looking for flavorful, tender potatoes punctuated by crunchy bits of onion and celery. An ideal dressing would have both a hint of sweetness and a measure of acidity.

The Potatoes

Recipe writers and home cooks are divided on which potatoes are best for potato salad. Most insist on waxy Red Bliss or boiling potatoes, which hold their shape well during cooking. Some like golden-fleshed, moderately starchy Yukon Golds, while a minority maintain a preference for russets. I boiled up each of these common supermarket candidates and made bare-bones potato salads for a panel of tasters. Obviously, the potatoes differed texturally. But they had one thing in common: They were all incredibly bland.

While developing other recipes for potato salad, the test kitchen has found that seasoning the potatoes while they're hot maximizes flavor.

COOK'S EXTRA gives you free recipes and information online. For our recipe for Garlicky Potato Salad with Basil, visit www.cooksillustrated.com and key in code 4043. For our hard-cooked eggs recipe, key in code 4044. This information will be available until August 15, 2004.

Russets absorb dressing better than other potatoes, and their starchy texture makes for a rich, slightly crumbly salad.

For my next round of tests, then, I splashed the hot potatoes with white vinegar before proceeding with my recipe. The russets, being the driest, sponged up the vinegar and tasted great. In contrast, the other potatoes were still a little too mild tasting after the vinegar soak. Although russets were called for in but a small minority of recipes, their capacity to soak up vinegar gave them a lot of credibility with me, as it allowed their flavor to shine through the inevitable cloak of mayonnaise. Yes, they do crumble a bit when mixed, but tasters found this quality charming, not alarming.

I next experimented with possible stand-ins for the plain white vinegar. Lemon juice seemed out of place in potato salad, and pickle juice wasn't acidic enough. Cider vinegar, with its distinctively fruity flavor, was dismissed, as was red wine vinegar. Two tablespoons of white vinegar got the most votes for its clean, clear acidity.

Next I had to determine how to prep the potatoes. Those boiled in their skins were rich and earthy; those peeled and cut before being boiling exhibited slightly less flavor. But peeling and cutting steaming hot potatoes (a requirement if the potatoes are to be properly seasoned) is a tricky proposition. Thankfully, once the potatoes were dressed, the flavor differences between those boiled with and without their jackets were barely noticeable.

Now I wanted to see if I could further develop that flavor by spiking the boiling water. A quartered onion and smashed garlic clove went nearly undetected, as did chicken broth. I added a few glugs of vinegar to a pot of boiling potatoes, wondering if it would be more effective than seasoning them postcooking. After nearly an hour of simmering, the potatoes were still not tender. A quick consultation with our science editor reminded me that acid reinforces the pectin in potatoes, making them resistant to breaking down on exposure to heat. I decided to leave well enough alone and stick with salted water as the boiling medium.

The Dressing

I wanted a classic mayonnaise-based dressing but also thought it worthwhile to investigate variations. Using pure mayonnaise as the control, I made three other mixtures in which I substituted buttermilk, sour cream, and yogurt for half of the mayonnaise. Tasters opted for the traditional choice of unadulterated

The Dye Tells the Story

RUSSET | RED BLISS

We soaked cubes of boiled russet and Red Bliss potatoes in vinegar colored with food dye for 20 minutes. The vinegar penetrated deep into the russet but did not make it much past the exterior of the Red Bliss.

mayonnaise. Just ½ cup dressed 2 pounds of potatoes perfectly.

In the crunch department, celery is a must, and one rib fit the bill. Garlic added a likeable sting but was determined inappropriate for the master recipe. Among scallions, shallots, and red, yellow, white, and Vidalia onions, red onion was the winner for its bright color and taste.

I also considered pickles—in my opinion, a mandatory ingredient. My colleagues agreed. Bread and butter, dill, and kosher pickles were in the running with gherkins and sweet pickle relish. Each had its devotees, but I decided on pickle relish, which requires no preparation and gives the potato salad a subtle sweetness.

I was nearing the end of recipe development when I hit upon an unusual finding. My intuition told me to test celery seed, a seasoning that has fallen out of favor. The seed of a type of wild celery known as smallage, celery seed didn't merely add strong celery flavor but also provided an underlying complexity and depth. Potato salad made without celery seed tasted hollow in comparison. Now I won't make potato salad without it.

Next I pitted dry mustard (ground mustard seed) against prepared mustard. The dry mustard added pungency to the salad, while the prepared mustard fell flat. Paprika's only contribution was color, so I nixed it. Salt, pepper, and minced fresh parsley played their usual role of sharpening the other flavors. Hard-cooked eggs created some controversy, considered obligatory by some and a mistake by others—I leave the choice to the cook.

One last note. It may seem obvious, but it makes sense to mix the dressing first, then fold it into the potatoes. Several recipes I had tested instructed the cook to add the dressing ingredients one by one; this led to excess mixing, which turned the potatoes to mush. With careless potato salads a thing of the past, burgers, ribs, and fried chicken, beware—this one may grab all of the attention at the next BBQ.

ALL-AMERICAN POTATO SALAD

SERVES 4 TO 6

Note that this recipe calls for celery seed, not celery salt; if only celery salt is available, use the same amount but omit the addition of salt in the dressing. When testing the potatoes for doneness, simply taste a piece; do not overcook the potatoes or they will become mealy and will break apart. The potatoes must be just warm, or even fully cooled, when you add the dressing. If you find the potato salad a little dry for your liking, add up to 2 tablespoons more mayonnaise.

2   pounds (3 to 4 medium) russet potatoes, peeled and cut into ¾-inch cubes
    Salt
2   tablespoons distilled white vinegar
1   medium celery rib, chopped fine (about ½ cup)
2   tablespoons minced red onion
3   tablespoons sweet pickle relish
½   cup mayonnaise (see note)
¾   teaspoon powdered mustard
¾   teaspoon celery seed
2   tablespoons minced fresh parsley leaves
¼   teaspoon ground black pepper
2   large hard-cooked eggs, peeled and cut into ¼-inch cubes (optional)

1. Place potatoes in large saucepan and add water to cover by 1 inch. Bring to boil over medium-high heat; add 1 tablespoon salt, reduce heat to medium, and simmer, stirring once or twice, until potatoes are tender, about 8 minutes.

2. Drain potatoes and transfer to large bowl. Add vinegar and, using rubber spatula, toss gently to combine. Let stand until potatoes are just warm, about 20 minutes.

3. Meanwhile, in small bowl, stir together celery, onion, pickle relish, mayonnaise, powdered mustard, celery seed, parsley, pepper, and ½ teaspoon salt. Using rubber spatula, gently fold dressing and eggs, if using, into potatoes. Cover with plastic wrap and refrigerate until chilled, about 1 hour; serve. (Potato salad can be covered and refrigerated for up to 1 day.)

Spice Rubs for Grilled Steak

Do you need a dozen pan-toasted ingredients for a top-notch spice rub?

⪴ BY GARTH CLINGINGSMITH ⪤

A grilled steak is simple enough, but sometimes you want to dress it up a bit and—aye—there's the rub. You can look to the supermarket shelf, which displays rubs from celebrity chefs containing a dozen or more ingredients, or you can follow one of those "empty the spice cabinet" recipes that usually require a trip to the market. The question before me was this: Was there such a thing as a simple spice rub recipe for steaks that really does the trick? I set out to find it.

My first step was to round up the usual suspects: 24 spices, herbs, seeds, and chiles that show up most often in spice rubs. I wanted to test each of them to see how heat affected their flavor. Because I wanted to replicate the intense heat of the grill, I toasted the spices over medium-high heat in a small skillet until they had darkened a shade, about two minutes. This seemed fair when you consider that each side of a steak spends about three minutes over the hottest coals.

I settled in with a clipboard, a pencil, a spoon, and a large glass of water. The spices fell into three categories: the delicious, the decent, and the dogs (see box). I learned that savory spices hold up well over heat, while garlic, whether powdered or granulated, turns putrid and bitter. Aside from cinnamon, which becomes more complex, sweeter spices such as nutmeg, cloves, and cardamom lose any pleasant attributes.

Peppers and chiles benefit from high heat, with one glaring exception: paprika. It is one of the most frequently used spices in rubs, yet this finely ground red pepper turns very bitter. Because relatively few spices taste better when heated, I realized that a five-ingredient rub (made with carefully chosen ingredients) is actually preferable to a pantry-emptying rub.

Many proponents of spice rubs profess the benefits of toasting whole versions of all spices and grinding them fresh. To our great surprise, the flavor of steaks rubbed with freshly toasted and ground spices was indistinguishable from that of steaks rubbed with preground, untoasted spices. The intense heat of the grill does the toasting for you and obliterates any subtle differences between freshly ground and preground spices.

The one exception to this finding was black pepper, which is best ground to order. The quick and easy solution is to use an electric coffee grinder devoted to this purpose. Therefore, in any rub recipe calling for black pepper, you can also use whole spices (mustard or coriander seeds, for example) without extra effort. Simply measure all of the ingredients into the hopper and grind.

While these rubs can be thrown together quickly, you can get yourself through the entire grilling season by doubling or tripling the recipes. If kept in an airtight container away from light and heat, these rubs will maintain potency for six months.

While a spice rub is meant to be a quick, last-minute addition, most recipes direct you to rub the steak hours in advance. To test this advice, I rubbed steaks two, six, 12, and 24 hours prior to grilling. Rubs that sat on the steaks for more than two hours actually lost some of their bright kick. Steaks rubbed more than six hours before hitting the coals developed an unpleasant texture. I got the best results by lighting the coals and then rubbing the steaks. Eight- to 12-ounce steaks easily take 2 teaspoons of rub per side, but this is a vague rule of thumb. Simply sprinkle on enough rub to cover the steak, and gently pat it to adhere.

Best Spices for Rubs

To simulate the effects of grilling, common ingredients in spice rubs were toasted separately and tasted. We divided the spices into three categories. **Good:** Intense heat makes these ingredients taste more complex. **Fair:** Extreme heat does not adversely affect these ingredients. **Poor:** High heat renders these spices nearly tasteless, extremely bitter, or medicinal.

GOOD	FAIR	POOR
Allspice	Cocoa	Cardamom
Ancho chile	Coffee	Celery seed
Black pepper	Coriander	Cloves
Chipotle chile	Dill seed	Garlic, powdered
Cinnamon	Fennel	or granulated
Cumin	Star anise	Nutmeg
Mustard seed	Tarragon	Oregano
	Thyme	Paprika
		Rosemary

CHILE-CUMIN SPICE RUB
MAKES ABOUT ¹/₃ CUP

3 dried chipotle chiles, stemmed, seeded, and cut into rough pieces
2 dried ancho chiles, stemmed, seeded, and torn into rough pieces
1 tablespoon ground cumin
1 tablespoon table salt
2 teaspoons sugar

Grind chiles in dedicated spice grinder until powdery. Whisk together ground chiles and remaining ingredients in small bowl until combined.

COCOA-CUMIN-ALLSPICE RUB
MAKES ABOUT ¹/₃ CUP

1 tablespoon unsweetened cocoa
4 teaspoons ground cumin
2 teaspoons ground allspice
4 teaspoons black peppercorns
2 teaspoons table salt

Grind all ingredients in dedicated spice grinder until no whole peppercorns remain.

TARRAGON–MUSTARD SEED RUB
MAKES ABOUT ¹/₃ CUP

3 tablespoons dried tarragon
2 tablespoons yellow mustard seeds
2¼ teaspoons black peppercorns
1 tablespoon table salt

Grind all ingredients in dedicated spice grinder until no whole peppercorns remain.

PEPPERY CORIANDER AND DILL SPICE RUB
MAKES ABOUT ¹/₃ CUP

2 tablespoons black peppercorns
2 tablespoons coriander seeds
1 tablespoon dill seed
1½ teaspoons red pepper flakes
2½ teaspoons table salt

Grind all ingredients in dedicated spice grinder until no whole peppercorns remain.

STAR ANISE AND COFFEE BEAN SPICE RUB
MAKES ABOUT ¹/₃ CUP

6 pods star anise
2 tablespoons whole coffee beans
1 tablespoon black peppercorns
2 teaspoons table salt
1 teaspoon sugar

Grind all ingredients in dedicated spice grinder until no whole peppercorns remain.

Discovering Texas Beef Ribs

A tour of Texas barbecue joints revealed that ribs are about intense meat flavor—not just smoke and spice. But can a backyard cook replicate this Lone Star classic?

∋ BY JULIA COLLIN DAVISON ∈

In Texas, good beef ribs are the secret handshake between experienced grillers. With a price tag of roughly $2 a pound and availability at nearly every butcher counter (they are the scrap bones from trimming rib-eye steaks), beef ribs manage to maintain a cool, cultlike obscurity only because their more popular porky brethren hog all the attention. Cost and anonymity aside, it is their huge meaty flavor—combined with spice, smoke, and fire—that epitomizes beef barbecue for many serious Texans. Wanting in on the beef rib secret, I doubted whether I would be able to figure it out myself in the cold, graffitied alley that runs behind the test kitchen here in Boston.

Reckoning that I'd better get a sense of what authentic Texas beef ribs taste like before I fired up the grill, I spent a hot day driving around Austin and neighboring towns to check out some of the country's best rib joints and roadside stands. Sampling plates of beef ribs throughout the day, I was repeatedly surprised by how much they weren't like what I thought of as barbecued ribs. The meat was not fall-off-the-bone tender but actually required a small toothy tug, and the immense, meaty flavor of the ribs was relatively unadorned by spice rubs and sticky sauces. In fact, if I hadn't been looking for evidence of a spice rub, I might have missed it all together. Served dry with a vinegary dipping sauce on the side, the ribs did not boast a lot of smoke flavor, either; instead, it served as a backdrop for the incredible beefy flavor.

How were these surprisingly flavorful ribs—basically bones lined with juicy steak trimmings—produced? That became my problem. The various barbecue chefs I talked to at each stop simply set dials and pushed buttons on gargantuan, electric smokers outfitted with automated temperature controls. I flew home having learned nothing of value in terms of backyard cooking in a simple kettle-style grill, but at least I knew exactly what I was looking for: potent meat flavor with a bit of honest Texas chew.

Shop, Prep, and Rub
Back in Boston, my first task was to track down beef ribs at my local supermarket. Known to

Texas beef ribs have a distinct taste and texture. They are meaty (rather than spicy) and chewy (rather than fall-off-the-bone tender).

butchers as beef back ribs (not to be confused with beef short ribs), they were in fact widely available; I probably had been reaching over them for years. Because these ribs are often considered scrap bones (especially by Yankee butchers), the real challenge is finding any with a decent amount of meat (see "Where's the Beef?" on page 14), and I learned the hard way that skimpy ribs are simply not worth cooking.

There is a membrane with a fair amount of fat that runs along the backside of the bones, and I tested the effects of removing it, scoring it, and leaving it alone. A number of the recipes I had looked at provided detailed instructions on how to remove the membrane using a screwdriver (no joke), but I found this step to be wholly unnecessary, as it resulted in drier meat. Scoring the membrane with a sharp knife also failed to wow tasters; now the ribs presented relatively dry meat as well as a shaggy appearance. The best results—the juiciest meat with the most flavor—were had by

means of the easiest route: simply leaving the membrane in place. The fat not only bastes the ribs as they cook but also renders to a crisp, baconlike texture, which one old local told me is called candy—and a real Texan never trims away the candy.

Moving on to the rub, I remembered the comments of one Austin cook, who said, "It's not about what you put on beef ribs that makes the difference, it's what you leave off." Using a simple mixture of salt, pepper, cayenne, and chili powder, I found that a mere 2 teaspoons rubbed into each rack were all that it took to bring out the flavor of the meat. I then tested the effects of rubbing the slabs and refrigerating them, both wrapped in plastic and unwrapped, on wire racks for two days, one day, and one hour versus the effects of rubbing a slab and cooking it straight away. Surprisingly, I found that the differences in flavor were not the result of the rub's having infiltrated the meat but rather the result of the aging of the beef. Here in the test kitchen, we have generally found that aged beef roasts take on a pleasant hearty flavor. In this case, however, the aged ribs were a bust. They tasted sour and smelled tallowy. I did make one useful discovery, though: Ribs left at room temperature for an hour cooked through more evenly.

Smoking in the Alley
The next question was how to turn my kettle grill into a backyard smoker. The first step was choosing the correct fuel. Hardwood charcoal was out; briquettes burn cooler and longer, making them perfect for barbecue. I had already discovered that cooking the ribs directly over the briquettes didn't work—the ribs burned long before they had cooked through and turned tender. I needed indirect heat, and there were two ways to get it. I could bank all of the coals on one side of the grill, or I could create two piles on opposite sides. A single pile on one side of the grill proved best, providing a slow, even fire that was easy to stoke with fresh coals and left more room for the ribs.

In Texas, barbecue fanatics can be particular about the kind of wood they use to create smoke, so I tested the three most popular varieties: hickory, mesquite, and green oak. The green oak had

Barbecue experts have plenty of theories as to exactly what goes on inside a covered grill, but agreement is hard to come by. In search of wisdom rather than witchcraft, I wanted to see if I could scientifically determine the best way to lay a fire. What, once and for all, really is the best way to arrange the coals to secure evenly, thoroughly, deeply barbecued meat?

To answer this question, I outfitted a Weber kettle grill with five temperature probes, four around the edges of the grill and one in the center (at bottom of photo). Through holes drilled in the lid, I attached these probes—or thermocouples—to a computer data recorder (at top of photo) that would measure the temperature inside the grill every minute for up to two hours. After running more than a dozen tests over a six-week period, I arrived at some answers.

Because barbecue is by definition slow cooking over low heat, the high temperatures produced by so-called direct heat (cooking directly over a pile of coals) are unacceptable. What's wanted is indirect heat, and, in a kettle grill, you can produce indirect heat in one of two ways: by banking two piles of coals on opposite sides of the grill or by banking one pile on one side.

My computer data showed that splitting the coals between two sides produced worrisome temperature spikes. This was unacceptable if the goal was to maintain a near-constant temperature. Moreover, the temperature at different sites in the grill showed significant variation.

If anything, I expected the variation in heat distribution with the single-banked coals to be even worse. With the exception of the probe placed directly over the fire, however, the probes in this case produced temperature readings that were within a few degrees of each other. This was surprising considering that one probe was about

We drilled holes in our kettle grill so we could snake thermocouples from a computer data recorder to the fire.

twice the distance from the fire as the other three. This was also good news, as it meant that a large part of the cooking area was being held at a pretty constant temperature. The single-banked method also showed almost no heat spikes and held the temperature between the ideal (for barbecue) 250 and 300 degrees for the longest period of time.

The results of these tests, then, seemed clear: It's best to have a single pile of coals rather than two piles, because one source of heat produced steady, evenly distributed heat, while two sources produced greater temperature variation.

But this wasn't the only thing I learned. Barbecue experts often recommend placing the lid vent (or vents) away from the fire, so this is what we'd been doing during testing. Was it really part of the reason why the pile of banked coals was providing even, steady heat? Sure enough, when I placed the open vent directly over the fire, the fire burned hotter and faster. With the vent in this position, a direct convection current was formed inside the egg-shaped Weber kettle. When the vent was placed away from the fire, a more diffuse convection current ensured a more even distribution of heat. Also important was the degree to which I opened the lid vent. When the vent was opened up completely, the fire burned much hotter, and the heat was less even throughout the grill. The vent is best kept partially cracked. (Close the vent completely, of course, and you risk snuffing out the fire.)

The final, and most important, thing I learned was also probably the most obvious: When you open the lid to check on the progress of your barbecue, you lose all of the even heat distribution that you have worked so hard to establish. Above all, resist the temptation to peek. —John Olson, Science Editor

---

a clean, gentle smoke that was mild and pleasant, but this wood was hard to find. Dried hickory chunks offered a similar flavor profile and were easy to locate at a hardware store. Mesquite, on the other hand, had a fake, pungent flavor that tasters universally hated. I then wondered if chips (rather than chunks) wrapped in a foil packet were as good. No, they reduced the heat of the charcoal (the aluminum foil acted as a shield), whereas the chunks extended its burning power, acting as a fuel source.

Not wanting the meat to taste too smoky, I then tested the difference among using one, two, and three medium-size (about 2 ounces each) chunks (all soaked in water, as dry chunks burn rather than smoke). One chunk was too little, three was too many, but two was just right. I tried

adding both chunks to the fire right at the beginning versus adding just one and letting it burn out before adding the second. Tasters favored the ribs smoked steadily during the entire cooking time, which is how an electric smoker works. These ribs had a more complex flavor than those that were bombarded with lots of smoke at the beginning.

The Secret Handshake

Inspired by the temperature-controlled smokers I saw in Texas, I decided to use an indoor oven to test various cooking temperatures. I would then apply what I'd learned back outside on the grill. I tested more than 15 combinations of time and temperature until I got it right. The first thing I learned was that the cooking temperature should never exceed 300 degrees. Higher temperatures

render too much fat and turn the meat dry and stringy. Yet the temperature should not dip below 250 degrees. Then the fat won't render, the meat stays tough, and the ribs never achieve that signature roasted beefy flavor. The ideal temperature, then, was a range of 250 to 300 degrees, and the ideal time was about 2½ hours, which causes some, but not all, of the fat to render and makes the ribs juicy, tender, and slightly toothy. When cooked any longer, as is the case with pork ribs, the meat disintegrates into messy shreds, taking on a sticky, pot-roasted sort of texture that any real Texan would immediately reject.

Now I was ready to go back to the grill and add the finishing touches. The first problem was maintaining a constant temperature. The solution was to count out exactly 30 briquettes (and one wood chunk) to start, which brought the grill

Where's the Beef?

Be careful when shopping for beef ribs—some ribs will yield poor results when barbecued. We prefer partial slabs (with three or four bones) that are very meaty.

TOO SKIMPY
The butcher trimmed too much meat from this slab; you can see the bones.

TOO SMALL
"Shorties" are cut in half and don't offer much meat.

TOO BIG
A whole slab (with seven ribs) is hard to maneuver on the grill.

JUST RIGHT
This partial slab has a thick layer of meat that covers the bones.

up to 300 degrees. Over the next hour, the grill cooled to 250 degrees, and it became necessary to add another 20 briquettes along with the second wood chunk. I also found that the top vents should be open two-thirds of the way and positioned at the side of the grill opposite from the wood chunk, so that the smoke is drawn across the grill, not straight up and out.

So, yes, you can make authentic Texas ribs at home, with big beef flavor, great chew, and just a hint of smoke and spice. The secret handshake? Confidence. Let the wood and smoke do their work without constant peeking and checking. Don't mess with Texas ribs.

TEXAS-STYLE BARBECUED BEEF RIBS
SERVES 4

It is important to use beef ribs with a decent amount of meat, not bony scraps; otherwise, the rewards of making this recipe are few. For more information about what to look for when buying ribs, see the photos on page 14. Because the ribs cook slowly and for an extended period of time, charcoal briquettes, not hardwood charcoal (which burns hot and fast), make a better fuel. That said, do not use Match Light charcoal, which contains lighter fluid for easy ignition. For the wood chunks, use any type of wood but mesquite, which can have an overpowering smokiness. It's a good idea to monitor the grill heat; if you don't own a reliable grill thermometer, insert an instant-read thermometer into the lid vent to spot-check the temperature. Except when adding coals, do not lift the grill lid, which will allow both smoke and heat to escape. When barbecuing, we prefer to use a Weber 22-inch kettle grill.

4	teaspoons chili powder
½	teaspoon cayenne
2	teaspoons salt
1½	teaspoons ground black pepper
3–4	beef rib slabs (3 to 4 ribs per slab, about 5 pounds total)
1	recipe Barbecue Sauce for Texas-Style Beef Ribs (recipe at right)

1. Mix chili powder, cayenne, salt, and pepper in small bowl; rub ribs evenly with spice mixture. Let ribs stand at room temperature for 1 hour.

2. Meanwhile, cover 2 large wood chunks (see note) with water and soak 1 hour. Drain wood chunks. Open bottom grill vents. Using chimney starter, ignite 30 briquettes (about one-third large chimney, or 2 quarts) and burn until covered with thin coating of light gray ash, about 10 minutes. Empty coals into grill, then bank coals against one side of grill, stacking them 2 to 3 coals high; place 1 soaked wood chunk on top of coals. Position grill grate over coals, cover grill, and adjust lid vents two-thirds open. Heat grate until hot, about 5 minutes; scrape grill grate clean with grill brush. Position ribs, meat-side down, on cool side of grill (they may overlap slightly); cover, positioning lid so that vents are directly above ribs. (Temperature on thermometer inserted through vents should register about 300 degrees.) Cook until grill temperature drops to about 250 degrees, about 1 hour. (On cold, windy days, temperature may drop more quickly, so spot-check temperature. If necessary, add 5 additional briquettes to maintain temperature above 250 degrees during first hour of cooking.)

3. After 1 hour, add 20 more briquettes and remaining wood chunk to coals; using tongs, flip ribs meat-side up and rotate so that edges once closest to coals are now farthest away. Cover grill, positioning lid so that vents are opposite wood chunk; continue to cook until dinner fork can be inserted into and removed from meat with little resistance, meat pulls away from bones when rack is gently twisted, and meat shrinks ½ to 1 inch up rib bones, 1¼ to 1¾ hours longer. Transfer ribs to cutting board and let rest 5 minutes; using chef's knife, slice between bones to separate into individual ribs. Serve, passing sauce separately.

TEXAS-STYLE BARBECUED BEEF RIBS
ON A GAS GRILL

On a gas grill, leaving one burner on and turning the other(s) off simulates the indirect heat method on a charcoal grill. Use wood chips instead of wood chunks and a disposable aluminum pan to hold them. On a gas grill, it is important to monitor the temperature closely; use an oven thermometer set on the grate next to the ribs and check the temperature every 15 minutes. Try to maintain a 250- to 300-degree grill temperature by adjusting the setting of the lit burner.

1. Follow recipe for Texas-Style Barbecued Beef Ribs through step 1.

2. Cover 3 cups wood chips with water; soak 30 minutes, then drain. Place wood chips in small disposable aluminum pan; set pan on gas grill burner that will remain on. Turn all burners to high, close lid, and heat grill until chips smoke heavily, about 20 minutes (if chips ignite, extinguish flames with water-filled squirt bottle). Scrape grill grate clean with grill brush; turn off burner(s) without wood chips. Position oven thermometer and ribs, meat-side down, on cool side of grill. Cover and cook 1¼ hours, checking grill temperature every 15 minutes and adjusting lit burner as needed to maintain temperature of 250 to 300 degrees.

3. Using tongs, flip ribs meat-side up and rotate so that edges once closest to lit burner are now farthest away. Cover and continue to cook and check/adjust grill temperature until dinner fork can be inserted into and removed from meat with little resistance, meat pulls away from bones when rack is gently twisted, and meat shrinks ½

to 1 inch up rib bones, 1 to 1½ hours longer. Transfer ribs to cutting board and let rest 5 minutes; using chef's knife, slice between bones to separate into individual ribs. Serve, passing sauce separately.

Grilling 101

A little know-how and some practice are all that's required to meet the challenges of grilling. BY REBECCA HAYS

The problem with (and the fun of) grilling is that it is unpredictable: flare-ups, a gust of wind, and a fire that is too cool or too hot are just a few of the occurrences that call for adjustments from the outdoor cook. To improve your chances of success, keep the following tips and techniques handy the next time you fire up the grill.

GRILLING EQUIPMENT

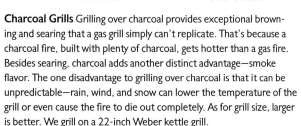

CHARCOAL GRILL   GAS GRILL

Charcoal Grills Grilling over charcoal provides exceptional browning and searing that a gas grill simply can't replicate. That's because a charcoal fire, built with plenty of charcoal, gets hotter than a gas fire. Besides searing, charcoal adds another distinct advantage—smoke flavor. The one disadvantage to grilling over charcoal is that it can be unpredictable—rain, wind, and snow can lower the temperature of the grill or even cause the fire to die out completely. As for grill size, larger is better. We grill on a 22-inch Weber kettle grill.

Gas Grills In terms of convenience and dependability, a gas grill can't be beat. A gas grill is consistent, delivering the same results day in and day out. Gas grills are roughly three times more expensive than charcoal grills, so it pays to shop carefully. Make sure to buy a gas grill with at least two burners to facilitate cooking over indirect heat. In past *Cook's* tests, gas grills made by Weber have come out on top.

Chimney Starter Look for a large chimney starter capable of holding 6 quarts of charcoal. Fill the bottom of the starter with crumpled newspaper, set the starter on the bottom rack of a kettle grill, fill the main compartment with as much charcoal as directed in a given recipe, and light the newspaper. When the coals are well lit and covered with a layer of gray ash, dump them onto the rack, using long-handled tongs to move the briquettes into place, if necessary.

GRILLING TECHNIQUES

Grilling: Quickly cooking relatively thin cuts of food (steaks, chops, fish, and chicken parts) directly over a hot or medium-hot fire (around 500 degrees Fahrenheit, and in some cases even hotter). Charcoal grilling is always done with the lid off. When cooking with gas, the lid must be kept down to contain the heat.

Grill-Roasting: An alternative to oven-roasting that involves indirect cooking over moderate heat (300 to 400 degrees) with the lid on. Whole chickens and turkeys and tender cuts such as beef tenderloin and pork loin are grill-roasted.

Barbecuing: Slowly smoking tough, thick cuts (ribs, brisket, or pork shoulder rubbed with dry spices) over a low fire (250 to 300 degrees). This method tenderizes the meat and adds authentic smoky barbecue flavor.

Charcoal To test the assertion that charcoal type influences flavor, we grilled steaks and zucchini over three fires built with the following: hardwood charcoal, regular charcoal briquettes, and Match Light, a Kingsford product infused with lighter fluid to guarantee rapid ignition. The flavor differences in the steaks were nearly imperceptible, but the delicate zucchini was a different story, with the zucchini grilled over Match Light tasting oddly bitter. In separate tests with delicate foods—chicken, fish, and vegetables—grilled over fires started with lighter fluid, tasters also detected harsh, acrid flavors. Consequently, we like to steer clear of both Match Light and lighter fluid. Hardwood charcoal is the best choice for grilling because it burns hot and fast, while slower burning briquettes are optimal for grill-roasting and barbecuing.

THREE TYPES OF FIRES

Single-Level Fire
Delivers direct, moderate heat. Used with fairly thin foods that cook quickly.
USE FOR: Fruits, vegetables, fish and shellfish, hamburgers, and kebabs.
TO BUILD: Arrange lit charcoal evenly in the grill.
GAS-GRILL EQUIVALENT: Adjust all burners to high for a very hot fire, or turn the burners to medium after preheating.

Two-Level Fire
Allows the cook to sear foods over a very hot section of the grill and to finish the cooking over a medium-hot section so that the exterior doesn't char.
USE FOR: Chops (pork, lamb, and veal), steaks, turkey burgers, bone-in chicken legs and thighs, and thick fish steaks (mahi-mahi and swordfish).
TO BUILD: Arrange some lit coals in a single layer on half of the grill. Leave the remaining coals in a pile.
GAS-GRILL EQUIVALENT: Leave one burner on high or medium-high and turn the other(s) to medium or medium-low.

Modified Two-Level Fire
Ideal for foods that are susceptible to burning but require a long cooking time. Can also be used to create an especially hot fire when grilling small, thin cuts of meat.
USE FOR: Bone-in chicken breasts, boneless chicken breasts and thighs, sausages, flank steak, pork tenderloin, rack of lamb, and butterflied leg of lamb.
TO BUILD: Pile all of the lit coals onto one side of the grill, leaving the other side empty. We often cover foods on the cool part of the grill with a disposable aluminum pan to trap the heat and create an ovenlike cooking environment.
GAS-GRILL EQUIVALENT: Leave one burner on high and turn the other burner(s) to medium-low.

ILLUSTRATION · JOHN BURGOYNE

COMMON GRILLING PROBLEMS AND HOW TO SOLVE THEM

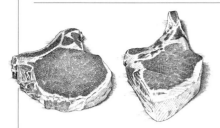

PROBLEM: Grilled foods are dry.
Charcoal smoke adds great flavor, but it also tends to dehydrate food.
SOLUTION: Generally speaking, thicker foods are easier to grill than thinner ones, so shop for moderately thick chops, fish fillets, and steaks. It's often beneficial to brine foods (especially lean poultry, pork, and shrimp) that will be cooked over charcoal.

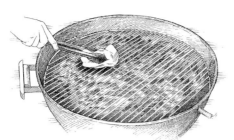

PROBLEM: Burgers and fish stick to the grill.
SOLUTION: It is essential to heat the grill and then scrape it clean with a grill brush before each use. Grilling on a grill grate clogged with burnt, stuck-on food from last night's dinner is akin to cooking in a dirty pan. In addition, we recommend oiling the grill grate to keep foods from sticking. We've found that the easiest method is to dip a wad of paper towels in vegetable oil, grasp the oiled towels with tongs, and rub the oil over the hot cooking grate.

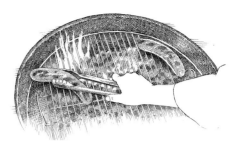

PROBLEM: The food chars before it cooks through.
SOLUTION: Build a fire that has hot and cool spots so that you can sear food over the hotter area and then cook it through without scorching on the cooler area. Flare-ups are common when grilling high-fat foods like sausages and skin-on chicken. At the first sign of flames, move foods to a cooler part of the grill. Also, don't apply barbecue or other sticky sauces until the last minutes of cooking (or pass sauces at the table).

How to Judge the Temperature of a Fire

You can get a good idea of just how hot a fire is by holding your hand 5 inches above the grill grate and counting the number of seconds you can comfortably leave it there.

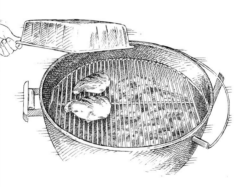

INTENSITY OF FIRE	TIME	USE FOR
Hot	**2 seconds**	Flank steak, shrimp, scallops
Medium-hot	**3–4 seconds**	Steaks, burgers, chops, fish, vegetables, fruit
Medium	**5–6 seconds**	Grill-roasting
Medium-low	**7 seconds**	Barbecuing

PROBLEM: Charcoal-grilled food has an off, stale smoke flavor.
SOLUTION: Don't use the grill cover every time you grill. It may have a buildup of soot and resinous compounds that can impart unwelcome flavors. When grilling steaks, chops, or chicken parts, for instance, build a fire that's big enough to cook the food through quickly, covering food with a diposable aluminum pan if you need to trap heat to cook food through. When you want to barbecue or grill-roast for a prolonged period of time, the lid must be used. (The smoky flavor from wood chips or chunks generally masks any off flavor that the lid may impart.)

PROBLEM: It's difficult to monitor the temperature when grill-roasting and barbecuing.
SOLUTION: A grill thermometer can be inserted through the lid vents of a charcoal grill. To measure the temperature of the spot where the food is being cooked, rotate the lid so that the thermometer is close to the food and away from the fire. Do not let the thermometer stem touch the food.

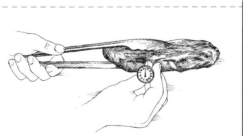

PROBLEM: It's difficult to gauge doneness.
SOLUTION: Grilling is an inexact cooking technique, and it is sometimes necessary to adjust timing to account for cool or windy conditions. Taking the temperature of food with an instant-read thermometer is the best way to tell if it's done. Pick up a steak or chop with a pair of tongs and insert the tip of a thermometer through the side of the meat until most of the shaft is embedded in the meat and not touching any bone. Because most grills have hot spots, you can't assume that every burger, steak, or piece of chicken will be done at the same time—check each one.

When Is It Done?

The temperatures in this chart reflect our opinion with regard to palatability. Meat should come off the grill when it is 5 to 10 degrees shy of the desired final internal temperature listed below, as the temperature will continue to rise for several minutes (see page 3 for more information). Note that the U.S. Department of Agriculture recommends cooking ground meat to 160 degrees; roasts, steaks, and chops to 145 degrees; and poultry to 180 degrees to eliminate potential food-borne pathogens.

	RARE	MEDIUM-RARE	MEDIUM	WELL-DONE
Red Meat (BEEF, LAMB, VEAL)	125°	130°	140°	160°
Pork	*	*	145°	160°
Chicken (WHITE MEAT)	*	*	*	160°
Chicken (DARK MEAT)	*	*	*	165°

Fish (Check for doneness by nicking the flesh with a paring knife; most fish should be opaque at the center. Tuna and salmon can be cooked until just translucent at the center.)

*Not recommended

Grilled Glazed Salmon

A burnt, stuck-to-the-grill crust and flavorless interior are the reality of glazed salmon.
With 50 pounds of salmon and gallons of briquettes, we set out to solve both problems.

≥ BY BRIDGET LANCASTER ≤

I was always confident in my ability to produce great grilled salmon. With its firm, meaty texture and rich, buttery interior, the salmon on my grill had at least a chance of coming off that hot grate moist and in one piece. Then one day I tried my hand at grilled glazed salmon and watched as my dinner (as well as my bravado) went up in smoke. *Sticky* was the operative word here as the glazed salmon gripped the grill grate for dear life and could only be torn off in many tiny pieces. Not that it was actually worth getting off the grill, mind you, because each of those tiny pieces was charred beyond recognition. When it comes to grilled glazed salmon, you can call me chicken.

So why glaze (and inevitably ruin) an otherwise perfect piece of fish? Well, because truly great glazed salmon off the grill is a thing of beauty, both inside and out. As if working double duty, the sweet glaze not only forms a glossy, deeply caramelized crust, but it also permeates the flesh, making the last bite of fish every bit as good as the first. This was the salmon that I wanted to re-create—sweet, crisp, moist, and oh-so-flavorful—and I was willing to ruin a few more fish to get there.

I knew I needed all the help I could get, and I went straight to cookbooks in hopes of direction. The first choice was easy. When confronted with fillets, steaks, and whole sides, I was going with the fillets for ease of grilling (ever try flipping a whole side?) and ease of eating (who wants to eat around all those salmon steak bones, anyway?). The next choice was glazing method, and here things were less clear. I could try using a marinade to flavor the fish. I could try brushing the fish with a thick glaze before throwing it on the grill. Finally, I could simply grill the fish plain and apply the glaze afterward. I fired up the grill and got to work.

Flavor Inside, Crust Outside

After testing, there was no doubt that marinating gave the salmon flavor. Soy sauce was chosen for its ability to season the fish through and through, while vinegar (another standard marinade ingredient) was omitted, as it broke down the salmon until it was too fragile to hold its shape on the grill. In my perfect world, the marinade would also work as

A glaze made with just soy sauce and maple syrup adds a thick, flavorful crust to grilled salmon.

a glaze of sorts, with the sugars caramelizing once they hit the hot grill. In fact, tests demonstrated that the marinated salmon failed to produce any kind of crust. Increasing the amount of sugar only served to make the salmon too sweet. Taking a cue from some brush-on glaze recipes, I tested more viscous sweeteners, such as maple syrup, honey, and molasses. While the molasses was rejected for its bitter flavor, the maple syrup and honey worked like a dream. With a thicker marinade, the sweet flavors clung to the salmon rather than dripping through the bars of the grate, and a crust (however thin) was beginning to form.

Using a marinade alone wasn't going to produce the thick crust I wanted, however. The next step was to brush the marinated salmon with a much thicker glaze—a winning combination of soy sauce and maple syrup—very similar to the marinade. Yep, here was a crust—a burnt, stuck-to-the-grill crust—not what I was after. Instead, I basted the salmon with this glaze a few moments after it hit the hot grill. Better. Not as charred, not as sticky, but still not acceptable. Not sure where else to turn at this point, I thought it might be time to examine the fire.

Catch and Release

Few things are more frustrating than trying to pull the daily catch off the grill in one piece. But there's no shortage of equipment, gadgets, or plain old advice intended to help you get around this problem. After testing them all, using both sturdy salmon fillets and more fragile flounder, we found that the best method requires equipment that you probably own already. Methods are listed in order of effectiveness.

TOOL: OILED WAD OF PAPER TOWELS
METHOD: Using long-handled tongs, dip towels in vegetable oil and brush over heated grill grate.
RESULTS: Most failsafe way to keep fish from sticking to grill.

TOOL: COOKING SPRAY
METHOD: Spray cold grate before heating.
RESULTS: Worked well, although part of one fillet needed some prodding.

TOOL: OIL ON THE FISH
METHOD: Oil fish before placing on hot grill.
RESULTS: Mixed reviews. Although fish released well, flare-ups were a problem.

TOOL: LEMON SLICES
METHOD: Place lemon on grate, then place fish on top.
RESULTS: Mixed reviews. Although fish did not stick to grill, lemon slices kept fish from developing exterior color. Worked well for fragile fish, though, when browning is not important.

TOOL: STAINLESS STEEL SCREEN MATERIAL
METHOD: Place mesh on grate, then place fish on top.
RESULTS: Not bad. Worked well when sprayed with vegetable oil spray. Fish must be rapidly removed from screen after being grilled, as it will begin to stick.

TOOL: FISH BASKET
METHOD: Place fish in oiled fish basket.
RESULTS: Not recommended. Salmon stuck to basket. Doesn't work with glazing because one can't get at caged salmon to brush it.

TOOL: GRILL GRATE
METHOD: Tested enameled steel, cast-iron, and stainless steel grates.
RESULTS: When it comes to types of grill grates, fish is nondiscriminatory. It will stick to any surface. Best to use the oiled grate method with any of these grill grate materials. —B.L.

The Salmon Three-Step

Up to this point, I had been cooking the salmon in a pretty traditional way. I was searing the fish skin-side down, then skin-side up over a hot fire; the superhot grill grate helped to keep the fish from sticking. The problem now was that the hot fire was causing my sweet glazed salmon to burn.

After trying more temperate medium and low fires (both of which failed), I tried a two-level fire. Piling the hot briquettes one-high on one side and two-high on the other, I seared the marinated salmon over the high heat. I then brushed the salmon with some of the glaze and pulled it to the cooler side of the grill to cook through. This was a big improvement, with a decent crust.

But I was still having a problem. When started skin-side down, the fillet buckled, causing the other side to cook unevenly. The solution was to start the salmon skin-side up, flip it to sear the skin side, brush on some glaze, and then flip it again to finish cooking on the cool side of the grill. The downside of this approach was that the grill had to be well oiled to prevent sticking, a step that is not optional. The good news was that I had an incredible crust, built in two layers, that was both sweet and substantial. All that was left to do was to brush the grilled salmon with more glaze before serving. Gilding the lily, perhaps, but with a high-gloss shine and potent flavor within, this fish never looked (or tasted) so good.

GRILLED GLAZED SALMON
SERVES 4

Scraping the grill grate clean will help prevent the salmon from sticking. Also, be sure to oil the grate just before placing the fillets on the grill.

1	recipe glaze (recipes follow)
1/3	cup soy sauce
1/3	cup maple syrup
4	salmon fillets (about 8 ounces each), each about 1 1/2 inches at thickest part
	Ground black pepper
	Vegetable oil for grill grate
	Lemon wedges for serving

1. Measure 2 tablespoons glaze into small bowl and set aside.
2. Whisk soy sauce and maple syrup in 13 by 9-inch baking dish until combined; carefully place fillets flesh-side down in single layer in marinade (do not coat salmon skin with marinade). Refrigerate while preparing grill.
3. Using chimney starter, ignite about 6 quarts (1 large chimney, or 2 1/2 pounds) charcoal briquettes and burn until covered with layer of light gray ash, about 15 minutes. Empty coals into grill; build two-level fire by stacking two-thirds of coals in one half of grill and arranging remaining coals in single layer in other half. Position grill grate over coals, cover grill, and heat until grate is hot, about 5 minutes; scrape grill grate clean with grill brush.
4. Remove salmon from marinade and sprinkle flesh liberally with pepper. Using long-handled grill tongs, dip wad of paper towels in vegetable oil and wipe hot side of grill grate. Place fillets flesh-side down on hot side of grill and cook until grill-marked, about 1 minute. Using tongs, flip fillets skin-side down, still on hot side of grill; brush flesh with glaze and cook until salmon is opaque about halfway up thickness of fillets, 3 to 4 minutes.
5. Again using long-handled grill tongs, dip wad of paper towels in vegetable oil and wipe cooler side of grill grate. Brush flesh again with glaze, then turn fillets flesh-side down onto cooler side of grill; cook until deeply browned, crust has formed, and center of thickest part of fillet is still translucent when cut into with paring knife, about 1 1/2 minutes. Transfer fillets to platter, brush with reserved 2 tablespoons glaze, and serve immediately with lemon wedges.

GRILLED GLAZED SALMON ON A GAS GRILL

1. Follow recipe for Grilled Glazed Salmon through step 2.
2. Turn all burners on gas grill to high; cover and heat until very hot, about 15 minutes. Scrape grill grate clean with grill brush. Turn all but 1 burner to medium-low. Remove salmon from marinade and sprinkle flesh liberally with pepper. Using long-handled grill tongs, dip wad of paper towels in vegetable oil and wipe hot side of grill grate. Place fillets flesh-side down on hot side of grill and cook until grill-marked, 1 to 2 minutes. Using tongs, flip fillets skin-side down, still on hot side of grill; brush flesh with glaze, cover grill, and cook until salmon is opaque about halfway up thickness of fillets, 3 to 4 minutes.
3. Again using long-handled grill tongs, dip wad of paper towels in vegetable oil and wipe cooler side of grill grate. Brush flesh again with glaze, then turn fillets flesh-side down onto cooler side of grill; cook until deeply browned, crust has formed, and center of thickest part of fillet is still translucent when cut into with paring knife, about 2 minutes. Transfer fillets to platter, brush with reserved 2 tablespoons glaze, and serve immediately with lemon wedges.

MAPLE-SOY GLAZE

Stir together 2 tablespoons soy sauce and 1/4 cup maple syrup in small saucepan; bring to simmer over medium-high heat and cook until slightly thickened, 3 to 4 minutes.

HONEY-MUSTARD GLAZE

Stir together 2 tablespoons soy sauce and 1/4 cup honey in small saucepan; bring to simmer over medium-high heat and cook until slightly thickened, 3 to 4 minutes. Off heat, whisk in 3 tablespoons Dijon mustard.

MAPLE-CHIPOTLE GLAZE

Offer lime wedges instead of lemon when serving.

Stir together 2 tablespoons soy sauce, 1/4 cup maple syrup, and 1 teaspoon minced chipotle chile in adobo in small saucepan; bring to simmer over medium-high heat and cook until slightly thickened, 3 to 4 minutes. Off heat, whisk in 2 tablespoons lime juice.

RECIPE SHORTHAND: GRILLING GLAZED SALMON

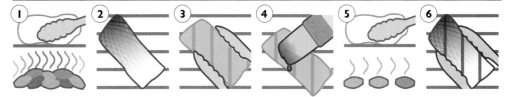

1. Rub oiled paper towels over hot side of grill. **2.** Place salmon flesh-side down at 45-degree angle to grill grate. **3.** With tongs, carefully flip salmon skin-side down. **4.** Brush flesh side of salmon with glaze. **5.** Rub oiled paper towels over grate on cooler side of grill. **6.** Carefully flip salmon flesh-side down onto cooler side of grill.

RECIPE TESTING: The Soft, the Sticky, and the Good

Here's how we solved two common problems that came up during recipe testing.

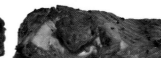  

TOO SOFT
Salmon that was marinated for more than 30 minutes became mushy and fell apart on the grill.

TOO STICKY
When we skipped the step of oiling the grill grate, the salmon stuck terribly.

JUST RIGHT
With a short marinating time and a thorough oiling of the grill, our salmon came off the fire intact.

All-Season Fresh Tomato Salsa

Could we develop a recipe that would work with any tomato—even a bland supermarket specimen?

⊱ BY NINA WEST ⊰

Backyard, farm-stand, and supermarket summertime tomatoes alike should be sweet, juicy, and ready for top billing in a fresh tomato salsa. But even in the midst of tomato season, some can be less than stellar. Complicating matters, salsa's popularity has opened the door to versions employing extravagant (smoked paprika) and extraneous (canned tomato juice) ingredients, relegating fresh tomatoes to a minor role. One such recipe had me fishing around—literally—in water for miniscule pieces of tomato, while another used four different chiles but only one measly tomato. I wanted a fresh, chunky Mexican-style salsa, or *salsa cruda*, that would emphasize the tomatoes; the other traditional flavors—lime, garlic, onion, chile, and cilantro—would have supporting roles. I also wanted to get the texture just right for scooping up and balancing on a tortilla chip.

Simply combining salsa ingredients in one bowl for mixing and serving turned out to be a bad idea. The tomatoes exuded so much juice that the other ingredients were submerged in liquid within minutes. The first step, then, was to solve the problem of watery salsa. Peeling and seeding tomatoes are often employed to remove excess moisture. Peeling, however, removed the structure that kept the diced pieces intact, resulting in a salsa that was too mushy. Seeding diminished the tomatoes' flavor, and tasters did not mind the presence of seeds. So much for peeling and seeding.

I recalled that here in the test kitchen we often salt tomatoes to concentrate flavor and exude liquid. This technique was promising, but because much more surface area was exposed when the tomatoes were diced, the salt penetrated too deeply and broke them down too much. I was left with mealy, mushy tomatoes, and the salsa was just as watery as before. Dicing the tomatoes larger to expose less surface area was out of the question; the tomato pieces would be too large to balance on a tortilla chip. Taking round slices of tomatoes, salting them, and then dicing them after they had drained was just too much work.

Frustrated, I diced a few tomatoes whole (skin, seeds, and all), threw them into a colander, and walked away. Thirty minutes later, to my surprise, a few tablespoons of liquid had drained out; after a few shakes of the colander, the tomatoes were chunky and relatively dry. I found that in fewer than 30 minutes, not enough liquid drained out, whereas more time didn't produce enough additional juice to justify the wait. Overall, I found that really ripe tomatoes exude more juice than less ripe supermarket tomatoes. This simple technique, with minimal tomato prep, had accomplished a major feat: It put all tomatoes, regardless of origin, ripeness, or juiciness, on a level—and dry—playing field.

With the main technique established, I fixed the spotlight on the supporting ingredients. Red onions were preferred over white, yellow, and sweet onions for color and flavor. Jalapeño chiles were chosen over serrano, habanero, and poblano chiles because of their wide availability, slight vegetal flavor, and moderate heat. Lime juice tasted more authentic (and better) than red wine vinegar, rice vinegar, or lemon juice. Olive oil, while included at the beginning of the recipe testing process, was rejected later on when tasters found it dulled the other flavors.

I also investigated the best way to combine the ingredients and rejected all but the simplest technique. Marinating the tomatoes, onion, garlic, and chile in lime juice resulted in dull, washed-out flavors and involved extra bowls and work. I tried letting the drained tomatoes, onion, chile, garlic, and cilantro sit for a bit before adding the lime juice, sugar, and salt. Now the flavors of the chile and onion stole the show. It was much more efficient to chop the chile, onion, garlic, and cilantro and layer each ingredient on top of the tomatoes while they drained in the colander. Once the tomatoes were finished draining, the chile, onion, garlic, cilantro, and tomatoes needed just a few stirs before being immediately finished with the lime juice, sugar, and salt, and then served.

FRESH TOMATO SALSA
MAKES ABOUT 3 CUPS

Heat varies from jalapeño to jalapeño, and because much of the heat resides in the seeds, we suggest mincing the seeds separately from the flesh, then adding minced seeds to taste. The amount of sugar and lime juice to use depends on the ripeness of the tomatoes. The salsa can be made 2 to 3 hours in advance, but hold off adding the salt, lime juice, and sugar until just before serving. The salsa is perfect for tortilla chips, but it's also a nice accompaniment to grilled steaks, chicken, and fish.

1 1/2   pounds firm, ripe tomatoes, cut into
        3/8-inch dice (about 3 cups)
1   large jalapeño chile, seeded (seeds reserved
        and minced; see note), flesh minced
        (about 2 tablespoons)
1/2   cup minced red onion
1   small garlic clove, minced (about 1/2 teaspoon)
1/4   cup chopped fresh cilantro leaves
1/2   teaspoon salt
        Pinch ground black pepper
2–6   teaspoons juice from 1 to 2 limes
        Sugar to taste (up to 1 teaspoon)

1. Set large colander in large bowl. Place tomatoes in colander and let drain 30 minutes. As tomatoes drain, layer jalapeño, onion, garlic, and cilantro on top. Shake colander to drain off excess tomato juice. Discard juice; wipe out bowl.

2. Transfer contents of colander to now-empty bowl. Add salt, pepper, and 2 teaspoons lime juice; toss to combine. Taste and add minced jalapeño seeds, sugar, and additional lime juice to taste.

> **COOK'S EXTRA** gives you free information online. For the results of our tasting of tortilla chips, visit www.cooksillustrated.com and key in code 4046. This information will be available until August 15, 2004.

STEP-BY-STEP | CUTTING TOMATOES FOR SALSA

1. Cut each cored tomato in half through the equator.

2. Cut each half into 3/8-inch-thick slices.

3. Stack two slices, cut them into 3/8 inch strips, then into 3/8-inch dice.

Freeform Fruit Tart

Few things are better than a summer fruit pie, but that takes time and skill. We wanted an easy recipe with a short list of ingredients that would produce an extra-flaky crust.

⇒ BY ERIKA BRUCE ⇐

Whoever coined the expression "easy as pie" probably never made one. Every summer I find myself in a quandary: Should I put myself through the ordeal of making a double-crust pie, or should I take the easy way out and whip up a cobbler or crisp instead, thus avoiding the need to roll out the dough, to transfer it (in one, untorn piece) from countertop to pie plate, and to press and crimp it in place? So a cobbler or crisp it usually is—but nothing can take the place of a buttery, flaky crust paired with juicy summer fruit. What I needed was a lazy recipe, one that produced both crust and fruit with half the work.

A freeform tart—a single layer of buttery pie dough folded up around fresh fruit—seemed the obvious solution. But I quickly discovered that this method was not troublefree. Without the support of a pie plate, tender crusts are prone to leak juice, and this results in soggy bottoms. A quick glance at a couple of dozen recipes revealed that many bakers solve this problem by making a sturdier (and so tougher) dough. Several recipes skirted the tough-crust issue by utilizing a different sort of dough. Cookielike crusts, short and sandy in texture, were common. However, these recipes usually include sour cream, cream cheese, egg yolk, and/or cornmeal—ingredients that mask the pure flavor of simple pie dough. Because I was keen on a flaky, delicate pie pastry, I knew I had my work cut out for me.

Just Flour, Fat, and Water

Reverting to a standard formula of flour, fat, and water, I made crusts with both shortening and butter and with butter alone. I preferred the latter, but there was a limit as to just how much butter I could use. A ratio of 2 parts flour to 1 part butter resulted in a weak, leaky crust, which I attributed to too much fat and too little flour. Doughs made with too little butter, however, were crackerlike and edging toward tough. I settled on 10 tablespoons of butter to 1½ cups of flour, which provided the most buttery flavor and tender texture without compromising the structure.

I tried mixing the dough with a food processor, with a standing mixer, and by hand. The latter two methods mashed the butter into the flour and produced a less flaky crust. Quick pulses with the food processor "cut" the butter into the flour so that it remained in distinct pieces. After

This rustic summer fruit tart tastes every bit as good as a hard-to-prepare pie—and the crust is even flakier.

this step, I added water tablespoon by tablespoon through the food processor feed tube. I knew I had added enough when a small bit of dough held its shape when pinched.

Further testing revealed that doughs with large lumps of butter needed a lot of water to come together. Once baked, these crusts were very flaky but weak; as soon as the chunks of butter melted, the fruit juices found their escape hatches. Alternatively, doughs in which the butter was processed to fine crumbs required very little water. They yielded crusts that were more sturdy but also short and mealy (similar to cookielike crusts). Because I was after the long, fine layering of a flaky crust without a lot of leaking, I mixed the butter somewhere in-between—to about the size of coarse bread crumbs—just big enough to create the steamed spaces needed for flakiness.

Leave It to the French

The next step in most recipes involves lightly working the dough into a cohesive mass and patting it into a disk before chilling (to firm the butter) and then rolling it. Obligingly, I followed their lead, but I was getting disappointing results.

The tart still had a bad habit of leaking juice that then burned on the baking sheet. I tried coating the bottom of the dough with a layer of egg white, sprinkling crumbs (bread, cookie, and nut) under the fruit, and adding thickeners to the fruit (flour and cornstarch). Each method had its advantages, but none was a winner.

Then I remembered a French technique in pastry making called *fraisage*. It refers to the process of smearing the dough with the heel of your hand, thereby spreading the butter pieces into long thin streaks between skeletal layers of flour and water. Now my crust was more sturdy (the melted butter left behind no gaping holes), but it was also incredibly flaky, interspersed with long layers that I could pull apart with my fingers. It reminded tasters of classic French pastries such as palmiers and sacristans, which are made with multilayered puff pastry. Now I had the ideal crust: flaky but strong enough to contain the bubbling fruit juices during baking.

As final refinements to the recipe, I tried adding lemon juice, sugar, and salt to flavor the dough. Lemon juice made the crust too tender, as acid breaks down the protein structure in flour.

WITH FRAISAGE   WITHOUT FRAISAGE

We found that fraisage—the technique of smearing dough on the counter—was necessary in this recipe. What happens if you omit this key step? Something like the crust on the right, which has short flaky layers and is prone to leaking; the dough had lumps of butter that when melted in the oven left behind holes that weakened the walls of the crust. The crust on the left has long flaky layers and is far less prone to leaking. The fraisage creates long streaks of butter (rather than lumps) that make for a stable yet tender crust.

Sugar and salt both improved the flavor, but I was surprised to see that even a small amount of sugar had detrimental effects on the texture, making the crust more brittle. I decided to sprinkle sugar on top of the dough before baking instead. Brushing the dough with water before sprinkling on the sugar was an easy way to make it adhere.

Shape and Bake

I rolled out my dough to different thicknesses and found that 3/16 inch (about the height of three quarters) was ideal: thick enough to contain a lot of fruit but thin enough to bake evenly and thoroughly. Three cups of fruit were mounded in the center, leaving a 2½-inch border. The dough was then lifted up and back over the fruit (the center of the tart remains exposed) and loosely pleated to allow for shrinkage. The bright summer fruit needed only the simple addition of sugar; neither butter nor lemon juice was required. The amount of sugar varied from 3 to 5 tablespoons, depending on the type of fruit.

I baked the tart on the center rack of the oven at 350, 375, 400, and 425 degrees. Baking at the lower temperatures took too long; it also dried out the fruit and failed to brown the crust. At too high a temperature, the crust darkened on the folds but remained pale and underdone in the creases, and the fruit became charred. Lowering the rack and setting the oven to 400 degrees

generated the ideal time and temperature for an evenly baked, flaky tart. The last small but significant step toward a crisp crust was to cool the tart on a wire rack; this kept the crust from steaming itself as it cooled.

Thus, with a satisfying crunch of my knife, I cut myself a wedge of tart. For the effort expended, the reward was remarkable: a toothsome, flaky crust crackling around each bite of sweet summer fruit. And it was definitely easier than pie.

FREEFORM SUMMER FRUIT TART
MAKES ONE 8-INCH TART, SERVING 6

The amount of water that the dough will require depends on the ambient humidity; in a dry environment, it may need more water, in a humid environment, less. The dough can be made ahead and refrigerated overnight or tightly wrapped in two sheets of plastic wrap and frozen for up to one week. If at any point the dough becomes soft, sticky, and difficult to work with during rolling, chill it until it becomes workable.

Though we prefer the tart made with a mix of stone fruits and berries (our favorite combinations were plums and raspberries, peaches and blueberries, and apricots and blackberries), you can use only one type of fruit if you prefer. Peeling the stone fruit (even the peaches) is not necessary. Taste the fruit before adding sugar to it; use the lesser amount if the fruit is very sweet, more if it is

tart. However much sugar you use, do not add it to the fruit until you are ready to fill and form the tart. Once baked, the tart is best eaten warm, or within 3 or 4 hours, although leftovers do reheat well in a 350-degree oven. Excellent accompaniments are vanilla ice cream or lightly sweetened whipped cream or crème fraîche.

Dough
- 1½ cups (7½ ounces) unbleached all-purpose flour, plus additional for work surface
- ½ teaspoon salt
- 10 tablespoons (1¼ sticks) cold unsalted butter, cut into ½-inch cubes
- 3–6 tablespoons ice water

Fruit Filling
- 1 pound peaches, nectarines, apricots, or plums
- 1 cup berries (about ½ dry pint)
- 3–5 tablespoons sugar, plus 1 tablespoon for sprinkling

1. **FOR THE DOUGH:** In food processor, pulse flour and salt to combine, about three 1-second pulses. Scatter butter pieces over flour, then pulse until texture resembles coarse bread crumbs and butter pieces about the size of small peas remain, ten to twelve 1-second pulses. Sprinkle 1 tablespoon water over mixture and process 1 second; repeat until dough begins to form small curds and holds together when pinched with fingers. Empty dough onto work surface; dough will be crumbly (if dough has large dry areas, sprinkle additional 2 teaspoons water over dry areas and incorporate by gently fluffing entire amount of dough with fingers). Using bench scraper, gather dough into rough mound about 12 inches long and 4 inches wide (mound should be perpendicular to edge of counter). Beginning from farthest end, use heel of a hand to smear about one sixth of dough against work surface away from you. Repeat until all dough has been worked. Using bench scraper, gather dough again and repeat. Dough should now be cohesive. Form dough into 4-inch disk, wrap in plastic, and refrigerate until cold and firm but malleable, about 1 hour.

2. **FOR THE FILLING:** During last 30 minutes of chilling, prepare fruit. Halve and pit stone fruit

Making the Dough

1. Cut chilled butter into flour and salt until mixture resembles coarse bread crumbs.

2. Add water and pulse until mixture consists of curdlike pieces that hold together when pinched.

3. Turn dough onto work surface and gather into rough 12 by 4-inch mound. Smear dough bit by bit.

4. Using bench scraper, gather dough again into 12 by 4-inch mound.

5. Repeat smearing of dough with heel of hand until it is cohesive.

6. Gather and shape dough into 4-inch disk.

1. For an even circle, roll in short motions, working from center outward and moving dough ¼ turn after each roll.

2. Pile fruit in center of dough, leaving 2½-inch border around fruit.

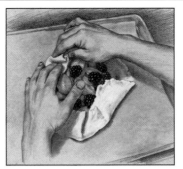

3. Working your way around dough, gently pull up sides and create fold every 2 inches.

4. Working quickly, brush top and sides of dough with water and sprinkle with 1 tablespoon sugar.

and cut into ½-inch-thick wedges. Gently wash and dry berries. Combine fruit in medium bowl (you should have about 3 cups); set aside. Adjust oven rack to lower-middle position and heat oven to 400 degrees.

3. **TO ASSEMBLE AND BAKE:** (If dough has chilled longer than 1 hour and is cold and hard, let stand at room temperature 15 to 20 minutes before proceeding.) On large sheet of parchment paper lightly dusted with flour, roll dough to 12-inch round about ³⁄₁₆ inch thick, dusting with flour as needed. (If dough sticks to parchment, gently loosen and lift sticky area with bench scraper and dust parchment with additional flour.) Slide parchment and dough onto baking sheet and refrigerate until cool and firm yet pliant, 15 to 30 minutes (if refrigerated longer and dough is hard and brittle, let stand at room temperature until pliant).

4. Sprinkle fruit with sugar and toss gently to combine. Remove baking sheet with dough from refrigerator. Mound fruit in center of dough, leaving 2½-inch border around edge. Carefully grasp one edge of dough and fold up outer 2 inches over fruit, leaving ½-inch area of dough just inside of fold free of fruit. Repeat around circumference of tart, overlapping dough every 2 to 3 inches; gently pinch pleated dough to secure, but do not press dough into fruit. Working quickly, brush dough with water and sprinkle evenly with 1 tablespoon sugar. Bake until crust is deep golden brown and fruit is bubbling, 50 to 55 minutes. Cool tart on baking sheet on wire rack 10 minutes. Using offset or wide metal spatula, loosen tart from parchment and carefully slide tart off parchment onto wire rack; cool until warm, about 30 minutes, or to room temperature, about 1 hour. Cut into wedges and serve.

FREEFORM SUMMER FRUIT TARTLETS

Follow recipe for Freeform Summer Fruit Tart, dividing dough into 4 equal portions before rolling out in step 3. Roll each portion into 7-inch round on parchment paper; stack rounds and refrigerate until cool and firm, yet pliant. Continue with recipe from step 4, mounding one quarter of fruit in center of dough, leaving 1½-inch border around edge. Carefully grasp one edge of dough and fold up outer 1 to 1¼ inches of dough over fruit, leaving ¼-inch area of dough just inside of fold free of fruit. Transfer parchment with tart to rimmed baking sheet. Repeat with remaining fruit and dough. Brush dough with water and sprinkle each tartlet with portion of remaining 1 tablespoon sugar. Bake until deep golden brown and fruit is bubbling, 40 to 45 minutes. Cool tartlets on wire rack 10 minutes. Using offset or wide metal spatula, loosen tartlets from parchment and transfer to wire rack; cool until warm, about 20 minutes, or to room temperature, about 45 minutes. Serve.

TESTING EQUIPMENT: **Pastry Brushes**

A good pastry brush is hard to maintain. Most quickly degrade into a stained, shaggy mess. Hoping to find one that could swab barbecue sauce, brush garlic oil, delicately paint pastry with egg wash, and still clean up free of stains, lingering odors, or stiff greasy bristles, we ran eight brushes through a series of kitchen tests.

In terms of bristles, we found that no material can compete with the quality and feel of natural boar's hair. While often not labeled as such, most gold-colored bristles are made from boar's hair. These bristles are also available in black, a color that is easier to spot on food if a bristle falls out. Avoid brushes with nylon bristles, which are usually clear. We found that these bristles lack absorbency and tend to clump. Silicone bristles (which are usually very thick and black) are both nonabsorbent and overly flexible. We even tried a bundle of goose feathers tied together with butcher's twine. Not bad for applying an egg wash, but definitely not made to last.

We preferred pastry brushes with handles and collars made of plastic or rubber. These brushes are dishwasher-safe and make swollen, cracked wooden handles a thing of the past. Traditional paintbrush-style brushes with wooden handles and metal collars tend to have pockets of space under the collar that trap oil and off flavors.

Only one brush, the Oxo Good Grips, successfully combined the tradition of boar's hair bristles with the more modern design of a dishwasher-safe plastic handle and a tight-fitting rubber collar that made no room for grease. It was the clear winner of our tests. –Garth Clingingsmith

BEST BRUSH
The Oxo Good Grips combines traditional boar's hair bristles with a modern, dishwasher-safe handle.

RUNNER-UP BRUSH
The Carlisle brush works well, but its wooden handle can't go in the dishwasher.

SILLY BRUSH
The Sili Gourmet brush has thick, nonabsorbent bristles. We had to scoop up egg wash and oil when using it.

COLLARLESS BRUSH
Without a collar, the bristles in the Calphalon brush fell out after three washings.

STINKY BRUSH
The Ateco brush trapped oils under the collar. After a few weeks, this brush started to smell.

COOK'S EXTRA gives you free information online. For the results of our tests of rolling pins, visit www.cooksillustrated.com and key in code 4047. This information will be available until August 15, 2004.

Improving Peach Cobbler

Bad peaches, soggy biscuits, and syrupy filling were just three of the problems we had to solve in resurrecting this simple summer dessert.

⇒ BY KEITH DRESSER ⇐

If I were to write a TV ad for the perfect peach cobbler, I would sing the praises of its honeyed taste and silky texture, all the while showing softly filtered shots of the bright days of summer. After all, this classic marriage of cobbler topping and sweet, fresh fruit is worth advertising; so few modern cooks serve it, and yet it is easy enough to throw together at the last minute. What could be more appealing than warm cobbler dough atop rich, juicy peaches?

The reason most cooks have not made peach cobbler recently is the usual one: The promise is better than the reality. For starters, peaches are unpredictable. Some turn mushy if cooked a bit too long, while others exude an ocean of overly sweet juices. The topping is also problematic, ranging from tough, dry biscuits to raw, cakey lumps of dough. In worst-case recipes, it is both hard and crusty on top and soggy on the bottom. So what's a home cook to do?

The Problem with Peaches

My initial tests told me two things: The peaches should be peeled to avoid any unpleasant leathery bits of skin, and they should be cut in relatively large pieces to avoid development of a peach mush during baking. Another way to avoid the mush, I learned, was to choose ripe yet firm peaches, which better withstood the rigors of baking. (Save those soft, super-ripe peaches for eating out of hand.) What proved to be the most perplexing problem was the wide variation in juiciness from peach to peach, which sometimes resulted in a baking dish overflowing with liquid.

In my first attempt to solve this problem, I tried parcooking the peaches by means of roasting or sautéing, thus removing excess juices. But this was a dead end, as I discovered that most of the juices are not released until the peaches are almost fully cooked—something that necessarily happens after the peaches have been joined with the cobbler topping. Next I thought to draw on a technique used to make another American dessert classic—strawberry shortcake—in which the fruit is macerated in sugar to draw out its juices. Sugar did indeed draw off some of the moisture from the peaches, but I quickly discovered that I needed to replenish

Sugaring the sliced peaches and draining the excess juice ensures a crisp biscuit topping.

the cobbler with some of the liquid that had been drained away. Starting with 1 tablespoon, I added the drawn juice back to the filling. In the end, ¼ cup of the drawn juice had to be added back to guarantee a juicy cobbler that would have the same amount of liquid every time.

Because tasters greeted overly sweet cobbler fillings with comments such as "tastes like it came from a can," I settled on a scant ¼ cup of sugar, just enough to do the job without making the filling syrupy. To thicken the peach juices, I tried cornstarch, pulverized tapioca, flour, and arrowroot. Each starch thickened the juices admirably, but the high price and limited availability of arrowroot disqualified it. Tapioca, too, was out of the running because of its propensity to leave behind hardened starch granules (tapioca works better in a double-crust pie, where the pastry traps juices and helps to steam the granules until they dissolve). Flour, meanwhile, gave the filling a pasty quality. Cornstarch it was, then. A mere teaspoon was the perfect amount, giving the filling body without overwhelming the delicate texture of the peaches. Wondering if the fruit would benefit from the addition of other flavors, I conducted a battery of tests, using ingredients such as lemon juice, almond extract, Triple Sec, ginger, and cardamom. Lemon juice was the only keeper, as it helped to brighten the peach flavor; the other additions were only distractions.

Getting to the Top

There were many choices for the topping other than biscuit dough, but none of them were as appealing (see "Recipe Testing" below). The next step was to select the style of biscuit topping: rolled or dropped. Rolled biscuits had a nice light texture,

RECIPE TESTING: Searching for the Right Cobbler Topping

Some recipes for peach cobbler stray far and away from the traditional biscuit topping. Here's a look at some of these alternatives, with comments from tasters.

COOKIELIKE CRUST
Our tasters felt this "sweet," "sandy" topping was "not right for a cobbler."

CAKELIKE BATTER
Tasters thought this "dumplinglike" topping looked more like clafouti and called it "pasty" and "doughy."

FLAKY PASTRY TOPPING
Making a topping similar to pie dough was a lot of work, and the peaches sitting under it were "gluey."

Anatomy of a Peach

A number of cobbler recipes call for removing the dark red flesh that surrounds the pit of the peach. Wondering what impact this would have on my cobbler, I made two versions—one with the red part of the peaches removed, the other with it intact. While the latter had an appealing reddish blush, I was surprised to find that it also had a bitter taste. The cobbler made with cleaned peaches tasted better. So if you see red once the peaches have been pitted (not all peaches will have this red flesh), take a few extra seconds to scoop it out and discard it. –K.D.

but I wondered if there was an easier way. Drop biscuits (a wet dough is dropped by spoonfuls onto the fruit) were certainly easier to prepare than rolled biscuits, and they had an attractive rustic and craggy appearance. Tasters found drop biscuits too dense, however. The compromise was a biscuit recipe in which the butter is cut into the flour (as it is with rolled biscuits) but which also contains a little more dairy, making the dough more moist. Now I could avoid the rolling and cutting but still get the light texture of a traditional biscuit.

In testing the "fat" component of the biscuit, I tried vegetable shortening and cream cheese, but tasters quickly discarded these in favor of butter, which not only improved the flavor of the biscuits but also aided in browning. For dairy, I tested the usual suspects—heavy cream, half-and-half, milk, and buttermilk—and received mixed results. Tasters liked the tang of the buttermilk biscuits but the cakier, more substantial crumb produced by richer dairy products (the cream and the half-and-half). The simple solution was to use whole milk yogurt. These biscuits had plenty of tangy flavor and a texture that resembled that of the biscuits made with half-and-half.

Moving on to the leavener, I found that a combination of baking powder and soda was best. An egg, tasters decided, made the biscuits too heavy, but they did like biscuits with a bit of sugar, which both added flavor and helped to crisp the exterior. I tried spices such as cinnamon, nutmeg, and ginger as well as lemon zest but decided that the biscuits ought to be a quiet backup for the show-stealing peaches. (Lemon zest did work nicely with a cornmeal biscuit variation, however.)

Assembling and Baking

Up until this point, I had been placing the fairly moist biscuit dough on top of the raw peaches and then baking the cobbler at 425 degrees—a technique that was producing gluey biscuits that were slightly raw in the center. Investigating a technique similar to one employed in our Sour Cherry Cobbler recipe (July/August 2001), I tried partially baking the peaches before adding the topping, hoping that the hot fruit would jump-start the cooking process. It did. The biscuits were much better, and the fruit was no longer overcooked. Finally, to further enhance the biscuits' crispness, I sprinkled the tops with sugar before they went into the oven. I

now had a peach cobbler recipe that was reliably good, whether I was using juicy or not-so-juicy fruit. In fact, it was ready for prime time.

FRESH PEACH COBBLER
SERVES 6

If your peaches are firm, you should be able to peel them with a sharp vegetable peeler. If they are too soft and ripe to withstand the pressure of a peeler, you'll need to blanch and shock them before peeling (for detailed instructions, see Kitchen Notes, page 31). In the biscuit topping, low-fat or nonfat plain yogurt can be used in place of whole milk yogurt, but the biscuits will be a little less rich. If you live in an arid climate, the biscuit dough may require up to an additional tablespoon of yogurt for it to form a cohesive dough. Do not prepare the biscuit dough any sooner than the recipe indicates; if the unbaked dough is left to stand too long, the leavener will expire and the biscuits will not rise properly in the oven. This recipe can be doubled to serve a crowd. Use a 13 by 9-inch baking dish and increase the baking times in steps 2 and 4 by about 5 minutes. Serve the warm cobbler with vanilla ice cream or whipped cream. Leftovers can be reheated in a 350-degree oven until warmed through.

Filling
2½	pounds ripe but firm peaches (6 to 7 medium)
¼	cup (1¾ ounces) sugar
1	teaspoon cornstarch
1	tablespoon juice from 1 lemon
	Pinch salt

Biscuit Topping
1	cup (5 ounces) unbleached all-purpose flour
3	tablespoons plus 1 teaspoon sugar
¾	teaspoon baking powder
¼	teaspoon baking soda
¼	teaspoon salt
5	tablespoons cold unsalted butter, cut into ¼-inch cubes
⅓	cup plain whole milk yogurt

1. Adjust oven rack to lower-middle position and heat oven to 425 degrees.

2. **FOR THE FILLING:** Peel peaches (see note), then halve and pit each. Using small spoon, scoop out and discard dark flesh from pit area

(see "Anatomy of a Peach"). Cut each half into 4 wedges. Gently toss peaches and sugar together in large bowl; let stand for 30 minutes, tossing several times. Drain peaches in colander set over large bowl. Whisk ¼ cup of drained juice (discard extra), cornstarch, lemon juice, and salt together in small bowl. Toss peach juice mixture with peach slices and transfer to 8-inch-square glass baking dish. Bake until peaches begin to bubble around edges, about 10 minutes.

3. **FOR THE TOPPING:** While peaches are baking, in food processor, pulse flour, 3 tablespoons sugar, baking powder, baking soda, and salt to combine. Scatter butter over and pulse until mixture resembles coarse meal, about ten 1-second pulses. Transfer to medium bowl; add yogurt and toss with rubber spatula until cohesive dough is formed. (Don't overmix dough or biscuits will be tough.) Break dough into 6 evenly sized but roughly shaped mounds and set aside.

4. **TO ASSEMBLE AND BAKE:** After peaches have baked 10 minutes, remove peaches from oven and place dough mounds on top, spacing them at least ½ inch apart (they should not touch). Sprinkle each mound with portion of remaining 1 teaspoon sugar. Bake until topping is golden brown and fruit is bubbling, 16 to 18 minutes. Cool cobbler on wire rack until warm, about 20 minutes; serve.

BLUEBERRY-PEACH COBBLER WITH LEMON-CORNMEAL BISCUIT TOPPING

Follow recipe for Fresh Peach Cobbler, using 2 pounds peaches and tossing 1 cup fresh blueberries (about 5 ounces) into peach juice/cornstarch mixture along with peaches in step 2. In biscuit topping, substitute 2 tablespoons stone-ground cornmeal for equal amount flour and add ½ teaspoon grated lemon zest to food processor along with dry ingredients in step 3.

TECHNIQUE |
DROP THOSE COBBLES

Place the biscuits too close to one another and they will bake up doughy. To avoid this problem, stagger the rows of biscuits slightly.

The Bottled Water Wars

Are we out of our minds to pay 35 cents per glass for bottled water?

BY DAWN YANAGIHARA

It is rather baffling that a substance as fundamental and as abundant as water can form the basis of an astonishingly large business. In 2003, bottled water sales ballooned to $8.3 billion in the United States alone. Per capita consumption is more than 22 gallons, nearly double what it was only a decade ago, and sales and consumption of bottled water are only expected to grow further. To meet the demand, retailers have stocked their shelves with a multitude of brands, both domestic and foreign, many donning labels that suggest pristine alpine springs or crisp, clean mountain air. That the bottles differ in labeling is clear; what is less apparent is the extent to which they differ in taste. To better understand what—if anything—distinguishes one bottled water from another, we conducted a blind tasting.

We arrived at nine brands that covered the still-water spectrum—both domestic and imported. We also included a water not expressly meant for drinking, ultrapure plasma-grade water. Used in sensitive chemistry applications, this water is double-distilled and virtually free of all minerals and impurities. We reasoned that by including in the tasting water in its near-purest form, we might gain some insight into what makes water taste good—purity or impurities, in a manner of speaking.

Bottled Water Primer

There are several types of bottled water, but three categories stand out: spring water, artesian water, and purified water. A bottle labeled "spring water" must contain water that came from an underground water formation that flows naturally to the earth's surface. The location of the source must be identified. The water is collected either at the spring or through a hole that has been made to tap the source that feeds the spring. Spring water is sometimes bottled without additional treatment (this is particularly true of European bottled waters), but domestic bottlers often use carbon filtration to remove odors, micro- or ultrafiltration to remove fine particles and impurities, and/or ultraviolet light or ozonation to disinfect the water.

Some producers tap several springs, bottle each separately, and yet sell all under the same brand name. This means that a bottle of brand X purchased on the East Coast may not be from the same source as a bottle of brand X purchased on the West Coast. This practice is common among domestic producers and better allows suppliers to meet demand and minimize the cost of transport. But it also means that the flavor profiles of the

same brand may differ from one region of the country to another. Many European and foreign producers bottle water from a single source—and are proud of it.

Of the nine brands we assembled for our tasting, six were spring waters. Two of these, Poland Spring and Arrowhead, are bottled under the agency of Nestlé Waters North America, which, with nearly a dozen brands to its name, holds the largest share of the bottled water business in the United States. Danone Waters of North America sells Volvic and Evian (the best-selling imported water). The final two spring waters were Dannon, the sixth-best-selling bottled water, and Crystal Geyser, the seventh bestseller.

Artesian water differs from spring water in that its source must be an underground formation known as a confined aquifer. The water is sandwiched between—or confined by—a top and bottom layer of impermeable rock. When the aquifer is tapped, natural internal pressure causes the water to flow. Is artesian water better than "regular" spring water? Not necessarily. While the U.S. Environmental Protection Agency says that water from artesian aquifers is often cleaner because the confining layers of rock and clay impede the movement of contaminants, there is no guarantee that artesian water is any more pure—or otherwise better—than spring water. The only artesian water in the tasting was Fiji, which is indeed imported from the Fiji Islands in the Pacific and is the second-best-selling imported brand.

Spring water and artesian water both contain dissolved solids (or minerals) such as calcium, magnesium, sulfates, silica, and chlorides. Mineral water is spring or artesian water that naturally contains at least 250 parts per million (ppm) of total dissolved solids (TDS). Evian was the only mineral water in the tasting, although it is not marketed as such. (A laboratory analysis conducted by *Cook's* did show that our sample of Fiji had TDS of more than 250 ppm, but to qualify as a mineral water, the water must, through repeated analysis, be shown to consistently contain 250 ppm of TDS. According to Fiji, its water has TDS of 210 ppm.)

Two purified waters—Pepsi-Cola's Aquafina and Coca-Cola's Dasani—were part of our tasting. Aquafina is the best-selling brand of bottled water in this country, and

Dasani is number two. What is purified water? The simple definition is that purified water has been processed to remove contaminants and minerals before being bottled. The source is often a municipal water supply. Pepsi and Coke tap municipal water sources in various parts of the country and filter the water in a process called reverse osmosis. Reverse osmosis removes most of the impurities, and the water is left nearly bereft of minerals. Such a tight filtration process means that no matter what the source, the taste of purified water is likely to be consistent from bottle to bottle.

Purified water is frequently criticized for being merely a highly filtered version of what flows when you open the home tap. Coke claims, however, that consumers are much more concerned about

What about Tap Water?

We were curious to see how the top- and lowest-rated bottled waters would fare against tap water, so we organized a second tasting in which we sampled Volvic (first place), Poland Spring (last place), Boston tap water, samples of water from the Metropolitan Water District (MWD) of Southern California in Los Angeles (because it has won awards in its category at international water tastings), and tap water from a residence in Los Angeles County.

Volvic and the MWD water were equally well liked, earning identical scores and accolades such as "fresh" and "clean." Poland Spring came in next, besting Boston tap water, which tasters described as metallic, musty, and stale. Residential Los Angeles County water was so chlorinated that it stopped tasters in their tracks. Why would the MWD water be so good and the residential water so bad? The MWD is a water wholesaler, and the water it has to offer is not necessarily the water that flows from area faucets. A phone call to the MWD revealed that it was, in fact, not the source of the residential tap water that we tasted.

RATING TAP WATER

Water from a home faucet in Los Angeles (right) tasted terrible, but a sample sent to us by the local water authority (left) rivaled the best bottled water.

What, then, did we learn from this tasting? That tap water can rival even the best bottled water, but that even our least-favorite bottled water was superior to water culled straight from two not-so-excellent taps in Boston and Los Angeles. –D.Y.

COOK'S ILLUSTRATED

26

TASTING BOTTLED WATER

Twenty-three tasters sampled nine different brands of bottled water. Tasters sampled the waters in different orders to eliminate the effects of palate fatigue. The waters were tasted at room temperature, which allows odors and flavors to be more perceptible than when tasted chilled. Tasters assessed the odor, flavor, and aftertaste of each sample, then rated each on a 10-point scale. Total dissolved solids (TDS) analysis was conducted by an independent laboratory; amounts listed below may not be identical to amounts given by producers. All bottled waters are recommended; they are listed in order of preference.

RECOMMENDED

VOLVIC Natural Spring Water
SOURCE: CLAIRVIC SPRING, VOLVIC, FRANCE
➤ **$1.29/1-liter bottle**
TDS: 137 ppm
Tasters had a clear preference for this water, calling it very fresh, pure, and clean, with slight mineral flavors. One taster wrote, "smooth and velvety," while another declared it a favorite because it "tastes like water."

FIJI Natural Artesian Water
SOURCE: VITI LEVU, REPUBLIC OF FIJI ISLANDS
➤ **$1.59/1-liter bottle**
TDS: 260 ppm
Tasters appreciated the "nice and clean," "incredibly drinkable," "unadulterated" quality of this water. One taster hailed it as "perfect." It was also described as having a hint of sweetness and mineral flavor. A few detractors called it "dull."

DANNON Natural Spring Water
SOURCE: SPRINGS IN BELLEFONTE, PA.; GRAND PRAIRIE, TEXAS; ANAHEIM, CALIF.; HIGH SPRINGS, FLA.; MOUNT SHASTA, CALIF. (sample tasted was from Bellefonte, Pa.)
➤ **$0.53/25-ounce bottle**
TDS: 200 ppm
"Pure," "clean," "fresh," and "smooth" were the accolades. A couple tasters noted a sweetness. Negative comments included "stale" and "flat."

AQUAFINA Purified Drinking Water
SOURCE: MULTIPLE MUNICIPAL WATER SUPPLIES
➤ **$0.99/1-liter bottle**
TDS: 30 ppm
Most tasters found this water to be sweet, but there agreement ended. Comments like "fresh" and "lively" were countered with criticisms like "metallic" and "artificial."

DASANI Purified Water
SOURCE: MULTIPLE MUNICIPAL WATER SUPPLIES
➤ **$1.19/1-liter bottle**
TDS: 80 ppm
Nearly half of the tasters found this water to have distinct mineral flavors ("like licking a geode," said one). Though it was described as "clean," some found it "harsh."

ARROWHEAD MOUNTAIN Spring Water
SOURCE: MULTIPLE SPRINGS IN THE U.S. AND CANADA
➤ **$1.09/1-liter bottle** (available in California, Arizona, and Nevada)
TDS: 120 ppm
Comments ranged from positive ("nice taste" and "silky") to moderate ("not bad") to decidedly negative ("yuck, tap water"). Some tasters commented that this water had an aftertaste, and one said that the flavor "lingers on and on."

EVIAN Natural Spring Water
SOURCE: CACHAT SPRING, EVIAN, FRANCE
➤ **$1.69/1-liter bottle**
TDS: 340 ppm
This was a controversial water. "Soft and smooth" and "refreshing" were praises. "Heavy" and "creamy" were criticisms. Most agreed that this water had a notable sweetness and strong mineral flavors.

CRYSTAL GEYSER
SOURCE: SPRINGS IN BENTON, TENN.; MOUNT SHASTA, CALIF., OLANCHA PEAK, CALIF. (sample tasted was from Benton)
➤ **$0.49/25.3-ounce bottle**
TDS: 180 ppm
Tasters mustered little excitement—positive or negative—about this water. "Pretty neutral and clean" and "a bit dull, but relatively clean" typified comments.

POLAND SPRING
SOURCES: SPRINGS IN HOLLIS, FRYEBURG, POLAND SPRING, AND POLAND, MAINE (sample tasted was from Hollis)
➤ **$0.89/1-liter bottle** (available in the Northeast)
TDS: 50 ppm
This water was criticized for tasting "unnatural" and having "off flavors." More temperate tasters commented that it was "basic" but uninteresting. Several tasters noted a saltiness.

---

taste than source. Toward that end, after reverse-osmosis processing, Coke adds minerals back to the purified water to obtain optimal taste. Pepsi does not add minerals to Aquafina.

By contrast, a spring water's flavor profile is organically derived. As the water journeys from its origin as rainwater or snowmelt to the spring, a process that can take years, it travels through layers of rock, clay, gravel, and/or sand that filter out impurities. As the impurities are filtered out, the water also acquires dissolved minerals that in their specific combinations give the water its signature flavor.

What It Boils Down To

The only water that tasters unanimously rejected was the ultrapure plasma-grade water, which earned the lowest possible score because of its flat, vapid flavor. Though this water is of course unavailable to consumers as drinking water, it did teach us something. Ostensibly, when it comes to water, absolute purity is a liability, not an asset. Some mineral content makes water likable.

Is spring water better than purified municipal water? The two purified waters we sampled, Aquafina and Dasani, earned respectable scores, coming in fourth and fifth, and beat out four spring waters. But they were not in the winners' circle. Two spring waters and the one artesian water in the tasting swept the pack, with win, place, and show. Volvic, a spring water from France, was the clear winner, with Fiji, the artesian water, close behind.

What should you buy? While most of our tasters will now purchase Volvic or Fiji when given the option, our results show that the flavor differences between bottled waters are not great. Unlike the differences between brands of chocolate or barbecue sauce, the distinctions between brands of bottled water are so modest that you are unlikely to be disappointed with any of those that we tasted.

Do You Really Need a Santoku Knife?

Is there something better than the classic chef's knife?
We tested 10 of these trendy Japanese knives to find out.

⇒ BY MARYELLEN DRISCOLL ⇐

The santoku has long been the Japanese equivalent of a chef's knife. But only recently has this knife gained America's attention, when Food Network chef Rachel Ray talked it up on national television as her favorite all-purpose knife. Because the classic 8-inch chef is still the workhorse in our test kitchen, we couldn't help but wonder if this was a case of media-inspired hype. Or could the santoku really be as good as promised?

What is a santoku knife? Compared with a classic chef's knife, the santoku is typically shorter and has a thinner blade, a stubbier tip, and a straighter edge. It is thought to have evolved from the narrow, rectangular Japanese vegetable knife and may be called an Asian or oriental chef's knife.

To find out whether the santoku is in fact multipurpose, we bought 10 models and ran them through a series of tests, using the Forschner Victorinox chef's knife (the winning model from our July/August 1999 rating) for comparison. The tests included preparing onions, garlic, carrots, tomatoes, and boneless chicken breasts. We assessed each knife in terms of precision, control, sharpness of blade, efficiency, and comfort.

Of the 10 knives tested, prices ranged from as low as $27 to as high as $140. The blades were made from a variety of materials, from the conventional high-carbon stainless steel to the exotic, including ceramic and a titanium silver alloy. But the most evident difference between the knives was the range in blade size, from 6 to 7 inches. That single inch proved significant in test performances.

Forget Shorty

In the onion test, the smaller knives verged on the ridiculous. The 6-inch blades were so short that the hands holding those knives ended up knuckle-deep in chopped onion. Interestingly, while most of the knives recommended in the chart (page 29) scored well at this task, only one, the Kershaw Shun, was preferred over the Forschner chef's knife.

The santoku really shined in tasks requiring more delicate or precise knife work, such as thinly slicing carrots. Compared with the chef's knife,

Chef's knife

Santoku knife

WHAT'S THE DIFFERENCE?
A santoku has a stubbier tip, a straighter cutting edge, and a shorter, thinner blade.

the thinner blade of the santoku was able to cut through the dense carrot more smoothly. The narrower the blade, the less food material has to be moved out of the way as the blade slices. A thicker blade requires more force, as it acts more like a wedge. The shorter santoku blade proved advantageous here as well. The tip of a chef's knife often feels remote and somewhat out of control, especially for beginning cooks. In contrast, the closer proximity of the santoku's tip (as well as its straighter design) gave our testers a greater sense of control.

The santokus were also well liked for butterflying boneless chicken breasts. Testers indicated that the smaller—but not too small—size of the santoku and the less tapered tip made the knife easier to manage. The narrowness of the blade also seemed to help reduce friction.

For mincing, the curve of the blade was the main factor mentioned by testers. Those santokus with straighter edges tended to feel more jarring, meeting the cutting board abruptly and interrupting the flow of motion instead of smoothly rocking back and forth. These knives were deemed more single purpose, best at slicing. Santokus with more curve could rock with more fluidity. A few testers preferred the curved santoku to the chef's knife, but most testers gave the chef high marks for its fluid rocking motion, which is the essence of mincing and chopping.

The sliced tomato test revealed a lot about the sharpness of each knife. Testers found that the knives made of high-carbon stainless steel were sharpest. While the Kyocera's ceramic blade was respectably sharp, its small size was a deterrent, as was the fact that if you dropped it at a certain angle, the tip would break off. The Boker, made of a titanium silver alloy, was disappointingly

COOK'S EXTRA gives you free information online. For our rating of inexpensive chef's knives, visit www.cooksillustrated.com and key in code 4048. This information will be available until August 15, 2004.

Hollowed-Edge Santokus

Many santokus are available with either a standard or a granton blade, the latter being hollow-ground and incorporating oval recesses along the blade. (This design was originally intended to make slicing meat easier.) Granton blades are often advertised as "nonstick."

Unfortunately, we quickly learned that these knives are not exactly nonstick. Minced garlic and cucumber slices cling vigilantly to the sides of a granton-style blade. However, as master bladesmith Bob Kramer explained to us, the hollows do help break the surface tension between the food and the blade surface. The hollows create air pockets between the breadth of the blade and the food, thus reducing the drag, or friction, between the two. So it was no coincidence that the two knives with the tallest hollows, the MAC and the Kershaw Shun, seemed to show the biggest decrease in friction when tested against their standard-edge versions. Even then, however, the differences didn't bowl us over.

A santoku with a granton edge typically costs $10 to $20 more than one with a standard edge. Knives with granton edges can be sharpened, although it takes a little more care because once sharpened into the hollows, the blade becomes slightly thinner. Given the less-than-eye-opening differences, we prefer santokus with the cheaper standard edge. –M.D.

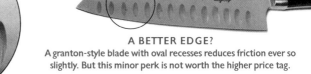

A BETTER EDGE?
A granton-style blade with oval recesses reduces friction ever so slightly. But this minor perk is not worth the higher price tag.

RATINGS
GOOD: ★★★
FAIR: ★★
POOR: ★

Seven magazine staffers and one kitchen intern evaluated each knife for its performance in a variety of specific tasks as well as for its handle and blade design. The testers ran the gamut in terms of knife skills—from beginner to advanced—as well as hand size and strength. Only one tester was left-handed. Knives are listed in order of preference based on testers' average overall scores for each knife.

PRICE: Prices paid in Boston-area stores, in national mail-order catalogs, and on Web sites.
PERFORMANCE: Knives were used to chop and dice onions, mince and slice garlic, thinly slice and julienne carrots, slice tomatoes, and butterfly boneless, skinless chicken breasts. Scores from individual tests were averaged to create an overall performance rating.
BLADE: Testers rated blades for sharpness and curvature. Blades that were sharp and thin (but not flimsy) were preferred. Curved blades were able to handle a greater variety of tasks and received higher ratings.
HANDLE: Testers rated handles for balance and comfort. Snug grips that didn't become slippery when greasy or wet were preferred, as were knives with handles that felt balanced with the blade.
BLADE MATERIAL/LENGTH: Most of the knives had blades made from high-carbon stainless steel. One had a ceramic blade; another a blade made from a titanium silver alloy. Testers generally found the high-carbon stainless steel blades to be the sharpest. Blade length was measured from the tip to the point where the blade meets the handle; longer blades were preferred.
TESTERS' COMMENTS: Observations about design or performance in specific tests.

FAVORITE KNIFE

	TESTERS' COMMENTS
MAC Superior Santoku BLADE MATERIAL/LENGTH: High-carbon stainless steel/6½ inches PRICE: $55.00 PERFORMANCE: ★★★ BLADE: ★★★ HANDLE: ★★★	Ideal bridge between cramped, smaller santokus and larger chef's knife. Admired for being most sharp and responsive, this knife was especially nimble, easy to control, and precise. As one tester gushed, "great with everything."

RECOMMENDED

	TESTERS' COMMENTS
Kershaw Shun Classic Santoku model DM-0702 BLADE MATERIAL/LENGTH: High-carbon stainless steel/6½ inches PRICE: $89.99 PERFORMANCE: ★★★ BLADE: ★★★ HANDLE: ★★★	Cadillac of group, this knife felt "sturdy" and "solid." Curvature of blade made it good at rocking while mincing, and tip was sharp and decisive. Bulge on right side of handle was uncomfortable for left-handed tester.
Wüsthof Grand Prix Oriental Cook's BLADE MATERIAL/LENGTH: High-carbon stainless steel/6⅔ inches PRICE: $69.99 PERFORMANCE: ★★ BLADE: ★★★ HANDLE: ★★★	"Super-accurate" at thin slicing and fine mincing. Straight blade created abrupt "see-saw" effect when rocking to mince or chop. One camp applauded light feel—"like a smaller, quicker chef's knife." Others deemed it flimsy. Sharp, but not exceptionally so.
Global Oriental Cook BLADE MATERIAL/LENGTH: High-carbon stainless steel/7 inches PRICE: $78.00 PERFORMANCE: ★★★ BLADE: ★★★ HANDLE: ★	Could have been perfect if not for narrow, sleek stainless steel handle that made grip feel "all over the place." Sharp blade with markedly curved edge and tapered tip were more like a chef's knife than santoku.
Zwilling Henckels Four Star Santoku BLADE MATERIAL/LENGTH: High-carbon stainless steel/7 inches PRICE: $64.95 PERFORMANCE: ★★★ BLADE: ★★ HANDLE: ★★★	Sharp, relatively thick blade made this knife a strong, substantial slicer, but blade's flat curve made rocking motion shallow and somewhat jarring. Knife generally had awkward, less maneuverable feel.
Oxo Good Grips MV55-PRO Santoku BLADE MATERIAL/LENGTH: High-carbon stainless steel/6½ inches PRICE: $27.00 PERFORMANCE: ★★ BLADE: ★★ HANDLE: ★★	Decent sharpness and maneuverability but best suited to slicing. Stubby, cleaver-shaped blade felt somewhat "dead" at rocking motion needed for mincing and coarse chopping. Fat handle was liked by many for its soft, grippy feel.

NOT RECOMMENDED

	TESTERS' COMMENTS
Kyocera Ming Tsai Santoku BLADE MATERIAL/LENGTH: Ceramic/6 inches PRICE: $140.00 PERFORMANCE: ★★ BLADE: ★★ HANDLE: ★★	Notably sharp, short blade performed delicate knife work respectably but, overall, "too small to be of much use." White ceramic blade made it tricky to see white food (such as garlic) when working on white plastic board.
Füri Pro East/West BLADE MATERIAL/LENGTH: High-carbon stainless steel/7 inches PRICE: $69.95 PERFORMANCE: ★★ BLADE: ★ HANDLE: ★	Blade was dull, fat, stubby, and "kind of clumsy"—more like a cleaver. Decent rocking motion but lacked capacity for delicate and precise work. Molded stainless steel handle too large and cumbersome.
Boker Cera-Titan I Santoku BLADE MATERIAL/LENGTH: Titanium silver alloy/6½ inches PRICE: $127.50 PERFORMANCE: ★★ BLADE: ★★ HANDLE: ★	"Feather-light," flimsy, short, and, ironically—given steep price—cheap in feel was overall consensus. Difficult to control and shallow, abrupt rocking motion were common complaints.
Forschner Santoku BLADE MATERIAL/LENGTH: High-carbon stainless steel/6 inches PRICE: $35.36 PERFORMANCE: ★ BLADE: ★ HANDLE: ★	Most testers found teeny "hobbit" size uncomfortable and difficult to control. Not enough clearance under handle, so even those with small hands banged their knuckles when blade came in full contact with cutting board.

dull. The blade was also unnervingly thin and extremely flexible. There was little trend in terms of the best handles. Unobtrusive designs that allotted a clean, comfortable grip were preferred. For most of the testers, the slick look of stainless handles, featured on the Füri and Global, translated to a slick grip as well.

And the Winner Is . . .

While testers liked most of the santokus, only two—the MAC and the Kershaw Shun—were consistently preferred over the Forschner chef's knife in the tests. But given how much we like the Forschner (and the fact that many chef's knives are inferior to this brand), the santokus certainly held their own. But you could argue that our tests were rigged in favor of the santokus. In preliminary testing, we tried to halve acorn squashes, and only a couple of the santokus could manage this basic task. The blades were simply too thin and too short. We also avoided cutting up a whole chicken because manufacturers warned that santoku blades were too thin to cut through bone. A chef's knife can handle both of these chores easily.

Is the era of the chef's knife at an end? No. The chef's knife is more versatile than the santoku. If you are going to have only one type of knife in your kitchen, it should be a chef's knife. That said, our testers felt that the santoku is indeed better at precision slicing: The blade is shorter, thinner, and easier to manage. Stick with the chef's knife for more substantial tasks.

We heartily recommend the MAC Superior Santoku knife—it performed well and was one of the cheapest models tested. But use this santoku to complement—not to replace—your chef's knife.

≥ BY DAWN YANAGIHARA ≤

Bottled Water for Cooking?

Drinking bottled water out of hand (or glass) is one thing, but cooking with it seems extravagant. We wondered if it could be worth the extra expense and so chose three applications—a simple Italian bread, lemon ice, and hot brewed tea—and tried them with Boston tap water, Volvic (our top-rated bottled water, see page 27), and Evian (in which our tasters detected a distinct mineral flavor).

No differences could be detected in the three loaves of bread, and while there were slight flavor differences in the lemon ices, none was a clear favorite. Likewise, little difference was detected in the teas, except that the batch made with Evian left behind mineral deposits in the pot used to boil the water and the tea itself contained tiny lumps (for more information on this phenomenon, see Notes from Readers, page 2).

While we can't say with certainty that using water that is abjectly awful wouldn't make a difference in your cooking, we can say that just about any potable water works. Keep in mind, though, that the quality of tap water can vary from season to season; if yours is particularly "fragrant" or "off," consider filtering it before use in recipes or uncapping some bottled water.

Lighten Up

Hellmann's Mayonnaise (or Best Foods if you're west of the Rockies) was the winner of our March/April 2003 mayonnaise tasting, and its skinnier cousin, Hellmann's Light, was right on its heels. What about using this light mayo in our All-American Potato Salad (page 11)? In a tasting, we thought the regular, full-fat version tasted richer, more

THE LOWDOWN ON MAYO
Light Hellmann's is nearly as good as our favorite mayo, regular Hellmann's.

flavorful, and more balanced. But we liked Hellmann's Light almost as well.

And what about in a cooked application, where mayonnaise serves as a binder and isn't a featured flavor? An excellent excuse to fry up some crab cakes, we thought (we also made tartar sauces with the two mayos). Only one astute taster detected any differences in the crab cakes. The tartar sauces were another story. The sauce made with light mayonnaise was noticeably softer in texture and sweeter and leaner in flavor, but it wasn't objectionable.

Our Conclusion: Though its half-the-calorie/half-the-fat handicap (or advantage, depending on your perspective) sacrifices some flavor in mayo-centric recipes, light mayonnaise can do everything that regular can do.

Separation Anxiety

While some stone fruits, such as freestone peaches, easily part with their pits, others, such as cling peaches and nectarines, hold on to theirs as if for dear life. When faced with a clinger, there are a couple of strategies that can be employed.

The first is to use a paring knife to cut the flesh into wedges, all the way around the fruit. You then reinsert the blade of the knife into one of the cuts and, using your thumb to steady the wedge against the flat of the blade, pry the wedge free of the pit. The first slice is always the hardest to remove; subsequent slices are usually pried free with relative ease.

If you find that the fruit is absolutely intractable, then resort to strategy number two, which incurs some waste and will give you imperfect slices: With the fruit sitting stem-side down for stability, cut the flesh from the pit with vertical swipes of a chef's knife, leaving the pit encased in a squared-off column of flesh.

A Sweeter Nightshade

When developing our recipe for Fresh Tomato Salsa (page 20), we purchased tomatoes by the flat and stored them at room temperature. As the week progressed, we noticed that the salsas were becoming sweeter and more flavorful.

To confirm these findings and check the impact of refrigeration on ripening, we purchased flats of tomatoes on a Monday. As soon as they arrived, we put some in the fridge, stored some at room temperature, and turned the remainder into salsa. This salsa was hardly worth the effort; fresh from the store, the color of the tomatoes was peaked and the flavor vegetal and bland.

On Wednesday, things were beginning to look up, at least for the room-temperature tomatoes. The salsa made from them was more vivid in both color and flavor. The refrigerated tomatoes, however, showed no signs of ripening.

On Thursday, the tomatoes kept at room temperature were at their peak. They yielded to gentle pressure and had deepened in color. The salsa made with them was bright red, sweet, and flavorful. And the

TEST KITCHEN TIP: Split Decision

We've found store-bought split chicken breasts to be problematic. Some are so sloppily cut that the tenderloins are missing, some retain only tiny shreds of tattered skin, and some packages contain wildly divergent sizes. Consequently, for our Thai Grilled Chicken (page 9) and other such recipes, we advise purchasing whole breasts and splitting them yourself.

The basic method for splitting a chicken breast is to simply push a chef's knife through the skin, flesh, and bone. While this method is straightforward, sometimes the split breasts end up lopsided, and sometimes both lobes are marred by unruly bits of bone and cartilage around which a knife and fork must eventually navigate. Enter a classic technique for splitting a chicken breast. It involves the removal of the keel bone and cartilage that divide the breast, thereby making the chicken easier to eat. This method takes a few extra minutes, but we think it's time well spent.

Begin by trimming the rib sections (a chef's knife will suffice, but kitchen shears are particularly well suited to this task). Then, with the breast turned skin-side down on a cutting board, use a chef's knife to score the membrane down the center along the length of the breast. Pick up the breast and, using both hands and some force, bend back the breast lobes, forcing the keel bone to pop out. Now, grasp the keel bone, and pull it free. (On occasion, the cartilage breaks. If this happens, just dig in with your fingers, grip the remaining piece, and pull it out.) Finally, use a chef's knife to halve the breast down the center at the seam, applying force near the top to cut through the wishbone.

 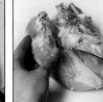 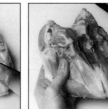  

I. Trim rib sections.   **2.** Score membrane.   **3.** Pop out keel bone.   **4.** Pull out keel bone.   **5.** Halve breast.

KITCHEN SCIENCE: The Mystery of the Yellow Biscuit

You might think that all baking powders are the same. Past kitchen tests have pitted various brands against each other, and we concluded that they all worked just fine.

We decided to see if we would get the same outcome with our Tall and Fluffy Buttermilk Biscuits (page 7) and prepared the final recipe with five brands of baking powder. We were surprised by the results. Although no brand emerged as a clear favorite, we noticed significant differences in the appearance of the biscuits. Some were quite yellow, while others were snow white. What was going on?

We thought we might learn something from the pH of the biscuits, and we did. Our pH meter indicated a variation of 6.9 (more acidic) to

We tested our buttermilk biscuits with five brands of baking powder. All worked just fine, but biscuits made with a double-acid (or double-acting) brand, such as Clabber Girl, were yellower (and slightly taller) than biscuits made with a single-acid brand, such as Featherweight, which were bright white.

8.2 (more alkaline). Biscuits made from Clabber Girl, for instance, yielded very tall but decidedly yellow biscuits with a pH of about 8. Featherweight, on the other hand, produced very white biscuits that were reduced in height and had a finished pH of about 7. It turns out that double-acid (also called double-acting) powders such as Clabber Girl have a greater tendency to yield yellow biscuits. This color change aside, there's no reason to avoid using two-acid powders. Moreover, they do provide better oven rise. –John Olson, Science Editor

---

chilled tomatoes? Still as hard as rocks, orange-red, and in no way improved.

By Friday, though, overripeness had begun to set in. The tomatoes stored at room-temperature had a few squishy spots and a slightly mealy texture. The refrigerated ones were a lost cause; we wrote them off.

The Lesson Here: If you're stuck buying grocery-store tomatoes, a little patience pays off. A few days to ripen at room temperature—not in the fridge—can mean the difference between tasteless and toothsome tomatoes.

Peel Out

Fuzzy skin is no problem when eating a fresh peach out of hand. But when baked into a dessert like our Fresh Peach Cobbler (page 25), fuzzy peach skin becomes leathery flap, and so it must be removed. If your peaches

X MARKS THE SPOT
Cut an X in the bottom of a peach before blanching. After shocking in ice water, the peach nearly peels itself.

are firm enough, a sharp vegetable peeler can make quick work of peeling, but if they are soft and can't take the pressure, the easiest way to remove the skin is to blanch them in boiling water and then shock the peaches in ice water. But for how long should the peaches be blanched? Too long and the flesh becomes mushy, not long enough and the peel will still resist removal. And the timing will vary depending on the ripeness of the peach.

One way to tell when you should pull a peach from boiling water is to score the bottom with an X before blanching and then watch the skin around the X for signs of splitting and tearing during blanching. After 30 to 60 seconds, the peach should be ready. Remove it from the boiling water with a slotted spoon and plunge it into an ice water bath to stop the cooking. Once the peach has cooled, pull it from the ice water and use a paring knife to help peel back the slippery skin. Start peeling at the X, and the skin should come off in large strips.

RECIPE UPDATE: READERS RESPOND

Brown Sugar

Infrequent bakers often find a hard, sugary brick in their pantry when they reach for brown sugar. A new product aims to alleviate this problem. Domino Brownulated is a granulated, pourable light brown sugar with a light, dry texture. Readers wondered if it could be used interchangeably with traditional light brown sugar.

To find out, we made two batches of **Thin, Crispy Chocolate Chip Cookies** (March/April 2001), the first with traditional light brown sugar and the second with Brownulated. The first batch of cookies was sweeter and crisper than the second, which were drier, cakier, and less sweet. We quickly figured out why the two batches were so different. We had measured by volume, and the lighter, airier Brownulated sugar was taking up more room in the measuring cup than the damp traditional light brown sugar, which we packed as we measured it. It turns out that 1 cup of Brownulated sugar weighs just 5 ounces, whereas 1 cup of packed regular brown sugar weighs 7 ounces. Once we used equal amounts of the sugars *by weight*, the cookies were similar. Use this equivalency to determine how much Brownulated sugar is needed in any given recipe.

Pan Preparation

Our recipes can sometimes seem fussy, especially when it comes to preparing pans. With our **Chocolate Mousse Cake** (November/December 2002), for instance, you must grease the pan, dust it with flour, and line the bottom with parchment paper. Once this cake comes out of the oven, you must run a knife around the edges of the pan. Skeptical readers wondered if these steps were really necessary. We baked four cakes to find out.

When we declined to grease and flour the springform pan, the cake souffléed above the rim and hardened there; it clung to the pan as we removed the sides to reveal an unattractive and unevenly baked specimen. When we omitted the parchment lining, we lost 1/8 inch of cake as we pried the pan bottom off the supermoist cake. When we failed to run a knife around the

BAKED IN
UNPREPARED PAN

BAKED IN GREASED &
FLOURED PAN

edge after baking (which helps ease sticking as the cake contracts and cools in the pan), the top and sides remained suspended at rim level while the center fell far below, creating a chocolate crater. Clearly, the five minutes it takes to prepare a pan properly is a wise investment of time. For our Chocolate Mousse Cake recipe, visit **Cook's Extra** at www.cooksillustrated.com and key in code 4049.

Low-Sodium Meat Tenderizer

We have found in several recipes that traditional soy sauce can tenderize beef and chicken (see **Better Beef and Broccoli Stir-Fry** (September/October 2003), **Investigating Steak Tips** (May/June 2003), and **Chicken Stir-Fries** (May/June 2004). Some readers asked if low-sodium soy sauce would produce similar results. We found that while the flavor of meat marinated in low-sodium soy sauce was good, the meat marinated in regular soy sauce was better, with a pronounced soy flavor; the texture of the latter was also more tender. To guarantee tender, flavorful meat, we'd reach for regular soy sauce. But if you use the low-sodium variety, the meat will still be far better than meat that has not been marinated. –Compiled by Nina West

IF YOU HAVE A QUESTION about a recently published recipe, let us know. Send your inquiry, name, address, and daytime telephone number to Recipe Update, Cook's Illustrated, P.O. Box 470589, Brookline, MA 02447, or to recipeupdate@bcpress.com.

≥ BY GARTH CLINGINGSMITH ≤

NEW PRODUCT: Calphalon One

Calphalon has a new line of cookware, known as Calphalon One, that's been heavily advertised as combining "the best qualities of both traditional metal and nonstick cookware." Made by infusing an anodized aluminum pan with an advanced release polymer, these hybrid pans are not cheap—a 12-inch skillet costs $125—but if one pan really can do the work of two, why not give it a try? We did, running a series of tests that pitted the Calphalon One skillet against our favorite traditional and nonstick skillets, both All-Clad.

The Calphalon One proved strong as a traditional skillet. Seared steak and salmon showed superior color and crust development. After searing the steak, we noted the amount of fond (the residue of browned meat that sticks to the pan), which can be deglazed for a rich, flavorful pan sauce. Although nonstick pans are notoriously poor at developing fond, the Calphalon One had no trouble passing this test, easily rivaling our favorite All-Clad traditional pan.

Calphalon's new pan did not fare so well in the nonstick category. When we sautéed fish fillets lightly coated with flour in a small amount of oil, some scraping was required to flip the fillets. But the pan really fell down when it came to several other tasks best suited for a nonstick skillet. Both hash browns and a stir-fry with chicken that had been coated in oil, flour, and cornstarch had to be abandoned. This pan's only likeness to a nonstick pan appeared to be in the sink, where it cleaned up as easily as a nonstick if given a brief soak.

PULLING DOUBLE DUTY?

The new Calphalon One rivals the best traditional skillet but can't compete with a true nonstick pan.

WEAR & TEAR: Adjustable Measuring Cups

In our March/April 2004 issue, we heralded the virtues of the Wonder Cup, which effortlessly measures—and releases—such hard-to-measure ingredients as molasses, shortening, and peanut butter. But as we passed ours through the dishwasher nearly every day in the test kitchen, the measurement delineations started to fade. We called the maker of the Wonder Cup and learned that the numbers are applied with food-grade ink and a unique cylindrical silk-screening process that can withstand gentle hand washing but not the extremes of a dishwasher. Whoops.

ALL WASHED OUT

After many washings, the measurement lines on our Wonder Cup (left) faded from their original clarity. We found that the Adjust-A-Cup (right) works just as well and is dishwasher-safe.

Fortunately, the Wonder Cup's popularity has prompted many copycats. One that stands out is KitchenArt's Adjust-A-Cup, which is marked with an epoxy-type ink that is safe for the dishwasher and withstands moderate scrubbing. Available in 1- and 2-cup capacities and in an array of materials, from plastic to stainless steel, these cups are ruggedly constructed with a very tight seal between plunger and tube. Prices start at $3.59 and go up to $10.99 for a model with a flashy chrome finish.

EQUIPMENT UPDATE: Vegetable Peelers

Since our 1998 rating of vegetable peelers, the Oxo Good Grips has become a standard in our test kitchen. Could Oxo outdo itself? It did. As part of its new line of products called the I-Series, Oxo has introduced a peeler with replaceable blades.

We found the I-Series peeler to be exceptionally sharp and liked its slender handle (the decidedly

OXO   MESSERMEISTER

The Oxo I-Series peeler is our new favorite. The Messermeister peeler works wonders with delicate fruit, but the handle is smaller than we'd like.

unslender handle of the earlier model was our only gripe with that peeler). The new peeler is heavier than the original, but the balance of the extra weight falls to the blade end, so this peeler seems to require less effort on the part of the cook.

The replaceable blades (much like razor blades that click on and pop off) would seem to be a great idea, but in the test kitchen we've found that a peeler can take years to become dull and that it can then be easily realigned with a sharpening steel—in the same fashion as a knife—by essentially "peeling" the steel. (Use this method if you've got the Good Grips peeler and would rather not upgrade.)

Another new peeler that recently made its way to our kitchen has a serrated blade. Made by Messermeister, this peeler is exceptional in its ability to peel peaches, other ripe stone fruits, and tomatoes, a difficult task for even the sharpest of peelers. We loved it for prepping the Fresh Peach Cobbler on page 25, but the handle is too small for cooks with average- or larger-than-average-size hands.

(Visit **Cook's Extra** at www.cooksillustrated .com for the results of our original testing of vegetable peelers. Key in code 4050.)

PRODUCT REDESIGN: Weber Genesis Gas Grills

One of our two top-pick gas grills (rated in July/ August 2003) just got better. The Weber Genesis Silver A has relocated its thermometer to the center of the grill, a more telling position. An under-the-lid swinging basket has been added, as has an additional tool holder, a front condiment tray, and a swing-up work surface. The two-burner Silver A's price increases to $379.

Sources

The following are mail-order sources for items recommended in this issue. Prices were current at press time and do not include shipping and handling. Contact companies directly to confirm up-to-date prices and availability.

PAGE 3: MUDDLER
➤ Rösle Muddler: $15, item #229641, **Sur La Table** (1765 Sixth Avenue South, Seattle, WA 98134-1608; 800-243-0852; www.surlatable.com).

PAGE 9: PORTABLE GAS GRILLS
➤ Thermos Grill2Go: $149.99, item #613191, **Target** (available at stores nationwide and at www.target.com).
➤ Weber Q Portable Gas Grill: $179.99, item #514652, **Target**.
➤ Coleman Road Trip Sport: $169.99, item #504048, **Target**.

PAGE 23: PASTRY BRUSH
➤ OXO Pastry Brush: $4.49, item #470528, **Kitchen Etc.** (32 Industrial Drive, Exeter, NH 03833; 800-232-4070; www.kitchenetc.com).

PAGE 29: SANTOKUS
➤ MAC Superior Santoku Knife, 6½ inch: $55, item #4368, **A Cook's Wares** (211 37th Street, Beaver Falls, PA 15010; 800-915-9788; www.cookswares.com).

PAGE 32: VEGETABLE PEELERS
➤ Oxo I-Series Swivel Peeler: $9.99, item #995944. Oxo I-Series Replacement Blades: $4.99, item #995985. Both at **Kitchen Etc.**

➤ Messermeister Peeler: $5.50, item #154005; **Sur La Table**.

PAGE 32: CALPHALON SKILLET
➤ Calphalon One Infused Anodized Omelette Pan, 12 Inch: $124.99, item #1025956; **Kitchen Etc.**

PAGE 32: MEASURING CUPS
➤ Adjust-A-Cups: $4.99–$10.99, **KitchenArt** (4420 Helton Drive, Florence, AL 35630; 800-239-8090; www.kitchenart.com).

RECIPES
July & August 2004

www.cooksillustrated.com

Get all 11 years of *Cook's Illustrated* magazine and a free gift!

Join www.cooksillustrated.com today and gain access to 11 years' worth of recipes, equipment tests, and food tastings . . . at any time and from anywhere! Plus, as a *Cook's Illustrated* subscriber, you're offered a 20% discount.

Free Gift: As a paid member, you'll also get *The Essential Kitchen: 25 Kitchen Tools No Cook Should Be Without*. This downloadable online guide produced by the editors of *Cook's Illustrated* provides recommendations on the best cookware, tools, and gadgets for your kitchen. Simply type in the promotion code **CB44A** when signing up online.

Here are a few of the many things available at our site:

Best Recipes: Eleven years' worth of recipes developed in America's Test Kitchen.
Cookware Reviews: Every cookware review published since 1993, plus many reviews never seen in *Cook's*.
Ingredient Tastings: A decade of taste-test results, offering recommendations on everything from ketchup and mayonnaise to canned tomatoes, baking chocolates, and salt.
Online Bookstore: Cookbooks from the editors of *Cook's*, plus much more.

AMERICA'S TEST KITCHEN TV SHOW

Join the millions of home cooks who watch our TV show, *America's Test Kitchen*, on public television every week. For more information, including recipes and a schedule of program times in your area, visit www.americastestkitchen.com.

Grilled Glazed Salmon, 19

Thai-Style Grilled Chicken with Spicy Sweet and Sour Dipping Sauce, 9

Tall and Fluffy Buttermilk Biscuits, 7

All-American Potato Salad, 11

Spice Rubs for Grilled Steak, 12

Texas-Style Barbecued Beef Ribs, 15

Fresh Tomato Salsa, 20

Fresh Peach Cobbler, 25

Freeform Summer Fruit Tart, 22

PHOTOGRAPHY: CARL TREMBLAY, STYLING: MARIE PIRANO

Ribier

Muscat

Crimson Seedless

Perlette

Autumn Royal

Black Marroo

Concord

Flame Seedless

Red Globe

Champagne

Thompson Seedless

GRAPES

COOK'S
ILLUSTRATED

Grilled Beef Tenderloin
Salt, Rest, and Grill

How to Bake Chicken Breasts
Juicy Meat and Crisp Skin

Tasting Spaghetti Sauces

Ultimate Sticky Buns

Rating Hand Mixers
Can They Handle Cookie Dough?

Pineapple Upside-Down Cake

Lasagna Bolognese
Faster and Simpler

www.cooksillustrated.com

$5.95 U.S./$6.95 CANADA

0 74470 62805 7

10

CONTENTS

September & October 2004

COOK'S ILLUSTRATED
www.cooksillustrated.com

HOME OF AMERICA'S TEST KITCHEN

Founder and Editor	Christopher Kimball
Executive Editor	Jack Bishop
Senior Editors	Maryellen Driscoll
	Dawn Yanagihara
Editorial Manager, Books	Elizabeth Carduff
Art Director	Amy Klee
Test Kitchen Director	Erin McMurrer
Senior Editors, Books	Julia Collin Davison
	Lori Galvin
Senior Writer	Bridget Lancaster
Managing Editor	Rebecca Hays
Associate Editors	Matthew Card
	Keith Dresser
Science Editor	John Olson
Web Editor	Keri Fisher
Copy Editor	India Koopman
Test Cooks	Stephanie Alleyne
	Erika Bruce
	Sean Lawler
	Diane Unger-Mahoney
Assistant Test Cooks	Garth Clingingsmith
	Charles Kelsey
	Nina West
Editorial Assistant	Elizabeth Wray
Assistant to the Publisher	Melissa Baldino
Kitchen Assistants	Nadia Domeq
	Maria Elena Delgado
	Ena Gudiel
Kitchen Interns	Barbara Akins
	Katie Archambault
	Lori Bullock Floyd
	Julia Humes
	Cali Todd
Contributing Editor	Elizabeth Germain
Consulting Editors	Shirley Corriher
	Jasper White
	Robert L. Wolke
Proofreader	Jean Rogers
Vice President Marketing	David Mack
Sales Director	Leslie Ray
Retail Sales Director	Jason Geller
Corporate Sponsorship Specialist	Laura Phillipps
Sales Representative	Shekinah Cohn
Marketing Assistant	Connie Forbes
Circulation Director	Bill Tine
Circulation Manager	Larisa Greiner
Products Director	Steven Browall
Direct Mail Director	Adam Perry
Customer Service Manager	Jacqueline Valerio
Customer Service Representative	Julie Gardner
E-Commerce Marketing Manager	Hugh Buchan
Marketing Intern	Ian Halpern
Vice President Operations	James McCormack
Senior Production Manager	Jessica Lindheimer Quirk
Production Manager	Mary Connelly
Book Production Specialist	Ron Bilodeau
Production Assistants	Jennifer McCreary
	Jennifer Power
	Christian Steinmetz
Systems Administrator	Richard Cassidy
WebMaster	Aaron Shuman
Production Web Interns	Lauren Feinberg
	Lauren Pettapiece
Chief Financial Officer	Sharyn Chabot
Controller	Mandy Shito
Office Manager	Saudiyah Abdul-Rahim
Receptionist	Henrietta Murray
Publicity	Deborah Broide

PRINTED IN THE USA

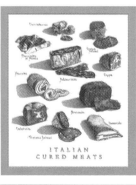

Italian Cured Meats (Salumi) *Salumi* is the word Italians use to label their wide variety of cured meats. Prosciutto di Parma is a cured ham known for its balance of sweet and salty flavors. Culatello is also made from the leg of a pig but is pressed into a 2-inch square and streaked with several lines of fat. Coppa is made from pork shoulder and is more marbled than prosciutto. Bresaola is made from beef loin and is extremely lean. Salamis are made from seasoned ground meat that is stuffed into casings (like sausage) and then aged. Genoa and Toscano salamis look similar and are both made from finely ground pork, but the latter is larger and flavored with garlic. Schiacciata salami is flattened into an oblong shape and comes dolce (sweet) or piccante (spicy). Cacciatorini are small rustic salami designed to fit easily in hunters' pockets, where they serve as a portable lunch. Pancetta, like bacon, is made from the belly of the pig, but it is not smoked. After being aged, it is cooked and added to soups and pasta sauces as a seasoning. Guanciale is used in a very similar manner, but it is made from pig jowls and has a stronger pork flavor.

COVER (*Squash*): Elizabeth Brandon, BACK COVER (*Italian Cured Meats*): John Burgoyne

For list rental information, contact: ClientLogic, 1200 Harbor Blvd., 9th Floor, Weehawken, NJ 07087; 201-865-5800; fax 201-867-2450.
Editorial Office: 17 Station St., Brookline, MA 02445; 617-232-1000; fax 617-232-1572. Subscription inquiries: call 800-526-8442.
Postmaster: Send all new orders, subscription inquiries, and change of address notices to Cook's Illustrated, P.O. Box 7446, Red Oak, IA 51591-0446.

NATURAL DISASTERS

The worst hailstorm on record for Washington County lasted an hour and a half and cut a swath so violent that it scythed 200 acres of new hay, bruised cows, and left so much ice in one farmer's driveway that he couldn't get out to the main road without using a plow. After the ensuing downpour, hail was washed down into the valleys, leaving mounds of frozen slush more than 3 feet high. January thaws and heavy rain took out half the culverts in town a few years ago, and back in the early '90s, a small twister worked its way down our mountain valley, uprooting huge maples and oaks along its path. There was a lot of firewood that year.

As a child, I remember standing high up on Red Mountain in the Bartlett Lot, looking down the valley toward New York State and seeing a large plume of smoke coming up from Colonel Vaughn's farm. Some green hay had spontaneously combusted, and the milking barn was turned into ashes and blackened concrete in mere hours. Just two years ago, the Wilcox Dairy south of Manchester went up in smoke, and the West Farm on Tate Hill Road was burned to the foundation last fall. I once ran into a local man who was excavating a cemetery back in the woods, claiming that he had discovered a mass grave. He told me that a hundred years ago, in a bad influenza epidemic, the dead were laid out like cordwood by the road and were picked up by horse-drawn carts and buried together. The same fate awaited many of those involved with the Shays Rebellion in the 1780s. They hid out on top of Egg Mountain (a short walk from our farm), and many died of the flu.

Just recently, the town gossip included a divorce; whispers about a bad traffic accident involving a teenage girl; a horse that fell on a rider, crushing her leg; and the deaths of Georgie, who was living up at Susy's place

in a converted barn, and Roy McBride, who had moved to Florida some years back but had kept his small red house next to the old Smith farm. Of course, over the years one collects heartbreaking stories of tractor accidents, hunters mistaking friends for deer, logging mishaps, and automobiles that collide with moose. I can point out more than a few crosses with flowers erected by the side of the road.

Those of us who grew up in the country often regard our own childhoods as accidents waiting to happen, as parents were less protective back then. In the summer, as a young farmhand, I was chased by a bull, frequently stepped on by a 1-ton draft horse, and worked alongside corn choppers, Farmall tractors, and hay balers so dangerous that I'm surprised I still have both arms. My first horse was a Morgan that had a nasty habit of stopping cold on the edge of embankments (I kept going) or loping under large, low-hanging boughs (I stopped cold). Other days, I would take off with my .22 and a sandwich into the mountains to explore abandoned camps with rotten floors and half-fallen ceilings. After supper and a few doses of Jim Beam, my mother often took my sister and I on wild rides up Southeast Corners Road in a surplus army Jeep that skidded and sluiced over the gravel and loose fill. It's a wonder we survived.

My own kids seem to live a more protected life. They've fallen off horses, survived an overturned canoe in the Battenkill, and made their share of visits to the emergency room after swallowing staples, fracturing a leg, drinking a half-bottle of cough syrup, and suffering a short list of other childhood injuries. Real disasters seem more distant. We recently heard of a family that

Christopher Kimball

lost two sons to sudden heart failure and a freak car accident in the next town that ended the lives of a mother and her two children. It is unbearably tragic but not threatening, as if you could hear the distant rumble of a gathering storm without actually seeing it. For now, the weather report for our mountain valley remains sunny.

Families endure all sorts of other, more minor tragedies. When I ask Charlie if he wants to play with his train set, he looks at me with a slightly pitying look and says, "No, it's OK, Dad," in an effort to soften the blow. Or I yell at Caroline for losing control of her horse and she spends the rest of the day alone, her pride having suffered. Many things are natural enough: the longing for a neighbor recently buried, or grief taken in hand and measured out in small bits over a lifetime. But it is also natural to be hopeful, to sense a homecoming in the faint scent of wood smoke drifting up the valley and think well of the future despite the present.

On occasion, Adrienne and I have the good sense to sit on the porch after dinner when all of the good and bad add up to nothing much, if you call watching fingered shadows steal across our lower meadow nothing. It's for certain the end of a perfect day, a day that will soon be lost to history as the cool Vermont twilight steals down from the darkening woods. It's natural to forget how good a day it was, thinking that tomorrow will be just as fine, an easy replacement, if you will. But, being older and perhaps just a bit wiser, we'll sit awhile and watch the last minutes of this day ebb into night and try to commit it to memory. One just never knows what the future may bring.

FOR INQUIRIES, ORDERS, OR MORE INFORMATION:

www.cooksillustrated.com

At www.cooksillustrated.com, you can order books and subscriptions, sign up for our free e-newsletter, or renew your magazine subscription. Subscribe to the Web site and you'll have access to 11 years of *Cook's* recipes, cookware tests, ingredient testings, and more.

COOKBOOKS

We sell more than 40 cookbooks by the editors of *Cook's Illustrated*. To order, visit our bookstore at www.cooksillustrated.com or call 800-611-0759 (or 515-246-6911 from outside the U.S.).

COOK'S ILLUSTRATED Magazine

Cook's Illustrated magazine (ISSN 1068-2821), number 70, is published bimonthly by Boston Common Press Limited Partnership, 17 Station Street, Brookline, MA 02445. Copyright 2004 Boston Common Press Limited Partnership. Periodicals postage paid at Boston, Mass., and additional mailing offices, USPS #012487. POSTMASTER: Send address changes to Cook's Illustrated, P.O. Box 7446, Red Oak, IA 51591-0446. For subscription and gift subscription orders, subscription inquiries, or change-of-address notices, call 800-526-8442 in the U.S. or 515-247-7571 from outside the U.S., or write us at Cook's Illustrated, P.O. Box 7446, Red Oak, IA 51591-0446.

NOTES FROM READERS

⇒ COMPILED BY INDIA KOOPMAN ⇐

The Matter of Pan Size

Your recipe for Lemon Pound Cake in the March/April 2002 issue calls for a pan size of 9 by 5 inches. Does this measurement refer to the bottom of the pan or the top? The sides of loaf pans often angle outward, so the top measurement is larger than the bottom measurement.

ELIZABETH MCCARTHY
SAN MATEO, CALIF.

➤ Loaf pans, like other bakeware and cookware, are measured across the top, from one inside edge to the other. Depth is measured from the bottom inside of the pan to the top of the lip, with the measure held perpendicular to the pan bottom.

According to the Cookware Manufacturers Association, the generic term "loaf pan" can apply to pans measuring anywhere from 7½ by 3¾ inches to 11 by 7 inches. Our recipe was developed in the pan that won our September/October 2000 rating of loaf pans, the Baker's Secret, which measures 9⅛ by 5⅛.

For the results of our loaf pan ratings, visit **Cook's Extra** at www.cooksillustrated.com and key in code 5041.

Your question made us curious to see how our Lemon Pound Cake would turn out if made in slightly larger or smaller pans. After making the cake in our standard pan as well as in an 8½ by 4½ pan and a 10 by 5 pan, we found the greatest variation in outcome with the larger pan. The ideal cake (see photo below right), baked in our standard pan, shows a nicely domed cake with a fissure running through the top—a telltale sign of a classic pound cake. The cake baked in the smaller pan looked much the same; it just rose a bit higher, as would be expected given the smaller volume of the pan. The cake baked in the 10 by 5 pan, however, had a flat top with no fissure (see photo below left). This larger, flatter cake was also a bit dry. Being a good inch shorter than the

PAN WAS TOO BIG   PAN WAS JUST RIGHT

The cake at left, baked in a pan too large for the recipe, didn't rise well and was dry. The cake at right, baked in the proper pan size, rose well, developed a classic pound cake fissure on top, and was moist.

other two cakes, it needed less time to cook and so was overdone when we took it out of the oven at the suggested cooking time of 50 minutes.

Lighter, Fluffier Pancakes

I add soda water and powdered buttermilk to my pancake batter instead of liquid buttermilk. It always turns out light and fluffy pancakes. Have you tried it?

ONLINE READER

➤ We're familiar with your suggestion of using sparkling water (and even beer or ginger ale) in pancake recipes and thought we should finally give it a try. To do so, we made our recipe for Light and Fluffy Pancakes (January/February 1996), substituting the requisite amounts of sparkling water and powdered buttermilk for the ¾ cup of liquid buttermilk called for in the recipe. We noticed straight away that the batter made with sparkling water was much more bubbly, almost lively. While we wouldn't describe the resulting pancakes as lively, we did find them to be lighter than those made according to the regular recipe, which are already pretty light. Readers looking for the ultimate in light and fluffy pancakes should try a batch made with sparkling water. For our recipe, you'll need 3 tablespoons of powdered buttermilk, which is available in the baking ingredients aisle in most supermarkets.

Béchamel Made Even Easier

I just read your test results on whether or not it's important to scald milk (March/April 2004). Whenever I make a béchamel—or any other sauce or gravy where liquid is added to a fat and flour mixture and then stirred to thicken—I always heat the liquid first. I do this in a measuring cup in the microwave—thereby eliminating the extra dirty pan—and the result is that the sauce comes together and thickens almost immediately when the liquid is added. This saves lots of stirring time and seems such an obvious thing to do. My question is whether there's any reason not to do it.

JOAN VOGAN
SUGAR LAND, TEXAS

➤ In the test you mention, we learned that scalding milk or not before using it to make béchamel doesn't make a difference in the quality of the finished sauce. Starting with either will get you to the same end point: a thickened white sauce that might be used for anything from the base for a chowder to the sauce for spinach lasagna. But what we realized after trying your suggestion is that heating

the milk in the microwave does get you to that end point with less effort and in less time. In fact, in microwaving the 3½ cups of milk required for the béchamel in our spinach lasagna recipe (also in the March/April 2004 issue), we shaved about 3 minutes off the 10-minute cooking (and stirring) time. As you say, heating the milk in a measuring cup—which you need to use anyway—spared us the need to dirty another pan.

A Fishy Skillet

I like to sear tuna and salmon in my cast-iron skillet, but I don't like the fish flavor that seems to arise when I cook something else in the same pan later. Short of dedicating a pan to fish, is there any way to get rid of the fishy taste and smell?

BRANDON FOX
RICHMOND, VA.

➤ After frying up more than 3 pounds of salmon and trying at least one-half dozen ways to eliminate the smelly evidence—using kosher salt, baking soda, lemon juice, and various combinations thereof—we were stumped. Scrubbing with baking soda and rubbing with lemon juice and kosher salt helped to diminish the smell, but not enough to keep an egg subsequently fried in the pan from smelling like fish oil.

Frustrated, we resorted to a method we had hoped to let lie: a scrub with hot water and a small amount of dishwashing detergent. Many cooks refuse to use detergent on their cast-iron cookware, arguing that scrubbing with detergent will remove the valuable seasoning that takes so long to build up. Be that as it may—and in the test kitchen we have cooks on both sides of the argument—this method was easy and effective.

One last thought we had was to heat some vegetable oil in the pan, reasoning that a new hot fat might work best to release—or at least mask—the odor of the old fishy fat. This technique—pouring enough oil in the pan to coat the bottom (about ¹⁄₁₆ inch), heating until it started to smoke, then taking the pan off the heat and letting it cool to room temperature—was almost completely effective, and we recommend it for those cooks who don't want to use detergent on their cast iron.

Is this a lot of work? Yes. So if you fry oily fish frequently, we recommend that you set aside one skillet (a new 10-inch costs only about $15) for that purpose. Either that, or the next morning fry some bacon in your pan before you use it to fry eggs. The rendered bacon fat works just as well as vegetable oil, and the bacon has so much flavor that we couldn't detect any fishy flavor.

A Better Bottle for Water?

I found it curious that in your bottled water tasting (July/August 2004) you didn't address the question of what sort of plastic it comes in—opaque (HDPE, like the containers that milk comes in) or clear (PET). Personally, I wish milk still came in glass bottles. I swear I can taste plastic in milk from a plastic container.

LYNN POWER
SOMERVILLE, MASS.

➤ To eliminate any possibility that the type of plastic used to bottle water might influence flavor, in our tasting we sampled only waters bottled in plastic made from PET (polyethylene terephthalate). Although representatives of the bottled water industry uniformly claim that both plastics typically used to bottle water—PET and HDPE, or high density polyethylene—are of equal quality, anecdotal reports as well as a bottled water tasting conducted by *Consumer Reports* have indicated that water bottled in HDPE often doesn't seem to taste as good as water bottled in PET. Curious to see if we could taste a difference, we decided to conduct our own blind tasting.

In this tasting were two of the brands in our July/August tasting, Arrowhead and Poland Spring, with samples of each in HDPE and PET bottles. The results were curious. Tasters liked the Arrowhead PET and HDPE waters equally well, but they distinctly preferred the Poland Spring water from the PET bottle, with some finding the samples from the HDPE bottle to taste "stale" or to have "a strong plastic aftertaste." Our tasting results, then, are inconclusive.

There is, however, a very strong argument being made for PET by one constituency, and the bottled water industry is paying attention. According to Jane Lazgin of Nestlé Waters North America, which owns both the Arrowhead and Poland Spring brands, consumers prefer the hard, clear PET plastic traditionally used for smaller bottles and have been requesting it in the larger-size jugs and containers, which have until recently been made from less expensive HDPE plastic. Nestlé, for one, will now be offering its larger gallon-size jug in both PET and HDPE for some of its 13 brands. The fact that only two of the nine brands we sampled in our initial tasting are available in HDPE containers also attests to the growing popularity of PET.

Tuna in a Pouch Gets Cheaper

In your write-up of canned tuna versus pouch tuna in the May/June 2003 issue, you say it costs more per ounce for the pouch tuna, which your tasters preferred. But you didn't account for the fact that half of the 6-ounce can consists of the "packing medium"—water or oil—which most people I know pour down the drain. The 7.06-ounce pouch, on the other hand, is 100 percent usable. If you redo the math, you'll find that the price difference per ounce between the can and the pouch is pretty minimal.

MARK M. DENITTIS, CHEF INSTRUCTOR
JOHNSON & WALES UNIVERSITY
PROVIDENCE, R.I.

➤ StarKist solid white albacore in spring water, our favorite canned brand, costs $1.39 for a 6-ounce can or, it would seem, 23 cents per ounce. StarKist chunk white albacore, our highest rated tuna in a pouch, costs $2.89 for a 7.06-ounce pouch, or about 41 cents per ounce. But once we drained off the water from the canned tuna, we found that a 6-ounce can contained just 3½ ounces of tuna. That brought the price for the canned tuna up to about 40 cents per ounce. So we now recommend the StarKist pouch tuna with no caveats at all. Tasters found it fresher tasting and more moist than canned, and its cost is the same.

For the results of our tasting of tuna in a pouch, visit **Cook's Extra** at www.cooksillustrated.com and key in code 5042.

Perplexed by Pyrex

After publishing a quick tip in our May/June 2004 issue that calls for microwaving bulk popcorn in a microwave-safe bowl, we got several notes from readers wanting to know if they could use a Pyrex bowl. The answer is no. Pyrex is sold as "microwave-safe," but a list of restrictions on the Pyrex Web site includes a warning against using Pyrex to pop popcorn in the microwave. This applies to both bulk popcorn and "microwave popcorn" purchased in bags.

Another warning on the site applies to our acorn squash recipe (see page 13). The warning directs the cook to "add a small amount of liquid" to Pyrex-ware before "baking foods that release liquids while cooking." We cook our squash in the microwave, but this warning applies to such foods when cooked in either a conventional or a microwave oven.

In the case of both the popcorn and the squash, the warnings reflect Pyrex's vulnerability to shattering when exposed to extreme changes in temperature (the steam from the popcorn and the searingly hot liquid from the cooking squash would be the culprits). More information on the safe use of Pyrex can be accessed through World Kitchen, now the owner of the Pyrex brand. Go to www.worldkitchen.com.

As for our quick tip on popcorn, we've found that you can safely use a brown paper lunch bag instead of a bowl. Add ¼ cup bulk popcorn to the bag and fold the bag over several times to close. Depending on the power of your microwave, the popcorn will take between two and six minutes to pop. Check its progress frequently.

WHAT IS IT?

This gadget belonged to my late grandmother. My grandparents owned a restaurant from the 1940s through the 1960s, and I assume it was originally used there. It appears to be used for portioning out some mystery ingredient.

SALLY OLSEN
GREEN BAY, WIS.

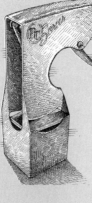

➤ Your unusual gadget—which is used to portion out cubes of ice cream rather than the familiar well-rounded scoops—has an interesting history that involves none other than the entrepreneurial Ray Kroc, the man who came up with the idea of franchising the hamburger stand that we now know as McDonald's. The square ice cream scoop, called the Dip It, was one of the many business schemes Kroc pursued before striking gold with McDonald's.

Made of stainless steel, the Dip It has two arms that measure about 4½ inches each. The square end of the device is dipped into a container of ice cream, the ice cream packed in, and a straight edge used to square off the cube. The handle, which sits next to a spring-loading mechanism, is squeezed to release the ice cream (see illustration at right). According to the book *McDonald's: Behind the Arches* by John F. Love (Bantam, 1986), the selling points of this scoop were more precise portion control and ease of use. The test kitchen, however, didn't find the Dip It easy to use. Loading the scoop was awkward, and turning out a perfect cube was a challenge. Practice might eventually make perfect, but the test kitchen found the Dip It to be a gimmick—and certainly not a gold strike.

The Dip It, an ice cream scoop dispensing cubes rather than round scoops, was one of many products dreamed up by Ray Kroc before he struck gold with McDonald's.

Quick Tips

≳ COMPILED BY ERIKA BRUCE ≲

Easier Cake Removal

Often interrupted while trying to bake in the kitchen, Jean Olsen of Palo Alto, Calif., sometimes allows her cakes to cool while still in the greased pans, and she then has trouble getting them out. By carefully running the cake pan over low heat on the stovetop, she melts the grease that was initally spread on the pan bottom. The cake pops out easily when the pan is flipped over. Jamie Kalakay of Nantucket, Mass., found that this technique also works well for loosening stubborn Bavarians, flans, and crème caramels.

Quicker Cutting

Chris Sroka of Minneapolis, Minn., found a creative use for his pizza cutter. During breakfast, when his young grandchildren are waiting impatiently for their French toast, pancakes, or waffles, he uses a pizza cutter to cut them neatly and quickly into bite-size pieces.

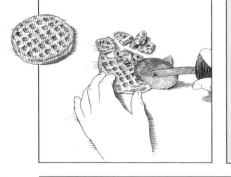

Kitchen Organization

We are always looking for better ways to organize our kitchen. Here are four tips from readers that we found very useful.

A. To avoid a messy cleanup when using her standing mixer, Mary Flack of Schulenburg, Texas, puts a plastic serving tray (like the kind found in cafeterias) under the mixer. Not only is it easier to slide the mixer on the countertop, but any mess can be easily cleaned up with a quick rinse of the tray.

B. Carroll McNeill of Cupertino, Calif., utilizes her deep kitchen drawers by stacking cutlery trays on top of each other. For easy access, she uses the top tray for the items that she uses most often (everyday utensils, such as can openers, spatulas, and large spoons) and the bottom tray for less frequently needed items (such as spreaders, skewers, straws, and chopsticks). It's a simple matter to grasp the top tray and lift it aside when access to the bottom layer is desired.

C. Tired of playing hide-and-seek with spices stored in his kitchen cabinet, Mike Ehlenfeldt of Charlestown, N.H., found a simple way to keep them organized. By arranging the spices in labeled rectangular baskets alphabetically or according to type, he can quickly identify their location and retrieve whatever he needs by pulling down the appropriate basket.

D. Ann Neilson of Los Angeles, Calif., keeps her refrigerator neat and organized by keeping a permanent marker and masking tape handy. Every time a new bottle or jar is opened or leftovers are packaged up, she writes the date on a piece of tape and sticks it to the side of the container in a highly visible spot.

A.

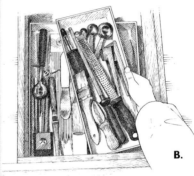

B.

C.

D.

Neater Cheese Grating

Donna Maderer of Quincy, Mass., uses a clean plastic bag (a large zipper-lock bag or a grocery store shopping bag) to hold both grater and cheese. By placing the bag around the grater and the cheese, she can grate cheese with clean hands and eliminate flyaway bits. Leftover grated cheese is ready for storage in a handy bag.

Saving Fresh Ginger

Fresh ginger is often sold in large pieces that may not be used up in one recipe. Not wanting any to go to waste, Susan Brown of Gatineau, Quebec, figured out an easy way to extend its shelf life.

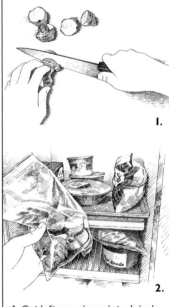

I.

2.

1. Cut leftover ginger into 1-inch pieces and place them in a zipper-lock bag.
2. Store the bag in the freezer for one month or longer. Whenever fresh ginger is needed, simply pull a piece from the freezer, allow it to thaw, peel it, and then grate or chop as required.

Catching Oil Drips

A. To prevent unsightly oil stains on pantry shelves, Pat Ware of Fostoria, Mich., wraps a clean sweatband around the middle of her bottle of oil to catch drips. When the band becomes too dirty, she cleans it in the washing machine.

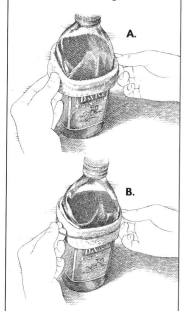

B. Alternatively, a band of folded paper towels can be fastened around the bottle with a rubber band and simply thrown away when dirty.

Juicing Citrus

When Lori Factor-Marcus of Malden, Mass., needs just a little lemon or lime juice—not enough to warrant use of a juicer—she employs the following method.

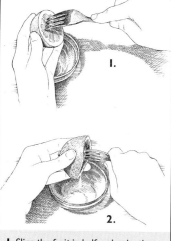

1. Slice the fruit in half and poke the flesh a few times with a fork.
2. Stick the fork in the citrus and twist, just as you would with a reamer.

Speedy Dough Rising

Lynn McHugh of Roanoke, Va., was looking for an easy way to speed up the bread-making process. She hit pay dirt with a microwavable neck wrap, the kind normally used to relieve stress. When wrapped around a bowl of dough, it provides just enough extra heat to gently nudge the dough into rising in about half the time.

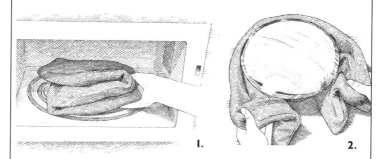

1. Heat the neck warmer in the microwave for 1 to 2 minutes.
2. Fit the warmer snugly around the bowl of dough.

Tea-bag Stand-Ins

Two readers learned how to manage quite nicely without a ball or sieve designed to capture loose tea by putting a paper coffee filter to use.

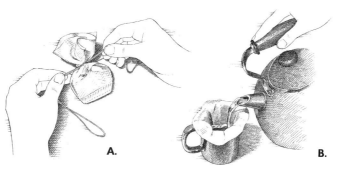

A. Rachel Platter of Chicago, Ill., places her tea (or an herbal blend—chamomile flowers, mint, and so forth) in the center of the filter, then gathers the edges and ties them with cooking twine. When trimming the twine, she leaves a little extra length to use in pulling the bag out of the cup or teapot when it is done steeping.

B. Francis Lam of Elmhurst, N.Y., has an alternative method for making just one mug of tea: Line the mug with a cone-shaped coffee filter large enough to extend over the rim of the mug. Fold the filter over the rim to secure, then fill with loose tea and add hot water. When finished steeping, just pull out the filter and squeeze gently, as you would a regular tea bag.

Cleaning Mushrooms

Susan Asanovic of Wilton, Conn., found the perfect tool for cleaning all of those hard-to-reach spots on mushrooms. No need for those cute little specialty brushes—a clean, soft-bristled toothbrush provides a comfortable handle, and the small head slips easily under the gills to capture every stray bit of dirt. A run through the dishwasher cleans the soiled brush.

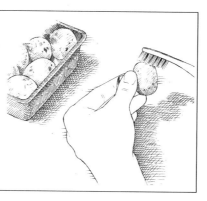

Mincing Chiles

Jean Kelly of Boston, Mass., found a quick way to season her dips and sauces with chipotle peppers or pickled jalapeño chiles. She simply puts a small amount of chile into the well of a garlic press and squeezes.

Nonskid Cutting Boards and Cakes

A. After lining her new kitchen cabinets with nonskid shelf liner, Patricia Babiarz of Dallas, Texas, came up with a good way to use the leftover material. She cut it into pieces that fit perfectly under her cutting boards, thus stopping them from slipping and sliding. When the makeshift mats are not in use, she just rolls them up and stores them neatly in a kitchen drawer.

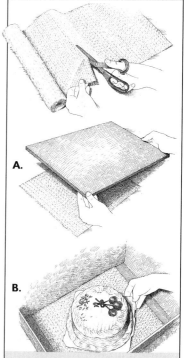

B. Caitlin Campbell of Richmond, Calif., uses nonskid shelf liner to safely transport cakes, casseroles, and other large serving dishes. She lines the bottom of the cake carrier, box, or other container with a small piece to keep the contents from sliding into the walls of the carrier while in transit.

Grill-Roasted Beef Tenderloin

With a whole tenderloin going for as much as $180, uneven cooking, bland flavor, and a tough outer crust just don't cut it. Could we do it cheaper and better?

≥ BY BRIDGET LANCASTER ≤

I'm not one to part easily with money, but I will on occasion break the bank and buy a couple of beef tenderloin steaks to throw on the grill. The tender, buttery interior is the big draw for me, and the combination of a healthy seasoning and the flavor from the charcoal grill is a perfect solution to a rather mild-tasting (boring) piece of meat. Recently, at the prospect of feeding a large crowd (and not crazy about the idea of standing over a hot grill, flipping a dozen steaks), I ordered a whole beef tenderloin from my local supermarket. Six pounds of perfectly trimmed tenderloin later, I had shelled out a jaw-dropping $167.94 (that's $27.99 per pound), questioned my sanity, and headed for home.

I heated up the grill and gingerly placed my new, most valuable possession over the hot coals. Even though I watched it like a hawk, I couldn't get the tenderloin to cook evenly. The exterior was charred and tough; the interior of the fat butt end was pink and the thinner tail end was beyond well-done. Worst of all, because I was able to season only the exterior of the tenderloin, the interior was bland and flavorless. Maybe I should have stuck to steaks after all.

Crying into my can of Coors, I wondered if there was a way to take this mammoth and insanely expensive cut of beef and grill it to absolute perfection. My expectations were high: an even, rosy pink throughout; a browned, crusty exterior; and well-seasoned, grilled flavor. Nothing less would do. And, after having spent nearly $170 on a complete flop, I was determined to find a cheaper alternative.

Sticker Shock

At local supermarkets, I learned, whole beef tenderloin isn't a meat case–ready item. Most butchers I talked to said they keep the tenderloins in the back to be cut for filets, so if you want one, you've got to ask for it. When you do ask for whole tenderloin, it will usually come "peeled," which means that the outer layer of fat and silver skin (tough muscle sheath) has been removed. These peeled tenderloins ran anywhere from $13.99 per pound for Choice grade meat to an even more astounding $32.99 per pound for Prime grade at a high-end butcher—that's

A perfect tenderloin from the grill starts with smart shopping and finishes with a two-level fire.

$200 dollars for a 6-pound roast. At that price, I expected the butcher to come to my house, grill the meat for me, wash the dishes, and throw in a back rub.

A few days later, I went shopping at a wholesale club. No longer just a place to buy giant cans of beans, most wholesale clubs sell meat as well. I soon found myself eye-to-eye with a case full of Cryovac'ed, Choice grade, whole tenderloins. If the mountain of meat hadn't caught my attention, the price sure would have. Weighing in at about $9 per pound, these tenderloins were one-third the cost of the roast I had bought from my butcher. I grabbed as many as I could pack into the giant shopping cart and headed back to the kitchen.

I soon discovered the one downside of using the wholesale club tenderloins: They came "unpeeled," so a fair amount of trimming, tugging, and prying was necessary to rid the meat of its fat and silver skin. But I had to be judicious, as I found my trimmings could weigh more than 1½ pounds, including the loss of some valuable meat. The best way to trim one of these tenderloins was

to first peel off as much fat as possible with my hands; the fat came away clean and took very little of the pricey meat with it (see the illustrations on page 7). Next I got out my flexible boning knife (a sharp paring knife works well in a pinch) and removed the silver skin, the muscle sheath that would otherwise cause the tenderloin to curl up on the grill. Last, I took the advice of many cookbooks and tucked the narrow tip end of the tenderloin under and tied it securely. This tuck-and-tie step gave the tenderloin a more consistent thickness that would allow it to grill more evenly.

Was this extra 20 minutes of preparatory work worth the effort? You'd better believe it! Tenderloin is by no means a "cheap" piece of meat, but this time it didn't empty my wallet. (See the Tasting box on page 8 for detailed information on price versus quality.)

Beef Season

While some love beef tenderloin for its "mild" beef flavor, others scoff at it for exactly the same reason. I found myself in the latter camp and felt that the tenderloin could use a flavor boost. Many recipes suggested marinades, spice rubs, or herb crusts. Tasters rejected the marinated tenderloins for their weird, spongy texture. Spice rubs made the beef taste too much like barbecue (if I wanted BBQ, I'd buy a cheap rack of ribs), while herb rubs were too powerful for such a tame cut of meat. I was looking for a way to enhance the beef flavor, not mask it.

Then a colleague turned me on to a recently heralded technique in which the tenderloin is salted and left to sit overnight in the fridge. The theory goes that the salt penetrates the meat all the way to the center, seasoning the tenderloin throughout. Sure enough, the salted-overnight beef was seasoned through and through, but at quite a cost. The meat had turned a sickly brown-gray (even when the center was cooked to medium-rare), and the texture was webby, like that of an undercooked pot roast (see photo on page 7).

For my next round, I salted two more tenderloins. I wrapped both in plastic and refrigerated one for four hours, the other for one hour. Although both were markedly better than the overnight-salted tenderloin, the winner was the beef that had been salted for only one hour. Given

When Should You Salt Meat?

Salting meat is nothing new; it was used centuries before refrigeration as a method of preservation. Recently, though, there has been a renewed chorus of voices singing the praises of the simple salt rub, sometimes applied the night before cooking. It's not so hard to see why salt might make a tough cut more palatable, but would this technique improve pricey tenderloin?

We found that salting the meat an hour before cooking gave the roast a beefier flavor. A four-hour salt produced much the same results, but salting the roast the night before cooking was not desirable. The loin turned brown at the surface and lost some of its legendary texture. But why?

Anyone who lives in a cold climate knows that the salting of roadways causes cars to rust. This is due to salt's ability to promote oxidation (the removal of electrons) from iron. Salt can also help to oxidize myoglobin, an iron-containing protein that gives meat its red color. The brown color of the tenderloin that had been salted overnight indicated that a significant amount of the myoglobin had been oxidized and its red color lost.

Perhaps the poor color could be excused if the procedure had produced phenomenal flavor. In fact, the opposite was true; the meat was stringy and the flavor was tired. In addition to oxidizing the myoglobin, the salt had drawn water from the meat, causing it to look thready, as if it had been overcooked. Moreover, some of the mild but juicy beef flavor normally associated with tenderloin was lost; a new dull taste had developed. In the case of tenderloin, which is beautifully textured and delicately flavored out of the package, there is really no good reason to salt for extended periods. –John Olson, Science Editor

OVERNIGHT SALTING
Looks like overcooked pot roast

ONE-HOUR SALTING
A tender, juicy, and flavorful roast

just enough time to season the meat without compromising the texture, the salt brought out a decidedly beefier flavor. Even better was letting the salted tenderloin sit on the countertop rather than refrigerating it. The big tenderloin lost some of its chill, and it grilled at a more even rate.

Up to this point, I had been grilling the tenderloin directly over the hot fire, an approach that burned the crust before the interior had cooked through. I tried a more moderate heat. Now the exterior was no longer scorched, but the outer inch of meat was approaching well-done before the interior cooked.

In a forehead-slapping moment, it struck me that I was grilling the tenderloin as if it were a steak and not what it was—a roast. So I set up the grill for grill-roasting, in which indirect heat is used to cook the meat. I piled the coals up on one side the grill, leaving the other side empty, then placed the tenderloin over the empty side, covered the grill, and left it alone. About 45 minutes later, I knew that I was on to something. The indirect heat had cooked the tenderloin evenly from tip to tip (OK, so the very ends were more well-done), and the meat had taken on a mild, smoky flavor from spending so much time exposed to the hot coals. But I missed the crust that came with searing the meat. The solution was to sear the tenderloin over the hot coals before switching to the cooler (coal-free) side to finish grilling. This was it: a remarkable, well-browned crust and a rosy pink interior. To impart more smoky flavor, I tried adding soaked wood chunks to the fire. Smoky was just what I got; there was no denying that this meat had been grilled.

When I cut into a tenderloin right off the grill, it gave off a lot of juice—not a good idea with such a lean piece of meat. The easy solution was to let the meat rest for 10 to 15 minutes before cutting, but during this rest period the meat rose from medium-rare (about 135 degrees) to medium-well (over 150 degrees). I next removed the tenderloin from the grill when the meat was still rare. After resting, the roast was incredibly juicy, with a rosy pink interior, a beautiful dark brown crust, and a smoky, seasoned flavor—all of which was worth every cent I had paid for it.

GRILL-ROASTED BEEF TENDERLOIN
SERVES 10 TO 12

Once trimmed, and with the butt tenderloin (the lobe at the large end of the roast) still attached, the roast should weigh 4½ to 5 pounds. If you purchase an already-trimmed tenderloin without the butt tenderloin attached, begin checking for doneness about 5 minutes early. If you prefer your tenderloin without a smoky flavor, you may opt not to use wood chips or chunks. Serve as is or with either of the sauces on page 8.

- 1   beef tenderloin (about 6 pounds), trimmed of fat and silver skin (see illustrations 1 through 6), tail end tucked and tied at 2-inch intervals
- 1½   tablespoons kosher salt
- 2   tablespoons olive oil
- 1   tablespoon ground black pepper

1. About 1 hour before grilling, set tenderloin on rimmed baking sheet and rub with salt. Cover loosely with plastic wrap and let stand at room temperature. Cover two 2-inch wood chunks with cold water and soak 1 hour; drain.

2. About 15 minutes before grilling, open bottom grill vents. Using large chimney starter, ignite about 6 quarts (1 large chimney, or 2½ pounds) charcoal briquettes and burn until covered with layer of light gray ash, about 15 minutes. Empty coals into grill; build modified two-level fire by arranging coals to cover one half of grill, piling them about 3 briquettes high. Set wood chunks

STEP-BY-STEP | TRIMMING THE TENDERLOIN

Although wholesale clubs offer whole beef tenderloins at an affordable price, most come "unpeeled," with the fat and silver skin (a tough membrane) intact. Here's how to trim a tenderloin for the grill. Expect to lose between 1 and 1½ pounds during the trimming process. A boning knife is the best tool for this task.

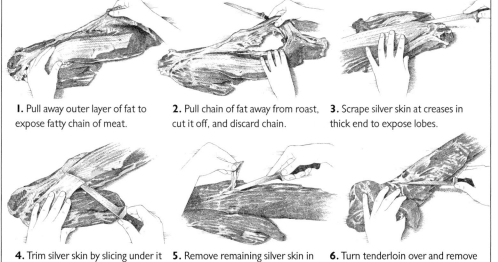

1. Pull away outer layer of fat to expose fatty chain of meat.

2. Pull chain of fat away from roast, cut it off, and discard chain.

3. Scrape silver skin at creases in thick end to expose lobes.

4. Trim silver skin by slicing under it and cutting upward.

5. Remove remaining silver skin in creases at thick end.

6. Turn tenderloin over and remove fat from underside.

on coals. Position grill grate over coals, cover grill, and heat grate until hot, about 10 minutes; scrape grill grate clean with grill brush.

3. Coat tenderloin with oil and sprinkle all sides with pepper. Grill tenderloin on hot side of grill directly over coals; cook until well browned, about 2 minutes, then rotate one quarter turn and repeat until all sides are well browned, total of 8 minutes. Move tenderloin to cooler side of grill and cover, positioning lid vents over ten-derloin. Cook until instant-read thermometer inserted into thickest part of tenderloin registers 120 degrees for rare, 16 to 20 minutes, or 125 degrees for medium-rare, 20 to 25 minutes.

4. Transfer tenderloin to cutting board and tent loosely with foil; let rest 10 to 15 minutes. Cut into ½-inch-thick slices and serve.

GRILL-ROASTED BEEF TENDERLOIN ON A GAS GRILL

If you're using a gas grill, wood chips are a better option than wood chunks.

1. Follow step 1 of recipe for Grill-Roasted Beef Tenderloin, substituting 2 cups wood chips for wood chunks and soaking chips 20 minutes. Drain chips, place in small disposable foil pan, and cover with heavy-duty foil; poke 6 holes in foil and set aside.

2. About 20 minutes before grilling, place wood chip tray on primary burner (burner that will remain on during grilling); position cooking grates. Turn all burners to high, cover grill, and heat until very hot, about 20 minutes. Scrape grill grate clean with grill brush.

3. Uncover tenderloin, coat with olive oil, and sprinkle all sides with pepper. Place tenderloin on side of grate opposite primary burner. Grill tenderloin over burner(s) without wood chips until well browned, 2 to 3 minutes, then rotate one quarter turn and repeat until all sides are well browned, for total of 8 to 12 minutes. Turn off all burners except primary burner (tenderloin should be positioned over extinguished burner). Cover and cook until instant-read thermometer inserted in thickest part of tenderloin registers 120 degrees for rare, 16 to 20 minutes, or 125 degrees for medium-rare, 20 to 25 minutes.

4. Transfer tenderloin to cutting board and tent loosely with foil; let rest 10 to 15 minutes. Cut into ½-inch-thick slices and serve.

ROMESCO SAUCE
MAKES ABOUT 2 CUPS

1–2 slices white sandwich bread
3 tablespoons slivered almonds, toasted in small dry skillet over medium heat until beginning to brown, about 4 minutes
1 jar (12 ounces) roasted red peppers, drained (about 1¾ cups)
1 small ripe tomato (4 ounces), cored, seeded, and chopped medium
1 large garlic clove, minced or pressed through garlic press (about 1 generous teaspoon)
2 tablespoons extra-virgin olive oil
1½ tablespoons sherry vinegar
¼ teaspoon cayenne
Table salt

1. Toast bread in toaster at lowest setting until surface is dry but not browned. Remove crusts and cut bread into rough ½-inch pieces (you should have about ½ cup).

2. Process bread and almonds in food pro-cessor until nuts are finely ground, 10 to 15 seconds. Add red peppers, tomato, garlic, oil, vinegar, cayenne, and ½ teaspoon salt. Pulse, scraping down side of bowl as necessary, until mixture has texture similar to mayonnaise, 20 to 30 seconds. Adjust seasoning with salt; transfer mixture to bowl and serve. (Can refrigerate in airtight container up to 2 days; return sauce to room temperature before serving.)

CILANTRO-PARSLEY SAUCE WITH PICKLED JALAPEÑOS
MAKES ABOUT 1½ CUPS

This sauce will discolor if left to sit for too long; it's best served within 4 hours of making it.

2–3 slices white sandwich bread
1 cup extra-virgin olive oil
¼ cup juice from 1 to 2 lemons
2 cups lightly packed fresh cilantro leaves
2 cups lightly packed fresh flat-leaf parsley leaves
¼ cup drained pickled jalapeño slices, chopped medium (about 3 tablespoons)
1 large garlic clove, minced or pressed through garlic press (about 1 generous teaspoon)
Table salt

1. Toast bread in toaster at lowest setting until surface is dry but not browned. Remove crusts and cut bread into rough ½-inch pieces (you should have about 1 cup).

2. Process bread, oil, and lemon juice in food processor until smooth, 10 to 15 seconds. Add cilantro, parsley, jalapeños, garlic, and ¼ tea-spoon salt. Pulse until finely chopped (mixture should not be smooth), about ten 1-second pulses, scraping down bowl as necessary. Adjust seasoning with salt; transfer to bowl and serve.

Building a Better Stuffed Baked Potato

Could we avoid the usual crunchy vegetables and soggy potato skin?

⇒ BY BRIDGET LANCASTER AND ERIN MCMURRER ⇐

Packed with cheese, vegetables, and savory meats, a stuffed baked potato walks a fine line between being a big snack and a one-dish meal. Although found everywhere from drive-through windows to chain restaurants, these spuds have resisted our efforts to make them successfully at home, ending up soggy bottomed and stuffed with heavy, greasy fillings.

Starting from the bottom up, we learned that an extra step—scooping out the pulp of the baked potatoes and drying the emptied skins in the oven—made for a crisp shell to house our fillings. When it came to the fillings, however, the problems were not as easily solved. We found that raw vegetables exuded too much liquid. Crunchy broccoli and crisp cabbage softened and became more flavorful when cooked first. Smoky bacon also had to be cooked to a crisp to shed most of its heavy fat before going into the potato.

Just a few tablespoons of butter were necessary to crisp the vegetables and sauté the fillings—any more added heaviness to the mix. To bind the filling, we turned to sour cream and half-and-half, which together provided a luxurious texture without making the filling too greasy.

As for the cheese (we wouldn't think of baking potatoes twice without it), our attempts at any kind of restraint led us to dissatisfaction. We settled on about 2 cups (about ¼ cup per potato half), but the key here was to mix half of the cheese in with the filling, sprinkle the other half on top, and brown the potatoes under the broiler until golden and crisp.

BAKED POTATOES FOR TWICE-BAKED POTATOES

Adjust oven rack to middle position; heat oven to 400 degrees. Scrub, dry, and lightly rub 4 russet potatoes (8 to 9 ounces each) with vegetable oil. Bake potatoes on foil-lined baking sheet until skewer can be inserted into and removed from potatoes with little resistance, 60 to 70 minutes (do not turn oven off). Cool potatoes on baking sheet about 10 minutes.

TWICE-BAKED POTATOES WITH BROCCOLI, CHEDDAR, AND SCALLIONS

SERVES 4 AS A MAIN COURSE OR 8 AS A SIDE DISH

I	recipe Baked Potatoes
4	tablespoons unsalted butter (melt 2 tablespoons)
6	cups broccoli florets (from 2-pound bunch) cut into ½- to 1-inch pieces, stems discarded

Table salt
I	teaspoon juice from I lemon
¼	teaspoon powdered mustard
6	ounces sharp cheddar cheese, shredded (2 cups)
3–4	scallions, sliced thin (about ½ cup)
½	cup sour cream
¼	cup half-and-half
	Ground black pepper

1. While potatoes are baking, heat 2 tablespoons butter in 12-inch skillet over medium-high heat until foam subsides; add broccoli and ½ teaspoon salt and cook, stirring occasionally, until lightly browned, about 2 minutes. Add 2 tablespoons water; cover and cook until crisp-tender, about 1 minute. Uncover and continue to cook until water evaporates, about 1 minute. Transfer to bowl and stir in lemon juice.

2. Halve each potato lengthwise. Using soup spoon, scoop flesh from each half into bowl, leaving about ⅜ inch thickness of flesh. Place shells cut-sides up on baking sheet and return to oven until dry and slightly crisp, about 10 minutes.

3. Meanwhile, mash potato flesh with fork until smooth; stir in melted butter, ¾ teaspoon salt, powdered mustard, 1 cup cheese, scallions, sour cream, half-and-half, and pepper to taste, then stir in broccoli.

4. Remove shells from oven; heat broiler. Mound filling into shells; sprinkle with remaining 1 cup cheese and broil until spotty brown, 6 to 10 minutes. Cool 5 minutes; serve.

TWICE-BAKED POTATOES WITH BACON, CABBAGE, AND CHEDDAR

SERVES 4 AS A MAIN COURSE OR 8 AS A SIDE DISH

Tender savoy cabbage is our first choice, but the soft outer leaves from a head of regular green cabbage can also be used.

I	recipe Baked Potatoes
8	ounces bacon (8 strips), cut into ½-inch pieces
3	tablespoons unsalted butter (melt 2 tablespoons)
6	cups savoy cabbage (about ¾ pound) cored and sliced into ½ by 1-inch pieces
	Table salt
2	teaspoons red wine vinegar
6	ounces sharp cheddar cheese, shredded (2 cups)
3–4	scallions, sliced thin (about ½ cup)
½	cup sour cream
¼	cup half-and-half
	Ground black pepper

1. While potatoes are baking, fry bacon in 12-inch skillet over medium heat until crisp, 8 to 10 minutes. Using slotted spoon, transfer bacon to paper towel–lined plate; pour off all but 1 tablespoon bacon fat. Add 1 tablespoon butter to bacon fat; heat over medium-high until melted, then add cabbage and ½ teaspoon salt and cook, stirring occasionally, until cabbage begins to wilt and is lightly browned, about 2 minutes. Add ½ cup water, cover, and cook until crisp-tender, 5 to 7 minutes; uncover and continue to cook until water evaporates, about 30 seconds. Transfer to bowl and stir in vinegar.

2. Follow step 2 of Twice-Baked Potatoes with Broccoli, Cheddar, and Scallions.

3. Meanwhile, mash potato flesh with fork until smooth; stir in melted butter, cabbage, ½ teaspoon salt, ¼ cup bacon, 1 cup cheese, scallions, sour cream, half-and-half, and pepper, to taste.

4. Follow step 4 of Twice-Baked Potatoes with Broccoli, Cheddar, and Scallions, sprinkling filling with both remaining cheese and remaining bacon.

TWICE-BAKED POTATOES WITH HAM, PEAS, AND GRUYÈRE

SERVES 4 AS A MAIN COURSE OR 8 AS A SIDE DISH

I	recipe Baked Potatoes
3	tablespoons unsalted butter (melt 2 tablespoons)
¾	pound baked deli ham, sliced ¼ inch thick and cut into ¼-inch cubes
I	cup frozen peas
6	ounces Gruyère cheese, shredded (2 cups)
½	cup sour cream
¼	cup half-and-half
2	tablespoons whole-grain mustard
	Salt and ground black pepper

1. While potatoes are baking, heat 1 tablespoon butter in 12-inch skillet over medium-high heat until foaming; add ham in even layer and cook, without stirring, until lightly browned, about 2 minutes. Stir and cook 30 seconds longer. Off heat, stir in peas; transfer mixture to large plate.

2. Follow step 2 of Twice-Baked Potatoes with Broccoli, Cheddar, and Scallions.

3. Meanwhile, mash potato flesh with fork until smooth; stir in melted butter, ham mixture, 1 cup cheese, sour cream, half-and-half, mustard, and salt and pepper to taste.

4. Follow step 4 of Twice-Baked Potatoes with Broccoli, Cheddar, and Scallions.

Solving the Problem of Baked Chicken Breasts

Nothing is worse (or more common) than baked chicken breasts—chalky, sour meat topped with rubbery, flaccid skin. Could we make this simple dinner item worth eating?

> BY ELIZABETH GERMAIN <

At their best, roasted bone-in, skin-on chicken breasts ought to provide moist, tender, seasoned meat and crisp brown skin. But white meat lovers will pass up a leg for a breast any day, even when less than ideal. Despite the demand, recipes for plain roasted chicken breasts are in short supply. I wondered why. Research showed that even the simplest recipes included flavoring ingredients. Minimalists add herbs, lemon, or mustard; others enhance with olives, capers, sesame, or honey.

I tested a half-dozen recipes. Not even the most potent of ingredients could disguise the consistently bland and dry meat. "Like eating cardboard," said one taster. The skin on all of the breasts proved equally disappointing. Hints of crispness were overshadowed by mostly fatty, rubbery skin. My goal was to create a simple recipe for plain roasted chicken breasts that would yield perfectly cooked meat and skin. I envisioned a quick and easy recipe, perfect for a weeknight meal.

False Start

A field trip to local supermarkets confirmed what *Cook's* has concluded before: Bone-in, skin-on chicken breasts are best bought whole. Purchasing already split breasts presents problems worth avoiding. These precut, prepackaged breasts vary widely in size and often contain specimens with torn and missing skin or meat. Better to take control and cut the breast yourself. One-and-a-half-pound whole breasts proved best. They are readily available, the portion size is good, and they are large enough for the skin to crisp when the meat is cooked through.

Any long-time reader of this magazine also knows that *Cook's* likes to brine chicken. A full-strength quick brine (30 minutes) worked best for the roasted meat, but the skin was soggy. To solve this problem, I would have to air-dry the breasts on a rack in the refrigerator, something that made no sense for a Tuesday-night supper. After conducting a number of additional failed tests—including removing the skin before brining, stretching it over a rack, and freezing it—I ditched the notion of brining and air-drying altogether and directed my efforts toward a simpler, quicker solution. (Stretching the skin

For crisp skin and juicy meat, roast whole chicken breasts and carve the meat off the bone at serving time.

and freezing it was a smashing success—"the skin is almost like cracklin' pork rinds," said one taster—but it's too much trouble for what ought to be a simple dinner.)

Fresh Start

I started over, this time asking myself if cutting the whole breasts before roasting them, as I had been doing, was a good idea. I split two raw breasts and roasted them along with two unsplit breasts. I was shocked by the results. This simple notion—roasting whole instead of split breasts—turned out to be a major discovery, one that dramatically improved the juiciness of the meat. The explanation? Whole breasts retain more of their juices than cut breasts, which have more avenues for moisture loss. But waiting to cut through the breastbone until after cooking (the chicken must be cut for serving) presented problems: uneven halves, unattractive pieces, and chicken that was

not easy to eat. Carving the meat entirely off the bones and serving it fanned on the plate was a simpler, more attractive alternative.

In terms of oven temperature, I tested heat levels from 350 degrees up to 500 degrees. The visual difference was glaring when the breasts emerged from the oven. The skin on the breasts roasted at 350 was pale yellow and rubbery looking; the skin roasted at 500 was burnt. Neither tasted great, though breasts from the hotter ovens were better. In the end, 450 degrees proved best. The meat was still juicy and the skin color improved, but the skin still wasn't as crisp as desired. And, occasionally, fat dripped from the chicken into the baking pan, smoking up the kitchen.

Getting Close

To solve the problem of smoking, I switched from my 13 by 9-inch Pyrex pan to a stainless roasting pan fitted with a rack. Still, a shallow layer of fat formed, causing some smoke. The good news was that I had unwittingly discovered another secret of perfectly baked chicken. By getting the breasts up off the pan bottom, the rack allowed heat to circulate underneath them. The result was more even, quicker cooking and juicier meat. Inspired by the rack, I tried creating a natural rack by pulling out the rib cage on each side of the whole breast so that it could stand up on its own. It worked! Instead of curling under the breast, the edges of the breast now fanned outward and allowed for better air circulation. But the smoke ensued. I tried one more time, this time using a broiler pan. Bingo—the fat dripped below the rack, which shielded it from the heat. Roasting was now smokefree, the meat was juicier, and the broiler pan was easy to clean up as long as I covered the bottom with foil.

One problem, however, remained: mediocre skin. I knew from earlier tests that separating the skin from the meat allows hot air to circulate more freely under the skin, renders more fat, and produces crispier skin. I tried several approaches, including slashing the skin and severing it everywhere but along the breastbone, before determining that a one-sided pocket opening worked best. Using my fingers, I gently pulled apart the bottom edge and used a spoon to open up a cavity. This

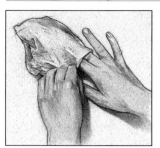

1. Gently lift skin at bottom of breast to create small pocket for butter.

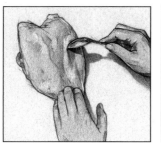

2. Using teaspoon, place butter in center of meat. Pressing on skin, spread butter evenly over meat.

3. Gently pull out rib cage from each side of breast to create a stable base.

method minimized skin shrinkage and allowed the skin to roast to a deep golden brown. Now the color of the skin was appealing, but a crispy texture remained elusive.

I had been rubbing oil on the skin, as it helped with browning and crisping. Now I tried rubbing some under the skin as well. "Yes! The skin is finally blistering and crisp," said my colleagues. Next I tried butter instead of oil. The response? "The skin is ultra-crisp," and "The meat seems better flavored and juicier." The butter helped to keep the delicate breast meat juicy while adding flavor. I tried rubbing softened butter on top of the skin as well, but the cold skin caused the butter to seize up, making spreading difficult. So I stayed with the oil on top of the skin.

Finally, I turned to the salt. Having rejected brining, I had been seasoning the outer breasts liberally with salt and pepper. I now tried salting under the skin. "Yes," said tasters, "the meat is better seasoned and juicier." As I was already rubbing on butter, I tried adding the salt to the butter to make the seasoning easier. It worked.

At last I had perfectly roasted plain chicken breasts. And my recipe was just as easy as—and even quicker than—some of the simplest I had tested. Here was the secret formula: Roast a whole breast, use a very hot oven, allow air to circulate under the breastbone and under the skin, and use modest amounts of oil, butter, salt, and

pepper. This technique also made it easy to add flavors by simply flavoring the butter—as long as I avoided sugar and honey, which made the skin burn, or too much ground spice (more than a teaspoon), which created a gritty texture. Best of all, I now have a simple recipe that produces white meat so good that even lovers of dark meat may take notice.

ROASTED CHICKEN BREASTS
SERVES 4

To make sure that the breasts cook at the same rate, purchase two similarly sized whole breasts (not split breasts) with skins fully intact. Whole chicken breasts weighing about 1½ pounds work best because they require a cooking time long enough to ensure that the skin will brown and crisp nicely. If you do not own a broiler pan, use a roasting pan fitted with a flat wire rack. This recipe can easily be increased by 50 or 100 percent. If you do increase it, just make certain not to crowd the chicken breasts on the broiler pan, which can impede the browning and crisping of the skin.

2   tablespoons unsalted butter, room temperature
2   whole bone-in, skin-on chicken breasts (about 1½ pounds each), patted dry with paper towels and trimmed of excess fat
    Table salt

Ground black pepper
1   tablespoon vegetable oil

1. Adjust oven rack to middle position; heat oven to 450 degrees. Line bottom of broiler pan with foil, place broiler pan rack on top; set aside. In small bowl, mix ½ teaspoon salt and butter until combined. Sprinkle underside of chicken breasts liberally with salt and pepper. Following illustrations 1 through 3 at left, gently loosen bottom portion of skin covering each breast. Using small spoon, place a quarter of softened butter under skin, directly on meat in center of each breast half. Using spoon, spread butter evenly over breast meat. Rub skin of each whole breast with 1½ teaspoons oil and sprinkle liberally with pepper. Set chicken breasts on broiler pan rack, propping up breasts on rib bones.

2. Roast until thickest part of breast registers 160 degrees on instant-read thermometer, 35 to 40 minutes. Transfer chicken to cutting board and let rest 5 minutes. To carve, follow illustrations 1 through 3 below. Serve immediately.

ROASTED CHICKEN BREASTS WITH GARLIC, ROSEMARY, AND LEMON

Follow recipe for Roasted Chicken Breasts, mixing 2 minced medium garlic cloves, 2 teaspoons minced fresh rosemary leaves, and 1 teaspoon grated lemon zest into softened butter along with salt.

ROASTED CHICKEN BREASTS WITH CHIPOTLE, CUMIN, AND CILANTRO

Follow recipe for Roasted Chicken Breasts, mixing 2 teaspoons minced chipotle chiles in adobo, 1 teaspoon ground cumin, and 2 teaspoons chopped fresh cilantro leaves into softened butter along with salt.

ROASTED CHICKEN BREASTS WITH OLIVES, PARSLEY, AND LEMON

Follow recipe for Roasted Chicken Breasts, mixing 1 tablespoon chopped pitted kalamata olives, 1 teaspoon grated lemon zest, and 2 teaspoons chopped fresh parsley leaves into softened butter along with salt.

ROASTED CHICKEN BREASTS WITH HERBS AND PORCINI MUSHROOMS

In small bowl, cover 2 tablespoons dried porcini mushrooms with boiling water; let stand until mushrooms soften, about 15 minutes. Using fork, lift mushrooms from liquid and chop fine (you should have about 4 teaspoons). Follow recipe for Roasted Chicken Breasts, mixing porcini, 1 teaspoon minced fresh thyme leaves, and 1 teaspoon minced fresh rosemary leaves into softened butter along with salt.

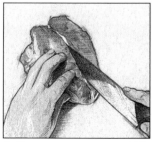

1. To remove meat, cut straight down along one side of breastbone.

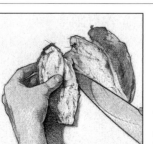

2. Run knife down along rib cage to remove entire breast half.

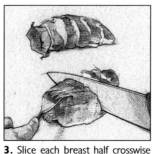

3. Slice each breast half crosswise on bias, making thin slices.

How to Cook Acorn Squash

Tired of mealy, stringy squash that takes an hour to bake? We wanted it faster and better.

⇒ BY REBECCA HAYS ⇐

The popularity of acorn squash has always mystified me. After what seems like eons in the oven, it inevitably lands on the table with little flavor and a dry, grainy texture. Perhaps the appeal resides in its spherical shape—the hollowed-out halves are perfect receptacles for melted butter and sugar—but this feature doesn't make up for the dry, cottony flesh. Yet acorn squash can be quite good, if not outright delicious, when prepared properly. At its rare best, it is characterized by a sweet, almost nutty taste and moist, smooth flesh. Could I solve this culinary challenge and do it relatively quickly?

High-Tech(nique)

Most cookbook authors recommend baking acorn squash in a covered dish, while a few suggest somewhat unconventional methods, including steaming, boiling, braising, and baking. Steamed and boiled chunks of peeled squash cooked quickly but turned out mushy and waterlogged. Braising resulted in a soggy, stringy texture that was all the more disappointing given the arduous task of peeling the squash before cooking it. The baked squash were just as expected: dry, very dry.

I was running out of hope until I found a recipe on the Internet that suggested microwaving, a cooking method we avoid at all costs here in the test kitchen because of its finicky nature and its poor powers of flavor enhancement. Nonetheless, I shoved aside my concerns about committing culinary heresy and nuked a couple of squash. When I tasted a forkful, I became a believer. It was tender and silky smooth, with nary a trace of dryness or stringiness. I was so surprised (and pleased) with the results that I repeated the test once, and then again. When subsequent tries produced identical outcomes, I seemed to have no choice but to use the microwave to cook the squash.

Hammering out the details was easy: Microwave on high power for 20 minutes (give or take a few, depending on the model used—see "Are All Microwaves Created Equal?" on page 13), and the squash is perfectly cooked. It was best to halve and seed the squash before cooking; whole pierced squash cooked unevenly. Last, I learned that when added before cooking, salt seemed to better permeate the squash. Now I had a 20-minute recipe and vastly improved results!

A 20-minute recipe yields creamy squash with a golden brown glaze.

Why was the microwave such a success? Our science editor explained that as microwaves (which, like radio waves, are electromagnetic), enter food, water molecules in the food begin to vibrate, and this activity generates heat evenly and efficiently, for quick cooking. In effect, the microwave was steaming the squash in its own juices. In contrast, a conventional oven uses dry, hot air to slowly heat food from the outside in, causing dehydration and a less desirable texture, especially on the outer edges.

Sweet Stuff

The one important issue I had left to tackle was the topping, or flavoring, for the squash. My colleagues were loud and clear about what they wanted: a classic butter and sugar glaze. Dark brown sugar is the most common choice and was named the best sweetener, with maple syrup a runner-up. Other options (honey, granulated sugar, and light brown sugar) were either not sweet enough or didn't provide the familiar flavor that we wanted. I limited the amount of brown sugar to 3 tablespoons—enough to provide ample sweetness but not so much that I'd be tempted to serve the squash with a scoop of vanilla ice cream. An equal amount of butter made the best complement.

One problem remained. The squash was still lacking the sticky, caramelized glaze that forms when it is oven-baked. Passing the buttered and sugared squash under the broiler for a few minutes after microwaving was the way to go. Many cooks, myself included, have the habit of simply placing a pat of butter in the cavity of the squash and then adding a coating of sugar. A better method, I found, was to melt the two ingredients, along with a pinch of salt, on the stovetop for a smooth, cohesive mixture.

By using the microwave and broiler, I was now able to produce squash with great texture and flavor. Not bad for 20 minutes' work.

SHOPPING: How to Buy and Store Acorn Squash

As I halved, seeded, and cooked more than 50 squash for this story, I noticed significant differences in quality, depending on where I purchased the squash, how I stored it, and how long I kept it. Some were richly flavored, with deep, golden orange flesh, while others were spongy and pale. Here's what I learned. –R.H.

SEASON Acorn squash is domestically in season from July through November. When purchased in the off-season, the squash, which during those months is usually imported from Mexico, is likely to be more expensive. Squash that had spent weeks in transit cooked up dehydrated, fibrous, and pasty in the test kitchen.

WEIGHT Squash should be hard and heavy for its size, an indication that it contains a lot of moisture and has not been sitting on the supermarket produce shelf for weeks.

COLOR The most popular variety of acorn squash is green, though gold and white varieties are spottily available. Gold or orange tinges on the rind of green squash are not indicators of ripeness but rather a mark of where the fruit touched the ground during growing (and was therefore untouched by sunlight).

STORAGE Acorn squash should be stored at cool room temperature, not in the refrigerator. When I stored squash for a few weeks in the refrigerator, chill damage set in, causing the flavor and texture to deteriorate.

Getting Squash Ready to Microwave

If your microwave is spacious enough to accommodate it, a 13 by 9-inch microwave-safe baking dish works well for containing the squash halves. Otherwise, a large, wide microwave-safe bowl can be used. If using a bowl, position the squash with cut sides facing out.

ACORN SQUASH WITH BROWN SUGAR
SERVES 4

Squash smaller than 1½ pounds will likely cook a little faster than the recipe indicates, so begin checking for doneness a few minutes early. Conversely, larger squash will take slightly longer to cook. However, keep in mind that the cooking time is largely dependent on the microwave. If microwaving the squash in Pyrex, the manufacturer recommends adding water to the dish (or bowl) prior to cooking. See Notes from Readers, page 3, for an explanation. To avoid a steam burn when uncovering the cooked squash, peel back the plastic wrap very carefully, starting from the side that is farthest away from you.

- 2 **acorn squash (about 1½ pounds each), halved pole to pole and seeded**
  Table salt
- 3 **tablespoons unsalted butter**
- 3 **tablespoons dark brown sugar**

1. Sprinkle squash halves with salt and place halves cut-sides down in 13 by 9-inch microwave-safe baking dish or arrange halves in large (about 4-quart) microwave-safe bowl so that cut sides face out (see photo at left). If using Pyrex, add ¼ cup water to dish or bowl. Cover tightly with plastic wrap, using multiple sheets, if necessary; with paring knife, poke about 4 steam vents in plastic wrap. Microwave on high power until squash is very tender and offers no resistance when pierced with paring knife, 15 to 25 minutes. Using potholders, remove baking dish or bowl from oven and set on clean, dry surface (avoid damp or cold surfaces).

2. While squash is cooking, adjust oven rack to uppermost position (about 6 inches from heating element); heat broiler. Melt butter, brown sugar, and ⅛ teaspoon salt in small saucepan over low heat, whisking occasionally, until combined.

3. When squash is cooked, carefully pull back plastic wrap from side farthest from you. Using tongs, transfer cooked squash cut-side up to rimmed baking sheet. Spoon portion of butter/sugar mixture onto each squash half. Broil until brown and caramelized, 5 to 8 minutes, rotating baking sheet as necessary and removing squash halves as they are done. Set squash halves on individual plates and serve immediately.

ACORN SQUASH WITH ROSEMARY–DRIED FIG COMPOTE

1. Follow recipe for Acorn Squash with Brown Sugar, omitting brown sugar/butter mixture. While squash is cooking, combine 1 cup orange juice; 4 dried black figs, chopped medium (scant ½ cup); ½ teaspoon minced fresh rosemary; 1 tablespoon dark brown sugar; ¼ teaspoon ground black pepper; and ⅛ teaspoon salt in small saucepan. Simmer rapidly over medium-high heat, stirring occasionally, until syrupy and liquid is reduced to about 3 tablespoons, 15 to 20 minutes. Stir in 1 tablespoon butter.

2. Continue with recipe to fill and broil squash halves, substituting fig compote for brown sugar/butter mixture.

TECHNIQUE | TWO WAYS TO CUT SQUASH SAFELY

 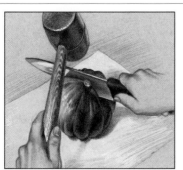  

Knife and Rubber Mallet: 1. Set squash on damp kitchen towel to hold it in place. Position knife on rind of squash. **2.** Strike back of knife with rubber mallet to drive knife into squash. Continue to hit knife with mallet until knife cuts through squash.

Metal Bench Scraper and Hammer: 1. Set squash on damp kitchen towel. Position bench scraper on rind. **2.** Strike handle of bench scraper with hammer to drive blade into squash. Continue to hit bench scraper with hammer until blade cuts through squash.

Lasagna Bolognese Simplified

Could we adapt and simplify this northern Italian classic for the American kitchen?

⋟ BY SEAN LAWLER ⋞

In most American lasagnas, the meat is merely an afterthought—bits of sausage or hamburger lost in gooey layers of cheese and tomato sauce. In an authentic lasagna Bolognese, however, meat is the main idea. Three kinds of meat, in fact: beef, pork, and veal simmered until tender and delicately sweet in a slowly reducing sauce of milk, wine, and tomatoes. This rich sauce is bound between thin sheets of pasta with a creamy béchamel sauce and Parmesan cheese. Hold the mozzarella and ricotta, please.

The unrivaled richness of this northern Italian classic may elicit objections from dieters, but certainly not from the poor cook who slaved over it. He or she has likely been up since dawn rolling out fresh pasta sheets and tending an all-day meat sauce, and thus feels entitled to indulge. In this case, the poor cook was me. I made several of these monsters, using our existing recipes for fresh pasta dough, béchamel, and the meat sauce, or *ragù*, and managed to get them on the table in just under . . . six hours. I was told they were delicious. I was too tired to taste them.

Lasagna Bolognese was never going to be a quick Tuesday-night supper, but there had to be a way to make it something less than an all-day affair. The ragù was a time-consuming but largely unattended labor. It was the kneading, rolling, cutting, blanching, shocking, and drying of the lasagna noodles that was the most arduous task. The test kitchen had already developed several recipes that put no-boil noodles to good use, and, though purists might consider it a sacrilege, I could not resist their convenience.

Use Your Noodle

Sticking close to our existing sauce recipes for now, I prepared a lasagna with five layers of no-boil noodles. I followed the assembly guidelines of a traditional lasagna Bolognese recipe, spreading ⅔ cup of ragù over each layer, followed by several tablespoons of Parmesan and béchamel, the flour-thickened cream sauce that "glues" the layers together. The top layer of noodles was then coated with a thin layer of béchamel and more cheese to prevent the noodles from drying out in the oven. I followed the instructions on the package of noodles, baking for 50 minutes, covered with foil for all but the last 10 minutes.

No-boil noodles and a quick meat sauce turn an all-day Italian recipe into a manageable project that yields excellent results.

My worries about the pasta had been unfounded. The taste and texture of the noodles were fine. (Lasagna Bolognese with homemade pasta is indeed better—and traditional—but the extra labor put this recipe into the "once in a lifetime" category.) Noodles aside, though, the dish had come out dry as a bone, and when I peeled back the layers I discovered nothing but dried-out bits of meat and the chalky white remains of a béchamel. The no-boil noodles had absorbed most of the moisture, leaving none behind in the sauce. Increasing the quantity of the meat sauce didn't make the dish any saucier; there was simply more dried-out meat between the noodles.

While developing a recipe for spinach lasagna (March/April 2004), the test kitchen had presoaked no-boil noodles in hot tap water. Thinking that this technique might help to solve the dry sauce problem (the noodles might absorb less liquid during cooking), I tested it. This lasagna, made with noodles that had been soaked for five minutes, was slightly saucier but still nowhere close to saucy enough—a few drops in a drought. During 10- and 15-minute soaks, the

noodles absorbed even more water but then proceeded to turn flabby and mushy in the oven. So a five-minute soak was helpful, but I would have to make other adjustments.

Keep Your (Sauce) Cool

I now turned back to the preparation of the ragù, which traditionally is simmered for hours to evaporate excess moisture and produce a thick, rich sauce. Because I needed extra moisture in this lasagna, this last step seemed counterproductive. Abbreviating this final step not only would save hours but also would leave me with a wetter sauce. Thinking along the same lines, I thinned out the béchamel by doubling the quantity of milk.

To say that this idea didn't work out as planned would be an understatement. No-boil noodles expand during cooking, which means that when the lasagna is assembled, there is quite a bit of space around the edges of the pan. The thin sauce ran off the noodles and puddled in this space, carrying chunks of meat with it. This problem worsened in the oven, and the result, to put it mildly, was an unattractive lasagna with a sunken center and blown-out edges erupting with ground meat.

What I needed was a sauce that was stiff enough to stay put between the noodles during assembly but that also had enough moisture to rehydrate the noodles in the oven. One afternoon, as I was reheating a batch of the previous day's ragù, I noticed that the cold sauce seemed quite thick—too thick, in fact, to be spread easily across the noodles. But when gently warmed to just above room temperature, the texture of the sauce was much closer to what I'd been looking for. As for the béchamel, it also thickened considerably as it cooled, and I found that it performed its adhesive duties more readily in this state.

As the ragù cooled, however, some of the excess liquid separated out from the sauce, leaving it looking watery and greasy. What if I were to use a small portion of the cooled béchamel to thicken the ragù, then assemble the lasagna as before? Even before the lasagna went into the oven, I knew I was onto something. Adding just ¾ cup of the cooled béchamel to the ragù kept the water and fat in emulsion. Thickened, but easy to spread, the sauce now stayed in place between the noodles as they expanded, yet it still contained enough moisture to cook the noodles. Finally, I had made a perfectly respectable lasagna Bolognese in about two hours using no-boil noodles, a far cry from the usual all-day affair. Almost as good as the authentic northern Italian dish—and I wasn't too tired to eat it!

LASAGNA BOLOGNESE, SIMPLIFIED
SERVES 8

For assembly, both the meat sauce and the béchamel should be just warm to the touch, not piping hot. Both sauces can be made, cooled, and refrigerated up to 2 days ahead, then gently reheated until warm. In terms of flavor and texture, we find that Barilla no-boil noodles are the closest to fresh, but this recipe will work with all major brands of no-boil noodles.

Meat Sauce (Ragù)
1	medium carrot, peeled and roughly chopped
1	medium celery rib, roughly chopped
1/2	small onion, roughly chopped
1	can (28 ounces) whole tomatoes with juice
2	tablespoons unsalted butter
8	ounces ground beef, preferably 90 percent lean
8	ounces ground pork
8	ounces ground veal
1 1/2	cups whole milk
1 1/2	cups dry white wine
2	tablespoons tomato paste
1	teaspoon table salt
1/4	teaspoon ground black pepper

Béchamel
4	tablespoons unsalted butter
1/4	cup all-purpose flour
4	cups whole milk
3/4	teaspoon table salt

Noodles and Cheese
15	sheets (9 ounces) no-boil lasagna noodles
4	ounces Parmesan, grated (2 cups)

1. **FOR THE MEAT SAUCE:** Process carrot, celery, and onion in food processor until finely chopped, about ten 1-second pulses, scraping down bowl as necessary; transfer mixture to small bowl. Wipe out food processor workbowl; process tomatoes and juice until finely chopped, six to eight 1-second pulses. Heat butter in heavy-bottomed Dutch oven over medium heat until foaming; add carrot, celery, and onion and cook, stirring occasionally, until softened but not browned, about 4 minutes. Add ground meats and cook, breaking meat into 1-inch pieces with wooden spoon, about 1 minute. Add milk and stir, breaking meat into 1/2-inch bits; bring to simmer and cook, stirring to break meat into small pieces, until almost all liquid has evaporated, 20 to 30 minutes. Using potato masher or wooden spoon, break up any remaining clumps of meat

(no large pieces should remain). Add wine and bring to simmer; cook, stirring occasionally, until liquid has evaporated, 20 to 30 minutes. Stir in tomato paste until combined, about 1 minute; add chopped tomatoes, salt, and pepper. Bring to simmer, then reduce heat to medium-low and cook until sauce is slightly thickened, about 15 minutes. (You should have about 6 cups meat sauce.) Transfer meat sauce to bowl and cool until just warm to touch, about 30 minutes.

2. **FOR THE BÉCHAMEL:** While meat sauce simmers, melt butter in medium saucepan over medium heat until foaming; add flour and cook, whisking constantly, until thoroughly combined, about 1 1/2 minutes; mixture should not brown. Gradually whisk in milk; increase heat to medium-high and bring to full boil, whisking frequently. Add salt, reduce heat to medium-low, and simmer 10 minutes, stirring occasionally with heatproof rubber spatula or wooden spoon, making sure to scrape bottom and corners of saucepan. (You should have about 3 1/3 cups.) Transfer béchamel to bowl and cool until just warm to touch, about 30 minutes.

3. **TO ASSEMBLE AND BAKE:** Adjust oven rack to middle position; heat oven to 425 degrees. Place noodles in 13 by 9-inch baking dish and cover with very hot tap water; soak 5 minutes, agitating

noodles occasionally to prevent sticking. Remove noodles from water, place in single layer on kitchen towel, and pat dry. Wipe out baking dish and spray lightly with nonstick cooking spray. Stir béchamel to recombine; mix 3/4 cup warm béchamel into warm meat sauce until thoroughly combined.

4. Distribute 1 cup béchamel-enriched meat sauce in baking dish. Place three noodles in single layer on top of sauce, arranging them close together, but not touching, at center of pan. Spread 1 1/4 cups béchamel-enriched meat sauce evenly over noodles, spreading sauce to edge of noodles but not to edge of dish (see illustration 1 below). Drizzle 1/3 cup béchamel evenly over meat sauce (illustration 2). Sprinkle 1/3 cup Parmesan evenly over béchamel. Repeat layering of noodles, béchamel-enriched meat sauce, béchamel, and cheese 3 more times. Place final 3 noodles on top and cover completely with remaining béchamel, spreading béchamel with rubber spatula and allowing it to spill over noodles (illustration 3). Sprinkle evenly with remaining Parmesan.

5. Spray large sheet foil with nonstick cooking spray and cover lasagna; bake until bubbling, about 30 minutes. Remove foil, increase heat to 450 degrees, and continue to bake until surface is spotty brown, about 15 minutes. Cool 15 minutes; cut into pieces and serve.

Two Common Lasagna Problems

THE CENTER DOES NOT HOLD
If the meat sauce is too thin, it will pool at the edges, resulting in a lasagna with a sunken center. Thickening the ragù with some béchamel solves this problem.

THE DISH IS TOO DRY
Use plenty of sauce and cover the dish with foil to avoid a dry lasagna. Soaking the no-boil noodles in hot water before using them also helps.

STEP-BY-STEP | ASSEMBLING THE LASAGNA

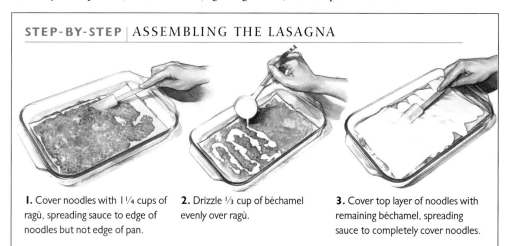

1. Cover noodles with 1 1/4 cups of ragù, spreading sauce to edge of noodles but not edge of pan.

2. Drizzle 1/3 cup of béchamel evenly over ragù.

3. Cover top layer of noodles with remaining béchamel, spreading sauce to completely cover noodles.

Guide to Buying & Preparing Chicken

Whole birds taste better than packaged parts and cost less, so it makes sense to cut up chicken at home. Here's all you need to know to master this basic skill and to buy a good chicken. BY SEAN LAWLER

BUYING THE RIGHT-SIZE BIRD

Producers breed chickens to "plump out" (an industry term indicating that the breast meat is thick and plump) at different ages, depending on the desired weight of the slaughtered bird. We have found that certain sizes (usually described by producers with the terms below) work better for certain recipes.

  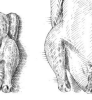 

POUSSIN	CORNISH GAME HEN	BROILER/FRYER	ROASTER

Poussins are baby chickens that weigh about 1 pound. Generally available only at specialty stores or butchers, they are ideal for one person.

Cornish Game Hens are slightly older than poussins and weigh between 1 and 2 pounds. Larger game hens will serve two people, but these birds are usually mass-market brands that lack the flavor of the smaller poussins.

Broiler/fryers are the standard supermarket chicken—and our favorite. They generally weigh between 3 and 4 ½ pounds and will serve four people. All *Cook's* recipes using whole birds are developed with chickens from this category.

Roasters generally weigh between 5 and 8 pounds. Despite their name, we do not recommend roasting birds this large, as the outer layers of meat tend to overcook before the meat near the bone reaches a safe internal temperature. When feeding a crowd, we prefer to buy two broiler/fryers.

TASTING

We tasted 3½- to 4-pound chickens from nine widely available producers. Supermarket chickens range from budget birds raised on factory farms to pricier fowl with ambiguous labels—"organic," "free range," "all natural"—proclaiming the virtues of their diet and lifestyle. These terms mean different things to different producers, and, as our tasting demonstrated, they are not reliable indicators of flavor or texture. Neither is price.

Tyson, a mass-produced bird, came in third, ahead of birds costing twice as much. Perdue, the other mass-produced brand in our tasting, came in dead last. The best-tasting chicken was a kosher bird from Empire. Tasters found it to be the most juicy and well seasoned of the bunch. During the koshering process, the Empire chicken is covered with salt to draw out impurities. This leads to a juicier, more flavorful bird that never needs to be brined to pump up flavor or juiciness. If your supermarket doesn't carry kosher chickens, brining can improve the quality of just about any chicken, even last-place Perdue.

For the full results of our tasting of chicken, visit **Cook's Extra** at www.cooksillustrated.com and key in code 5043.

HIGHLY RECOMMENDED
EMPIRE KOSHER Broiler Chicken
➤ **$2.29/lb.**
Tasters found this bird to be the most flavorful of the tasting, calling it "perfectly seasoned," with meat that was "moist" and "tender."

RECOMMENDED
BELL & EVANS Fresh Young Chicken
➤ **$2.69/lb.**
Raised on an all-vegetable, antibiotic-free diet, this chicken was praised for meat that tasted "clean" and "fresh."

TYSON Fresh Young Chicken
➤ **$1.29/lb.**
Some tasters liked the "firm" texture, others found it slightly "mealy." Nevertheless, Tyson outscored chickens that cost twice as much.

BRINING

Innumerable tests have shown that soaking chicken in a saltwater solution prior to cooking produces juicy, well-seasoned meat. (The exception to this rule is a kosher bird.) To brine, add salt to cold water, stir to dissolve the salt, then immerse the chicken in the brine and refrigerate for the allotted time.

Formulating the Brine
Either of the two readily available brands of kosher salt can be substituted for the table salt in the formulas below. Because kosher salt is less salty than table salt, and because one brand of kosher salt is less salty than the other, the formulas must be adjusted. Substitute 1 cup of Diamond Crystal Kosher Salt or ¾ cup of Morton Kosher Salt for ½ cup of table salt.

	TABLE SALT	WATER	TIME
Whole chicken (3½– 4 lb.)	½ **cup**	½ **gallon**	**1 hour**
Chicken parts (bone-in)	½ **cup**	½ **gallon**	**30 min.**

Rinsing and Drying Brined Chicken
Once the chicken has been brined, it must be rinsed to wash away any excess salt that might remain on the skin. Brining does have one negative effect: The added moisture can prevent the skin from crisping when cooked. Letting brined chicken dry uncovered in the refrigerator remedies this problem. For best results, air-dry whole brined birds overnight. Brined chicken parts should be air-dried for several hours. Although this step is optional, if crisp skin is a goal, it's worth the extra time.

1. To rinse chicken, place on wire rack, set rack in empty sink, and use sink spray hose to wash off chicken. Blot chicken dry with paper towels.

2. To air-dry chicken, set rack with towel-dried chicken on rimmed baking sheet and place in refrigerator.

CUTTING UP A WHOLE CHICKEN

Even when a recipe calls for chicken parts, there are many advantages to purchasing a whole chicken and cutting it up yourself. Packaged chicken parts are generally mass-produced and are of a lower quality, so buying a whole chicken gives you the chance to buy a better bird. In addition, packages of chicken parts often come from different chickens of different sizes; as a result, the pieces may cook unevenly. To top it off, whole chickens generally cost less per pound and provide trimmings that are perfect for freezing to make homemade stock.

The Legs

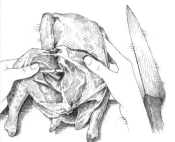 

1. Cut through skin around leg where it attaches to breast. Using both hands, bend leg back to pop leg joint out of its socket.

2. Cut through broken joint to separate leg. Cut very close to back, so that tender, meaty "oyster" is removed along with leg.

3. Note line of fat separating thigh and drumstick. Cut through joint at this line.

The Wings

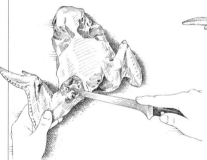 

1. Bend wing out from breast and cut through joint to separate.

2. Cut through cartilage around wing tip to remove it. Freeze tips and use to make your next batch of homemade chicken stock.

3. A triangular flap of skin connecting two halves of chicken wing can make it awkward to eat. Cut straight through center joint; two smaller pieces will cook up crispier and be easier to eat.

The Breast

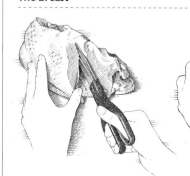 

1. To separate whole breast from backbone, cut through ribs with kitchen shears, following vertical line of fat from tapered end of breast up to socket where wing was attached.

2. With whole breast skin-side down on cutting board, center knife on breastbone, then apply pressure to cut through and separate breast into halves.

3. If you purchase one whole, bone-in chicken breast, you may need to trim rib sections with kitchen shears.

TIPS FOR HANDLING CHICKEN

Containing Raw Chicken
Avoiding cross-contamination when washing and drying raw chicken can be a challenge. To contain the chicken, wash it in a colander, then pat dry while it's still in the colander. When done, simply transfer the chicken to your cooking vessel, then wash your hands and the colander with hot, soapy water.

Saving Your Back
Don't stop butchering once you've removed the legs, wings, and breast—hack the back into 2-inch pieces with a cleaver and then freeze it (along with wing tips) to make homemade stock.

Getting a Grip on Raw Chicken
Raw chicken is slippery, which makes cutting it up hazardous. Get a firmer grip by using a folded wad of paper towels to hold the chicken in place.

Seasoning Raw Chicken
Touching the salt shaker or pepper mill after you've handled raw chicken can lead to cross-contamination. To avoid this, mix the necessary salt and pepper in a ramekin before handling the chicken.

Perfecting Mexican Rice

'Arroz a la Mexicana' promises bright flavor and a pilaf-style texture, but it rarely delivers.

⇒ BY REBECCA HAYS ⇐

A cursory look at Mexican rice reveals a simple pilaf prepared by sautéing raw white rice in oil, then slowly cooking the grains in chicken broth flavored with pureed tomatoes, onion, and garlic. Some cooks finish the dish with a sprinkle of fresh chiles and cilantro. In Mexico, rice pilaf, or *sopa seca* (dry soup), often serves as a separate course, in the manner that Italians serve pasta; on the American table, it makes a unique side dish.

Yet for a basic dish with a remarkably short ingredient list, I found it vexing. Variable ingredient quantities and cooking techniques produced disparate results when I put a selection of recipes from respected Mexican cookbook authors to the test. Two of these recipes turned out soupy and greasy, spurring tasters to crack jokes about my "Risotto a la Mexicana" and "Mexican Porridge." These descriptions, along with my own taste buds, told me that these supersoggy, oily versions were off-track. Other recipes seemed misguided in terms of ingredient amounts. Some had just a hint of garlic, others tasted of tomato and nothing else, and one was overtaken by pungent cilantro.

To my way of thinking, the perfect version of this dish would exhibit clean, balanced flavors and tender, perfectly cooked rice. It would be rich but not oily, moist but not watery. In search of this ideal, I returned to the test kitchen with some basic questions in mind: What is the proper ratio of liquid to rice for a moist but not brothy dish? Would canned tomatoes provide more balanced flavor than fresh? Could I skip the sautéing step and still end up with an agreeable texture? Could I add any ingredients that would improve the basic recipe?

The Cooking Medium

The liquid traditionally used in this dish is a mixture of chicken broth and pureed fresh tomatoes (plus a little salt); experiments with a variety of

COOK'S EXTRA gives you free recipes online. For a variation of Mexican rice with charred vegetables, visit www.cooksillustrated.com and key in code 5044. This recipe will be available until October 15, 2004.

The oven is key to perfectly cooked Mexican rice, and a final garnish of minced chiles, cilantro, and lime completes the flavor of the dish.

ratios helped me to settle on equal parts of each. With too much tomato puree, the rice tasted like warm gazpacho; with too little, its flavor waned. Though past *Cook's* recipes for pilaf have called for less liquid, I found that when pulpy tomatoes make up a portion of the fluid, a 2:1 ratio of liquid to rice produces just the right texture.

Each and every recipe I consulted called for fresh tomatoes, and when I pitted rice made with canned tomatoes against rice made with fresh, the reason for using the latter crystallized for me. Batches made with fresh tomatoes tasted, well, fresh. Those made with canned tomatoes, however eye-catching, tasted overcooked and too tomatoey; the rice should be scented with tomatoes, not overtaken by them. To capture the one benefit of canned tomatoes—an intense, tomato-red color—I stirred in an untraditional ingredient: tomato paste. Mexican rice often

appears washed out, and the tomato paste gave it an appealing hue while adding a little flavor to boot.

The Rice

The usual method for making Mexican rice is to sauté rinsed, long-grain white rice (tasters rejected less traditional short- and medium-grain rice) in oil before adding the cooking liquid. Rice that was rinsed indeed produced more distinct, separate grains when compared with unrinsed rice. While some recipes call for only a quick sauté, cooking the rice until it was golden brown proved crucial in providing a mild, toasted flavor and satisfying texture. As for the amount of oil, I experimented with a wide range, spanning from 3 tablespoons to 1¼ cups. When I essentially deep-fried the rice in copious amounts of oil, as more than one recipe suggested, the rice was much too oily; even straining off excess oil from the rice, as directed, didn't help, and it was a messy process. Insubstantial amounts of oil made rice that was dry and lacking richness. One-third of a cup seemed just right—this rice was rich but not greasy. Canola oil was favored over the comparatively pungent olive oil.

I had questions about whether to sauté other components of the recipe, such as the aromatics and the tomato pulp. I tried multiple permutations and landed on a compromised technique of sautéing a generous amount of garlic and jalapeños, then mixing in a raw puree of tomato and onion. This technique produced the balanced yet fresh-tasting flavor I was after; it also allowed me to process the onion in the food processor along with the tomatoes rather than having to chop it by hand.

I was having trouble achieving properly cooked rice on the stovetop. The grains inevitably scorched and then turned soupy when I attempted a rescue with extra broth. In the past, I've converted rice recipes from finicky to infallible by baking the rice, and testing proved that this recipe would be no exception. Still, as I baked batch after batch of rice, I was frustrated by cooking times that were inconsistent. Most batches contained a smattering of crunchy grains mixed in with the tender ones. Prolonged cooking didn't solve the problem; what did was stirring the rice partway through cooking to reincorporate the tomato mixture, which had been settling on top of the pilaf. With this practice in place, every last grain cooked evenly.

Extras

Some Mexican cooks stir peas and blanched, diced carrots into the finished rice, but my tasting panel rejected that option, preferring a simpler mixture. While many traditional recipes consider fresh cilantro and minced jalapeño optional, in my book they are mandatory. The raw herbs and pungent chiles complement the richer tones of the cooked tomatoes, garlic, and onions. When a little something still seemed missing from the rice, I thought to offer wedges of lime. A squirt of acidity illuminated the flavor even further.

MEXICAN RICE
SERVES 6 TO 8 AS A SIDE DISH

Because the spiciness of jalapeños varies from chile to chile, we try to control the heat by removing the ribs and seeds (the source of most of the heat) from those chiles that are cooked in the rice. Use an ovensafe pot about 12 inches in diameter so that the rice cooks evenly and in the time indicated. The pot's depth is less important than its diameter; we've successfully used both a straight-sided sauté pan and a Dutch oven. Whichever type of pot you use, it should have a tight-fitting, ovensafe lid. Vegetable broth can be substituted for chicken broth.

- 2 medium ripe tomatoes (about 12 ounces), cored and quartered
- 1 medium onion, preferably white, peeled, trimmed of root end, and quartered
- 3 medium jalapeño chiles
- 2 cups long-grain white rice
- ⅓ cup canola oil
- 4 medium garlic cloves, minced or pressed through garlic press (about 4 teaspoons)
- 2 cups low-sodium chicken broth
- 1 tablespoon tomato paste
- 1½ teaspoons table salt
- ½ cup minced fresh cilantro leaves
- 1 lime, cut into wedges for serving

1. Adjust oven rack to middle position and heat oven to 350 degrees. Process tomatoes and onion in food processor until smooth and thoroughly pureed, about 15 seconds, scraping down bowl if necessary. Transfer mixture to liquid measuring cup; you should have 2 cups (if necessary, spoon off excess so that volume equals 2 cups). Remove ribs and seeds from 2 jalapeños and discard; mince flesh and set aside. Mince remaining jalapeño, including ribs and seeds; set aside.

2. Place rice in large fine-mesh strainer and rinse under cold running water until water runs clear, about 1½ minutes. Shake rice vigorously in strainer to remove all excess water.

3. Heat oil in heavy-bottomed ovensafe 12-inch straight-sided sauté pan or Dutch oven with tight-fitting lid over medium-high heat, 1 to 2 minutes. Drop 3 or 4 grains rice in oil; if grains sizzle, oil is ready. Add rice and fry, stirring frequently, until rice is light golden and translucent, 6 to 8 minutes. Reduce heat to medium, add garlic and seeded minced jalapeños; cook, stirring constantly, until fragrant, about 1½ minutes. Stir in pureed tomatoes and onions, chicken broth, tomato paste, and salt; increase heat to medium-high and bring to boil. Cover pan and transfer to oven; bake until liquid is absorbed and rice is tender, 30 to 35 minutes, stirring well after 15 minutes.

4. Stir in cilantro and reserved minced jalapeño with seeds to taste. Serve immediately, passing lime wedges separately.

RECIPE SHORTHAND: KEYS TO GREAT MEXICAN RICE

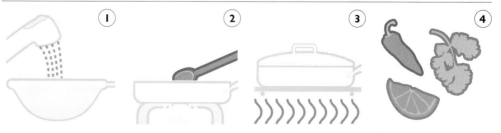

1. Rinse rice in mesh strainer until water runs clear. This ensures separate grains. **2.** Fry rice until light golden brown for rich, toasty flavor. **3.** For even cooking, bake rice in oven. **4.** Finish with fresh flavors—lime, cilantro, and chiles.

Sesame Noodles with Chicken

We set out to eliminate sticky noodles, gloppy sauce, and lackluster flavors.

⋟ BY JULIA COLLIN DAVISON ⋞

Toasted sesame seeds are ground into the sauce for extra flavor and are also used as a garnish.

Much like a Chinese finger trap that lures by appearing to be a toy, sesame noodles are not what they seem. You may think of them as merely a humble bowl of cold noodles, but don't be fooled—just one bite and you're hooked on these toothsome noodles with shreds of tender chicken, all tossed with the fresh sesame sauce. And now you've got a real problem: Once you get the hankering, good versions of this dish can be hard to find. The cold noodles have a habit of turning gummy, the chicken often dries out, and the sauce is notorious for turning bland and pasty. I wanted a recipe that could not only quell a serious craving but could do it fast.

Though drawn to the softer texture of fresh Asian-style noodles, I conceded that dried spaghetti could serve as a second-string substitute. The trouble with both types of noodle, however, was that after being cooked and chilled, they gelled into a rubbery skein. After trying a number of ways to avoid this, I found it necessary to rinse the noodles under cold tap water directly after cooking. This not only cooled the hot noodles immediately but also washed away much of their sticky starch. To further forestall any clumping, I tossed the rinsed noodles with a little oil.

Boneless, skinless chicken breasts are quick to cook and easy to shred; the real question is how to cook them. The microwave seemed easy in theory, but I found the rate of cooking difficult to monitor—30 seconds meant the difference between overdone and underdone. Many

recipes suggested poaching the chicken in water or broth, but this chicken had a washed-out flavor. Nor was roasting the answer; it caused the outer meat to dry out before the interior was fully cooked. Cooking under both gas and electric broilers, however, worked perfectly. The chicken cooked through in minutes, retaining much of its moisture and flavor.

To be authentic, the sesame sauce should be made with an Asian sesame paste (not to be confused with Middle Eastern tahini), but most recipes substitute peanut butter because it's easier to find. Somewhat surprisingly, tasters preferred chunky peanut butter over smooth, describing its flavor as fresh and more peanutty. I had been making the sauce in a blender and realized that the chunky bits of peanuts were being freshly ground into the sauce, producing a cleaner, stronger flavor. I found the flavors of both fresh garlic and ginger necessary, along with soy sauce, rice vinegar, hot sauce, and brown sugar. I then stumbled on the obvious way to keep the sauce from being too thick or pasty: Thin it out with water.

Although the sauce was tasting pretty good, tasters still complained that there was not enough sesame flavor. Tossing the rinsed pasta with toasted sesame oil helped a bit, as did garnishing the noodles with toasted sesame seeds. But tasters were still not satisfied; they wanted more. Finally, I tried adding some of the toasted sesame seeds to the sauce. Blended into the sauce along with the chunky peanut butter, the sesame seeds added the final kick of authentic sesame flavor we were all hankering for.

SESAME NOODLES WITH SHREDDED CHICKEN
SERVES 4 TO 6 AS A MAIN DISH

We prefer the flavor and texture of chunky peanut butter in the sauce; in particular, we like conventional chunky peanut butter because it tends to be sweeter than natural or old-fashioned versions.

- ¼ cup sesame seeds
- ¼ cup chunky peanut butter
- 2 medium garlic cloves, minced or pressed through garlic press (about 2 teaspoons)
- 1 tablespoon minced fresh ginger
- 5 tablespoons soy sauce
- 2 tablespoons rice vinegar
- 1 teaspoon hot sauce (such as Tabasco)
- 2 tablespoons lightly packed light brown sugar
  Hot water

- 1½ pounds boneless, skinless chicken breast halves
- 1 tablespoon table salt
- 1 pound fresh Asian-style noodles or 12 ounces dried spaghetti
- 2 tablespoons Asian sesame oil
- 4 scallions, sliced thin on diagonal
- 1 medium carrot, grated

1. Toast sesame seeds in medium skillet over medium heat, stirring frequently, until golden and fragrant, about 10 minutes. Reserve 1 tablespoon sesame seeds in small bowl. In blender or food processor, puree remaining 3 tablespoons sesame seeds, peanut butter, garlic, ginger, soy sauce, vinegar, hot sauce, and sugar until smooth, about 30 seconds. With machine running, add hot water 1 tablespoon at time until sauce has consistency of heavy cream, about 5 tablespoons; set blender jar or workbowl aside.

2. Bring 6 quarts water to boil in stockpot over high heat. Meanwhile, adjust oven rack to 6 inches from broiler element; heat broiler. Spray broiler pan top with vegetable cooking spray; place chicken breasts on top and broil chicken until lightly browned, 4 to 8 minutes. Using tongs, flip chicken over and continue to broil until thickest part is no longer pink when cut into and registers about 160 degrees on instant-read thermometer, 6 to 8 minutes. Transfer to cutting board and let rest 5 minutes. Using 2 forks, shred chicken into bite-size pieces and set aside. Add salt and noodles to boiling water; boil noodles until tender, about 4 minutes for fresh and 10 minutes for dried. Drain, then rinse with cold running tap water until cool to touch; drain again. In large bowl, toss noodles with sesame oil until evenly coated. Add shredded chicken, scallions, carrot, and sauce; toss to combine. Divide among individual bowls, sprinkle each bowl with portion of reserved sesame seeds, and serve.

SESAME NOODLES WITH SWEET PEPPERS AND CUCUMBERS

Core, seed, and cut into ¼-inch slices 1 medium red bell pepper; peel, halve lengthwise, seed, and cut crosswise into ⅛-inch slices 1 medium cucumber. Follow recipe for Sesame Noodles with Shredded Chicken, omitting chicken, adding bell pepper and cucumber to noodles with sauce, and sprinkling each bowl with portion of 1 tablespoon chopped fresh cilantro leaves along with sesame seeds.

The Ultimate Sticky Buns

These bakery favorites are often too sweet, too big, too rich, and just too much.
We wanted sticky buns that were impressive, not excessive.

> BY DAWN YANAGIHARA <

Sticky buns are things of breakfast-time debauchery. In bakeries, they are often plate-size buns, warm and glistening, heady with brown sugar and spices. In my opinion, anything less than a great one is not worth its calories. A sticky bun should be neither dense nor bready. The crumb should be tender and feathery and the sticky glaze gently chewy and gooey; the flavor should be warm and spicy, buttery and sweet—but just enough so that devouring one isn't a feat. Home bakers rarely attempt them, probably because sticky buns, like many other sweet yeasted breads, are a project, requiring a substantial time commitment. The results ought to be beyond edible—they should be irresistible.

A collection of recipes turned up all manner of sticky buns. Of those that I tried, one was too lean—more like a sugar-soaked baguette. One was cakey, with an insubstantial crumb, and it had a meager amount of sticky goo. Another was doughy and had a hard sugar veneer. The most laborious recipe resulted—some 18 hours later—in overly rich sticky buns that weren't worth the time or the effort. Those recipes that contained nuts, which were baked beneath the buns, had in common soggy, steamy pecans or walnuts that contributed little to either flavor or texture.

Dough Nut

The basic MO for sticky buns starts with a sugary glaze mixture that is put into a baking dish. The dough, after its first rise, is rolled, filled, and cut into buns. The buns are set on top of the glaze mixture, allowed a second rise, then baked, inverted, and devoured.

I began this multi-component preparation with the dough. From the start I knew that a lean dough, made with only flour and water, was out. It was an anomaly anyway. Most recipes involved fairly rich doughs, with milk, butter, eggs, and sugar in addition to the requisite flour, yeast, and salt. First off, I tried different liquids. Water, milk, and buttermilk all worked, but the buttermilk dough was vastly superior to the others. In the baked buns, the tanginess of the buttermilk translated into a flavor complexity that the others simply lacked; its acidity, though not overt, made for a nice counter to the sugary sweetness. Both flavor and texture were rich without being heavy, and the crumb was tender and light. Nonfat and

These sticky buns rise twice and receive two glazes (one before baking, the other after), but they are worth the wait.

low-fat buttermilk alike succeeded, as did, to my surprise, powdered buttermilk (which is added as a dry ingredient, with water being substituted for the buttermilk).

For the four or so cups of flour in the dough, I tested varying quantities of butter and finally settled on 6 tablespoons. It turned out that melted (rather than softened) butter was not only easier to use but yielded superb results. Next I experimented with eggs, starting with none and increasing to four whole (included were yolk and white permutations as well). Without eggs or with too few, the texture of the buns lacked substance; the crumb was too soft and yielding, like a squishy sandwich bread. Egg-rich versions—namely, those made with three eggs—were the favorite. These were moist, with a nice, light, open crumb. They were also tender and yet had substantial chew.

The rest of the dough fell into place. One-quarter cup of sugar gave it a light sweetness, and a hit of salt boosted flavor. One packet of instant yeast (2¼ teaspoons) worked to get the dough rising in a timely manner without leaving a distinct yeastiness in its wake (as an overabundance

of yeast would). Bread flour didn't outperform all-purpose flour, so all-purpose it was.

After the dough's first rise, or fermentation, it is rolled out into a rectangle and filled. The contents of the spiced sugar filling, which creates the swirl in the shaped buns, were quickly settled. Brown sugar beat out granulated because it had more presence; its color is darker and its flavor more assertive. A healthy dose of ground cinnamon and a dash of ground cloves added warmth and fragrance.

Glaze-Crazed

Most recipes specify dark brown sugar for use in the glaze as well as the filling, but before too long I dropped dark brown sugar in favor of light brown for the glaze. During baking, dark brown sugar took on too much color, and, though it tasted fine, it made the buns look unattractive.

At this point, progress slowed. In the batches I baked, the glaze invariably cooked up treacherously sticky and far too firm—ideal for ripping out dental work (which it did in fact do for one unfortunate taster). In combination with ¾ cup of brown sugar, I tried different amounts of butter—2, 4, 6, 8, and even 10 tablespoons.

We tested dozens of recipes and found that several recurring problems plagued most of them.

RUNAWAY GOO
Immediately after baking, the glaze is molten and will run off the buns if the pan is inverted too soon.

UNDERBROWNED
When baked in a glass Pyrex baking dish, the surface of the buns appears underbaked in color and texture.

SEEMINGLY BURNED
Using dark brown sugar in the glaze results in dark, almost burnt-looking sticky buns.

I increased and decreased the brown sugar. I tried adding water to the glaze mixture. I shortened baking times and lowered oven temperatures so that the glaze faced less heat (heat is what causes it to cook and harden). All to no avail. I tried adding a dose of corn syrup. The glaze showed some improvement—it had a softer, chewier texture—but it was still rather stiff and taffylike, and it lacked fluidity. With a thick, unctuous but pourable classic caramel sauce in mind (one made from caramelized sugar and heavy cream), I tried adding heavy cream—just 2 tablespoons—and it worked like magic. The topping was now sticky, gooey, and just a bit saucelike. The downside to the cream was that it had a slight dulling effect on the flavor of the caramel, but my tasters and I—and our fillings, bridges, and crowns—could live with that.

I tried different oven temperatures, and a 350-degree oven worked best, as did a 13 by 9-inch baking pan. Yet the buns were still far from perfect. They had a tacky, doughy, underdone surface, and the caramel glaze was a couple of shades too light. One cookbook author suggested placing the baking dish on a preheated baking stone, a step that vastly improved the evenness of browning and allowed the bottoms of the buns (which, bear in mind, later become the tops) to bake through in spite of all the goo that they sat in. With the pizza stone in play, though, the baking pan's material was no longer incidental (see box at left for details).

At first, I was inverting the hot sticky buns out of the pan as soon as they were done. After a few batches, though, I finally realized the merits of allowing them to cool for about 10 minutes before inversion. When hot, the caramel glaze was so molten that it quickly ran off the buns and pooled on the platter. Cooled for just a bit, however, the glaze was viscous enough to generously blanket the surface.

Oh, Nuts
According to tasters, the sticky buns were close to being great, but they were missing something—nuts, pecans, in particular. Instead of sprinkling chopped toasted pecans over the glaze in the baking dish, where I knew they would turn soggy, I introduced them to the filling. No good. Encased in the dough rather than sitting beneath it, the once toasty, crisp pecans still turned soggy.

I recalled a recipe that had included an unusual postbake glaze. At first the idea of still more glaze seemed superfluous (enough sugar already!), but then I realized that it could set a sort of precedent for a topping . . . a toasted pecan topping. I formulated a mixture of more glaze ingredients—butter, light brown sugar, and corn syrup for fluidity—to which I added toasted chopped pecans and some vanilla for good measure. The relatively small amount of sugar in this topping gave the nuts some cohesion without oversweetening matters. Crowned with pecans, the sticky buns had achieved greatness.

STICKY BUNS WITH PECANS
MAKES TWELVE 3½-INCH BUNS

This recipe has four components: the dough that is shaped into buns, the filling that creates the swirl in the shaped buns, the caramel glaze that bakes in the bottom of the baking dish along with the buns, and the pecan topping that garnishes the buns once baked. Although the ingredient list may look long, note that many ingredients are repeated. If not using a pizza stone or nonstick baking dish, see "Baking the Buns" at left. Leftover sticky buns can be wrapped in foil or plastic wrap and refrigerated for up to 3 days, but they should be warmed through before serving. They reheat quickly in a microwave oven (for 2 buns, about 2 minutes at 50 percent power works well); they can also be put into a 325-degree oven for about 8 minutes.

Dough
- 3 large eggs, room temperature
- ¾ cup buttermilk, room temperature
- ¼ cup granulated sugar
- 1¼ teaspoons table salt
- 2¼ teaspoons instant yeast
- 4¼ cups (21¼ ounces) unbleached all-purpose flour, plus additional for dusting work surface
- 6 tablespoons unsalted butter, melted, cooled until warm

Caramel Glaze
- 6 tablespoons unsalted butter
- ¾ cup (5¼ ounces) packed light brown sugar
- 3 tablespoons light or dark corn syrup
- 2 tablespoons heavy cream
- Pinch table salt

Cinnamon-Sugar Filling
- ¾ cup (5¼ ounces) packed light brown sugar
- 2 teaspoons ground cinnamon
- ¼ teaspoon ground cloves
- Pinch table salt
- 1 tablespoon unsalted butter, melted

Pecan Topping
- 3 tablespoons unsalted butter
- ¼ cup (1¾ ounces) packed light brown sugar
- 3 tablespoons light or dark corn syrup
- Pinch table salt
- 1 teaspoon vanilla extract
- ¾ cup (3 ounces) pecans, toasted in skillet over medium heat until fragrant and browned, about 5 minutes, then cooled and coarsely chopped

---

1. Spread hot glaze in baking dish.

2. Sprinkle dough with filling.

3. Roll dough into tight cylinder.

4. Firmly pinch seam to seal.

5. Cut cylinder into 12 buns.

6. Arrange buns in prepared dish.

pressed against one another, about 1½ hours. Meanwhile, adjust oven rack to lowest position, place pizza stone (if using) on rack, and heat oven to 350 degrees.

6. Place baking pan on pizza stone; bake until golden brown and center of dough registers about 180 degrees on instant-read thermometer, 25 to 30 minutes. Cool on wire rack 10 minutes; invert onto rimmed baking sheet, large rectangular platter, or cutting board. With rubber spatula, scrape any glaze remaining in baking pan onto buns; let cool while making pecan topping.

7. **FOR THE TOPPING:** Combine butter, brown sugar, corn syrup, and salt in small saucepan and bring to simmer over medium heat, whisking occasionally to thoroughly combine. Off heat, stir in vanilla and pecans until pecans are evenly coated. Using soup spoon, spoon heaping tablespoon nuts and topping over center of each sticky bun. Continue to cool until sticky buns are warm, 15 to 20 minutes. Pull apart or use serrated knife to cut apart sticky buns; serve.

1. **FOR THE DOUGH:** In bowl of standing mixer, whisk eggs to combine; add buttermilk and whisk to combine. Whisk in sugar, salt, and yeast. Add about 2 cups flour and butter; stir with wooden spoon or rubber spatula until evenly moistened and combined. Add all but about ¼ cup remaining flour and knead with dough hook at low speed 5 minutes. Check consistency of dough (dough should feel soft and moist but should not be wet and sticky; add more flour, if necessary); knead at low speed 5 minutes longer (dough should clear sides of bowl but stick to bottom). Turn dough out onto lightly floured work surface; knead by hand about 1 minute to ensure that dough is uniform (dough should not stick to work surface during hand kneading; if it does stick, knead in additional flour 1 tablespoon at a time).

2. Lightly spray large bowl or plastic container with nonstick cooking spray. Transfer dough to bowl, spray dough lightly with cooking spray, then cover bowl tightly with plastic wrap and set in warm, draftfree spot until doubled in volume, 2 to 2½ hours.

3. **FOR THE GLAZE:** Meanwhile, combine all ingredients for glaze in small saucepan; cook over medium heat, whisking occasionally, until butter is melted and mixture is thoroughly combined. Pour mixture into nonstick metal 13 by 9-inch baking dish; using rubber spatula, spread mixture to cover surface of baking dish. Set baking dish aside.

4. **TO ASSEMBLE AND BAKE BUNS:** For filling, combine brown sugar, cinnamon, cloves, and salt in small bowl and mix until thoroughly combined, using fingers to break up sugar lumps; set aside. Turn dough out onto lightly floured work surface. Gently shape dough into rough rectangle with long side nearest you. Lightly flour dough and roll to 16 by 12-inch rectangle. Brush dough

with 1 tablespoon melted butter, leaving ½-inch border along top edge; with butter remaining on brush, brush sides of baking dish. Sprinkle filling mixture over dough, leaving ¾-inch border along top edge; smooth filling in even layer with hand, then gently press mixture into dough to adhere. Beginning with long edge nearest you, roll dough into taut cylinder. Firmly pinch seam to seal and roll cylinder seam-side down. Very gently stretch to cylinder of even diameter and 18-inch length; push ends in to create even thickness. Using serrated knife and gentle sawing motion, slice cylinder in half, then slice each half in half again to create evenly sized quarters. Slice each quarter evenly into thirds, yielding 12 buns (end pieces may be slightly smaller).

5. Arrange buns cut-side down in prepared baking dish; cover tightly with plastic wrap and set in warm, draftfree spot until puffy and

OVERNIGHT STICKY BUNS

If you like, sticky buns can be made and shaped the night before and then refrigerated. The next morning, set the baking dish in a warm-water bath to speed the dough's rise.

1. Follow recipe for Sticky Buns with Pecans; after forming and arranging buns in baking pan, cover pan tightly with plastic wrap and refrigerate 10 to 14 hours.

2. Place baking pan in warm-water bath (about 120 degrees) in kitchen sink or large roasting pan for 20 minutes. Remove from water bath and let stand at room temperature until buns look slightly puffy and are pressed against one another, about 1½ hours. About an hour before baking, adjust oven rack to lowest position, place pizza stone on rack (if using), and heat oven to 350 degrees.

SCIENCE: **Designer Yeast**

Lesaffre, the producer of Red Star and SAF yeast, also makes a line of yeast called Nevada Gold Label that is designed for high-sugar doughs, and we thought that an ideal candidate on which to test it would be our sweet sticky buns. After baking two batches of rolls, we found that this special yeast worked, decreasing the time required for the first rise by 33 percent and the second rise by 45 percent when compared with the standard SAF instant yeast. In total, this saved us more than an hour in rising time. Our curiosity was piqued.

It's not easy being single-celled yeast. Precious little separates their insides from the harsh world at large—no skin, no fat, just a membrane. Most bakers consider sugar food for yeast, but sugar in too high a concentration can be a killer. Yeast placed in a high-sugar dough can undergo osmotic stress, in which water wants to flow out of the yeast and into the dough, causing the yeast to dry out.

Nevada Gold Label yeast is designed to withstand this stress better than regular yeast. The dough we made with it performed particularly well in the second rise, when the rolls were shaped, cloaked in sugar, and exposed to the air—definitely a harsh environment for a moisture-loving organism. If you bake a lot of sweet breads, you may want to keep some Nevada Gold Label on hand. —John Olson, Science Editor

SWEET YEAST
Nevada Gold Label yeast performs especially well in our sticky bun recipe. See page 32 for mail-order information.

Pineapple Upside-Down Cake

This simple skillet dessert deserves better than bland flavors and soggy cake.

⇒ BY ERIKA BRUCE ⇐

As soon as canned pineapple became readily available in this country, in the early 1900s, the pineapple evolved from a once-exotic symbol of hospitality into the latest food trend. This fruit really came into its own when it appeared on top of the pineapple upside-down cake. The recipe was based on the simple technique of cooking fruit in sugar and butter in a heavy skillet (usually cast iron), topping it with cake batter, then baking it. To serve, the cake was turned "upside down."

Things have changed since the days of canned pineapple rings studded with Day-Glo cherries. Juicy and sweet fresh pineapples are widely available. The big surprise is that fresh, high-quality pineapple has not revitalized upside-down cake. In fact, when I tested modern recipes that call for fresh pineapple (after having tested and dismissed Dole's canned pineapple version as bland), I quickly discovered that the juiciness of the fresh fruit turned the cake soggy. If it was to make a comeback, this dessert would need a topping of caramelized pineapple, coated (not swimming) in thick syrup.

Starting at the Top

The topping ingredients were the same in most recipes: half a pineapple, ¾ cup of light brown sugar (dark brown sugar turned black in the oven), and 4 tablespoons of butter. Also the same was the basic technique for preparing it: Melt the butter, stir in the sugar, add the pineapple. The result was a topping with little caramelized flavor.

Because the pineapple was so juicy, it steamed in the oven and remained pale. I tried sautéing the pineapple, butter, and sugar to develop color, but again the juice from the pineapple turned the mixture to soup and prevented browning. Determined to caramelize the topping, I continued to cook it and thereby evaporate the extra liquid. But this approach took so long that the butter eventually burned and the fruit became shriveled and chewy. Removing the butter from the equation, I cooked the pineapple in the sugar alone. When the fruit turned golden brown and became infused with syrup, I strained it out and returned the syrup to the skillet. Now I could reduce the syrup until it thickened and started to color (but not burn) and add the butter at

Fresh pineapple makes a better topping for this classic cake than canned fruit, but it requires adjustments to the recipe.

the end. Using this method, I could control the moisture in the pineapple (by cooking the syrup more or less) and develop a smooth caramel.

But when I assembled all of the elements of the cake, I discovered that the conservative ration of just half a pineapple had been cooked down to a mere garnish. To make the topping an integral part of the cake, I would have to use a whole pineapple. In my first attempt, I also doubled the amounts of butter and brown sugar. Now I had

too much sauce. In the end, I was able to increase the sugar by just ¼ cup and to decrease the butter—to just 3 tablespoons.

Only one problem remained: Using a whole pineapple made it nearly impossible to fork my way through the solid layer of rings without smashing the cake. I traded elegance for practicality and cut the fruit into bite-size pieces, creating a mosaic design that made the cake easier to eat.

Getting to the Bottom

Because butter cake had the best flavor of the cakes I'd tried in preliminary testing, I started there, with a standard recipe of 1½ cups all-purpose flour, 1½ teaspoons baking powder, 8 tablespoons unsalted butter, 1 cup granulated sugar, 2 whole eggs, and ½ cup whole milk. Even with my new and nicely thickened topping, the juices from the pineapple quickly turned this classic cake into a gummy, saccharine, cloying mess.

The easiest thing to fix was the sweetness of the cake, so I reduced the sugar by ¼ cup. Next I removed a few tablespoons of milk, which alleviated some of the gumminess. To lighten the texture, I tried increasing the baking powder by ¼ teaspoon, but the cake became too light and cottony and lost its structure, crumbling all over the plate. I tried cake flour instead of all-purpose, but this, too, weakened the structure of the cake to the point where it was unable to hold up the heavy layer of glazed fruit. Adding a third whole egg allowed the cake to maintain its structure, but its texture became rubbery. Adding just a yolk (instead of a whole egg) turned the cake into a dense pound cake. Finally, I tried the only other alternative, just an egg white, which succeeded in lightening the texture without compromising the structure.

RECIPE TESTING: **Problem Cakes**

TOO DARK	TOO SOUPY	NOT ENOUGH FRUIT

During our initial recipe testing, we noticed that dark brown sugar added flavor to the topping, but it also made for a murky appearance (left). Fresh, uncooked pineapple combined with sugar and butter led to a soggy topping (middle). Many recipes skimped on the fruit, making the pineapple more garnish than topping (right).

Higher oven temperatures of 375 or 400 degrees burned the outside of the cake while leaving it raw in the center. The steady, even heat of 350 degrees was the best option. Once baked, the cake was best left in the pan for 10 minutes before being flipped onto a serving platter. This was just enough time for the cake to set up and for the syrup of the topping to thicken slightly.

As far as I was concerned, this cake needed no garnish, but some of my colleagues thought whipped cream might do nicely. Fine with me—just as long as you hold the maraschino cherries.

PINEAPPLE UPSIDE-DOWN CAKE
MAKES ONE 9-INCH CAKE, SERVING 8 TO 10

For this recipe, we prefer to use a 9-inch cake pan with sides that are at least 2 inches high. Alternatively, a 10-inch ovensafe skillet (cast iron or stainless steel) can be used to both cook the pineapple and bake the cake. If using a skillet instead of a cake pan, cool the juices directly in the skillet while making the batter; it's OK if the skillet is warm when the batter is added.

Pineapple Topping
- 1 medium ripe pineapple (about 4 pounds), prepared according to illustrations below (about 4 cups prepared fruit)
- 1 cup (7 ounces) packed light brown sugar
- 3 tablespoons unsalted butter
- 1/2 teaspoon vanilla extract

Cake
- 1 1/2 cups (7 1/2 ounces) unbleached all-purpose flour
- 1 1/2 teaspoons baking powder
- 1/2 teaspoon table salt
- 8 tablespoons (1 stick) unsalted butter, softened but still cool
- 3/4 cup (5 1/4 ounces) granulated sugar
- 1 teaspoon vanilla extract
- 2 large eggs plus 1 egg white, room temperature
- 1/3 cup whole milk, room temperature

1. Lightly spray 9-inch round, 2-inch deep cake pan with nonstick cooking spray; set aside.

2. **FOR THE PINEAPPLE TOPPING:** Combine pineapple and brown sugar in 10-inch skillet; cook over medium heat, stirring occasionally during first 5 minutes, until pineapple is translucent and has light brown hue, 15 to 18 minutes. Empty fruit and juices into mesh strainer or colander set over medium bowl. Return juices to skillet, leaving pineapple in strainer (you should have about 2 cups cooked fruit). Simmer juices over medium heat until thickened, beginning to darken, and mixture forms large bubbles, 6 to 8 minutes, adding any more juices released by fruit to skillet after about 4 minutes. Off heat, whisk in butter and vanilla; pour caramel mixture into prepared cake pan. Set aside while preparing cake. (Pineapple will continue to release liquid as

it sits; do not add this liquid to already-reduced juice mixture.)

3. **FOR THE CAKE:** Adjust oven rack to lower-middle position and heat oven to 350 degrees. Whisk flour, baking powder, and salt in medium bowl; set aside.

4. In bowl of standing mixer fitted with flat beater, cream butter and sugar at medium-high speed until light and fluffy, 3 to 4 minutes. Reduce speed to medium, add vanilla, and beat to combine; one at a time, add whole eggs then egg white, beating well and scraping down bowl after each addition. Reduce speed to low; add about one-third of flour mixture and beat until incorporated. Add half of milk and beat until incorporated; repeat, adding half of remaining flour mixture and remaining milk, and finish with remaining flour. Give final stir with rubber spatula, scraping bottom and sides of bowl to ensure that batter is combined. Batter will be thick.

5. **TO BAKE:** Working quickly, distribute cooked pineapple in cake pan in even layer, gently pressing fruit into caramel. Using rubber spatula, drop mounds of batter over fruit, then spread batter over fruit and to sides of pan. Tap pan lightly against work surface to release any air bubbles. Bake until cake is golden brown and toothpick inserted into center of cake comes out clean, 45 to 50 minutes. Cool 10 minutes on wire rack, then place inverted serving platter over cake pan. Invert cake pan and platter together; lift off cake pan. Cool to room temperature, about 2 hours; then cut into pieces and serve.

COOK'S EXTRA gives you free recipes online. For two variations of our pineapple upside-down cake, visit www.cooksillustrated.com and key in code 5046. These recipes will be available until October 15, 2004.

STEP-BY-STEP | PREPARING THE PINEAPPLE

1. Slice 1 inch off top and bottom. Standing pineapple on one end, cut off strips of skin from top to bottom.

2. Quarter pineapple lengthwise. Place each quarter on its side and cut out light-colored piece of core.

3. Cut pineapple lengthwise into 3/4-inch strips. Turn 90 degrees and cut crosswise into 1/2-inch pieces.

Tomato Paste in a Jar

Many brands of tomato sauce are not much more than reconstituted tomato paste.
Could we find a jarred tomato sauce with fresh taste and a good balance of flavors?

≥ BY MARYELLEN DRISCOLL ≤

I was cramming my shopping cart with jars of pasta sauce to stock up for a taste test when a young, sophisticated-looking couple stopped in front of the sauce display. The fellow began to speak emphatically in Spanish. I thought for sure he was telling his girlfriend, "Buy this rubbish and we're through." But I understood enough to realize that he was instructing her on which brands to avoid. Then he pointed out what he considered the absolute best. It was the winning sauce from a *Cook's* blind tasting five years ago. Good call.

Since that tasting, published in the March/April 1999 issue, a slew of new brands of jarred pasta sauces have emerged, making for a booming $1.4 billion market. Considering that even the winner of that tasting, Barilla, didn't exactly sweep tasters off their feet—it won for being the freshest tasting of a not very fresh tasting lot—we wanted to find out if any of the new players could do better. We narrowed the lineup to the following: the winner of the last jarred pasta sauce tasting (Barilla), the nation's three top-selling brands (Prego, Classico, and Ragù, respectively), and five of the most widely available newcomers to the market since the 1999 tasting. All of the sauces were either marinaras or the brand's most basic tomato and herb–style sauce.

The Shipping News

From our perspective, the challenge of making a good-tasting jarred pasta sauce is to preserve a fresh tomato flavor. In the 1999 tasting, we learned that the lack of freshness among jarred sauces can be credited to the common practice of using tomato paste, reconstituted with water, as the primary tomato ingredient instead of a fresher product, such as canned diced tomatoes. Made from tomatoes that are cooked for several hours until reduced to a thick, spreadable consistency, tomato paste is a highly concentrated product.

Why do most jarred pasta sauce manufacturers prefer to use tomato paste—and in relatively large quantities? Robert Graf, president of the California League of Food Processors, helped to clear this up. (He ought to know; California grows 10 million tons of tomatoes in a typical year, supplying 35 percent of the world's processed tomatoes.) His explanation was simple

Where Are the Tomatoes?

NICE & CHUNKY   SMOOTH BUT BLAND

We spooned equal amounts of each sauce in the tasting into a strainer and then rinsed the sauce under running water to see what would be left. Our top-rated sauces, including Bertolli (in left strainer), showed off nice chunks of tomatoes, even after being rinsed for about 45 seconds, while the low-rated sauces washed away to almost nothing. The Ragù (in right strainer) left behind only tomato skin, herbs, and bits of diced vegetables.

enough: Most jarred pasta sauces are manufactured east of the Rockies, and fresher-tasting products, such as diced or crushed tomatoes, contain a lot of water. "Water," he said, "is very expensive to ship." It is therefore much cheaper to ship tomato paste and reconstitute the paste with water at the manufacturing plant as a first step in making the jarred sauce.

Another advantage of using tomato paste is that its low water content makes it extremely shelf-stable compared with fresh tomatoes. Its long shelf life gives manufacturers a larger window of time during which they can turn "tomatoes" into sauce.

Fresher Means Better

The good news is that some manufacturers, such as Patsy's, Bertolli, and Barilla, do use fresher tomato products. Each of them uses some fresher form of canned tomatoes, such as diced or freshly pureed, as their main tomato ingredient (although some tomato paste may be used as a secondary ingredient). This difference delivered not only winning flavor but a pleasant chunky consistency instead of the smooth, ketchuplike texture of most other sauces in the tasting.

To get a better handle on the differences between a "tomato paste" sauce and one made with less-processed tomatoes, we ran a small experiment. We took a portion of each sauce and rinsed it with water in a fine-meshed sieve until all of the soluble ingredients were rinsed away. A reputable portion of tomato chunks remained in the sieves with the favored sauces (see example, far left). But woe to the tomato paste sauces that displayed only meager bits of tomato flesh (see example, immediate left). With one sauce, little beyond flecks of herbs, tomato skin, and dehydrated onion could be observed.

But Will the Kids Like It?

Any household with children is more apt to stock a jarred pasta sauce than one without (69 percent versus 53 percent, respectively, according to one industry source)—which begs the question, Which sauce do kids like best? To find out, we brought in a group of 19 fifth and sixth graders from the Atrium School in Watertown, Mass., who were happy to take the job seriously. Their favorite, as predicted, was the sauce with nearly twice as much sugar (from corn syrup) as the others. Prego, which had 13 grams per serving versus an average 7 grams among the other sauces, inspired such comments as "zippy good blend" and "I'm in heaven, I'm in heaven!" But there is good news for parents who prefer not to buy such sugary tomato sauces. The panel's second choice (third place for the adults) was Barilla, which they appreciated for its "tomatoey" chunky texture. The only brand that got a thumbs down was Ragù, which one taster described as "not spicy, too smooth, not tomatoey enough, not happy!" –M.D.

TASTING JARRED PASTA SAUCES

Twenty-four tasters from the magazine staff sampled nine jarred pasta sauces (labeled by number so that they could not identify the brand). The sauces were served warm with bowls of cooked ziti on the side. Samples were tasted in different orders by different tasters, with one sample repeated as a control to confirm the validity of the test. The tasters rated each sample from 1 to 10, placing them in categories of recommended and not recommended. Samples were also scored for freshness of tomato flavor, sweetness, saltiness, degree of herbal flavor, and desirability of consistency. The sauces are listed in order of preference based on overall scores from tasters.

RECOMMENDED

PATSY'S Marinara ➤ **$8.49 for 24 ounces**
Garlic lovers rallied around this marinara, said to be the very same sauce served at the popular Patsy's Italian Restaurant in New York City. In addition to the garlic, which is added fresh (not in a powder), the sauce had an equally strong herbal punch and an "OK balance of acid, sweetness, and salt." The chunky tomato texture was a good reflection of this sauce's "reasonably fresh" tomato essence. But talk about sticker shock: Patsy's was more than three times the price of most other sauces.

BERTOLLI Tomato & Basil Pasta Sauce ➤ **$2.49 for 26 ounces**
Tasters thought that this sauce had the freshest flavor. As one taster summed it up, "bright, zesty tomatoes, with some depth of flavor." The texture was "meaty," with an agreeable balance of tomato chunks and puree. Herbs and spices were evident but not assertive.

BARILLA Marinara ➤ **$2.29 for 26 ounces**
The top jarred sauce in our 1999 tasting, Barilla held its own among sauces new to the market for being one of the freshest in flavor. Many tasters said they would like the sauce more if it wasn't so heavily seasoned with oregano. The oregano notwithstanding, the sauce had good balance and a pleasant chunky texture.

RECOMMENDED WITH RESERVATIONS

EMERIL'S Home Style Marinara Pasta Sauce ➤ **$4.29 for 25 ounces**
More than one taster likened this famed chef's marinara to pizza sauce. There was no "Bam!" This was instead a balanced, "plain and simple" sauce that some found "not very interesting" and even "kinda boring." The texture was that of a smooth puree.

RECOMMENDED WITH RESERVATIONS (CONT.)

PREGO Traditional Pasta Sauce ➤ **$2.29 for 26 ounces**
As America's top-selling jarred pasta sauce, Prego was the favorite in our kids' tasting (see page 26). Its heavy oregano taste was popular with many tasters but a "dried-herb nightmare" for others. More than one taster picked up on the corn syrup used as the sweetener.

CLASSICO Sweet Basil Marinara ➤ **$2.39 for 26 ounces**
This familiar-tasting national top seller wasn't a favorite, but it was ranked among those considered decent enough. A cooked tomato paste flavor contributed to a noted sweetness and thick, pastelike texture. It "tastes like nondescript pasta sauce from a jar," noted one taster.

BUITONI Marinara ➤ **$2.99 for 26 ounces**
Another jarred sauce that was strong on oregano and likened to pizza sauce. It did have a relatively good balance of flavors, but the flavorless, crunchy bits of something unidentifiable—possibly celery—were troubling to munch on.

NOT RECOMMENDED

RAGÙ Marinara ➤ **$2.29 for 26 ounces**
More than one taster said that this sauce tasted as if it came from a tin can. The absence of favorable comments was striking: "might as well be tomato paste," "extremely salty," and tastes "heavily cooked/cooked for days," "like V-8," and "more like tomato soup," with a texture like ketchup.

COLAVITA Marinara Sauce ➤ **$4.69 for 26 ounces**
A little doctoring with salt and sugar (neither of which is listed in the ingredients) might have saved this ultrabland sauce that tasted "waaay too tomatoey"—"like a can of crushed tomatoes." The herbs were also too understated.

Another key to a good jarred pasta sauce turned out to be balanced flavor. Many sauces couldn't get it right, overdosing on the dried herbs or loading up on sweetener (sugar or corn syrup) and salt. When comparing the amount of sodium and sugar in the sauces, it was readily apparent that the top three contained only moderate amounts of both. Colavita was the perfect example of a potentially good sauce that missed its mark by way of unbalanced flavor. It was the only other sauce in the tasting that wasn't made primarily of tomato paste—containing whole and crushed canned tomatoes—but it also contained absolutely no added salt or sugar. Tasters felt that it tasted incomplete, more like canned tomatoes than pasta sauce.

No Miracle in a Jar

There has not, then, been a revolution in the making of jarred sauces. The options for a half-decent jarred sauce, however, have broadened—albeit slightly. Given this finding, we continue to plead the case—as we did in 1999—that a quick homemade marinara remains a far better option.

As for convenience, our favorite Simple Tomato Sauce requires little more than pantry ingredients (we like to add fresh basil), and it takes about the same amount of time to prepare as it takes to cook a pot of pasta. But on nights when any cooking task seems arduous, you now know which jarred sauces won't thoroughly disappoint.

COOK'S EXTRA gives you free recipes online. To get our recipe for Simple Tomato Sauce, visit www.cooksillustrated.com and key in code 5047. This recipe will be available until October 15, 2004.

Are Hand-Held Mixers History?

Is there any reason to purchase a hand-held mixer in this age of all-purpose (but expensive) standing mixers?

⇒ BY MARYELLEN DRISCOLL AND GARTH CLINGINGSMITH ⇐

In head-to-head competitions in our test kitchen, standing mixers always outperform held-held mixers. Simply put, a standing mixer offers greater flexibility and versatility. The most obvious difference is brute force. Any decent standing mixer can knead bread dough, but even the best hand-held mixer fails miserably at this task. A standing mixer also frees up the cook to take on other tasks.

While these two advantages are dramatic, for many day-to-day uses, hand-held and standing mixers are actually quite similar. When making cake batters and cookie doughs, whipping cream, and beating egg whites, we have found that a hand-held mixer can yield the same results as a standing mixer—albeit a little more slowly.

In addition, a hand-held mixer is much cheaper than a standing mixer, and it's compact and easily transported. If your workspace or budget is restricted, a hand-held mixer can prove most valuable—especially if you're willing to forgo bread making and to stand by the bowl as the mixer does its work. But this calculation makes sense only if you invest in a good hand-held mixer—and that's easier said than done.

A Mix of Troubles

Over the years, we've been disappointed by many hand-held mixers; they can be little more than glorified whisks. And who hasn't encountered the disconcerting smoky odor of a hand-held mixer's motor as the beaters slog their way through a particularly stiff dough? These experiences notwithstanding, the promise of a good hand-held mixer—reliable performance easily had, and at a low cost—beckoned. And so we assembled eight leading models to see if we could separate the wimps from the workhorses.

Lack of power isn't the only complaint we've had with hand-held mixers. With a standing mixer, splattering isn't much of an issue because the whisk sits deep in the bowl. A hand-held mixer, however, can spray both the counter and the cook as the beaters whirl away. When whipping cream, we found that most mixers splattered on some level, but the best mixers kept the mess in the bowl; the worst managed to propel flecks of cream up to eye level, which was not appreciated.

All of the mixers were able to beat egg whites to stiff peaks. The main discrepancy resided in the "feel" of the mixer as it beat the whites; some felt

unwieldy (and thus received a rating of "fair" on this task), while others felt controlled (and were rated "good").

Making pound cake seemed the perfect test for a mixer's effectiveness at creaming. Traditional pound cake contains no chemical leaveners; its rise comes from creaming the butter and sugar until they are light and fluffy. Proper aeration is the key to avoiding an overly dense cake. The eight mixers tested made pound cakes that rose to heights within ¼ inch of one another—a range so negligible that this test counted for little in the overall ratings.

Power Crunch

The test that really separated the winners from the losers was mixing peanut butter cookie dough. Unlike chocolate chip cookie dough, which is easy enough to mix by hand if necessary, thick, stiff peanut butter cookie dough requires a determined motor. Of the eight mixers tested, only the KitchenAid and Braun did not hesitate once the dry ingredients were added to the sticky mix of peanut butter, eggs, and butter. Four of the mixers struggled but ultimately managed to tough it out as the dough began to come together or the mixing speed was increased. Two models could not complete this task and landed at the bottom of our ratings.

Somewhat to our surprise, wattage was not a good indicator of power. Of the mixers that fell

into the run-of-the-mill category, one had the highest wattage of all eight mixers tested, another the lowest. KitchenAid, the maker of our winning mixer, did not even post the machine's wattage on its box or in its literature.

Because so many consumers judge the power of an appliance by its wattage, we asked KitchenAid about this. A representative explained that unlike most manufacturers, who use AC (alternating current) motors, KitchenAid uses a DC (direct current) motor, which it believes to be less heavy and less noisy than AC motors. The company also claims that this motor is more energy-efficient and requires less wattage to operate. (KitchenAid would not disclose the exact wattage required.) In sum, the KitchenAid representative said, wattage is not always the best measurement of power when buying small electrical appliances. Our science editor explained that wattage is a measure of input—the amount of power a motor is taking in to operate. If a motor is not designed to work efficiently, it can require more input, or wattage, without necessarily delivering more output—that is, a stronger performance.

Design Matters

Secondary to power—although still significant—was design. Most of the mixers weighed in at around 2 pounds, 2 ounces, but some felt much heavier than others and were more fatiguing to use. For example, mixers with angled handles let

---

Choosing Your Beater

In recent years, many manufacturers have abandoned the old-style beaters with flat tines and a center post for a more streamlined wire beater without the hard-to-clean center post. Some still offer both styles, while others are also throwing in a bonus whisk attachment. One model in our testing offered all three. How do you know which attachment to use when? Here's what we found.

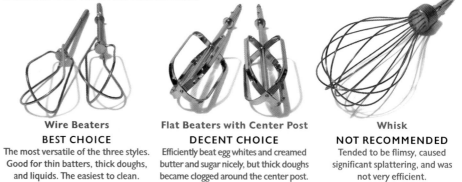

Wire Beaters
BEST CHOICE
The most versatile of the three styles. Good for thin batters, thick doughs, and liquids. The easiest to clean.

Flat Beaters with Center Post
DECENT CHOICE
Efficiently beat egg whites and creamed butter and sugar nicely, but thick doughs became clogged around the center post.

Whisk
NOT RECOMMENDED
Tended to be flimsy, caused significant splattering, and was not very efficient.

RATING HAND-HELD MIXERS

We tested eight hand-held mixers, evaluating each according to the following criteria. Mixers were categorized as highly recommended, recommended, or not recommended based on the ratings they earned for performance and design. They are listed in order of preference.

PRICE: Prices paid in Boston-area stores, national mail-order catalogs, and on Web sites.

ATTACHMENTS: While tests of different beater styles revealed some differences (see box on page 28), wire beaters were considered the most versatile and effective. Dough hooks and nonmixing attachments, such as choppers, were not tested.

WHIPPING CREAM: Mixers able to whip heavy cream to stiff peaks with little to no splattering outside of the bowl were rated good.

BEATING EGG WHITES: Mixers able to beat egg whites to stiff peaks quickly and without feeling unwieldy were rated good.

POUND CAKE BATTER: Mixers were rated for their ability to cream butter and sugar. Because all of the cakes rose to within a negligible ¼ inch of one another in height, all were rated good.

PEANUT BUTTER COOKIE DOUGH: Mixers that could easily mix a thick, stiff peanut butter cookie dough were rated good. Those that slowed at the task but were able to complete the mixing process were rated fair. Mixers that could not complete this job were rated poor.

DESIGN: Well-balanced mixers, with easy-to-operate controls, were rated good.

TESTERS' COMMENTS: Additional observations about the mixers' design, ease of use, or performance in specific tests.

HIGHLY RECOMMENDED

	TESTERS' COMMENTS
KitchenAid 7 Speed Mixer Model KHM7T PRICE: $69.99 ATTACHMENT: wire beaters WHIPPING CREAM: ★★★ BEATING EGG WHITES: ★★★ POUND CAKE: ★★★ COOKIE DOUGH: ★★★ DESIGN: ★★★	Never slowed or hesitated when mixing stiff peanut butter cookie dough. Compact size, digital display for speeds, and smooth touch-pad speed control made it a pleasure to operate; on/off switch was welcome safety feature. Mixing action notably "neat," "smooth," and "controlled" compared with that of others.
Braun MultiMix 4-in-1 Model M880 PRICE: $49.99 ATTACHMENTS: wire beaters, dough hooks, hand blender shaft, and chopper WHIPPING CREAM: ★★★ BEATING EGG WHITES: ★★★ POUND CAKE: ★★★ COOKIE DOUGH: ★★★ DESIGN: ★★	Perhaps better named Brawn, was one of just two mixers that worked through thick cookie dough without slowing. Angled design of wire beaters seemed to grab and whip up egg whites to stiff peaks, working faster than any other mixer with wire beaters. More angled handle with narrower grip would have been more comfortable.

RECOMMENDED

	TESTERS' COMMENTS
Bosch TurboBeat Hand Mixer Model MFQ 2100 PRICE: $65.00 ATTACHMENTS: wire beaters, dough hooks WHIPPING CREAM: ★★★ BEATING EGG WHITES: ★★★ POUND CAKE: ★★★ COOKIE DOUGH: ★★ DESIGN: ★★★	Beater design similar to Braun's and thus extremely efficient at whipping. Motor was quiet—"like a modern-day sewing machine"—and overall operation felt smooth. Beaters slowed some when making cookie dough, but increasing speed took care of this. Straight handle compromised comfort slightly.
Cuisinart SmartPower Electronic Hand Mixer Model HTM-7L PRICE: $49.99 ATTACHMENTS: wire beaters, whisk WHIPPING CREAM: ★★★ BEATING EGG WHITES: ★★★ POUND CAKE: ★★★ COOKIE DOUGH: ★★ DESIGN: ★★★	On/off switch, digital touchpad display, and good overall balance were clear design strengths. Didn't "bite into the cookie dough," however, requiring mixer to be pushed through dough, at which point beaters turned but didn't appear to be blending anything.
Black & Decker PowerPro Model MX85 PRICE: $19.99 ATTACHMENTS: wire beaters, insertable spatula WHIPPING CREAM: ★★★ BEATING EGG WHITES: ★★★ POUND CAKE: ★★★ COOKIE DOUGH: ★★ DESIGN: ★★	This mixer struggled some and motor began to smell when mixing peanut butter cookie dough. Increased speed helped, but mixer still had to be pushed through dough, as beaters didn't grab it. We don't recommend using spatula attachment that inserts alongside beaters. Beater eject button was difficult to operate.
Oster Easystore Hand Mixer Model 2491 PRICE: $24.99 ATTACHMENTS: flat beaters, dough hooks WHIPPING CREAM: ★★★ BEATING EGG WHITES: ★★★ POUND CAKE: ★★★ COOKIE DOUGH: ★ DESIGN: ★★	Except for failure at cookie dough test, performance was top-notch. This mixer splattered least of all tested while whipping cream, "swooped" egg whites into stiff peaks, and neatly creamed butter and sugar in center of bowl. We loved retractable cord but found handle hard to hold.

NOT RECOMMENDED

	TESTERS' COMMENTS
Hamilton Beach Power Deluxe 6 Speed Mixer 62695 PRICE: $24.99 ATTACHMENTS: wire beaters, flat beaters, whisk WHIPPING CREAM: ★★ BEATING EGG WHITES: ★★★ POUND CAKE: ★★★ COOKIE DOUGH: ★ DESIGN: ★★	Square edges on wire beaters clanged and rattled against sides of bowl. Splatters from whipping cream reached eye level, and beaters repeatedly bogged down in cookie dough as motor emitted burning odor. We liked handle grip, but mixer felt back-heavy and vibrated noticeably during use.
Farberware Preferred Hand Mixer Model FPHM600 PRICE: $29.99 ATTACHMENTS: wire beaters, flat beaters, dough hooks WHIPPING CREAM: ★★ BEATING EGG WHITES: ★★ POUND CAKE: ★★★ COOKIE DOUGH: ★★ DESIGN: ★	While there was some bogging down of beaters during cookie dough test, our biggest complaint was this mixer's tendency to fling ingredients around and out of bowl. Handle was so thick that even tester with large hands struggled to maintain his grip. Beaters were difficult to eject.

you relax your elbow at your side. Those with horizontal handles (parallel to the machine's body) made it necessary to lift your elbow in order to hold the machine upright. This posture quickly proved tiring. Balance of weight and the shape of the handle grip also affected fatigue. The number of speeds didn't seem nearly as important as the range of power within those speeds. The Braun, for instance, with just three speeds, outperformed many models with seven speeds.

Both the KitchenAid and the Cuisinart came with an on/off switch, which we considered a welcome safety mechanism—just in case the machine gets plugged in before the beaters are inserted. We were also big fans of Oster's retractable cord (press a button and the cord automatically winds into the mixer's housing). A round cord design was also preferred to a flat cord with a crease up the center, because the former is much easier to wipe clean.

Overall—and as expected—most of the mixers tested had their shortcomings. But the KitchenAid was the total package: powerful, quiet, controlled, and compact. It was a pleasure to use. It also came with the highest price tag: $70. Braun, the runner-up, was cheaper by $20, but lacked the KitchenAid's finesse. Considering the KitchenAid's versatility and the fact that our favorite standing mixer sells for about $250, maybe $70 isn't so unreasonable after all.

KITCHEN NOTES

⇒ BY DAWN YANAGIHARA ⇐

Supercool

If you're in a rush to get a sauce, soup, or stew from hot to not so hot, so that you can put it in the fridge for storage, the best thing to do is get it out of the pot that it was cooked in and into a wide, shallow receptacle, such as a baking dish or large bowl. This increases the surface area, thereby speeding cooling. If you care to further fast-forward cooling, surround the food-filled receptacle with some ice water in the kitchen sink and stir the contents occasionally. Once cooled, the contents can be transferred to a storage container and put into the fridge.

Buttermilk Goes Bust

In our Sticky Buns (page 22), using room-temperature buttermilk helps the dough rise more quickly than using icebox-cold buttermilk.

Allowing it to sit out on the counter is one way to get the buttermilk to shake its chill. The microwave presents a quicker option, but don't plan on microwaving the buttermilk with the same gusto as you would plain milk. With heat—at about 90 degrees, in our experience—buttermilk easily curdles and separates.

For the many batches of buns that we made, we successfully brought the buttermilk to room temperature by microwaving it for 30 to 40 seconds at only 30 percent power. Because the area in contact with the measuring cup heats more quickly than the center, it's a good idea to stir once or twice.

Picking a Pineapple

The usual advice for choosing a juicy, ripe pineapple is to look for gold-colored skin and to see if leaves can be easily plucked from the crown (if they can, the fruit is supposed to be ripe). A bit of research uncovered cautionary notes warning that color is not a reliable indicator of ripeness because some pineapple varieties are green even when ripe. That said, the majority of pineapples in grocery stores are varietals that *can* be judged by color. Included in this group, and now quite common, are extra-sweet varieties from Costa Rica. When we selected pineapples for our Pineapple Upside-Down Cake (page 25), we looked for Costa Rican fruit with yellow-orange skin (or with at least patches of color). We also sought out fruits that gave slightly to gentle pressure, had a fresh crown of leaves, felt heavy for their size, and, most important, had a lively, bright fragrance. We avoided those that were uniformly green and uniformly solid, that displayed blemishes or bruises, or that had an overripe, fermented aroma. Honestly, we had a pretty good batting average.

And the leaf-pulling tip? Hogwash. We encountered pineapples with easy-to-pluck leaves that were sour and undoubtedly underripe.

Oodles of Noodles

Noodle shopping for Sesame Noodles with Shredded Chicken (page 20) turned up two different brands of fresh Asian-style noodles available in supermarkets nationwide: Nasoya and Azumaya. Both are sold in the refrigerated produce section, typically near the tofu.

Nasoya and Azumaya alike put their names on packaged noodles of two different widths, one thin and one wide. Look for Nasoya's Chinese Style Noodles or Azumaya's Asian Style Noodles. Both represent thin-cut noodles, the type we used in developing our recipe. Which of these two brands do we prefer? When we cooked them up, the Azumaya noodles were slightly larger and more substantial than the slender Nasoya noodles, but both worked well and were well liked.

Sugar-Packed

When a *Cook's* recipe, such as our Sticky Buns, calls for "packed brown sugar," that really means firmly packed. But as we learned after asking five test kitchen staffers to pack brown sugar into a 1-cup dry measure, "firmly packed" can mean different things to different people. Their packed cups of brown sugar ranged in weight from 6¾ ounces to 8 ounces, although on average they weighed 7 ounces, the same as 1 cup of granulated sugar.

For those readers who do not own kitchen scales, we thought it would be helpful to describe the act of packing brown sugar: Fill the cup with sugar until mounded, then, using your fingers, a spoon, the back of another measuring cup, or the flat of an icing spatula, compress the sugar until no air pockets remain and

---

KITCHEN SCIENCE: **The Truth about Cutting Boards and Bacteria**

The Bac Story

In 1994, a research report was published that proved to be the opening salvo in a long battle over which material was more sanitary for cutting boards, wood or plastic. The researchers found that fewer bacteria could be recovered from wooden boards infected with live cultures than from plastic boards treated the same way. These results caused the researchers to question the prevailing view that plastic was more sanitary than wood; some have further interpreted the data to mean that wood is, in fact, a safer material for cutting boards. In a report that followed, researchers at a U.S. Department of Agriculture (USDA) lab concluded that beef bacteria on polyethylene and wooden cutting boards had statistically similar patterns of attachment and removal. Even so, the idea that wood is more sanitary than plastic persists and was recently reaffirmed in the food section of the *New York Times*.

So What's on Your Cutting Board?

We wanted to get our own perspective on the problem, so we asked four staff members to donate their used boards, two wooden and two plastic. We found very little bacteria growing on these boards when we sampled them, so we took the boards to a local lab to have them artificially inoculated with bacteria. The procedure worked as follows: A drop of the medium containing millions of bacteria was placed on the boards, the boards were left to sit for 40 minutes to allow for absorption of the bacteria, and an attempt was then made to remove the bacteria. In repeated tests, between 6.0 percent and 8.1 percent of the bacteria were recovered from the plastic and between 1.3 percent and 6.2 percent from the wood. Given that the number of bacteria recovered from each type of board was well into the hundreds of thousands, there was little to assure us that one material was much safer than the other.

Soap and Water to the Rescue

Scrubbing the boards with hot soapy water was a different story. Once the contaminated boards had been cleaned, we recovered an average of 0.00015 percent from the plastic and 0.00037 percent from the wood—or fewer than 100 bacteria from each board. In a related test, we were able to transfer bacteria from contaminated, unwashed boards made from both wood and plastic to petri dishes using potatoes and onions. But our most surprising discovery by far was that the bacteria could persist on unwashed boards of both types for up to 60 hours!

What, then, is the truth about cutting boards? Both plastic and wooden boards can hold on to bacteria for long periods of time. Both plastic and wooden boards allow for transference of bacteria to other foods. Luckily, we found that scrubbing with hot soapy water was an effective (though not perfect) way of cleaning both kinds of boards; the USDA also recommends the regular application of a solution of 1 teaspoon bleach per quart of water. Simply put, maintenance, not material, provides the greatest margin of safety.

–John Olson, Science Editor

In the test kitchen, we employ instant yeast in our yeast-leavened breads and batters. We prefer instant yeast to active dry because it does not require warm liquid to be activated. Moreover, teaspoon for teaspoon, instant yeast contains more living cells and results in a quicker rise. But instant yeast isn't always sold as "instant yeast." It often goes by gimmicky marketing names that suggest a speedier rise or by the term "bread machine yeast," which implies a very specific use. No wonder it causes so much confusion, even among seasoned bread bakers.

Here's a quick review of the yeasts on the market that really are instant. Despite their misleading names, all of these yeasts will work in any recipe calling for instant yeast.
➤ **SAF:** Bread Machine Yeast (in jars), Gourmet Perfect Rise (in packets), Instant Yeast (in vacuum-packed bricks).
➤ **RED STAR:** Bread Machine Yeast (in jars), Quick-Rise Yeast (in packets).
➤ **FLEISCHMANN'S:** Bread Machine Yeast (in jars), Rapid Rise Yeast (in packets). If you're still in doubt, look at the ingredient list on the label. Instant yeast available to consumers usually contains ascorbic acid, whereas active dry does not.

Despite their names, all of these products contain the same thing: instant yeast.

Cook's Extra gives you free additional information online. To read a thorough investigation of yeast—instant and otherwise—visit www.cooksillustrated.com and key in code 5048. This information will be available until October 15, 2004.

the sugar can be compressed no more (but be reasonable—don't strain a muscle). If the cup isn't completely filled, add more sugar and compress again; if it is then mounded, push or scrape off the excess so that the sugar is level with the sides of the cup.

The Way the Meat Crumbles

When making the meat sauce for our Lasagna Bolognese (page 15), we found it important to break up the ground meat as it cooked. If left with large meat chunks, the sauce didn't allow the pasta to form neat, compact layers. Most cooks use the edge of a wooden spoon to break up chunks during cooking, but we discovered that a potato masher (see illustration) is much more efficient.

A quicker way to crumble meat

Kneading by Hand

In the test kitchen, a standing mixer or a food processor is the machine of choice for mixing and kneading bread doughs. But some cooks don't own either, and a hand-held mixer is simply too lightweight (see page 28). Using your hands, of course, is certainly an option.

Over the years, we've found that the following method works with most bread doughs. Start by mixing the wet ingredients in a large bowl. Add about half of the flour called for and mix with a wooden spoon until combined. Stir in the remaining flour, leaving aside ¼ to ½ cup. At this point, the mixture should form a shaggy dough.

Turn the dough onto a lightly floured work surface and knead, adding the reserved flour as needed, until the dough is no longer sticky. Most doughs, including the one for our Sticky Buns, will require 10 to 15 minutes of kneading by hand. Expect to get a good upper-body workout, but your efforts will pay off. As long as you resist the temptation to add too much flour, hand-kneaded dough yields Sticky Buns (and other breads) that compare favorably with buns made from machine-kneaded doughs.

Chocolate Chips or Bars?

When a recipe calls for chocolate, we usually reach for quality bar chocolate, but several readers wondered if instead they could use chocolate chips in our **Chewy, Fudgy Triple Chocolate Brownies** (May/June 2000). The idea is appealing. Chips require no prep, whereas chopping up a block of bar chocolate makes a mess. We baked four batches of brownies—one with bittersweet bar chocolate, one with semisweet bar chocolate (the recipe calls for either), a third with commonly available semisweet chips, and a fourth with bittersweet chips.

Surprisingly, the texture and appearance of all four pans of brownies were the same. There were, however, slight differences in flavor. While the brownies made with either form of bittersweet chocolate (chips or bar) were generally preferred for their complexity, brownies made with semisweet bar chocolate were preferred over those made with semisweet chips, and the bittersweet bar also won out over the bittersweet chips. In the end, though, sweetness level (bittersweet versus semisweet) was more important than the form of the chocolate (bar versus chip). We had especially good results with Ghirardelli Double Chocolate Chips, which are made with bittersweet chocolate.

Cool-Weather Barbecue

In the dead of winter, it's difficult to maintain the constant grill temperature necessary for barbecuing. That's why several readers wrote wondering if there was a way to make our **Baby Back Ribs** (July/August 2002) indoors.

We found that making ribs in the oven worked. We kept the cooking temperature constant at 275 degrees, elevated the ribs on a rack, and cooked them, alternately flipping the ribs and rotating the pan every 30 minutes, for three hours, at which point the ribs were nice and tender. The problem with these ribs was their lack of smoky, grilled flavor. Adding liquid smoke to the brine or smoked paprika to the rub amounted to interesting ideas that didn't pan out. To make matters worse, without the smoke, the flavor of the original recipe became unbalanced; it was overly salty. Cutting back on the strength of the brine (we used just ¼ cup of table salt and ¼ cup of sugar) helped put the flavors back in balance. As for a good hit of smoke, our advice is to serve the ribs with a smoky barbecue sauce.

Phyllo Trouble

We stock a large size of phyllo in the test kitchen, and, because we thought it was the only size available, we were surprised to hear that some readers were having a hard time fitting all of the filling from our **Quick Apple Strudel** (September/October 2003) into their pastry sheets. It turns out that Athens phyllo, the most common brand, is available in two sizes. Both are 1-pound packages, with the larger size containing 20 sheets measur-

Smaller sheets of phyllo (top) are best for baklava, while larger sheets (bottom) are better for strudel.

ing 14 by 18 inches and the smaller size containing 40 sheets measuring 14 by 9 inches—exactly half the size of the larger sheets.

For the strudel recipe, our preference is still for the larger sheets. If you can find only the smaller sheets, divide the filling evenly and make two smaller strudels. While news of the smaller phyllo required some problem solving when it came to our strudel recipe, we found that it simplified things when we tried it with our **Baklava** (March/April 2004). The smaller size phyllo fits quite well into the bottom of a 13 by 9-inch pan, thus eliminating the step in which the larger sheets of phyllo are to be cut in half.

– Compiled by Nina West

IF YOU HAVE A QUESTION about a recently published recipe, let us know. Send your inquiry, name, address, and daytime telephone number to Recipe Update, Cook's Illustrated, P.O. Box 470589, Brookline, MA 02447, or to recipeupdate@bcpress.com.

PRODUCT REDESIGN
Pyrex Serveware

The winner of our rating of 13 by 9-inch baking pans in the March/April 2004 issue—Pyrex—now comes in a dressier version. Pyrex Serveware is designed with outer surfaces that resemble a woven basket. The changes are strictly aesthetic. The original 13 by 9-inch (or 3-quart) Pyrex Bakeware costs less than $9, while the new Serveware is closer to $12. Performance differences between the two lines are nonexistent, but spillovers are more difficult to remove from the Serveware's textured outer surface. We'll stick with the original and save some money and cleanup time.

NEW PRODUCT
Cordless Hand-Held Mixer

Many cooks use a hand mixer to whip cream, beat a few egg whites, or pull together a quick cookie dough. We wondered if a cordless newcomer could compete with the mixers rated on page 29.

Black and Decker's $30 Gizmo Twist Mixer is a battery-powered, hand-held mixer with a single beater attachment. While it could whip cream nearly as quickly as a typical hand mixer with two beaters, beating egg whites was a lengthy chore, and the mixer strained once the egg whites thickened and approached stiff peaks. The manufacturer did not recommend the Gizmo for anything thicker than pancake or waffle batter, and we soon found

The convenience of this battery-operated mixer can't compensate for its lack of power.

out why. It lacks oomph. We tried making cookies, but the Gizmo's single beater just couldn't grab the butter to cream with the sugar in the fashion of a traditional hand mixer with two opposing beaters. Adding other ingredients to the bowl caused the Gizmo to grind to a halt.

Black and Decker's Power Pro hand mixer, which has a cord and was rated in this issue, costs just $19.99, yet it rated well for whipping cream and egg whites and also managed to handle cookie dough and pound cake batter. In the end, we found a cord to be less of a hindrance than an uncharged battery and poor performance.

NEW PRODUCT
All-Clad Lasagna Pan

The All-Clad Stainless Steel Roti is our top-rated roasting pan (see the January/February 1999 issue). But in the test kitchen, we also make use of a smaller version of this pan, the Petit Roti. Neither pan comes cheap, usually priced at $260 and $210, respectively. Given their eye-popping price tags, we were curious when All-Clad recently introduced a "Gourmet Accessory" Lasagna Pan that looks suspiciously similar to the Petit Roti but sells for just $100. Could this new pan be a bargain hunter's dream come true? To find out, we put the two smaller pans up against each other in a series of tests that included roasting a 12-pound turkey, making gravy on the stovetop, and roasting carrots.

At 15 by 12 inches, the lasagna pan boasts an extra inch in length and width over the Petit Roti, providing ample room for the turkey and easily straddling two burners for making gravy. Browning of the roasted carrots was equally modest in both pans. The Petit Roti has distinctive vertical handles (as does the big roasting pan). The lasagna pan's handles extend horizontally, thus requiring more oven space but still affording a sure grip.

Finding the pans to be nearly identical in terms of both appearance and performance, we called All-Clad to confirm our suspicions. They were confirmed. We learned that both pans are basically the same.

The $100 price of the lasagna pan is a promotional, introductory price that will be subject to rising along with the pan's popularity, according to All-Clad. What then appears to be a luxury item for—of all things—lasagna is actually a great multipurpose buy. With the exception of cooking a huge bird, the lasagna pan makes a fine (and inexpensive) roasting pan.

This All-Clad Lasagna Pan can double as a roasting pan and costs half as much as the very similar All-Clad Petit Roti.

DO YOU REALLY NEED THIS?
Nonstick Oven Liner

Our Sticky Buns reminded us of the mess that can overflow a baking pan and stick to the bottom of the oven. For $25, Chef's Planet offers a Teflon-coated mat that fits on the bottom rack of the oven and can be run through the dishwasher for cleanup. Sounds great, right?

We put this product to the test by spilling some fruit filling and caramel on it in a hot oven and letting them bake on for 15 minutes. We mistakenly damaged the liner in this first test because of what turned out to be inadequate instructions, which direct the cook to "place the Chef's Planet Ovenliner on the bottom of your electric oven, under the element. For gas ovens, place the Ovenliner on the bottom rack." Well, our test kitchen ovens are electric, but the heating element is hidden beneath the oven floor. A call to Chef's Planet confirmed what we had already found out: Placing a

liner on the floor of such an oven causes it to overheat and damages its Teflon coating. The next time around we placed the liner on the bottom rack of our electric oven, and it performed well. Cleanup, however, was not quite as easy as the manufacturer promises; a short soak and a good scrubbing were needed.

We conducted a third test with aluminum foil and afterward simply tossed it in the trash when we were done. It remains our liner of choice.

Sources

The following are mail-order sources for particular items recommended in this issue. Prices were current at press time and do not include shipping and handling. Contact companies directly to confirm up-to-date prices and availability.

page 23: SWEET DOUGH YEAST
● SAF Nevada Gold, 15.86 oz.: $6.50, item #1491, The Baker's Catalogue (P.O. Box 876, Norwich, VT 05055-0876; 800-827-6836; www.bakerscatalogue.com).

page 25: PINEAPPLE GADGET
● Vacu Vin Pineapple Slicer: $14.95, item #68924, Sur La Table (P.O. Box 34707, Seattle, WA 98184-1608; 800-243-0852; www.surlatable.com).

page 29: HAND-HELD MIXERS
● KitchenAid 7 Speed Ultra Power Plus Hand Mixer: $69.99, item #107128, Kitchen Etc. (32 Industrial Drive, Exeter, NH 03833; 800-232-4070; www.kitchenetc.com).
● Braun MultiMix Hand Mixer with Hand Blender Attachment: $49.99, item #255093, Kitchen Etc.

page 32: PYREX SERVEWARE
● Textured Oblong Baking Dish, 3 Quart: $11.99, item #934604, Kitchen Etc.

page 32: LASAGNA PAN
● All-Clad Stainless Lasagna Pan: $99.95, item #59906, Cutlery and More (645 Lunt Avenue, Elk Grove Village, IL 60007; 800-650-9866; www.cutleryandmore.com).

RECIPES
September & October 2004

Mexican Rice, 19

Twice-Baked Potatoes with Broccoli, Cheddar, and Scallions, 9

Lasagna Bolognese, 15

Roasted Chicken Breasts, 11

Acorn Squash with Brown Sugar, 13

www.cooksillustrated.com

Get all 11 years of *Cook's Illustrated* magazine and a free gift!

Join www.cooksillustrated.com today and gain access to 11 years' worth of recipes, equipment tests, and food tastings . . . at any time and from anywhere! Plus, as a *Cook's Illustrated* subscriber, you're offered a 20% discount.

Free Gift: As a paid member, you'll also get *The Essential Kitchen: 25 Kitchen Tools No Cook Should Be Without*. This downloadable online guide produced by the editors of *Cook's Illustrated* provides recommendations on the best cookware, tools, and gadgets for your kitchen. Simply type in the promotion code **CB49A** when signing up online.

Here are a few of the many things available at our site:

Best Recipes: Eleven years' worth of recipes developed in America's Test Kitchen.
Cookware Reviews: Every cookware review published since 1993, plus many reviews never seen in *Cook's*.
Ingredient Tastings: A decade of taste-test results, offering recommendations on everything from ketchup and mayonnaise to flour, yeast, and salt.
Online Bookstore: Cookbooks from the editors of *Cook's*, plus much more.

Sesame Noodles with Shredded Chicken, 20

Grill-Roasted Beef Tenderloin, 7

AMERICA'S TEST KITCHEN TV SHOW

Join the millions of home cooks who watch our show, *America's Test Kitchen*, on public television every week. For more information, including recipes and a schedule of program times in your area, visit www.americastestkitchen.com.

Pineapple Upside-Down Cake, 25

Sticky Buns with Pecans, 22

PHOTOGRAPHY: CARL TREMBLAY, STYLING: MARY JANE SAWYER

Cacciatorini

Prosciutto
di Parma

Genoa
Salami

Pancetta

Schiacciata

Coppa

Culatello

Bresaola

Guanciale

Toscano Salami

ITALIAN
CURED MEATS

COOK'S
ILLUSTRATED

Perfect Turkey
We Test Everything

Rating Food Processors
Should You Spend $35 or $280?

"New" Butter Tasting
As Good as Land O' Lakes?

Balsamic Chicken

Gravy Illustrated
No Grease, No Lumps

Chocolate Walnut Tart

Spritz Butter Cookies
Testing Cookie Presses

Smashed Potatoes
Belgian Beef Stew
Blue Cheese Salads
Pan-Roasted Pork Tenderloin
Marinated Mushrooms

www.cooksillustrated.com

$5.95 U.S./$6.95 CANADA

0 74470 62805 7

1 2>

CONTENTS

November & December 2004

www.cooksillustrated.com

HOME OF AMERICA'S TEST KITCHEN

Founder and Editor	Christopher Kimball
Executive Editor	Jack Bishop
Senior Editor	Dawn Yanagihara
Editorial Manager, Books	Elizabeth Carduff
Art Director	Amy Klee
Test Kitchen Director	Erin McMurrer
Senior Editors, Books	Julia Collin Davison
	Lori Galvin
Senior Writer	Bridget Lancaster
Managing Editor	Rebecca Hays
Associate Editors, Books	Matthew Card
	Keith Dresser
Associate Editor	Sandra Wu
Science Editor	John Olson
Web Editor	Keri Fisher
Copy Editor	India Koopman
Test Cooks	Stephanie Alleyne
	Erika Bruce
	Sean Lawler
	Jeremy Sauer
	Diane Unger-Mahoney
Assistant Test Cooks	Garth Clingingsmith
	Charles Kelsey
	Nina West
Editorial Assistant, Books	Elizabeth Wray
Assistant to the Publisher	Melissa Baldino
Kitchen Assistants	Nadia Domeq
	Maria Elena Delgado
	Ena Gudiel
Kitchen Interns	Barbara Akins
	Katie Archambault
	Lori Bullock Floyd
	Julia Humes
	Cali Todd
Staff Photographer	Daniel van Ackere
Contributing Editor	Elizabeth Germain
Consulting Editors	Shirley Corriher
	Jasper White
	Robert L. Wolke
Proofreader	Jean Rogers
Vice President Marketing	David Mack
Sales Director	Leslie Ray
Retail Sales Director	Jason Geller
Corporate Sponsorship Specialist	Laura Phillipps
Sales Representative	Shekinah Cohn
Marketing Assistant	Connie Forbes
Circulation Director	Bill Tine
Circulation Manager	Larisa Greiner
Products Director	Steven Browall
Direct Mail Director	Adam Perry
Customer Service Manager	Jacqueline Valerio
Customer Service Representative	Julie Gardner
E-Commerce Marketing Manager	Hugh Buchan
Marketing Intern	Ian Halpern
Vice President Operations	James McCormack
Senior Production Manager	Jessica Lindheimer Quirk
Production Manager	Mary Connelly
Book Production Specialist	Ron Bilodeau
Production Assistants	Jennifer Power
	Christian Steinmetz
Systems Administrator	Richard Cassidy
WebMaster	Aaron Shuman
Production Intern	Mark Pasierb
Chief Financial Officer	Sharyn Chabot
Controller	Mandy Shito
Office Manager	Saudiyah Abdul-Rahim
Receptionist	Henrietta Murray
Publicity	Deborah Broide

PRINTED IN THE USA

DRIED FRUIT From the everyday apple to the seasonal peach and tropical pineapple, most fresh fruits can be dried and enjoyed when they are out of season. Drying changes a fruit's flavor and concentrates its sweetness. For instance, prunes (stylishly referred to these days as dried plums) taste more like molasses-infused raisins than fresh plums. Thompson seedless grapes are dried in different ways to become both golden (also known as Sultanas) and black raisins, both of which taste very different from the fresh grape. In a twist of logic, dried currants are descended from tiny Zante grapes rather than fresh currant berries. Dried fruits aren't simply dehydrated and packaged; some undergo an additional processing to prevent oxidation and browning. Apricots are often sulfured and easily distinguished by their bright yellow-orange color. (Unsulfured apricots have a deep, dark brown color.) Tart cranberries, like some varieties of sour cherries, are often sweetened before being packaged. Dates, on the other hand, contain so much concentrated sugar that they can seem candied rather than dried. Among the different varieties of figs suitable for drying are the dark-purple, California-grown Black Mission and the pale, plump Turkish Smyrna.

COVER (*Pears*): Kate Mueller, BACK COVER (*Dried Fruit*): John Burgoyne

For list rental information, contact: ClientLogic, 1200 Harbor Blvd., 9th Floor, Weehawken, NJ 07087; 201-865-5800
Editorial Office: 17 Station St., Brookline, MA 02445; 617-232-1000; fax 617-232-1572. Subscription inquiries, call 800-526-8442.
Postmaster: Send all new orders, subscription inquiries, and change of address notices to Cook's Illustrated, P.O. Box 7446, Red Oak, IA 51591-0446.

JULIA CHILD 1912–2004

Loss is unpredictable. At the time we lose someone—a family member, a friend, a national figure—we never know exactly what we are going to miss the most. The wit? The comfortable familiarity? The moral compass? The ability to lead? We certainly miss Kennedy's unshakeable optimism, King's righteous oratory, and Audrey Hepburn's playful dignity. What, then, will we miss most about Julia Child?

For many, the first and last thing will be the voice. She ascended into the pantheon of beloved national figures as a bit of an eccentric, an imposing tower of willful culinary domination. The juxtaposition of Julia's unstoppable can-do enthusiasm, her physical stature, the subject at hand—an ugly, massive "loup de mer" or a row of chickens to be roasted—was not comedic but it was startling. It reminded one of other rather odd but endearing American figures: Eleanor Roosevelt, Abraham Lincoln, and perhaps Ross Perot.

Yet I suspect that Julia's winning charm, her physical presence, even her beloved French cooking, may not survive through the ages. I have always thought of Julia's entrance onto the national scene as unfortunate timing. Women were leaving their homes for careers by the millions. America was just getting serious about becoming a fast-food nation. Agribusiness was in high gear. And, most of all, French cooking was on its last legs. For more than a century, fancy French cooking had made an uneasy partnership with our own pioneer culinary arts. Fannie Farmer, among others, deftly presented us with this marriage of the continental gourmet to the country bumpkin. And by the 1960s, the future of classic French cooking was certainly in doubt. By the 1980s, Alice Waters, Larry Forgione, Jeremiah Tower, and many others would be leading an American culinary revolution that goes on today.

So, in the midst of a culinary Three Mile Island, Julia arrived to save us from ourselves. Her popularity belied her topic. Yet she prevailed with a strong sense of tradition, of culinary history, and of the complexities of great cooking. The rest of America was busy throwing off the shackles of the past and, with them, the notion that there was something to learn from it. We wanted bright lights and Julia offered us hard work and anonymity. We wanted instant gratification and Julia told us that a good stock took time. We celebrated the young and the beautiful and Julia presented us with an image that defied the times. This, in effect, was a recipe for disaster, and yet she turned it into a great success.

Over the years, Julia defied us at every turn. Diets were anathema to Julia because they implied that food was harmful. She had no truck with the organic and natural food movements—hadn't American agriculture fed the world? Yes, butter and cream could be reduced, but then the dish would not be worth eating.

And, yes, Julia was a real character. At one particularly poorly lit Italian restaurant where we dined shortly before her move to California, she constantly demanded more light so that she could see her food properly. When it was not forthcoming, she simply dipped into her large purse, took out a flashlight, and proceeded to inspect the rather insipid offering as if it were a corpse.

But to focus on these minor eccentricities is to miss the point. Julia Child provided what America really wants from its celebrities: She endured. She never took up the banner of "meals in minutes." She never offered a recipe for "lite" cheesecake. She never allowed her name to be used in the promotion of any commercial enterprise. She never wavered in her convictions. And she stood the test of time. She told America to look to the past and not to discard the wisdom of the ages. And she then proceeded to lead her life based on those simple, enduring principles.

Despite our infatuation with the moment, I think we knew that Julia was right. Yes, America loves those who struggle against the odds. But, in the end, the greatest among us also have to walk a righteous path. And Julia's instincts always pointed her in the proper direction. She was in a battle with the strongest and most dangerous of our cultural currents. Yet she held her head high, had no regrets, and dined thoughtfully off centuries past while the rest of us were grabbing a bite from the takeout window.

For all of these reasons and more, we will miss Julia terribly. But for many of us, those who followed in her footsteps in later years, there is the Julia of kindness, the lady who would get to know each and every star-struck buyer at a book signing—even if it took hours. When interrupted during a restaurant meal, she would be gracious and unhurried in her attentions. When she was with Paul, her beloved husband, she deflected attention from herself to him—to his paintings, to his life story. Here was a woman who launched a thousand culinary ships, who gave so many of us the confidence and inspiration to do good work in the kitchen.

It feels as if we have lost the best of us in recent years—as if these great men and women were descended from a race of people who walked the earth in strides too long for our time. Who now will demand the best of us, demand that we speak to our better instincts? Who will save us from ourselves? Yes, I can look back wistfully and say, "I knew Julia Child. I cooked with her. I knew her as a friend." But that's not good enough for Julia. She would politely suggest, with a twinkle in her eye, that we turn on the stove, grab a knife, and start preparing a proper dinner, the type of food that would satisfy our souls, not just our physical needs.

She did the cooking all those years. Now it is our turn. As if faced with the loss of a parent, we no longer have someone to encourage us, to tell us how we are doing. I think that Julia would ask, as any good mother would, that we pull up our socks, roll up our sleeves, and shrug off childish appetites in pursuit of excellence. It would be a great tribute to Julia to do this well, not in memory of her but for ourselves, for history, and for the bright promise of hard work and devotion to principle that has built the American dream.   – Christopher Kimball

FOR INQUIRIES, ORDERS, OR MORE INFORMATION:

www.cooksillustrated.com

At www.cooksillustrated.com, you can order books and subscriptions, sign up for our free e-newsletter, or renew your magazine subscription. Subscribe to the Web site and you'll have access to 12 years of *Cook's* recipes, cookware tests, ingredient tastings, and more.

COOKBOOKS

We sell more than 40 cookbooks by the editors of *Cook's Illustrated*. To order, visit our bookstore at www.cooksillustrated.com or call 800-611-0759 (or 515-246-6911 from outside the U.S.).

COOK'S ILLUSTRATED Magazine

Cook's Illustrated magazine (ISSN 1068-2821), number 71, is published bimonthly by Boston Common Press Limited Partnership, 17 Station Street, Brookline, MA 02445. Copyright 2004 Boston Common Press Limited Partnership. Periodicals postage paid at Boston, Mass., and additional mailing offices, USPS #012487. POSTMASTER: Send address changes to Cook's Illustrated, P.O. Box 7446, Red Oak, IA 51591-0446. For subscription and gift subscription orders, subscription inquiries, or change-of-address notices, call 800-526-8442 in the U.S. or 515-247-7571 from outside the U.S., or write us at Cook's Illustrated, P.O. Box 7446, Red Oak, IA 51591-0446.

Good Old Lard

When you wrote about flaky pie crust and healthier alternatives to Crisco (May/June 2004), why didn't you test the very best shortening, which is good old lard?

PAT OWSLEY
HORSESHOE BEND, IDAHO

➤ Like most other bakers, we had long ago dismissed lard as not being very good for you because of its saturated fat content. But as several readers pointed out to us, lard is now considered to have a healthier profile than partially hydrogenated vegetable shortenings like Crisco, which contain trans fats, considered the most damaging dietary fats of all. According to Walter Willett, professor at the Harvard University School of Public Health's Department of Nutrition, lard is about as good (or bad) for you as butter.

That's good to know, but we still had a problem with lard from a culinary point of view. Several of our test cooks have complained about the poor quality of the lard sold in supermarkets. To confirm the validity of their concerns, we made a pie crust with supermarket lard. While the crust was flaky, the taste was off. Out of the box, the lard had a slightly sour smell that tasters could also detect in the baked pie crust. But this was not the end of the road for lard.

In our research, we came across the term *leaf lard*, and wherever we encountered it, high praise followed. Leaf lard, often called kidney fat, is rendered from the fat that lines the abdominal cavity of the pig. According to Dr. David Meisinger of the National Pork Board, leaf lard is considered to be of higher quality than the fat from any other part of the pig. We contacted the maker of the supermarket lard we had purchased and learned that it was indeed not leaf lard but could have been rendered from any type of pork fat—the back, the belly, and so on. A search for leaf lard led us to Dietrich's Meats (see Sources on page 32).

After baking with this product, we finally understood why so many readers had written to us in pretty passionate defense of lard. The pie crust made with Dietrich's leaf lard was extremely tender and flaky, but what most distinguished it from pie crusts made with supermarket lard (or Crisco) was its rich, almost savory flavor. Straight

from the container the Dietrich's lard smelled sweet and pleasant, almost nutty, and it contributed these qualities to the pie crust. Dietrich's is a small, family-owned enterprise that raises its own pigs on a diet of grain—mostly corn—that the family grows itself. While we can't vouch for all leaf lard, this product is far superior to what you might buy in the supermarket.

For a real holiday treat, you can simply substitute an equal amount of lard for the vegetable shortening called for in most any pie crust recipe, including ours. (For our pie dough recipe, see **Cook's Extra**, below.)

Imitation Cider Vinegar

I have been choosing Heinz Apple Cider Vinegar over other brands because I thought it was better quality and had a better flavor. I was quite surprised to note that my last purchase was labeled "Apple Cider Flavored Distilled Vinegar." Is this plain white vinegar with flavoring?

JEAN MEAD
WINFIELD, W.V.

➤ We, too, were surprised to learn about this product, which is an alternative to Heinz's regular cider vinegar. We learned from Heinz that the Apple Cider Flavored Distilled Vinegar was developed for food service customers, but this product is also available at many supermarkets. Sold only by the gallon, the flavored distilled vinegar costs $3.89. Heinz's regular cider vinegar, which is not sold by the gallon, costs $2.12 per quart, which would work out to about $8.50 per gallon. So the real thing costs more than twice as much as its imitator, but is the savings worth it?

We tasted both vinegars straight from their bottles and in one of the salad dressings in this issue. The flavored product is made from distilled white vinegar to which apple juice is added. And that's exactly what it tastes like—rather flat, a little medicinal, and sweet. This product has none of the mouth-puckering tartness that you get with real cider vinegar,

READING THE FINE PRINT

Check labels closely to make sure you get real cider vinegar.

which is made solely from apple cider. So the next time you shop, check the labels carefully, and remember that the real thing doesn't come in gallon-size containers.

What a Muddle

In the July/August 2004 issue, we ran an illustration of a "muddler"—a tool that looks like a small baseball bat and is used to crush herbs and fruit in a cocktail glass. Seems like we may have enjoyed one too many of these cocktails ourselves. The muddler is pictured upside down; the working end is the flat-edged end, not the rounded end, as depicted.

Where's the Chile Heat?

In your recipes for Chicken Biryani (March/April 2004) and Fresh Tomato Salsa (July/August 2004), you direct readers to reserve or add the seeds from chiles to control the "heat" or add "fire" to the dish. It is my understanding that the seeds themselves don't contain any heat but that it is in the pith of the chile.

MICHAEL FITZHENRY
CAMBRIDGE, MASS.

➤ Chiles get their "heat"—or "pungency," as the experts like to say—from a group of chemical compounds called capsaicinoids, the best known of which is capsaicin. To figure out where most of these compounds reside, we donned rubber gloves and separated the outer green-colored flesh, the inner whitish pith (also called membranes or ribs), and the seeds from 40 jalapeños. We then sent the lot to our food lab. As it turned out, there were just 5 milligrams of capsaicin per kilogram

Where does the chile store most of its heat—in the dark flesh, the white pith, or the seeds?

of green jalapeño flesh (not enough to really make much impact on the human tongue), 73 mg per kg of seeds, and an impressive 512 mg per kg of pith.

The reason why the seeds registered more heat than the flesh is simply because they are embedded in the pith; they are essentially guilty—or hot—by reason of association. From now on, then, when we want to carefully mete out the fire in our salsa or biryani, we'll do it by means of the pith. The seeds will just be along for the ride.

COOK'S EXTRA For our Basic Pie Dough recipe, go to www.cooksillustrated.com and key in code 6048. This recipe will be available until December 15, 2004. For the complete results of our tests of nutmeg mills and graters, go to www.cooksillustrated.com and key in code 6049.

Safe Nutmeg Grating

As a follow-up to your review of spice grinders (May/June 2004): What's the best/safest/easiest way to grind nutmeg? I've found that most nutmeg graters invite ground fingers and don't work that well. Any other ideas?

LUISA BALDINGER
SANTE FE, N.M.

☞ Before testing nutmeg graters, we ran a couple of tests to see if grating fresh nutmeg is worth the effort. We found that in something like a béchamel sauce or egg nog, where there are no other spices to compete with it, fresh-ground nutmeg contributes a distinctively heady flavor that we really like. In baked goods that call for lots of spices, however, such as spice cookies, we found that the signature flavor of fresh-ground nutmeg was lost; ground nutmeg from a jar works just fine in such recipes.

With the holiday season and egg nog in mind, then, we purchased the following: three nutmeg mills, which work just like pepper mills and so keep your fingers completely safe; a new-style grater from Zyliss designed especially to keep your fingers out of harm's way; an old-style nutmeg grater; and a Microplane grater for spices.

Only one of the mills—the Cole & Mason acrylic mill—produced a neat and even grind in good time. It is pricey, though, at $21.54. The new Zyliss Nutmeg Grater, which costs $14.99, does protect your fingers, but it produced painfully little grated nutmeg. To use it, you put a whole nutmeg in a plastic hopper, secure the spring-loaded cap on top, then slide the cap back and forth to grate the nutmeg. The oldest-style nutmeg grater comes in the form of a metal cylinder; the curves are intended to keep your fingertips away from the teeth as you grate. We tested one from Norpro that cost just $2, but it brought our fingers perilously close to the grating teeth.

Microplane takes the idea of a cylinder even further. In addition to a comfortable handle, this $7.95 grater has a slender, tightly curled, 5-inch-long grating surface that provides a good margin of safety for your fingertips. It also produced mounds of nutmeg in no time flat and can also be used for grating nuts and chocolate. Perhaps not as elegant as the Cole & Mason for garnishing an egg nog, it is

MICROPLANE
Effective new twist on an old-style grater.

COLE & MASON
Expensive, but perfect for garnishing eggnog.

ZYLISS
Interesting idea, but not much output.

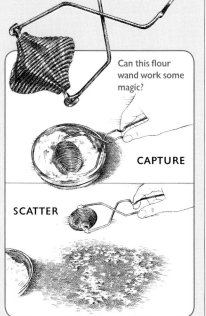

WHAT IS IT?

Do you know where can I get one of these things? A friend of mine uses it for dusting flour when making pie dough and such. Kind of cool. She inherited it from her grandmother but has no idea how (or when) her grandmother came to own it.

JILL FLANAGAN
NORTH READING, MASS.

☞ You can buy this item—known variously as a flour wand, duster, or mini sifter—from several online sources, the cheapest being Cooking.com (see Sources on page 32 for details). As you seem to know, the wand is often used to dust a work surface evenly with flour when rolling out pie or cookie dough.

To use the metal 9-inch wand, you hold the "arms" between your thumb and forefinger, press them together to open the rounded, spiral-wired cage, dip the open cage into a bowl of flour, then release pressure on the "arms" to let the cage close, thereby capturing a tablespoon or so of flour. You're then ready to dust the work surface by again squeezing the "arms" to open the cage and shaking the wand enough to let the flour pass through. While well-practiced bakers can scatter flour by hand just as easily, we found that novices appreciated the help in creating a smooth and even coating of flour. The wand can also be used to decorate the top of a cake with confectioners' sugar or to coat a pizza peel with cornmeal.

Can this flour wand work some magic?

CAPTURE

SCATTER

nonetheless our top choice based on price, ease of use, and output. (See **Cook's Extra**, page 2, to access the complete testing results.)

What's a Sauté Pan to Do?

In the January/February 2001 issue of the magazine, the pans you rated as "sauté" pans all had straight sides. Then, in the May/June 2004 issue, in "Mastering the Art of Sauté," you say that straight-sided pans are ill-suited for sautéing. Sloped sides, it seems, are "perfect." So what do I buy?

IRENE R. SMITH
MCLEAN, VA.

☞ Unfortately, different cookware manufacturers use different terms for the same sort of pan; one manufacturer may call a slope-sided pan a sauté pan, whereas another will call a slope-sided pan a fry pan (or omelet pan or skillet). At *Cook's*, we use the term *sauté pan* when writing about a pan with straight sides and a lid and the term *skillet* when writing about a pan with sloped sides. That said, our advice is to choose one pan or the other based on the recipes you plan to cook with it, not its name.

A pan with sloped sides is best for sautéing. The sloped sides make it easier for the cook to maneuver the food. The sloped sides also facilitate evaporation, which in turn speeds browning. Examples of foods well suited to the slope-sided pan are thin fish fillets, chicken or veal cutlets, pan-seared steaks, hamburgers, and shrimp scampi. A pan with straight sides is well suited for pan-frying (in which the food actually sits in a shallow pool of oil) and for braising, in which the food cooks in liquid and is covered for at least part of the time. Foods that do well in straight-sided pans include poached fish, pan-fried chicken, and braised chicken.

Note that a sloped-side pan has no substitutes. In many recipes, however, you can use a Dutch oven in place of a straight-sided pan, so the latter is nice to own but not essential.

Film Canisters and Food Storage

Several readers wrote in to express their concern over the safety of using 35 mm film canisters to store mayonnaise and other condiments when going on a picnic, as suggested in a quick tip in our July/August 2004 issue. According to Mary Keith, food and nutrition agent at the University of Florida Extension in Tampa, Fla., film containers are not made of food-grade plastic, so it's not advisable to use them to store any type of food. Furthermore, washing the canisters will not make them safe for food. Safer storage options for picnics are the smallest-size plastic yogurt containers or the gift-pack-size glass jars with a screw-top lid used for some jams and jellies. Just make sure to pack the jars between layers of napkins or inside paper cups to make sure they don't break during transport.

Quick Tips

⋟ COMPILED BY ERIKA BRUCE ⋞

Keeping Parchment in Place

Spooning soft cookie dough onto a baking sheet layered with parchment can be a frustrating matter indeed, as the parchment has a propensity to curl up and become unruly. Michelle Bruno of Snohomish, Wash., found a clever solution to this problem: Grab four refrigerator magnets and place one over each corner of the parchment. Make sure to return the magnets to the fridge before baking the cookies.

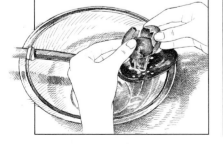

Separating Eggs

Some cooks find it awkward to crack an egg perfectly down the middle and then juggle the yolk between the shell halves to release all of the white. Linda P. Lee of Marysville, Wash., came up with a clever way to avoid this step: Wrap a rubber band around the handle of a large slotted spoon. Set the spoon over a small bowl by resting the tip of the spoon and the rubber band on opposite edges of the bowl. Crack each egg over the spoon, and watch the whites slip through the holes into the bowl while the yolk stays in the spoon.

No More Greasy Hands

When Flora Barrett of Chesapeake Beach, Md., needs shortening or butter to grease a pan, she keeps her hands clean inside a plastic sandwich bag.

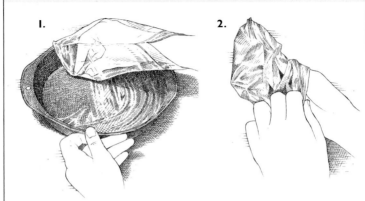

1.
2.

1. Wearing the bag like a glove, grease the pan.
2. When finished, remove the bag by turning it inside out and neatly discarding it. No more messy paper towels!

Quick Filtered-Water Chill

To avoid waiting for filtered water to chill in the refrigerator, Jennifer Martin of Burke, Va., adds ice to the filtration pitcher reservoir before refilling with tap water.

Holding Mashed Potatoes

Finishing the mashed potatoes at the same time as the roast, the gravy, and the green beans can become quite a juggling act. Gayl Beck of Allendale, Mich., frees up some of those precious few last minutes (and some valuable stovetop space) by making her mashed potatoes a couple of hours ahead of time and keeping them warm in a slow cooker on the low setting. All they need is a quick stir before serving.

Quick Dough Wrapping

While preparing batches of pie dough for the holidays, Peg Syverson of Austin, Texas, hit on a time-saving trick that keeps her hands and the counter clean.

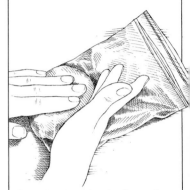

Once the dough is mixed, transfer it directly from the bowl to a large zipper-lock bag. Shape the dough into a disk through the outside of the bag, and chill until ready to use.

Instant Homemade Cocoa

Brenda Locklear of Wilmington, N.C., gave us the idea for making quick individual servings of homemade hot cocoa. We adapted our recipe (from January/February 1997), omitting the dairy component, to make a cocoa "base."

To make four servings, whisk together 6 tablespoons Dutch-processed cocoa, 5 tablespoons sugar, a pinch of salt, 1 teaspoon vanilla extract, and 1 cup water in a small saucepan. Heat mixture over low heat for two minutes, stirring frequently. Cool to room temperature, then store in the refrigerator in an airtight container for up to three weeks. Multiply the recipe as needed.

When the mood strikes for a nice hot cup of cocoa, simply add 3 to 4 tablespoons of the cocoa base to 8 ounces of hot milk and stir.

Send Us Your Tip We will provide a complimentary one-year subscription for each tip we print. Send your tip, name, and address to Quick Tips, Cook's Illustrated, P.O. Box 470589, Brookline, MA 02447, or to quicktips@bcpress.com.

Measuring Ahead of Time

During the holidays, many bakers find themselves making multiple batches of cookies, cakes, and quick breads. Erika Deru of Arvada, Col., found smart ways to save some time during this process. She measures out and labels all of the recipes ahead of time, storing the dry ingredients in zipper-lock bags on the counter and wet ingredients in plastic containers in the refrigerator. When it's time to bake, everything is ready to be mixed.

Sauce-Thickening Tip

Paul Morand of Essexville, Mich., found that children's "sippy cups"—the plastic cups that have lids complete with drinking spouts—come in handy when making sauces.

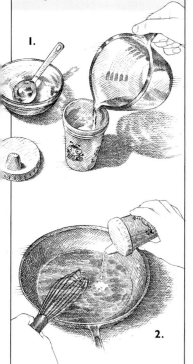

1. Place equal parts cold water and cornstarch (or starch of choice) into the cup, and replace the lid.
2. Shake vigorously, then pour the mixture through the spout into the sauce, little by little, until the sauce has reached the desired thickness.

Flatter Countertops

Tiled countertops may look attractive, but they are not especially practical when it comes to baking. To avoid rumpled rolled cookie or pie dough (not to mention a floury mess between the cracks of the tile), Suzie Barnhart of Akron, Ohio, places a flexible cutting board over her bumpy tile countertop to create a smoother surface.

Tips for Oven-Fried Bacon

A couple of readers had some great tips on how to improve on our Oven-Fried Bacon recipe (January/February 1998).

A. Carolyn Hopke, of Granite City, Ill., minimizes cleanup. She lines her baking sheet with wide foil (18 inches), covering the entire surface, including the sides. She then cooks and drains the bacon, as per recipe instructions, and allows the baking sheet and any remaining grease to cool completely. Cleanup is easy: Just roll up the soiled foil and discard.

A.

B. For another flavor dimension, Cathy Friedman of Natick, Mass., makes maple-glazed bacon. When the bacon has reached a nice golden brown shade and is almost done, she pours off most of the grease and drizzles maple syrup over each strip. She then returns the tray to the oven and continues cooking for 2 to 3 minutes, or until the maple syrup begins to bubble.

B.

Makeshift Splatter Screen

Many cooks are turned off from sautéing because of the greasy mess that can spread around the stovetop, especially when browning meat. For those who don't own a splatter screen, Jennifer Williamson of Charlestown, Mass., came up with an easy alternative: Simply invert a large-mesh strainer over the skillet during the splattering phase of cooking, and the mess will be cut down significantly.

Easier Chocolate Chopping

Most home cooks don't own a fancy chocolate fork, used to break up large blocks of chocolate into more manageable pieces. Erika Schuster of Portland, Ore., found a way to improvise one. Using the sharp two-tined fork from her meat-slicing set and a secured cutting board, she presses straight down into the chocolate. The chocolate breaks into neater pieces than when cut by a knife, and a lot less effort is required.

Neater Dusting with Powdered Sugar

When a small item like a cookie or a piece of cake calls for a dusting with powdered sugar, Jeannie Eddy of Saratoga Springs, N.Y., finds that her mesh tea-ball strainer works wonders. Filled by a quick scoop into the sugar, it is much neater and easier to use than a sifter and won't create a dust storm.

Magazine Recipe Stand

Judith Kalish, of Brighton, Mass., found a clever way to keep her magazine recipes in plain view (and out of harm's way) while cooking by placing the open magazine in an empty napkin holder.

Grilling 101

Improving Carbonnade

Why is this simple Belgian beef stew so hard to make well?

≫ BY THE COOK'S ILLUSTRATED TEST KITCHEN ≪

A basic beef stew can be altered in dozens of ways, usually by adding more ingredients to the pot. But can you go the other way and strip beef stew down to its bare bones (or, to be more precise, to its beef)? If you trade the carrots and potatoes for a mess of onions and add a good dose of beer (instead of red wine) as part of the braising liquid, you've created a simple Belgian beef stew called *carbonnade à la flamande*. Beef, beer, and onions have a natural affinity—think burger, onion rings, and a beer. In a carbonnade, the heartiness of beef melds with the soft sweetness of sliced onions in a lightly thickened broth that is rich, deep, and satisfying, with the malty flavor of beer.

Thorough browning of the meat is the first step in making any beef stew, including carbonnade.

We made several versions of carbonnade and discovered that making a poor one is easy. Some stews were so gussied up that it was hard to notice all but the most serious flaws. But stews stripped down to the three main ingredients were primed for failure—any mistake really stood out. After several trials, we wound up with batches of tasteless beef and onions in a pale, one-dimensional broth.

We decided on a basic method that would serve as a springboard for arriving at an improved recipe. Beef is browned and set aside, onions are sautéed in the empty pot, flour is sprinkled over the onions, liquid is added, the beef is returned to the pot, and the pot simmers in the oven. Now we had to figure out the best cut of beef, the best way to cook the onions, and the right type of beer.

The Beef

Nearly every recipe we consulted recommended cubed chuck roast. To check this recommendation, we tested a dozen cuts of beef and hit upon an unusual winner. Blade steaks (also called top blade or flatiron steaks) are small, long, narrow, steaks cut from the shoulder (or chuck) area of the cow. Most blade steaks have a decent amount of fat marbling, which gives them good flavor as well as a tender texture. A perfect choice, we thought, for carbonnade. One taster described the blade steak in carbonnade as "buttery," a quality that is well suited to this stew. If you cannot find a blade steak, however, any chuck roast will do. Just be sure to avoid the round, the portion of the rear leg from the knee to the hip. It has less fat than the chuck (the forequarter of the animal), and our tasters weren't wild about the flavor.

The Onions and Beer

Onions—and lots of them—go into a traditional carbonnade. Two pounds was the right amount for a generous pot of stew (made with 3½ pounds of beef). We tried white and red onions, but both were cloyingly sweet. Thinly sliced yellow onions tasted the best. The onions are lightly browned before being incorporated into the stew—if they are over-caramelized, they disintegrate after two hours of stewing.

To deepen their gentle sweetness, we thought to add a spoonful of tomato paste while sautéing the onions, a trick we had used in other recipes. This simple (if untraditional) ingredient dramatically improved the flavor. (We also tried brown sugar but found it too sweet.) A sprinkling of salt helped the onions release their moisture, which kept the flavorful *fond* (brown bits) from burning and helped to loosen the bits from the pot during deglazing. Garlic is not an ingredient in all carbonnade recipes, but we liked it, adding two minced cloves to the onions only after the onions had cooked to make sure the garlic didn't burn.

Key to the cuisine of Belgium is beer, its national drink. Belgians routinely pour beer into dishes at times when other cooks might uncork a bottle of wine. Cooking with wine is fairly straightforward; most reasonable choices work just fine in a stew. Cooking with beer is a different story. Beers of the light, lager persuasion, popular in America but not traditional in carbonnade, lack potency and result in pale, watery-tasting stews. We tried a number of dark beers and found that reasonably dark ales, very dark ales, and stouts made the richest and best-tasting carbonnades (for individual flavor profiles of a variety of beers, see the tasting "Beer for Carbonnade" on page 7).

While the braising liquid for carbonnade is typically beer, beef stock is sometimes added. We made carbonnades with beer as the only liquid, but they lacked backbone and were sometimes overwhelmingly bitter, depending on the type of beer used. Canned beef broth made for a tinny taste, whereas chicken broth didn't provide enough depth. Equal parts chicken and beef broth plus beer, however, created a stew with solid, complex flavor. Fresh thyme and bay leaves were natural additions, and cider vinegar perked things up with sweet-and-sour tones.

With a blade steak, plenty of yellow onions, and a rich, dark beer, we made the simplest of all stews, carbonnade, finally come to life. It's even better than a burger with onion rings.

Beef Stew 101

Keep these key points in mind when making carbonnade or any beef stew.

1. Select meat from the chuck. We particularly like blade steak and chuck eye roast, which have the best texture and flavor for stewing.

2. Cut your own stew meat from a whole roast or steaks. Packages of stew meat contain multiple cuts (some not desirable) and pieces of varying size.

3. Brown the meat thoroughly. Drying the beef on paper towels and cooking it in batches will help to sear it properly and create a flavorful fond.

4. Thicken the stew with flour, sprinkled over sautéed aromatics. Cooking the flour for a few minutes eliminates a raw floury taste.

5. Simmer the stew in the oven. The oven heats more gently and evenly than the stovetop does.

6. Cook the stew for a long time. At least 2 hours of slow moist cooking ensures tender meat.

CARBONNADE À LA FLAMANDE
(Belgian Beef, Beer, and Onion Stew)
SERVES 6

Top blade steaks (also called blade or flatiron steaks) are our first choice, but any boneless roast from the chuck will work. If you end up using a chuck roast, look for the chuck eye roast, an especially flavorful cut that can easily be trimmed and cut into 1-inch pieces. Buttered egg noodles or mashed potatoes make excellent accompaniments to carbonnade.

3½	pounds top blade steaks, 1 inch thick, trimmed of gristle and fat and cut into 1-inch pieces (see illustrations 1 through 3)
	Table salt and ground black pepper
3	tablespoons vegetable oil
2	pounds yellow onions (about 3 medium), halved and sliced about ¼ inch thick (about 8 cups)
1	tablespoon tomato paste
2	medium garlic cloves, minced or pressed through garlic press (about 2 teaspoons)
3	tablespoons all-purpose flour
¾	cup low-sodium chicken broth
¾	cup low-sodium beef broth
1½	cups (12-ounce bottle or can) beer
4	sprigs fresh thyme, tied with kitchen twine
2	bay leaves
1	tablespoon cider vinegar

1. Adjust oven rack to lower-middle position; heat oven to 300 degrees. Dry beef thoroughly with paper towels, then season generously with salt and pepper. Heat 2 teaspoons oil in large heavy-bottomed Dutch oven over medium-high heat until beginning to smoke; add about one-third of beef to pot. Cook without moving pieces until well browned, 2 to 3 minutes; using tongs, turn each piece and continue cooking until second side is well browned, about 5 minutes longer. Transfer browned beef to medium bowl. Repeat with additional 2 teaspoons oil and half of remaining beef. (If drippings in bottom of pot are very dark, add about ½ cup of above-listed chicken or beef broth and scrape pan bottom with wooden spoon to loosen browned bits; pour liquid into bowl with browned beef, then proceed.) Repeat once more with 2 teaspoons oil and remaining beef.

2. Add remaining 1 tablespoon oil to now-empty Dutch oven; reduce heat to medium-low. Add onions, ½ teaspoon salt, and tomato paste; cook, scraping bottom of pot with wooden spoon to loosen browned bits, until onions have released some moisture, about 5 minutes. Increase heat to medium and continue to cook, stirring occasionally, until onions are lightly browned, 12 to 14 minutes. Stir in garlic and cook until fragrant, about 30 seconds. Add flour and stir until onions are evenly coated and flour is lightly browned, about 2 minutes. Stir in broths, scraping pan bottom to loosen browned bits; stir in beer, thyme, bay, vinegar, browned beef with any accumulated juices, and salt and pepper to taste. Increase heat

to medium-high and bring to full simmer, stirring occasionally; cover partially, then place pot in oven. Cook until fork inserted into beef meets little resistance, about 2 hours.

3. Discard thyme and bay. Adjust seasonings with salt and pepper to taste and serve. (Can be cooled and refrigerated in airtight container for up to 4 days; reheat over medium-low heat.)

STEP-BY-STEP | TRIMMING BLADE STEAKS

1. Halve each steak lengthwise, leaving gristle on one half.

2. Cut away gristle from half to which it is still attached.

3. Cut trimmed meat crosswise into 1-inch pieces.

TASTING: Beer for Carbonnade

When making carbonnade, purists will settle for nothing less than a traditional copper-colored Belgian ale with fruity, spicy aromas and a pleasant hoppy bitterness. But is it the only choice?

To find out, we pulled together nine different styles of beer, ranging from a dark, full-bodied stout to a nonalcoholic brew. We even included Bud Light (after all, it was already in the fridge).

After a few hours in the oven, the flavors you taste straight from the bottle are concentrated and easily recognized in this stew. Our tasters preferred beers that possessed plenty of sweetness matched with moderate bitterness. Light-bodied beers, like Bud Light, were noted for a mild sweetness but lacked the contrasting bitterness to make a balanced, full-flavored stew. On the other hand, brews with a high degree of bitterness often did not have enough sweetness. This was the case with Sierra Nevada's Pale Ale, which came across as singularly bitter. –Garth Clingingsmith

BEST CHOICE

Chimay Pères Trappistes Ale-Première
$9.49 for 25.4-ounce bottle
➤ The Belgians have had this right the whole time. This traditional Trappist ale was "rich and robust" and brought out a "very deep flavor" with a "dark chocolate finish."

THE OTHERS (IN ORDER OF PREFERENCE)

➤ **Newcastle Brown Ale, $7.49 for six-pack** This English ale was noted for its low sweetness and bitterness, which allowed for "lots of malt" flavor.

➤ **O'Doul's Amber (Nonalcoholic), $4.99 for six-pack** This nonalcoholic beer was the dark horse favorite. A fruity sweetness brought out "rich beefiness."

➤ **Anchor Steam, $8.69 for six-pack** "Grassy, barley" notes made a very "hearty" stew, but this beer pushed the bitter limits.

➤ **Samuel Adams Boston Lager, $7.29 for six-pack** "Black pepper" and "sweet spices" dominate this premium lager, alternately described as "burnt" or "molasses-sweet."

➤ **Guinness Extra Stout, $7.29 for six-pack** The archetypal stout bordered on "bitter and burnt," but a high degree of sweetness countered for a vigorously flavored carbonnade.

➤ **Sierra Nevada Porter, $7.99 for six-pack** This beer lacked enough contrasting sweetness. Several tasters likened this stew to "espresso."

➤ **Bud Light, $5.29 for six-pack** "Boring," not bitter, not sweet, and not very flavorful. Stew was "flat."

➤ **Sierra Nevada Pale Ale, $7.99 for six-pack** This beer is good straight from the bottle but made a stew that was "bitter" and "sour."

Rethinking Marinated Mushrooms

Do marinated mushrooms have to be slimy, watery, and, well, pretty much inedible?

⇒ BY BRIDGET LANCASTER ⇐

An unorthodox recipe, which starts on the stovetop, yields the best results.

Marinated mushrooms should taste good. As a classic Italian antipasto, foraged wild mushrooms are potent with earthy flavor. Blended with the right combination of bright acidity, heady herbs, and the nap of a fine olive oil, each bite packs a punch. But today most marinated mushrooms have morphed into little more than white button mushrooms soaked in bottled Italian dressing for days on end. The result is slimy, rubbery, brown orbs—hardly the life of the party.

Be that as it may, marinated mushrooms are still inexplicably popular (just try to find an hors d'oeuvres tray without them), and so it was time to get to work. My goals were clear: I wanted to get rid of that slippery, rubbery texture; I wanted a balance of flavor from oil and vinegar; and, above all, I wanted to make the mushrooms taste like mushrooms again.

Wild mushrooms aren't a produce-case regular, so I tested what was readily available—namely, portobellos, cremini (baby portobellos), and the ubiquitous white button. When all was said and done, I had eliminated the portobellos because of their spongy texture. Cremini got the thumbs up for flavor, but if I was going to be practical, the recipe could not ignore the white button mushroom.

Simply marinating raw mushrooms for any length of time was a no-go—they ended up slippery and slimy with no mushroom flavor. Boiling the mushrooms in a vinegar bath only compounded the problem; these mushrooms were not only slimy but tough, too. Poaching the mushrooms in oil worked a bit better, but the whole dish was watery and bland.

It was clear that I would have to think outside the box, so I tried a few dry heat methods instead, hoping the excess moisture would have a chance to evaporate. Spread out on a sheet pan and roasted in a hot oven, the mushrooms expelled their liquid and began to intensify in flavor. But I still felt that the flavor could be bigger.

And so I turned to my good old 12-inch skillet. The mushrooms were crowded in the pan and exuded a lot of liquid—so much so that I worried that this flood wouldn't reduce sufficiently, but I was wrong. With the heat cranked up, the liquid reduced down until it formed a potent glaze with concentrated mushroom flavor. And if that wasn't good enough, the seven or so minutes that it took to reduce the liquid produced a tender yet "al dente" mushroom, with no slime in sight. How easy could it get?

Oh yeah, I almost forgot. These were supposed to be marinated mushrooms, not sautéed mushrooms. I chose my base ingredients. Olive oil was in for its flavor, and it paid to use the good stuff—the fruitier the better. Typically, recipes call for white or red wine vinegar, but these vinegars were too harsh, making the mushrooms taste more pickled than marinated. Champagne, balsamic, and rice vinegars fell to a similar fate, but the fresh flavor of lemon juice fit perfectly.

Simply soaking the sautéed mushrooms in the vinaigrette wasn't cutting it; days passed before the mushrooms fully absorbed its flavors. I went back to my sautéing step and added a little lemon juice, which reduced nicely into the mushroom glaze. What a difference! Now the mushrooms started to take on a marinated flavor in only minutes instead of days. But if lemon juice was good, how about additional ingredients like garlic or onions or shallots? Yes and no. Yes, tasters liked the shallots and garlic (onions were deemed too strong), along with the sweet flavor from a red bell pepper, but sautéing the vegetables gave the whole dish a dull, stewed flavor.

I decided to add the vegetables to the cooled mushrooms. I tossed the whole lot together and came back to taste an hour later. Not bad, but two hours was better, three hours even better, and four hours . . . well, you get the point; the magic number turned out to be six. Thanks to the lemon juice, the bite from the raw shallots and garlic had mellowed and the flavors permeated the mushrooms. All that was left to do was to add a final shot of fresh lemon juice and olive oil as well as a chopped herb to brighten the mushrooms. I now had tender, balanced marinated mushrooms with no slip and no slime, and they actually (gasp) tasted like mushrooms.

MARINATED MUSHROOMS
MAKES ABOUT 3½ CUPS

Skillet size limits the yield of this recipe; if you would like to double it, cook the mushrooms in two separate batches but marinate them together. Thyme, parsley, or basil makes a good last-minute addition—use only one, however, not all three.

- 3 tablespoons extra-virgin olive oil, plus 1 tablespoon for finishing
- ⅛ teaspoon red pepper flakes
  Table salt
- 1 pound cremini or white button mushrooms, cleaned, left whole if small, halved if medium, quartered if large
- 2 tablespoons juice from 1 lemon, plus 1 tablespoon for finishing
- 1 medium garlic clove, sliced very thin
- 1 large shallot, chopped fine (about ¼ cup)
- ¼ small red bell pepper, chopped fine (about ¼ cup)
- 1 teaspoon minced fresh thyme leaves or 1 tablespoon chopped fresh parsley or basil leaves
  Ground black pepper

1. Heat 3 tablespoons oil, red pepper flakes, and ½ teaspoon salt in 12-inch skillet over medium-high heat until shimmering but not smoking. Add mushrooms and 2 tablespoons lemon juice; cook, stirring frequently, until mushrooms release moisture, moisture evaporates, and mushrooms have browned around edges, about 10 minutes. Spread mushrooms in single layer on large plate or rimmed baking sheet; cool to room temperature, about 20 minutes. When cooled, transfer mushrooms to medium bowl, leaving behind any juices. Stir garlic, shallot, and bell pepper into mushrooms, cover with plastic wrap, and refrigerate at least 6 or up to 24 hours.

2. Before serving, allow mushrooms to stand at room temperature about 1 hour. Stir in remaining 1 tablespoon olive oil, 1 tablespoon lemon juice, and thyme and adjust seasonings with salt and pepper just before serving.

The Last Word on Roast Turkey

Since we introduced the brined turkey in 1993, we have tested dozens of techniques for producing the perfect Thanksgiving bird. Here's what really works.

≥ BY REBECCA HAYS WITH JOHN OLSON AND GARTH CLINGINGSMITH ≤

In the test kitchen, we've been in pursuit of perfect turkey recipes for more than a decade. Countless birds have been oven-roasted, grill-roasted, and high-roasted, with careful evaluations of brining, air drying, basting, and trussing along the way. This year, we revisited our existing recipes to answer your questions and summarize 11 years of kitchen research.

What's the basic formula for brining? Does it change depending on the size of the turkey?

➢ A four-hour soak in a solution of 1 cup of table salt per gallon of water does the job for moderately sized 15-pound turkeys, but we were curious to see if the salt levels should be adjusted for smaller and larger birds. We soaked lightweight, middleweight, and heavyweight birds in brines with salt levels ranging from ½ cup to 4 cups and then refrigerated each bird for four hours. After roasting the birds, we asked tasters to give us their impressions of white and dark meat carved from each one. Apart from a distaste for the meat brined in the weakest and strongest solutions, tasters found most permutations to be acceptable. In fact, after several attempts, we found that consensus was nearly impossible to come by; tasters just weren't very sensitive to minor variations in salt levels. Even for a rather large or small bird, then, our standard formula—1 cup of table salt per gallon of water—is just fine.

My schedule would work better with an overnight brine rather than a four-hour brine. What adjustments should I make?

➢ For an overnight brine, halve the salt—use ½ cup table salt per gallon of water.

If a bird spends more or less time in the brine than recommended, what will happen?

➢ We didn't find significant differences in birds brined for an hour or two longer than our standard four-hour or overnight brine; but if you go much beyond that, the bird will be too salty. And if you brine a turkey for only two or three hours, you won't get all the benefits of brining (moisture retention, thoroughly seasoned meat, and a

The perfect holiday bird—with crisp skin and tender, juicy meat—is possible, if you follow our foolproof game plan.

better ability to withstand hot oven temperatures, which is essential for crisp skin).

I prefer to use kosher salt, not table salt, when brining. How do I adjust the recipe?

➢ Because kosher salt is less dense than table salt and one brand of kosher salt is even less dense than the other, our standard formula must be adjusted. Substitute 2 cups of Diamond Crystal Kosher Salt or 1½ cups of Morton Kosher Salt for 1 cup of table salt.

How does koshering differ from brining?

➢ Though their purposes are quite different, koshering and brining have similar effects on turkey meat. While brining consists of a single soak in salt water, the koshering process involves several steps. The turkey is first soaked in water for one-half hour. Then it is heavily salted and placed on an incline for about an hour to encourage the removal of blood. Finally, the bird is showered with final rinses of cold water. Because both koshering and brining encourage the absorption of water and salt, we do not recommend brining a bird that has been koshered.

Why do I sometimes see a "fresh" turkey being sold in a freezer case at the market?

➢ According to the U.S. Department of Agriculture, poultry that has never been stored below 26 degrees Fahrenheit can be labeled "fresh." While this temperature is below the freezing point of water (32 degrees), it is not cold enough to freeze enough of the water in the bird for it to qualify for the USDA's definition of "frozen." The USDA considers poultry that is "still pliable and yields to the thumb when pressed [to be] consistent with consumer expectations of 'fresh' poultry. Any turkey that has fallen below 26 degrees should be stored at or below 0 degrees and must be labeled "frozen" or "previously frozen."

How much salt is in kosher and natural birds? What would happen if I brined a self-basting bird?

➢ We get a lot of questions about salt concentrations in treated birds. We sent a skinless breast from each of five turkeys (see the list on page 10) to our lab for sodium analysis. Note that 1 percent sodium by weight translates to about 1.9 teaspoons table salt in every pound of turkey.

What's in a Name?

What is the difference between basted, kosher, and natural turkeys, and which tastes best?

➤ Self-basting, kosher, and natural turkeys are the types most often available to consumers. Traditionally processed frozen turkey is labeled "basted" or "self-basting." This means that it has been injected with a solution intended to make it more flavorful and tender. The components of this solution, which vary from company to company, are listed on the labels of these turkeys. Expect to see ingredients as innocent as turkey broth and as dubious as emulsifiers and artificial flavors. While tasters liked the texture and extreme juiciness of these birds, they also noted many off and unnatural flavors.

Kosher turkeys are processed mostly by hand and according to kosher law. (See the question on koshering versus brining on page 9.) Tasters generally preferred the juiciness of a brined, natural bird to the drier texture of a kosher turkey.

"Natural" turkeys are untreated fresh turkeys. This broad category includes free-range birds raised on small organic farms as well as birds raised for large commercial enterprises that are neither organic nor free-range. We tasted two "natural" birds: a Butterball Fresh Young Turkey and a Plainville Farms Young Turkey, a regionally available "veggie grown" bird. We brined these turkeys to level the playing field with the koshered and injected birds. While the Butterball had a juicy texture, its flavor paled next to that of the Plainville Farms turkey. (A Plainville Farms turkey that was not brined, however, was very bland. Locally grown, "all-natural" turkeys almost always need the moisture that brining provides.)

Local, 'Natural,' and Fresh
➤ **Plainville Farms**
For perfectly seasoned meat with "honest and real" flavor, choose a fresh turkey from a small regional producer and brine it yourself.

Nationwide, 'Natural,' and Fresh
➤ **Butterball Fresh**
These mass-produced turkeys are nationally available, but they lack flavor—be sure to brine them.

Kosher
➤ **Empire Kosher**
Hand-processing often leaves these salt-treated birds with a good number of feathers still attached. They taste great without brining.

'Basted' and Frozen
➤ **Butterball Frozen**
Never brine this "mild and boring" bird, which has already been injected with salt.

Readying the Bird: Air Drying & Trussing

You sometimes recommend air drying. Is it necessary?

➤ If you have the time and refrigerator space, air drying produces extremely crisp skin and is worth the effort. After brining, rinsing, and patting the turkey dry, place the turkey breast-side up on a flat wire rack set over a rimmed baking sheet and refrigerate, uncovered, 8 to 24 hours. Proceed with the recipe.

Do I have to truss the bird?

➤ Trussing with kitchen twine is done to keep the legs of the turkey from splaying during cooking. We recommend an easier approach, pictured at right.

TO AIR DRY: Place the brined and rinsed bird on a rack set over a rimmed baking sheet and refrigerate for at least 8 hours.
NO-FUSS TRUSS: Don't bother with complicated trussing. Instead, secure the legs by tucking the ankles of the bird into the pocket of skin at the tail end. Tuck the wings behind the bird.

- **Fresh turkey brined for 4 hours** (1 cup of table salt per gallon of water): 0.22 percent sodium by weight
- **Fresh turkey brined for 12 hours** ($\frac{1}{2}$ cup of table salt per gallon of water): 0.21 percent sodium by weight
- **Unbrined self-basting frozen turkey:** 0.27 percent sodium by weight
- **Brined self-basting frozen turkey:** 0.34 percent sodium by weight
- **Frozen kosher turkey:** 0.16 percent sodium by weight

The short answer to your question? Don't brine a self-basting turkey; it will be unpalatably salty.

On Thanksgiving, my refrigerator is packed. Is there a way to brine outside the refrigerator?

➤ A large, foodsafe container (such as a cooler) can be used to hold the turkey if the refrigerator is not an option. It is important to thoroughly clean and sanitize the container before and after use. Because the container is not going to be stored in the refrigerator, you must add a sufficient number of ice packs or bags of ice to maintain a temperature below 40 degrees. Choose a container that's large enough to keep the bird completely submerged.

What's your stance on stuffing?

➤ Most of the time, we roast unstuffed birds. Cooking the stuffing in a stuffed bird to a safe internal temperature takes quite a while and usually results in overcooked meat. If it wouldn't be Thanksgiving without a stuffed turkey on your table, you can reduce the roasting time (and the risk of dry turkey) by heating the stuffing before spooning it into the cavity of the turkey. Heat the stuffing in the microwave on high power until very hot (120 to 130 degrees), or 6 to 8 minutes. See **Cook's Extra** on page 9 for our stuffed roast turkey recipe.

I don't have a roasting rack. What should I do?

➤ A V-rack is important for two reasons. First, the rack holds the turkey in position during roasting and keeps it from rolling to one side or the other. Second, it elevates the meat above the roasting pan, allowing air to circulate and promoting even cooking and browning. If you don't own a V-rack, cooking grates from a gas stove can be used to create a makeshift roasting rack. Wrap two stove grates with aluminum foil and then use a paring knife or skewer to poke holes in the foil so that juices can drip down into the pan as the bird roasts. Place the grates in the roasting pan, leaning them against the sides of the pan so that the bottoms of the grates meet to create a V shape. Roast the turkey as usual.

Do I really have to turn the bird during roasting?

➤ Repeatedly rotating a hot turkey during the frenzied preparation of a holiday meal is troublesome at best and ultimately not worth it, we decided, for the minimal extra browning provided. Still, one flip protects the delicate breast meat during the first half of the cooking time and results in meat that is more moist—and that is worth the bother.

TECHNIQUE

FLIPPING THE TURKEY

With a towel or potholder in each hand, grasp the turkey and flip it over, placing it breast-side up on the rack. Take care to protect your hands from hot juices that will run out of the turkey.

TAKING THE TEMPERATURE

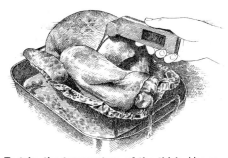

To take the temperature of the thigh: Use an instant-read thermometer, inserted into the thickest part of the thigh away from the bone, to determine when the leg meat is done.

To take the temperature of the breast: Insert the thermometer at the neck end, holding it parallel to the bird. Confirm the temperature by inserting the thermometer in both sides of the bird.

Do I have to baste the bird?

➤ Yes, but only at the outset. Brushing the turkey with butter before roasting is very little extra work, contributes to browning, and adds a mild buttery flavor. Conversely, basting during roasting is an unnecessary extra step. As a matter of fact, basting in the last hour of roasting can actually turn crisp turkey skin soft.

How do I know when the turkey is done?

➤ Getting an accurate temperature reading on a turkey can be a challenge. In several instances, we recorded temperatures that varied by as much as 20 degrees when taken in the same spot on the same bird at 10-second intervals. To reduce the margin of error as much as possible, follow the procedures illustrated above when taking the temperature of the bird. Roast the turkey until the legs move freely and the thickest part of the breast registers 165 degrees and the thickest part of the thigh registers 170 to 175 degrees on an instant-read thermometer.

Thirty minutes seems like a long time to rest the turkey after roasting. Is it really necessary?

➤ Yes. Resting allows for the redistribution and reabsorption of the juices in the meat. This makes for ultramoist, flavorful meat while also giving the bird a chance to cool for easier carving. Skip this

step and you'll both burn yourself and end up with a flood of juices on your carving board, not to mention dry turkey. To get an idea of how much juice is lost by slicing the meat too soon, we roasted six skin-on turkey breasts and weighed them. We sliced three straight from the oven and waited 30 minutes to slice the others. On average, we found that the rested turkeys weighed 2 to 3 percent more than the unrested turkeys, which translates to a great deal of juice saved. Plan on a 30-minute rest for most birds and up to 40 minutes for very large birds.

ROASTED BRINED TURKEY
SERVES 10 TO 22, DEPENDING ON TURKEY SIZE

We offer two brine formulas: one for a 4- to 6-hour brine and another for a 12- to 14-hour brine. The amount of salt used in each brine does not change with turkey size. If you're roasting a kosher or self-basting turkey, do not brine it; it already contains a good amount of sodium.

Rotating the bird from a breast-side down position to a breast-side up position midway through cooking helps to produce evenly cooked dark and white meat. If you're roasting a large (18- to 22-pound) bird and are reluctant to rotate it, skip the step of lining the V-rack with foil and roast the bird breast-side up for the full time. If making gravy, scatter 1 cup each of coarsely chopped onion, celery, and carrot as well as several fresh thyme sprigs in the roasting pan at the outset; add 1 cup water to keep the vegetables from burning.

Table salt
1 turkey (12–22 pounds gross weight), rinsed thoroughly, giblets and neck reserved for gravy, if making (see page 16)
4 tablespoons unsalted butter, melted

1. Dissolve 1 cup salt per gallon cold water for 4- to 6-hour brine or ½ cup salt per gallon cold water for 12- to 14-hour brine (see chart at right) in large stockpot or clean bucket. Add turkey and refrigerate for predetermined amount of time.

2. Before removing turkey from brine, adjust oven rack to lowest position; heat oven to 400 degrees for 12- to 18-pound bird or 425 degrees for 18- to 22-pound bird. Line large V-rack with heavy-duty foil and use paring knife or skewer to poke 20 to 30 holes in foil; set V-rack in large roasting pan.

3. Remove turkey from brine and rinse well under cool running water. Pat dry inside and out with paper towels. Tuck

tips of drumsticks into skin at tail to secure (see photo on page 10); tuck wing tips behind back. Brush turkey breast with 2 tablespoons butter. Set turkey breast-side down on prepared V-rack; brush back with remaining 2 tablespoons butter. Roast 45 minutes for 12- to 18-pound bird or 1 hour for 18- to 22-pound bird.

4. Remove roasting pan with turkey from oven (close oven door to retain oven heat); reduce oven temperature to 325 degrees if roasting 18- to 22-pound bird. Using clean potholders or kitchen towels, rotate turkey breast-side up; continue to roast until thickest part of breast registers 165 degrees and thickest part of thigh registers 170 to 175 degrees on instant-read thermometer, 50 to 60 minutes longer for 12- to 15-pound bird, about 1¼ hours for 15- to 18-pound bird, or about 2 hours longer for 18- to 22-pound bird. Transfer turkey to carving board; let rest 30 minutes (or up to 40 minutes for 18- to 22-pound bird). Carve and serve.

All-Purpose Guide to Roasting Turkey
Brining
Use the brining formulas below no matter the size of your turkey. Two gallons of water will be sufficient for most birds; larger birds may require three gallons. See page 9 for information on substituting kosher salt for table salt.

	QUICK Brine	OVERNIGHT Brine
TABLE SALT per gallon water	1 cup	½ cup
REFRIGERATION TIME	4 to 6 hours	12 hours or overnight, not to exceed 14 hours

Serving Sizes, Roasting Temperatures, and Roasting Times
Use the times below as guidelines; gauge doneness according to internal temperatures. Roast the turkey until the legs move freely and the thickest part of the breast registers 165 degrees and the thickest part of the thigh registers 170 to 175 degrees on an instant-read thermometer.

If cooking an 18- to 22-pound bird, you may choose not to rotate the bird; in that case, roast it breast-side up for the entire cooking time.

	12–15 lb	15–18 lb	18–22 lb
NUMBER OF SERVINGS	10–12	14–16	20–22
OVEN TEMPERATURE	400°	400°	425°, reduce to 325° after 1 hr
BREAST-SIDE DOWN ROASTING TIME	45 min	45 min	1 hr
BREAST-SIDE UP ROASTING TIME	50–60 min	1 hr, 15 min	2 hr
RESTING TIME	30 min	30 min	35–40 min

Smashed Potatoes

When there's no gravy and the potatoes have to stand on their own, lots of home cooks 'smash' them. But good smashed potatoes are hard to find.

⋑ BY ERIKA BRUCE ⋐

S ilky smooth mashed potatoes are at their best when topped with a rich holiday gravy or when napped with a highly seasoned pan sauce. Either way, it's a partnership, a question of the whole being greater than the sum of its parts. But there are times when there is no gravy to be had, and that's when smashed potatoes are just the thing. Their bold flavors and rustic, chunky texture give them the brawn to stand on their own, whether served with a grilled steak or a roast chicken.

Unfortunately, most recipes for this dish are plagued by a multitude of variations and refinements. Running the gamut from lean and mean to dangerously close to mashed (no skin, no texture, no oomph), smashed potatoes suffer from an identity crisis. I wanted chunks of potato textured with skins and bound by rich, creamy puree. Sturdy and robust, these were going to be potatoes worth fighting for.

Choosing, Cooking, Smashing
The only thing I was absolutely sure of was that I wanted the skins on. After all, these are supposed to be gutsy spuds, not white tablecloth social climbers.

Using the test kitchen's standard add-ins—melted butter and half-and-half—I smashed my way through five different varieties of potato: russet, all-purpose, Yukon Gold, medium-size Red Bliss, and tiny new potatoes (with red skins). The russets and all-purpose potatoes had strong potato flavor, but their dry texture caused them to crumble quickly when smashed, and their skins were too thick and tough against the soft, mealy flesh. The texture of the butter-colored Yukon Golds was slightly firmer, but these potatoes were still fluffy enough to break down. The two red varieties fared much better; their compact structure held up well under pressure, maintaining its integrity. The thin skins were pleasantly tender and paired nicely with the chunky potatoes. Clearly, this dish was meant for moist, low-starch potatoes. But because the tiny new potatoes had too high a ratio of skin to flesh, the medium-size Red Bliss won out.

I cooked the Red Bliss both whole and cut into 1-inch chunks (each time starting them in

An unusual ingredient gives smashed red potatoes just the right tang and texture.

cold water for best texture). Even though cutting the potatoes reduced the cooking time, the end result was leaden, soggy smashed potatoes with diluted potato flavor. Cooked whole, the potatoes retained their naturally creamy texture, as less potato surface was exposed to the water. I cooked the unpeeled potatoes in plain water, in salted water, in milk, and in stock. The latter two seemed wasteful, as neither did much to improve the flavor, and the salted water outdid the plain water, penetrating the skins and heightening the potato flavor. Next I added garlic and herbs (fresh rosemary and thyme, dried bay leaves) to the cooking water. Even though I wanted an assertive dish, the garlic flavor was just too strong; it was reserved for a recipe variation. Of the herbs, the bay leaf imparted the most complementary flavor, adding depth.

While a potato masher and fork are good tools for making chunky mashed potatoes, they took the smashed potatoes a little too far, smoothing out the rough, uneven chunks of potato that define this dish. I took a cue from the recipe

name, grabbed a plain old wooden spoon, and began smashing each potato with the back of it. If they were cooked just right, they burst apart, splitting the skins when they broke. This was even easier once the potatoes had dried for a few minutes so that their skins were no longer slippery. Then, making the spoon serve double duty, I used it to stir in the remaining ingredients. In fact, this technique was so simple that it even worked with a stiff rubber spatula, a better tool for folding in ingredients.

Unlikely Secrets of Success
With my key ingredient and basic technique settled, I turned to the other component that would make these potatoes really stand out: the dairy. Using only butter and half-and-half with the mildly flavored Red Bliss resulted in flat-tasting smashed potatoes. To boost the flavor I tried sour cream, trusted partner of the baked potato. Sour cream alone didn't give the potatoes enough body, so I tried supplementing it with both half-and-half and heavy cream. Both of these additions served only to dull the acidity of the sour cream—which I liked. I turned to tangier products such as yogurt and buttermilk. After making batches of sour, watery potatoes, I realized this was the wrong approach. I needed something tangy yet creamy that would bind the potatoes in terms of both flavor and texture. A fellow test cook suggested the rather unconventional cream cheese. Surprisingly, ½ cup of cream cheese—and no sour cream—gave these savory potatoes just the right touch of tang and creaminess. All they needed now was some butter to add richness, and 4 tablespoons was just the right amount for a deeper flavor without greasiness.

Then, as happens often in recipe development, I was confronted with a last-minute surprise. After my sensational smashed potatoes sat in the pot for a few minutes, their luscious texture went from creamy and smooth to dry and unpalatable. The potatoes had quickly absorbed what little moisture the butter and cream cheese had to offer. Not wanting to make the potatoes any richer, I tried a little milk and then chicken broth to moisten the potatoes. Both improved the texture, but they also diluted the potato flavor.

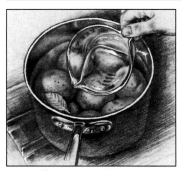

1. For the best flavor and texture, boil whole, skin-on potatoes. Leave a measuring cup nearby as a reminder to reserve some cooking liquid.

2. While the potatoes are drying, whisk together the cream cheese and butter.

3. When smashing the potatoes, use a spatula or large wooden spoon; both work better than a potato masher or fork. Smash just until the skins are broken.

4. Fold the cream cheese mixture into the potatoes gently, adding more reserved cooking liquid if the potatoes look dry.

Then I thought of a technique the test kitchen favors when making thick pasta sauces: Some of the water used to cook the pasta is reserved, and, if the sauce becomes too thick, the pasta water is added until the desired consistency is achieved. I applied this concept to my thick smashed potatoes, using the potato cooking water (nicely seasoned with salt and bay leaf and thickened with potato starch). I started with ¼ cup and added more as needed until I had a unified and creamy consistency. Just thick enough to be scooped up with a fork, these potatoes were thinner in terms of texture but not flavor.

In our standard mashed potato recipe, we found it important to add the melted butter before the half-and-half (the butter coats the potatoes' starch molecules with fat, which keeps them from soaking up too much liquid from the half-and-half and turning leaden). I wondered if the order in which I added the cream cheese, butter, and cooking water to the smashed potatoes would make a difference. In fact, I found that in adding each ingredient separately I overworked the potatoes, making them gluey and dense. It was better to mix them together first and then gently fold them into the smashed potatoes all at once.

To finish seasoning the potatoes, I added a little more salt and a dash of freshly ground black pepper. Tasters thought something green and fresh would be nice, so I tried parsley, scallions, and chives. The parsley was a bit dull and the scallions were too oniony, but the sprinkling of chopped fresh chives brightened the flavor just enough.

Finally, I had rediscovered the self-sufficient alternative to those needy mashed potatoes. Cream cheese and a little added cooking water, paired with the right kind of potato, were the secrets to smashed potatoes with big flavor and creamy texture. This quick, no-fuss side dish would complement any casual dinner. In fact, they're so tasty, I might even serve them as the main course.

SMASHED POTATOES
SERVES 4 TO 6

White potatoes can be used instead of Red Bliss, but their skins lack the rosy color of Red Bliss skins. Try to get potatoes of equal size; if that's not possible, test the larger potatoes for doneness. If only larger potatoes are available, increase the cooking time by about 10 minutes. Check for doneness with a paring knife.

    2   pounds Red Bliss potatoes (about 2 inches in
        diameter), unpeeled and scrubbed
        Table salt
    1   bay leaf
    4   tablespoons unsalted butter, melted and warm
    ½   cup cream cheese (4 ounces), room temperature
        Ground black pepper
    3   tablespoons chopped fresh chives (optional)

1. Place potatoes in large saucepan and cover with 1 inch cold water; add 1 teaspoon salt and bay leaf. Bring to boil over high heat, then reduce heat to medium-low and simmer gently until paring knife can be inserted into potatoes with no resistance, 35 to 45 minutes. Reserve ½ cup cooking water, then drain potatoes. Return potatoes to pot, discard bay, and allow potatoes to stand in pot, uncovered, until surfaces are dry, about 5 minutes.

2. While potatoes dry, whisk melted butter and softened cream cheese in medium bowl until smooth and fully incorporated. Add ¼ cup of reserved cooking water, ½ teaspoon pepper, chives (if using), and ½ teaspoon salt. Using rubber spatula or back of wooden spoon, smash potatoes just enough to break skins. Fold in butter/cream cheese mixture until most of liquid has been absorbed and chunks of potatoes remain. Add more cooking water 1 tablespoon at a time as needed, until potatoes are slightly looser than desired (potatoes will thicken slightly with standing). Adjust seasonings with salt and pepper; serve immediately.

SMASHED POTATOES WITH BACON AND PARSLEY

Halve 6 slices bacon lengthwise, then cut crosswise into ¼-inch pieces. Fry bacon in medium skillet over medium heat until crisp and browned, about 8 minutes. Using slotted spoon, transfer bacon to paper towel–lined plate; reserve 1 tablespoon bacon fat. Follow recipe for Smashed Potatoes, substituting 1 tablespoon bacon fat for equal amount butter, substituting 2 tablespoons chopped fresh parsley for chives, and reducing salt added to cream cheese mixture to ¼ teaspoon. Sprinkle individual servings with portion of fried bacon.

GARLIC-ROSEMARY SMASHED POTATOES

Heat 4 tablespoons butter in small skillet over medium heat; when foaming subsides, add ½ teaspoon chopped fresh rosemary and 1 medium garlic clove, minced or pressed through garlic press. Cook until just fragrant, about 30 seconds; set skillet aside. Follow recipe for Smashed Potatoes, adding 2 medium peeled garlic cloves to potatoes in saucepan along with salt and bay; substitute butter/garlic mixture for melted butter, add whole cooked garlic cloves to cream cheese along with butter mixture, and omit chives.

Two Styles of Potatoes

MASHED POTATOES   **SMASHED POTATOES**

The extra effort of a food mill or ricer is needed to achieve the soft, creamy texture that is characteristic of mashed potatoes. More rustic in appearance but quick and easy to prepare, smashed potatoes are perfect for a weeknight supper.

Pan-Seared Pork Tenderloin

How could we add flavor and juiciness to this lean, dry, often overcooked cut of meat?

⪢ BY BRIDGET LANCASTER ⪡

Give me slices of moist, rich pork roast any day. But pork tenderloin, well, I can take it or leave it. Partly because this incredibly lean cut dries out so quickly, but mostly because it's so darn flavorless, I'm not inclined to give this piece of pork a second chance. But even I have to admit that the tenderloin has its advantages. This boneless roast is easy to prepare, and it cooks very quickly.

Over the years, the test kitchen has found that pork tenderloin is especially suited to the grill: A hot charcoal fire adds flavor. Unfortunately, grilled pork tenderloin doesn't translate well to the kitchen oven. Not willing to suffer through a supper of mediocre pork (or to grill in a parka), I set out to discover an indoor cooking method that would equal the grill.

Cooking Challenge

Figuring that oven temperature was the key to success, I started out with a moderate oven (375 degrees) and worked my way up (475 degrees) and down (250 degrees) the temperature scale. Unfortunately, none of these temperatures was a winner. Cooler ovens produced evenly cooked tenderloins, but they had a pallid, spongy appearance. Confident that a blast of intense heat would give me the seared, crusted exterior I was looking for, I placed the tenderloins inside the oven, closed the door, and waited expectantly. I got color, but it was spotty at best. Even worse, these boneless tenderloins had become as dry as a bone.

Having been let down by the oven, I thought I would try the stovetop. I seared whole tenderloins and was heartened by the brilliant crust that formed on the exterior of the pork. But when I cut into the meat, it was nearly raw.

Wanting to retain the crust and cook the meat through to the center, I tried another approach. This time I started the tenderloins over a high flame, turning them until evenly browned, then placed the lid on the pan, lowered the flame to almost nil, and hoped that the ambient heat would cook the pork through. A few minutes later, I pulled the tenderloins out of the pan. The tenderloins had steamed in the covered pan. The crust was gone, and the meat was spongy.

A marriage of searing and roasting has worked

Searing on the stovetop guarantees browning, and removing the silver skin keeps the roasts from bowing.

well for me in the past (it's the best way to cook up a thick pork chop), and it was clearly time to revisit this method. I heated up a little oil in my skillet, cooked the tenderloins to golden perfection, then slid the pan into a 475-degree oven to finish cooking. Not bad. This time the tenderloins came out of the oven deeply colored and evenly cooked, but the meat was on the dry side. I tried lowering the oven in a series of tests until it hit 400 degrees. The meat was still deeply colored but less dry. Tests subsequently revealed that it was best to take the pork out of the oven when the internal temperature was between 135 and 140 degrees. After a 10-minute rest, the temperature climbed to between 145 and 150, and the meat retained lots of juices. (Note that the U.S. Department of Agriculture suggests a final temperature of 160 degrees. The choice is yours, but we find 160-degree pork to be unpalatable.)

Flavor Boosting

Although the golden crust now contributed flavor, I wanted more. My first thought was marinating. Marinated tenderloins turned wet and spongy, and after a few minutes in a hot skillet they were swimming in a pool of juice, which prevented browning. Brining, a method in which lean cuts of meat

are soaked in a salt and water solution (sometimes fortified with a little sugar), yielded similarly disappointing results.

I decided to try dry rubs with various combinations of salt and spices. Sometimes the best solution is the simplest; in the end, a healthy dose of salt and pepper did the trick. When I had time, I found that letting the salt and pepper sit on the pork for just 15 to 30 minutes allowed the seasonings to permeate the meat.

Gazing into the bottom of my dirtied skillet, I realized that a pan sauce was a natural. While the seared and roasted tenderloins were resting before being carved, I began to build the sauce. After twice burning my hand on the hot-from-the-oven skillet handle, I opted for a safer technique, transferring the seared tenderloins to a sheet pan to finish in the oven. This technique also came with a great benefit. In the 10 or so minutes that the tenderloins spent in the oven, I had time to reduce vinegar or wine down to a glaze or to caramelize onions and garlic in the empty pan. While the tenderloins rested, I finished the sauce with fresh herbs or mustard and swirled in butter as well. Now I had a richly flavored sauce fit to accompany my golden-crusted, juicy pork tenderloins, and all in less than 30 minutes.

PAN-SEARED OVEN-ROASTED PORK TENDERLOINS
SERVES 4

"Enhanced" pork—pork that has been injected with water, salt, and sodium phosphate—does not brown well owing to the extra moisture. We prefer natural pork tenderloins that have not been injected. Because two are cooked at once, tenderloins larger than 1 pound apiece will not fit comfortably in a 12-inch skillet. Time permitting, season the tenderloins up to 30 minutes before cooking; the seasonings will better penetrate the meat. The recipe will work in a nonstick or a traditional (not nonstick) skillet. A pan sauce can be made while the tenderloins rest (recipes follow);

COOK'S EXTRA gives you free recipes online. For two pork tenderloin variations, go to www.cooksillustrated.com and key in code 6043. These recipes will be available until December 15, 2004.

if you intend to make a sauce, make sure to prepare all of the sauce ingredients before cooking the pork.

> 2 pork tenderloins (12 to 16 ounces each), trimmed of fat and silver skin
> 1¼ teaspoons kosher salt
> ¾ teaspoon ground black pepper
> 2 teaspoons vegetable oil

1. Adjust oven rack to middle position; heat oven to 400 degrees. Sprinkle tenderloins evenly with salt and pepper; rub seasoning into meat. Heat oil in 12-inch skillet over medium-high heat until smoking. Place both tenderloins in skillet; cook until well browned, 1 to 1½ minutes. Using tongs, rotate tenderloins ¼ turn; cook until well browned, 45 to 60 seconds. Repeat until all sides are browned. Transfer tenderloins to rimmed baking sheet and place in oven (reserve skillet if making pan sauce); roast until internal temperature registers 135 to 140 degrees on instant-read thermometer, 10 to 16 minutes. (Begin pan sauce, if making, while meat roasts.)

2. Transfer tenderloins to cutting board and tent loosely with foil (continue with pan sauce, if making); let rest until internal temperature registers 145 to 150 degrees, 8 to 10 minutes. Cut tenderloins crosswise into ½-inch-thick slices, arrange on platter or individual plates, and spoon sauce (if using) over; serve immediately.

DRIED CHERRY–PORT SAUCE WITH ONIONS AND MARMALADE
MAKES ENOUGH TO SAUCE 2 TENDERLOINS

> 1 teaspoon vegetable oil
> 1 large onion, halved and sliced ½ inch thick (about 1½ cups)
> ¾ cup port
> ¾ cup dried cherries
> 2 tablespoons orange marmalade
> 3 tablespoons unsalted butter, cut into 3 pieces
> Table salt and ground black pepper

1. Immediately after placing pork in oven, add oil to still-hot skillet, swirl to coat, and set skillet over medium-high heat; add onion and cook, stirring frequently, until softened and browned about the edges, 5 to 7 minutes (if drippings are browning too quickly, add 2 tablespoons water and scrape up browned bits with wooden spoon). Set skillet aside off heat.

2. While pork is resting, set skillet over medium-high heat and add port and cherries; simmer, scraping up browned bits with wooden spoon, until mixture is slightly thickened, 4 to 6 minutes. Add any accumulated pork juices and continue to simmer until thickened and reduced to about ⅓ cup, 2 to 4 minutes longer. Off heat, whisk in orange marmalade and butter, one piece at a time. Adjust seasonings with salt and pepper.

GARLICKY LIME SAUCE WITH CILANTRO
MAKES ENOUGH TO SAUCE 2 TENDERLOINS

This assertive sauce is based on a Mexican sauce called *mojo de ajo*. A rasp-style grater is the best way to break down the garlic to a fine paste. Another option is to put the garlic through a press and then finish mincing it to a paste with a knife. If your garlic cloves contain green sprouts or shoots, remove the sprouts before grating—their flavor is bitter and hot. The initial cooking of the garlic off heat will prevent scorching.

> 10 garlic cloves, peeled and grated to fine paste on rasp-style grater (about 2 tablespoons)
> 2 tablespoons water
> 1 tablespoon vegetable oil
> ¼ teaspoon red pepper flakes
> 2 teaspoons light brown sugar
> 3 tablespoons juice from 2 limes
> ¼ cup chopped fresh cilantro leaves
> 1 tablespoon chopped fresh chives
> 4 tablespoons unsalted butter, cut into 4 pieces
> Table salt and ground black pepper

1. Immediately after placing pork in oven, mix garlic paste with water in small bowl. Add oil to still-hot skillet and swirl to coat; add garlic paste and cook with skillet's residual heat, scraping up browned bits with wooden spoon, until sizzling subsides, about 2 minutes. Set skillet over low heat and continue cooking, stirring frequently, until garlic is sticky, 8 to 10 minutes; set skillet aside off heat.

2. While pork is resting, set skillet over medium heat; add pepper flakes and sugar to skillet and cook until sticky and sugar is dissolved, about 1 minute. Add lime juice, cilantro, and chives; simmer to blend flavors, 1 to 2 minutes. Add any accumulated pork juices and simmer 1 minute longer. Off heat, whisk in butter, one piece at a time. Adjust seasonings with salt and pepper.

Mastering Turkey Gravy

Here's how to take the guesswork (and the lumps) out of America's favorite pan sauce—and produce perfect gravy every time. BY SEAN LAWLER

The turkey is carved, the potatoes are mashed, the family is starving—now is not the time to be hovering over the stove, fussing like a mad scientist with bulb basters and tiny bottles of suspicious brown liquid. But with so many items on the menu for holiday dinners, busy cooks often neglect the gravy until the last minute. Is it any wonder that it turns out lumpy, pasty, and pale? But gravy need not cause so much stress. In fact, much of the work can (and should) be done ahead of time.

EQUIPMENT

Sauce Whisks

Asking a balloon whisk to reach into the "corners" of a pan is usually a stretch. To find out what sort of whisk would be better suited to making sauces, such as gravy (page 17), we rounded up 12 models in various shapes and sizes. We prepared gravy, béchamel, and a steak pan sauce with each whisk.

A WINNING WHISK
This whisk is our favorite for making everything from turkey gravy to béchamel.

Many of the more unusual whisks did a good job—but they could do only one job. Square-headed whisks reached into the right angles of pots, but they were awkward when used for anything else. Coil-type whisks deglazed pans with aplomb, but they couldn't handle much volume and were easily clogged by thicker sauces. We settled on a "skinny" balloon whisk as the best choice for sauces. Shape is key here. The tight radius of the tines can dig a roux out of the corner of a pan. The long, relatively straight wires can even scrape a sauce from the sides of a pan. When tilted on its side, this whisk covers a wide swath of pan for efficient deglazing. We recommend a whisk measuring between 10 and 12 inches—too long to be lost to the bottom of a Dutch oven but too short to tilt out of most small pans. Some flexibility is necessary, so avoid a whisk with very stiff wires.

We found five whisks that met these criteria. Our favorite was the Best Manufacturers 12-Inch Standard French Whip ($9.95). This long whisk boasts an agile set of tines and a comfortable handle that is light enough to keep this whisk from tipping out of shorter saucepans. – Garth Clingingsmith

Roasting Pans
BEST ROASTING PAN
A roasting pan with a heavy bottom is a must when deglazing, which is done over stovetop burners. We've tested nearly a dozen, and our two favorites are made by All-Clad. The Petit Roti is fine for a small turkey, whereas the larger Roti is necessary for a turkey that weighs more than 12 pounds.

BEST ROASTING PAN
The All-Clad roasting pan is our top choice for turkey and more.

DISPOSABLE ROASTING PAN
A disposable foil roasting pan is fine for catching flavorful turkey drippings, but it can't be put on the stovetop to deglaze. If using a disposable foil roasting pan, just strain and defat the pan drippings and add them to the gravy to taste.

INGREDIENTS

What's in That Bag?
No need to fear that mysterious little bag that comes inside the turkey cavity—it contains the makings for a flavorful gravy. The turkey neck and the "giblets," or internal organs, are mechanically separated, washed, and then repackaged during turkey processing precisely for the purpose of making gravy. Here's what's in the bag:

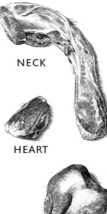

NECK

HEART

GIZZARD

LIVER

NECK
The *neck* is the large, elongated muscle with a bone through the center. It contains some very flavorful meat. Cut it into several pieces for easy browning, then simmer it in the broth. Discard after straining the broth.

GIBLETS (HEART, GIZZARD, AND LIVER)
The *heart* is the small, oblong, dark-colored organ. Brown it along with the neck and gizzard, then simmer it in the broth. Reserve after straining the broth, then dice and return to the gravy before serving.

The *gizzard* is the reddish, spherical organ. It is a grinding organ from the bird's digestive tract, recognizable by a butterfly-shaped strip of connective tissue. Cut the gizzard in half, brown it along with the heart and neck, then reserve it after straining the broth. Dice the gizzard and return it to the gravy along with the heart.

The *liver* is the soft, brownish, flat organ. Because the liver tends to impart a characteristically strong flavor, we don't recommend using it to make gravy.

Broth: Watch Out for Salt
Because making gravy involves simmering, which concentrates flavors, it's important to tread lightly with salt. That includes using a low-sodium chicken broth. In fact, we recommend cutting the commercial broth with water to reduce the overall salt level of the gravy. (A 2:1 ratio of broth to water works best.) After sampling a dozen leading brands of chicken broth, tasters found broths from Swanson to be the best. Broth sold in aseptic packages undergoes less heating than broth sold in cans, and we found that the former tastes better.

BEST CHICKEN BROTH
Swanson Natural Goodness

Thickener: Flour, Not Cornstarch, Means No More Lumps
Cornstarch is notorious for clumping when added to a hot liquid. And once it does clump, all the whisking in the world won't smooth things out. This is why we recommend thickening gravy with a roux (made with flour and butter). As long as you add liquid to the roux in small increments, lumps will not be a problem.

ILLUSTRATION: JOHN BURGOYNE

BEST TURKEY GRAVY

MAKES ABOUT 6 CUPS

This recipe makes enough gravy to accompany a 12- to 14-pound turkey, with leftovers. If you are roasting a very large bird and want to double the recipe, prepare the gravy in a Dutch oven. White wine adds a welcome note of acidity to gravy, but in a pinch you can use more chicken broth in its place.

1   tablespoon vegetable oil
     Reserved turkey giblets and
     neck
1   onion, unpeeled and chopped
4   cups low-sodium chicken
     broth
2   cups water
2   sprigs fresh thyme
8   parsley stems
3   tablespoons unsalted butter
¼   cup all-purpose flour
1   cup dry white wine
     Table salt and ground black
     pepper

STEP ONE: Make the broth.
TIMETABLE: 1 to 2 days in advance.

STEP TWO: Make the roux and thicken the broth.
TIMETABLE: 1 day in advance or while turkey roasts.

STEP THREE: Deglaze the roasting pan and add the drippings to the gravy.
TIMETABLE: While the turkey rests on the carving board.

STEP ONE Make the broth

Good gravy starts with turkey stock, but few home cooks have the time to make homemade. With turkey trimmings and an onion, you can quickly doctor store-bought chicken broth into a flavorful base for gravy.

 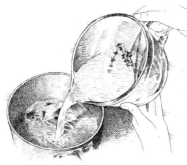 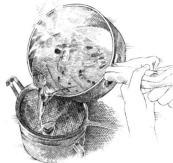

1. Sauté and sweat. Heat oil in large saucepan over medium-high heat. Brown turkey giblets and neck for 5 minutes. Cook onion for 3 minutes. Cover and cook over low heat for 20 minutes.

2. Simmer and skim. Add chicken broth and water, scrape pan bottom, and bring to boil. Add herbs and simmer, skimming foam from surface, for 30 minutes.

3. Strain and cool. Pour broth through fine-mesh strainer. Reserve and dice heart and gizzard. Refrigerate broth and diced giblets until ready to use.

STEP TWO Make the roux and thicken the broth

A nutty brown roux (made with butter and flour) thickens and flavors the turkey broth. The roux also adds deep brown color, so you won't need artificial gravy helpers, such as Gravy Master or Kitchen Bouquet.

 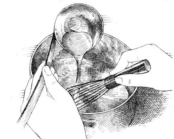 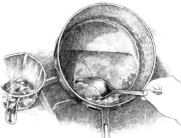

4. Cook roux. Melt butter in large saucepan over medium-low heat. Whisk in flour. Cook, stirring constantly, until nutty brown and fragrant, 10 to 15 minutes. Bring reserved turkey broth to simmer.

5. Add broth. Gradually add hot turkey broth to roux. Vigorous and constant whisking at this point is key to avoiding lumps. Reserve 1 cup of broth for deglazing roasting pan (see #9).

6. Simmer gravy. Simmer gravy, stirring occasionally and skimming scum from surface with spoon, until thickened, about 30 minutes. Set aside, covered, until turkey is done.

STEP THREE Deglaze the pan and add the drippings to the gravy

Browned vegetables and drippings in the roasting pan used to cook the turkey are the final flavor enhancers for gravy. Add 1 cup each of chopped onions, carrots, and celery along with fresh thyme sprigs and 1 cup of water to the roasting pan before the turkey goes into the oven.

7. Strain drippings. Pour drippings through mesh strainer set over measuring cup. Let liquid settle until fat rises to top. Return vegetables in strainer to roasting pan.

8. Defat drippings. Tilt measuring cup and use wide, shallow soup spoon to skim fat off surface. Reserve defatted drippings. Return gravy in saucepan to simmer.

9. Deglaze pan. Place roasting pan over two burners at medium-high heat. Add wine and reserved 1 cup broth and scrape up browned bits in pan. Boil until liquid reduces by half, 5 minutes.

10. Finish gravy. Strain roasting pan liquid into gravy, pressing on solids to extract all liquid. Add defatted drippings to taste. Stir in giblets and serve.

Balsamic Braised Chicken

Italians have long paired balsamic vinegar and chicken. But given the poor quality of most supermarket vinegar, we wondered if this was indeed a match made in heaven.

⇒ BY JOHN OLSON ⇐

Balsamic vinegar runs the gamut from single-malt scotch (old and sophisticated) to moonshine (young and harsh), depending on how it is made. Used in cooking, it has the same range. It can deepen the flavor of a dish, add a quick splash of welcome contrast, or it can overpower, say, simple greens with an unwelcome double-barreled hello, a syrupy sweet-and-sour handshake that the Italians refer to as *agrodolce*. The good news is that the pairing of chicken and balsamic vinegar has plenty of precedent in Italian cooking and that for the most part this partnership has been a success.

Recipe research quickly uncovered the simple truth: There is no standard method for putting these two ingredients together. Some recipes marinate chicken in balsamic, others add it during cooking, and a few just drizzle in a little at the end. Nor is there any uniformity in the quantity of balsamic called for; using a few teaspoons for seasoning appears to be just as acceptable as using a half cup to make a base for a sauce. The one notable constant among these recipes is their call for a strong taste element in addition to sweet and sour—salty bacon or capers, for example—that will make the match complete.

Building a Recipe

For starters, the chicken was going to be braised, a slow, low-heat method that involves a covered pan and a small amount of liquid. I quickly realized that chicken thighs would be the best choice for braising. For a flightless bird, the breast muscles are little more than filler; the hard-working muscles are in the legs, especially the thighs. These tough muscles, laced with fat and connective tissue, both provide a robust flavor (good for pairing with balsamic vinegar) and resist overcooking, something to which breast meat is particularly susceptible.

I began my testing using a standard braising recipe: Brown the thighs and remove them from

Basic chicken stew gets a big boost in flavor from balsamic vinegar that's been reduced to a syrupy glaze.

the pot; sauté onion and garlic; add balsamic vinegar, tomatoes, and broth; return the chicken (with the skin removed) to the pot; and bake in a 350-degree oven with the lid on for about an hour. The results were mediocre at best, but I had learned that tomatoes are a key ingredient (they help balance the flavor of the vinegar). Eager to remove my dish from the mediocre category, I wondered if bacon or pancetta might add interest. Neither panned out, but anchovies did perk up the flavor a bit. Even so, I was still well short of a great recipe.

There is nothing new about using wine in a braise, but I had been reluctant because I wanted the balsamic vinegar to be the star. (Balsamic vinegar is traditionally produced from white Trebbiano grapes and is then aged in barrels. Some of its flavors are akin to those of a hearty wine.) Desperate for more and better flavor, I tested the recipe with three different wines: a medium white wine, a dry red wine, and Italian Marsala. The verdict was unanimous: Red wine offered the fullest flavor without being too sweet, and the dish was inarguably better than it had been without the wine.

At this point, I felt that the braising liquid was substantial enough but could nonetheless use a few choice herbs and spices. I tested hot red pepper flakes, clove, fennel, thyme, and bay leaf. Fennel and clove both tasted out of place, but most everyone in the kitchen liked the addition of thyme, bay, and red pepper. I also experimented with fresh oregano, marjoram, and rosemary. Rosemary was too resinous (except if added very late in the process), and neither the marjoram nor the oregano made much of a mark on the strong-tasting braising liquid. Now the recipe was quite good, but there was a problem with the balsamic vinegar. It was supposed to be the main event but had become merely a casual bystander.

Less Is More

From the start, I had been adding ¼ cup of vinegar at the beginning of braising, simply accepting the mild balsamic note in the finished dish. One remedy might be to drizzle a little balsamic into the sauce just before serving. This certainly made the dish more tart, but it did not enhance the overall standing of the vinegar. Well, I thought, why not just add more to start? When

Reduction Deduction

STRAIGHT FROM THE BOTTLE   **REDUCED BY HALF**

A quick simmer concentrates and improves the flavor and consistency of inexpensive balsamic vinegar from the supermarket. Straight from the bottle, the vinegar runs right off the pan (left). Once reduced by half, it lightly coats the pan (right).

COOK'S EXTRA gives you free recipes online. For our polenta recipe, go to www.cooksillustrated.com and key in code 6044. This recipe will be available until December 15, 2004.

Cheap or Fancy?

Would expensive vinegar make our chicken braise taste better? We tried two brands we like a lot—one cheap and one not so cheap. In the end, we preferred the inexpensive 365 Organic Every Day Value ($4.99 for 500 milliliters) to the Cavalli ($24.99 for 500 milliliters), which lost its complexity in our recipe.

I doubled the amount in the braising liquid to ½ cup, the balsamic flavor became pronounced, but the chicken became dull colored and thready, ill effects from the newly increased acidity of the braising liquid. Not wanting to end with a chicken sauerbraten, I had to find a new method.

In the past, our cooks have found that reducing supermarket balsamic vinegar (that is, simmering on the stovetop for several minutes to drive off excess moisture) goes a long way toward improving its flavor. For my next test, I reduced ½ cup of vinegar by half. Simply drizzling the reduced vinegar over the chicken before serving was haphazard and ineffective. Adding the reduced vinegar directly to the finished braising liquid, however, did the trick. Here was the balsamic flavor I had been looking for all along: silky, smooth, and soothing.

Finally, I was curious to see if higher quality balsamic vinegar would be even better when reduced. The supermarket product is a far cry from the $150 bottles that contain the "good stuff," balsamic vinegar that has been aged for many years. My first test was to purchase a better quality $25 bottle of balsamic and substitute it for the economical supermarket vinegar I had been using. Now the braising liquid was thick and sweet—too sweet, according to most tasters. The reason for this result is that when a good balsamic vinegar is aged, water is allowed to evaporate, concentrating the flavor. In a sense, older balsamic is already partially reduced. I could have tried a less concentrated reduction of the good vinegar, but adapting a recipe for use with high-quality vinegar would be difficult, as the sweetness and thickness can vary from brand to brand. (Supermarket balsamics are thin, like regular red wine vinegar.)

At this point, I stopped my tests with the high-end vinegar. Simmering such a vinegar might well be considered high crime in Italy. All the time and effort expended to create its subtle flavor balance would be wasted, as boiling destroys it. (This is not a problem with the cheap stuff.)

My last piece of business was to inject some

freshness and color into the dish. I had gotten many comments on the overall "dull and stewed" nature of the tomatoes and onions. I thought that fresh greens such as kale, spinach, or Swiss chard might liven things up. Spinach wilted away to a flavorless mass, while kale never really joined the party, behaving more like a garnish. Chard was a happy median between the two; it stood up to the hearty flavors of the braise and added a touch of its own earthy bitterness. With the addition of greens, I felt that the strong flavor of the balsamic had finally come into balance with that of the chicken, tomato, anchovy, garlic, and red wine. Here was sweet, sour, bitter, hot, herbal, and meaty—all in one dish.

BRAISED CHICKEN WITH SWISS CHARD, TOMATOES, AND BALSAMIC VINEGAR
SERVES 4

When browning the chicken, avoid overcrowding the pot—brown the thighs in two batches if all eight do not fit comfortably. If you like the flavor of rosemary, a sprig can be added with the Swiss chard in step 4, then discarded before serving. You don't need an expensive balsamic vinegar for this recipe. The $4.99 winner of our 2001 tasting, 365 (the house brand at Whole Foods Markets), works perfectly. Polenta is an excellent accompaniment to this hearty braise. See **Cook's Extra** on page 18 for our recipe.

8	bone-in, skin-on chicken thighs (about 3 pounds), trimmed of excess fat and skin
	Table salt and ground black pepper
1	tablespoon olive oil
1	large onion, halved and sliced ¼ inch thick (about 2 cups)
1	tablespoon tomato paste
3	medium garlic cloves, minced or pressed through garlic press (about 1 tablespoon)
1	anchovy fillet, minced (about 1 teaspoon)
1	can (14½ ounces) diced tomatoes, drained
2	cups low-sodium chicken broth
¼	cup dry red wine
¼	teaspoon red pepper flakes
1½	tablespoons chopped fresh thyme leaves
1	bay leaf
12	ounces Swiss chard, washed and dried
½	cup balsamic vinegar

1. Adjust oven rack to lower-middle position; heat oven to 350 degrees. Sprinkle both sides of chicken thighs with salt and pepper. Heat oil in nonreactive Dutch oven over medium-high heat until shimmering but not smoking; add chicken thighs skin-side down and cook without moving them until skin is crisped and well browned, 10 to 12 minutes. Using tongs, turn chicken pieces and brown on second side, about 5 minutes longer; transfer thighs to large plate.

2. Pour off all but 1 teaspoon fat from pot. Add

onion and tomato paste and cook over medium heat, stirring occasionally and scraping bottom of pot with wooden spoon, until tomato paste begins to darken, about 4 minutes (if bottom of pot becomes very dark and sticky, stir in 1 to 2 tablespoons water). Add garlic and anchovy and cook, stirring constantly, until fragrant, about 1 minute. Stir in tomatoes, chicken broth, and wine, scraping up browned bits with wooden spoon. Add red pepper flakes, thyme, and bay. Remove and discard skin from chicken thighs, then submerge chicken bone-side up in liquid, adding any chicken juices accumulated on plate. Increase heat to high, bring to simmer, cover, then place pot in oven. Cook until chicken offers no resistance when poked with tip of paring knife but meat still clings to bone, 40 to 55 minutes.

3. While chicken cooks, trim stems from Swiss chard (see "Preparing Chard," below). Cut stems crosswise into ¼-inch pieces; halve leaves lengthwise, then cut crosswise into ¼-inch-thick strips. Set stems and leaves aside separately. Also while chicken cooks, simmer balsamic vinegar in 8-inch nonreactive skillet over medium-high heat until thick, syrupy, and reduced to ¼ cup, 3 to 5 minutes (begin measuring volume when vinegar begins to cling to sides of saucepan). Set vinegar reduction aside.

4. Using slotted spoon, transfer chicken to plate and tent with foil; discard bay leaf. Bring liquid in Dutch oven to simmer over medium-high heat; add chard stems and cook, stirring occasionally, until almost tender, about 8 minutes. Add chard greens and cook until wilted, about 2 minutes. Stir about ⅓ cup sauce into balsamic reduction to loosen, then stir mixture into sauce; adjust seasoning with salt and pepper. Return chicken and accumulated juices to sauce, cook until heated through, about 2 minutes, turning chicken once or twice. Use slotted spoon to transfer chard to serving dish or individual bowls; place chicken thighs on chard, then spoon sauce over. Serve immediately.

TECHNIQUE

PREPARING CHARD

Hold each leaf at the base of the stem over a bowl filled with water and use a sharp knife to slash the leafy portion from either side of the thick stem.

Holiday Spritz Cookies

That golden-swirled kiss of a holiday cookie often ends up bland, gummy, and tasteless.
Why can't spritz cookies taste as good as they look?

≥ BY ERIKA BRUCE ≤

It's the peak of the festive holiday season, and you find yourself at yet another party, standing next to one more long buffet table. You spy a towering plate of cookies and instinctively reach for the golden-swirled kiss—only to discover a bland, gummy, stick-to-the-roof-of-your-mouth impostor. But this is not the way spritz cookies were meant to be. Scandinavian in origin, they are the most simple of butter cookies, their distinct design created by the pressing, or *spritzing*, of a very soft dough through a piping bag or a cookie press. Whichever the vehicle, the shaping technique allows for an extremely buttery dough (they don't have to be rolled out), which translates into light, crisp cookies.

A victim of vanity to be sure, the spritz cookie has been subject to all manner of insult by recipe writers intent on finding shortcuts to a more shapely cookie. And the worst offenders have produced the most attractive cookies. Their crime? Using vegetable shortening in place of butter, which makes the cookies flavorless and waxy. Recipe writers who do use butter often add so many eggs (to keep the cookies from spreading in the oven) that the cookies bake up soft and chewy rather than light and crisp. Yet another tactic used to guarantee a shapely cookie is to add an excess of confectioners' sugar to the dough. The confectioners' sugar, which is laced with cornstarch, makes the cookies pasty.

The Ingredient List

The foundation for the spritz cookie is a dough that is soft enough to press or pipe yet sturdy enough to hold its shape in the oven. And it must be made with butter, and lots of it. Starting with a nice even two sticks of butter and ¾ cup granulated sugar, I found that I could add no more than 2 cups of flour before the dough got too stiff. From here, I tested the use of eggs, as many recipes varied in this regard. With no eggs, the cookies were like shortbread—buttery, but too tender and crumbly, with an ill-defined shape. One whole egg resulted in chewy, tough cookies. By adding only yolks, I got more tender cookies that also retained their shape. But even two yolks were one too many, resulting in greasy, eggy-tasting cookies; just one yolk made them tender, crisp, and sturdy.

But a mere yolk did not contribute enough liquid to make a smooth, workable dough. Adding more butter didn't solve the problem, so I turned

A pastry bag can produce cookies in countless shapes and sizes, but we had decent luck with a cookie press, too.

to dairy, trying milk, half-and-half, and heavy cream. Each improved the texture of the dough, but the milk and half-and-half caused the cookies to spread in the oven. The cookies made with heavy cream—and just 1 tablespoon of it—not only held their shape but were also the most flavorful.

Fearing that I might be missing out on some helpful (rather than harmful) innovation happened upon by another baker, I tested some additional ingredients. I added baking powder, presumably for a lighter, airier texture; instead, the dramatic rise and puff in the oven obliterated the precise "spritz" shape I was after. As for flour, the softer, more finely milled cake flour resulted in a cookie that was tender to the point of being pasty. A similar result ensued when I added a small amount of cornstarch to all-purpose flour, a common technique for tenderizing baked goods. Superfine sugar, a finer version of granulated sugar, gave the cookies a tighter crumb, something sought after in cookies that are rolled flat and cut out but not in a spritz cookie. Granulated was still the sugar of choice, but a

few tasters complained that the cookies were too sweet. Reducing the sugar to ⅔ cup tamed the sweetness and brought the butter flavor to the foreground. I was now satisfied that these cookies needed no secret ingredient; all they needed were a few simple ingredients gathered in the proper proportions.

The Method

The standard technique for mixing this dough involves creaming, or whipping the butter and sugar together until light and fluffy, before adding the other ingredients. The large, sharp-edged crystals of granulated sugar allow pockets of air to be whipped into the butter, and these pockets expand in the heat of the oven, producing a light, crisp texture. Because these cookies contain no leavener and only one egg yolk, they rely on this action for their ethereal texture. Creaming was also essential for producing a dough light enough to easily press into cookies.

Most home bakers turn to a cookie press to shape spritz cookies. Having trained as a pastry chef, I am more comfortable with a pastry bag. A testing of cookie presses did uncover a winner—the Wilton Comfort Grip Cookie Press (see page 21)—but an all-purpose pastry bag does have its advantages. It allows for fancier shapes (stars, rosettes, and "S" shapes are generally beyond the reach of a press), and the bag also provides more control and freedom of motion. I prefer to use a pastry bag, but it's hard to argue with the convenience of a good cookie press.

Oven temperature had a direct impact on the

Shining Stars

| PERFECT: | PUNY: |
| From a Pastry Bag | From a Press |

A traditional piping bag gives the baker more control over the size and shape of the cookies, providing for a more attractive result. A cookie press offers less control and makes small, squat cookies.

1. Make C-shape with one hand and hold piping bag. Fold bag over that hand about halfway down, insert tip, and scrape dough into bag.

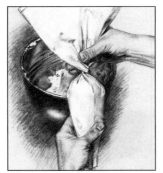

2. When bag is about half full, pull up sides, push down dough, and twist tightly while again pushing down on dough to squeeze out air.

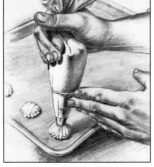

3. Grab bag at base of twist. Using other hand as guide, hold tip at 90-degree angle about ½ inch above baking sheet and squeeze to form shape.

texture of the cookies. If it was too low, the cookies became dry and crisp all the way through. Too high and the outside crisped while the inside remained soft. Tasters preferred a slight variation in texture, which was perfectly achieved at the moderately high temperature of 375 degrees.

I concluded that great spritz cookies weren't so complicated after all. No shortcuts, no gimmicks—just simple ingredients and the right technique—made my holiday wish come true.

SPRITZ COOKIES
MAKES ABOUT 6 DOZEN 1½-INCH COOKIES

If using a pastry bag, use a star tip to create the various shapes. For stars, a ½- to ⅝-inch tip works best, but for rosettes and "S" shapes, use a ⅜-inch tip (measure the diameter of the tip at the smallest point). To create stars, hold the bag at a 90-degree angle to the baking sheet and pipe the dough straight down, as shown in illustration 3, above; stars should be about 1 inch in diameter. To create rosettes, pipe the dough while moving the bag in a circular motion, ending at the center of the rosette; rosettes should be about 1¼ inches in diameter. To create "S" shapes, pipe the dough into compact "S's"; they should be about 2 inches long and 1 inch wide. If you make an error while piping, the dough can be scraped off the baking sheet and repiped.

We had the best results baking these cookies one sheet at a time. When reusing a cookie sheet, make sure that it has completely cooled before forming more cookies on it. Unbaked dough can be refrigerated in an airtight container for up to 4 days; to use, let it stand at room temperature until softened, about 45 minutes. Baked cookies will keep for more than a week if stored in an airtight container or zipper-lock bag.

- 1 large egg yolk
- 1 tablespoon heavy cream
- 1 teaspoon vanilla extract
- 1 cup (2 sticks) unsalted butter, softened (about 70 degrees)
- ⅔ cup (about 4¾ ounces) sugar
- ¼ teaspoon table salt
- 2 cups (10 ounces) unbleached all-purpose flour

1. Adjust oven rack to middle position; heat oven to 375 degrees. In small bowl, beat yolk, cream, and vanilla with fork until combined; set aside.

2. In standing mixer, cream butter, sugar, and salt at medium-high speed until light and fluffy, 3 to 4 minutes. Scrape down bowl with rubber spatula. With mixer running at medium speed, add yolk/cream mixture and beat until incorporated, about 30 seconds. Scrape down bowl. With mixer running at low speed, gradually beat in flour until combined. Scrape down bowl and give final stir with rubber spatula to ensure that no flour pockets remain.

3. If using cookie press to form cookies, follow manufacturer's instructions to fill press; if using pastry bag, follow illustrations 1 through 3 to fill bag. Press or pipe cookies onto ungreased baking sheets, spacing them about 1½ inches apart. Bake one sheet at a time until cookies are light golden brown, 10 to 12 minutes, rotating baking sheet halfway through baking time. Cool cookies on baking sheet until just warm, 10 to 15 minutes; using metal spatula, transfer to wire rack and cool to room temperature.

SPRITZ COOKIES WITH LEMON ESSENCE

Follow recipe for Spritz Cookies, adding 1 teaspoon lemon juice to yolk/cream mixture in step 1 and adding 1 teaspoon finely grated lemon zest to butter along with sugar and salt in step 2.

ALMOND SPRITZ COOKIES

Grind ½ cup sliced almonds and 2 tablespoons of flour called for in Spritz Cookies in food processor until powdery and evenly fine, about 60 seconds; combine almond mixture with remaining flour. Follow recipe for Spritz Cookies, substituting ¾ teaspoon almond extract for vanilla.

TESTING EQUIPMENT: Cookie Presses

For those of us lacking a steady hand or experience with a pastry bag, a cookie press would seem indispensable for making attractive spritz cookies. These inexpensive tools promise to produce consistently shaped cookies in record time. We tested six models to see if they lived up to their word.

Old-fashioned cookie presses rely on a screw-driven plunger to press the dough through cut dies, resulting in dozens of possible shapes. In our tests, these presses were awkward to use, especially with buttery hands. The one electric press we tested was even worse. The production of uniform cookies depended on split-second timing; hold down that power button too long or release it too soon—by what seemed like a millisecond—and you ended up with a cookie swollen to unrecognizable proportions or a cookie so puny it was destined to burn.

A third style of cookie press relies on a triggered, ratcheting mechanism. One click of the ratchet yields a perfect cookie every time. Our favorite press of this kind, the Wilton Comfort Grip Cookie Press, was nearly goofproof and allowed us to make dozens of cookies in just minutes. This sort of press does have its limitations, however. Its one-cookie-at-a-time design restricts it to "drop" cookies. It is extremely difficult to produce an elongated cookie, for example, with this sort of press. Even for a novice baker, a pastry bag is better suited for making fancier shapes. But it's hard to argue with the convenience of a good cookie press, especially if volume and uniformity are your main concerns.
–Garth Clingingsmith

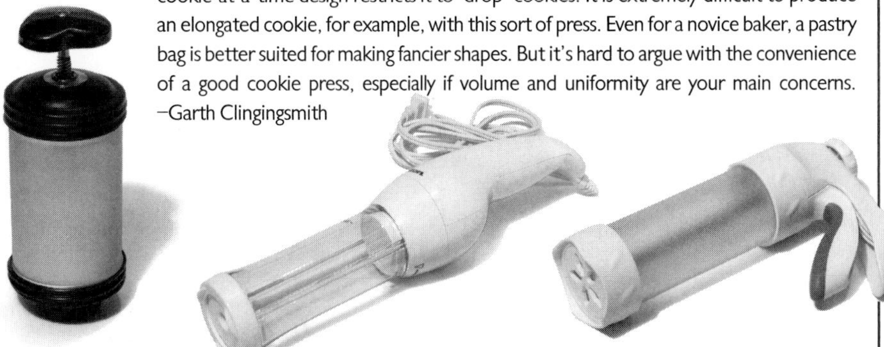

SLIP AND SLIDE
A screw-driven plunger was nearly impossible to use with buttery hands.

ELEC-TRICKY
This huge electric contraption was difficult to operate and a pain to clean.

TRIGGER HAPPY
A trigger mechanism yields perfectly uniform cookies in record time.

Chocolate Caramel Walnut Tart

This holiday tart is a winner, as long as the star ingredients sing in harmony, not discord.

≥ BY SEAN LAWLER ≤

Dark and complicated, the chocolate caramel walnut tart wants nothing to do with its good-natured neighbors on the holiday dessert tray. While the pies and cookies all sing sugar and spice, this decadent tart answers on the black keys: deep, dark chocolate, the sharp tang of caramel, and the bitter, earthy crunch of walnuts.

Considering the natural affinity of its main ingredients, a chocolate caramel walnut tart would seem a hard recipe to botch. Forced to share space in a slim tart shell, however, this tight trio doesn't always live in harmony. Some of the tart recipes I tested relegated the walnuts to a mere garnish and sprinkled them over chilled chocolate fillings with textures that ran the gamut from soft pudding to cold butter. Other recipes placed the nuts at the fore, but these were simply uptown knockoffs of pecan pie; any real walnut flavor was buried beneath a gooey flow of corn syrup–based filling, and the chocolate seemed an afterthought.

To make certain each element received the proper emphasis, I decided to take a layered approach to tart building. Starting with a prebaked shell, I wanted a layer of walnuts draped with soft caramel topped with a smooth layer of rich, dark chocolate—firm enough to slice neatly but neither dense nor overpowering. In short, I wanted a Snickers bar dressed up for the holidays.

A Tough Nut to Crack

The test kitchen had already developed a reliable recipe for pâte sucrée (sweet tart pastry), so my first test was to replace some of the flour in this recipe with ground nuts to boost flavor. Unfortunately, the nuts made the dough extremely fragile and nearly impossible to transfer to the tart pan. By reducing the amount of butter (to account for the lesser quantity of flour and the extra fat from the ground walnuts), I was able to produce a firmer, less crumbly crust, but this did nothing to improve the tart's scruffy appearance once baked. Part of the solution was to simply form-fit the dough into the tart pan by hand, reforming and reshaping the scraps as needed. So much for professional pastry techniques. But the finished baked tart still lacked

the sharp, elegant lines I was after. My first thought was to adjust the liquid ingredients—1 egg yolk and 1 tablespoon of cream—hoping that less fat might produce a more clearly defined baked crust. I used half an egg white (or 1 tablespoon) in place of the cream. Problem solved. Now I had a crisp crust with sharp, sturdy edges.

But I wondered what to do with the other half of the egg white. Then I thought of an old cookbook tip. When the next tart shell came out of the oven, I brushed it with the remaining egg white, which is supposed to act as a moisture barrier between filling and crust, keeping the crust crisp, especially if served the next day. It worked.

Build a Better Tart

My starting point for the caramel walnut filling was a caramel sauce developed for a previous issue of *Cook's*. I made minor adjustments in the quantity of heavy cream to produce a filling that was sliceable but still soft and slightly gooey.

The layer of chocolate ganache was not so simple. I tested various ratios of chocolate, cream, and butter, but tasters repeatedly noted that the chilled ganache was too dense and dominated the flavor of the walnuts and caramel. Efforts to lighten it by increasing the quantities of cream and butter resulted in a ganache that was too soft to slice. The

answer was to lighten the chocolate mixture with eggs and then bake it on top of the layer of caramel-walnut filling (instead of simply pouring ganache over the tart and chilling to firm its texture).

As far as baking the tart, a 300-degree oven was the winner, with a baking time of about 25 minutes. The key visual clue was to wait until the surface of the chocolate was set even if the contents below were a bit wobbly. The tart will continue to cook out of the oven. A long three-hour chill was necessary to firm up the caramel layer and prevent oozing during slicing.

The smooth chocolate surface of the baked tart needed a decorative garnish of walnuts. A sprinkle of plain toasted walnuts, whole or chopped, appeared lackluster. A better solution was to coat a handful of whole walnut halves with the caramel sauce, fishing them out with a slotted spoon before adding in the chopped nuts for the filling. Arranged neatly around the perimeter of the tart, they made for an easy and elegant final touch.

CHOCOLATE CARAMEL WALNUT TART

MAKES ONE 9-INCH TART, SERVING 12 TO 16

The nuts used in the crust, in the caramel filling, and as a garnish must all be toasted; the entire amount can be toasted together on a baking sheet in a 375-degree oven until fragrant and golden brown, 8 to 10 minutes. For cutting clean slices, dip the blade of the knife in warm water and wipe with a kitchen towel before making each cut.

Walnut Crust

- 1 large egg, separated
- ¼ teaspoon vanilla extract
- ½ cup toasted walnuts (2½ ounces), see note
- ½ cup (2 ounces) confectioners' sugar
- 1 cup (5 ounces) unbleached all-purpose flour
- ⅛ teaspoon table salt
- 5 tablespoons cold unsalted butter, cut into ½-inch cubes

Caramel-Walnut Filling and Garnish

- ¼ cup water
- 1 cup (7 ounces) granulated sugar
- ⅔ cup heavy cream
- 3 tablespoons unsalted butter, cut into 3 pieces
- ½ teaspoon vanilla extract
- ½ teaspoon juice from 1 lemon
- ⅛ teaspoon table salt
- 16–18 toasted walnut halves, plus 1 cup (5 ounces) toasted walnuts, coarsely chopped (see note)

Layers of caramel and chocolate custard are baked in a nut-flavored crust and topped with candied walnut halves.

Chocolate Filling

- 2 large egg yolks
- 1 tablespoon plus ⅓ cup heavy cream
- ⅓ cup whole milk
- 5 ounces semisweet chocolate, chopped fine
- 2 tablespoons unsalted butter, cut into 4 pieces

1. **FOR THE CRUST:** Beat egg white in bowl with fork until frothy; remove 1 tablespoon egg white to second bowl and whisk in yolk and vanilla. Process nuts and sugar in food processor until finely ground, 8 to 10 seconds. Add flour and salt and pulse to combine. Scatter butter pieces over flour mixture; pulse to cut butter into flour until mixture resembles coarse meal, about fifteen 1-second pulses. With machine running, add egg yolk mixture and process until dough forms ball, about 20 seconds. Transfer dough to large sheet plastic wrap and press into 6-inch disk; wrap dough in plastic and refrigerate until firm but malleable, about 30 minutes.

2. Roll out dough between 2 large sheets lightly floured plastic wrap to 13-inch round, about ⅛-inch thick (if at any point dough becomes too soft and sticky to work with, slip dough onto baking sheet and freeze or refrigerate until workable). Place dough round on baking sheet and freeze until stiff and cold, about 15 minutes (or refrigerate about 30 minutes). Meanwhile, evenly spray 9-inch tart pan with removable bottom with nonstick cooking spray.

3. Remove dough from freezer; discard top sheet plastic wrap but keep dough on baking sheet. Following illustrations above, line tart pan with dough. Freeze dough-lined tart pan until firm, about 30 minutes. (Can be wrapped tightly in plastic wrap and frozen up to 1 month.)

4. Meanwhile, adjust oven rack to middle position; heat oven to 375 degrees. Set dough-lined tart pan on baking sheet. Spray 12-inch square foil with nonstick cooking spray and press foil inside chilled tart shell; fill with pie weights. Bake until light golden brown, about 30 minutes, rotating halfway through baking time. Carefully remove foil and weights and continue to bake until golden brown, about 5 minutes longer. Cool on baking sheet on wire rack about 5 minutes, then brush hot crust with reserved egg white. Reduce oven temperature to 300 degrees.

STEP-BY-STEP | A NEW WAY TO HANDLE TART DOUGH

This novel method works with any tart, although it is especially helpful when working with a delicate dough.

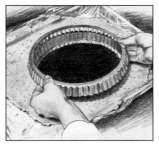

1. Invert tart pan (with bottom) on top of dough round. (Removable bottom will drop onto dough.) Press on tart pan to cut dough.

2. Pick up baking sheet, carefully invert it, and set tart pan down on counter right-side up. Remove baking sheet and peel off plastic wrap.

3. Roll over dough edges with rolling pin to cut. In a few minutes, the dough will slip into bottom of pan. Gently ease and press dough into pan.

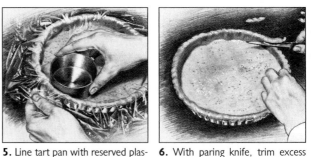

4. Roll dough scraps into ¾-inch rope (various lengths are OK). Line fluted edge of tart pan with rope(s) and gently press into fluted sides.

5. Line tart pan with reserved plastic wrap. Using measuring cup, gently press dough to even thickness. Sides should be ¼ inch thick.

6. With paring knife, trim excess dough above rim of tart pan; discard scraps.

5. **FOR CARAMEL-WALNUT FILLING AND GARNISH:** While crust is cooling, pour water into medium heavy-bottomed saucepan; add sugar to center of pot to keep granules from adhering to sides of pot. Bring to boil over medium-high heat, covered, swirling pan once or twice to dissolve sugar. Uncover pot and continue to boil, without stirring, until sugar is deep amber, begins to smoke, and registers about 375 degrees on instant-read or candy thermometer, 5 to 10 minutes. Remove pan from heat. Carefully add about half of cream; mixture will sputter and steam. Add remaining cream and let bubbling subside. Return pan to low heat and stir with heatproof rubber spatula until caramel is smooth. Add butter and stir until melted. Remove pan from heat; stir in vanilla, lemon juice, and salt.

6. Add walnut halves to caramel and stir to coat; let stand until caramel is slightly thickened, about 8 minutes. Using slotted spoon and allowing excess caramel to drain back into saucepan, transfer walnuts to wire rack set over baking sheet; set aside. Stir chopped walnuts into caramel, then pour mixture evenly into tart shell. Refrigerate, uncovered, on baking sheet until caramel is firm and does not slip when pan is tilted, about 20 minutes.

7. **FOR CHOCOLATE FILLING:** Whisk yolks and 1 tablespoon cream in small bowl. Bring milk and remaining ⅓ cup cream to simmer in small saucepan; off heat, add chocolate and butter. Cover pan and let stand until chocolate is mostly melted, about 2 minutes. Using spatula, stir mixture until smooth; stir in yolk mixture. (Chocolate should be thin and pourable; if too thick to pour evenly, set saucepan over low heat to warm mixture.) Pour filling into caramel-filled tart shell, tilting tart pan as necessary to evenly distribute chocolate to edges of tart. Bake on baking sheet in 300-degree oven until tiny bubbles are visible on surface and chocolate layer is just set (if pan is gently shaken, filling will appear very wobbly because caramel layer is warm), about 25 minutes. Set baking sheet with tart on wire rack; arrange caramel-coated walnut halves on surface of tart, around perimeter. Cool tart until just warm, about 30 minutes, then refrigerate, uncovered, until chocolate is firm, at least 3 hours or up to 24 hours.

RECIPE TESTING: Common Mishaps

TORN DOUGH
Do not attempt to transfer the dough to the tart pan all in one piece. The fragile pastry tears easily.

MISSHAPEN CRUST
Unless the tart shell is weighted down with pie weights as it bakes, the sides will slope inward and collapse.

LIQUID CENTER
If the finished tart is not chilled for at least three hours, the caramel filling will not set up properly.

Holiday Salads with Blue Cheese

Blue cheese makes an interesting dinner guest, inviting a wide range of other ingredients—sweet, tart, bitter, and crunchy—to the table.

⋛ BY REBECCA HAYS ⋜

Like a well-spoken dinner guest, blue cheese is intense, complex, and sophisticated. But pair the life of the party with a dull companion (tender lettuce leaves) and the dinner magic all but disappears.

The trick to including blue cheese in a salad, I found, is to have a free hand when introducing other flavors and textures; strong cheese really shines when tasted with sweet, tart, bitter, and crunchy ingredients. A good shot of vinegar gave necessary tartness to the dressing, and a spoonful of honey performed double duty, both tempering the acidity of the vinegar and highlighting the saltiness of the cheese. As for the greens, tasters particularly liked bitter radicchio and peppery arugula mixed with milder lettuces. Sweetness and holiday crimson tones come from dried fruit (cherries), fresh fruit (apple), or beets. Good tooth-sinking texture comes by way of crunchy chopped toasted nuts, fresh celery slices, or a flurry of fried shallots. With balanced, flavorful salad recipes at the ready, guess who's coming to dinner?

SALAD WITH FENNEL, DRIED CHERRIES, WALNUTS, AND ROQUEFORT
SERVES 6 AS A FIRST COURSE

We tried a half-dozen varieties of blue cheese and all were acceptable, but tasters favored rich, creamy Roquefort. If you prefer to use a very mild and mellow blue cheese, we recommend Danish blue; if you prefer a sharp and piquant one, try Stilton.

- 2 teaspoons honey
- 3 tablespoons red wine vinegar
- 1/2 cup dried sweetened cherries or cranberries
- 3 tablespoons extra-virgin olive oil
  Table salt and ground black pepper
- 1 small fennel bulb, trimmed of stalks and sliced very thin (about 1 1/2 cups), fronds chopped coarse (about 1/4 cup)
- 1 small head red or green leaf lettuce, washed, dried, and torn into bite-size pieces (7 cups)
- 1 small head radicchio, quartered, cored, and cut crosswise into 1/8-inch-wide strips (about 3 cups)
- 1/2 cup chopped walnuts, toasted in medium skillet over medium heat until fragrant, about 4 minutes
- 6 ounces Roquefort, crumbled (about 1 1/2 cups)

1. Whisk honey and vinegar in medium microwave-safe bowl; stir in cherries. Cover with plastic wrap, cut several steam vents in plastic, and microwave on high until cherries are plump, about 1 minute. Whisk in oil, 1/4 teaspoon salt, and 1/8 teaspoon pepper; while mixture is still warm, add sliced fennel bulb and toss to combine. Let cool to room temperature.

2. Toss lettuce, radicchio, fennel fronds, and dried cherry/fennel mixture in large bowl; adjust seasonings with salt and pepper. Divide salad among individual plates; top each with portion of nuts and Roquefort. Serve immediately.

SALAD WITH APPLE, CELERY, HAZELNUTS, AND ROQUEFORT
SERVES 6 AS A FIRST COURSE

Use a dishtowel to rub the skins from the hazelnuts while still hot. Blanched slivered almonds can be substituted for hazelnuts.

- 1 tablespoon honey
- 3 tablespoons cider vinegar
- 3 tablespoons extra-virgin olive oil
- 1/4 teaspoon table salt
- 1/8 teaspoon ground black pepper
- 1 sweet red apple, such as Braeburn or Fuji, cored and sliced very thin (about 2 cups)
- 2 celery ribs, sliced very thin on bias (about 1 1/4 cups)
- 1 medium head red or green leaf lettuce, washed, dried, and torn into bite-size pieces (about 9 cups)
- 1/4 cup loosely packed torn fresh parsley leaves
- 1/2 cup hazelnuts, toasted in medium skillet over medium heat until fragrant, about 4 minutes, then skinned and chopped fine
- 6 ounces Roquefort, crumbled (about 1 1/2 cups)

1. Whisk honey, vinegar, oil, salt, and pepper in small bowl until combined. In medium bowl, toss apple and celery with 2 tablespoons vinaigrette; let stand 5 minutes.

2. Toss lettuce, parsley, and remaining vinaigrette in large bowl; adjust seasonings with salt and pepper. Divide greens among individual plates; top each with portion of apple/celery mixture, nuts, and Roquefort. Serve immediately.

SALAD WITH ROASTED BEETS, FRIED SHALLOTS, AND ROQUEFORT
SERVES 6 AS A FIRST COURSE

Use paper towels to rub the skins from the cooked and cooled beets.

- 3 small or 2 medium beets (about 12 ounces), washed and trimmed of root tips and stems
- 3 medium shallots, sliced thin and separated into rings (about 1 cup)
  Table salt and ground black pepper
- 2 tablespoons all-purpose flour
- 6 tablespoons extra-virgin olive oil
- 2 tablespoons sherry vinegar
- 2 teaspoons honey
- 1 large bunch arugula, washed, dried, trimmed of stems, and torn into bite-size pieces (about 6 cups)
- 1 medium head butter lettuce, washed, dried, and torn into bite-size pieces (about 7 cups)
- 6 ounces Roquefort, crumbled (about 1 1/2 cups)

1. Adjust oven rack to lower-middle position; heat oven to 400 degrees. Wrap each beet in foil and bake until paring knife can be inserted and removed with little resistance, 50 to 60 minutes. Unwrap beets; when cool enough to handle, peel and cut beets into 1/4-inch-thick wedges and place in medium bowl.

2. While beets are roasting, toss shallots with 1/4 teaspoon salt, 1/8 teaspoon pepper, and flour in medium bowl. Heat 3 tablespoons oil in 12-inch nonstick skillet over medium-high heat until smoking; add shallots and cook, stirring frequently, until golden and crisped, about 5 minutes. Using slotted spoon, transfer shallots to plate lined with triple layer of paper towels.

3. Whisk remaining 3 tablespoons oil, vinegar, honey, 1/4 teaspoon salt, and 1/8 teaspoon pepper in small bowl until combined. Add 1 tablespoon vinaigrette to beets, season beets to taste with salt and pepper, and toss to combine.

4. Toss arugula, lettuce, and remaining vinaigrette in large bowl; adjust seasonings with salt and pepper. Divide greens among individual plates; top each with portion of beets, fried shallots, and Roquefort. Serve immediately.

COOK'S EXTRA gives you free recipes online. For Salad with Roquefort, Avocado, Tomatoes, and Bacon, go to www.cooksillustrated.com and key in code 6041. This recipe will be available until December 15, 2004.

The All-Purpose Food Processor

Some models cost almost $300, while others are sold for relatively small change. Do the big bucks guarantee a better machine? And what about all those attachments?

BY GALEN MOORE AND GARTH CLINGINGSMITH

It has been seven years since we last put food processors through their paces. Although the basic concept hasn't changed much (plastic bowl with whirring blade), almost all of the models we tested back in 1997 have. Our new lineup included five mid- to high-priced models ($140 up to $280), plus three models at $70 or less. The high-priced models come with various attachments that are supposed to turn the machine into everything from a juicer to a blender. Do the attachments justify the extra cost? Could the back-to-basics models handle most kitchen tasks with ease? Should any food processor cost almost $300? We went into the test kitchen to find out.

Cheaper Models Get a Workout

What should a food processor—at minimum—be able to do? For starters, it ought to chop, grate, and slice vegetables; grind dry ingredients; and cut fat into flour for pie pastry. If it can't whiz through these tasks, it's wasting counterspace. The cheaper models failed most of these basic tests.

Using the Black & Decker Power Pro 11 ($48), our testers had to forcefully ram carrots through a grater attachment so dull that the back of the slicer blade, on the reverse side of the disk, was as likely to catch the carrot as the grater. At least one-third of our carrots were torn into mangled slices by the dull back of the blade. Test cooks agreed: We couldn't use this machine for carrot cake or grated carrot salad.

Another bargain-basement food processor, the two-speed Hamilton Beach PrepStar ($35), runs quieter and is better designed than its predecessor, the 70650. It performed well on the grating test, producing clean shreds of carrot and cheddar that were almost indistinguishable from those produced by machines costing three to four times as much. Slices of potato, however, came out like wedges—paper-thin on one side, up to ⅛ inch thick on the other. The coarse action of the Hamilton Beach slicing blade tore pulp and seeds out of tomatoes, leaving just a thin ring of mangled flesh and skin.

The Oster Inspire ($70) was a tad better than the two other inexpensive models tested, but it still flubbed some basic food processor chores. For instance, this machine was unable to chop onions, carrots, or celery without brutalizing them.

Considering that these cheaper food processors had a hard time with basic tasks, we had little hope that they could manage more challenging jobs, such as kneading bread dough or pureeing soup. Sure enough, the cheaper models lived down to their reputation when it came to making pizza dough. We turned off the Hamilton Beach processor after 51 seconds, when flour and water were barely incorporated, as other cooks in the test kitchen looked up with alarm at the smell of acrid smoke and the horrendous sound of the straining motor. The Oster and the Black & Decker got the job done, but their motors, too, began to grind down as the dough came together, smelling of smoking grease and what we could only guess was melting plastic. After 90 to 100 seconds in these processors, the doughs that emerged were adequate, but we wondered how many crusty pizzas we could enjoy before we'd have to buy a new machine. As for pureeing soup, all three bargain machines leaked soup from the bottom of the bowl. (The puree itself turned out OK.)

In the end, then, we cannot recommend any of the three cheaper food processors we tested. It was time to open our wallet and check out the more expensive machines.

Spending More Money

The two stars of the food processor world have always been the KitchenAid (we tested the Professional 670, $280) and the Cuisinart (we tested the relatively new Prep 11 Plus, $200, as well as the original Pro Custom 11, $160). We also checked out the Bosch 5000 ($139) and the Bosch 5200 ($200).

The two Bosch machines made an interesting pair in the testing, as the less expensive machine sometimes stood up to its brawnier cousin. When it came to chopping vegetables, the cheaper Bosch 5000 did a better job. Both models have the same bowl size and blade design, but the 4-speed motor in the 5200 didn't seem to cut the vegetables at all; it just kind of flogged them around the bowl. The 5000's simpler 2-speed motor was more effective. However, when it came to pureeing soups, both models were standouts. The rounded bowl and cone-shaped blade attachment enabled both models to puree 5 cups of mock soup perfectly, without leaking a drop. Cup measurements on the side of the workbowl perplexed us, however. According

---

TESTING NOTES: **Parsley and Pie Dough**

PERFECT PARSLEY

UNUSABLE MUSH

PERFECT PIE DOUGH   **DECENT PIE DOUGH**

With its mini-bowl filled to the brim, the KitchenAid produced chopped parsley that was dry and largely unbruised (left). In contrast, with more room to bat around the same 2 cups of parsley, the regular bowl on the KitchenAid turned out useless green mush (right). Parsley received much the same rough treatment in the regular-size bowls of the other food processors tested.

Both Cuisinart models produced dough with an even consistency of coarse sand and pea-sized lumps of butter, without clumps (left). In contrast, the Bosch 5000 yielded a dough that clumped in places and smeared on the blade (right). Because the blade on this machine (and the rest of the models tested) did not stop on a dime, it was easy to overprocess the fat and flour.

25

RATING FOOD PROCESSORS

TOP CHOICE   BEST VALUE

KITCHENAID   CUISINART PRO

CUISINART PREP

BOSCH 5000

OSTER

BOSCH 5200   BLACK & DECKER   HAMILTON BEACH

Each of eight food processors was put through a total of 11 tests to evaluate its performance at various food processor tasks. Special attachments were evaluated separately (see page 27 for details). The food processors are listed in order of preference based on their overall scores in the following tests.

PRICE: Prices paid in Boston-area stores, national mail-order catalogs, and on Web sites.

BOWL CAPACITY/BASE WEIGHT: We chose models with a capacity of 11 cups, or as close as possible. If a manufacturer did not make an 11-cup model, we tested its largest food processor. Base weights (as measured in the test kitchen) ranged from just under 5 pounds to more than 12 pounds. We found a correlation between heavier bases and superior performance.

GRATING/SLICING: We grated cheddar cheese and carrots and sliced plum tomatoes and potatoes. We looked for dry, consistent shreds and clean, even slices.

CHOPPING: We chopped parsley as well as a mixture of celery, carrots, and onions. We looked for a dry, even mixture of same-sized pieces. With the exception of the KitchenAid (which comes with a mini-bowl insert), all models fared poorly on the parsley test.

GRINDING: We processed whole walnuts to the texture of coarse cornmeal and a loaf of stale bread to bread crumbs. Minimal processing should produce dry ground nuts and even bread crumbs.

PASTRY DOUGH: We pulsed together vegetable shortening, butter, and dry ingredients, looking for coarse, yellow crumbs and pea-sized chunks of butter after about ten 1-second pulses.

BREAD DOUGH: We doubled our recipe for pissaladière dough (see March/April 2004 issue) for a load with 4 cups of flour. We looked for a smooth, satiny dough in less than 90 seconds.

SOUP PUREE: We tested how much liquid the workbowl could handle, then pureed a mock-soup mixture of water and steamed broccoli. We checked for leaks and passed the resulting puree through a coarse sieve, looking for unprocessed chunks. Any leaks or large chunks resulted in a poor rating.

TESTERS' COMMENTS: Observations about design or performance in specific tests.

RATINGS
GOOD: ★★★
FAIR: ★★
POOR: ★

RECOMMENDED

		TESTERS' COMMENTS
KitchenAid Professional 670, KFP670WH PRICE: $279.99 BOWL CAPACITY: 11 cups BASE WEIGHT: 12 lb 1 oz	GRATING/SLICING: ★★★ CHOPPING: ★★★ GRINDING: ★★★ PASTRY DOUGH: ★★★ BREAD DOUGH: ★★ SOUP PUREE: ★★	The prep whiz: chopped and sliced as cleanly and evenly as a carefully wielded knife—and a lot faster. Comes with a mini-bowl attachment that makes quick work of parsley; bigger bowls in other models beat parsley into a sorry, bruised state. Leaked slightly during the puree test.
Cuisinart Pro Custom 11, DLC-8S PRICE: $159.99 BOWL CAPACITY: 11 cups BASE WEIGHT: 10 lb 9 oz	GRATING/SLICING: ★★★ CHOPPING: ★★ GRINDING: ★★★ PASTRY DOUGH: ★★★ BREAD DOUGH: ★★★ SOUP PUREE: ★★	The original Cuisinart has changed little since its 1973 debut, but it handled every test (except bread dough) just as well as the newer, more expensive Cuisinart. In fact, it was better than the newer Cuisinart at grating and slicing and making pie dough. The feed tube design is "a pain."
Cuisinart Prep 11 Plus, DLC-2011 PRICE: $199.99 BOWL CAPACITY: 11 cups BASE WEIGHT: 11 lb 3 oz	GRATING/SLICING: ★★ CHOPPING: ★★ GRINDING: ★★★ PASTRY DOUGH: ★★★ BREAD DOUGH: ★★★ SOUP PUREE: ★★	This redesigned Cuisinart has some nice new features. The ultimate machine for bread: Under a heavy load of dough, it purred like a Mercedes. Fruit and vegetable processing was less than perfect, however. Testers weren't wild about the feed tube design on either this or the Pro Custom model, although they are the widest on the market.

RECOMMENDED WITH RESERVATIONS

Bosch 5000, MCM 5000 UC PRICE: $139 BOWL CAPACITY: 12 cups BASE WEIGHT: 6 lb 2 oz	GRATING/SLICING: ★★ CHOPPING: ★★ GRINDING: ★★ PASTRY DOUGH: ★★ BREAD DOUGH: ★★ SOUP PUREE: ★★★	Didn't perform any task exceptionally well, but didn't fail miserably at any task, either. If you can live with less-than-perfect but still passable potato slices and pastry doughs, you might buy this model and save a few dollars. Inexplicably, this model struggled on the easiest test—grinding bread crumbs.

NOT RECOMMENDED

Oster Inspire 3200 PRICE: $69.99 BOWL CAPACITY: 10 cups BASE WEIGHT: 10 lb 15 oz	GRATING/SLICING: ★★ CHOPPING: ★ GRINDING: ★★★ PASTRY DOUGH: ★★ BREAD DOUGH: ★★ SOUP PUREE: ★★	This unit almost got a passing grade—until it brutalized the carrots, celery, and onions in the chopping test. If you want a food processor and absolutely can't afford anything more expensive, this one is the best of the really cheap choices. Just use a knife to chop veggies.
Bosch 5200, MCM 5200 UC PRICE: $199.99 BOWL CAPACITY: 12 cups BASE WEIGHT: 6 lb 5 oz	GRATING/SLICING: ★ CHOPPING: ★ GRINDING: ★★★ PASTRY DOUGH: ★★ BREAD DOUGH: ★★ SOUP PUREE: ★★★	Surprisingly bad performance during chopping, slicing, and grating tests, but several of its extra attachments—blender, whip, and juicer—proved useful. Nice extras, but designers seem to have forgotten about core functions.
Black & Decker Power Pro 11, FP 1500 PRICE: $47.99 BOWL CAPACITY: 10 cups BASE WEIGHT: 4 lb 15 oz	GRATING/SLICING: ★ CHOPPING: ★ GRINDING: ★★★ PASTRY DOUGH: ★★ BREAD DOUGH: ★ SOUP PUREE: ★	Although it mimics the look and feel of a high-end food processor, even simple tasks proved too much for the Black & Decker, and forget about more difficult tasks such as making bread dough or pureeing soup.
Hamilton Beach PrepStar, 70550R PRICE: $35 BOWL CAPACITY: 8 cups BASE WEIGHT: 5 lb 2 oz	GRATING/SLICING: ★ CHOPPING: ★★ GRINDING: ★★★ PASTRY DOUGH: ★★ BREAD DOUGH: ★ SOUP PUREE: ★	Fine if you use a food processor once a year, at Thanksgiving, to grind bread crumbs for stuffing. Otherwise, mediocre-to-poor performance on every other test. You don't get what you don't pay for.

to these markings, a 5-cup measure of liquid would be equivalent to 2 pints. In terms of other tasks, neither Bosch machine was great at making pizza dough or pie pastry.

One selling point of the 5200 is the attachments it comes with, several of which received high marks (see "Attachment Disorder," at right). We concluded that the 5200's failure with vegetables could not be overlooked, despite its top-notch pureeing performance and its array of useful accessories. As one tester put it, "If the machine can't slice potatoes, who cares if the juicer works?" The 5000 received a higher score because it is cheaper and because it's able to handle vegetables—a core activity—handily.

The Big Guns

It was now time to move on to the big guns: KitchenAid and Cuisinart. After even a cursory examination, it was clear that more money does buy a better, more heavy-duty processor. The KitchenAid and Cuisinart blades are among the sturdiest and appear to be the sharpest. Their motors had more weight, ran quieter, and did not slow down under a heavy load of bread dough.

Speaking of dough, the dough-mixing features included with the newer Cuisinart Prep 11—a special blade and a separate speed for dough—proved well conceived. At the dough-mixing speed, the motor purred; it was quiet enough to allow for normal conversation. The original Cuisinart model, the Pro Custom 11, produced a result of equal quality but took a little longer to get there. (As with the KitchenAid and Bosch processors, this task put an audible strain on the motor.)

The Pro Custom 11, however, did the best job with pie pastry, as the blade stops spinning almost immediately once the pulse button is released. Other blades took a second or two to spin down. Because it usually takes about 10 pulses to cut fat into flour, a 2-second spin-down after each pulse can make a significant difference in the finished texture of the dough (see testing notes box on page 25). Other machines, especially the Cuisinart Prep 11 and KitchenAid, did a good job with pastry, but the Pro Custom 11 yielded perfect pie dough.

When it came to pureeing soups, neither the KitchenAid nor the two Cuisinart models could compare with the Bosch food processors, which handled twice as much liquid and did not leak. The KitchenAid leaked slightly under the blade and has a small bowl capacity. The two Cuisinarts didn't leak, but they produced imperfect purees and their bowl capacities are even smaller.

What, then, should you buy? If you are partial to Cuisinart, it turns out that the classic (and somewhat cheaper) model, the Pro Custom 11, is a better value, clearly outperforming the newer Prep 11 Plus in the vegetable tests and slightly outperforming its successor in the pie pastry test. Bread bakers, however, might want to go with the newer, more expensive model, which mixes bread dough superbly. And what about the KitchenAid, priced an eye-popping $280, a full 40 percent more than the top-of-the-line Cuisinart? First off, it is the hands-down winner with vegetable preparation; the Cuisinarts really don't measure up in this regard. But the KitchenAid was only second-best compared with the two Cuisinarts when making dough.

And what, then, have we learned since our last rating of food processors? Seven years and about a thousand dollars later, we have concluded that KitchenAid and Cuisinart are still the machines to beat. If vegetable prep is important to you, buy the KitchenAid. If you don't care too much about vegetable prep, the Cuisinarts perform all other tasks as well as (or better than) their pricier competition.

Attachment Disorder

Many food processors come with attachments. As you might expect, some are completely useless, while others are surprisingly well designed. The Bosch 5200 garnered top honors for attachments that we would really want to own. (It wasn't very good at some basic tasks, though.) Here's a rundown on the attachments we tested. All attachments were included with the food processors.

JUICER & JUICE EXTRACTOR

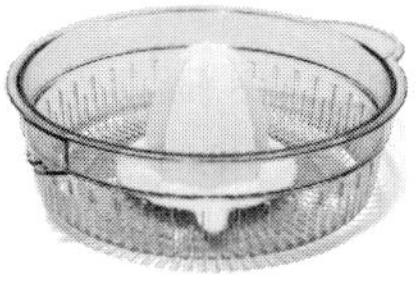

FOOD PROCESSOR: Bosch 5200

PURPOSE: Juice all kinds of fruits and vegetables.

TESTERS' COMMENTS: Juiced carrots with ease, but apple peels caused some hesitation. The citrus juicer was thorough and worked with both large and small fruits.

CITRUS JUICER

FOOD PROCESSOR: KitchenAid

PURPOSE: Juice oranges and grapefruits.

TESTERS' COMMENTS: Produced pulpy "home-style" orange juice but was too wide to handle lemons or limes.

WHIP

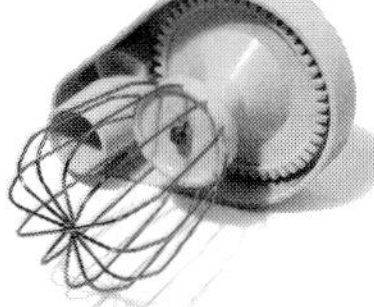

FOOD PROCESSOR: Bosch 5200

PURPOSE: Beat cream, egg whites, or batters.

TESTERS' COMMENTS: Whipped cream to stiff peaks just as fast as a good hand mixer.

COMPACT COVER

FOOD PROCESSOR: Cuisinart Pro Custom 11

PURPOSE: This separate lid without a standard feed tube or pusher is designed for use when kneading, chopping, mixing, or pureeing.

TESTERS' COMMENTS: Much easier to clean than wide feed tube.

BLENDER

FOOD PROCESSOR: Bosch 5200

PURPOSE: Make smoothies and pureed soups.

TESTERS' COMMENTS: Handled smoothies and soup capably.

BREAD DOUGH BLADE & BREAD SPEED SETTING

FOOD PROCESSOR: Cuisinart Prep 11 Plus

PURPOSE: Modulates speed according to the dough consistency when kneading.

TESTERS' COMMENTS: Produced satiny dough, perfectly free of lumps, in less than 60 seconds without any audible strain on motor.

DOUGH HOOK

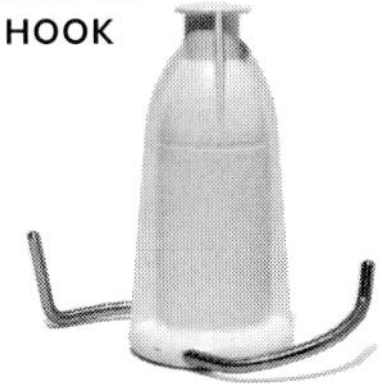

FOOD PROCESSOR: Bosch (both models)

PURPOSE: Special blade attachment with raised ends designed for kneading dough.

TESTERS' COMMENTS: Fine performance but no better than the regular blade that comes with these machines.

FOOD FINGERS

FOOD PROCESSOR: Black & Decker

PURPOSE: Metal claw that clips into feed tube is designed to hold a single vegetable, such as a carrot, for slicing or grating.

TESTERS' COMMENTS: Bizarre and useless.

MINI-BOWL & CHEF'S BOWL

FOOD PROCESSOR: KitchenAid

PURPOSE: The mini-bowl (seen here) is designed to handle small jobs; the chef's bowl fits inside the regular workbowl.

TESTERS' COMMENTS: The mini-bowl proved essential when chopping herbs; the chef's bowl lets the cook handle two jobs without any dishwashing in between.

CONTINUOUS FEED CHUTE

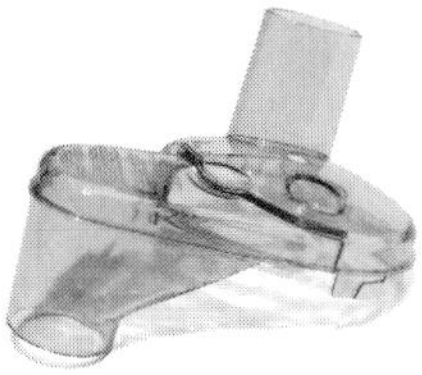

FOOD PROCESSOR: Hamilton Beach

PURPOSE: Supposed to propel sliced or shredded ingredients out of the workbowl. Think Salad Shooter.

TESTERS' COMMENTS: Useless. Chute mutilated potato slices and got jammed full of grated cheese.

The Fat Wars

The American food industry is not content with simply selling a natural, high-quality food product—butter. It wants us to buy 'healthier' and 'premium' alternatives, too.

BY JACK BISHOP AND GARTH CLINGINGSMITH

The American food industry loves to replace delicious, natural products (take butter, for example) with substitutes made from cheap ingredients that require processing (margarine) in an effort to increase profit margins and market share. These new products are often sold under the dubious guise of claims that they are "healthy"—low fat, low sugar, low carb—and the strategy has proven enormously successful. In 1909, butter outsold margarine by a factor of 15 to 1; by 1993, margarine was outselling butter by nearly 3 to 1. Here in the test kitchen, we are usually immune to the charms of "new" and "improved" products, but two recent developments have given us pause to reconsider. First, premium butters (with higher percentages of milk fat) are now widely available in supermarkets. Second, the margarine industry has lately introduced "healthier" spreads that do not contain trans fats, ostensibly making them a more attractive alternative to butter. We purchased 11 premium butters and six new butter substitutes and headed to the test kitchen. Here is what we learned.

Margarine Gets a Makeover

Margarine has long been touted as a healthier alternative to butter, which has two to three times as much saturated fat. Until recently, that pitch has been working. But margarine has had a rough time of late. During the 1990s, more and more health experts started to sound the alarm about margarine, especially the solid versions sold in sticks. Margarine is vegetable oil that has been turned into a solid by means of a process called partial hydrogenation, the same process used to make vegetable shortenings such as Crisco. While margarine contains less artery-clogging saturated fat than butter, it also contains much more trans fat, which is a product of partial hydrogenation. Researchers have warned that trans fats may be more dangerous than saturated fat. (Saturated fat is thought to raise total cholesterol, both the "good" kind, known as HDL, and the "bad" kind, known as LDL, but trans fats are thought to raise bad cholesterol while lowering good cholesterol—a nutritional double whammy.) In general, the more solid the margarine, the more trans fats it contains.

During the past decade, per capita consumption of margarine has declined by about 25 percent. In contrast, butter consumption has climbed more than 10 percent since 1997. As might be expected, the margarine industry is fighting back. It has responded with a new generation of spreads—sold in tubs rather than sticks—that don't contain trans fats. (A product qualifies as "margarine" if it is 80 percent fat, like most butters; it's considered a "spread" if it's less than 80 percent fat.) Some spreads even contain additives that are supposed to reduce cholesterol. Because these butter substitutes contain little or no hydrogenated oil, however, gums, emulsifiers, and/or tropical oils (which are naturally solid at room temperature) must be used to make them solid. These products (we tested five of them) are designed for more than just spreading on toast; most manufacturers claim that they can also be used in baking and cooking.

In our tasting, we also included Land O' Lakes Soft Baking Butter with Canola Oil. Although not really a butter substitute, this product doesn't qualify as a true butter, either. The pitch is pretty simple. Any avid baker knows that successful cakes and cookies often start with butter brought to room temperature. Soft Baking Butter is designed for cooks who would rather not wait an hour. We also wanted to see how these new products stacked up against real butter, so we threw two of them into the test: Land O' Lakes regular unsalted butter and Land O' Lakes Ultra Creamy, the company's entry into the boutique butter business.

The first taste test was simple enough: We spread each product on toast. The butter substitutes were clear losers. Several spreads tasted like fake movie-theater popcorn butter, and one reminded us of fish. When choosing a spread for toast, we'll stick with the real thing. Next, we melted the products over green beans and used them to sauté chicken cutlets. To our surprise, Land O' Lakes Soft Baking Butter actually bested the two real butters in both applications. We surmise that the small percentage of canola oil in the baking butter makes it melt better and protects against burning when used for cooking on the stovetop. Two of the butter substitutes, Olivio and Smart Balance, also received decent scores in these tests.

In the shortbread test, our panel had no trouble picking out the two real butters. Tasters thought that the Soft Baking Butter made mediocre shortbread, and the other butter substitutes fared much,

---

Rating Butter Alternatives

Sixteen tasters sampled six butter substitutes in four tests: straight from the package, melted over green beans, sautée with chicken cutlets, and baked into shortbread. We included regular unsalted Land O' Lakes and unsalted Land O' Lake Ultra Creamy (our favorite high-fat butter) in all four tests. The real butters were the overall winners. The butter substi tutes are listed in order of preference based on their overall scores.

RECOMMENDED

➤ **LAND O' LAKES Soft Baking Butter with Canola Oil, $4.69 for 16 ounces** Straight from the package, this "presoftened" butter was "salty," "greasy," and "bland." Despite its labeling as a "baking butter," it showed more promise in savory dishes, besting regular butters in the green bean and chicken tests.

RECOMMENDED WITH RESERVATIONS

➤ **LEE IACOCCA'S OLIVIO, $1.69 for 15 ounces** This spread contains olive oil and is endorsed by Lee Iacocca of Chrysler fame. It rivaled butter in the green bean and chicken tests but elicited comments such as "fishy," "oily," and "rancid" when tasted plain.

➤ **SMART BALANCE Buttery Spread, $2.29 for 16 ounces** This spread performed well in the chicken sauté, where it promoted decent browning. But in the plain tasting, panelists complained loudly about its "fake" fruity and vegetable notes and "slippery texture."

NOT RECOMMENDED

➤ **BENECOL Spread, $4.99 for 8 ounces** According to the label, this spread with plant stanol esters is "proven to significantly reduce cholesterol." But, as one taster said, it tastes "like solidified fryer oil."

➤ **SOY GARDEN Spread, $2.19 for 16 ounces** This spread reminded tasters of "rancid mayonnaise." Terrible plain and in shortbread, but less offensive in the green bean and chicken tests.

➤ **SPECTRUM Naturals Spread, $2.19 for 10 ounces** This canola oil spread refused to melt over beans and made awful shortbread. Tastes like "Jell-O married with fake movie popcorn butter."

COOK'S ILLUSTRATED

28

TASTING PREMIUM BUTTERS

Twenty tasters sampled six salted butters and seven unsalted butters in separate tastings. The butters were allowed to come to room temperature, and tasters were encouraged to sample the butters plain in order to experience their melting properties directly on the tongue. Tasters also spread the butters on baguette slices. One brand was offered twice in each tasting, as a control to confirm the validity of the tests. **The butters are listed in order of preference, but all brands are recommended.**

SALTED BUTTERS

RECOMMENDED

LAND O' LAKES Ultra Creamy Salted Butter
➤ **$2.89 for 8 ounces**

This high-fat butter was lighter tasting than some of the other samples but very pleasantly creamy and smooth. A few tasters picked up a "hint of fruitiness," and it had a good salt punch.

LAND O' LAKES Regular Salted Butter
➤ **$3.69 for 16 ounces**

This "regular" butter was liked for its clean, rich flavor and creamy mouthfeel. Most tasters considered it "a little light on flavor" but smooth and pleasant. The salt was pronounced.

LURPAK Slightly Salted Danish Butter
➤ **$3.99 for 8 ounces**

This Danish butter carried a "subtle, delicate nut flavor" and "slight tang." As one taster noted, the "flavor is sweet and complex, but it doesn't have the staying power of some others."

LE GALL BEURRE DE BARATTE DE BRETAGNE Butter with Fleur de Sel
➤ **$6.99 for 8.82 ounces**

Dense in texture, with unexpected nuggets of sea salt, this French butter had "pretty big flavor" and noticeable tang, but it was "intensely salty."

VERMONT BUTTER & CHEESE COMPANY Salted Cultured Butter
➤ **$3.29 for 8 ounces**

Most tasters welcomed the "nice tangy finish" of this cultured butter. "I'd spend money on this," wrote one fan. Another considered it "so buttery it almost tastes artificial."

KERRYGOLD Pure Irish Butter
➤ **$2.59 for 8 ounces**

This vivid yellow Irish butter was described as "very rich" and "savory." More than one taster picked up a "grassy" essence, while a couple thought it tasted somewhat musty.

UNSALTED BUTTERS

RECOMMENDED

LAND O' LAKES Ultra Creamy Butter
➤ **$2.89 for 8 ounces**

This butter was "rich," "lush," and "tangy," with a creamy mouthfeel. More than one taster picked up on subtle lemony notes. It has a fuller flavor than its salted counterpart.

PRÉSIDENT Unsalted Butter
➤ **$2.99 for 7 ounces**

This French butter was "very rich but not terribly complex." Or, as one taster noted, "It's not like 'wow' in the mouth." Still it received reputable scores, being well liked for its clean flavor.

CELLES SUR BELLE Premium Churn Unsalted Butter
➤ **$5.29 for 8.82 ounces**

This French butter was extremely neutral in flavor, with little richness but an overall pleasant, clean taste.

LAND O' LAKES Unsalted Sweet Butter
➤ **$3.69 for 16 ounces**

This supermarket standard was "bland upfront, with a slight, creamy finish." It melted too quickly for some tasters.

ORGANIC VALLEY European Style Cultured Butter
➤ **$2.99 for 8 ounces**

As one taster noted, the tangy flavor of this cultured American butter "takes getting used to . . . good, just different." This butter had a slightly grassy flavor and was one of the creamiest.

PLUGRÁ European Style Unsalted Butter
➤ **$4.99 for 8 ounces**

An American brand popular with chefs, Plugrá was considered "best in show" by a few tasters but less creamy by others.

JANA VALLEY Imported Sweet Cream Butter
➤ **$1.99 for 8.825 ounces**

This reasonably priced Czech butter was more milky than creamy, which made it seem a little lean.

---

much worse. In this test, real butter was a slam-dunk. Our results were decisive: The margarine industry just can't compete with natural, unprocessed, no-additives butter in terms of flavor. It's not nice to fool Mother Nature.

A Premium for Butter?

All right, but what about the "premium" butters? The principal differences between "regular" butter and "premium" butter are fat content and price. According to U.S. Department of Agriculture standards, all butter must consist of at least 80 percent milk fat. (The rest is mostly water, with some milk solids, too.) Because fat costs money, regular butters rarely contain more than 80 percent. Premium butters have a milk fat content of 82 to 88 percent, which is typical of European butters. They are often called "European-style."

Traditionally, butter was made from cream that had been allowed to sit for a few days and sour slightly before it was churned, giving the butter a subtly tangy and slightly acidic character. Some present-day butter makers attempt to reproduce this flavor by adding a bacterial culture to the cream before agitating it into butter. We included two of these "cultured" butters in our lineup, in addition to nine high-fat butters that were not cultured. As a benchmark, we included regular Land O' Lakes butter. We divided these butters into two categories: salted and unsalted. In a preliminary tasting, we discovered that the differences between various premium butters were subtle and nearly disappeared once you started to bake or cook with them. As a result, we only tasted premium butters straight from the package.

Among the salted butters, Land O' Lakes Ultra Creamy was the winner, followed by regular Land O' Lakes butter, which easily held its own against butters costing twice as much. As for the unsalted butters, Land O' Lakes Ultra Creamy was again the winner, although two French butters were close runners-up. This time the regular Land O' Lakes butter finished in the middle of the pack. So, yes, the Land O' Lakes Ultra Creamy butter is a winner (especially for spreading on toast, where its rich flavor can be appreciated), but you can save money and be quite happy with the company's regular, cheaper product as well.

KITCHEN NOTES

⋛ BY DAWN YANAGIHARA ⋜

How to Slice It: Onions

A couple of years back, in reference to our Caramelized Onions recipe (January/February 2002), we said it made no difference whether the onions were sliced against or with the grain. We still agree with that assertion; caramelized onions form a sticky, cohesive mass, so appearance and texture aren't issues. But the question of how to slice onions for a braise, such as our Carbonnade (page 7), in which the onions are in liquid, generated some debate in the test kitchen. While some argued that it doesn't matter how they're sliced, others insisted that slicing with the grain (pole to pole, that is) is preferable.

A couple of carbonnades later, we can tell you that the way in which the onions are sliced makes no difference in flavor, but it does affect appearance. Sliced against the grain, the onions were mousy and lifeless and seemed to have disintegrated a fair amount with cooking. They also looked, according to one critic, "wormy," meaning that the slices looked as if they consisted of small connected segments. Sliced with the grain, the onions had more presence and became a more significant component of the braise. They also seemed to retain some shape and texture (however soft) and were more pleasing to the eye.

To slice an onion with the grain, trim off both ends, then halve the onion pole to pole. Remove and discard the skins, set one half on its flat side, and slice it pole to pole.

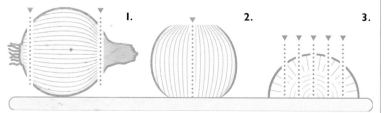

I. Trim off both ends of onion. **2.** Turn onion onto cut end and slice in half, pole to pole. **3.** Peel each half, place cut-side down, and slice with the grain (pole to pole).

Hard-Headed

The heads of garlic now available in grocery stores are a far cry from the plump, lusty knobs that were available in the summer. Indeed, by this time of year, the domestic garlic season has passed, and we find that when shopping, some attention is required to avoid purchasing garlic that is spoiled or desiccated. The test kitchen's advice: Go for the loose garlic, not the heads sold packaged in little cellophane-wrapped boxes that don't allow for close inspection. Look for heads with no spots of mold or signs of sprouting. Take a whiff. It should not smell unusually fragrant or fermented—signs of spoilage, to be sure. Finally, squeeze the head in your hand. If you feel hollow skins where cloves used to reside or if the head feels at all spongy or rubbery, pass it up—it should feel firm and solid.

Refresher Course

If your bunch of parsley or cilantro is looking a little weary, there's an easy way to refresh it (and, in the process, wash it). Lop off the stems, submerge the leaves in a bowl of ice water, then swish them around to loosen any dirt and grit. Let them stand for 5 to 10 minutes, until they perk up and regain their lost vitality. To drain, instead of pouring the whole lot into a colander or salad spinner basket, which will upset the grit settled in the bottom of the bowl, lift the greens out of the water using your hands, leaving the dirt behind. Note: If your parsley or cilantro is utterly limp and lifeless, it is probably beyond resurrection.

Carbonnade Alternative

For our Carbonnade recipe, we like the flavor and particularly the texture of top blade steaks; with braising they become meltingly tender. These steaks are cut from a larger piece of meat called the boneless top blade roast. If you procure this roast—instead of the steaks—don't begin cutting it into 1-inch pieces in a haphazard manner. We found that the simplest way to prepare it for this stew is to first trim it of exterior fat. Next, because a sheet of gristle spans the entire length of the roast and is difficult to remove as a single unit, cut the roast crosswise into 1-inch-thick steaks, then trim the steaks of gristle, as shown in the illustrations on page 7.

TOP BLADE ROAST
Another good option for stews.

Bagging It

To make our Spritz Cookies (page 21), you can use a cookie press made expressly for cookie making, or you can use a pastry bag that costs a fraction of the price and has numerous uses in the kitchen. If you go the way of the bag, allow us to make a couple of recommendations before you make a purchase.

Some pastry bags are very thick and heavy; we prefer thin, supple

---

KITCHEN SCIENCE: **Dishwasher Dilemma**

In our September/October 2004 issue, we looked at the effectiveness of a soap and hot water scrub in removing bacteria from a cutting board. Because a large number of households rely on the dishwasher to clean and sanitize kitchen equipment and tableware, we thought an investigation of this appliance was in order.

There are several standards for assessing dishwasher performance. We used the guideline (American National Standard 184) for residential dishwashers published by NSF International, a standards development organization. The guideline uses a sliding standard in which the surface temperature of items in the dishwasher must be held longer if the temperature is lower. For example, a surface temperature of 160 degrees must be held for 39 seconds, while a temperature of 143 degrees needs to be held for an hour to ensure effective sanitation.

The Tape Test With these criteria in mind, I sent 12 co-workers home with two types of thermal tape, one that could register 140 degrees and the other 160 degrees. (The tapes change color if they reach the specified temperature.) I asked everyone to affix the thermal tape to a plate and an additional item. The results were surprising. We had two dishwashers that did not reach 140 degrees and clearly failed this safety test. Five dishwashers were almost-certain passes (the temperature exceeded 160 degrees, and we assume that they maintained this temperature for at least 39 seconds). We also had five possible passes (the highest temperature was between 140 and 160 degrees, but we were unable to gauge the time spent at 143 degrees or higher).

Conclusions We did find a trend in our study. Older dishwashers did not perform as well as newer washers. The two dishwashers that failed the test were eight and 12 years old, while the top performers were less than three years old (there was one exception, but it was a high-end brand). Fortunately, every dishwasher has several advantages over a simple soap and hot water scrub in the sink, and heat is only one of them. Most dishwasher detergents contain sanitizing agents, and the action of water jets does a lot to remove unwanted material. That said, our tests suggest that a newer dishwasher is more likely than an older model to reach a higher temperature and to provide a greater margin of safety.
–John Olson, Science Editor

SHOPPING: Crème de la Crème

When a *Cook's* recipe calls for cream, it's almost always for heavy cream. But when shopping for heavy cream, the temptation always exists to pick up a carton of whipping cream instead. A pint of it costs about 30 cents less than a pint of heavy cream, and they're pretty much the same thing—or are they?

As it turns out, the two creams differ in fat content. Heavy cream must contain at least 36 percent milk fat, whipping cream at least 30 percent. To find out what effect this difference in fat has on a recipe, we made two caramel sauces. The one made with whipping cream had a noticeably thinner texture and leaner flavor than the one made with heavy cream. The results were the same for chocolate sauces.

The Fat Matters Past tests support these findings. In Crème Brûlée (November/December 2001), custards made with whipping cream lacked the velvety, lush texture of those made with heavy cream. Even when it was whipped into whipped cream, we preferred the flavor, texture, and staying power of heavy cream (see Notes from Readers, May/June 2002).

All told, then, substituting whipping cream for heavy cream will probably not yield calamitous results (this is especially true in recipes like the one for our Spritz Cookies, where only a tablespoon is required), but the best results will be had by using heavy cream whenever it's called for.

---

ones that have less bulk when gathered and twisted (as they are when you use them). We found a diswasher safe bag that we liked from Wilton (www.wilton.com; item #404-5168). The 16-inch Featherweight Decorating Bag is available for $7.59.

Disposable pastry bags are also an option. Because they're sold several to a package, they are particularly useful if you want to pipe numerous shapes or designs without first having to empty the bag in order to change tips. These are available from Cooking.com. A 10-pack of 12-inch bags made by Ateco costs $2.95 (item #148371). Prices do not include shipping.

With a Grain of Salt
Kosher salt, with its coarse grain, is superb for seasoning foods because it's easy to sprinkle it evenly with your fingers. Our experience has shown that in baking, however, that coarseness can be problematic. Breads and cakes—items that involve the addition of a good amount of liquid or moisture—can usually be made successfully with kosher salt. But in baked goods that contain nominal amounts of liquid (such as Spritz Cookies, page 21), we find fine-grained table salt to be preferable because its diminutive grain is more easily distributed and dissolved.

In the Spritz Cookies and in pie pastry made with kosher salt, the salinity was noticeably harsh and uneven. With each bite, small bursts of salt could be tasted wherever the undissolved salt grains happened to land on the tongue. That's not to say, however, that kosher salt—if it is the only type of salt on hand—cannot be used in baking. If you use Diamond Crystal Kosher salt, use twice the amount of table salt called for (by volume, kosher salt is less dense than table salt) and be sure to rub the granules between your fingers before adding the salt to the other ingredients. This breaks down the granules for even dissolution and dispersal.

As for Morton Coarse Kosher, we advise against using this salt in baking. These salt granules are so dense and hard that they resist being crumbled between the fingers. If Morton Kosher is the only salt on hand, use 1½ times the amount of table salt called for and, before using it, break down the granules by crushing them in a small bowl or saucer with the back of a spoon.

KOSHER FOR BAKING?
We've figured out how to use these salts in cookies and pie crusts.

RECIPE UPDATE: **READERS RESPOND**

Creaming Equipment

Several readers asked if they could prepare our **Chocolate Bundt Cake** (January/February 2004) in a food processor. We were skeptical because this recipe employs the creaming method of mixing to incorporate air and produce a light, fluffy batter. We returned to the test kitchen to compare cakes made with a standing mixer (as per the recipe), a hand mixer, and a food processor.

We had no problem creaming the butter and sugar efficiently in the standing mixer. With a hand mixer, we had to almost double the creaming time (from three to about six minutes) to achieve a light and fluffy mixture. With a food processor, it was almost impossible to achieve this texture, though the ingredients did incorporate into a homogenous batter quite quickly.

The standing mixer cake had the best height, while the cake made with the hand mixer was shorter and the one made in the food processor shorter still. This proved that the standing mixer was the most efficient at incorporating air into the batter. As far as texture and flavor went, we were hard pressed to choose a favorite between the two cakes made with the mixers. The food processor cake, however, was distinguished by its greasy, spotty, and supertough exterior.

Low-Fat Fry?

The allure of our **Oven Fries** (January/February 2004) is that they require far less oil than their deep-fried cousins. But a few readers wrote to ask whether all 5 tablespoons of the oil in our recipe were necessary; as they noted (and as we acknowledged in the article), this amount of oil puts the oven fries out of the running for low-fat status. After cooking a few batches, we found it was possible to get away with a bit less oil. We had the best results when we generously coated the pan with cooking spray and tossed the fries with 2 tablespoons of vegetable oil. Although these fries were not quite as well browned as those made with 5 tablespoons of oil, their exterior was acceptably crisp and the interior creamy. The cooking spray also made it a breeze to flip the fries and remove them from the pan.

ORIGINAL FRY

LOW-FAT FRY

Our original oven fries (top) are deep golden brown. Cutting the fat in half yields good fries that are not quite as deeply browned (bottom).

Make-Ahead Wine Reduction

Reducing a liquid to concentrate flavors is a worthwhile but time-consuming effort. And so readers wanted to know if they could prepare our slow red wine reduction ("**Pan Sauces 101**," May/June 2003) ahead of time and freeze it.

As written, the recipe calls for reducing 1 cup of wine. Thinking big, we tripled the recipe so it could be made with a whole bottle of wine to yield 6 tablespoons of concentrated wine reduction, enough for three or four pan sauces. Did our experiment work? Yes, it did. And here's how you can repeat it: Along with the bottle of wine, you will need ⅓ cup each minced carrot, shallot, and white mushrooms; 3 sprigs of parsley; and 1 small bay leaf. Combine all of the ingredients in a 12-inch skillet and cook, without simmering (the mixture should steam but not bubble), until reduced to 3 cups (30 to 35 minutes). Strain and return the liquid to a clean skillet. Continue to cook over low heat, without simmering, until reduced to 6 tablespoons, 1½ to 2 hours.

Place the wine reduction in a small plastic storage container and freeze until needed. The wine reduction will freeze in a slushy consistency, so you'll easily be able to scoop out by tablespoon the amount you need for a sauce recipe.

– Compiled by Nina West

IF YOU HAVE A QUESTION about a recently published recipe, let us know. Send your inquiry, name, address, and daytime telephone number to Recipe Update, Cook's Illustrated, P.O. Box 470589, Brookline, MA 02447, or to recipeupdate@cooksillustrated.com.

EQUIPMENT UPDATE
Stain Removers

Nearly a year ago, we tested 16 stain removers and found oxygen-based powders, such as Oxi-Clean, to be the most effective (see January/February 2004). But there's a new kid on the block. Tide's Buzz Ultrasonic Stain Remover by Black & Decker ($49.99) uses a wand that emits ultrasonic waves to "knock" stains out of fabric and onto a "stain catcher pad" below—without any washing.

The Buzz promises to work on any stain (fresh or old), so we soiled a couple of cotton shirts with an array of notorious stain makers: ketchup, chili, beets, coffee, mustard, chocolate, and red wine. The stains on one shirt were treated immediately, and the shirt was then washed. The second shirt was stained, washed with regular laundry soap, and fully dried prior to our attempts to remove the stains with Buzz.

The initial novelty of the gently humming wand quickly turned tedious. The wand covers very little area, and unless we exerted significant downward pressure, little happened. Still, we managed to have some luck with the fresh stains. Ketchup, chili, and beet stains disappeared under the wand, and coffee, mustard, chocolate, and red wine stains lightened considerably (but were not removed). When it came to the dried-on stains, however, the Buzz was completely ineffective.

Given the product's poor showing with old stains and the continued expense of detergent refill packs ($4.99 for 10 ounces) and pads ($4.99 for 15), we gave it a thumbs down.

ULTRASONIC STAIN REMOVER
Can you really wave away stains?

NEW PRODUCT
Plastic Disposable Baking Pans

Recently, we noticed disposable plastic baking pans in supermarket aisles. Curiosity overcame our initial skepticism, so we decided to give these new items a test.

We chose two plastic options—Glad Ovenware (two pans for $3.99) and Reynolds Pot Lux Cookware (one for $2.79)—and tested them alongside a disposable aluminum pan, Hefty's EZ Foil (two for $4.99). The pans measured at least 12 by 9 inches. As a benchmark, we also included our favorite standard baking pan, made by Pyrex (see March/April 2004). We baked raspberry squares, cornbread, and lasagna in each pan.

HOT PAN
Can plastic baking pans withstand the heat?

All three disposable pans were surprisingly solid performers, although the Pyrex pan, which costs just $9 and will last for years, is clearly the best option. The plastic pans are basically nonstick, so they were just the thing for sticky raspberry squares and gooey lasagna. The plastic pans were also sturdy enough to allow us to cut the food right in the pan with a knife. By comparison, the foil pan was incredibly flimsy when filled, and it was much easier to slice right through it. In the cornbread test, however, the disposable aluminum pan came out on top for its better browning.

The plastic pans cannot withstand temperatures above 400 degrees, so make sure your oven is properly set and calibrated. We found that placing the plastic pans on a metal baking sheet not only ensured safe passage into and out of the oven but also promoted better, more even browning.

Overall, we preferred the sturdier plastic pans to the flimsy foil pan, and Glad Ovenware is the better bargain.

DO YOU REALLY NEED THIS?
Coffee Toddy

Cold brewing with the Toddy Coffee Maker ($33.99) promises a milder cup of java with less acidity and caffeine. Steep a full pound of coffee in 9 cups of cold water for 10 to 12 hours and you end up with a carafe of coffee concentrate that can be diluted with hot water for a cup of coffee or ice for iced coffee. We found the Coffee Toddy very easy to use, but what about the coffee? Could it compete with traditional brews?

Nearly all tasters noted the even, balanced flavor of the cold-brewed coffee. That mildness was either received as a pleasant break from coffee's usual bitterness or frowned upon as "kiddy coffee" or "coffee on training wheels." A few tasters felt they could drink this milder brew without the milk and sugar they use to tame regular coffee. Because the Coffee Toddy produces enough concentrate to make sixty-four 4-ounce cups of hot coffee, we tested its staying power. Sealed in its airtight carafe, the concentrate was still producing clean-tasting coffee after eight weeks.

While most tasters said they would still prefer to make a fresh pot every morning, iced coffee enthusiasts or coffee drinkers looking for an exceptionally mellow brew will find the Coffee Toddy pretty appealing.

COLD BREW
The Coffee Toddy promises a kinder, gentler brew.

RECIPES

November & December 2004

Carbonnade à la Flamande, 7

Roasted Brined Turkey, 11

Salad with Roasted Beets, Fried Shallots, and Roquefort, 24

Braised Chicken with Swiss Chard, Tomatoes, and Balsamic Vinegar, 19

Marinated Mushrooms, 8

Pan-Seared Oven-Roasted Pork Tenderloins, 14, and Smashed Potatoes, 13

www.cooksillustrated.com

Get all 11 years of *Cook's Illustrated* magazine and a free gift!

Join www.cooksillustrated.com today and gain access to 11 years' worth of recipes, equipment tests, and food tastings . . . at any time and from anywhere! Plus, as a *Cook's Illustrated* subscriber, you're offered a 20% discount.

Free Gift: As a paid member, you'll also get *The Essential Kitchen: 25 Kitchen Tools No Cook Should Be Without.* This downloadable online guide produced by the editors of *Cook's Illustrated* provides recommendations on the best cookware, tools, and gadgets for your kitchen. Simply type in the promotion code **CB411A** when signing up online.

Here are a few of the many things available at our site:

Best Recipes: Eleven years' worth of recipes developed in America's Test Kitchen.
Cookware Reviews: Every cookware review published since 1993, plus many reviews never seen in *Cook's*.
Ingredient Tastings: A decade of taste-test results, offering recommendations on everything from ketchup and mayonnaise to flour, yeast, and salt.
Online Bookstore: Cookbooks from the editors of *Cook's*, plus much more.

AMERICA'S TEST KITCHEN TV SHOW

Join the millions of home cooks who watch our show, *America's Test Kitchen*, on public television every week. For more information, including recipes and a schedule of program times in your area, visit www.americastestkitchen.com.

Spritz Cookies, 21

Chocolate Caramel Walnut Tart, 22

PHOTOGRAPHY: CARL TREMBLAY, STYLING: MARY JANE SAWYER